for Santha, always

GRAHAM HANCOCK

Night of Sorrows

War God 3

CORONET

First published in Great Britain in 2017 by Coronet
An imprint of Hodder & Stoughton
An Hachette UK company

1

A CIP catalogue record for this title is available from the British Library

Hardback ISBN: 978 1 444 78841 9
Trade Paperback ISBN: 978 1 444 78842 6
Ebook ISBN: 978 1 444 78843 3

Typeset in Minion Pro by Palimpsest Book Production Ltd,
Falkirk, Stirlingshire

Printed and bound by Clays Ltd, St Ives plc

Hodder & Stoughton policy is to use papers that are natural,
renewable and recyclable products and made from wood grown in
sustainable forests. The logging and manufacturing processes are expected
to conform to the environmental regulations of the country of origin.

Hodder & Stoughton Ltd
Carmelite House
50 Victoria Embankment
London EC4Y 0DZ

www.hodder.co.uk

Part I

Chapter One

Monday 2 November–Saturday 7 November 1519

The god had told Moctezuma to follow his heart, to search within and find the path to glory.

But when he searched within, as he did every waking moment, as he did even in his haunted, agitated dreams, he found . . . nothing.

So he waited . . .

And he watched.

His spies followed the *tueles*, some mingling with their retinue, and through relays of runners he received twice-daily reports on the progress of their march towards Tenochtitlan. They had drafted two thousand *tamanes* from amongst the survivors of Cholula to carry their baggage and were supported by a thousand Tlascalan warriors under Shikotenka himself. Disturbingly, Moctezuma had been informed that a thousand warriors from Ishtlil's rebel Texcocan faction now also marched under their banner. On the other hand their Totonac lackeys had deserted them and were making their way back to their home cities of Cempoala and Huitztlan – the latter lying adjacent to the town the white-skins had established on the coast – and settled with more than two hundred of their soldiers.

This settlement of the *tueles* was judged to be too strongly fortified – fire-serpents were mounted all around the stockade – for a direct attack to be made on it with any chance of success. However, Moctezuma's cousin Qualpopoca, newly appointed to the rank of general, suggested an alternative plan to lure part of the garrison out into the open. The plan appealed to Moctezuma's sense of justice so strongly that he at once sent Qualpopoca on his way, leading a punitive expedition of four regiments at a forced march. First they were to overtake and destroy the returning Totonac contingent; then they were to proceed to Cempoala and brutally reimpose the tribute payments suspended some months before. Since the *tueles* had made commitments to defend the Totonacs against the Mexica, the commander of their garrison near Huitztlan would be honour-bound to send out a relief-column which Qualpopoca would then annihilate.

Contemplating what he hoped would be an easy victory over a small contingent gave Moctezuma some pleasure, but he was filled with fear by his spies' reports of the advance on Tenochtitlan of the main force of *tueles*. By the second day of their march they seemed unstoppable, having already ascended the Tlalmanalco pass between Popocatépetl and Iztaccihuatl. There, without hesitation, they took the turning Moctezuma's younger brother Cuitláhuac had suggested should be blocked and began a rapid descent towards the Mexica heartland. 'They came grouped, they came assembled,' said the spy who brought the news to Moctezuma, 'they came raising dust. The gleam of their metal lances was seen from far away, their metal swords made a rippling line like a flume and their metal shirts and helmets clanked. Some of them marched all in metal, shining men of metal whose very appearance struck the eye with terror, while their great dogs of war went ahead of them, panting, their nostrils gaping and foam dripping from their mouths.'

They passed the second night on the slopes of the mountain on the outskirts of the town of Huehuecalco in rest houses belonging to the *pochteca* guild. Here plentiful food was stored. Shortly after their arrival there, in the early evening, a group of Moctezuma's spies approached them, pretending to be locals filled with innocent curiosity, and the lord Malinche told them through his woman Malinal: 'Let it be known that these men who accompany me do not sleep by night; if they sleep at all it is a little during the day. By night they are at arms, and whoever they see afoot or entering where they are, they kill at once, and I am power-less to prevent it. Therefore make it known to all your people and tell them that after the sun sets no one is to come where we are or he will die.' To this he added, in a tone Moctezuma was coming to know well: 'I should be sorry for any that might be killed.'

The spies felt obliged to test this threat and five of their number crept into the *tueles'* camp after dark. Horrible screams were heard and none returned to join the others.

Guided by his heart, Moctezuma attempted a new ruse on the third day of the *tueles'* march. Just outside the town of Amecameca, he arranged for them to be intercepted by a huge and splendid delegation led by . . . himself! Or rather not by himself but by an impersonator, the nobleman

Tziuac, who did greatly resemble him and who was carried forward to the *tueles* on the sumptuous royal litter pretending to be him and wearing the rich and distinctive clothes that normally only he was allowed to wear.

Since Malinche had repeatedly said his own king required an eye-witness description of the Great Speaker, Moctezuma hoped he might be satisfied by this encounter and agree to turn back. Moreover it even seemed the trick might work when Malinche asked Tziuac: 'Are you perhaps Moctezuma?'

'Yes, I am your servant,' the impersonator replied. 'I am Moctezuma.'

Translating these words, the accursed woman Malinal burst into loud and offensive laughter and spoke to Malinche in his language, at which he too laughed before giving a threatening reply to Tziuac: 'Go home, imposter! Who do you take us to be? You cannot lie to us. You cannot mock us, or confuse us, or flatter us, or trick us, or bedazzle us, or cast mud in our eyes, or destroy us, or make us turn back. You are not Moctezuma! He is there, in his city! So go now and tell him I know who he is and where he is, and that he will never be able to hide from me or take refuge anywhere. Is he perhaps a bird that can fly away? Or will he tunnel under the earth? Will he somewhere enter a mountain hollowed within? For I will see him! I will look upon his face! I will listen to his words and hear them from his own lips!'

Even so the white-skins did not disdain to receive the rich presents that Tziuac brought them – golden banners, precious feather streamers of gold and a hundred golden necklaces. When they were given these gifts, the messenger told Moctezuma: 'They smiled and rejoiced in unseemly ways. As if they were monkeys they seized upon the gold, their bodies swelled with greed and they went about lifting on high the golden banners; they went moving them back and forth, displaying them, babbling and talking gibberish. In truth, lord, they hungered mightily for gold, they stuffed themselves with it, lusting after it, grubbing at it until they were glutted like the food animals they travel with – those filthy and disgusting animals resembling our peccaries that they call "pigs".'

The third and fourth nights of their journey the *tueles* rested in Amecameca, where Malinche, whose behaviour the spies described as 'sly and cunning', flattered Moctezuma's vassals. 'He showed them great affection,' said the spies. 'He warned them and persuaded them to be his friends. He described you, your lordship – oh great Moctezuma forgive us for reporting these words – as a tyrant. He said he had not come to do them harm but to liberate them from oppression, promising them freedom from vassalage if they would support him.'

On the fifth day, relentless and unstoppable, the *tueles* were on the move again, intending to spend the night in the city of Chalco where they would come for the first time to the shore of Lake Texcoco. In a state of panic and despair, Moctezuma continued to search his own heart, as Hummingbird had commanded, but the path that would lead him to glory stubbornly refused to present itself. It was in desperation, therefore, that he sent out four new magicians, freshly recruited to his court after their predecessors' execution and Acopol's death, ordering them to cast their spells on the *tueles* before they could reach Chalco.

Then disaster struck. Waiting to intercept the advancing white-skins, the four novices were confronted on the outskirts of Chalco by a hunched, elderly man, blinded by cataracts, who spoke to them in a strange, droning, roaring voice like a swarm of angry bees. 'What have you come to gain here?' he roared. 'What do you yet require? What is Moctezuma trying to do? Has he still not recovered his wits? Does he still tremble and beg, since he knows he has abandoned the common folk and committed a multitude of sins with his lust for human sacrifice. That crime of wickedness was long ago forbidden by the great god Quetzalcoatl who now returns in glory to avenge all those Moctezuma has cruelly and needlessly slain.'

The magicians were so overawed that they attempted to construct a shrine of earth and a seat of couch-grass for the mysterious soothsayer, but he reproved them, saying: 'Why in vain have you come walking here? Never more will Tenochtitlan exist. It will be destroyed. It will be left in ruins. Turn about! Look what is going to befall the Mexica!'

'And did you turn?' asked Moctezuma. His voice was a whisper. He was shivering uncontrollably, utterly consumed by an awful and overwhelming dread.

'We turned, lord, and we saw terrifying visions. We beheld all the temples and pyramids, all the great buildings, all the houses of Tenochtitlan burning and beset by fighting. But when we sought to question the old man further, lord, he had vanished into thin air as though he had never existed . . .'

This prophecy of Tenochtitlan's destruction coincided so completely with Moctezuma's own intuitions of impending doom that he did not even have the strength to be angry with the magicians, who had aborted their mission without confronting the *tueles* and returned to Tenochtitlan at once. He sat before them with a bowed head, dejected, hopeless, and after a long while he heard his own voice say, as though it came to him from a very far place: 'We are finished, my friends. There is no hope for us now. No hope for our nation. Shall we run away? Shall we climb the mountains and try to escape when our old men and old women and our innocent little children lack the strength to save themselves? No! We will be judged and punished. And however it may be, and whenever it may be, we can do nothing but wait.'

On reflection, however, he decided to make one last appeal to the *tueles*' now legendary greed for gold. To this end he sent Cuitláhuac, bearing gifts, to meet them at Chalco . . .

On Friday 6 November, after an unhurried five-day march from Cholula, the Spaniards passed the night in the town of Chalco on the extreme southeastern shore of Lake Texcoco where the city of Tenochtitlan was concealed from their view by an intervening neck of higher land. The following morning, Saturday 7 November, as the troops were mustering for the sixth day of their advance, a large group of Mexica appeared – ten noblemen and the usual train of bearers.

Armoured by her beauty, tall and lithe, with glowing skin, full, sensual lips, big, dark eyes and straight black hair that fell almost to her waist, Malinal advanced with Alvarado, Sandoval, Díaz, Mibiercas and La Serna, to meet the delegates at the edge of town where they'd been detained by the sentries. In their midst, carried on the shoulders of eight bearers, themselves all in the regalia of minor chiefs, was a princely litter richly decorated with plates of gold and precious stones. A canopy of green plumes hid its occupant from view, but now the screen parted and a jolt of shock, as though she'd been struck by lightning, passed through Malinal's body as she recognised the tall, angular figure, the high, flat brow, the liquid brown eyes, the sculpted cheekbones and the long prominent nose of Moctezuma's younger brother, Cuitláhuac.

Mastering herself, she walked directly to the palanquin and looked Cuitláhuac in the eyes, something that clearly made him uncomfortable. 'Lord Cuitláhuac,' she said. 'We meet again, in rather different circumstances than before. Then I was at your mercy and you threatened me with death should I ever return to Tenochtitlan. Will you dare to repeat that threat, I wonder, now I have the greatest warriors in the world at my back?'

Cuitláhuac's voice was soft but filled with menace. 'Whore!' he said. 'I was told you'd become the tongue of these foreign devils, but couldn't believe even you would be so disloyal as to lead their army to our gates.'

'I owe no loyalty to you, Cuitláhuac, or to your master Moctezuma, and it is not I, but the gods who ordain all things, who have sent this army to you. If the Mexica had served the gods well, and ruled this land gently, without human sacrifice, as you were long ago commanded, you would have nothing to fear.'

'Bah!' Cuitláhuac whisked the screen of feathers closed. 'Take me to the man they call Malinche. My words are for him not for you.'

Wearing his finery of long leather boots, a fine Toledo broadsword strapped over a rich purple doublet, a black velvet cloak with knots and buttons of gold, and a large gold medallion suspended from a thick gold chain around his neck, Cortés was waiting in the audience chamber of the spacious manor, built around a grassy courtyard, where the Spaniards had spent the night. Thirty-six years old, but radiating an air of worldly experience that made him seem far older, he was deeply tanned with a long oval face, a generous forehead and black hair cropped short military style. A beard followed the firm edge of his jaw and covered his chin; a long moustache decorated his upper lip. Disconcertingly, his eyes were different sizes, shapes and colours – the left being large, round and grey, the right being smaller, oval, and so dark it was almost black.

He was standing by the window deep in discussion with his officers, Velázquez de Léon and Diego de Ordaz, but moved into the centre of the room as Cuitláhuac, dressed in an ankle-length robe of red and blue feathers, stepped down from the palanquin.

'Who's this splendid fellow?' Cortés asked Malinal.

'Cuitláhuac,' she said quietly, 'brother of Moctezuma himself.'

'Is it significant – that he's sent his brother?'

'Yes. He's the second man in the kingdom. Moctezuma trusts him very much. He must have something important to say.' She used an eye movement to indicate the bearers standing behind the group of nobles. 'Looks like they brought you more presents, Hernán.'

Cortés rubbed his hands together. 'Good. Let's get on with it.'

When the introductions were over, Cortés seated himself on his folding chair with Malinal as usual on a stool by his knee, and Pepillo standing by to clarify weaknesses in her Castilian. Cuitláhuac, too, was provided with a stool, slightly lower, Malinal was pleased to note, than her own, while the other Mexica delegates squatted on their heels on a grass mat on the floor. Cuitláhuac then summoned the bearers forward and a dazzling array of gold and silver gifts was laid out – mostly gold plates and goblets but also heavy gold figurines of animals and birds, and a collection of fifty gold necklaces, pectorals and pendants. Alvarado, eyes gleaming, handled everything and pronounced the total value of the gift at close to forty thousand pesos.

'Malinche,' Cuitláhuac addressed Cortés, 'this present is sent to you by our lord the great Moctezuma, who says he is sorry you have endured so many hardships in travelling from far distant lands to see him, and he tells you again, as he has told you before, that he will give you much more gold and silver and precious stones as a tribute to your king and yourself and the *tueles* of your company, provided you do not visit Tenochtitlan. He therefore begs you to advance no further, but to return whence you came, and he will send to the town you have established on our coast a great quantity of gold and silver and precious stones for your king, and to you he will give four loads of gold, and to each of your brothers-in-arms one load. Your entry into Tenochtitlan is, however, forbidden. All his vassals are in arms to prevent it. What is more, there is only the narrowest of roads, and no food there for you to eat.'

'Can you believe this clown?' Cortés said to Malinal when she and Pepillo finished rendering Cuitláhuac's weak and foolish speech into Castilian. 'This is what? The fourth or fifth time they've tried to buy us off? Do they really imagine we'd come all this way and then turn back now?'

'Especially when they keep showing us how much gold they have,' chortled Alvarado.

'What are the white-skins saying?' demanded Cuitláhuac.

'They're discussing your offer,' Malinal replied smoothly, 'but I can tell you now you might as well try to stop an ocean tide from rising as stop these warriors coming to Tenochtitlan.'

'Tell the feathered fool this,' Cortés said to Malinal. 'Tell him I'm amazed and disappointed that the lord Moctezuma, who constantly proclaims himself to be our friend and is said to be such a great prince, should be so changeable as to invite us to visit Tenochtitlan one day and then tell us to stay away on another. How can he possibly imagine it is right, since we're now so near to his city, for us to turn back without fulfilling our king's commands to see him? If Moctezuma had sent messengers and ambassadors to some great lord like himself, and if after nearly

9

reaching the palace of that great lord those messengers and ambassadors should turn back without delivering the message they carried, what sort of reception would he give them when they returned into his presence with such a tale?'

When Malinal had translated this, and before Cuitláhuac could say anything in response, Cortés answered his own question: 'He would consider them a pack of worthless cowards, and our king would undoubtedly think the same of us. So please understand, Lord Cuitláhuac, that we are determined at all costs to visit Tenochtitlan and the great Moctezuma must make no more attempts to put us off. I *will* see him and I *will* speak with him and explain the purpose for which I've come here – something I can only do in person. As for his pathetic excuse that he doesn't have enough supplies to feed us, let him know we are men who can exist on very little and that we're already on our way. We will sleep tonight in Iztapalapa,' Cortés concluded, 'and tomorrow we will enter Tenochtitlan. We expect Moctezuma to welcome us!'

His voice rose to a hoarse shout on these last words, and Cuitláhuac stared at him aghast as Malinal gave the translation.

'Well,' Cortés demanded roughly, 'does the feathered fool have anything to say?'

'The lord Malinche wishes to know if you have any response for him, Lord Cuitláhuac?'

'I will consult with the Great Speaker and you will be informed of his answer when you reach Iztapalapa tonight,' Cuitláhuac replied.

The members of the Supreme Council were already gathered in the House of the Eagle Knights when Cuitláhuac returned to Tenochtitlan in the early afternoon and reported that Malinche, the leader of the *tueles*, was adamant. He and his warriors would spend the night in Iztapalapa and proceed to Tenochtitlan in the morning using the causeway, six miles in length, that connected the two cities across the waters of Lake Texcoco.

'Give the order, lord,' said Cuitláhuac, 'and I will have every bridge on the causeway removed and our armies ready to descend upon the white-skins in vast numbers by land and by canoe. We can still destroy them before they reach the sacred soil of Tenochtitlan.'

Seated on his plinth in the centre of the great assembly room, Moctezuma thought about it. Were the *tueles* truly gods, or some strange species of men, as many of his advisers, Cuitláhuac amongst them, now believed? If they were gods then they were warrior gods, gods of darkness, gods of destruction, as they had proved in Cholula – and their transformation from gods of peace was a just and fitting punishment, sent down on Moctezuma from heaven, for his own failure to obey the ancient code of Quetzalcoatl. Such gods could not be destroyed! Such gods could not be defeated! On the other hand, if they were men, then they were possessors of magic, weavers of spells, who could overcome the most powerful sorcerers, as they had also proved in Cholula, and crush to powder the greatest of armies, as they had demonstrated first against the Chontal Maya and later against the Tlascalans who now marched in their train. Such men could not be destroyed! Such men could not be defeated!

'I thank you, brave and loyal Cuitláhuac,' Moctezuma said, 'for your advice and for your courage, but I must tell you I feel the hand of fate upon me and I do not believe it will benefit us to resist. I have therefore made my decision. You are to return at once to Iztapalapa and await the arrival of the *tueles* there, and honour them and inform them that I invite them to enter Tenochtitlan. When they advance along the causeway from Iztapalapa tomorrow I will go out to greet them and welcome them into our sacred city . . .'

'Great Lord,' it was Cacama, King of Texcoco, who spoke, 'this is a wise decision, and one I myself have always advocated. If these *tueles* are men as they claim, and if they are ambassadors of a powerful foreign king as they tell us, and as I personally believe, then it is right and proper for you to welcome them into Tenochtitlan and hear the messages they bring, and perhaps great advantages in trade and a valuable military alliance will come to us from a treaty of peace with their kingdom.'

'Thank you, Cacama,' replied Moctezuma, 'for your kind and heartening words. Let us hope you are correct and our encounter with the *tueles* tomorrow will indeed be to our advantage. But again I must repeat that I feel the hand of fate in this matter and am certain in my heart that the sun is setting on our days of power.' With tears welling up in his eyes he turned to address the whole room: 'Oh mighty lords, it is fitting that we all be gathered here to receive the *tueles*, and therefore I wish to find solace with you. I wish to greet you now and also bid farewell to you. How little we have enjoyed the realms our ancestors bequeathed to us! They – mighty lords and kings – left this life in peace and harmony, free of sorrow and sadness! Woe to us! Why do we deserve this? How did we offend the gods? How did this come to pass? Whence

11

came this calamity, this anguish? Who are these who have come? Whence have they come? Who showed them the way? Why did this not happen in the times of our ancestors? There is only one remedy: you must make your hearts strong in order to bear what is about to happen, for the *tueles* are at our gates and will enter our city tomorrow and we cannot prevent this.' Streams of tears were flowing down his cheeks now, huge sobs rising in his chest. 'Let us beg these gods to have pity,' he concluded, 'if not upon ourselves then upon the poor, upon the orphans and widows, upon the children and the aged.'

And so saying, amidst a stunned silence, he rose from his plinth and left the room weeping, going directly to the north stair of the great pyramid and climbing, climbing, towards the dark door of the temple of Huitzilopochtli.

'They are strange people,' said Bernal Díaz. 'Their love of human sacrifice, their cannibalism, their devil worship – all these things say they are savages. But in other ways they're highly advanced – witness their architecture, their engineering, their agriculture, their textiles, their goldsmiths. If their military science is of the same order as the skill it took to build this causeway, then we'll be in trouble if we have to face them in battle.'

Díaz was marching at the head of his company of fifty with La Serna and Mibiercas at his side as usual, and the three of them had spent much of the day discussing the enigma of the Mexica.

'Their weapons are inferior,' said Mibiercas dismissively. 'Stone will never be a match for steel. And from what we've seen so far they lack the *espirit de corps* of our Tlascalan allies.'

'Besides,' offered La Serna, 'Cortés could talk a nun out of her virginity, and at the rate he's been going with their embassies I'll wager he'll talk them into surrendering to us without a fight!'

After leaving Chalco, itself a town of no more than six or eight thousand people, though boasting many very large and well-made palaces and temples, they had marched along the southern shore of Lake Texcoco, where a filament of that great body of water trended approximately west to east for some ten miles, and approximately north to south for two miles. The causeway that now bore the entire Spanish army spanned the narrowest point of this filament, leapfrogging from its southern to its northern shore by way of an island which, it seemed, was named Cuitláhuac after the Mexica nobleman whose embassy Cortés had received that morning.

Construction of the causeway, Díaz reckoned, must have been a mighty feat – one that would have taxed the best engineers of Europe – for it was made of solid stone, deeply founded in the bed of the lake, paved with precisely cut stone slabs and wide enough for ten men to march abreast. Each of its two sections – from the southern shore to the island, and from the island to the northern shore – was a mile in length, and at regular intervals of three hundred paces there were gaps, overpassed by hump-backed bridges of sturdy wooden planks, to allow the free circulation of the waters of the lake. The bridges were cunningly designed in interlocking sections that would make them easy to remove, and each of them required six good paces to cross – a distance too great, Díaz reckoned, for most men or horses to jump. It would be easy for the Mexica to deny the use of the causeway to any attacking enemy by the simple expedient of removing the bridges.

Darting around the causeway as the Spaniards marched were hundreds of tiny watercraft, crowded with Indians in brightly coloured clothes, who had come to ogle at the strangers or, in some cases, to offer food, textiles or ornaments for barter. They made a gay spectacle, filling the air with their excited chatter, and while there was nothing obviously threatening about their manner, their sheer numbers were daunting. The shores of the lake were likewise densely populated with many towns and villages dotted amongst stately forests of tall trees, their leaves glowing in autumnal reds and golds, separated here and there by cultivated orchards radiant with ripe and inviting fruits and by well-tended fields, criss-crossed by irrigation canals and bearing an abundant crop of tall yellow maize. Much in this idyllic landscape spoke to Díaz of his own farming heritage in the Castilian countryside north of Medina del Campo, but there was also much that was new to him. Remarkably, the Indians had even created ingenious floating gardens to exploit the surface of the lake itself, some as large as fifty paces on each side, made of dense mats of the plaited and twisted roots of numerous different species of exotic plants, overlaid with rich soil dredged from the lake bottom and planted with fruits, flowers and maize.

The more he saw of all this, the more Díaz found himself praying La Serna was right and Cortés could indeed somehow talk the Mexica into surrender – or, if not surrender, at least a peaceful acceptance of the alien presence in their midst. For, friendly as the multitudes pressing in on them might seem today, he did not think it would take much – perhaps no more than a single word from Moctezuma – to transform them into a screaming, determined horde of enemies who would throw themselves in endless waves upon the Spaniards until, worn down by sheer numbers, they finally succumbed and were borne away for sacrifice.

Díaz's uncomfortable sense of a looming cataclysm behind the brash colours and insistent curiosity of the Indians continued to mount as the little Spanish force completed its crossing of the causeway and set off, standards flying, to march the last four miles into the city of Iztapalapa. The mob thronging round, pressing in from both sides of the highway and threatening to disrupt the integrity of the squares, bore an increasingly hostile and arrogant mien, and at last Cortés responded with two volleys of musket fire into the air that drove the gaping sightseers back. Thereafter, for the remainder of the march, the pikemen were ordered to kill any who came too close. 'Don't let them get familiar with us,' Cortés yelled, and Díaz heard him instructing Malinal to tell the Indians: 'These men are gods. If you mingle with them you will die.'

After that, with the pressure on the column somewhat reduced, Díaz found himself gazing in awe at the ever more amazing sights that presented themselves – towns and villages built half on land and half on stilts extending far out into the lake, with pyramids and temples made of beautifully dressed stone rising out of the water like ensorcelled visions from the tale of Amadis. 'Is this all a dream?' La Serna asked at one point, and Mibiercas replied, 'perhaps it is, Alonso. I've never seen or imagined I would see any such things. It seems like an enchantment.'

Cortés rode at the head of the column, with Malinal walking at his right stirrup and Pepillo at his left. Ranged out on either side, also on horseback and in full armour, were Alvarado, Sandoval, Davila, Velázquez de Léon, Olid and Ordaz. They made, Cortés knew, a formidable sight, with the rest of the cavaliers in a tight mass behind followed by the ranks of marching foot soldiers in perfect order, swords and pikes gleaming.

The outskirts of Iztapalapa stretched before them, a town of soaring towers and pyramids set amidst countless thousands of fine houses, as good as the best in Spain. Many were built on the dry land that sloped down from here towards the main body of Lake Texcoco, and many more were carried on stilts far out into the lake itself, which was fifteen miles wide from east to west at this point, dotted with islands, and seemed to stretch at least thirty miles further to the north, surrounded on all sides by towering, snow-capped mountains.

But what immediately caught Cortés's eye amongst the many splendours that lay ahead, and caused him to halt the column there on the road so he could take the sight in properly, was an immense city, built in part on an island and in part on water, lying far out in the midst of the lake – six miles or so due north, he guessed. It was a city that in every respect dwarfed Iztapalapa, a city that appeared to float above the sparkling wavelets as though it were a mirage, a city joined to the shore by a long causeway, straight and wide, that beckoned him into its midst – a city overshadowed by a gigantic pyramid, its four levels painted green, red, turquoise and yellow, that even at this distance seemed to pulse out tidings of threat and menace across the waters.

'Tenochtitlan?' he asked Malinal.

'Yes,' she said, 'Tenochtitlan, which you have crossed vast distances and conquered many enemies to reach.'

'And the pyramid? Is it the shrine of that demon from hell they call Hummingbird?'

'It is. There, on the summit, I was offered up for sacrifice. From there I made my escape and began the journey that brought me to your side.'

'God sent you to us, Malinal.'

'If you say so my lord . . .' She seemed to hesitate. 'My lord . . . there is something I must tell you . . .'

'Wait.' Cortés rested his mailed fist on her shoulder to silence her. 'Looks like Moctezuma has sent us a welcoming committee.'

Advancing towards them from the centre of Iztapalapa, surrounded by a retinue of at least a hundred men, was the same golden palanquin with a screen of green feathers that had brought Cuitláhuac to them in Chalco earlier.

Malinal studied Cuitláhuac's patrician face as he addressed Cortés: 'Malinche,' he said with the pained expression of a man required to smell something foul, 'we have come here, I and these chieftains, to place ourselves at your service, and to see you receive everything you require for yourself and your companions, and to take you on the morrow to our city Tenochtitlan, which you must consider your home – for so our lord, the great Moctezuma, has commanded. He asks you to pardon him for not coming with us himself, but he remained behind in his palace because of ill-health, and not from lack of goodwill towards you.'

Cortés's response was to embrace Cuitláhuac warmly in the Spanish fashion, even though he already knew very well – for Malinal had told him – that close physical contact with members of the Mexica royal

15

family was forbidden under pain of death in a law that Moctezuma himself had promulgated just the year before. But, like everything else Cortés did, this act, which caused Cuitláhuac to recoil as though confronted by a viper, was calculated. In this case his purpose was to demonstrate not only to Cuitláhuac and his delegation of puffed-up noblemen, but also to the crowds of spectators who lined the road into Iztapalapa, that the famous Malinche was above all laws made for mortal men, and could and would do whatever he wished to whomsoever he wished. Moreover, he did not content himself simply with an embrace, but went further and caressed Cuitláhuac as though he were a woman, and then added insult to injury by giving him three of the common blue glass beads, which, though a novelty to the Mexica, were practically without value to the Spaniards who carried huge quantities of them for barter.

With these formalities over, Cuitláhuac was then lifted back into his palanquin, Cortés hoisted himself into Molinero's saddle, and the whole assembly, with the Mexica nobles leading the way and the Spanish column following, proceeded in stately fashion into the heart of Iztapalapa. 'Well,' Cortés asked Malinal, 'what do you think? Are we safe or should we prepare to be attacked by these treacherous bastards?'

'Safe,' said Malinal, 'for tonight anyway. I watched Cuitláhuac closely. He hates me and he hates you. If he were the Great Speaker we'd have been attacked and destroyed long ago, but he doesn't have that power. Moctezuma had ordered him to show us hospitality and treat us well. He wants to kill us all but he'll never disobey his brother.'

'Then we're safe so long as I can continue to dominate Moctezuma and bend him to my will.'

'Unless there's some sort of rebellion against him.'

'And is there anyone capable of leading such a rebellion?'

'Very few would ever dare to challenge the Great Speaker. Perhaps Guatemoc, Cuitláhuac's own son?'

'The bastard who took Sandoval prisoner?'

'Yes, that one.'

'But we've not seen him since.'

'Most likely out of favour with Moctezuma now.'

'Then long may it stay that way,' smiled Cortés.

Following the Mexica nobles in their feathered robes and elaborate headdresses, the Spanish column was now marching down a wide avenue lined with grand houses. Every house had a flat roof, and every rooftop was packed with spectators, waving brightly coloured streamers, who cheered mightily and gave vent to high-pitched ululations as the conquistadors passed by.

'So we enter Tenochtitlan tomorrow, my lord?' asked Malinal. She had grown accustomed to addressing her lover formally in public, as he preferred, keeping his name and other terms of endearment for their private times together.

'Yes.'

'And you still intend to take him prisoner when we're inside the city?'

'I will judge the moment, but that is my plan, and when I have him I will make him my puppet and rule his empire through him.'

'I pray that moment will come soon, lord.'

Malinal's tone alerted Cortés: 'You mentioned earlier there was something you had to tell me,' he said.

'Yes, lord. I did not want to trouble you with this until I knew for sure we reach Tenochtitlan in time. Before she left us, Tozi told me of a wicked sacrifice planned by Moctezuma.'

'Ah yes, Tozi. Strange little thing. What happened to her? Where did she go?'

'She and the old man Huicton have been very busy these past days, working to disturb Moctezuma. In Chalco they staged a "prophecy" that will terrify him. They're playing their part to do the will of God.'

Cortés's interest visibly quickened: 'The will of God?'

Malinal had chosen her words carefully.

'An end to human sacrifice – the high purpose for which God sent you here. In just nine days Moctezuma will begin a sacrifice for the birthday of the demon Huitzilopochtli. This will be no ordinary sacrifice, my lord! Ten thousand young girls, all virgins, now fill the fattening pens of Tenochtitlan. Moctezuma plans to kill them all.'

'Dear God!' exclaimed Cortés. 'Ten thousand?'

'Ten thousand innocent children! Many teams of sacrificers will work four days and nights to take their hearts. The pyramid, the plaza – all bathed in blood. Such a thing the Mexica did before, long time ago but keep records, know how long will take to complete their work. Killing to begin dawn on sixteenth November and end dawn on twentieth November, first day of the Mexica month of Panquetzaliztli. That is birthday of Huitzilopochtli.'

Cortés was nodding grimly, his eyes fixed on the distant pyramid. 'That doesn't give us long,' he said, 'just eight days after we enter the city

17

tomorrow. I'll do everything I can, Malinal, everything in my power, but I can't promise we'll be in a position to halt this abomination in time.'

Malinal felt her heartbeat rising, and a rush of anger. 'You must halt it, lord! You must find a way. Fail in this, fail God, fail yourself!'

'The failure will be worse if I bring this expedition to ruin through hasty, ill-judged actions. I *will* stop the human sacrifices of the Mexica, you have my word on that, but to do so in eight days may be asking too much, even of God.'

'But lord,' Malinal felt suddenly desperate. 'You enter Tenochtitlan tomorrow. You have power to save lives of ten thousand women. You must save them!'

'Enough!' Cortés barked, and his voice was suddenly harsh and cruel. 'I'll think on what you've said but I'll hear no more on the matter now.'

Up ahead the group of Mexica nobles had come to a halt before an immense palace of wood and stone, set amidst bright gardens, close to the shore of Lake Texcoco. Cuitláhuac stepped down from his palanquin, and with two minor chiefs sweeping the ground at his feet he walked back to Cortés. 'Malinche,' he said. 'Here you will rest for the night and tomorrow you will see the face of the great Moctezuma.'

Moctezuma had spent the afternoon in silence, seated cross-legged before the idol in the inner sanctum of Hummingbird's temple. He had considered asking High Priest Namacuix to provide him with a large dose of *teonaná-catl* but had decided, finally, that on this occasion he would meditate without the aid of the sacred mushrooms – not in yet another vain attempt to summon Huitzilopochtli himself, but with the intention of searching deep within his own heart as the god had commanded him to do.

In this way, little by little, as his emotions grew calm in the silence and his thoughts fell into order, Moctezuma felt a reawakening of hope. It was not too late. Hummingbird might yet join the fight on his side, as he had always promised he would, and give him victory over the *tueles*. In a very few days the great sacrifice of the ten thousand virgins now being fattened in the pens would begin. If that magnificent holocaust could tempt Huitzilopochtli back, as the war god had given Moctezuma reason to believe it would, then all was not lost and the white-skins could still be destroyed. Despite the reverses and strange omens of recent months, Moctezuma remained confident that none – neither *tueles* nor men – could stand against the might of the Hummingbird when he was nourished with sufficient quantities of precious blood and beating hearts.

Sensing the idol glaring down at him, its black eyes burning into him where he sat on the floor, Moctezuma sought deep within for the path to glory. The fog that had clouded his mind for so long cleared and he saw and understood at last what he must do. Tomorrow, after the white-skins had entered Tenochtitlan, the heart of Hummingbird's power, he would quarter them in the vacant palace of his late father Axayacatl at the foot of the great pyramid in the very shadow of Hummingbird's temple. There he would show them gentle and generous hospitality and offer them many words and tokens of peace and friendship to lull them into a false sense of security, while all the time readying his armies in secret. Then, on the day the sacrifice of the virgins began, after first cutting all the causeways so there could be no escape, he would throw every warrior under his command at the white-skins to seize them as prisoners for sacrifice and destroy them utterly, together with their war animals and their fire-serpents.

Surely their *tuele* blood, mingled with the blood of ten thousand virgins, would be most gratifying to Hummingbird?

Moctezuma looked up expectantly at the great stone idol and into its obsidian eyes.

Was he imagining? Or did he see there a glint of sly intelligence and approval?

It was early evening, the last rays of the setting sun still lit up the sky, and Bernal Díaz was taking a turn around the beautiful gardens of the palace by the lakeshore where the Spaniards were quartered. The palace itself was spacious enough to accommodate the entire army with ease. Two storeys high, it was well made of cut stone ashlars, with floors and beams of cedar and other fragrant woods, and boasted many great rooms, courts and patios shaded with awnings of woven cotton – the whole edifice so large and so beautiful that it compared favourably with any of the great royal residences of Europe.

The gardens were immense, laid out in regular squares interconnected by paths, and bordered by trellises supporting creepers and aromatic shrubs that filled the air with heady perfumes. Aqueducts and canals carried fresh water into all parts of the grounds, and many local fruit trees and rose bushes flourished. Remarkably a channel had been cut from the lake, through which Díaz saw a number of large canoes entering into the heart of the gardens to take on and offload produce and, as he continued his walk, the sound of birdsong drew him to an aviary stocked with many different species of tropical birds, seemingly selected for the brilliance and dazzling colours of their plumage. Finally, in the midst of a vast orchard, he came to a great artificial pool of mortared stone measuring four hundred paces along each side with steps leading down to the water at several points to allow inspection of the many varieties of fish it contained and the aquatic birds that paddled on its surface and the elegant fountains that diffused an ethereal and cooling mist.

Taking in this fantasia of sights and sensations, as the dusk gathered and the sound of cicadas mingled with birdsong in the evening air, Díaz caught himself wondering again if La Serna had been right and they were all in the midst of some bizarre and far-fetched dream? Or had Mibiercas come closer to the mark when he'd spoken of an enchantment?

And if perchance all this were not a dream or an enchantment, but truly the work of human hands, then how could a few hundred Spaniards possibly hope to prevail against a civilisation great enough to create such marvels? Díaz was a man of stolid temperament, not given to flights of fancy, but just for a moment, as day became night and the lights of distant Tenochtitlan sparkled out across the waters of the lake, he thought: *We are pygmies in a land of giants; what fools we have been ever to imagine we might conquer here.*

That night, in his dreams, Cortés stood atop the great pyramid of Tenochtitlan with Saint Peter. Beside them, about waist high and two paces in diameter, was a mossy block of green jasper. Its smooth, convex surface was caked with dried blood. Placed next to it was a smouldering brazier filled with glowing coals, and a huge cylindrical drum covered with the diamond-patterned skins of serpents. Behind, its doorway also stained with blood and decorated with grotesque carvings, was a dark, narrow temple, very tall, with an elaborate structure like a huge comb or crest on its roof. Beyond the doorway, dimly lit by torches, rooms were faintly visible. There was something ominous, something dreadful, about these rooms, but Saint Peter directed Cortés's gaze away from them and drew his attention instead to the teeming island metropolis that lay spread out far beneath them, anchored to the land at north and south and west by stately causeways.

'I have brought you safe through many dangers,' the saint said, 'as I promised I would, and now your moment has come. Because I have laid my hand on him, Moctezuma quakes in fear of you and tomorrow he will open the gates of this city to you without a fight, like a virgin bride surrendering to her husband.'

'Thank you, Holiness. I am grateful . . .'

'Yet now in your triumph you face your greatest danger,' the saint warned. 'The woman Malinal whom I sent you to help secure your victory is tempting you to an act of foolishness.'

Cortés pointed to the bloodstains on the curved block of jasper and to the flaming brazier. 'Holiness, she wishes me to intervene to prevent the sin of human sacrifice.'

'And so you will, my son, and so you will, but all in good time. If you meddle in the great offering that is planned for the coming days, disaster will follow.' The saint paused and his tongue, curiously red and pointed, darted out between his lips. 'It is too soon for you to take such an extreme measure – and you know this in your heart, my son. Try to prevent it as the woman Malinal asks, and the entire populace of this great city will rise against you as one man and your little army will be crushed. Then everything you have fought for will be lost and your very name will be erased from history.'

'Am I then to stand by, Holiness, and let it happen? Such a thing seems unworthy of a Christian.'

'Unworthy, perhaps, but necessary. It is ultimate victory you seek here, and with it the cessation of all human sacrifice forever. You will not achieve that lofty goal, and you will not succeed in imposing the faith of Christ upon these benighted people, if you act foolishly and recklessly now. But bide your time, choose your moment well, and victory will be yours.'

The saint stepped closer to Cortés and placed a huge calloused hand on his shoulder, sending a shiver of ecstasy through his body. 'These things I have spoken to you,' he said, 'that in me you might have peace. In the world you shall have tribulation, but be of good cheer; I have overcome the world.'

Chapter Two

Sunday 8 November 1519

Before he went out to meet them in person and set the royal eyes upon them for the first time, Moctezuma wanted an account of the bearing and battle order of the *tueles* as they advanced from Iztapalapa on to the great causeway that would lead them into Tenochtitlan. For this purpose he had chosen the runner Achitometl, who was not only amongst the most fleet of foot of all his messengers, but also the most intelligent and gifted with words. Moctezuma had already been carried in his palanquin to the city gates at the northern end of the causeway. There, leaving his retinue of two hundred of the highest lords in the land outside in the morning sun, he rested in the guardhouse, attended by Cacama, king of Texcoco, Totoqui, king of Tacuba, and faithful Teudile. Moctezuma reclined on a divan specially brought here for the purpose, Cacama and Totoqui were seated on stools, and Teudile stood fussing with jugs of fruit drinks, chilled with ice from the mountains, cups of foaming chocolate, and various snacks and delicacies offered to them by flocks of servants.

The chatter of the lords outside suddenly stilled, there came the sound of bare feet running on paving stones, the door was thrust open by the guards, a shaft of bright sunlight lanced through and Achitometl entered, a handsome youth, lean and strong, long hair falling to his shoulders. Despite the six-mile run he had barely broken a sweat and his breathing was unlaboured as he fell to his knees, head bowed.

'Tell us,' said Moctezuma, 'of the *tueles*. Have they left Iztapalapa? Are they already on the causeway?'

'They are, sire,' replied Achitometl. 'Guided by Lord Cuitláhuac and his entourage, I saw them move forth attired and arrayed for war. They girt themselves; they bound on their battle dress. They disposed their deer in order, sire, arranged in rows, put in line.

'Four men mounted on deer came first, came leading the others, constituting the vanguard. They advanced, continually turning their heads about, facing the people who lined the causeway, looking hither and thither, scanning every side. Likewise their unnatural dogs also came ahead. They came sniffing at the feet of the crowd, putting fear into their hearts. Each one came panting, continually panting.

'After the vanguard of deer-riders and dogs, lord, came the one who bore the standard upon his shoulders. He came continually shaking it; he went making it circle; he went tossing it from side to side. It came continually stiffening in the breeze; it came rising like a warrior. Smartly did it twist; it came twisting as it raised itself; it came twisting and filling itself out.

'Then behind him came the bearers of metal swords. Their metal swords went flashing and each bore on their shoulders their shields – shields of metal, shields of wood, shields of leather.

'The third group was of deer, each carrying a soldier, each with his metal armour, his leather shield and his metal sword. Each deer had bells and the bells resounded and the deer gave tongue with a sound like "*neigh . . . neigh . . . neigh*". Much did they sweat, these great war deer; it was as if water fell from them. And the flecks of foam from their mouths fell in large drops on the ground; they fell on the ground in drops like suds of *amolli* soap. And as they advanced, heavily did their hooves beat. There was a pounding as if stones were cast.

'The fourth group was of those with metal bows; in the arms of the bowmen their metal bows went resting, and their quivers went hung at their sides or passed under their arms, each one well filled, crowded with metal bolts.

'The fifth group likewise was of deer-riders; their array was the same as I have told of the others.

'The sixth group were those with fire-serpents. They carried the fire-serpents on their shoulders. Some came with them extended and just before they entered on to the causeway they fired them into the air. They each exploded, they each crackled and thundered, they each disgorged smoke. Smoke was spread diffusely, smoke darkened, smoke massed all over the ground. By its fetid smell it stupefied the crowds who watched; it robbed them of their senses . . .'

Moctezuma was sitting upright on his divan. 'Where is their commander?' he asked. 'The one called Malinche?'

'He came directing from the rear, lord, like our *tlacateccatl*, the battle ruler, the battle director. He rode on a great war deer, all clad in metal armour, and surrounding him, scattered about him, close to his side, knowing him, went his brave warriors, his insignia bearers who were like our shorn ones, our Cuahchics, the strong ones, the intrepid ones.'

'And what of the Tlascalans?' Moctezuma asked. 'And the men of Ishtlil? Does Malinche presume to bring our mortal enemies into the heart of our city?'

Achitometl bowed his head further: 'They come, lord, pressing close behind Malinche, the thousand of Ishtlil and the thousand of Tlascala, all placed under the command of the lord Shikotenka himself. They come arrayed for war, each in his cotton armour, each with his shield, his *macuahuitl* and his bow. Each one's quiver is filled, crowded with feathered arrows. They come with knees bent, loosing cries, loosing shrieks while striking their mouths with their hands, whistling and singing their war songs, but many amongst them, lord, bear burdens in carrying frames, some in cages, some in deep baskets, and some draw the great metal fire-serpents of the *tueles* on wooden chariots, those fire-serpents that strike dead a thousand men at a single blow.'

Moctezuma stood and paced restlessly around the guardhouse. Now he had the whole picture in his mind, it was bad.

It was as bad as it could possibly be.

Never before had a foreign army been granted admission to the sacred city of the Mexica, but the arrival of the *tueles* had brought his spirits so low he had allowed himself to be browbeaten into agreeing to this anathema, even permitting the loathsome Shikotenka and his picked warriors to enter with them.

Yet this was no defeat, he reminded himself. This was a trap! And in a few days he would spring that trap and the *tueles* would die and Shikotenka would die, and the balance of the one world would be restored.

'We're walking into a trap,' growled Panitzin, glancing back over his muscular shoulder. 'You know that, don't you?' Nicknamed 'Tree' for his massive size, stolid features, dark skin and wild, tangled hair, his long stride kept him always a little ahead of the rest of the Tlascalan contingent.

'And what's more we're walking into it humping all this stuff for the white men,' complained Chipahua who indeed, like Tree and Shikotenka, bore a huge pannier on his back fully loaded with items of military equipment belonging to the *tueles*. Chipahua's big, bald head, smooth and domed on top, narrowed somewhat at the temples, but widened again to accommodate his prominent cheekbones and full, fleshy face. The jagged gaps in his front teeth, where he'd been struck full in the mouth some months before by a Mexica war club, gave him an expression of permanent ferocity.

Shikotenka shifted his own burden into a more comfortable position and grinned broadly. 'Stop moaning, brothers, it's the price of getting us into Tenochtitlan to end Moctezuma's rule. I'd hump this shit a lot further than six miles for the pleasure of snatching that bastard's city from him.'

Dressed only in a loincloth and sandals, his thick black hair drawn back from his brow in long, matted braids, Shikotenka's chest, abdomen, legs and arms were criss-crossed with the scars of battle wounds received in hand-to-hand combat against the Mexica. At thirty-four, he had already been a warrior for eighteen years. The experience showed in the flat, impassive planes of his face and the determined set of his wide sensual mouth, which masked equally the cold cruelty and calculation of which he was capable, as well as the bravery, resolve and inspired flights of rash brilliance that had led to his election, less than a year before, as the battle king of Tlascala.

Last night in Iztapalapa, Cuitláhuac had sought to persuade Malinche not to bring any of the Tlascalan or rebel Texcocan warriors into the Mexica capital. 'They are our hated foes,' he'd said. 'Our people are fearful they'll cause trouble.' The argument grew heated and, seeing it was becoming a sticking point, Malinche had improvised – something that Shikotenka had noticed was characteristic of the man. 'There's nothing to fear,' he'd said. 'My Tlascalans and Texcocans aren't soldiers but bearers. I need them to carry our provisions and equipment.'

The statement was patently untrue, but Malinche had underpinned it by dismissing all two thousand Cholulans who'd served as the expedition's *tamanes* during the past days, claiming he was unsatisfied with their work and sending them out of Iztapalapa at once. Eventually, after much further argument and persuasion, and obtaining permission by messenger from Moctezuma himself, Cuitláhuac had backed down, though not without spitefully insisting he expected to see Shikotenka carrying his share of the baggage.

They were now about a mile into the march, and the towers and pyramids of Tenochtitlan loomed ever larger ahead. The great crowds of curious Mexica lining the sides of the causeway, though not overtly hostile towards the Spaniards, murmured furiously as Shikotenka and his men went by. Many of the Tlascalans responded with war cries and whistles and verses of martial songs, while some brandished their weapons when the mob pressed too close.

'What I don't get,' said Tree shoving an impetuous Mexica youth out of his way, 'is what we're expected to do once we're inside.'

'It's simple,' said Shikotenka. 'We support Malinche, as we promised we would.'

'But support him to do what?' asked Chipahua. 'When one fly follows another into the spider's web, both get eaten.'

'Except,' said Shikotenka, 'that it's Malinche who's the spider here, and Moctezuma who's the fly.'

'Sure you're right about that?' asked Tree.

'I'm sure,' said Shikotenka. 'You saw how they defeated us in Tlascala. They'll do the same here.'

Shikotenka had many misgivings but chose not to share them.

First and foremost, Tree was right. Tenochtitlan was a gigantic, malevolent trap from which they might never escape. Despite the formidable fighting skills of the Spaniards, despite their flinty resolve, despite their murderous weapons and their willingness to use them, the fact was they would be grievously outnumbered and disadvantaged in the heart of the enemy capital and could be confined there at a snap of Moctezuma's fingers by the simple expedient of removing the bridges from the causeways. True the Great Speaker had so far shown himself singularly lacking in the courage or initiative needed to make such a hostile move, but if that should change, or if he had the wisdom to delegate military command to a spirited warrior like Guatemoc, then a fight to the death would ensue – a fight that Shikotenka did not think even the Spaniards could win.

Secondly there was the wider meaning of all this. Suppose, against all odds, everything did go Malinche's way in Tenochtitlan? Suppose today was the beginning of the end of Mexica dominance of the one world?

What then?

Would Tlascala ascend, as Malinche had promised? Would the rebel Texcocans of Ishtlil ascend? Would the Totonacs be rewarded for the services they too had provided? And would they all, ever afterwards, live in peace and harmony together, growing fatter and richer day by day under the wise and benevolent rule of the *tueles*?

Somehow Shikotenka did not think so.

Having seen the Spaniards in action and confronted them in war, he knew they were capable of cruelties just as hideous as any the Mexica had inflicted during their two hundred years of mastery. Indeed, in his opinion, the greed of these strange and cold-hearted white-skinned men was so monstrous, and their will to power so unruly, that they would sweep everything and everyone away, like autumn leaves, until nothing at all was left of the one world as it once had been. Its gods, its customs, its poetry, its songs, its stories, its paintings, its grand buildings, even its dreams would be gone, its blood would be sucked dry, its wealth would be taken up piece by piece and sent across the seas in the great boats of the *tueles*, its people would be enslaved, or worse still would forget completely who they were, until in the end there was nothing left but dreary devastation, overlooked by churches filled with images of Christ writhing on his cross. Already there were many amongst the Tlascalans who were abandoning the old ways, the old beliefs, and falling on their knees to worship this tortured god with his pious, life-denying teachings that despised all joy and scorned all laughter.

So was it right, Shikotenka asked himself, even though the overthrow of Moctezuma and the collapse of Mexica hegemony were goals that every loyal Tlascalan sought, for him to have put himself and his warriors at the disposal of the Spaniards, going so far as to carry their baggage like humble *tamanes*, to bring all this about?

He looked up and saw Malinche riding nearby amongst his captains, an awesome predator who, strangely and paradoxically, he both hated and loved. He shook his head to banish his dark imaginings. He had given his word to the Spanish leader when they'd settled the peace before the Hill of Tzompach, and he'd kept faith with him until now, even rescuing him from what otherwise would have been certain disaster in Cholula by putting fifty thousand Tlascalans into the field to halt the approach of a vast Mexica army. So it was too late to turn back, too late to have second thoughts. Shame might whisper secretly in his heart, but the only honourable thing to do – and he would do it! – was press on and strive for victory.

Barefoot, shamefully disguised in a commoner's short rough cloak, his handsome, hook-nosed face concealed beneath a hood, Moctezuma's fiery and rebellious nephew Guatemoc had broken the terms of his house arrest on the family estate at Chapultepec and crept away to witness the arrival of the white-skins in Tenochtitlan. To go into the city itself would have been unwise – there were too many checkpoints and Moctezuma's secret police were everywhere – so he had trekked south along the western shore of Lake Texcoco and positioned himself amidst a stand of trees on a deserted hilltop outside Tacuba, where he had an unimpeded view of the progress of the white-skinned bandits along the Iztapalapa causeway.

He recognised his father's palanquin at the head of the procession, surrounded in a bright splash of feathers and costly textiles by the usual entourage of nobles who accompanied Cuitláhuac whenever he officiated at state occasions. Then, after a decent interval of a hundred paces, came the *tueles'* vanguard, four men in gleaming metal armour on the backs of their great deer. Behind them strode a standard bearer, making a pretty sight twirling his banner in the air, letting the freshening breeze catch it in billows, and then six more groups, each separated by an interval of twenty paces, blocks of deer-riders interspersed amongst blocks of foot soldiers, their armour and weapons shining. Last of all, in a great noisy mass – their cries and ululations carrying clearly across the water – came the rearguard and baggage train made up of a thousand treacherous Texcocans and a thousand Tlascalans in their distinctive red and black war cloaks. At this distance Guatemoc could not make out individual faces, but he had received intelligence that Shikotenka was there – his heart no doubt filled with insolent pride at the hitherto unimaginable prospect of Tlascalan warriors entering Tenochtitlan in triumph.

From his vantage point Guatemoc could see the entire length of the causeway extending spear-straight across the lake from its start at Iztapalapa on the south shore to its terminus at Tenochtitlan six miles to the north. The *tueles* had already passed the junction two miles north of Iztapalapa where a spur of the causeway branched off west to the town of Coyoacan and would now march a further two and a half miles due north from there until they came to Acachinanco, a massive ceremonial plaza in the midst of the lake, from which rose up two tall stone towers, resplendent with banners, where Mexica heroes returning from battle were always officially greeted. Still a mile and a half short of the gates of Tenochtitlan itself, the plaza was also known affectionately as Malcuitlapilco, meaning 'the tail end of the file of prisoners', because the line of eighty thousand victims awaiting sacrifice had stretched as far as this point on the causeway during the inauguration of Hummingbird's great pyramid thirty years earlier. There were all sorts of symbolic reasons why it made sense for Moctezuma to receive the *tueles* beneath the twin towers and, sure enough, just as the thought came to him, Guatemoc

28

saw the city gates swing open and the advance party of the Great Speaker's retinue begin to stream south along the causeway to prepare the welcoming ceremony.

Welcoming ceremony, Guatemoc thought. *What a disgrace!* If he'd had his way Malinche and his gang of marauders would not be welcomed with garlands and gold as the coward Moctezuma no doubt intended, but with knives, spears and *macuahuitls* and the implacable hatred of half a million enraged citizens.

Indeed, if he'd had his way, Malinche would not have reached Tenochtitlan at all! He should have been wiped from the face of the earth before he ever left the steamy lowlands of the coast and never – never! – allowed to approach the Mexica heartland.

Guatemoc ground his teeth in frustration. Unfortunately he'd not had his way. Instead he was skulking in these woods on top of this miserable hill in stinking commoner's clothes and about as far from all influence as it was possible for a prince of the blood to be.

Still, something must be done about the rank betrayal of Mexica honour that was now underway, and it fell to him to do it.

Fighting the Tlascalans on their moors and mountainsides had been bad enough, Sandoval thought, and it was little short of a miracle the Spanish had triumphed there, but Cortés must be mad to imagine they could pull off the same trick against the Mexica in the much more complex, dangerous and unpredictable urban environment that lay ahead.

Sandoval was short with a broad, deep chest. His curly chestnut hair had receded almost to his crown, making him look peculiarly high-browed, but as though to compensate he had grown a chestnut beard, quite well maintained, that covered most of the lower half of his face. Supremely self-assured on horseback, he had the bandy legs of a man who'd spent most of his life in the saddle, but his confidence was badly shaken now – because even at this distance Tenochtitlan looked far bigger than any of the great cities of Spain, dwarfing Toledo, Barcelona, Madrid and even Seville. Moreover it seemed not only much bigger, but also incomparably finer, with its castellated fortresses, its hundred pyramids and its gigantic royal dwelling places. How marvellous it was to gaze on them, all stuccoed, carved and crowned with different types of merlons, painted with animals, covered with stone figures – a strange and alluring mixture of beauty and horror, with the hellish pyramid of the war god towering at the heart of it all!

And so many people! Giving off an offensive smell and generating a threatening babel of shouts, cries and whistles, mingled with a continuous murmur of mumbling and chatter, countless thousands crowded the sides of the great causeway, leaving barely enough room for the Spanish column to pass. Countless thousands more had crossed the lake in fleets of dugout canoes, some so large they carried upwards of sixty passengers and cargo. These primitive craft, many of which skimmed close to the causeway or passed beneath its bridges so their occupants could gape up at the marching Spaniards, betrayed a level of boat-building technology far inferior to that of Europe. On the other hand, the causeway itself was a marvel of engineering. Its wooden bridges were placed at somewhat greater intervals, five hundred paces or more, than those on the narrower and shorter but still spectacular causeway they'd crossed yesterday, and spanned greater distances – ten or twelve paces wide, Sandoval guessed. As they came to yet another of these bridges, the iron-shod hooves of their horses ringing hollowly, he turned to Pedro de Alvarado, Cortés's undisputed second in command, who was riding beside him in the vanguard.

'What do you think, Pedro?' Sandoval asked. 'Could you jump this gap if you had to?'

Thirty-four years old, broad-shouldered and strong, but light on his feet with the easy grace of a practised fencer, Alvarado's thick blond hair hung to his shoulders and an extravagant blond moustache, elaborately curled and waxed, decorated his upper lip. Fine featured, with a firm chin, a long straight nose and a duelling scar running from his right temple to the corner of his right eye, he didn't seem to have considered the problem. 'Why would I have to?' he asked. 'The bridge is solid enough.'

'A day might come,' Sandoval offered, 'when Moctezuma orders all the bridges cut.'

'Ha!' Alvarado exclaimed. 'I see what you're getting at!' He looked back, judging the gap they'd just crossed. 'Bucephalus at full stretch could do it,' he said, 'and I reckon I might make such a leap on foot if I had a good enough run-up – but I'll hazard I'm the only man in this army that could!'

Sandoval must have looked sceptical, for Alvarado added sulkily: 'Don't doubt me, Gonzalo. I'm not given to idle boasts.'

Now that Sandoval had put the idea into his head, Alvarado had to admit the bridges did represent a serious problem. He studied the next one carefully as they rode over it and saw it was built from interlocking sections that could easily be removed. The Indians loved ambushes and it would be a typical cunning trick to lure the Spaniards into Tenochtitlan, trap them there and slaughter them.

On reflection, though, Cortés was a more cunning and conniving bastard by far than any Indian could ever hope to be, and had been gathering intelligence on the Mexica capital for months, so obviously he must have thought this all through and had no doubt worked out a solution long ago.

Hernán always had a solution for everything, which was why Alvarado was, by and large, happy to be second in command of this expedition. It meant he could leave all the big questions and difficult decisions to his friend and get on with what he did best, namely killing people and winning gold, enterprises that brought him enormous pleasure. Hernán's unreasonable concern for the local savages, which had begun months before when they'd landed at Cozumel, had fortunately ended there as well and, since then, at Potonchan and in Tlascala, the battles had come thick and fast, with no quarter given and exemplary cruelty – which was all the Indians understood – not only allowed but encouraged. Alvarado had relished every moment! As to gold, matters had been less satisfactory until they'd reached Cholula where the temples and palaces had yielded at least a hundred thousand pesos' worth of treasures for his personal horde. Of course every man was supposed to put their loot into the common pile, of which twenty per cent, 'the king's fifth', was reserved as a tax for the royal treasury and – following the usurious deal struck at the time of the founding of Villa Rica – a further twenty per cent was supposed to be set aside for Cortés. Alvarado had supported the deal out of solidarity with his friend but had never considered that its terms applied to himself. 'Yours we share,' was his private motto, 'but mine I keep.'

He looked up along the causeway. Tenochtitlan, that city of dreams with its seemingly inexhaustible supplies of gold horded by a weak and foolish emperor, now lay less than two miles distant, its gates flung wide like the legs of a woman eager to be pleasured. The welcoming committee of colourful Mexica nobles was already out in force, gathering with streamers and banners about half a mile ahead at a point where the causeway broadened into a ceremonial plaza dominated by a pair of tall and gaily decorated towers.

Now, from out the gates, a palanquin emerged, borne shoulder-high, glinting with gold and the iridescent sparkle of the costly green feathers the Mexica reserved for their royal family. Since the only other palanquin on the causeway was Cuitláhuac's, it followed that this one advancing in solemn procession must be occupied by Moctezuma himself.

Cortés had remained with the rearguard of the Spanish column to ensure he was not kept waiting for Moctezuma to arrive. He would come to the front only when the emperor was sighted. Alvarado tapped Sandoval on the arm. 'Looks like Mucktey's on his way,' he said. 'Better ride back and tell the caudillo to be ready.'

Cortés walked Molinero forward through the column with Malinal in her accustomed place at his right stirrup and Pepillo, under strict instructions to note and record all events, at his left. By the time they had caught up with Alvarado, Velázquez de Léon, Olid and Sandoval, the vanguard had already reached the point where the causeway broadened into an impressive plaza, three hundred paces square and built, like the causeway itself, of massive blocks of stone solidly founded on the lake bed. At the northern edge of this plaza, just before it narrowed again into the final section of causeway leading into the city, loomed two huge stone towers with merloned battlements where a large group of splendidly attired Mexica nobles had gathered. Beyond them, still on the causeway, and about as far north of the towers as Cortés was presently south of it, Alvarado pointed out the plumed golden palanquin that he assumed must contain Moctezuma. 'Is that him do you think,' Cortés asked Malinal, 'or another imposter?'

'This time it is Moctezuma himself,' Malinal replied. 'See the manner of the people – ' and she indicated the crowds filling the plaza, whose chatter had ceased and who stood deadly quiet on either side of the central avenue, their eyes turned down and their faces pale. 'To look on the Great Speaker means death,' she explained.

As they moved through the eerily silent throng, the nobles beneath the towers came forward to greet them, a hundred to the left and a hundred to the right, flanking both sides of the walkway. Still with Malinal and Pepillo at his side, Cortés nudged Molinero ahead of the other four riders and the whole welcoming committee dropped to their knees as one man and performed the 'eating dirt' ceremony, putting their hands to the ground and then to their mouths. They were all barefoot, Cortés noticed, and each wore a loincloth, a broad, richly dyed cotton mantle with feather embroidery that flowed down over their shoulders, collars and bracelets of turquoise mosaic also embellished with feathers, and lip and ear plugs of gold and precious stones.

The twin towers were now less than fifty paces ahead and, looking up, Cortés saw Moctezuma's palanquin being carried into position between them, borne on the shoulders of eight men in costly robes – 'all chiefs,' Malinal said. Their feet were bare and they proceeded at a dignified pace, their eyes turned towards the ground. A few steps in front of them were three other high officers of state, also barefoot and with downcast eyes, who painstakingly swept the surface of the walkway with long-handled brooms. Leading the procession, carrying a golden staff, was the familiar hollow-cheeked figure of Moctezuma's steward Teudile, wearing his conical headdress and his long black robe spangled with silver stars.

Cortés felt calm, ready for anything, reminding himself that the man he was about to meet, about whom he had heard so much, and whose character he had come to know from a hundred reports and descriptions, was not some powerful European monarch but the half-savage ruler of a barbarian nation, whom he had played like a fish on a line for the past eight months and who was about to jump into his net.

The royal procession came to a halt between the towers, and two lords, one of whom Cortés recognised as Cuitláhuac, the other a young man whom Malinal identified as Cacama, the imposter king of Texcoco, emerged from the shadows and stood with heads bowed beside the palanquin as the canopy of feathers was pulled back and a tall, lean figure stepped down, dressed in a purple cloak of fine cotton with embroidered ends tied in a knot around his neck. In the same moment Cortés dismounted from Molinero and walked forward with Malinal and Pepillo, telling Alvarado and Sandoval to follow close behind on foot.

The distance between the two groups was less than twenty paces, and although there was nothing obviously infirm about Moctezuma, who might be about fifty years of age and paler skinned than most of his brethren, it was noticeable how Cuitláhuac and Cacama gave him their arms to lean on as the three of them advanced over cloaks that fawning retainers threw down before them. Cortés also observed that of the thousands of Indians present, including the highest nobles of the land, Moctezuma was the only one whose feet were shod; his beautifully made sandals, sprinkled with pearls and precious stones, had gold soles, and were bound to his rather slim and effeminate ankles with gold-embossed thongs. Likewise amongst the thousands of Indians present, Cortés noted with a flush of pride and affection that his own exceptional, courageous and extraordinary Malinal was the only one who held her head high, refused to lower her eyes and looked straight at Moctezuma without fear.

Malinal was not surprised when Cortés stepped in close to Moctezuma and attempted to embrace him. Nor was she surprised that Cuitláhuac and Cacama were shocked by this sacrilege and leapt to restrain the Spaniard, or by the rasp of steel as Alvarado and Sandoval both half drew their swords. Cortés told them to sheathe their weapons and had Malinal hastily explain to Moctezuma that such embraces were the normal form of greeting in his own land, but that if the monarch preferred they could simply shake hands.

'What does Malinche mean "shake hands"?' asked Moctezuma. There was, Malinal saw, a kind of evasive recognition in the monarch's glance as he put the question. Undoubtedly he remembered her – indeed Teudile had long ago made a point of telling her so – but it was equally obvious he didn't want to acknowledge this officially now.

'He means he will extend his hand to you,' Malinal replied, keeping her own expression deliberately neutral. 'This is also how men greet one another in his land. You are to extend your hand to him and you and he will clasp each other's hands and then you will be friends.'

Cortés, who had a mocking look in his eye, already had his hand out, and now tentatively Moctezuma reached out his own which Cortés took and shook vigorously. There came a great cheer from the Spanish ranks, and ten of the musketeers fired their weapons in the air, causing hundreds of the spectators and guards to throw themselves to the ground while a chorus of screams rose up and Moctezuma, Cuitláhuac and Cacama cowered back in terror.

In the confusion, Cortés favoured Malinal with a sardonic wink: 'Tell the great Moctezuma to forgive my men's high spirits,' he said, 'but this is also a custom in my land, and a salute, when two leaders meet.'

While Malinal was giving the translation, two of the expedition's great armoured war dogs came bounding up, one of the tribe the Spaniards called mastiff, the other of the tribe called wolfhound, and began sniffing first at Moctezuma's feet and then, with increasing enthusiasm, at his crotch. Cacama and Cuitláhuac tried to push the heavy animals away, but were rebuffed with menacing snarls, and Moctezuma gave a little whimper of fear. Remembering the murdering bully he'd been the last time she saw him, hacking out women's hearts on top of the great pyramid,

Malinal felt a thrill of wild, vengeful joy as the Great Speaker's eyes, almost pleading, swivelled towards her.

'Tell his Excellency,' Cortés suggested, 'to stand very still.' He looked back over his shoulder. '*Vendabal*,' he yelled, 'at the double please,' and in an instant the hunchbacked dog handler appeared from the Spanish ranks and dragged the two animals away.

'My apologies, sire,' Cortés said insincerely, as Moctezuma glared at him in bewilderment, 'our war dogs like to tear men to pieces so you've had a lucky escape. Now please, accept this gift which is but poor recompense for the many kindnesses you have showered upon us during our long journey to reach you.' And with that he took off the necklace of cheap freshwater pearls and cut-glass beads scented with musk that he'd chosen this morning after he and Malinal had risen from their bed, placing it ceremoniously round Moctezuma's neck.

Although beardless like all the Indians, Moctezuma did have six or eight wispy hairs dangling from his delicate, somewhat receding chin, a shining obsidian disk in each of his earlobes, a blue stone labret decorated with the figure of a hummingbird suspended from his lower lip and a turquoise ring passed through his septum. His nostrils twitched around this ring and he recoiled when Cortés gave him the necklace, his soft brown eyes darting from side to side, but then he smiled uncertainly and fingered the pearls and beads before turning to whisper to an aide.

'What's he whispering about?' Cortés asked Malinal.

'Nothing bad,' she replied. 'You'll see.'

The aide beckoned a servant carrying a vase of flowers, who now shuffled forward, his head bowed. With curious delicacy Moctezuma delved amongst the flowers with long, graceful fingers and extracted a gold neckband. Set in its midst was the shell of a crawfish, and connected to it a chain of heavy gold links, from which hung eight solid gold pendants, each a span in length and made with the most delicate workmanship to resemble the same species of crawfish. 'Twenty thousand pesos at least,' Alvarado commented enviously to Sandoval, as Moctezuma placed this opulent collar over Cortés's head and settled it round his neck, but then at a signal from the Mexica leader, servants came forward with similar, though smaller and less ornate, collars, which they placed around the necks not only of Alvarado and Sandoval but also of Velázquez de Léon and Olid as well. The four of them burst into smiles and happy laughter.

'I have gifts for all your men,' Moctezuma said gravely through Malinal, 'which shall be presented when we bring you to your quarters.'

'So you are really he?' asked Cortés, wanting to be sure. 'You are really Moctezuma?'

'Yes, I am Moctezuma,' the monarch replied, and Malinal added in Spanish: 'I'll vouch for him. He is the bastard he claims to be.'

Now Moctezuma was speaking again, addressing Cortés: 'And you are really he, the lord Malinche?'

'Yes, I am he.'

'Then I am not dreaming,' Moctezuma continued in an oddly wistful and poetic tone. 'I am not walking in my sleep. I have seen you at last! I have met you face to face. I was in agony for five days, for ten days, with my eyes fixed on the Region of Mystery, and now you have come out of the clouds and mists to sit on your throne again. You have come back to us as was long ago foretold, you have come down from the sky. You have come to govern your city of Tenochtitlan, which for an interval I have watched and guarded for you. Welcome to your land, my lord.'

When Malinal, with some help from Pepillo, had finished the translation, Cortés suppressed a smile and replied: 'Tell Moctezuma I have wanted to see him for a long time, and now I have seen his face and heard his words, I love him well and my heart is contented. Tell him I am his friend and he has nothing to fear.'

Knowing Malinal's deep and abiding hatred for the Mexica leader, Cortés had no difficulty imagining the revulsion she must feel at having to translate such flowery and ingratiating words. But during the long march to Tenochtitlan they'd sat up late many nights discussing how this encounter was to be handled, and he'd reassured her that – although he would do and say anything necessary to get the Spanish army into Tenochtitlan – it was his unwavering purpose to overthrow Moctezuma and take his empire from him. Nothing had changed and, contrary to the promise he had just made, the Mexica leader did, indeed, have a great deal to fear.

Now the initial formalities were over, Moctezuma repeated that quarters awaited the Spaniards and their Indian allies in the heart of the city. 'The Lord Cuitláhuac will lead you to your residence,' he said, 'and I will see you again there.' Then, with ponderous dignity, he ascended to his palanquin, vanished behind the curtain of flowers and feathers and, with Teudile walking ahead, was borne off northward towards Tenochtitlan.

Soon afterwards, Cuitláhuac also climbed into his palanquin, which set out at once towards the city, and Cortés mounted up on Molinero again and gave the signal to advance.

The Spanish army resumed its march, its drummers and trumpeters playing a rousing tattoo.

'You ever been to Venice?' Le Serna asked.

'No,' said Díaz.

'Nor I,' said Mibiercas.

All three had gained battlefield experience in the Italian wars before taking ship to Hispaniola and Cuba, but it turned out the fighting had never taken any of them near the fabled 'floating city' ruled by the doges.

'I reckon this Tenochtitlan is the Venice of the New Lands,' said La Serna, 'but I'll wager it's five times as large and ten times as beautiful.'

Having passed through the main gates, they were marching in the ranks of swordsmen down a great avenue lined with gigantic houses, all built on dry land – no doubt the original island upon which Tenochtitlan had been founded. But at intervals of several hundred paces, sometimes less, the avenue was crossed by bridges spanning manmade canals, alongside which further immense and beautiful residences had been constructed, extending away to east and west as far as the lake. All these noble dwellings, both those on the avenue and those along the canals, were constructed from regular blocks of a polished red stone, somewhat like red marble, and reared above them to a great height. All had flat roofs upon which grew luxuriant flower gardens in a riot of bright colours, overhanging, yet not completely disguising, the surrounding stone parapets that turned every one of them, Díaz realised, into a fortress. And although these roof gardens were today occupied by curious, seemingly friendly crowds, waving and calling out now that the emperor and his retinue had passed from view, it was not difficult to imagine how these same crowds might one day turn hostile and rain down arrows, spears and stones upon the Spaniards should they ever be forced to retreat from the city.

Looking left and right as they crossed the bridges, Díaz noted that the canals, like the lake itself, were filled with a busy traffic of canoes loaded with people and produce, and that every house had a doorway constructed at water level where more canoes were moored. Nor did the canals end at the margins of the original island; rather they continued far out into the lake, providing the only thoroughfares between thousands of poorer houses of wood and adobe built on stilts. From there the eye was drawn out further across the sparkling waters to the hazy distance, where jagged, snow-capped mountains reached for heaven and bestowed upon the whole scene the glamour of some remote fairyland.

As well as by the canals, the great avenue along which the Spaniards marched was broken from time to time by airy squares with bubbling fountains, vibrant, noisy market places bordered by porticos of stone and stucco, and here and there by pyramids and temples scattered amongst the palatial houses. The greatest pyramid of all, however, its four levels painted respectively green, red, turquoise and yellow, now loomed dead ahead, surrounded at a distance by a high wall penetrated by a pair of towering gates presently held open by a squad of spear-carrying guards dressed in distinctive scarlet cloaks. Coming closer, Díaz saw the wall was decorated with reliefs depicting huge bronze, green and blue serpents, their gaping jaws set with long fangs and their heads plumed with crests of feathers.

As they approached the serpent wall, with the hideous mass of the great pyramid looming beyond it, Malinal's head began to thud and she felt a deep pain at the centre of her chest as though monstrous talons plucked at her heart. It was clear now that Cuitláhuac, whose palanquin bobbed fifty paces in front of them on the shoulders of its bearers, was going to lead them directly into the sacred precinct. The residence Moctezuma had prepared for the Spaniards must therefore be either a wing of his own sprawling palace or, more likely, the empty palace of his father Axayacatl, where Cuitláhuac had taken Malinal and Tozi to be washed and clothed after they'd been reprieved from death on the great pyramid.

Malinal still walked at Hernán's stirrup. 'My lord,' she said, 'I don't know if I have the courage to go within.'

'You have the courage, Malinal,' Cortés said, and for a moment he rested his hand reassuringly on her shoulder. 'You're braver than anyone else I know.'

'I faced death in this place, my lord, and in the most horrible way; I fear the Mexica and their cruelty.'

'Fear is their weapon, my love. They've used it to lord over this land for too long. We're here to end all that. While I live, you have my promise no one will harm you.'

'What if they kill you, my lord?'

'They won't. I'm here to triumph. You'll see.'

He said it with such calm, quiet confidence that Malinal felt her panic subside as quickly as it had come. Hernán Cortés was by no means invulnerable, and certainly no god, but she had seen him triumph at Potonchan and again at Tlascala and Cholula through sheer force of will and the ruthless application of cunning and power. She trusted – she had always trusted – that he would triumph here also.

Passing through the great gates, Molinero's hoofs slipped on the polished flagstones of the sacred plaza, and it seemed for a dangerous moment the great warhorse would fall – a terrible omen – but Cortés quickly regained control. As though by some irresistible force, Malinal felt her eyes drawn up the steep steps of the south face of the pyramid, which towered directly ahead at the centre of the plaza with the loathsome temple of Huitzilopochtli crouching like a malignant toad on its summit. But she also registered the squat rectangular House of the Eagle Knights standing in the plaza near the base of the pyramid, offset a little to the east of the steps, and to her left and right just within the gates the barred enclosures of two large fattening pens. These had previously held male prisoners but now, as Tozi had warned her, Malinal saw they were filled exclusively with females, mostly young girls, many crowded close to the bars watching the entry of the Spanish army with dull, hopeless eyes.

Cortés had seen them too. 'These are the virgins Moctezuma plans to sacrifice?' he asked.

'Some of them, not all! There are five such pens around the plaza. Every one of them filled to make the great basket of ten thousand virgins he'll offer to the god eight days from today . . . You have to stop him, lord.'

'We've discussed this already. What you ask will not be easy so soon after we enter the city. It could put us at war with the Mexica before we've consolidated our position.'

'Still I ask it, lord. In the name of God.'

Cortés's mouth had set in a thin line; he made no answer as they crossed the plaza, passing the southwest corner of the great pyramid on their right, and then, on their left, the western gates leading on to the Tacuba causeway, along which Malinal and Tozi had made their escape on the awful night of the last great holocaust. They had not reached the causeway through the gates, however, but through a postern at the rear of the palace of Moctezuma's father Axayacatl – and it was to this gigantic edifice, as Malinal had suspected, that Cuitláhuac was now leading the Spaniards. Empty for many years, and used only occasionally for state functions, it was nonetheless kept fully staffed and furnished and contained hundreds of rooms, including several vast ceremonial halls. It was more than large enough to accommodate the little Spanish army and their two thousand Tlascalan and Texcocan auxiliaries.

Cuitláhuac's palanquin now came to a halt in front of the imposing main entrance, guarded by a dozen spearmen, and the lord descended. Cortés too dismounted, signalled to Alvarado, Velázquez de Léon, Olid and Sandoval to follow, and strode forward with Pepillo and Malinal. As they walked, a presentiment of horror once again overtook Malinal, and her eyes were drawn to the nearby fattening pen in the northwest corner of the plaza, filled like the others with young girls, their grimy faces pressed to the bars. The intervening months fled away and in her imagination she was once again a prisoner there awaiting death. Her footsteps faltered and Cortés took her by the arm, as Cuitláhuac and his retinue of nobles led them through the massive portico into the ornate and spacious courtyard beyond, planted with graceful trees and flower gardens, bubbling with clear, freshwater fountains and encompassed by the four principal wings of the palace.

At the centre of the courtyard, alone beneath a tall ceiba tree, stood Moctezuma.

'Malinche,' Moctezuma said gravely. 'You are weary. Rest now from the hardships of your journey and the battles which you have fought, for I know full well what has happened to you from Potonchan to here, and I also know how those of Cempoala and Tlascala, some of whom are here with you, have told you much evil about me. Believe, I beg you, only what you see with your own eyes, for those are my enemies, and some were my vassals, and have rebelled against me at your coming and said things to gain favour with you. Here you are in your own house, Malinche, and so are your brothers. Rest after your fatigues, for you have much need to do so, and in a little while I will visit you again.'

Then, without another word or backward glance, he left the courtyard with Cuitláhuac by his side, and a group of servants who had been standing fearfully nearby, heads lowered, shuffled forward and indicated they were there to attend to all the Spaniards' needs and that refreshments would be served immediately.

Watching Moctezuma go, Cortés decided he was a strange, effete sort of character, uncertain about what manner of creatures he was now dealing with – gods who descended from the sky at one moment, or men who fought battles, grew tired and had bodily needs at the next. Still, he had to admit the emperor was also oddly delicate and considerate, indeed almost civilised, in his own savage way. Great jugs of cooled drinks accompanied by copious dishes of turkey and tortillas were already being offered to the Spanish soldiers and Indian allies who were now gathering in large numbers in the courtyard, and – a nice touch this! – someone had also thought to provide heaps of grass for the horses.

But Cortés felt too restless to eat, since it was already mid-afternoon and the first order of business was to inspect the palace, decide on accommodations for the army and the Indian allies, and post guards and artillery. Telling the men to be at ease and enjoy the repast, he therefore summoned Malinal, Sandoval, and Francisco de Mesa, his chief of artillery, and set off on a tour, bringing Pepillo along to take notes.

Each of the palace's four wings rose to two storeys and was more than a hundred paces in length and thirty deep, with the rear elevation of the western wing forming part of the enclosure wall of the plaza as a whole. This was the only sector of the edifice that directly adjoined the busy streets of the city, and Malinal pointed out the postern, guarded by a pair of Mexica spearmen, through which she and Tozi had made their exit into a narrow alley, and thence on to the Tacuba causeway, some months before. It was an obvious weak point, Cortés thought. 'Take a note, Pepillo,' he said. 'We'll need our own guards on this at all times.' Malinal then led the way to the small door at the northern end of the east wing where she and Tozi had entered the palace that same night. Two more spearmen were on sentry duty here. 'We'll replace them with our own men,' Cortés commented, and again Pepillo made a note.

Next they visited the main entrance portico in the middle of the east wing where the dozen spearmen they'd seen earlier were still on duty. 'Another note, Pepillo,' Cortés said. 'When we see Moctezuma again, remind me to ask him to remove these fellows. We'll all sleep a lot safer in our beds with our own men guarding the palace.' He then turned to Mesa. 'What do you think?' he asked. 'Shall we have some artillery here?'

'We can place one of the lombards in the courtyard to command the portico,' Mesa replied, 'and we won't go wrong if we flank it with a pair of falconets.'

'Very good,' said Cortés. 'What about the other eight falconets?'

'Up on the roof?' the artilleryman suggested.

'Let's go and take a look.'

Since the four wings of the palace were interconnected, they were covered by a continuous flat roof some fifty feet above the ground, protected at all points, Cortés was pleased to establish, by a solid parapet with towers and battlements. On the west side these fortifications commanded the adjoining quarter of the city, while on the other three sides they overlooked the sacred plaza with the great pyramid lying a few hundred paces to the east. 'Two falconets on each section of the roof?' Cortés asked.

'They'd be wasted up here,' said Mesa bluntly. 'We'd be able to hit the pyramid if we ever needed to, but we won't be able to depress the barrels far enough to command the plaza. Same goes for the city side as well.'

'Then how do we protect the roof? With scaling ladders they could get up here.'

'Cannon won't do it. If we come under sufficiently determined attack we'd need armed squads up here with pikes.'

'Pikes!' said Cortés. 'You hear that, Pepillo? We brought few enough anyway and most of those were smashed in the Tlascalan campaign. We'll need to have more made.'

They left the roof and turned their attention to the interior of the palace, which consisted, on both levels, of innumerable halls, chambers and antechambers, many of great size. The walls of the best apartments were hung with bright cotton draperies, while their wooden floors were strewn with aromatic rushes. Many of the rooms had been set aside as sleeping quarters. Some were obviously intended as dormitories, with rows of mats on the floor, and would serve for the Indian allies. But many others were furnished with fine beds with woven palm-leaf mattresses, coverlets and canopies of cotton, pillows of leather and tree-fibre, good eiderdowns and exquisite white fur robes. In still others there were low stools elaborately carved from single pieces of wood, and in one particularly enormous chamber at ground level facing the courtyard there were two impressive thrones, also carved from single pieces of wood and equipped with soft cushions. Adjoining was another even larger chamber, with many long refectory tables for dining, while additional facilities on the ground floor included a grand kitchen, certain rooms for the relieving of bowels, and two bath houses.

When he had completed his tour of inspection and was satisfied the palace was defensible and provided more than adequate quarters for the whole army, Cortés ordered a general muster in the plaza, at which the musketeers fired two volleys into the air and all the artillery was lined up and discharged. Although the cannon were not loaded with shot or ball, but only with hefty charges of powder, the richly clad nobles, armed knights outlandishly dressed as eagles and panthers, and filthy Mexica priests who'd gathered to watch the ceremony threw themselves to the ground and rolled about moaning with fear, clutching their ears and gazing in awe at the clouds of smoke that billowed forth from the guns and wreathed the base of the pyramid to the height of its first course in a thick, sulphurous haze.

At the same time, from the fattening pens, there rose a pitiful chorus of shrieks and cries that clutched at Cortés's heart, filling him with righteous anger and a reckless urge to take action.

Malinal's appeals, he realised, were having an insidious effect on his reason.

Proclaiming himself dead tired, Cortés had retired for a siesta immediately after the display of ordnance in the plaza, and was sleeping on his side naked under the cotton coverlet in the grand apartment he'd chosen for his personal residence. The apartment faced inwards to the palace courtyard, where the long shadows of the late afternoon were already deepening, and Malinal stood by the open shutters, watching the play of water in the fountains, lost in thought.

After a little while she sensed movement behind her and, feeling a hand fall gently on her shoulder, turned to kiss her lover, only to discover that Hernán still slept on the bed and Tozi was with her, holding a finger to her lips. 'How did you get in here?' Malinal whispered as they embraced. Tozi gave her a scornful look: 'After I saw Acopol's rotting head,' she said, 'all my powers returned. I come and go as I please.'

Malinal smiled. 'I thought so! Outside Chalco, it was you and Huicton, wasn't it, performing the trick of the vanishing soothsayer with his prophecy of doom for Tenochtitlan!'.

Tozi nodded: 'Yes, such things disturb Moctezuma deeply. I've been working on his fears, weakening his will. That's why he admitted the *tueles* to his city today.' She turned towards the bed, where Cortés muttered some words in his sleep and rolled on to his back. 'Is he ready to do his part?' she asked.

'He'll do his part sooner or later,' Malinal whispered. 'I've no doubt of that. He does intend to overthrow Moctezuma – he has no other plan! – but I don't know if he'll act in time to stop the coming sacrifices.'

Tozi's face had become fierce. 'He must!' she hissed. 'That's why we brought him here, you and I . . .'

43

'We brought him to end Moctezuma's cruel reign,' Malinal corrected. 'He says if he acts too fast now, before he's ready, the Spaniards could be defeated.'

'It's a risk he must take!' Tozi was furious; her voice rose and Cortés stirred again in his sleep.

'Hush,' Malinal whispered. 'Don't wake him.'

'He won't wake until I let him,' said Tozi. She padded silently on bare feet to the bedside and placed the palm of her hand on Cortés's brow. Immediately he became still again. She remained standing over him, not moving her hand, her eyes moving rapidly beneath closed lids.

For a hundred count there was silence, a silence charged with meaning, and Malinal watched, fascinated, as some strange, wordless communion seemed to pass between her friend and her sleeping lord. In the midst of it, Tozi gave a start and recoiled, then leaned forward again and looked down intently at Cortés. Finally she took away her hand. 'He is a man,' she said, 'not a god.'

'I already told you this many times when we were in Cholula,' Malinal whispered.

'He is not a god,' Tozi repeated, 'and Hummingbird has touched him.'

'But that's impossible. His own god, the god of the Christians, protects him.'

'No! He is in danger. Hummingbird exerts his power upon him.'

'How can you know this, Tozi?'

'I know it! Remember I too have been touched by the god.'

'Then you're in danger as well!'

'We're all in danger because we're all born into this world of created things with the freedom to choose between good and evil. The danger does not lie in the evil but in the choices we make. For Moctezuma it's already too late; he's chosen evil for so long, plunged his own heart so deep in darkness, he can never turn back.' Tozi looked down at Cortés, whose stern face was somehow gentle in sleep. 'Not so this lord!' she continued softly, almost tenderly. 'Hummingbird tempts him to evil every day, but there's still hope for him. It's the true battlefield of his life. We must help him to choose the good.'

'How do we do that?'

'Make him stop the sacrifices!'

'But I've tried.' Malinal felt desperate. 'I've tried, but he won't listen to me. He just gets angry.'

'Keep trying, even if it angers him, and tell him you want me by your side here in the palace.'

There came a grunt from the bed and Cortés sat up, wide awake, a look of puzzlement on his face. 'How did she get here?' he asked gruffly, staring at Tozi. 'And what are you both whispering about?'

'I sent word for her to come,' Malinal said. 'Surely you don't object, my lord? You know what Tozi and I went through together.'

'I know,' he said, rubbing his tousled hair with his hand, 'and I suppose I don't object.'

'I'd like her to stay here with us now, lord – here at the palace. I fear for her safety in the city.'

Cortés nodded, looking from one woman to the other. Eventually he smiled: 'Any friend of yours, Malinal, is a friend of mine. Of course she can stay. Call Pepillo and get him to find her a suitable room.'

Pepillo, who'd filled out and grown stronger in the past months so that he now felt almost a man, sat opposite Tozi at the end of one of the long refectory tables in the dining hall, the hundreds of rough, cheerful soldiers all around them paying them no more heed than if they were flies. Night had long since fallen, but the hall was brightly lit by burning torches fixed in brackets to the walls, and slaves assigned to serve the Spaniards bustled here and there, carrying dishes of food and jugs brimming with local fruit juices.

Pepillo was happy, filled with a bubbling joy, and realised this was because he was together with Tozi again. He'd grown attached to her during the ten days of her convalescence in Cholula, when they'd been almost continually in each other's company; he'd felt hurt and bewildered when she'd gone away with Huicton to do her mysterious witchy work in Tenochtitlan, and now he was simply grateful to be able to look at her and talk to her again and know she was safe from all the dangers that surrounded her. Her strange, alluring beauty made his heart beat faster, and filled his body with unfamiliar sensations and a delicious feeling of . . . of . . . He didn't know what! Everything about this experience was new to him and he thought he might be falling in love, but had to admit he had no idea what that involved or what he was supposed to do about it. All he knew was that she was the most wonderful, captivating, brave and interesting person he'd ever met, and she was his friend and he would cheerfully die for her.

'You can read other people's thoughts, can't you?' he asked her in his increasingly fluent Nahuatl.

'Yes,' she said. 'If I want to.'

'But I suppose they have to be thinking in Nahuatl for you to do that?'

Tozi considered the question. 'No,' she answered eventually. 'I don't speak Spanish, but if I want to know what you're thinking I can. Before thoughts become language they're feelings and emotions. They have shape. They have form. They even have colour sometimes.' She smiled shyly: 'So I know you like me a lot.'

Pepillo blushed.

'But don't worry.' Tozi smiled again. 'You're my friend. I trust you. It would be rude of me to go around reading your thoughts all the time and I don't – except maybe to help you when you're struggling for a word in Nahuatl. Otherwise I don't pry. I promise.'

'Oh good.' Pepillo laughed nervously. 'That's a relief!' He lowered his voice: 'I know you can make yourself invisible,' he said, 'because I saw you do it in Cholula, just for a moment, after we showed you Acopol's head. It was amazing. You didn't even have a shadow. You disappeared.'

'Acopol took away my powers. When I saw he was really dead, that the lord called Alvarado had killed him, my powers came back.'

Although they were speaking Nahuatl and none of the Spaniards could understand them, Pepillo reduced his voice to a whisper. 'How do you do it?' he asked. 'Make yourself invisible, I mean?'

'There must be an intention,' Tozi said. 'If I want very much to be invisible, if I make that the whole focus of my being, it will happen. And I've got better at it, more able to manage it, with training and practice.'

'But I can want to be invisible and it won't happen for me,' Pepillo objected. 'No matter how much I want it or how hard I try. So why can you do it and I can't? Where does your power come from?'

'I never knew the answer to that,' Tozi said, 'until Acopol imprisoned me under the pyramid in Cholula. I met my mother there in a vision and she told me our magic came from the source of all created things and that it has flowed through the female line of my family for ten thousand years. And she told me something else . . .' Tozi paused, looking suddenly frightened. 'She told me it can be used for good or evil, to magnify darkness or light as we choose.' She stuck out her stubborn lower lip. 'I chose goodness. I chose light . . .'

Just then there came a commotion at the door of the dining chamber and a group of Mexica lords swept in, followed, without announcement, by Moctezuma himself. Seeing him, Cortés, dressed in a fine doublet and hose, at once stood up; soon all the Spaniards were on their feet. The two leaders then shook hands and Moctezuma's steward Teudile announced, with Malinal translating, that presents would now be distributed to the *tueles* and to their Tlascalan and Texcocan *tamanes*. There was a buzz of conversation that fell to a hush as an army of servants entered and went around the tables, bestowing bundles of fine cotton clothing and two loads of cloaks on every common soldier – Spaniards and Indians alike, though the latter had been referred to by the demeaning word that meant 'bearers' – while each of the captains, Shikotenka amongst them, received gifts of heavy gold chains and three loads of cloaks of rich featherwork.

'Moctezuma seems so gentle,' Pepillo whispered to Tozi, 'and so generous. A real prince! Seeing him like this it's hard to believe all the stories of his cruelty.'

The corners of the girl's mouth turned down in an expression of extreme displeasure. 'I know the stories are true,' Pepillo added hastily. 'I'm just saying appearances can be deceptive.'

'You should see him as I have seen him,' Tozi said, 'when he's covered from head to foot in blood. Then he can't disguise the monster he really is.'

After the presents were distributed, the Mexica ruler asked if all the Spaniards were brothers and vassals of that great king across the ocean of whom Cortés had informed him so often through messengers.

'They are indeed brothers in love and friendship,' Cortés replied, 'persons of distinction and servants of our great king and lord.'

Moctezuma then asked for the names of the principal Spanish captains and the positions they occupied in Cortés's army, and one of the court artists, working with surprising accuracy and speed, made lifelike sketches of Cortés himself, Alvarado, Velázquez de Léon, Olid, Ordaz, Sandoval, Davila and others.

More pious speeches followed, in which Cortés explained that his lord, Don Carlos, Holy Roman Emperor and King of Spain, had sent him to this land with one purpose above all others, and that was to beg Moctezuma, about whom he knew everything, to become a Christian, so that his soul and those of all his vassals might be saved. In the coming days, he said, he would explain how this could be, and tell of the nature of the one true God, and how he should be worshipped, and also many other good things, excellent to know, which would profit Moctezuma and his people greatly.

When he had heard all this out, a grave expression on his face, Moctezuma rose and took Cortés by the hand and led him towards the adjoining audience chamber, beckoning Malinal. Cortés signalled for Pepillo to follow.

Other than that evasive movement of his eyes on the causeway that morning, Moctezuma had done nothing to suggest that the last time he'd met Malinal she had worn the paper garments of humiliation and he had held the obsidian knife of sacrifice in his hands. Indeed he honoured her – they all did! – by insisting on referring to Cortés not by his own name but as Malinche, literally 'the master of Malinal'.

Cortés and Moctezuma were now seated face to face on the two imposing thrones at the centre of the great audience chamber. Malinal had drawn up a stool at Cortés's knee, Pepillo stood to the side ready to assist her with the finer points of Castilian. As in the dining hall, torches made the room bright, and Malinal saw the faces of the two leaders clearly. Cortés's expression was frank, eager, confident, formally respectful, yet with a thinly veiled element of challenge and mockery. Moctezuma, whose name actually meant 'angry lord', did indeed look serious and severe. When you probed deeper, however, his slippery eyes, a certain weakness of his chin and the faintest tremor of his upper lip gave the game away. Although he had grown used to holding the lives of millions in his hands, the Mexica leader was deeply unsure of himself. Cortés, who was an excellent reader of men, had understood this vulnerability before they'd ever met and would be poised to exploit it tonight in every way he could.

'Malinche,' Moctezuma began, as though all the talk in the dining hall had never occurred, 'if I begged you heretofore not to come to Tenochtitlan, it was because I and my people were afraid of you, for you frightened us with your wild beards, and brought animals that swallow men, and we believed you had descended from heaven, and could call down the lightning and thunder, striking dead whomever you pleased. So what say you, Malinche – are you a god or a man?'

'I say what I have always said when your emissaries have asked me this question,' Cortés replied. 'I am a man of flesh and blood – as you are – and I serve my master Don Carlos, King of Spain, who reigns across the sea, of whom I spoke to you just now, and who is also a man of flesh and blood. It is he who has sent me to you.'

'And this is the truth, Malinche? You are not deceiving me? You have not come down from heaven?'

'I am not deceiving you, great Moctezuma. I am a man, mortal and substantial just as you are, and I have come here not from heaven but from a land called Spain that lies far away to the east, across the great ocean, in the direction of the rising sun.'

Moctezuma fell silent for a long while, his mobile, sensitive face seeming to reflect some inner turmoil. 'According to our traditions and histories,' he said eventually, 'the father of our nation, the divine Quetzalcoatl, fled to a land across the ocean long ages ago when our people wickedly drove him out, but he promised that he or his descendants would one day return. In the meantime my ancestors and I have ruled unworthily in his name, but we have always held that Quetzalcoatl himself, or god-like men descended from him who would be armed as you are, white of skin as you are, bearded as you are, would come and conquer us here and be our lords and take us again as his vassals. If you say you are not a god then I believe you, but because of the place from which you claim to come, namely from where the sun rises, and the things you tell us of the great king who sent you here, I believe and am certain that he is our natural lord, especially as you say he already knows everything about us.'

'Good,' Cortés said to Malinal, when she and Pepillo had translated these words. 'Let's do everything we can to encourage this notion of his that King Carlos is the lord whose return they've been expecting. Even better, let's see if we can get him to make some sort of formal statement swearing loyalty to the king, agreeing to be his vassal and accepting me as his envoy and representative here.'

'When we were in Tlascala,' Malinal remembered, 'Teudile told us Moctezuma was ready to do that.'

'I know, but I want to hear it from his own mouth in his own words. Go ahead and put the question to him. Ask him outright.'

Malinal's mind worked quickly, finding the right form of words. 'The lord Malinche,' she said to Moctezuma in Nahuatl, 'is happy you recognise his king as the natural lord of this land, descended from Quetzalcoatl with the divine right to rule here, and he asks for your formal pledge of vassalage to be given to him as deputy and envoy of his king.'

To her surprise Moctezuma immediately and easily – perhaps too easily – agreed. 'Nothing could please me more,' he told Cortés solemnly, 'than to be the vassal of your great king across the ocean, as I have already sent to you several times to say. I pledge my fealty to him and accept you as his delegate. Be assured also that I and all my people will obey you and hold you as our lord in place of that great sovereign, and that in all the land that lies in my domain, you may command as you will, for you shall be obeyed, and all that we own is for you to dispose of as you choose. Thus you are in your own country and your own house.'

Cortés beamed with pleasure and exclaimed, 'We've got him!' as Malinal gave the translation. Seeing her moment, her heart beating fast, she added in Spanish: 'Now would be the right time to urge the bastard to abandon the sacrifices he's planning.'

Cortés's face clouded over: 'Don't be a fool,' he said. 'That'll push him too far and undo all the good we've just done ourselves. I've told you not to press me on this, Malinal.' His expression changed again and he favoured Moctezuma with a smile. 'I will talk to him about our faith, though, some soft words, just to plant the seed.' He then launched into one of his familiar harangues about Christianity, in which, he said, as he had hinted earlier in the dining hall, it was his particular duty to instruct the Mexica leader. He hoped in due course, preferably sooner rather than later, that Moctezuma would come to understand and accept the doctrines of the only true religion on earth, and abandon his addiction to idols which were nothing more than manifestations of the devil and were leading him and all his people straight to hell.

Malinal had noticed over the past months that once Cortés got launched on this subject he often went much further than other gentler souls would have wished or advised. The good Father Olmedo, for example, frequently urged him not to be overhasty in his efforts at conversion, and to avoid unnecessarily offending the Indians. None of the peoples they had encountered, even the compliant Totonacs, had liked it or remained calm when first told their cherished and revered gods were in fact demons, and there was no reason to suppose Moctezuma would be any different.

Since Cortés could expect the Mexica leader to be offended, perhaps even outraged by what he was saying, Malinal put very little of the homily about Christianity into Nahuatl. Aware that Pepillo was listening, and trusting he would keep this manipulation secret, she had Cortés say instead that he had seen the thousands of young girls imprisoned in the fattening pens around the sacred plaza, knew these were victims awaiting sacrifice to the demon Huitzilopochtli, and required not only that they be set free, but that from this day forth no further sacrifices should be carried out anywhere in the Mexica empire.

Now it was the turn of Moctezuma's face to darken. 'The lord Malinche goes too far,' he said, 'and touches on matters of which he has no right to speak.'

'What's he saying?' Cortés asked. 'He looks angry.'

'He says you have no right to insult his gods.'

'Tell him I do have that right! He just accepted he's a vassal of the Spanish Crown. King Carlos absolutely requires his vassals in foreign lands to abjure the worship of devils and make good Christians of themselves!'

'You have agreed,' Malinal rebuked Moctezuma, 'to be the vassal of that great lord of the land where the sun rises, King Carlos, who, like his ancestor the divine Quetzalcoatl, forbids and denounces the sacrifice of humans. The lord Malinche, whom you have promised to obey, reminds you that the divine Quetzalcoatl ordered the people of this land to sacrifice only fruits and flowers, and requires you to do the same.'

The Great Speaker's expression was difficult to read. The anger was still there but something else had joined it as well. Could it be fear? Was it perhaps foreboding? Was it dismay? 'I will consider what has been requested of me,' he said, 'and I will take counsel with my god, for I have not forgotten – ' and now, for the first time, Malinal felt Moctezuma's eyes directly engage with hers – 'that it was Hummingbird himself who ordered you freed from the altar of sacrifice when last we met.'

His eyes slid away from her again and settled back on Cortés. 'The lord Malinche has suffered fatigue,' he said, his voice oddly flat and with a new undertone of menace. 'He has endured weariness, his journey has tired him. He should rest.' Then, with a rustle of robes, he rose to his feet, gathered his dignity about him, and strode towards the door.

'Oh dear,' said Cortés with a contemptuous grin. 'Have I offended the great Mucktey?'

Chapter Three

❖

9 November 1519–12 November 1519

The next morning, Monday 9 November, since Moctezuma had done him the honour of visiting him the day before, Cortés decided it would be appropriate to return the courtesy, and took a stroll across the sacred plaza to pay a call on Moctezuma. With him were his principal officers, Alvarado, Davila, Velázquez de Léon, Olid, Ordaz and Sandoval. The latter had been doing a captain's work and accepting a captain's responsibilities for months, but Cortés had only officially confirmed him in his new rank the previous evening. The solid and reliable Bernal Díaz, raised at the same time from ensign to lieutenant, was also in the party, together with Mibiercas and La Serna, both now ensigns. Lastly, for good measure, Cortés brought along his loyal sergeant García Brabo, Father Olmedo to represent the Church, Pepillo to take notes and assist with translation, and the indispensable Malinal, who shuddered visibly as their route took them past the fattening pen in the northwest corner of the plaza, where she and Tozi had been imprisoned, and thence past the northern stairway of the great pyramid, which she told him held terrible memories for her.

Moctezuma's palace occupied the northeastern corner of the plaza and extended southward as far as the eastern gates. An edifice of enormous size, it covered a much larger ground area than the palace of Axayacatl in which the conquistadors were housed, rose to two storeys and was built of mixed blocks of alabaster, jasper and red-veined black marble, decorated with gigantic images of eagles and panthers carved in high relief. Over the centre of the entrance portico was a symbol of an eagle holding a panther in its claws – the personal arms or device, Malinal explained, of Moctezuma himself. Squads of Mexica knights clad once again as eagles and panthers, and wearing fearsome helmets of painted wood made to resemble the heads of those creatures, were on duty.

52

It seemed the Spaniards were expected, for they were at once ushered inside and provided with an escort of four highborn officials dressed in white robes with scarlet and blue embroidery. These grandees then led them through a bewildering series of corridors, halls and gracious, verdant courtyards, open to the sky, in which crowds of nobles, minor chieftains and wealthy merchants loitered by bubbling fountains of crystal-clear water. Some, Malinal said, sought the favour of Moctezuma in legal judgments, others were here to petition for grants of land or commercial monopolies, and others waited patiently to conduct business with the many high state functionaries, government ministers, treasurers and accountants who had their seats here. Indeed, she explained, the sprawling ground floor of the palace was where all the administration of the empire was done, boasting more than a hundred large apartments serving as offices, but also chapels, kitchens, rooms for the families of senior staff, a vast armoury stocked with spears, bows and obsidian-edged wooden broadswords, and the studios of potters, goldsmiths, feather-workers and other craftsmen, whose responsibility it was to produce state regalia and furnishings.

Moctezuma's personal residence, his dining chamber, the residences of his wives and concubines, the apartments used from time to time by other members of the royal family, and a series of immense audience chambers and meeting halls, occupied the entire second storey, to which the Spaniards now ascended by means of a gracefully curved mahogany stairway. Here an air of spectacular opulence reigned, with intricately carved ceilings of fragrant wood overhead; floors strewn with rushes or carpeted with rabbit skins and in some cases feathers; walls decorated with brilliantly coloured cotton and ravishing feather draperies made to resemble birds, insects and flowers, and the smoke of incense rising everywhere from glowing thuribles, diffusing exotic perfumes throughout the palace.

'I keep asking myself if I'm dreaming,' Díaz said as they traversed a long corridor, its walls painted with beautiful landscapes. 'After the islands, I expected nothing but savagery in the New Lands, but these Mexica live like sultans . . .'

'And this is more like a sultan's harem than any palace I've ever seen,' Velázquez de Léon added, peering through an open doorway at a crowd of nubile, scantily dressed women lounging on cushions, who blushed and shrieked as the bearded Spaniards strode by, armour and swords clanking.

Eventually they were led into an antechamber, where the Mexica officials who'd guided them through the maze took off their sandals and covered their costly robes with coarse, maguey-fibre mantles that were hanging there. Cortés raised an eyebrow to Malinal: 'Why are they doing that?' he asked.

'They're getting ready to take us into Moctezuma,' Malinal said. 'Bare feet and maguey fibre are the marks of commoners. The highest nobles have to dress like this when they go before the emperor. Only members of the royal family can keep their finery on, but even they have to go barefoot.'

'I'll be damned if I'll put on peasants' clothes for that monkey,' scoffed Alvarado.

'And I won't take my boots off for him,' said Cortés. 'None of us will.'

Malinal spoke briefly to the officials. 'You won't have to,' she said. 'Moctezuma left word that you're all exempt.' She reached out for a mantle. 'I have to wear the maguey fibre though.'

'No!' said Cortés, surprised by how strongly he felt about this. 'You don't! That's a fine Valencia dress I've given you and you'll go in as you are.'

'Very well, my lord,' said Malinal with a small bow of her head. 'I suspect the emperor won't like it though.'

In the event Moctezuma, whom they found enthroned in his audience chamber with Cuitláhuac standing at his shoulder, made no issue about Malinal's clothing. Indeed, despite his show of anger the night before, he seemed in high good humour. He greeted the Spaniards affably, asking after their health and whether they were comfortable in the accommodations he had provided for them.

Cortés answered that they were more than satisfied, thanked the emperor for his hospitality, and asked permission to address him further on matters of religion.

'I have heard Malinche's views on human sacrifice,' Moctezuma said primly to Malinal, 'and told him I will give thought to his words. He must be patient.'

Her heart racing at the possible consequences of her subterfuge and the tangle of deceit and misdirection it was leading her into, she replied that her master wished to speak on other matters today.

'Very well,' said Moctezuma. 'He may proceed.'

Cortés then launched into a long and abstruse theological sermon covering favourite topics of his, such as the Trinity, the Virgin Birth, the Incarnation and the Atonement. Though she had heard his views on these subjects often enough, they taxed Malinal's powers of interpretation to the limit, making her very glad of Pepillo's help, provoking cavernous yawns from Alvarado and Velázquez de Léon and failing to persuade Moctezuma. 'My lord Malinche,' he said to Cortés, 'these arguments of yours about the three gods, the god who impregnated a mortal woman and the sacrifice of the god-man you call Christ have been familiar to me for some time. I've had reports of them from the ambassadors I've sent to you on your journey, and I've been told what you have preached in the towns you've passed through. But we have worshipped our own gods here from the beginning and we are very happy with them and know them to be good. No doubt yours are good also, but do not trouble to tell us any more about them at present.'

Undaunted, Cortés went on to inform the Mexica leader of the Christian view of the Creation of the world, related the stories of Adam and Eve, the Garden of Eden and the Fall of Man and spoke of the role of Satan, 'that great antagonist' in these matters. Warming to his theme he proclaimed that the idols the Mexica worshipped were not 'good' and not even 'gods' but merely disguised forms of Satan. This was dangerous territory, but since Malinal had not translated a word of Cortés's comments on the devil at the previous meeting, preferring to keep the focus on human sacrifice, she did so now.

'You are misinformed, Malinche,' Moctezuma replied with a frown. 'I have told you already that our gods are good. They have nothing to do with this Satan of yours.'

'They have everything to do with Satan!' Cortés responded. 'Your bloody sacrifices and revolting cannibal feasts are sufficient proof of that. Compare them for example with our pure and simple rite of mass.' Another rambling, abstract and often incomprehensible dissertation followed on the Eucharist, and the doctrine of transubstantiation, in the midst of which, as Malinal struggled to translate, Moctezuma suddenly began to laugh.

'What's Mucktey laughing at?' Cortés asked.

The Great Speaker wiped a tear from his eye. 'Malinche tries to convince me his religion is superior to ours,' he said. 'He condemns us for sacrificing humans and eating their flesh and blood. Have I understood him correctly?'

Malinal put the question to Cortés, who answered: 'Yes. Of course.'

'You have understood him correctly,' Malinal told Moctezuma.

'Yet their god, this Jesus Christ, was sacrificed by being nailed to a cross of wood and now Malinche tells me that when they go to their temples they eat the flesh and drink the blood of Christ.' The Mexica ruler laughed again, a high, repetitive braying sound. 'So I don't see,' he concluded, looking immensely pleased with himself, 'any difference between Malinche's religion and ours!'

When Malinal and Pepillo put this into Spanish, Cortés leaned forward, his face flushed. 'No!' he said. 'No! The man's deliberately misunderstanding me. We consume bread and wine in symbolic commemoration of the flesh and blood of Christ, not actual flesh and blood!'

But Moctezuma would hear no more of it. 'I grow weary,' he said. He looked at Alvarado, who was suppressing another yawn. 'And so, I think, do Malinche's captains. Let us therefore not talk further on these weighty matters today.'

It seemed Cortés was about to object, but Olmedo whispered urgently in his ear and with some obvious difficulty the caudillo restrained himself. 'Very well, Your Excellency,' he said, 'but we must return to this subject. Do you agree?'

'I agree of course,' said Moctezuma graciously. 'You may call on me here at any time. My guards will be instructed to admit you to my presence whenever you require. Meanwhile – ' a broad and generous smile – 'can I suggest you take advantage of your stay in this great city of ours to acquaint yourself with its many sights and wonders?'

Cortés allowed that this was precisely the favour he had intended to ask Moctezuma next.

'In that case,' said the Mexica ruler, 'I will appoint guides to show you everything.'

He clapped his hands and Teudile appeared from a side door and listened intently while Moctezuma told him to arrange the freedom of the city for the Spaniards. 'They may go wherever they wish,' he said. 'Nowhere is closed to them, except the temples of our gods.'

On the way out, Malinal overheard Olmedo and Cortés speaking in lowered voices. 'I've told you a hundred times,' the friar was saying, 'I don't want any forced conversions. The emperor has the mind of a scholar, not a savage. You must reach his heart through persuasion and example.'

Alvarado had also overheard and placed his hand on the hilt of his falchion. 'Persuasion and example be damned,' he said. 'I know a quicker way to get to a man's heart.'

*   *   *

Moctezuma's spies told him how eagerly Malinche and his soldiers took up his invitation to explore Tenochtitlan. A garrison of two hundred *tueles* remained behind to secure and guard their quarters in the palace of Axayacatl. The rest followed the numerous guides who had been put at their disposal and went about in groups of a dozen or so, visiting the city's many markets to barter for goods and trinkets and to acquaint themselves with the hordes of painted prostitutes who, lacking all shame, beckoned to them from street corners and doorways.

Meanwhile, following their meeting, Malinche himself spent much of the day tramping through the maze of streets south and east of the grand plaza. He seemed peculiarly interested in wells, of which there were very few, and also asked to be taken out for an excursion on Lake Texcoco in one of Moctezuma's large royal canoes. It was noted that in addition to the woman Malinal, and several officers, the page Pepillo went everywhere with Malinche, who kept him busy taking notes and making sketches. Finally, when the canoe docked shortly after sunset, Malinche and his entourage returned to their quarters in the palace of Axayacatl, closing and barring the gates behind them.

After hearing the spies' reports, Moctezuma felt his confidence growing. From the *tueles*' appetites and behaviour it was becoming increasingly obvious that they were men, afflicted by human frailties, and might prove much easier to defeat than he had expected. Looking back on the morning's meeting he was also pleased with the way he had defended the name of the Mexica gods, got the better of Malinche in their argument, and demonstrated the hypocrisy of his much-vaunted 'Christian' religion, which high-handedly condemned human sacrifice and cannibalism while being based on precisely these things.

All in all, when he retired to his chambers that evening, Moctezuma was more relaxed and sure of himself than he had been for a long while. Visited by two of his concubines, he achieved a prodigious erection as he contemplated the thousands of extra troops who were filing silently into the city under cover of darkness and taking up concealed positions in noble houses near the grand plaza, ready for the surprise attack on the *tueles* that he planned to coincide with the first day of the great sacrifices in honour of Hummingbird.

The next morning Malinche, with his usual group of companions and the infernal Malinal, returned to the palace, requesting yet another meeting. Moctezuma was taking his breakfast, a time at which he normally refused to be disturbed, but since it was essential to keep the Spaniards mired in a false sense of security, complacent in their power and suspecting nothing, he at once invited them to join him. Again he honoured them by waiving the requirement for them to wear commoners' overclothes and take their footwear off in his presence, and continued to refer to them to their faces as '*tueles*'. They were men and, what was more, their stink told him they were men who did not know the concept of a bath, but they had formidable skills and weapons and should not be underestimated. Until the moment when his forces burst from hiding and destroyed them utterly, it served his purpose for these bandits to think him such a fool that he would persist in believing they were gods even while they themselves never actually claimed to be anything other than men.

So he sat and joked with them for an hour while they relished the frozen juices and chilled shellfish he shared with them, expressing amazement that his relay runners were able to bring blocks of ice still intact from the mountains, and shrimps and lobsters still alive from the ocean to his table, in less than a day and a night. He asked them polite questions about their land of Spain and about the great monarch who ruled there, answered their enquiries about his gold and silver mines, and noticed how Malinche carefully stayed away from the controversial subjects of religion and human sacrifice.

After the Spaniards had left him to join their guides for another day of sightseeing in Tenochtitlan, Teudile entered the dining room. 'Sire,' he said. There was a ghastly smile on his corpselike face. 'A runner has arrived bringing tidings from General Qualpopoca!'

Qualpopoca! This must be news of the good general's manoeuvres at the coast, designed to punish the *tueles* who had remained there when Cortés had marched inland. Moctezuma could barely restrain himself: 'Well then,' he exclaimed, 'spit it out, man!'

With a flourish Teudile reached into the flared sleeve of his star-spangled gown, produced a leather-bound codex, unfolded the broadsheet it contained and placed it before Moctezuma.

The news was better than good. It was by far the best news in what had so far been a dismal year!

Feasting his eyes on the mixture of pictographs and painted images, sometimes giggling as he read passages aloud to Teudile, Moctezuma saw immediately that his strategy in sending Qualpopoca to the coast with four regiments to chastise the Totonacs of Cempoala for non-payment of tribute had worked perfectly. Just as he'd anticipated, the Spaniards had responded to appeals from the hard-pressed Cempoalans by sending out a relief column from the town they'd built and garrisoned near Huitztlan. Consisting of fifty Spanish foot soldiers, two large fire-serpents and two deer-riders, and supported by some ten thousand Huitztlan Totonacs, the column had been outnumbered and outmatched by Qualpopoca's thirty-two thousand seasoned Mexica warriors. The upshot was that the Totonacs had deserted in the heat of the battle and the Spaniards themselves had been forced into a disorderly retreat, during which six of their number had been killed and two captured and sacrificed.

Better still, it turned out that one of the sacrificed prisoners was none other than the commander of the Spanish garrison!

Flushed with success, Qualpopoca was on his way back to Tenochtitlan at a forced march to present the commander's head to Moctezuma. He could not match the speed of the relay runners, but in two more days he should reach the capital.

'You see, Teudile!' Moctezuma crowed. 'This proves we can beat them! When General Qualpopoca arrives I'll put him in charge of the forces we've assembled to destroy the Spaniards here. Meanwhile – ' he lowered his voice – 'Malinche must learn nothing about what's happened on the coast, and we must do nothing to raise his suspicions. We comply with his every wish! Do you understand?'

'I understand, lord. But what of his wish for us to abandon our gods and desist from human sacrifice?'

'Never, Teudile! Not while my heart beats in my chest! But we'll continue to mislead him, appear to give serious thought to what he has to say, take offence sometimes and then seem to reconsider, seeking all the while to delay, to keep him unawares until we're ready to strike. How many of our warriors are inside the city now?'

'More than fifty thousand already, lord. Another ten thousand will enter tonight. In four days we will have the full hundred thousand.'

'Good,' said Moctezuma grimly. 'It will be enough.'

He dismissed Teudile and stood by the window, gazing out across the plaza to the palace of Axayacatl, where a dozen Spaniards in their shining metal armour loitered by the entrance portico. They were relaxed, laughing at something, but even taking their ease like this Moctezuma had to admit they looked dangerous – and confident. Very confident.

Now their garrison on the coast had been attacked and the commander killed, he realised, it was too late to turn back.

A worm of doubt gnawed at his bowels.

* * *

After taking breakfast with Moctezuma at his palace on the morning of Tuesday 10 November, Cortés, with Malinal and Pepillo at his side, set out to explore areas north of the grand plaza that they had not had time to visit the day before. Sandoval, Davila and Bernal Díaz accompanied them under the guidance of royal escorts.

The layout of the city was defined by the original island, roughly rectangular in shape, four miles in length from north to south and three miles in width from east to west, on which it had been founded some two centuries earlier. The island had at first been the home of two separate Mexica city states, Tenochtitlan in its southern two-thirds and Tlatelolco in its northern third; however, it seemed the former had overcome and subjugated the latter some fifty years before. Each continued to maintain a somewhat separate national character, but from a military point of view Cortés quickly realised he could regard them as a single unit under the governance of Moctezuma with a total combined population, which might at any point be raised in enmity against the Spaniards, of somewhere close to five hundred thousand.

Although there were many markets in Tenochtitlan itself, the largest, about half a mile north of Moctezuma's palace, was in the quarter still known as Tlatelolco where an arcaded emporium twice the size of the great square at Salamanca catered to all the diverse needs of the immense city. The vast square was protected from the sun by a network of colourful awnings and, as the royal escorts forced a way for Cortés and his party through the crowded, noisy, well-shaded alleys dividing the stalls, he saw that each trade and merchandise had its own place reserved for it which, Malinal explained, no one else could take or occupy.

Here were slavers, with many male and female prisoners on sale. Some of the wretched captives, reminding Cortés of the plot Moctezuma had hatched against him in Cholula, were attached to long poles by means of collars round their necks, but others were left free and showed no inclination to abscond.

Here were dealers in gold and silver bullion, precious stones, feathers, cloaks and embroidered goods. Here were silversmiths and goldsmiths offering the fruits of their intricate labours – an octagonal plate, half of gold, half of silver, joined in the casting, a fish with hundreds of tiny silver scales and another of gold, a parrot of silver with moving tongue, head and wings, a monkey of gold with moving feet and head, holding a distaff in its hands so naturally that it seemed to be spinning. Here were feather-workers, masters of their craft, making butterflies, animals, miniature trees, flowers, herbs and rocks – all done with feathers. Here were those who traded in the skins of exotic animals. Here sisal cloth, ropes and sandals were on display, here coarse maguey-fibre cloth, and here fine cottons and fabrics manufactured from twisted threads.

One large area, a gorgeous splash of colour, was given over exclusively to birds – tame birds as household pets, birds of prey for hunting, others prized for their feathers – all kept in cages and sending up a tremendous racket of song.

Here was the section of the market devoted to fresh foods – kidney beans and sage, a vast range of aromatic herbs and spices, red and green chillies, many different kinds of vegetables and fruits, live turkeys and other fowl, rabbits, deer, ducks and dogs.

In another section women sold cooked food – little cakes, tortillas, honey, honey paste, meats and fish baked or fried in batter, tripe, pies and omelettes made from the eggs of many different kinds of birds.

Here was a line of stalls dealing exclusively with sawn and prepared timbers, boards, cradles, beams, blocks and benches. Nearby one could buy building materials – even complete palm-leaf roofs for houses. Elsewhere all kinds of pottery from big water jars to little jugs were being offered for sale. Rather surprisingly, there was even a section of the market that offered vast loads of human excrement – in great demand, Malinal said, for the curing of animal skins.

It seemed the Mexica made scant use of money. Other than coca beans, little T-shaped lengths of tin and even bundles of cloaks that were used to balance some exchanges, almost all the buying and selling was done by barter – a turkey for a sheaf of maize, a mantle for a bag of salt, and so on and so forth. Remarkably, despite the huge numbers of people involved, perfect order reigned throughout the whole vast market.

'Everyone's too afraid of Moctezuma to cause any serious trouble,' Malinal explained. She pointed to patrols of state officials, whose job it was to keep the peace, collect taxes and see no false measures were used, and to a well-shaded central dais where three judges sat to make instant decisions on any disputes. 'If someone tries to sell stolen goods, they'll have him executed on the spot, unless he gives up the person he bought them from. If anyone gives short weight he's fined and his measures are broken.'

Although Cortés put on the manner of a sightseer, his exploration of Tenochtitlan was primarily a military reconnaissance. If attacked by overwhelming numbers, he might need to get his men out of the island metropolis quickly, and to this end he was obliged to understand its layout and principal points of ingress and egress. Likewise if he was expelled and wished afterwards to retake Tenochtitlan by force, what were its main strengths and weaknesses and how might it most effectively be besieged?

The city was accessed from the mainland by three principal causeways. The first, entering from the south, Cortés had already studied when he had marched his army from Iztapalapa on 8 November, and again yesterday, 9 November, when he'd explored the southern quarter. Since the causeway was fully six miles in length, with numerous bridges, it posed nightmarish logistical challenges as an evacuation route and could effectively be discounted. The second, a mile or so north of the Tlatelolco market led to Azcapotzalco, with a spur going to Tepayacac. It was shorter – about four miles in length – but to reach it the Spaniards would first have to fight their way through the crowded narrow streets of the northern quarter, where every flat-roofed house would become a fortress from which missiles could be rained down on them.

It followed that the single viable escape route was the western causeway leading to Tacuba, which Malinal and Tozi had also used when they had fled the city many months earlier. Only two miles in length, it had the added advantage of opening less than half a mile from the Spanish residence in the palace of Axayacatl. Even so, like all the others, the Mexica could quickly transform it into a killing ground by the simple expedient of removing its series of wooden bridges to prevent escape, and swarming it from all sides with waterborne forces in massed canoes.

The same factors that made Tenochtitlan difficult to escape would also make it difficult to attack, should Cortés be obliged at some future date to besiege it. First and foremost, it would be almost impossible to starve the inhabitants out, even if the causeways were closed, because supplies could always be brought into them by canoe; indeed, even in peacetime, it was by water rather than by road that most produce reached the markets. The only way a besieging army could counter this would be to control Lake Texcoco itself, but to do that Cortés calculated he would need a fleet of at least four brigantines – a difficult proposition since the lake was two hundred miles from the sea and he had, besides, destroyed all but one of his expedition's ships!

On the positive side the lake was salt, its waters brackish, and Cortés quickly established that Tenochtitlan had very few freshwater wells – certainly not enough to supply even a fraction of the needs of its half million citizens. With their usual ingenuity and talent for engineering, the Mexica had solved this problem by piping huge quantities of potable water into the city from the mainland by means of a remarkable pair of aqueducts more than four miles long, which passed over the western quarter of the lake on stilts from the Chapultepec springs a few miles north of Tacuba.

On Wednesday 11 November, after what was becoming a regular morning visit to Moctezuma in his palace, Cortés rode out on horseback with Malinal, Alvarado, Sandoval and Ordaz to reconnoitre the springs. He found them, as he had expected, well defended by a permanent garrison of twelve thousand seasoned Mexica troops. Should he ever be obliged to mount a siege, therefore, he resolved that clearing out this garrison would be his first objective, followed by the destruction of the aqueducts at source.

But, Cortés reasoned, all such extreme measures could be avoided without further bloodshed if he could simply pull off the outrageous *coup de main* he'd dreamed up during the long march to Tenochtitlan – which was to capture Moctezuma, hold him hostage and govern his city, his empire and all his armies through him. The idea of seizing the Mexica ruler in his own palace, under the noses of his own bodyguard, in the heart of his own capital, and using him as a puppet, had at first seemed so insane that Cortés had never broached it with his captains, though he had discussed it with Malinal several times; but now, as the days went by and he came to understand what a hard nut Tenochtitlan might prove to crack, it began to appeal to him more and more.

At the same time his visit to the market, while filling him with respect for the huge productivity of the diverse and rich hinterland that fed the Mexica capital, had enhanced his understanding of the empire's dependence on decisions taken at the centre by Moctezuma and the army of administrators working from his palace. Unlike the hydra of old, which had one body and many heads, this vast domain appeared to have many bodies – its tributary states – but only one head. It began to seem increasingly possible that if he could control the head, he really could control all the rest without a fight.

To this end, therefore, without explaining to anyone what he had in mind, Cortés made a point of paying daily courtesy calls on Moctezuma in his palace, always taking along a number of his commanders and soldiers, always fully armed and armoured, so that such visits would come to seem normal. Separately he also made a practice of sending individual officers to the palace several times a day with smaller groups of men on one pretext or another. None of this seemed to arouse the least suspicion: the Spaniards were always welcomed, never kept waiting and never disarmed, and so long as Cortés stayed off the subject of religion, Moctezuma was always obliging and friendly, offering him drinks of foaming chocolate or chilled fruit juices while they sat in the audience chamber making small talk.

In some ways, Cortés thought, Malinal was becoming like a nagging wife, even more determined, once she got the bit between her teeth, than that hell-mare Catalina he'd left behind in Cuba. But whereas Catalina nagged about many trivial things – money (she always wanted more), the size and quality of her wardrobe (never big or good enough), Cortés's treatment of her swinish uncle Diego (he deserved gratitude and respect), the need for a new house, the need to return to court in Spain, the need for more slaves and servants, etc, etc – Malinal only nagged about one big thing. While continuing to perform brilliantly, indeed indispensably, as an interpreter, and continuing to offer bedroom pleasures that would have been quite inconceivable to the dull and unimaginative Catalina, Malinal never ceased to remind Cortés of the looming holocaust of human sacrifices to honour the birthday of the foul demon Hummingbird, whom Moctezuma worshipped as a god. The sacrifices were scheduled to begin in Tenochtitlan at dawn on Monday 16 November, four days before the start of the Mexica month of Panquetzaliztli.

On Thursday 12 November, Malinal took up the cudgels again as she and Cortés prepared for their regular morning visit to the palace. Standing naked, her gorgeous rump turned alluringly towards him, she suddenly asked, 'What is the meaning of the word "hypocrite", Hernán?'

He sensed a trap. 'It means,' he said, 'a person who pretends to have moral beliefs or principles he doesn't actually possess . . .'

'Someone who says one thing but does another?'

'Yes . . .'

'Then I suppose you are a hypocrite, Hernán. Everywhere you say human sacrifice is bad, human sacrifice is evil, you even freed victims from their cages in Cempoala and Tlascala, yet you do nothing about the biggest sacrifice of all that Moctezuma will make here.'

Cortés, who was pulling on his hose and doublet, sat down on the bed. 'Please, Malinal, we've been through this often enough and you know my answer. I'd like to intervene but the time is not ripe—'

64

'The excuse of a hypocrite! You're very good at the blah, blah about your Christian virtues – you do small, easy things quickly – but when you face a real challenge you suddenly want more time.'

Cortés saw she was crying – the typical trick of a woman trying to wear a man down, except he'd never seen Malinal cry before. He sighed in exasperation. 'In this case it's true,' he said. 'I do need more time. Moctezuma is becoming comfortable around us and we'll soon be able to take him unawares. But not yet! I can't risk it yet. We could lose everything we've worked for if I spring the trap too early.'

'Ten thousand lives will be lost if you don't!' she shouted.

First tears, now anger – and with him! Something Malinal had never shown before. But Cortés coldly ignored her. 'Get ready,' he said. 'We have work to do.'

His own anger was bubbling, but he kept it in check, in part because of the troubling dream that had afflicted him while they slept. He had not dreamed of Saint Peter since 7 November in Iztapalapa, but last night, 11 November, the Holy Father had returned to him again and in the same setting on top of the great pyramid of Tenochtitlan, a place Cortés knew only in his imagination, for Moctezuma had not yet permitted him to visit it. As before, the saint spoke sternly of the need for patience in the conquest of the city, urging Cortés not to meddle in the great holocaust that would begin on 16 November, but to make his move soon afterwards, even suggesting that the celebrations the Mexica would indulge in on 20 November, the last day of the sacrifices and the birthday of Hummingbird, might be the ideal moment to strike.

As before, Cortés sought confirmation: 'So I am to stand by, Holiness, and let the sacrifices proceed? Is this not unworthy of a good Christian and a soldier of God?'

And Saint Peter replied with the exact form of words he had used the last time: 'Unworthy, perhaps, but necessary.' Inspiring in Cortés a haunting sense of déjà vu, the saint then began to add: 'It is ultimate victory you seek here, and with it the cessation of all human sacrifice forever,' when another figure appeared on the summit of the great pyramid. This being, it seemed to Cortés, might be an angel, for she was winged and held in her hands a great shining sword. Yet her features were not those of angels he was familiar with from the paintings of Botticelli or Verrocchio, but of a young Indian girl, and her hair was not a mass of golden curls but hung black and straight to her shoulders. Indeed, this intruder who approached so fiercely, whirling her sword, had the likeness of Malinal's friend Tozi! And now, with a great shout, she came between Cortés and Saint Peter and drove the Holy Father back!

No angel this! The apparition, perhaps even Tozi herself, must be a demon in angelic guise. And surely no demon, however subtle, could possibly overthrow the rock on whom Christ built his Church, against whom even the utmost powers of hell could not prevail? Firm in his belief in the depths of his dream, Cortés felt first surprise, and then dismay, as the demon girl continued her advance unchecked and the saint's retreat became a rout. Expecting at any moment to see the onslaught stopped, the demon crushed and withered, consumed by righteous flames, surprise was replaced by heart-pounding fear, amazement and doubt as the saint took three further stumbling steps backwards, roaring incoherently now, his flesh rippling as though some great beast within were struggling to break free, his strong, upright, soldierly posture becoming horribly slouched and misshapen, his features coarsening, eyes bulging and glaring, jagged fangs and tusks streaked with gore appearing in his mouth, and a necklace of dripping human hearts and hands materialising around his neck.

It was at this point, in the depths of the night, that Cortés had awakened, sweating with fear, and Malinal, now so hurt and angry as bright morning sunlight flooded into their room, had reached out in her sleep to comfort him.

Both the dream, which had disturbed him deeply, and Malinal's disappointment that he would not intervene to prevent the coming sacrifices, still preyed on Cortés's mind a little later that morning of Thursday 12 November when they crossed the grand plaza with Alvarado, Father Olmedo, Pepillo, Olid, Sandoval and Díaz, presented themselves to the guards at Moctezuma's palace and were immediately ushered upstairs to one of the several polished audience chambers. There they found the emperor in conference with Cacama, the king of Texcoco and Totoqui, king of Tacuba, his counterparts in the great Mexica triple alliance. Cuitláhuac and Teudile were also in attendance.

'Welcome!' Moctezuma said, beaming widely and breaking off his conversation.

'Do we interrupt Your Excellencies?' Cortés asked. 'We can come back later if you wish.'

'Not at all,' said Moctezuma. 'You know I'm always happy and honoured to see you, Malinche.' He waved the Spaniards over while a servant brought stools. 'Come and join us, please.'

Some moments of inconsequential conversation followed, to which Cortés paid scant attention. The problem was his dream! Try as he might, he couldn't rid himself of its lingering atmosphere and implications. That Saint Peter should stumble and falter before little Tozi! And that his appearance should change in that horrible way, coming to resemble in general form the hideous deities of the Mexica, most notably and particularly the demon Huitzilopochtli himself. What, if anything, did it mean? Cortés hoped very much it meant nothing at all – that this was one of those dreams spoken of by Penelope in the *Odyssey* as coming through the gate of sawn ivory 'to deceive men' and not one of those coming through the gate of polished horn that 'bring true issues to pass when any mortal sees them'. For surely it could not be true, as the substance of the dream had clearly hinted, that Saint Peter and the monstrous demon worshipped by the Mexica were one and the same?

Surely this must be some deceit worked by that very demon?

And yet . . . And yet . . .

What Cortés could not get out of his mind was the way 'the Holy Father' had urged him to allow the sacrifices planned by Moctezuma to proceed. It made no sense for the good Saint Peter to take such a position, even if it was sound military strategy.

'. . . the bastard Moctezuma wants to know if you would enjoy that?'

With a start, Cortés realised Malinal was speaking to him; he'd been so absorbed in his own thoughts that even the modicum of attention he'd kept on the translated words of the Mexica leader had strayed and he'd missed something – possibly something important. He flashed a broad smile at Moctezuma. 'The bastard wants to know if I'd enjoy what?' he asked Malinal, adding, 'Sorry, must have drifted off there for a moment.'

Malinal's tone was filled with loathing. 'The bastard wants to know,' she repeated, 'if you would enjoy a guided tour of the royal zoo. He claims there's nothing like it in all the world. He says he keeps in it many rare and remarkable creatures gathered from deserts, jungles, mountains and swamps in all parts of the empire. He offers to show these wonders to you personally. Now, if you so wish.'

Cortés understood the repugnance Malinal must feel and which her voice betrayed. It was indeed disgusting that Moctezuma should be allowed to sit here, boasting of his prized collection of animals like some pampered child, when he was about to offer ten thousand human hearts to the devil.

The Mexica ruler was watching him expectantly, waiting for an answer.

No doubt it was a rare privilege indeed to be guided round the royal zoo by Moctezuma himself!

'Thank the bastard for his generous offer,' Cortés replied, 'but tell him I don't want to visit his zoo today. I'd like him instead to take us to the summit of the great pyramid and show us the temple of Hummingbird. Until now he has not allowed us to see these places but, if his gods are good, as he claims, he should have nothing to hide.'

Something sparked in Malinal's eyes as she heard the question and put it into Nahuatl. Olmedo sat forward nervously, obviously scenting trouble, and the Mexica lords looked on in stunned silence.

Moctezuma stood, beckoning Teudile to follow, and the two men walked to the other end of the huge room, where they whispered to one another urgently, out of earshot. When they returned, Moctezuma had a tight, unreadable smile on his lean, nervous face. 'Very well, Malinche,' he said. 'I will grant your request. If you are ready we can go at once.'

It had been a little more than two months earlier that Tozi had first learned of Moctezuma's vile plan to sacrifice ten thousand virgin girls to Hummingbird.

She'd used her powers of invisibility to enter the fattening pens at the base of the great pyramid, where those who were to be killed awaited their fate; indeed she'd found herself within the very pen where she and Malinal and poor Coyotl had not so long before been prisoners.

But things had changed.

When Tozi was held there it had contained females of all ages and sexual status; now it was filled exclusively with young, virgin girls. Moreover, it wasn't the only pen rededicated to this purpose. Two of the four pens on the other side of the plaza, which had previously held only male prisoners, had been emptied of their former inmates and now also housed young girls.

Eavesdropping on conversations amongst the guards, Tozi had quickly discovered what was going on.

Ten thousand virgins were being stockpiled for a mass holocaust that was scheduled to begin four days before the birthday of the war god Huitzilopochtli, to proceed at the rate of two thousand five hundred victims per day, and to culminate on the birthday itself – the first day of the Mexica month of Panquetzaliztli which, as Tozi had later learned, coincided with 20 November in the Spanish calendar. The sacrifices would therefore begin on 16 November, and since today was 12 November, that meant just four days remained to persuade Cortés to prevent the murders.

What made this suddenly all the more urgent was an ancient prophecy, related to her during her stay amongst the Huichol by the shaman-priest Nakawey, which stated:

'In the time of darkness will appear the harbinger of the light. She will fight against the evil one for the future of the world. By these signs you shall recognise her. She will be an orphan born of Aztlán. She will be a witch and the daughter of a witch. She will be a protector of children. She will be offered as a sacrifice to he who stands at the left hand of the sun, but she will escape this doom.'

Nakawey, whose name meant 'Owner of Stars and Water', had encouraged her to believe that she was the 'harbinger of the light' spoken of in the prophecy. After all, he'd argued, she fulfilled all the signs. She was an orphan born of Aztlán. She was a witch and a daughter of a witch. And she had indeed been offered as a sacrifice to Huitzilopochtli, 'he who stands at the left hand of the sun', but she had escaped this doom.

Tozi had asked what the prophecy meant for her, but the single practical suggestion that Nakawey could offer was that she should 'go and protect children'. She had heeded this instruction and it had brought her back to the fattening pens of Tenochtitlan two months before. Though she had long since given up hope of ever finding her lost protégé, Coyotl, her intention had been to spirit away any children she found there, and she had already identified a little mentally defective eight-year-old girl called Miahuatl as the first she would take, before she realised that the pens now held *only* virgin girls, and that rapid progress was being made towards accumulating a total of ten thousand sacrificial victims to die for the war god's birthday.

Now, on the date the Spaniards called 12 November, cloaking herself in invisibility in a greatly changed Tenochtitlan, Tozi sought out Miahuatl again, and found her, amazingly still alive, still sweetly and innocently simple, still in the same pen in the northwest corner of the sacred plaza, and growing fat. This was not a good sign. The Mexica were fastidious in ensuring that all the victims earmarked for the forthcoming sacrifices would reach the knife in the pudgy, overfed state thought desirable to the god.

So severely retarded that her vocabulary consisted only of a handful of words, Miahuatl had never asked any questions when Tozi materialised beside her, or when she had disappeared again equally abruptly, and

Tozi had always been careful to avoid attracting attention from the other inmates. Now, after an absence of two months, the child frowned in momentary puzzlement when Tozi suddenly appeared, then beamed in recognition and reached out her arms, fingers waggling, for a hug. Tozi knelt and wrapped her in a warm embrace, kissing her on both cheeks, before producing a small, brightly painted wooden object from the pack she wore on her back. 'This is for you,' she said, 'a present.'

Miahuatl's eyes opened wide as she saw the gift – a toy figure of an Itzcuintli, the hairless Mexica dog, harnessed to a toy sledge loaded with miniature sheaves of maize. An added detail was that the Itzcuintli was holding a cob of maize in its mouth.

'Look,' said Tozi, 'you can make the dog work – see here.' As she moved the model along the ground, pulling the sledge, leaving little parallel tracks in the earth floor, Miahuatl gave a little squeal of pure joy. 'Doggy,' she said, 'name?'

'You can name him! He's yours.'

Miahuatl was on all fours now, studying the dog's little painted face, frowning and pursing her lips in concentration. Finally she giggled and said: 'Moctezuma!'

Tozi couldn't conceal her surprise. 'Moctezuma? Why would you call the nice doggy that?'

But Miahuatl didn't answer. Her span of attention was short and she was already playing with the toy, moving it around as Tozi had done, the runners etching swirling patterns into the floor.

Tozi watched her for a moment, feeling miserable and angry. There were ten thousand virgin girls, most under twelve years of age, distributed across the five pens in the sacred plaza. They would all be carefully counted as they were led out for sacrifice to Huitzilopochtli and, if by chance the final tally proved one or five or a dozen less than the ten thousand promised to the god, then additional girls would be snatched from the streets or purchased in the slave market to make up the quota.

So to save one was to condemn another, and there was only one man who could save them all. That man was Cortés, whom the Mexica called Malinche, naming him after his 'tongue' Malinal; Cortés, armoured in his fearsome Spanish power, the perceived manifestation of Quetzalcoatl, the Plumed Serpent, and still believed by many to be none other than that god himself.

Yet Malinche was no god.

Malinche was mortal!

Malinche was weak!

Malinche was tempted!

For Malinche's mind, and soul, had already been tainted by Huitzilopochtli.

Last night Tozi had visited the Spanish leader in his dreams and had shown him the truth behind his illusions. She could only hope she had reached him in time.

Hearing a commotion in the sacred plaza, she left Miahuatl to her play and slipped invisibly out of the fattening pen.

A procession of more than thirty priests and nobles was ascending the northern stairway of the great pyramid. At the front, preceded by Teudile who was holding aloft the gold wand of state, was Moctezuma, in his purple robes. Ritual required the Great Speaker to pretend he lacked the strength to make the climb unaided, and he was supported today by Cuitláhuac and Cacama. Behind, throwing off attempts to offer them similar assistance, strode Cortés and Malinal, with four of the Spanish captains all in armour, the Spanish priest Olmedo and dear, sweet Pepillo.

Transparent, free as the air, Tozi followed them.

In his father's mansion at Chapultepec on the west bank of Lake Texcoco, Guatemoc paced back and forth like a caged beast. It was maddening to be barred from Tenochtitlan at the time of his city's greatest need, when it held in its bosom the most deadly and dangerous foe it had ever known.

Yesterday, after a runner had brought him news that Malinche had crossed the Tacuba causeway, Guatemoc had broken his curfew for the second time, again disguised as a commoner, and had gone as far as the springs to see what the enemy leader was doing there. The answer had immediately become clear. In full view of his moronic royal guides, the poisonous snake was scouting Tenochtitlan's most vulnerable points before attempting to seize the city!

He would make his move any day now, Guatemoc was certain of it, yet there had been a new development that gave at least some cause for cautious optimism.

Just as Moctezuma had his spies, so Guatemoc was informed by his own network of loyal brothers in arms who brought him reports of important political and military developments. That was how he knew this morning what he'd not known yesterday, namely that Moctezuma, against all odds, appeared to have grown a backbone! Acting on orders from the Great Speaker, the newly appointed General Qualpopoca, though a pampered sycophant in Guatemoc's opinion, had somehow succeeded in luring soldiers out from the *tueles*' fort near Huitztlan on the coast, and given them a thorough beating, thus weakening the garrison there. At the same time, Guatemoc had learned, more than twelve regiments, a hundred thousand of the best fighters the Mexica could put in the field, were being secretly brought into Tenochtitlan in preparation for a devastating surprise attack on Malinche and his forces some time in the next few days. The word was that Qualpopoca, now hastening back from the coast, would be put in charge of this vital operation, at which prospect Guatemoc felt a twinge of resentment – and concern. Despite his fluke victory, Qualpopoca was a fawning backscratcher with little battlefield experience, while Malinche, whatever else might be said about him, was a hardened, cunning and utterly ruthless warrior. Though the Mexica had the numbers, the outcome of a contest between these two men was by no means a foregone conclusion.

From the roof of the palace of Axayacatl, Shikotenka, Chipahua and Tree watched with interest as the procession led by Moctezuma climbed the northern stairway of the great pyramid. Everyone looked very serious, heads bowed, pace slow and measured, until some twenty steps from the top, Malinche and Alvarado suddenly set off at a jog, overtook the rest and reached the summit neck and neck, where they clapped one another on the shoulders, laughed loudly and stood arms akimbo, taking in the view over Tlatelolco and the northern quarter of the city.

'Speaker's not going to like that,' observed Chipahua.

'Disrespectful,' said Tree.

'Probably meant to be,' offered Shikotenka. 'I reckon Malinche's looking to start a fight.'

''Bout time someone did,' said Tree. 'We've been cooped up in this trap too long.'

A fight was coming all right, building the way a thunderstorm builds, thickening the air with the threat of imminent, massive damage. Shikotenka felt it in his guts; they all did. But, unlike the Spaniards who saw as much as their royal guides were willing to show them during daylight hours, the Tlascalans were required by Moctezuma to remain within the walls of the palace of Axayacatl at all times, on the pretext their presence in the city might provoke a riot.

So, gut feelings aside, they were deaf and blind and the Spaniards not much better.

As Moctezuma reached the top of the stairway, he let go of the arms of Cuitláhuac and Cacama and addressed Cortés. 'You must be tired after such a climb,' he said through Malinal.

'My comrades and I,' Cortés replied, 'are never tired by anything.'

Moctezuma frowned, then seemed to force his features into a more friendly aspect. 'Come,' he said, 'let me show you my city. I enjoy viewing it from here.'

'Of course, sire. An honour.'

But even as the Mexica ruler began to point to places of interest in the panorama below, and Cortés responded with polite comments, his mind wandered, absorbed and puzzled by the striking sense of remembrance that had gripped him from the moment he set foot on the summit platform. Though he'd never visited it, he recognised this place – knew it absolutely – from his dreams! This was where he'd stood with Saint Peter last night and a few nights before! Here was the same glowing brazier. Here beside it, and quite unmistakable, was the same convex block of green jasper, hideously caked with dried blood, but now also showing great splashes of fresh gore that ran down its sides and lay in rivulets and thick pools across the paving slabs, proclaiming murders done this very morning. Here was the huge cylindrical drum of serpent skins. And further back, looming over everything, was the tall, dark temple of his dreams, with its crested roof, and its sinister torch-lit rooms dimly visible beyond a doorway decorated with satanic carvings.

As well as the disturbing feeling of familiarity, the implications of which he was still wrestling with, all this filled Cortés with a simmering, righteous anger, seeming to beckon to him – much, perhaps, as the money-changers' tables had beckoned to Christ – to cleanse the temple. Yet still Moctezuma's voice rattled on, rendered into Spanish in the softer and gentler tones of Malinal and Pepillo, drawing attention to the gardens of the royal palace where a series of courtyards were overgrown with luxuriant trees and plants and filled with cages, 'Look, Malinche, my zoo, where you must remind me to take you on another day. There – see! – the House of Panthers, and there the House of Serpents, there the House of Hunting Birds, and there the House of Human Monsters.'

Next Moctezuma pointed with pride to the great *coatepantli*, the so-called 'serpent wall', which defined the boundaries of the grand plaza and separated it physically from the rest of Tenochtitlan. 'Look there, Malinche, see how the whole city surrounds and protects our sacred precinct, with this pyramid and temple at its heart, as the nest of an eagle safeguards its egg. And what a city! What a wonder that delights the eye! Follow the avenues, follow the canals, see how they intersect, every one at right angles; see how all is perfection, all is geometry. See our great market of Tlatelolco, which you have visited. See my people thronging there in their gay costumes to buy and to sell. See the flowers, Malinche, blooming from every rooftop! Is it not rightly said that ours is a city of flowers? And see our wondrous lake, teeming with fish, its surface embroidered by canoes and crossed by mighty causeways. See our rich and orderly fields beyond, golden with autumn maize. And see there, Malinche – ' at this Moctezuma pointed west and east across the blue waters – 'the cities of Tacuba and Texcoco, our allies and friends. Cacama here – ' another wave of the royal hand – 'is lord of Texcoco. And there – ' an expansive gesture that took in the shores vanishing into the distance around the whole northern sector of the immense lake – 'so many other towns and villages great and small; even I cannot name every one. See our forests, Malinche. See our lofty mountains, and see our volcanoes – there Iztaccihuatl and there Popocatépetl, crowned with snow and wreathed with smoke.'

'And pray tell,' Cortés asked, when Moctezuma at last paused for breath, 'what is this?' He pointed to the curved green jasper block they stood next to, blood pooling around its base.

'Ah,' Moctezuma replied, 'that is our *techcatl* – ' Malinal, with hatred in her voice, translated the word as 'execution stone' – 'where those honoured with the flowery death offer their hearts to our god.'

'Flowery death?' Cortés asked.

'It is the name we give to the exalted death by human sacrifice,' Moctezuma replied. 'Those who die in such a way pay all their debts to the gods.'

Cortés turned to Malinal: 'I have no idea what he means by that,' he said.

'The Mexica abuse words as they abuse people,' Malinal hissed. 'There is nothing flowery or honourable about death upon this stone. It is here they will rip open the breasts of the ten thousand virgins who are to die in the four days before the birthday of the demon Huitzilopochtli. It is here their hearts will be torn out and burnt upon that brazier.'

Cortés looked again at the blood on the flagstones. 'And today?' he asked.

'They kill three or four every morning as the sun rises,' Malinal explained.

'Dear God! What madness!'

Cortés turned back to Moctezuma: 'These so-called "flowery sacrifices" of yours are simply pretty words for the cruel and horrible murder of your fellow human beings.' He cast an angry glance at the entourage of priests and nobles clustered round the Mexica ruler. 'Tell me,' he said, 'is there a man among you who wishes to be killed? Certainly not! Well then, why do you put others to death so cruelly?'

Moctezuma's response was a furious diatribe in Nahuatl to which Malinal listened tight-lipped before telling Cortés: 'He does not wish to discuss this matter, my lord. He says you and he already talked of human sacrifices yesterday and there is much for you both to think on.'

'There's nothing to think on,' said Cortés. 'The souls of these poor savages are in jeopardy and we're obliged as Christians to do all in our power to save them.' He paused and beckoned Olmedo: 'What say you, Father? Don't you agree this platform would afford a most conspicuous position for the cross of Christ? I'm minded to ask permission to plant it here.'

'It would be a good thing if it were successful,' Olmedo replied, 'but I suggest this is not the proper time to speak of it. Frankly Moctezuma doesn't look as though he's in the mood to allow further liberties.'

Cortés thought about it. He sometimes found the friar too cautious, but patience was a virtue and this was probably wise counsel. In a few more days, if all went well, he would have Moctezuma in his power; once he did he would not only put a cross here, but tear down the vile temple and replace it with a beautiful Christian church. Forcing a smile he addressed the Mexica leader again: 'Your Lordship is a great prince,' he said, 'and worthy of even better things. I and my companions have enjoyed seeing your city and, now that we stand here before the temple of your god Huitzilopochtli, will you show us his face?'

Moctezuma, who still appeared mightily vexed, seemed taken aback by the question and said he must first consult with his priests. The discussion went on for some time and became animated. 'What's happening?' Cortés whispered to Malinal.

'Namacuix is against it,' she said.

'Namacuix?'

'That sneering bastard there. He's the high priest, but the Great Speaker outranks him.'

Eventually Moctezuma was back with Cortés: 'You may go in,' he said. 'You may all go in, but kindly show respect.'

Díaz felt privileged to be in Cortés's party for the climb of the great pyramid. The filthy, gore-smeared priests and the bloody evidence of recent sacrifices on the summit were routine enough not to surprise or disturb him, the extraordinary view of Tenochtitlan took his breath away, and he listened with interest as Moctezuma pointed out the city's many wonders. He did notice clusters of men at work around a number of the bridges on the western and the northern causeways, and was just beginning to wonder what this might mean – the implications were potentially ominous – when the conversation between the two leaders, which had been affable, turned nasty without warning. Tension suddenly filled the air, somewhat diffused by Olmedo; Moctezuma went into a huddle with his priests; and a few moments later they were all led inside the temple through a doorway framed by images of devils and long curved fangs, carved in high relief, that made it look like the jaws of hell.

What came next was beyond Díaz's darkest nightmares and imaginings – far worse than anything he'd seen in any of the other blood-smeared shrines on the long journey through Mexico.

It started with the hideous infernal smell of the place, a stench of putrid blood and flesh more intolerable than that of the filthiest slaughterhouses of Castile. Then, as his eyes adjusted to the light of the flickering torches that lit the first of the two rooms, Díaz saw each wall was lined to the ceiling with racks of long, horizontal poles on which, in neat rows, were spitted hundreds of human heads. Some were the heads of men, some of women, some of children. Some were freshly severed and still dripping blood, their eyes reflecting the flames and seeming half alive, but others were already starting to rot, the flesh writhing with maggots and oozing away from the bone.

'They take them away to make room for more when the racks are full,' Malinal was telling Cortés. 'They're moved to the House of Darkness on the east side of the grand plaza. You haven't seen it yet, but there are tens of thousands of skulls in there, piled up in a great mound.'

Cortés had his hand over his nose and said nothing as they stepped through another doorway into the second chamber. Here, as well as flickering torches set in brackets in the walls, which were splashed and caked with gore, a tier of high, narrow windows admitted shafts of light, revealing a coven of priests whose blood-clotted robes and hair made them seem the very ministers of Satan. Muttering their evil spells, they hunched protectively by the idol that crouched, squat and massive, at the far end of the room behind a glowing brazier.

Ah! Jesu! This idol, wreathed in shadows, glittering with jewels, was a terrible thing to behold. Carved from a block of red granite shot through with veins of dark quartz, it was so thick-bodied it created an illusion of shortness but, as Díaz approached it, walking behind Cortés, he realised it towered over both of them, tall as a bear, monstrous and bestial, resembling in part a man and in part some hideous plumed lizard or crocodile, its scales and feathers finished in jade and bedecked with gold and jewels, its gaping maw stuffed with horned tusks and keen-edged fangs, its eyes beads of gleaming obsidian. The idol's feet were adorned with fans of iridescent hummingbird feathers. In its right fist, which was fearsomely clawed, it gripped a golden bow, and in its left a dozen golden arrows. About its midriff was coiled a serpent, thick as a warrior's thigh, crafted from ropes of pearls and gemstones. Around the idol's neck, like some hellish shambles, hung a garland of freshly butchered human hearts and hands, interspersed with skulls, while three more hearts lay smoking on the brazier before it.

Cortés, who only rarely revealed his emotions to others, looked strangely pale and shocked, as though he had seen a ghost. By contrast Alvarado was visibly excited as he examined the bow and arrows and other ornaments of gold. 'Twenty thousand pesos at least,' Díaz heard him mutter. Olmedo's face was sad and grim in the flickering twilight of the chamber, Malinal's jaw was set and her fists were clenched tight by her side, Sandoval looked as though he might be sick, Olid's hand strayed to the hilt of his broadsword and Cortés pushed close to the idol, gazing up into its obsidian eyes as though transfixed. Finally he said: 'Friends, I believe we've seen enough here. The stench is unbearable. Let's get some fresh air.' Then abruptly he turned, stepped round the brazier, took Malinal by the elbow and strode from the room.

Díaz followed and, once outside, as Cortés and Moctezuma fell to talking again, he strode to the edge of the pyramid to take another look at the western and northern causeways. To his relief the parties of men he'd thought were working on the bridges had gone and there was a normal flow of pedestrian traffic in both directions.

Cortés was shaken by what he'd seen. The resemblance of the hideous idol of Huitzilopochtli to the transformed appearance of Saint Peter in his dream was truly disturbing. He told himself it was all an invention of the devil, yet he could not deny that a worm of doubt now gnawed at him. It was perhaps because of this, even though wisdom and strategy – and even Olmedo! – counselled otherwise, that he was unable to constrain himself a moment longer.

'Lord Moctezuma,' he said, signalling to Malinal that she should translate as he went along, 'I cannot understand how a prince as great and wise as Your Majesty can have failed to realise these idols of yours – ' he pointed accusingly at the temple of Huitzilopochtli – 'are not gods but evil things, the proper name for which is devils.'

'No, no, Hernán,' Olmedo whispered. 'Too soon! I thought we agreed.'

But Cortés ignored him. 'There is no God other than our Christian God,' he continued, 'and it is He whom you must serve and worship, oh great Moctezuma; not with the killing of men and abominable sacrifices, but only with devotion and prayer, as we Christians do.'

As Malinal gave the translation, Cortés saw the Mexica ruler's lean face growing red and congested with rage, but he had the wind in his sails now and would be damned if he would stop. 'So that I may prove this to you,' he said, 'and make it clear to all your priests, grant me one favour. Allow me to erect a cross here on the top of this pyramid, and let us divide off part of the sanctuary where the demon Hummingbird stands as a place where we can put an image of Our Lady, and then you will see how your false god shrinks before her and how grievously he has deceived you.'

If Moctezuma's anger was transparent, the high priest standing beside him was even more obviously furious and agitated, and the two men engaged in an urgent, whispered discussion. 'Namacuix wants us all killed here and now,' Malinal told Cortés.

'Ha!' said Alvarado, who was standing close. 'Just let the little monkey try.'

'And Moctezuma's not saying no,' Malinal added.

Cortés bared his teeth. 'What is he saying then?'

'"Not here, not now", something like that. I think he's forgotten I can understand him.'

Cortés considered the problem. He was beginning to regret his rash speech, not because he feared a fight, but because he wanted it – when it came – to be on terms entirely dictated by him. 'Not here, not now' actually suited him very well.

Yet it must be soon. This status quo with Moctezuma was too volatile to be maintained for much longer.

The Mexica leader was addressing him again: 'Lord Malinche, if I had known you were going to utter this outrage to my lord Hummingbird, I should never have admitted you into his presence. He is the god who has led the Mexica on to victory since we were a nation, and who gives us health and rain and sends the seed-time and the harvest in their seasons. We hold him to be very good and we are bound to worship and sacrifice to him, so I beg you, if you value your life, say not another word to his dishonour.'

Cortés decided to beat a strategic retreat. 'I think it's time,' he said cheerfully, 'for Your Majesty and ourselves to depart! Let us think on all that's been said and meet as friends tomorrow.'

Some of the tension went from Moctezuma's face and he seemed to relent: 'Very well, Malinche, come to me again in my palace in the morning and we will talk further. As for myself, I shall remain here a while longer. I must pray and offer sacrifices on account of the great sin I've committed in allowing you to climb to this eminence and enter the sanctuary and look upon the face of my god, and for the affront you have caused by speaking ill of him.'

Cortés feigned remorse. 'If that is so, Your Majesty, I ask your pardon. It seems in my zeal for my own religion I have wounded your feelings and offended your priests, and I regret this. I'll endeavour to be more considerate in future.'

After Malinal had given the translation, Moctezuma pursed his lips, nodded curtly, turned his back and walked towards the temple while Cortés led his men down the steep steps of the pyramid. 'I can't believe you actually apologised to that heathen,' complained Alvarado. 'It feels like we're running from a fight.'

'And so we are, Pedro, and so we are. But as Tacitus teaches, he that fights and runs away, may turn and fight another day.'

Chapter Four

⬥

12 November 1519–14 November 1519

By the time the Spaniards returned to their quarters in the palace of Axayacatl, it was close to noon. Since Cortés preferred to rule by consent, or at least give the appearance of doing so, he called an immediate council over lunch with all his senior captains to seek their opinion on what should be done about the deteriorating relationship with Moctezuma. The dispute and exchange of insults at the great pyramid left little room for doubt that the Mexica ruler was no longer overawed by the conquistadors as he had clearly been during their long and bloody progress from the coast, and had shown himself still to be when they had marched into Tenochtitlan. The privileged and seemingly secure position they had occupied couldn't be counted upon to last, and it was obvious the 'friendship' of the emperor was now little more than a façade.

'As every day goes by the danger deepens,' warned Davila. 'Mucktey may be as rich as Croesus but his treasury won't stand the expense of maintaining us here forever.'

'Nor will his people much longer bear the insult of having a foreign army in their midst,' added Olid.

'Particularly so,' agreed Sandoval, 'since we are not an army of angels! The devil makes work for idle hands and I'm getting reports of increasing numbers of incidents. Some of our men drunk on the local hooch, abusing shopkeepers. One case of alleged theft. If it weren't for the royal guides, it would have come to blows before now.'

'The Tlascalan presence is also a problem,' Malinal said. 'The Mexica hate them. Even though they're confined to the palace, everyone in the city knows they're here. I've heard troublemakers on the street corners saying they should take this chance to trap them and kill them.' She paused: 'More and more they say that about us as well.'

'When we were on the pyramid just now,' Díaz offered, 'while you

80

and Moctezuma were talking, Hernán, I took the opportunity to look around. My eyesight's good and I thought I saw work parties on some of the bridges on the causeways . . .'

'Meaning what?' asked Ordaz suspiciously.

'I don't know,' Díaz replied. 'I did think I saw them lifting sections of two of the bridges, but then we went into the temple and when we came out the men were gone and the bridges were functional with people moving normally across them.'

Velázquez de Léon was looking alarmed. 'Lifting sections!' he squawked. 'This changes everything, don't you see? They're obviously preparing to cut the causeways. I say we get out of here before they have time to finish the job.'

'Are you suggesting we should run?' asked Alvarado disbelievingly.

'Yes!' said Velázquez de Léon. 'Tonight, under cover of darkness, before they have a chance to stop us.'

'Nonsense!' laughed Alvarado. 'You're panicking.'

'Nonetheless, I don't like the sound of this,' said Ordaz, 'and we should consider our position carefully. Now we've learned what we're up against in Tenochtitlan I personally don't see how we can possibly seize power here – just a few hundred of us against hundreds of thousands! I'm not in favour of a sudden flight, but perhaps an open, agreed departure? I'd say Mucktey will be glad to see the back of us and will let us go without a fight.'

'If I may suggest, gentlemen,' interrupted mild-mannered Sandoval, 'we are jumping too quickly to unwarranted conclusions. It's taken us a great deal of time and effort to get ourselves into this city, and we should not think of leaving it because of an unconfirmed sighting, the meaning of which we do not know. I dare say you'd agree, Díaz?'

'Of course, yes! I'm not sure what I saw or what it means. It was probably routine maintenance, or nothing at all. In my opinion what we should do is investigate further. We certainly shouldn't run, either in secret or in the open! I'm not in favour of any such idea! For what it's worth my vote, having got this far, is to find a way to stay and conquer.'

Once again, thought Cortés, feeling suddenly weary, the old fault lines in his expedition between the party of his jealous enemy and rival Diego de Velázquez, governor of Cuba – cousin to Velázquez de Léon – and his own allies such as Alvarado, Sandoval and Díaz, were opening up as soon as danger loomed on the horizon. Predictably Olid would be the next to add his voice to those in favour of quitting the city and, while he was confident he would be able to ride out this squall of dissent and impose his will, as he always did, it was obvious he must act soon. Indeed, even if by some fluke the present uncomfortable stalemate could be preserved for a few weeks or months longer, even if the Spaniards were allowed to stay in the palace of Axayacatl and continued to be fed and maintained there, what did he gain? The sands were running through the hourglass and his greatest fear, though he voiced it to no one, was not that the Velazquistas would force him to abandon the expedition, but that Diego de Velázquez himself would find a way to wrest the prize of conquest from his hands before he had completed and consolidated it.

'Brothers,' Cortés said, 'let us not fall to quarrelling again. Díaz and Sandoval are right. This matter of the bridges must be investigated before we can know if it requires a response from us. We'll send out scouts to make a thorough reconnaissance this afternoon but, even if Mucktey does have some treacherous scheme to cut the causeways, I'd not counsel an abrupt retreat with the air of flight. The quickest way to draw our enemies down upon us, like wolves on the fold, and lose the support of our allies into the bargain, is to show timidity and loss of confidence. The only thing keeping us alive is our courage, our show of strength and our self-assurance. Sacrifice that and all will truly be lost.'

'Well, what do you propose then?' said Velázquez de Léon, with an aggressive thrust of his chin.

Cortés nodded. It was time to share the plan that he'd held back from his officers until now – a plan so audacious, indeed seemingly insane, that some amongst them would have begun to mutter against him and sow dissensions behind his back if he'd entrusted them with his intentions sooner than absolutely necessary.

'What I propose, gentlemen,' he said, 'is that at some opportune moment in the next days, we should march over to Mucktey's palace and bring him back here with us – by persuasion if possible, by force if necessary, but by all means we must get possession of his person.'

From jutting forward, Velázquez de Léon's large jaw now dropped, rather comically Cortés thought, almost to his chest. Sandoval and Díaz exchanged a glance of approval. Malinal had a sphinx-like smile on her face. Alvarado laughed and slapped his thigh. Olid and Davila both looked astonished.

'Hernán!' exclaimed Ordaz as the idea sunk in. 'Have you taken leave of your senses?'

'Most certainly not,' Cortés replied. 'In fact, I don't think I've ever thought more clearly in my life. What I'm suggesting will require luck and daring, but I've already prepared the ground and I'm certain we can pull this off.'

'But . . . but . . .' Velázquez de Léon was gasping like a fish. 'Even suppose we seize him and bring him hither, what then? Has it escaped your attention, Hernán, that we are in the midst of his city, surrounded by half a million of his people? They're not just going to accept this quietly—'

'They can be made to accept it!' Malinal cut in, her voice very calm and clear. 'Hear me, because I know the Mexica. What my lord suggests will work. It is the best hope for all of us, maybe our only hope.'

'It will work,' Cortés continued smoothly, 'because Mucktey is both a coward and an absolute despot. The habit of obedience to him is deeply ingrained here. He will be our hostage, but we will make him tell his ministers and his generals that it is his wish to be with us. To reinforce this impression we will allow him a show of sovereignty and give him liberty to hear suits, dispatch his affairs, attend to the government of his realms much as before, but all the time he will be our puppet and we will pull the strings. With this one audacious stroke we can make ourselves safe, conquer this land, and possess its treasures without ever having to fight another battle!'

Cortés looked around at his captains and knew he'd persuaded them.

As usual it was the thought of treasure that had carried the day.

Moctezuma expiated the sin of bringing Malinche to the temple by sacrificing two young boys to Huitzilopochtli. Invisible and undetected, but helpless to intervene, Tozi watched the ceremony with mounting fury. She'd hoped the Spanish leader might take immediate action after she'd shown him the truth of his dreams, and he'd raised her hopes by confronting Moctezuma, but then he'd suddenly backed down and practically grovelled at the end, promising to be more considerate in future.

Now two more children had died horrible deaths because of him, and if 'more considerate' meant he was going to do nothing about the coming sacrifices, then he really was no use to her. Although she knew Huicton was against it, arguing that an even worse ruler would take the throne and the sacrifices would proceed anyway, Tozi was beginning to think seriously about killing Moctezuma herself.

It wouldn't be difficult to slip into his bedchamber and slit his throat while he slept.

By mid-afternoon he was finished in the temple. Tozi followed him down the steps of the pyramid, accompanied his palanquin as he was carried to his palace, and watched him with flat hatred while he bathed, carefully washing the blood out of his hair and from under his finger-nails. The Great Speaker was in fact fastidiously, meticulously clean, often taking as many as four baths a day, but his soul, the only part of him that would survive this life and go on to judgement, was filthy beyond redemption.

After he had dressed – and he never wore the same clothes twice – he made his way to a private chamber overlooking a corner of the palace gardens, where he was served a jug of chocolate and took a seat in a tall, upright chair. Ever more strongly drawn to the idea of returning later with a sharp knife, Tozi was about to leave him when the doors swung open and Teudile entered the room. 'Sire,' said the steward, 'good news. General Qualpopoca has arrived from the coast. He asks for an immediate audience.'

'Does he bring me the head of the sacrificed Spanish commander?'

'He does, my lord.'

'Then show him up, Teudile!' Moctezuma rubbed his hands together. 'Let him come as he is. My successful general need not wear commoner's overclothes in my presence. We have plans to make, and I'm eager to see this trophy!'

Silent and invisible, Tozi stayed in the room, her mind working rapidly. She knew from her conversations with Malinal and Pepillo that the Spaniards had established a small fortified settlement on the coast near the Totonac town of Huitztlan. If one of Moctezuma's generals had arrived from the coast bringing the head of a Spanish commander he'd somehow been able to sacrifice, then it could only belong to the commander of that garrison, which must mean a battle had been fought there that the Spanish had lost. Since she was certain none of the Spaniards in Tenochtitlan knew anything about such a battle, this was valuable intel-ligence. It might even be enough to make Malinche do the right thing.

'Ah Qualpopoca!' Moctezuma remained seated but smiled a welcome as Teudile ushered the general into the room. He was a middle-aged, round-eyed, travel-stained man, who'd nonetheless, Tozi noticed, taken the time to oil his bald head and dust down his scarlet military robe. He had the smooth, unlined skin of a courtier, not a soldier, and in his small, fine, uncalloused hands, he clutched a basket of just the right size to contain a human head.

'Sit down, good Qualpopoca,' Moctezuma said, indicating a stool, 'and let me be the first to congratulate you on your great victory over these Spanish devils.'

'It was not enough, sire,' Qualpopoca admitted bashfully as he sat and balanced the basket on his knee. 'We only killed eight of them. More than two hundred of their garrison remain.'

'You're too modest, cousin! By capturing and sacrificing a Spanish commander, you've done something no one else, not the Chontal Maya, not even the Tlascalans, have been able to do. I'm very proud of you. Now, tell me – this is important – is the problem contained?'

'Contained? I'm not sure I understand, sire.'

'You've no doubt heard from Teudile that Malinche and some hundreds of his Spaniards are here with us in Tenochtitlan?'

'I've brought him up to date, sire,' said Teudile.

'We decided to let them in,' Moctezuma continued, 'because it will be easier to kill them here than anywhere else. But until we're ready, it's vital they don't learn about your victory. Tell me you've taken suitable steps to isolate their garrison at the coast and stop them getting messages out.'

Qualpopoca seemed to swell up with pride: 'Indeed, sire! The town the Spaniards built near Huitztlan is well fortified and will be difficult to take, but I have it surrounded by twenty thousand of my men. No one can enter or leave it.'

'Even by sea?'

'Even by sea, my lord. We've cut off their access to their harbour and burned the great boat they have moored there.'

'Excellent. What about the Totonacs?'

'They sent out some messengers, sire, but we caught and killed them all and we hold their chiefs hostage. I don't think they'll dare try again. The rest of my force, close to twelve thousand men, control Cempoala, Huitztlan and the hill towns. All the roads and passes are guarded.'

'Well done, cousin! You've thought of everything. It seems you're a natural general.'

'Thank you, sire. You honour me.'

Moctezuma glanced out of the window, then leaned forward and lowered his voice to a whisper which, in the silent room, Tozi nonetheless heard clearly: 'I'm assembling a force of a hundred thousand of our best men to destroy Malinche and his little army. Most are already here, in hiding in the city. I want you, Qualpopoca, to take charge of that force and make ready for an attack in four days' time to coincide with the first day of the great basket of sacrifices I plan in honour of Huitzilopochtli. Are you prepared to accept this commission?'

'Sire! Of course!'

'Then it is yours, cousin. Time is short, there's much to do, and it all must be done in secret. Secrecy is the essence of this. Complete secrecy! Under no circumstances can the Spaniards be allowed to learn of our plans. They mustn't even suspect what we intend.'

'I understand, sire.'

'Malinche is deadly and cunning as a snake, but he has one great weakness. He thinks me a fool and that makes him feel safe.' Moctezuma's eyes strayed to the basket on Qualpopoca's knees. 'You have something to show me, I think.'

Moctezuma felt a strange mixture of emotions as Qualpopoca carefully untied and raised the lid of the basket, reached inside, gathered a handful of long black hair and lifted out the large head of a Spaniard. The skin, visible on the brow and high cheekbones, was uncommonly white, but discoloured with livid patches, the beard was huge and thick and the stub of the neck, which had been severed not far beneath the chin, was ragged and moist with bloody slime. The eyes were wide open and star-tlingly blue.

Slowly Moctezuma stood up, edged over to where Qualpopoca still sat perched on his stool, and took the trophy from him. It was heavy. The hair, gripped in his right fist, was lank and oily, crawling with lice. The beard, which he now explored with the fingers of his left hand, was bristly and dense, like the rough pelt of a beast. The top half of the right ear, exposed where the long black locks were lifted into the skein from which the head was suspended, had been hacked off, though not recently for the injury was healed and showed an ugly mass of scar tissue around the ear itself, and in the flesh under the hairline along the side of the skull.

Moctezuma moved to the window and raised the dangling head to the light to study it better, realising as he did so that it made him afraid. The savage features, rendered all the more terrifying by death, hung before him like a curse or a prophecy of inescapable doom; those unnat-ural eyes, somehow filled with a horrible intelligence, glared at him in mute accusation, and the pale, snarling lips bared around yellow teeth spoke to him of the vengeance of the race of destroyers now housed so close by.

He shuddered. He could not bear to gaze on the apparition a moment longer. 'Here Teudile,' he beckoned his steward. 'Take this from me. Give it over to Namacuix and have him set it on the skull rack in the temple of Hummingbird. Our god will know what to do with it.'

Turning to Qualpopoca he said: 'Go with Teudile, good cousin. He will brief you on everything else you need to know about the disposition of our forces in the city and the timing, which must be exact, for the attack on Malinche.'

When they were gone, Moctezuma returned to his seat and brooded for a long while. He had thought the sight of the head would cheer him but it had, on the contrary, disturbed and depressed him. He began to fret that the anger he had shown Malinche this morning might lead the Spanish commander to suspect an attack was coming and put him on his guard.

Sleight of hand was needed to distract him.

Moctezuma meditated deeply on the matter. After some time – it was surely a gift from the gods! – the perfect solution presented itself.

It was late afternoon and Cortés had retired for his siesta when Malinal woke him. 'I'm sorry, Hernán,' she said, 'but there's something you have to hear. It's urgent.'

He sat up, looking irritable, wiping sleep from his eyes. 'What is it?' he grumbled. 'Can't it wait?'

'No. I have terrible news from the coast. It seems that Moctezuma's men have attacked the garrison at Villa Rica. Captain Escalante has been killed—'

'What?' Cortés roared, fully awake now. '*What?*'

'Juan de Escalante has been killed, Hernán. I know he was your friend. Your good friend. I'm so sorry.'

Cortés was out of bed, already dressing. 'Who brought this news?' he said. 'Where is he? Take me to him.'

Malinal shook her head. 'No messenger has come from the coast, Hernán. Villa Rica is surrounded and they can't break out. We know of this because of Tozi—'

'Tozi! What are you talking about? I don't trust her!'

'Why would you not trust her? I vouch for her, and her talents as a spy make her an asset to us . . .'

Cortés frowned.

'You know this, Hernán,' Malinal said, beginning to feel anxious. It was important that the story she had concocted with Tozi in the past hour be believed, and particularly important that Cortés should learn nothing of Tozi's witchcraft. 'She's helped Huicton for many years to gather intelligence for Ishtlil.'

Cortés face had softened. 'Yes,' he said. 'I remember.'

'Well, she hasn't stopped spying. She's very good at it. And these last days while she's been here with us, inside the sacred precinct, she's been spying on Moctezuma. That's why I asked you if she could stay with us again. It's easy for her to get into his palace from here.'

Strapping on his sword with angry, jerky movements, Cortés said: 'You didn't inform me that was her purpose.'

'I saw no need to trouble you, Hernán. We're all on the same side. Anyway, does it matter?'

'I want to question her myself.'

'She's just outside, in the hallway, with Pepillo.'

With an angry look, Cortés strode to the door and flung it open. Tozi and Pepillo were sitting on the floor of the corridor. Pepillo's face was grief-stricken, his eyes red and brimming with tears.

'They've killed Juan,' the boy now sobbed – and Cortés remembered how Escalante had become Pepillo's mentor, in many ways a father to him. 'The bastards have killed Juan.'

A little later, as dusk gathered, Cortés walked to the comfortable room he'd commandeered as his office in the north wing of the palace of Axayacatl. The torches fixed to brackets in the walls were already lit, providing good illumination, and normally at this hour he would have been dictating the next passages of his new letter to King Carlos V of Spain. This evening, however, Pepillo was too distraught to work, and besides there were matters that must be thought through.

First and foremost there was the fact that if Tozi had brought her incredible tale to him a day earlier he would have doubted its truth, suspecting she and Malinal had made it up to goad him into hasty action against Moctezuma. But since the decision to seize the Mexica ruler had ceased to be an aspiration and become a definite plan earlier this afternoon, that motive no longer applied.

Exactly how Tozi had learned of Escalante's fate still bothered him. What was completely convincing, however, was her description of poor Jean's head and of how, in removing it from the basket and handling it, Moctezuma had exposed the right ear beneath the long hair. Only someone who'd taken a close look at Escalante could have known, as Tozi did, that the top half of his ear had been cut off, and that it was an old wound and heavily scarred. Indeed it was because he was vain, and felt mutilated by this sword cut received at the Battle of Ravenna seven years before, that he had insisted on wearing his hair so unfashionably long. Now, of course, it was just possible that Tozi had been told of Escalante's disfigurement by Malinal or even Pepillo, but Cortés didn't believe for a moment that either of them would collude with such a plot to misinform him, especially so since Pepillo's sorrow and despair at the death of the good man who'd become a father figure to him, indeed who had adopted him as his legal heir, was quite obviously genuine.

Besides, there was a final detail of Tozi's account that could – and would! – in due course be checked. It seemed, after examining the head, that Moctezuma had passed it to his steward Teudile with the instruction that it was to be spitted on the skull rack in the temple of Hummingbird.

What was clear from the conversation Tozi claimed to have overheard between Moctezuma and his general – a man named Qualpopoca – was that Villa Rica was now surrounded and besieged by twenty thousand Mexica warriors.

And next came the gravest and most worrying part of the little spy's report. It seemed that Qualpopoca had this afternoon been placed in charge of a much larger force, a hundred thousand strong, gathered in secret in Tenochtitlan to attack Cortés and his men just four days from today!

All in all, then, this was a very nasty problem. But again, like every other problem the Spaniards faced, it could be solved at a stroke by taking Moctezuma hostage and making him order his forces to back away. Moreover, now Cortés knew the depths of the Mexica ruler's duplicity, and knew his extravagant hospitality to be an elaborate sham, he felt fully justified in seizing him. Under other circumstances, for the guest to turn on his apparently generous host in such a way would amount to a shameless betrayal that would be hard to explain to the Spanish king, but now, with the information Tozi had brought, Cortés had an unimpeachable pretext.

The only remaining question was when the deed was to be done. Although he had earlier made his captains feel the raid on the royal palace would be easy to carry out, he knew in his heart it was fraught with terrible risks and there were a hundred ways – a thousand! – in which it might go wrong. Ideally he would have liked several more days to continue to lay the groundwork and thoroughly brief and rehearse his team, but Tozi's news, combined with the hint of preparations to lift the bridges on the causeways noticed by Díaz, called for urgent pre-emptive action – perhaps even as soon as tomorrow. True, Tozi had said the attack on the Spaniards would not occur for another four days, which sounded like it was meant to coincide with the first day of the sacrifices to Hummingbird on 16 November, but who was to say that this deadline might not be brought forward?

Yet tomorrow, Friday 13 November, was an unlucky date, and the more he thought about it, the more sure Cortés felt that to make his move then would be to act from panic rather than reason, and thus almost certainly a mistake. At least one further reconnaissance of Moctezuma's palace would be wise, as would at least one more day in which numbers of Spaniards might congregate in the halls, courtyards and government offices in a way that was coming to be seen as routine.

Everything therefore pointed to Saturday 14 November as the day to strike.

Without noticing what he was doing, Cortés started to pace restlessly to and fro across the floor of his office, allowing his thoughts to turn to Escalante, feeling at last the pain of his loss. He'd been a good man and a good and loyal friend, and he'd died a foul death at the hands of the Mexica. Dear God! They'd *sacrificed* him! They'd opened his breast and torn out his heart! They'd cut off his head and put it in a basket so some monkey of a general could carry it from the coast and display it to Moctezuma!

Cortés pictured the scene and shuddered. They would pay a terrible price for this, he resolved – the general who'd done it, and Moctezuma who'd ordered it, and anyone else involved; all of them would pay a terrible price in blood and fire and humiliation. He opened the Bible that lay on his desk, thumbed through its pages until he came to the book of Deuteronomy, chapter thirty-two, and read aloud:

'For their vine is the vine of Sodom, and of the fields of Gomorrah; their grapes are grapes of gall, their clusters are bitter; their wine is the poison of dragons and the cruel venom of asps. Is this not laid up in store with me, and sealed up among my treasures? To me belongeth vengeance and recompense. Their foot shall slide in due time, for the day of their calamity is at hand, and the things that shall come upon them make haste.'

As he closed the book there came a knock at the door. 'Good evening,

Hernán,' said Sandoval. 'Moctezuma's steward Teudile is here. He requests a meeting with you. Something urgent.'

Cortés sat on one of the two thrones, with Malinal, as usual, at his knee on a stool. Pepillo, grief-stricken, was not present, Teudile preferred to stand. He had an oily smile on his gaunt, ghoulish face. 'Malinche,' he said. 'I have excellent news for you.'

'I always welcome excellent news.' Cortés leaned back, locked his fingers behind his head and imagined the pleasure it would give him to run his broadsword through the steward's skinny guts.

'The great Moctezuma,' Teudile continued, 'is ever gracious. In his wisdom and generosity he has decided to accommodate your request for a place to erect the cross of your god and the image of your god's mother. He regrets this cannot be on our great pyramid by the temple of Hummingbird as this will anger the priests and the people. But out of the love he bears for you, he permits you to build a chapel to your god here within the palace of Axayacatl, your own residence. You may take over any room of the palace you wish for this purpose, do with it as you choose, and place your cross and images within it – as many as you choose – and all of you may worship in it freely at any time you choose.'

Cortés's mind was racing. This truly was a gift from God! For as his men worked to set up and decorate the chapel tomorrow, many good reasons could be found for groups of them to make their way over to Moctezuma's palace with Malinal or Pepillo as interpreters – for example to visit the government offices and stores and workshops there to request materials, carpenters, craftsmen, and additional permissions for this and that. He himself would make at least two visits, accompanied by larger than usual contingents of officers and men, to thank Moctezuma in person for his generosity and to clarify certain points about the chapel. The Mexica were already used to seeing armed and armoured Spaniards about the palace, and this new project, sanctioned by the Great Speaker himself, should avert any suspicion about their increased numbers while at the same time allowing a proper reconnaissance and serving as a dress rehearsal for the manoeuvres needed to take Moctezuma prisoner the day after tomorrow.

'The Great Speaker is indeed generous,' Cortés said, giving Teudile a broad smile. 'I am happy to accept this gracious offer he has made. We will select a suitable room and start work on the chapel this very evening, and I will visit the palace in the morning to thank His Majesty in person.'

'The lord Moctezuma will be very happy that you are happy, and has asked me to repeat that which you already know, Malinche: namely that you are welcome in his presence at any time.'

With that, looking extremely pleased with himself, Teudile took his leave.

As Moctezuma took his breakfast, Teudile gave him a report on the activities of the Spaniards who had begun work on the chapel of their god. The previous evening, soon after the steward had brought them the news, the spies amongst the staff assigned to serve them had seen them thoroughly prospecting all the available chambers of the palace of Axayacatl. It had at first seemed they would select one of the large apartments on the second floor, and intense interest had been shown in several of these; finally, however, they had settled on the great room next to the dining hall on the ground floor that Cortés had previously used as his audience chamber. The twin thrones had been carried out soon after sunrise and since then their carpenter and a team of assistants had been busily at work there building a series of long benches, on which it seemed the Spaniards would sit when they worshipped. Other work crews had been detailed to paint the walls, and several times already that morning groups of Spaniards had visited the government offices in Moctezuma's palace with requests for supplies and the help of certain skilled craftsmen. Teudile had seen to it that these requests were cheerfully granted. 'All in all, sire,' he concluded, 'they seem content and preoccupied. If I may say so, sire, it was a stroke of genius on your part to distract them in this way from all other concerns.'

Moctezuma beamed. It had indeed been a stroke of genius.

His next visitor was Qualpopoca. The general seemed agitated, and once the formalities were over he launched straight into what was troubling him. 'If I may suggest, Your Majesty, I would like to propose a small revision of the plans you have made . . .'

Moctezuma felt a moment of affront. He did not like his plans being meddled with. But then he remembered Qualpopoca's victory at the coast. The man had a brilliant military mind. This, after all, was why he had given him the honour of implementing the Spaniards' doom. 'Very well,' he said, 'speak.'

'Thank you, sire. I have reviewed our troops already in the city and, although the one hundred thousand you have ordered are not yet fully mustered, I believe we already have enough – more than sixty thousand

– for a successful operation.' He wrung his hands. 'I recommend, sire, that we bring the date of the attack forward—'

'Bring it forward?'

'With respect, Your Majesty, I think it is dangerous for us to wait another three days. As each day passes and more troops enter the city, the danger grows that the Spaniards will see something and become suspicious. I also understand from Teudile that since this morning they have been fully engaged constructing a temple to their god in the palace of Axayacatl. I believe, while they are thus preoccupied, that we have the perfect opportunity to attack them. I believe, sire, we should strike tonight . . .'

'Tonight?' Moctezuma was dumbfounded and his heart began to beat irregularly. With the attack still three days away he had not yet allowed his imagination to dwell on the awful consequences that would follow if it should fail. But the prospect of everything happening tonight filled him with terror and apprehension. 'It cannot be tonight,' he mumbled. 'I have told you already I wish the attack on the Spaniards to coincide with the first day of the great festival of sacrifices I have arranged. Everything is in order and perfect as it is. The sacrifices are to begin in three days' time and will take four days to complete, thus culminating on the morning of Hummingbird's birthday, the first day of Panquetzaliztli. It is fitting that the first day of the sacrifices should also be the day the Spaniards meet their doom. I intend that we should take many prisoners and hold them ready for sacrifice to mark the climax of the ceremonies on the birthday of the god himself.'

'That will not change, sire.' Qualpopoca looked nervous but was persistent. 'You will still have your prisoners. All I am proposing is that we attack sooner than you had originally intended to minimise any danger of our plans being discovered.'

Moctezuma frowned: 'I don't like it, Qualpopoca. Hummingbird will surely aid us if we have already begun sacrificing to him when we attack the Spaniards. This is what I have always intended and what I have indeed promised to the god. If we attack before the appointed time I fear he may not so willingly bless the enterprise . . .'

Qualpopoca wrung his hands again: 'There is another matter, Your Majesty . . .'

'Yes, yes. What is it?'

'The Spaniards are very powerful, sire. I succeeded in killing eight of them at the coast, it is true, but even though they were greatly

93

outnumbered, they put up a fearsome fight and close to a thousand of my own men died.'

'Men always die in battle, Qualpopoca. Yet still you triumphed and you will triumph here.'

'I have no doubt of it, sire. Nonetheless, Malinche has a much larger force in the palace of Axayacatl than the column I attacked at the coast—'

'And you have a much larger force with which to attack him, particularly if you wait until the appointed time when the full one hundred thousand will be mustered.'

'True, Your Majesty, but Malinche is reputedly a great battle ruler, greater by far than the garrison commander whose head I brought you yesterday. In addition, we cannot usefully bring so many men to bear at one time in an attack on the palace of Axayacatl. I have done the calculations, sire! There is not space in the sacred precinct for a hundred thousand, and this problem will only become more pressing if the attack is to be conducted while the priests and populace are gathered to witness the splendid holocaust of the virgins. At the very least I foresee a bloody and messy battle and a very great risk that the fighting will spill out into the sacred precinct itself and interfere with, perhaps even stop, the sacrifices. That, surely, would not be pleasing to the god, sire . . .'

Moctezuma sighed and closed his eyes. Qualpopoca was a clever man – why else had he appointed him as general? – and these objections he was raising were no mere quibbles.

But tonight?

No! Tonight was too soon! The very idea of such precipitate action filled Moctezuma with terror and turned the blood in his veins to ice. Besides, another ten thousand of his most fearsome warriors, all Cuahchics, he had recalled from the war against Ishtlil, were scheduled to enter the city tonight, and could not be deployed for duty until tomorrow. It had always been his intention they should spearhead the attack on the Spaniards.

For a long while he remained silent, deep in thought, while Qualpopoca stood before him, his robe rustling as he shifted his weight nervously from foot to foot. Finally Moctezuma opened his eyes again. 'Good General,' he said. 'I have heard your words and I find much merit in them. To wait three days may be too long. I will meditate in the temple tonight and seek to approach the god. If he sees fit to speak with me I will request his approval to bring forward our attack on the Spaniards to tomorrow . . .'

'But, sire—'

'*No Qualpopoca!* Enough! There will be no attack tonight. I must consult the god.'

As he spoke Teudile entered the room. 'Sire,' he said, 'the lord Malinche is in the palace with a large delegation.' He looked at the breakfast dishes spread around the dining room, still warming on braziers. 'They will not all fit comfortably in here so I have shown them into your audience chamber. I hope that is satisfactory.'

Cortés, who had elected not to share the stunning news of Escalante's death and the siege of Villa Rica until a time of his choosing, had brought fifteen officers and men with him this morning of Friday 13 November. They were Velázquez de Léon, Olid, Ordaz, Alvarado, Sandoval, Díaz, Davila, Jerónimo Alanis, Pedro Gonzalez de Trujillo, Francisco de Saucedo, Mibiercas, La Serna, Sergeant García Brabo and two of his rough crew. Malinal was of course also present, Pepillo was there with his notebook, his face strained, and Father Olmedo came along as well, dressed in a freshly laundered white habit. Altogether, with Cortés himself, a total delegation of nineteen.

There would be more than that in the palace when they came to arrest Moctezuma tomorrow, but nineteen was sufficient to create a feeling of normality around such large numbers.

As they waited in the audience chamber for the emperor to finish his breakfast, they talked quietly amongst themselves about the astonishing discovery that had been made the previous evening after Teudile had called to convey Moctezuma's permission for the construction of a chapel in the palace of Axayacatl. This discovery, all were agreed, was another sign that God had blessed their enterprise, and it had quite cured Velázquez de Léon of his fit of nerves at the prospect of the causeways being cut!

While inspecting various rooms that might prove suitable for a place of worship, the carpenter Martin Lopez had come across something odd in one of the large second-floor apartments. There was a section of wall here on which the faint outline of a doorframe was visible, heavily covered by thick plaster. Lopez notified Bernal Díaz and another soldier, Francisco de Lugo, asking whether he should break through the plaster and see what lay beyond. They informed Cortés, who came at once, and didn't scruple to have the plaster façade smashed out with a sledgehammer.

Beyond lay a large concealed chamber heaped with the most

astonishing and breathtaking treasures! Here amongst wickerwork chests filled with splendid feather ornaments, as well as many items carved from the green stone prized by the Maya and the Mexica but of little interest to the Spaniards, were great clusters of golden necklaces numbering in the hundreds, countless gold and silver bars, piled in parallel stacks as high as a man, extending the full length of one wall, fifty large ceramic containers filled with grains of gold fresh from the mines, many large gold plates and cups, and sparkling mounds of precious jewels. Alvarado, his eyes gleaming, said he could not easily estimate the value of all this, but that it might equal or exceed the entire contents of the royal treasury of Spain.

Word spread quickly, the gold-hungry conquistadors could not be kept out and, rather than attempt to do so, Cortés arranged an orderly inspection of the hoard by every one of the men, while at the same time ensuring that none of the Indian slaves and servants appointed to attend to them were allowed close. Finally, when all the soldiers had feasted their eyes and emerged dumbfounded, he ordered the broken wall closed up again and swore everyone to secrecy. What they had stumbled on, Malinal said, was undoubtedly the fabled royal treasure of Axayacatl, concealed here by Moctezuma himself some years before and kept as a national reserve. Until they held the emperor safely as a hostage, it was imperative he did not learn the Spaniards had found it.

'Does Mucktey have a second treasure house in his own palace?' Cortés had asked.

'Certainly yes,' Malinal replied, 'at least as large as this one.'

'We'll all be rich as Croesus then,' grinned Alvarado, 'once we have the bastard in our hands.'

Their progress towards that objective seemed assured by the behaviour of Moctezuma, who now entered the audience chamber, his presence hushing all conversation, advanced across the room wreathed in smiles and treated Cortés and his men to the friendliest of welcomes, showing no suspicion whatsoever at the size of the delegation. When Cortés said they had come to thank him for his generosity in allowing them to establish a Christian chapel in the palace of Axayacatl, the emperor replied through Malinal that it was the least he could do. He only regretted, he said, that he had not immediately been able to grant their request to install the symbols of their faith in Hummingbird's temple. 'This was through no wish of my own, Malinche, but as you saw yesterday, my priests were offended, and I was obliged to support them. I am hopeful as we all get to know one another better that a great deal more will become possible.'

'He's lying,' Malinal said in an aside to Cortés.

'I know,' Cortés replied. 'We're all liars here.' He then kept a straight face as he told Moctezuma the Spaniards hoped to complete work on their new chapel tomorrow, Saturday 14 November, so that the following day, Sunday, a day sacred to all Christians, they could hold their first service there.

Moctezuma expressed satisfaction at this since, he said, he could see the Spaniards attached as much importance to their religion as the Mexica did to theirs.

More lies and platitudes were exchanged, and in due course the meeting was adjourned.

That night Cortés summoned the entire Spanish force to assemble in the newly converted chapel where the cross, a makeshift altar, and images of the Virgin had already been installed. The day had gone as well as he possibly could have hoped. He'd held a second meeting with Moctezuma that had proved as affable as the first, and groups of conquistadors, all armed, had gone in and out of the royal palace several times without attracting any untoward attention.

After a brief blessing from Father Olmedo, Cortés stood by the altar. 'Gentlemen,' he announced, looking out over the crowd of grimy, bearded, expectant faces, 'some of you, a few, are already privy to the plan I am about to reveal. To the rest it will come as a surprise, and for this I ask your forgiveness, but events have moved fast and the need, always, has been for the utmost secrecy.' He paused to let this sink in, his hand resting on a huge leather-bound Bible. There was a shuffle of feet, a few coughs, but otherwise dead silence.

'Let me begin with some hard truths,' Cortés said. 'Fact the first – you are all aware that our position here is a dangerous one. Our hosts, the Mexica, are savage and unruly heathens who cut out the hearts of their enemies and eat their flesh. Until now they pretend to be our friends, and greet us with smiles, but I think no one doubts that at any moment they might turn on us . . . Fact the second – we are in the midst of an island city with no route of escape other than along the three principal causeways leading to the mainland. In the past days we have seen evidence that our hosts plan to cut these causeways by removing the bridges and marooning us here.'

At this there were startled exclamations and a buzz of whispered conversation amongst the men. Cortés raised his hand and continued. 'Fact the third – I have received reliable information that huge numbers of Mexica troops, possibly as many as one hundred thousand, have entered Tenochtitlan under cover of darkness during these last nights. They can only be here for one reason, gentlemen, and that is to attack us.'

The response was louder this time, a threatening hubbub of angry voices. 'Be quiet, please,' Cortés shouted. 'There is worse to follow. Fact the fourth – some days ago our garrison at Villa Rica de la Veracruz was attacked and some of our men were killed, amongst them my dear friend Captain Juan de Escalante—'

There were shouts of outrage and calls for revenge which Cortés waved down with difficulty. 'Fact the fifth – not only was Juan killed, gentlemen, but he was sacrificed, his heart cut out and his head sent here to Moctezuma. I have firm evidence that it hangs now in the skull rack of that hideous temple of the devil whom the Mexica call Hummingbird.'

A stamping of feet, a roar of fury, the sound of swords being loosened in their scabbards. Cortés waited until the noise had abated a little. 'Fact the sixth – the Mexica plan the same fate for us all. I have reason to believe the attack they are preparing will be launched within the next three days, perhaps sooner . . .'

'Then let's attack the bastards first,' someone yelled. There was a chorus of loud and angry agreement.

'Exactly,' said Cortés as the room quietened again. 'That's why I've called you here tonight, but before we get on to that, let us remind ourselves of fact the seventh – as you all know, last night we found a vast treasure hidden away here in our own residence . . .'

Complete silence. Greedy, hungry looks exchanged.

'I think you will agree, gentlemen, that said treasure is *ours by right!*'

A huge, rolling roar of approval, more stamping of feet, 'ours by right', 'ours by right', repeated by multiple voices all around the chapel.

'If we are to carry it off, however,' Cortés continued after order had been restored, 'we cannot hope to do so in a fighting retreat across one or other of the causeways. Nor will some great battle here in the heart of Tenochtitlan serve our interests. We have triumphed against overwhelming odds before, but I believe there is a better way. This is the plan I am here to share with you tonight. It is a plan for which I have prepared the ground carefully and in secret. It is a plan, gentlemen, that will work . . .'

Complete silence fell once again. 'All right, Don Hernán,' came a gruff voice from the back of the room, 'no need to keep us in suspense!'

Cortés smiled and told them the plan.

Hernán Cortés spent the night in prayer before the cross in the newly made chapel. He could not sleep with so hazardous a venture before him – his own life and the lives of all his men at stake on a single throw of the dice.

He asked for guidance from Saint Peter, but received none.

Moctezuma passed the night before the idol in the temple of Hummingbird. He consumed a great quantity of *teonanácatl* mushrooms and sacrificed a three-year-old boy, but the god did not appear to him; as he returned to his palace in the grey light of dawn, he was still uncertain about what to do. Once again, it seemed, Hummingbird was testing him, and he must seek in his own heart for the path to glory.

As the last surge of mushroom power pulsed through his veins, he made his decision and summoned Qualpopoca to join him while he took his breakfast.

'Are you ready to make war?' he asked the general.

'I am ready, sire.'

'Then you have my authority to attack the Spaniards at midnight tonight, when we can be sure they will all be gathered in their quarters and most sleeping. Take them unawares with overwhelming force and be sure you do not fail. Against a man like Malinche there will be no second chance.'

'I understand, Your Majesty. I am honoured – deeply honoured – to be entrusted with this command, and I will not fail.'

Moctezuma felt his face twitch into a smile. 'One other thing, Qualpopoca . . .'

'Yes, sire.'

'Be sure not to kill them all, for I shall require many prisoners for sacrifice . . . Above all, I want Malinche and his witch woman Malinal.'

Bernal Díaz felt he was moving through a world of unreality, a world of the preposterous, as he crossed the grand plaza and passed under the giant portico of the palace of Moctezuma, nodding to the spear guards in their fearsome panther and eagle helmets. There were a hundred cannibal knights on duty here alone, hundreds more lining the corridors, in front of every doorway, patrolling the courtyards and the gardens, and an elite squad of fifty always in close attendance on Mucktey himself in whichever chamber of this giant labyrinth it took his fancy to park his royal arse. Reconnaissance estimated a total of two thousand guards standing watch throughout the palace at any hour of the day or night. Wasn't it therefore absurd, fantastical and insane for Cortés to imagine a handful of Spaniards could snatch the emperor from his lair and oblige him to accompany them to house arrest in their own rather smaller quarters? The palace of Axayacatl was by no means some safe, well-protected fortress where they would be invulnerable to attack, but merely an enclave in the heart of that immense and deadly hornets' nest called Tenochtitlan, with its half million inhabitants who would be stirred to fury by the deed they planned.

Yet desperate straits called for a desperate remedy, and Díaz was satisfied no other possible solution to their problems offered them a better chance of success, survival, and ultimate wealth than this act of madness they were now embarked upon.

He was one of a party of twelve. Just twelve! The others, as well as Cortés himself, were Alvarado, Sandoval, Olid, Ordaz, Velázquez de Léon, Davila, Mibiercas, La Serna, Malinal and Pepillo, who longed, perhaps more than any of them, to see justice served on Moctezuma. After the meeting that was to culminate in Mucktey's arrest had begun, more Spaniards would drop into the palace, seemingly independently, on other business, in groups of three and four at a time, bringing the total number to thirty. They would loiter there until the arrest party emerged with its royal prize and then reinforce them as they exited through the portico and re-crossed the plaza to the palace of Axayacatl.

This, in summary, was the plan Cortés had unveiled last night and on which all their lives depended.

It was mid-morning. Mucktey had already taken his breakfast, and they were shown up to the great audience chamber on the second floor where he had often met them before.

Moctezuma's heart pounded when Teudile informed him that Malinche and his witch Malinal were here to see him once more, with yet another delegation of Spaniards – a party of a dozen of them this time. As usual he would be obliged to entertain them and engage them in polite conversation. He was exhausted after his vigil in the temple, and his nerves were on edge at the prospect of the great night attack Qualpopoca was even now preparing to rid him of this army of parasites forever. Until then it was essential Malinche should suspect nothing, and this was why he had resolved, though he would have preferred otherwise, to meet the Spaniard whenever he required, distract him with flattery, load him with gifts, offer him one of his daughters in marriage to add to the illusion of peaceful security, and even feign an interest in his hideous religion if necessary.

'Very well, Teudile,' he said with a sigh. 'Show them in . . .'

Some time must be allowed for the other groups of Spaniards to assemble casually at the palace, so Cortés did not get straight to the point, but began with a long description of the works undertaken to prepare the chapel.

Malinal faithfully translated both men's words, her face a mask, her emotions in check. This was the moment she had waited for and worked for every day since she'd been stretched out on the stone of sacrifice beneath Moctezuma's knife on that night of blood and terror all those months before. This was her moment of vengeance. This was her moment of requital and she intended to have payment in full.

When Cortés had finished his account of the chapel, Moctezuma suddenly changed the subject: 'I tell you what, Malinche,' he said, all smiles, 'to cement our friendship and alliance I would like to give you one of my daughters to enjoy in marriage. I propose Xochipapolotl. She is a delicious fruit, not yet twenty and ripe for plucking. Your union will be blessed with many children.'

Cortés's manner turned serious: 'I am honoured, Your Majesty, but with regret I am already married – ' Malinal knew he did not mean her but his hated Spanish wife Catalina, who had remained behind on the island called Cuba – 'and my religion forbids me to take more than one bride. Besides, and this is the more important matter, I could not possibly marry or even consort with any woman who is not baptised a Christian.'

A shadow of anger, quickly hidden, crossed Moctezuma's face. 'In that case,' he said, 'I shall send my daughter to your priest Olmedo that he may instruct her in the ways of your faith.' A tense, strained smile. 'Meanwhile please accept these small gifts.' He reached down and opened a basket at his feet. It was filled with gold necklaces and bangles, amidst which sparkled heaps of loose jewels. 'Please share them amongst your-selves as you see fit.'

Some more moments passed as the Spaniards clustered round the basket with their usual display of unconstrained greed, squabbling over this or that item until Cortés took charge and made a distribution according to rank. When he was done and the basket was empty he turned back to Moctezuma. 'Thank you, Your Majesty, for your generosity, but now, though it pains me, I must place a matter of the utmost gravity before you.' As he spoke, Mibiercas and La Serna both drew their swords and strode to the closed doors of the antechamber, taking up positions on either side of them. Seeing this, Teudile seemed about to call out, but was immediately silenced by Díaz, who dealt him a single hard punch to the temple that stretched him unconscious on the floor.

'What is this?' Moctezuma gasped.

'You have betrayed my trust,' Cortés said harshly. 'Even while you sit here offering me your daughter and distributing jewels and speaking soft words of friendship and alliance, you are planning to kill me and all my men . . .'

The Mexica ruler gulped and began to protest but Cortés silenced him: 'Do not add lie upon lie, Your Majesty. I can see into the secret places of your heart and I have learned every detail of your treachery.' He then revealed that he knew his town of Villa Rica de la Veracruz had been surrounded and was being besieged by Mexica forces, and even worse that eight Spaniards from the garrison had been killed, amongst them his own close friend Juan de Escalante.

Moctezuma was babbling now, and Malinal's spirits soared at the look of absolute, abject terror on his face, and at the way he suddenly clutched his stomach as though in pain. He denied everything. It was not true, he said. His enemies, of which he had many, must have fed this false information to Malinche. Did Malinche not realise that he loved him and would never allow any harm to befall the Spaniards on the coast?

Malinal translated all of this for Cortés. When she was done, he sneered and addressed Moctezuma again: 'You make your predicament worse with these lies, Majesty. Please understand that I know everything. *Everything!* You cannot hide from me. You cannot deceive me. I know not only what I have told you, but also that your commander General Qualpopoca had Captain Escalante sacrificed and cut off his head, and I know that this Qualpopoca – a fat, bald man – visited you here in your palace two days ago and showed you the severed head of my friend, and I know that you yourself handled the head, holding it by its long black hair and that afterwards you sent it to be placed on the repugnant rack of skulls in the temple of that evil demon Hummingbird.'

It was pure joy for Malinal to see Moctezuma double over with stomach cramps, which he only with difficulty got under control, to see his brown skin turn ashen, to see his eyes widen and roll. And she knew exactly what the vicious worm was thinking as his bowels turned to water. He was thinking that Cortés could only know all this through magic! He was thinking he could only know it through sorcery! He was thinking these Spaniards were after all gods, as he had always feared, and not mere men as they pretended to be! And now, because such thoughts were swirling around in his mind like smoke, confusing his reason, and because he feared he would soil himself, and because he was very, very afraid of Malinche, he abruptly changed his story. Yes, it was true, Villa Rica had been attacked. Yes, it was true Escalante had been sacrificed and beheaded. Yes, it was true the head had been brought to him here. But none of this was his doing. Instead it was the work of rebels led by the wicked General Qualpopoca, who were attempting to take command of his army, to stage a coup against him, to overthrow him and to place on the throne instead the scheming Prince Guatemoc, who hated the Spaniards. Moctezuma had received Qualpopoca and accepted the head, pretending to be pleased by it when in fact he was outraged at what had been done, only so that he could better move against the general and Guatemoc, crush the rebellion and afterwards make full recompense to his good friend Malinche.

After this had all been translated, Cortés gave an ugly laugh. 'The great Moctezuma,' he said, 'should be ashamed of himself for concocting such a weak and feeble excuse and for lacking the courage to take responsibility for actions he himself has ordered. You did the same thing at Cholula, where you gave express commands for us to be killed, but afterwards sought to blame the affray on others. Because of my great affection for you, I overlooked your cowardly and perfidious behaviour at the time, but I am not prepared to do so again, particularly so – ' and at this Cortés's hand dropped to the hilt of his sword – 'because what I have already revealed to you is not all that you have done. I know also, Moctezuma, that you are gathering a force of a hundred thousand men to attack us here in Tenochtitlan, and that you have placed this force under the command of that same General Qualpopoca who you now say is a rebel and a plotter against you!'

At this another flood of excuses spewed from Moctezuma's mouth, even as he groaned with the pain of his unruly belly. He was, he said, dumbfounded. He had never authorised the general to take up arms against the Spaniards, or put any forces at his disposal. He would order the immediate arrest of Qualpopoca and Prince Guatemoc so they could be questioned, the truth brought out and the wrongdoers punished as they deserved.

Cortés listened to Malinal's translation with a wry, twisted smile. At the end of it he said: 'If what you say is true, great Moctezuma, you will be vindicated and shown to be blameless once the plotters are under arrest and a proper inquiry has been conducted. I therefore have a solution to propose to you, since I have no desire to start a war on this account, or to destroy your city. You must come quietly with us now to our quarters, making no protest. You may choose whichever apartments there you wish and you will be well served and attended, as in your own palace, while we look further into all these matters. But if you cry out, or raise any commotion, you will be immediately killed by these captains –' he indicated the armed and armoured Spaniards standing menacingly around him – 'whom I have brought here for this sole purpose.'

Moctezuma began to cry pitifully as Malinal put these words into Nahuatl and said through sobs, his thin chest heaving, tears streaming down his cheeks: 'My person is not such a one as may be taken captive, Malinche, and even if I should consent to such a degradation, my people would not tolerate it. When was it ever heard that a great emperor, like myself, willingly left his own palace to become a prisoner in the hands of strangers?'

Cortés's manner was immediately more soothing. 'You will experience nothing but respectful treatment from us, Your Majesty. You will be surrounded by your own household and courtiers, hold intercourse with your people as usual, and I will not impede in any way your command of your domains. In short, you should view this as nothing but a change of residence from one of your palaces to another – something that you after all do frequently enough.'

But Moctezuma was having none of it, and now resorted to offering hostages instead of himself – Chimalpopoca, his one legitimate son, who was sickly and only four years old, and the same daughter, Xochipapolotl, shortly before offered to Cortés in marriage.

Cortés rejected these craven, desperate gambits, as Malinal had known he would. 'Besides,' he told Moctezuma, 'if what you say is true and you face an imminent rebellion led by a senior general, and if even Guatemoc, a high prince of the royal family, is involved in the plot, then you will be safer guarded by Spaniards with all their weapons and martial skills, men who answer only to me, than you will be in your own palace. Surely you can see, Your Majesty, that you have no other choice? You must by all means come with us.'

Still Moctezuma refused and the argument went back and forth until Velázquez de Léon, who had been growing visibly more tense and agitated, his huge black beard quivering, suddenly lost patience and roared furiously: 'Why do we waste words on this barbarian? We have gone too far to recede now. Let us seize him and if he resists plunge our swords into his body, for if we don't look after ourselves now we shall all be dead men.'

'I'll second that!' said Alvarado, drawing his falchion from its scabbard with a rasp of steel, and there was a chorus of angry assent from the other captains.

Moctezuma was already shaking with fear, sweat oozing from his brow, tears still running down his cheeks, but Velázquez de Léon's fierce tone and the sight of Alvarado's falchion completely unmanned him and he turned beseechingly to Malinal. 'What is happening?' he asked. 'Why are these men so angry? Tell me what I must do.'

Soil yourself, you coward, Malinal thought. *I've seen you do it before. Don't you remember?* But she bit back her hate and derision. What mattered now was the objective, and she sensed that gentle persuasion at this point would work better than the true expression of her own feelings: 'Lord Moctezuma,' she said, 'I advise you to accompany these *tueles* immediately to their quarters and make no protest. I know they will honour you there as the great lord you are. But if you try to stay here a moment longer, they will certainly kill you.'

His face contorted with grief, Moctezuma's resistance all at once collapsed and he gave his agreement in a trembling voice so small it was barely audible. 'I shall do as the *tueles* require,' he said, 'only tell them not to kill me.'

'He accepts,' Malinal told Cortés. 'He'll come with us.'

It was as though the air had changed, a fresh breeze after a thunderstorm, and the atmosphere of tension and danger in the room began to subside. The Spaniards' stern faces broke into wide grins, showing their teeth through their beards. Teudile, who had perhaps been conscious for some time, sat up looking dazed.

Malinal had no idea what was going to happen next, how the transfer of the emperor from his own palace to the palace of Axayacatl was actually going to be achieved, but watched amazed as Moctezuma's pride took over and did the Spaniards' work for them. Since it was clearly impossible for the Great Speaker of the Mexica to be forced to act in any way against his will, his strategy was to pretend that the huge indignity he had just consented to was, in fact, something he very much wanted to happen – indeed something he himself had suggested. 'Ah, Teudile,' he said, 'I have consulted with our lord Hummingbird and I have learnt from him of a plot that has been laid against me by Prince Guatemoc and the faithless General Qualpopoca. To save my life I must take shelter for some time in the palace of Axayacatl with our friends the *tueles*. Go now and summon Cuitláhuac, but first inform him of this decision and prepare my palanquin and have it ready.'

'My lord, are you sure?'

'I am completely sure, Teudile – ' a ghastly smile from Moctezuma, even as his stomach rumbled threateningly – 'do not question me again. No one is to question me. This is a matter of life and death and my mind is made up.'

Malinal explained what was happening to Cortés, who allowed Teudile to leave the room. The tension began to build again but a short while later the steward was back, accompanied by Cuitláhuac, whose face bore an expression of intense suspicion and confusion. 'My lord . . .' he began, but Moctezuma would not allow him to go further: 'No, Cuitláhuac. No questions. The *tueles* are my friends, they are *our* friends, and they have offered to protect my life in the coming days while we deal with the plotters . . .'

'Plotters, my lord? What plotters?'

'I regret to tell you, Cuitláhuac, that I have evidence of a plot against me mounted by your son, Prince Guatemoc, my own nephew . . .'

'But, sire. That is impossible. I assure you—'

'Sadly, Cuitláhuac, it is not impossible. I have been informed of this by my spies and it has been confirmed by the highest authority, the *very* highest authority, the god Hummingbird himself, in whose temple I kept vigil last night. It is not to be doubted.' From the second finger of his right hand Moctezuma removed a large ring, set with a gemstone, on which was carved an image of the War God: 'Here is my signet, brother, and my command. When you have seen my person safely installed under the protection of the *tueles* in the palace of Axayacatl, you are to take this ring and by its authority you are to arrest Prince Guatemoc and General Qualpopoca. These are the ringleaders, Cuitláhuac! I require them to be brought to me for questioning. I further require any troops they have assembled – and I believe you will find the numbers are large – to be disbanded at once and dispersed to barracks outside the city where they are to await my orders.'

'But Your Majesty—'

'NO!' snapped Moctezuma. 'No questions. You will do as I command, Cuitláhuac. I am your sovereign and your lord. Do you understand what is required of you?'

'I understand, Majesty, and I will obey.'

While all this unfolded, Malinal gave a whispered commentary to Cortés who replied: 'My God, the man has thought of everything. I couldn't have served our cause better if I'd put my own words in his mouth. But is Cuitláhuac really going to accept this? It seems astonishing he'd agree to arrest his own son.'

'It's not so astonishing when you know the Mexica as well as I do,' Malinal replied. 'They're so used to obeying the Great Speaker, most of them wouldn't hesitate to kill their own children or their mothers or their wives if Moctezuma required it. I've seen it happen before, and Cuitláhuac has a reputation as a yes-man.'

Preceded by Teudile, resting on the arms of Cuitláhuac and Cortés, followed and surrounded by the rest of the Spaniards and by his own royal bodyguard, Moctezuma made his way to the ground floor of the palace and through the polished halls, where Sergeant García Brabo and other members of his tough squad, who'd been loitering as instructed in groups of three and four, joined them, radiating harm and violence. Not once was a challenge offered by any of the hundreds of Mexica sentries they passed, but again Malinal was not surprised. As usual the guardsmen had their eyes lowered in the presence of their emperor and they were, besides, entirely used to seeing him in the company of the Spaniards.

At the portico Moctezuma's ornate palanquin was already waiting, as well as the retinue of nobles who would carry it and accompany the emperor on his progress across the grand plaza to the palace of Axayacatl. They were obviously aware that something was amiss, and several of them did pluck up the courage to ask their monarch if all was well with him, if he really wanted to go, and even – in the case of two particularly daring souls – if he would like them to fight with the Spaniards. To all these inquiries Moctezuma gave convincingly reassuring replies – he was well, he did indeed wish to go with the Spaniards, and under no circumstances should they be fought as they were friends and allies whose protection he sought against an anticipated onslaught by rebels and plotters.

Many ordinary citizens of Tenochtitlan – nobles, merchants and a large group of commoners – were present in the sacred plaza at the time, come to offer their devotions to Hummingbird and other deities. When they saw the emperor emerge from his palace and climb into his palanquin, all of course fell to their faces on the paving stones, but as the procession passed a rumour spread amongst them, instigated, Malinal suspected, by some agent of Teudile, that the monarch was being carried off by force to the residence of the white men. Soon the crowd, its mood turning ugly, was trailing in pursuit of the procession, some of the Spanish rearguard were jostled, swords were drawn and violence seemed inevitable, until Moctezuma drew back the curtains of the palanquin, showed himself and ordered the mob to disperse.

It was, Malinal realised, the emperor's last chance to end this ignominious kidnapping and secure his liberty, but he let it pass him by through a pathetic but sadly characteristic mixture of cowardice and pride.

Moments later, when he stepped down in the courtyard of the Spanish quarters, Moctezuma was no longer a free man.

Malinal could only trust and hope he would never be free again.

Invisible, unseen by all, though her presence was suspected by both Malinal and Pepillo, Tozi witnessed the unmanning of Moctezuma with grim satisfaction. Particularly pleasing was the fact that her information about Qualpopoca's attack on Villa Rica, and the murder of its commander, had been instrumental in bringing forward the caudillo's plans to take Moctezuma hostage, and thus made it certain that the ten thousand virgin girls trembling in the fattening pens and earmarked for sacrifice would now be rescued.

By being present as a silent witness, Tozi had also learned something else of immediate and urgent importance.

Guatemoc, who had so passionately made love to her in his quarters at Chapultepec that secret night two months before – fierce, beautiful Guatemoc, to whom she had surrendered her virginity and to whom she had at last revealed her true identity as a witch – was in danger! The charges behind Moctezuma's arrest warrant were trumped up, of course, but Cuitláhuac was such a sycophant, and such a stickler for the rules and for authority, that he would probably go ahead, arrest his own son, and even preside over his execution when Moctezuma demanded it – as he surely would.

Accordingly, when Moctezuma had eventually been conveyed to the palace of Axayacatl and had been left securely in Spanish hands, it was Cuitláhuac Tozi watched as, stern-faced, he summoned two squads of the Great Speaker's personal guard, each fifty strong, and sent them on their way – one squad to proceed at the double to Chapultepec to detain Guatemoc and the other to detain Qualpopoca.

Tozi could run like a deer, and she ran now ahead of the Chapultepec squad, still cloaked in invisibility. By the time she'd crossed the Tacuba causeway they were a mile behind her. She grinned and lengthened her stride. She'd have plenty of time to warn Guatemoc.

Chapter Five

The weeks after 14 November 1519 . . . The calm before the storm

Day followed day.

The forces mustered to destroy the Spaniards obeyed Moctezuma's command and withdrew in good order to their barracks outside the capital.

Freeing ten thousand sacrificial captives, most under the age of twelve, caused problems – for these children, many of whom had been orphaned in the same raids in which they were seized, all had to be housed and cared for while ways were found to return them to the tribes and regions from which they came. At first there was outrage at the mass release, and the sense of some great affront to the gods was compounded, amongst a populace addicted to the spectacle of sacrifice, by the simultaneous liberation of many of the other victims held prisoner in pens around the Mexica capital. There were murmurs and protests amongst the nobles, rumours of riots and wars amongst the commoners, veiled threats from the markets to stop selling to the nest of foreign vipers in their midst, but day followed day and none of this materialised, as Cortés strengthened his grip on power and the great city returned to its business much as usual.

Though he continued to radiate confidence and assurance, Cortés was, in truth, very relieved that his desperate gambit had succeeded. 'You shouldn't be surprised,' Malinal told him. 'These people depend utterly on Moctezuma for every decision, and you hold him in your hands.' The titles and epithets by which the Mexica emperor was traditionally known, she said, gave some glimpse of this – for he was 'the heart of the city', 'a great ceiba tree', towering above all, in whose shade and under whose protection the populace rested secure, 'a wall, a barricade' against all enemies and disasters, 'the seat, the flute, the jaws, the ears' of the gods, and above all 'he who commands'. There was nothing surprising in the fact that, by controlling such a pivotal figure, Cortés was able to dominate the whole of Mexica society.

The arrest of Qualpopoca had been ordered by Cuitláhuac on the same day, Saturday 14 November, that Moctezuma himself became a 'guest' of the Spaniards in the palace of Axayacatl. Guatemoc escaped, fleeing the family estates barely an hour ahead of the squad sent to bring him in for questioning – tipped off, Malinal knew, by Tozi.

Moctezuma wanted to order the prince pursued and captured. Prompted by Malinal's gentle urging, however, Cortés refused. Guatemoc meant nothing to him, and besides, the crime of treason the prince had been accused of was entirely fictitious. Qualpopoca was a different case entirely. He was guilty of the attack on the Spaniards at the coast and had sacrificed Juan de Escalante, whose poor ruined head was retrieved from the skull rack on top of the great pyramid.

For that crime Cortés required vengeance. He resolved to exact it in a way that would set an example to all the citizens of Tenochtitlan and to the ruling elite who lorded it over them. Accordingly a royal procla- mation was issued by the now entirely compliant Moctezuma, and sent to the coast in the hands of fast relay messengers, calling off the siege of Villa Rica. With the proclamation was an order requiring all fifteen of the senior officers who had served under Qualpopoca and participated in the sacrifice of Escalante to return to the capital at once.

They arrived in Tenochtitlan on Monday 23 November where they were immediately arrested and confined with Qualpopoca in the dungeon of the palace of Axayacatl. There, now that he had them all assembled, Cortés put them to torture. As their fingernails and teeth were pulled out and the soles of their feet roasted over hot coals, every one of them insisted that the operations at the coast – the re-imposition of tribute on the Totonacs, the attack on the Spanish relief column, the deaths that had resulted, the capture, sacrifice and beheading of Juan de Escalante, and the subsequent siege of Villa Rica – had all been done on the direct orders of Moctezuma.

Cortés had their confession written out, signed and notarised, and on the morning of Tuesday 24 November he took it to Moctezuma, who had remained throughout under comfortable house arrest in the suite of rooms he had been given in the palace of Axayacatl. Since the conse- quences of an escape by the emperor were too awful to contemplate, Cortés had placed him under close watch, guarded day and night by rotating teams of sixty heavily armed conquistadors, but otherwise leaving him free, as he had promised, to conduct the routine administration of his kingdom. As a result Teudile and several other courtiers and ministers were with him, engaged in government business, when Cortés entered and told them through Malinal to leave.

As they scurried away, Cortés addressed Moctezuma very sternly and read out the confession of Qualpopoca and his accomplices, which Malinal translated into Nahuatl.

Predictably Moctezuma fell to making excuses – it was all lies, men under torture would say anything, and so on and so forth – but Cortés cut him short. 'I'm sorry, Your Majesty,' he said, 'I don't believe you and I do believe this confession which deeply implicates you in the killing and sacrifice of my brother Spaniards. You didn't do these deeds yourself but I have no doubt whatsoever they were done on your command, and since our king's ordinances prescribe that anyone causing others to be killed should himself be killed, it's obvious what punishment you deserve.'

At this Moctezuma burst into tears and fell to his knees begging forgiveness. Cortés watched him for a while, knowing what it meant to Malinal to see her enemy humbled in this way, but finally raised the broken emperor and embraced him. 'I hold you in such high regard,' he said, nodding to Malinal to translate, 'and my affection and concern for you are so great that – even though you're guilty – I'd do anything to save your life. So be of good cheer, Moctezuma! You have nothing to fear from me and you can rest assured I won't kill you today or ever. You're my friend, and we'll continue to rule this great country together for many years to come.'

Moctezuma was so deeply, pitifully grateful that he fell to his knees a second time to express his thanks, at which Cortés suddenly, in a very deliberate piece of theatre, became stern again. 'Nonetheless,' he said, 'you have committed a great crime that merits death and that cannot be atoned for, even by a monarch, without punishment.' He turned and signalled to Sergeant García Brabo and three of his toughs, who were waiting in the hallway; they now entered carrying chains, fetters and tools.

With a loud groan Moctezuma soiled himself, filthying his costly robe, filling the room with a sour stink.

'Dear God,' Cortés muttered, 'what now?'

'Fear affects him this way,' Malinal confided. 'A year ago I witnessed the same thing and he ordered me strangled. I haven't told you the story, but it was the beginning of all this for me.'

'Well he's just going to have to go as he is,' Cortés said. There was scorn in his voice. 'Take him, Brabo.'

With a look of disgust, avoiding the worst of the mess, the sergeant forced Moctezuma to the floor and held him in place with a headlock while the fetters were hammered round his ankles, then hauled him upright again and dragged him from the room, crying out in terror, his fouled robe clinging to his thighs, while Cortés and Malinal followed coldly, saying nothing.

The full guard of sixty soldiers then fell into place around Moctezuma, shuffling fearfully in his fetters and chains, and marched him through the corridors and courtyard of the palace of Axayacatl, out under the portico and into the bright sunlight of the grand plaza. There the entire Spanish army was lined up in full armour, guns and cavalry at the ready, in front of the great pyramid where Qualpopoca and his fifteen accomplices awaited, tied to stakes amidst heaped piles of wooden spear shafts, arrows and *macuahuitls* brought as kindling from the royal armoury.

As witnesses to the spectacle, Cortés had drafted in an audience of several thousand of the leading citizens of Tenochtitlan and a great crowd of commoners. It was a calculated risk: a possible rebellion in one pan of the scales; a scaring and memorable demonstration of Spanish power in the other. But, as Cortés had expected, the cowed and superstitious Mexica, lacking effective leadership, made no trouble, and now stood in complete silence as their emperor in his stained robe was paraded before them in irons and made to stand on a viewing platform flanked by his guards.

No explanation was given for Moctezuma's humiliation, but Cortés read out a short prepared statement on the self-admitted guilt of Qualpopoca and his accomplices. They had conducted, he said, an unprovoked attack on the Spanish garrison at Villa Rica, and murdered eight innocent Spanish soldiers, two of whom, including the garrison commander, Don Juan de Escalante, a man of great goodness and nobility, had been subjected to the forbidden rite of human sacrifice. In punishment for these crimes all the perpetrators would now be burnt to death on a fire made from their own weapons of war. A similar fate, Cortés concluded, would be inflicted without mercy on any who should dare to raise their hands against the Spaniards in the future. He paused to allow Malinal to give the translation then, at his signal, a dozen conquistadors with burning brands approached the woodpile and set it alight.

The flames were small at first, but soon they licked around the bare feet and legs of the victims, who shifted uncomfortably, apparently unable to believe what was happening to them, then strained against the chains that bound them to the stakes, then cringed and recoiled as though they hoped to avoid this dreadful doom. Soon they were begging for clemency, crying out in terror and finally howling and screaming in hideous pain as the fire slowly devoured their living flesh, turning the links of their chains red hot and taking hold of the deposits of fat under their skin until their own bodies became fuel for the flames and they were transformed into blazing candles.

Cortés made Moctezuma watch until the corpses of Qualpopoca and his officers were reduced to blackened, twisted logs the size of children, and then had the emperor marched back to his quarters, still in irons. An hour later he joined him there, finding him slumped speechless on the floor uttering low animal groans, and with great gentleness personally removed his chains and fetters, all the while expressing his regret at having been obliged to impose so harsh a punishment on him. Once again Moctezuma responded with tears and wretched gratitude to these little acts of kindness, at which Cortés embraced him and told him he loved him like a brother.

'You've crushed his spirit,' Malinal said as they left the emperor for the night.

'Like a bug under my boot,' Cortés replied.

Day followed day.

Tozi kept little Miahuatl with her. There was no one else to care for her since the girl's mother had long since been sacrificed; another mouth to feed, more or less, made no difference in the well-supplied palace with its legions of willing servants and slaves. Malinal was positively delighted and even Malinche seemed pleased, loftily citing a passage from his religious book, the meaning of which Pepillo later helped Tozi to understand: 'Let the little children come to me, and do not hinder them, for the kingdom of God belongs to such as these.'

The girl was a delight, always happy in her simple, innocent way, filling the corridors and courtyards of the palace with bubbling, joyous laughter.

By contrast, poor Pepillo – though struggling to appear normal and even cheerful – was burdened with a deep and abiding sorrow at the loss of his friend and mentor Juan de Escalante. His hound Melchior, constantly at his side, failed to bring him out of this state of grief, indeed seemed only to remind him of his other friend, after whom the dog had been named, killed at the Battle of Potonchan.

So it was sorrow upon sorrow, loss upon loss, for Pepillo. And Tozi, who herself had suffered so many sorrows and losses, was unable to help. She knew that the young Spaniard was attracted to her, that he was a virgin, and that she could most probably subdue his grief if she were to take him as her lover. But she also felt an unbreakable bond with Guatemoc and was determined that he would be the only lover she would ever have. It made her heart soar when she remembered how they'd renewed their union at Chapultepec on the afternoon of Cortés's coup against Moctezuma, and she found herself longing for him again now.

Before they'd parted company that afternoon, with the arrest squad only minutes away, Guatemoc had charged her to get word of what had happened to his friends Starving Coyote, Fuzzy Face, Big Dart, Man-Eater and Mud Head, and to ask them to come to him.

'How will they find you?' she'd asked.

'They'll find me,' he'd replied with a wink. 'We saw this coming. We've got a plan.'

Since then the five warriors had quietly vanished from Tenochtitlan.

Tozi took it as a good sign.

Day followed day.

More than a thousand Tlascalan children had been amongst those selected for Moctezuma's great sacrifice and, following their release, Shikotenka, battle-king of Tlascala, made it his mission to bring them home, together with hundreds of men and women of his nation held in fattening pens outside the sacred precinct.

Malinche was a conundrum, likeable and detestable at the same time, but he had done a great thing by freeing these prisoners and Shikotenka would never forget it. After bringing them back to Tlascala, however, and spending some wildly erotic nights with his wife Xilonen, whom he had not seen since mounting his decisive intervention on Cortés's side at Cholula, he found he was in no hurry to return to Tenochtitlan. The Spaniards were no longer in immediate danger there and could manage very well without his help. Five hundred Tlascalan warriors under Chipahua's command had remained in the Mexica capital, and Shikotenka sent Tree back with five hundred more to reinforce them.

They would be needed if hostilities broke out again, but for the moment Shikotenka intended to enjoy the peace.

* * *

Day followed day.

The peace still held in Tenochtitlan and Moctezuma continued with the appearance of governing his country while remaining at all times under Spanish guard. Malinal watched him closely, but he always insisted when asked by the nobles and warrior chiefs who came to call on him that his presence in the palace of Axayacatl was voluntary and that the god Huitzilopochtli himself had told him he must remain here.

To add to the illusion that all was well, and that he was truly a willing guest amongst friends, Cortés one day asked Malinal to remind Moctezuma of his offer to show him the great royal zoo with its House of Serpents, House of Panthers, House of Hunting Birds and House of Human Monsters. These attractions lay within the gardens of Moctezuma's own palace, still the administrative heart of the empire, and Cortés felt that a public visit where he was seen to be shown around by the amenable emperor would go far to cement the impression he wished to maintain.

Moctezuma was carried in his palanquin across the sacred plaza to the portico of his own palace, and then with two nobles sweeping the path in front of him and Teudile going ahead, he led Cortés – together with Malinal and an escort of thirty fully armed Spaniards – through the gardens and into the zoo.

The House of Human Monsters came first, its cages filled with freaks – a naked woman whose whole body was completely covered in thick, matted hair, another with pink eyes and snow-white skin, identical twins joined at the head, a man with two heads, another with a huge growth of wrinkled, doughy flesh hanging from his face, and also numerous dwarfs, hunchbacks and cripples. 'Why do you make a show of such poor souls?' Cortés asked.

'For my amusement,' Moctezuma replied. He seemed entirely to have recovered his dignity, despite his recent public humiliation; indeed he now behaved as though that moment of shame had never occurred. 'Do you not find them amusing?'

Cortés did not reply.

In the House of Hunting Birds, Alvarado, who had joined the party, was very excited to discover many different birds of prey. These it seemed were used by the Mexica for hunting in the same manner as falcons, eagles and goshawks in Europe. An animated conversation ensued, with the upshot that the emperor and Alvarado agreed to mount a hunting expedition the very next day.

'You know,' Malinal said to Cortés, as they came next to the roaring and snarling jungle creatures the Spanish called panthers and the Chontal Maya called *b'alam* – jaguars – 'that the Mexica used to feed the unwanted corpse parts of their sacrificial victims to these beasts?'

Alvarado had overheard. 'You mean the parts the bloody savages didn't wish to eat themselves!' he said.

Bloody savages, with whom you're nonetheless quite happy to go hunting, Malinal thought.

Cortés was looking genuinely curious: 'What do they feed them on now?'

'I've no idea,' said Malinal shuddering. She didn't like it here. The horrible bellows and grunts, and the rank, filthy smell of the animals, combined with the scaly slithers and hissing sounds emanating from the neighbouring House of Serpents made her feel she had entered an ante-chamber to that place the Christians called hell.

'I say, Moctezuma,' Alvarado asked, 'we'd like to know what you feed your beasts on, now we no longer allow you to butcher humans?'

Malinal put the question a little more delicately into Nahuatl. Moctezuma replied he was not informed on this subject, but since hundreds of zookeepers were present, having prostrated themselves at the passage of the royal party, it should not be too difficult to find the answer. He whispered to a retainer who in turn called out for Ichtaka, the chief of the zookeepers, Moctezuma explained, who had formerly been responsible for salvaging the remains of sacrificial victims thrown down the great pyramid.

An elderly grey-haired man lying a few paces away raised his head, scrambled to his feet, and with much bowing and scraping approached the emperor, who questioned him about the present diet of the large carnivores. 'Leftovers from the kitchens, Your Majesty,' he answered. 'Whatever you and the nobles and these *tueles* don't finish, that's what we feed to our beasts . . .' It seemed whereas there had previously been an overabundance of flesh in the zoo, there was now a dearth and the animals were going hungry. 'If I may make so bold,' Ichtaka suggested, 'it might be wise to order extra supplies of fresh deer meat from the hunters in future, or some of your collection, Your Majesty, might starve.'

But Malinal was no longer translating for Cortés and in fact could hardly pay attention at all. Lying by the path that wound its way past every cage and enclosure in the zoo, next to the place where Ichtaka had lain moments before, was a skinny little boy dressed only in a loincloth.

His face was still down, pressed into the earth as was proper when the emperor was near, but there was something hauntingly, eerily familiar about him.

Malinal felt the beat of her heart rising, drumming in her chest. Surely this could not be little Coyotl, Tozi's protégé, snatched away from them, lost and presumed sacrificed that same terrible night, many moons before, when Tozi and Malinal had escaped death at Moctezuma's hands?

'Coyotl,' Malinal said, her voice barely a whisper. 'Is that you?'

There was no response and she spoke louder: 'Coyotl? Are you Coyotl?'

This time the little boy looked up and suddenly there was no doubt and she was running towards him, scooping him from the ground, holding him in her arms, feeling his little arms wrapped around her head, kissing his cheeks, embracing him. 'Coyotl!' she cried. 'Coyotl! You're alive.'

'Malinal,' he answered, 'where is Tozi?'

'She's here in Tenochtitlan!' Malinal replied, half laughing, half crying. 'She's alive and she's well and she's safe. We're all safe!'

Slowly at first, then like a torrent pouring through a broken earth dam, Coyotl's words came out.

That dreadful night of the holocaust, when he and Tozi and Malinal had been brought to the great pyramid to die and he'd been separated from them, he'd been sure he would never see them again. The wicked priest Ahuizotl had placed him in line at the foot of the western stairway and right there, right then, he'd decided he was going to live. He was very small, no one really noticed him, and when Ahuizotl was gone he slipped out of the line, dived into one of the great piles of butchered torsos lying at the foot of the steps, burrowed down deep amongst the blood and the guts and waited . . . waited.

The following morning Ichtaka the zookeeper and his staff came with wheelbarrows to begin collecting the bodies to take to the zoo to feed to the animals. It was Ichtaka himself, kindly Ichtaka, who had found Coyotl and said to him, 'Shush! Say nothing! Lie still!' and bundled him into a barrow and covered him with butchered torsos and wheeled him away to a new life, making him an assistant, feeding him, housing him, giving him a job to do and responsibility and safety.

All this was told while Moctezuma and Cortés and the royal party looked on. Now Malinal turned to Cortés and said: 'Hernán, do you understand who this little boy is?'

A broad smile: 'Yes, my dear. I think I've got it. He's the brat you and

Tozi were imprisoned with in the fattening pen, awaiting your deaths at the hands of our friend Mucktey here . . .'

'And we escaped. We all escaped! All three of us. It's truly a miracle.'

'The hand of the Lord was at work, Malinal.'

'So you understand Coyotl has to come back with us, now, to our quarters? He has to stay with us. Tozi's going to be overjoyed!'

Cortés's smile grew wider. 'I see . . . One more child to add to our little orphanage then.'

He paused and seemed to reflect, an emotion Malinal did not recognise showed in his eyes and his smile drained away. 'So many children have died on this campaign,' he continued finally, 'some at my own hand. Yet the Good Book tells us it's better to be drowned in the depths of the sea than to hurt a child. I fear I have much recompense to make.'

'What is the lord Malinche saying?' Moctezuma asked.

Malinal showed him a cold face. 'Nothing that concerns you,' she told him.

Day followed day.

Guatemoc trekked north through Chichemec canyon country with Starving Coyote, Fuzzy Face, Big Dart, Man-Eater and Mud Head.

It was not a matter of fleeing an arrest warrant. Guatemoc was here – they were all here – because Tenochtitlan ruled by Malinche with Moctezuma as his creature was an unbearable and insufferable disgrace. The nation had to be cleansed of its alien usurpers and returned to the state of purity from which it had so tragically fallen. For this purpose, and to fulfil the solemn promise he had made to Tozi when she had saved him from Moctezuma's plot to poison him many months before, Guatemoc had persuaded his companions to join him on a sacred pilgrimage. Their purpose was to seek the lost land of Aztlán and the Seven Caves of Chicomoztoc, the home of the gods, the mystic place of origin of the Mexica and all other Nahua peoples, where legends spoke of masters of wisdom and workers of magic who they hoped might weave for them the spells of a new dispensation.

They had sworn a blood oath to follow this sacred quest to its end and return to purge Tenochtitlan or die in the attempt. Judging only from the numbers of savage Chichemec warriors shadowing them from the cliffs above, the latter outcome seemed more likely than the former, but a thing was not done until it was done.

Guatemoc bared his teeth in a snarl and unslung his *macuahuitl*.

Part II

Five months later

Chapter Six

⬥

Friday 22 April 1520

Pepillo retrieved his journal from its hiding place beneath the floorboards in a corner of his room, blew off the dust from its cover, placed it on his desk, and opened it.

His last entry had been written more than five months previously, on Thursday 12 November 1519, and documented the bold plan to take Moctezuma prisoner that Cortés had put before the assembled conquistadors that day.

Rereading the entry now, Pepillo smiled wistfully at the enthusiastic language he'd used – the language, and enthusiasm, of the time before his world had changed forever. Orphaned in infancy, reared by the Dominicans, he had never known a father's love or guidance until Juan de Escalante had taken him under his wing, and shown him kindness and given him a sword and taught him how to use it. But only a few hours after Cortés had told the men of his plan, Tozi had come with the news of Juan's brutal murder by the Mexica and – dear God! – that his severed head had been carried in a basket to Moctezuma.

Two days later, on Saturday 14 November, Moctezuma had been made captive, precisely as Cortés had designed. Pepillo had witnessed the abject capitulation of the Great Speaker of the Mexica with a grim sense of justice being done – but with no joy, for no matter how cruelly Moctezuma or his generals might be punished, it would not bring Juan back to life.

In the months that followed, nothing lifted Pepillo out of his misery. He was restless and Melchior was his constant companion on long walks around the streets of Tenochtitlan, the crowds parting and making way, with gasps of fear and downcast eyes, at the approach of the '*tuele*' and his 'dragon'. But neither the huge dog's boundless energy, nor the exotic sights and sounds of the Mexica city, provided the least comfort.

Even Tozi, whom Pepillo was sure he loved, seemed distant towards him now, and a few days before had left Tenochtitlan on an unexplained mission to the north. Apparently her purpose there was so urgent that she had not even bid him farewell, merely passing the word through Malinal that she would be gone for some time.

Pepillo's one source of real satisfaction since last November, the only time when everything, just for a little while, had seemed good and right again, was when Malinal and Tozi had been reunited with their little protégé Coyotl. If such a thing could happen, in this cruel world, then surely there was a force that worked for the good in all things, even though it did not always succeed?

Pepillo continued to grieve but allowed himself to be conscripted as a tutor to Coyotl and, not wishing to spread despair, began to make a greater effort to hide his feelings. He did all the work that was assigned to him and did not complain when, towards the end of January 1520, Cortés took him aside and told him that until further notice he was to serve as page to Moctezuma. 'I know you detest him,' Cortés had said, 'and with good reason, but he has asked for you personally and – things being the way they are – we'd better oblige him.'

'Things being the way they are' was a reference to the growing discord in relations between the Mexica and the Spaniards that had already resulted, shortly after the New Year, in the first open attempt at rebellion.

It was an exciting time, Pepillo realised, and an important time – a time that would have its place in history. And it was his responsibility to keep a journal to record notable events so that the caudillo could later confirm dates and details for his own letters and memoirs. Pepillo knew that he should be making daily entries, but could not overcome the deadening depression that still gripped him, and so – for months – he wrote nothing.

Well . . . such a state of affairs could not be allowed to continue, and Pepillo had awakened this morning, Friday 22 April, filled with new resolve. Poor Juan was dead and there was nothing to be done about it. He would always hold a special place for him in his heart but he would grieve no longer.

Turning to the next blank page in his journal he dipped his quill into the inkpot and wrote in his neat, firm hand: Friday the 22nd day of April, Year of Our Lord 1520.

He paused and collected his thoughts. He would not try to describe everything that had happened in the past five months, but certain key developments must be documented.

For example, in the first days of December 1519, troubled by the island location of Tenochtitlan, and the risk that the Indians might break the bridges on the causeways and hold the Spaniards prisoner in the capital, Cortés had given orders for four ships to be built on the lake. Twin-masted brigantines that could be propelled either by sail or by oars, they had to be capable, should an emergency arise, of taking three hundred men and horses to the mainland.

The entire project was placed under the direction of the expedition's chief carpenter and most experienced shipbuilder, Martin Lopez. Hundreds of native craftsmen seconded by Moctezuma also contributed their skills, many of the highest order, Lopez confided. The work proceeded with such speed that the ships, each a little over forty feet long and capable of carrying four falconets and seventy-five men, were completed and ready for action by Wednesday 17 February 1520.

Having the foresight and taking the initiative to get the brigantines built reflected well on Cortés, and offered great reassurance to all, but his distribution of the spoils of war was a source of continuous unrest and discontent. In July the previous year, before the conquistadors had begun their march from the coast to Tenochtitlan, he had persuaded the men to part with their shares of the booty thus far acquired by the expedition, and had sent it all across the ocean to King Charles in Spain to win his favour for the venture.

There had been no attempt to assess the value of the many rich acquisitions since then, including the richest acquisition of all – the treasure of Axayacatl that the Spaniards had found concealed in their quarters. On Wednesday 20 January 1520, therefore, after frequent requests from the men, Cortés announced a stocktaking. In addition to feathers and trinkets (held not to be worth counting), it showed the following substantial items, all below – indeed vastly below! – expectations:

Gold gained both in the form of 'presents' from Moctezuma, from the treasury of Axayacatl, and from items seized: 160,000 pesos;

Fine ornaments, jewellery and silver plate: 75,000 pesos.

At once a rumour spread that Cortés had either hidden away or falsely underestimated the amount of gold, the true value of which was claimed to exceed a million pesos. There was likewise a general feeling that the jewels acquired along the way must be worth much more than 75,000 pesos; some even suggested ten times as much.

The following week the caudillo called a muster, at which he not only insisted that his figures were correct, but also went on to reveal the deductions that would be made before any general distribution. It was noted by many that a large share of the deductions were to reimburse Cortés himself for expenses incurred in financing the fleet the year before, and to reimburse the full cost of sailors' wages, the food, the horses and all the ships. In addition there was the king's fifth, and Cortés's own fifth, awarded to him in perpetuity by the men at Villa Rica but now bitterly resented.

The upshot, after the cavaliers had received five hundred pesos apiece, with double pay also going to musketeers and crossbowmen, was that very little – indeed not more than a hundred pesos each – was left to distribute to the common soldiers.

Some were so insulted that they refused to accept it, and all were angry and disappointed. Meanwhile a quarrel broke out involving the cavalier Juan Velázquez de Léon, who, despite earlier difficulties, had been a close ally of Cortés since Villa Rica, and Gonzalo de Mexia, the officer responsible for calculating the king's fifth.

Mexia accused the cavalier of keeping certain pieces of plate aside for himself before they were submitted to the royal stamp.

Velázquez de Léon replied that the gold from which the plate was made had been a gift to him from Cortés on which no fifth was payable.

From words the parties came to swords, and Velázquez de Léon succeeded in stabbing Mexia. The affair might have ended fatally but for the intervention of Cortés, who placed the cavalier under arrest.

It was not the first time that Velázquez de Léon had been imprisoned by Cortés but, by early February, after a fortnight in chains, Cortés had released him again.

Meanwhile, the poison over the unfair distribution of the spoils, once so virulent amongst the common soldiers, had begun to seep away. Many were addicted to cards and had soon lost what little they had gained, losing interest in the matter of the size of their share at the same time. Besides, Cortés had made them another speech – all honeyed words, Pepillo recalled – in which he had said that whatever was in his possession was for them, and that he did not want his fifth but only the share that came to him as captain-general, and that if anyone needed anything he would give it to him. He reminded the men that the gold that had come their way so far was only a trifle, and that they could see what great cities there were, and what rich mines, and that they should be lords of them all and very rich and prosperous. In addition, he secretly gave golden jewels to some soldiers and made great promises to others, and he ordered that the food brought by Moctezuma's stewards should be divided equally amongst all the soldiers, receiving no greater share himself than the rest.

All this went down well with the men, as it usually did, and very quickly the insurrection over pay drew to a close.

But another storm was brewing in the first months of 1520, this time amongst the Indians. The instigator was Cacama, the ruler of Texcoco. Out of all Moctezuma's vassals, it was well known that he had been most in favour of admitting the Spaniards to Tenochtitlan the year before, arguing that if their motives were good then all would be well, and if they were bad then there were sufficient warriors at the Great Speaker's disposal to destroy them. Now, seeing the humiliating captivity of Moctezuma – and indeed it *was* humiliating, Pepillo conceded, no matter how Cortés tried to dress it up as free choice – Cacama reached the obvious conclusion. Regretting his earlier advice that the Spaniards should be admitted, he set about forming a confederacy with other leading Mexica vassals to rescue the Great Speaker. He called in particular upon the king of Nonoalco, the king of Tlacopan, and some others of high authority, all of whom shared his views, and all of whom commanded significant forces running into the tens of thousands. He then sent messengers to Tenochtitlan urging the nobility of the Mexica to rise up and join him.

Falling into a black rage, Cortés would have marched on Texcoco at once to smash Cacama's rebellion and to replace him on the throne with the rival claimant – his brother Ishtlil, whom Cortés anyway favoured. However, he was dissuaded from so precipitate a course of action by Moctezuma who claimed – truthfully as it turned out – to have several powerful Texcocan nobles in his pay. With their assistance, he insinuated, it would be easy to secure Cacama's person, and thus break up the rebellion, without need for violence.

Pepillo smiled, remembering how Cortés had relished the intrigue, saying it reminded him of Europe, where monarchs were in the habit of maintaining stipendiaries for similar purposes in the courts of neighbouring princes, and on Saturday 6 February he gave his assent to the plan.

A few days later Cacama was ambushed, seized, bundled into a canoe and paddled straight across the lake to Tenochtitlan, where Cortés put him in fetters. Moctezuma then ordered the arrest of the other vassal kings and chiefs who had entered into the confederacy with Cacama.

By the end of February 1520, they all sweltered in the same stinking prison, in a wing of Axayacatl's palace, that already held their unfortunate leader.

The caudillo's thoughts at this time, which he shared openly with the men, naturally turned to the resources of the vast land which the Mexica called the One World, and over which the Great Speaker ruled. Most urgently – where did the gold of the Mexica come from? Were there mines? Was it panned from rivers?

Cortés put the problem to Moctezuma, who offered to provide guides to the region of Chinantla where gold was obtained. The offer was gratefully accepted and, near the beginning of March, one hundred and twenty Spaniards, accompanied by native guides, were sent out under the command of Rodrigo Rangel, the oldest conquistador – although Pepillo did not believe that he'd been born, as he claimed, in the Year of Our Lord 1447. He was charged, once reaching Chinantla, to divide his force into prospecting parties of ten men each so that the region could be thoroughly explored.

Almost equally pressing was the need for a good, permanent port on the Atlantic coast. The Spanish settlement at Villa Rica de la Veracruz, for which Pepillo's mentor Juan de Escalante had given his life, would continue, for the moment, to serve its purpose, but it was now known that it was exposed to deadly tempests at certain seasons which rendered it unsuitable for shipping. What was needed was a sheltered natural harbour, and to this end Cortés sent a commission, consisting of ten Spaniards, several of them pilots, accompanied by Mexica guides, who descended to Veracruz. From there they made a careful survey southwards as far as the great river Coatzacoalcos, near the mouth of which a safe and suitable harbour was at last found. By mid-March a spot had been selected as the site of a fortified post, and before the beginning of April the caudillo had sent out Juan Velázquez de Léon, still grateful to him for his recent release from prison, at the head of a column of one hundred and fifty men with a commission to plant a colony there.

But at this moment when all seemed well, with a new and perchance more lucrative phase of the conquest stretching ahead, the caudillo had suddenly been moved by his obligations to the faith. Despite all his own exertions, and those of Father Olmedo, neither Moctezuma, nor his subjects, showed the slightest disposition to abjure their ancient beliefs, and even continued to perform human sacrifices, though these had been forbidden. It was not on the scale that Moctezuma had planned for the birthday of the War God – no great holocausts in the thousands! – but it was two or three victims every day, and Pepillo recalled how it had begun to wear on Cortés's conscience.

On Saturday 2 April 1520 he had taken action. Calling together Pedro de Alvarado, Bernal Díaz, Diego de Ordaz, Cristóbal de Olid, Alonso Davila, Andres de Tapia and others, and bringing Pepillo along as a witness and translator, he proposed to test the resolve of the Mexica priests guarding the great pyramid. It was all still vivid in Pepillo's memory, so he dipped the quill again in the inkpot and began to write:

We assembled in the plaza at the base of the pyramid, casually, as though taking a stroll. It was not an unknown thing. But then Cortés turned to the rest of us and said: 'Who will climb that pyramid? It's been five months since I was up there and I'd like to know if anything has changed.'

It was Bernal Díaz, a brave man, who volunteered. He'd been with Cortés on the previous climb in November 1519 and he mounted the steps confidently now, fully armed and armoured.

We observed that he was immediately followed by a gang of filthy priests yelling insults and warnings, but they did not dare to attack him or even to prevent him from climbing. When he reached the summit he entered the temple of the war god, remained within for some moments and emerged, again without provoking any attack.

'Come on, gentlemen,' said Cortés to the rest of us strolling in the courtyard.

We marched up the pyramid at once, weapons at the ready, only to be confronted at the summit by Namacuix, high priest of the Mexica, who had ascended out of sight up another of the four stairways. Shaking with exertion and fury, spittle jumping from his lips, the index finger of his left hand jabbing and pointing accusingly, he ordered us to be gone from the sacred *teocalli*. I translated his words as best I could, at which the caudillo said, 'Knock him down' and Cristóbal de Olid and Diego de Ordaz complied, wrestling Namacuix to the ground and pummelling him about the head and private parts with their boots and fists. Only when he was unconscious, and to all appearances dead, did they cease their onslaught.

Cortés rubbed his hands together eagerly. 'Onward, gentlemen!' he said. 'Let us show this so-called war god what we think of him.'

Then he marched forthwith into the temple of Hummingbird, past the grizzly skull racks in the antechamber and on, with the rest of us following, into the very sanctuary of the demon where the huge effigy of Huitzilopochtli stood.

Here the caudillo did something quite unexpected. Wielding an iron bar that it seemed he had brought with him for this very purpose, and shouting 'Something must we venture for the Lord', he leapt high in the air – de Tapia would afterwards describe it as 'a supernatural leap' – and brought the end of the bar down with great force upon the idol's monstrous head. The priests set up a demented wail as the caudillo punished the great stone statue again and again, breaking off chunks and splinters from it and striking sparks. The rest of us, in a righteous frenzy, echoing Cortés's refrain of 'Something must we venture for the Lord', ran wild through the temple, toppling other idols that stood within, and across the whole summit of the pyramid, intent on wrecking everything.

What stopped us was a messenger from Moctezuma bringing a request that we were to wait for him, please, and in the meantime to do no further damage to the idols. Soon afterwards Moctezuma himself arrived at the summit of the pyramid and asked: 'What is it that you want, Lord Malinche?'

'Great Speaker,' Cortés replied, 'I have often begged you to give up sacrificing human beings to your gods, who are false gods, but you have never done so. Now I must tell you that all my companions, and these captains who have come with me, will tolerate no further delay. We will permit no further sacrifices of human beings. It is our purpose here to remove your false gods from your temple and put Our Lady and a cross, and images of Our Lord, in their place, and have the walls washed clean of all blood and foul corruption and painted white . . .'

Moctezuma spoke in a lowered voice: 'Malinche! Why will you urge matters to an extremity? Do you want to destroy our whole city by stirring up an insurrection? My people will never endure this profanation of their temple and our gods will be enraged against us if we cease to sacrifice to them; I do not know if they will even spare our lives. I pray you to be patient for the present, and I will summon all my priests and see what they reply.'

Cortés was beyond compromise, his hand on the hilt of his sword. 'Let insurrection come if it will! We are ready for it! And

130

by all means I will urge matters to an extremity since that is the right thing to do before God.'

At this show of resolve, Moctezuma crumbled and agreed to halt the sacrifices for a few days while he discussed the matter with the priesthood. Meanwhile, he suggested, perhaps the gods of the Mexica could be placed on one side of the temple and the gods of the Spaniards on the other?

Cortés refused.

In that case, offered Moctezuma, he would do all that he could to accommodate our demands so long as we at least accepted that the Mexica could take their deities wherever they wished. To this the caudillo assented readily enough and three days later, on Tuesday 5 April, with silent efficiency, several hundred Mexica priests bearing ropes and rollers, maguey mats and mattresses, came to the pyramid and carried all the idols off.

A great cross was then erected on the summit platform, and another cross and images of Christ and the Virgin Mary were placed within the now empty temple of Huitzilopochtli. When these arrangements were complete, our whole army moved in solemn procession up the stairway of the pyramid.

Entering the sanctuary, and clustering round its portals, we listened to the service of mass performed by Father Olmedo. And, as the *Te Deum* rose towards heaven, the soldiers knelt, with tears streaming from their eyes, and poured forth their gratitude to the Almighty for this glorious triumph of the cross.

In the days following, Moctezuma became increasingly grim and preoccupied. Contrary to his normal practice, which was for me to attend him at all his meetings, he began to hold private conferences with various of his lords. I suspected a plot and informed Cortés, who arranged to call upon Moctezuma forthwith, accompanied by Malinal, Cristóbal de Olid and Alvarado.

All paid their respects to the Great Speaker, who then addressed them in these words: 'My lord Malinche and captains, I have terrible news. Our god Huitzilopochtli will communicate with me no longer, and I believe this to be on account of my great sin in withholding sacrifice and allowing the idols to be removed from his temple . . .'

'Not so!' Cortés protested. 'By abolishing sacrifice and cleansing the temple you did a marvellous thing, and you will see how my God, the one true God, protects you . . .'

131

Moctezuma shook his head sadly. 'I fear I will not be protected, Malinche. Although he no longer appears to me, the lord Hummingbird has spoken to my priests in vision and through them has commanded us to make war on you and capture you and sacrifice you all on his altar. I have reflected on this command. I cannot hold back my priests much longer and they have the people behind them. I therefore think it would be best that you should at once depart from this city before you are attacked, and leave no one behind. This, my lord Malinche, you must certainly do, for it is in your own interest. Otherwise you will be killed. Remember that your lives are at stake. I have only to lift my finger and every Mexica in the land will rise in arms against you.'

Saying nothing of his own true purpose – which was always and only for the total conquest and subjugation of this land – Cortés replied in soothing and diplomatic tones that he was grateful for the warning, but that at the moment he was troubled by two things. Item the first: he had no ships at the coast in which to embark his men and depart. Item the second: when this deficit had been remedied and the necessary ships had been built, Moctezuma would have to accompany the Spaniards on their voyage so that their great monarch, Don Carlos, Holy Roman Emperor and king of Spain, might see him.

Cortés begged Moctezuma, therefore, to restrain his priests and captains until sufficient ships could be built at the coast to carry off our entire army, and asked for royal carpenters to accompany Martin Lopez to Villa Rica, there to cut wood and begin work.

Moctezuma assigned the carpenters and urged Cortés to hurry up and not waste time in talk, but to get to work. For a little while longer, he promised, he would order his priests and captains not to foment disturbances in the city.

Cortés for his part ordered Lopez to make elaborate and highly visible preparations to build the ships, but covertly to interpose every possible delay. His hope, if he could stall long enough, was that reinforcements, and confirmation of the royal blessing upon his enterprise, would arrive from Spain, whence the expedition's emissaries Don Alonso Hernández Puertocarrero and Don Francisco de Montejo had been sent many months before to win royal favour.

To Pepillo, the hope seemed a slim one. 'Every precaution that prudence can devise has now been taken,' he wrote in his journal. 'The soldier, as he throws himself on his mat for repose, keeps on his armour. He eats, drinks, sleeps with his weapons by his side. His horse stands ready caparisoned, day and night, with the bridle hanging at the saddle-bow. The falconets and lombards are carefully planted so as to command the great avenues. The sentries have been doubled, and every man, of whatever rank, takes his turn in mounting guard. Though we are reluctant to admit it, the facts speak for themselves. Our grip on Tenochtitlan is failing. We are, effectively, in a state of siege.'

Chapter Seven

Saturday 23 April 1520

Day followed day, turmoil boiling beneath the surface of all things and yet still the appearance of calm lay over the city. Cuitláhuac was constantly at Moctezuma's side, as was faithful Teudile, their presence helping to preserve the illusion that the Great Speaker of the Mexica was at court and continued to manage every aspect of government. Meanwhile Namacuix, still brooding over the beating he'd received on the pyramid, kept up his incessant demands for the resumption of human sacrifices, to which Moctezuma, afraid of provoking Malinche, refused to accede. 'Hummingbird himself will show us the right moment,' he said. To this end he began to make daily visits to the Great Pyramid and to the now empty and thoroughly whitewashed – but as yet still standing! – temple of Huitzilopochtli. There he would sit in meditation, sometimes for hours, before the spot where the idol of the war god had towered until the One World had been turned head over heels.

And sometimes, as had long been his habit, Moctezuma would consume the visionary mushrooms called *teonanácatl* in the hope that the divine presence might once again bless him. From the day that he had lost control of his city, however, he had been greeted only by silence and emptiness as tokens of the god's profound disfavour, and was expecting nothing more on this day when the power of the mushrooms coursed through him and bore his spirit aloft and placed him suddenly and uncompromisingly in Hummingbird's presence.

The war god had an alien look about him. He had always been golden haired with dazzling bright skin, which gave him a certain 'Spanish' quality quite unlike the other gods of the Mexica. Today, however, he was also dressed – Moctezuma frowned to see it – in the rough habit of a Spanish friar, was standing at a raised lectern of the type that the Spaniards placed in their churches, and even wore around his neck a rosary instead of the usual garland of human hearts and hands.

'What troubles you, my son?' Huitzilopochtli whispered, and as he spoke the light infusing the scene brightened and Moctezuma saw that they were within a building with soaring arches and vaults much resembling the huge church – they called it a cathedral – that the Spanish were even now preparing ground for in the sacred precinct, abutting the Great Pyramid. Malinche had allowed Moctezuma to study the site drawings and plans, of which he was evidently very proud, and had informed him that they would require the eventual demolition of the pyramid and its replacement by further edifices dedicated to their own god.

But all such plans had now been put on hold and the prospect that they would ever be brought to fruition seemed to wither beneath Hummingbird's bright and penetrating gaze.

'My lord,' Moctezuma stuttered, 'is it truly you?'

A gale of laughter. 'If I am not me, then who am I, do you think?'

'But I am confused, Great Lord. I do not understand your clothing. I do not understand why you take on the manner of the Spaniards. I do not understand why you wear the rosary . . .'

'Because it is not given to you to understand such things, my dear Moctezuma.' Suddenly the god's voice rose: '*And because you exist in a permanent state of confusion*. Really, I wonder why I should bother with you at all, when it seems the Spaniards do my business of war so much better than you do. As always, however, you allow yourself to be deceived by the outward appearance of things. *Do you prefer me like this?*'

Moctezuma gasped. Hummingbird had shape-shifted in an instant into his monstrous form – as though his own granite idol that had once stood here, tall as a bear, wide as a door, its snarling mouth smeared with gore, had suddenly rematerialised in its accustomed spot, strutting and animated, its tusks dripping and its huge hands curled into claws.

'*I await your answer.*' The monster reared, its fangs gaping: '*Do you prefer me like this?*'

'Great Lord . . .' Moctezuma thought quickly: 'I prefer you in whichever form it pleases you to appear.'

'Such a cowardly answer,' Huitzilopochtli sneered. 'But predictable from a snivelling arse licker. I'm almost tempted not to tell you the good news I brought you . . .'

'Good news?'

Huitzilopochtli laughed again – a deep, reverberating belly laugh: 'You look pathetically hopeful. Is good news in such short supply here in Tenochtitlan?'

Even through his mushroom haze, Moctezuma was puzzled. How could good news *not* be in short supply? 'The *tueles*, Great Lord, their occupation of our city, their desecration of your temples, their opposition to sacrifice, their placing into captivity of myself . . .'

'Ah, yes, of course. Poor fellow, you've had a very difficult time.' Hummingbird took a giant step forward, swivelled in a blur of motion and clamped a huge hand to the top of Moctezuma's head, long thick fingers projecting over his brow and threatening his eye sockets.

'But look on the bright side,' the war god continued in a softer tone, 'things couldn't possibly get much worse.'

A ghastly grin: 'Or could they?'

Still gripping Moctezuma's head, he seemed to reflect, then added, quietly, as though talking to himself: 'Actually, they could get *much* worse. A great deal depends on what you do with the good news that awaits you, my fawning, weak, insipid Moctezuma.'

'What is this good news, Lord?'

'You'll find out soon enough, you anxious little man. Return to your quarters in the palace of Axayacatl! A messenger from the coast awaits you there. He brings you a mantle.'

With a cavernous yawn, Hummingbird vanished.

The war god – as always – spoke true. When Moctezuma returned to the palace, Teudile approached in a state of uncharacteristic excitement to inform him that a runner from the coast had arrived bearing a painted mantle containing information said to be 'of the greatest importance – a matter of life or death'. Teudile did not yet know the precise nature of the information, but even now the lord Cuitláhuac was in the throne room, questioning the runner and examining the mantle.

Though he showed no emotion, Moctezuma seethed inwardly that his younger brother should have had the first look at the mysterious mantle. If this was indeed, as he suspected, Hummingbird's 'good news', then surely it was meant for his eyes only?

There was also the question of the *tueles*. Could they have learned of the arrival of the messenger? Teudile assured him they had not. Other than the page Pepillo, who had been occupied on business for Cortés today, there was little oversight of what happened or what was said in Moctezuma's quarters, and a hundred messengers could come and go without being noticed.

Though somewhat mean by comparison with the many audience

chambers in Moctezuma's own palace, the throne room built by old Axayacatl was spacious and well lit. As Teudile swung open the big double doors, and as Moctezuma swept in, they saw Cuitláhuac and the half-naked runner down on the floor in an unseemly huddle over a large, boldly painted mantle.

'Possess yourself, man,' Moctezuma hissed to his brother. 'The floor's no place for one of royal blood.'

Cuitláhuac was already scrambling to his feet and dusting off his robe. He made no apology but attempted to launch straight into an explanation, pointing out various features of the painting to Moctezuma, who gave him the cold face, brushed aside his words and walked slowly around the outspread mantle.

What the paintings showed, quite unmistakably, was a fleet of Spanish ships! And not the eleven ships that Malinche had arrived in, and later scuttled, but no less than eighteen ships, of which five were shown thrown up on the coast and turned over on the sand.

The runner was still crouched, trembling on the floor, his head bowed, his eyes cast down. Moctezuma extended his right foot in its golden sandal to receive the kiss of fealty and demanded a full report. Cuitláhuac interrupted to say that he had already heard the report, assessed the matter, and that it would be his pleasure to summarise the salient points, but again Moctezuma silenced him. 'The message is for me, brother, and I will hear it.'

It took some time to extract all the details of the story from the fearful runner, but when he was finally done, and had been sent away to receive his reward – immediate execution, though he no doubt imagined something different! – Moctezuma was excited with what he had learned.

Just four days previously, the great new fleet of Spanish ships depicted in the paintings had been driven ashore by a storm near the town of Cuetlaxtlan on the Gulf of Mexico – indeed close to the very spot where Malinche had anchored the year before and where Moctezuma's ambassadors had first encountered him face to face. Five of the ships had foundered in the storm, as indicated in the paintings; however, only one of them was beyond repair and all their crews had survived.

Several attempts had been made by Moctezuma's officials in Cuetlaxtlan to reach an accurate count of the total number of Spaniards present with the new expedition. The runner reported that they certainly exceeded nine hundred – almost double Malinche's force – including eighty armed with the fire-serpents that the Spaniards called arquebuses, eighty of the deer-riders called cavalry, one hundred and twenty crossbowmen, and twenty of the big fire-serpents called cannons, each fully crewed.

Moctezuma's first concern had been that the new arrivals were reinforcements for Malinche – in which case all was surely lost! – but the runner quickly put his mind at rest. By great good fortune three of the caudillo's own men had defected from a larger group sent out to prospect for gold in the Chinantla region, and had been making their way towards the coast. When they heard of the arrival of a fleet packed with their compatriots, they hastened to greet them. Like many of the conquistadors these three were disaffected from Malinche, whom they accused of keeping too many of the spoils of war to himself, and they were quickly persuaded by the commander of the new fleet to throw in their lot with him. Better still, the defectors had mastered more than a smattering of the Nahuatl language and were able to act as interpreters in the discussions that soon followed between the Spanish commander, a man named Nar-Vez, and Pichatzin, Moctezuma's provincial governor in Cuetlaxtlan. The runner had memorised the content of the discussions and was able to report that the new arrivals were by no means reinforcements for Malinche. On the contrary, they had come to overthrow him and to release the suffering Mexica from the servitude he had imposed.

This was good news – Moctezuma's stomach rumbled a warning but he clenched and successfully held back the spasm until it passed. Indeed it was excellent news! The best news possible under the circumstances. Infuriatingly, however, it had taken four full days for the tidings – in the hands of a single runner – to reach him. If relays of runners had been used, as should have been the case with a matter of such importance, he would have had the news three days earlier and been able to take the appropriate action so much sooner.

And the appropriate action, he had no doubt – he could even hear the voice of Hummingbird prompting him! – was to welcome this new force of Spaniards and make common cause with their commander. After all, was it not a first principle of statesmanship that one's enemy's enemy was one's friend?

But first things first.

'Teudile,' Moctezuma said, beckoning his steward closer. 'We will need fast communication with Cuetlaxtlan. Send out ten full teams of our fleetest couriers today and ensure they all have fresh runners ready and waiting at every relay station. Separately send a message at once to our provincial governor in Cuetlaxtlan . . . His name is Pichatzin, I recall . . .'

'Great lord,' muttered Teudile, 'as ever you recall correctly.'

'Send a message to the good Pichatzin,' Moctezuma continued. 'He is to lavish every hospitality upon these new Spaniards. Let them be given shelter according to their wishes and their needs, plentiful food, the best clothing, the most beautiful women, and baskets of gold – whatever they require. He is to begin as soon as he receives the message and you must ensure that the message reaches him by noon tomorrow. I will tolerate no further delays.'

As Teudile left to go about his tasks, Moctezuma turned to Cuitláhuac. 'Sit with me, dear brother,' he invited. 'Let us now compose a message directly to the new Spanish commander, this Nar-Vez, at Cuetlaxtlan. It must also be delivered tomorrow. I will value your counsel on our strategy.'

Cuitláhuac puffed out his chest and, as was so often the case, stated the obvious as though disclosing a revelation: 'We must inform him of our condition here, under the knife of Malinche, and ascertain whether he truly comes to our aid.'

Moctezuma suppressed a sigh. Cuitláhuac was unfortunately typical of the gaggle of dimwits and yes-men who had surrounded him, never daring to contradict him, always seeking to guess his wishes and make them come true, since he had banished Guatemoc from court.

And then the thought struck him – *Guatemoc!*

Not seen in Tenochtitlan these past five months, the prince was rumoured to have travelled to the north and there to have discovered the secret entrance to the caves of Chicomoztoc, and to have last been seen vanishing within to take counsel with the masters of wisdom.

Another story said that he had been killed in battle.

But according to yet another, he had triumphed, and lived, and had been raised to chieftain by a wild Cichemec tribe, from amongst whose myriads he had been gathering and training an army with which to attack Cortés.

Whatever the truth, an obvious question was raised by every one of the rumours. How was it possible for dull and unimaginative Cuitláhuac to have fathered such a firebrand?

It was intriguing, was it not? Recalling that he had cuckolded his younger brother years before when the Lady Achautli was still fresh from the marriage bed, Moctezuma even wondered whether he himself might not after all be the real father of the prince – who would therefore not be his nephew but his son!

It was a strangely appealing notion, and, just for a moment, he felt bereft of Guatemoc's forthright criticisms, and the loss of his strong right arm, and wished he had not falsely accused the prince of complicity in Qualpopoca's aborted attack on Malinche.

Chapter Eight

Sunday 24 April 1520

As Gonzalo de Sandoval climbed the guard tower of the stockade that surrounded the little town of Villa Rica, under his command these past two and a half months, he reflected that he was thoroughly enjoying his life in the New Lands. He was liked and respected by almost all of his fellows, his cavalry skills were applauded as second to none, and the caudillo valued his soldiering so highly that he had been elevated to ensign at the very start of the expedition, then later to captain and finally, in February 1520, to the command of Villa Rica de la Veracruz, the conquistadors' outpost on the coast of the Gulf of Mexico.

And a truly vital outpost it was! Its existence was the very basis of the legality of their expedition, and it also constituted their one fall-back plan – their single escape route and hope of safety, if, as seemed increasingly probable, things should go badly wrong in Tenochtitlan.

Villa Rica had been left without a commanding officer following the killing of Juan de Escalante at the beginning of November 1519. At first the men were on high alert, besieged by Qualpopoca's troops, expecting another attack, but then came Cortés's coup against Moctezuma, the siege was lifted, Qualpopoca was arrested and burned, and the realisation dawned that Villa Rica was safe.

In December, Cortés had installed Alonso de Grado as the new commanding officer. Vain, self-satisfied, weak-willed and greedy, he set a poor example. Right away, standards of discipline began to slip, and continued to tumble over Christmas and the New Year, with multiple acts of disorder and insubordination further undermining a command structure that was already fragmented and in disarray after Escalante's death. Men began to slip away – not deserting, exactly, but voting with their feet to reinforce the conquistadors already in Tenochtitlan, where they too could enjoy the attractions and splendour of the Mexica capital. As a result, the original complement of two hundred and thirty men – who had been left to defend Villa Rica when Cortés had begun his march to Tenochtitlan in August 1519 – had been reduced to just seventy-three when Sandoval rode down to the coast in February 1520 to set things in order.

He found the fortress in a dangerous state of disrepair. Half of its falconets were so badly corroded that they could not be fired, an entire section of the palisade wall had collapsed without any attempt to replace it, and guard rotas had been all but abandoned, leaving the settlement effectively defenceless against any determined attack. Morale was at an all-time low, and the few remaining officers – two ensigns and a captain – did not have sufficient charisma and authority to re-impose discipline.

Sandoval had changed all that, and this morning of Sunday 23 April 1520, as he climbed the guard tower, he was able to look out over an intact and reinforced stockade bristling with clean and functioning cannon. He had sought to increase the number of men from the seventy-three he had inherited in February to a larger and more effective force of around one hundred and fifty. Cortés, however, had refused on the grounds that he was already badly overstretched in Tenochtitlan, having sent out various parties, totalling one hundred and twenty men in all, to prospect for gold, as well as an additional contingent of one hundred and fifty men, under Juan Velázquez de Léon, to establish a settlement and build a harbour near the mouth of the Coatzacoalcos River. Since there was rarely any point in trying to change the caudillo's mind once it was made up, Sandoval had therefore focused his efforts on improving the discipline and martial skills of his own seventy-three men. Although several of them were elderly, and several more were natural malingerers, the majority learned fast, and he was pleased and proud this morning, as reveille sounded, to see how efficiently and quickly they mustered.

From habit he looked out to sea. The hope that Puertocarrero and Montejo might have succeeded in their mission to Spain, and that a fleet carrying reinforcements might arrive at any time, was by no means absurd – yet today, as on all previous days, there were no ships to be seen.

Sandoval turned his attention inland; at a distance he estimated at a couple of miles, he saw a cloud of dust. He narrowed his eyes. What was this?

The dust plume moved steadily closer. Soon it was close enough to resolve its source.

Three riders were approaching, which in itself was no cause for worry, since men on horseback in this land could only be fellow Spaniards from the Tenochtitlan garrison paying a visit to Villa Rica.

Yet there was something odd about these three, was there not?

Sandoval prided himself on his eyesight but, as they drew rapidly closer, they seemed unfamiliar to him. One of them held a fluttering pennant, tied to the end of a spear. Sandoval squinted again, recognising the insignia on the pennant, and then suddenly, with a lurch in the pit of his stomach, he understood. These men had not come down to Villa Rica from Tenochtitlan! They had been sent by Diego de Velázquez, conqueror and governor of Cuba and the chief enemy and rival of Hernán Cortés.

The bad blood between the two men arose from a remarkable incident. Diego de Velázquez had been the instigator, and the principal financier, of the expedition to the New Lands. He had originally appointed Cortés, who was married to his niece, as his captain-general. But then, rightly suspecting and fearing the ambitions of the younger and more dynamic man, he had acted unilaterally to replace Cortés with another relative – the more compliant and fiercely loyal Pánfilo de Narváez. Learning of this manoeuvre on the very night he was to be deprived of office, Cortés had ordered the fleet to sail at once and had left the governor of Cuba fuming on the quay-side, spitting with rage and hungry for revenge and restitution.

'To arms!' Sandoval shouted.

Below in the courtyard, the men were dispersing from their muster and no doubt looking forward to their breakfast. Now they stared up at him in surprise.

'To arms!' he yelled again. 'Lock and bar the gate! Prime the cannon! Prepare for an attack.'

But no army followed behind the three riders, who could hardly mount an attack by themselves, and when they asked for admission, Sandoval felt it would be unchivalrous to refuse them. They proved to be Alfonso de Vergara, who wore the robes of a royal notary, Father Antonio Ruiz de Guevara, a priest, and Antonio de Amaya, a close relative of Diego de Velázquez and the bearer of the pennant. Once through the gates, they dismounted and announced, since it was the day of rest, that before stating their business they wished to worship in Villa Rica's church.

The church was a primitive, makeshift structure, consisting of an awning stretched over an altar and rows of benches. Sandoval, who'd so far refrained from greeting the visitors formally, waited until they were done with their prayers before strolling over to introduce himself. It became apparent that Father Guevara, a corpulent bald man, jowly and sweaty with a sneering air, would speak for them. With Villa Rica's entire garrison looking on, the priest barked out his name, and the names of his companions, before announcing grandly, and in a booming voice: 'We have come on behalf of Don Pánfilo de Narváez, recently landed along this coast at the command of Don Diego de Velázquez, governor of Cuba, with a fleet of eighteen ships, many heavy cannon and a thousand men including cavalry, crossbowmen and arquebusiers . . .'

Sandoval whistled. 'Sounds like an impressive armada,' he said, 'but even if what you say about your numbers is true, how do I know that you're not pirates? Can you prove to me that yours is a legally appointed expedition?'

Guevara stamped his foot. 'Stop wasting time, man! Of course our expedition is legally appointed.'

'On whose authority?'

'On the authority, as I have already stated, of His Excellency Don Diego de Velázquez, governor of Cuba, who has appointed Don Pánfilo de Narváez as captain-general in the conquest of these New Lands.'

'Well that is passing strange,' commented Sandoval, 'since we already have a legally appointed captain-general here, Don Hernando Cortés, as you know very well, and have no need of another.'

'Cortés,' said Guevara with a loud sniff, 'is a traitor to the Crown.'

Now this was *really* annoying. Silently cursing his modest stature and his bandy, cavalryman's legs, Sandoval drew himself up to his full height, stepped in close to the other man, and whispered in his ear: 'If you weren't a priest, I'd have you beaten for saying that. We of the company of Don Hernando Cortés are better servants of His Majesty than your precious Velázquez or Narváez will ever be.'

'What? What did you say?' Father Guevara had turned red in the face, his features contorted with rage.

'*I said* – ' this time Sandoval raised his voice to full parade-ground level – '*if you weren't a priest I'd have you beaten for your bad words about our caudillo* . . .'

As he spoke, however, Guevara strode brusquely past him and addressed the assembled men. 'Your officer here gives his loyalty to the traitor Cortés and is therefore a traitor himself. We are merciful and recognise that this is not the fault of you common soldiers. You will all be held blameless, so long as you go at once to pledge your obedience to Captain-General Narváez, the only lawful authority in this land.'

With a menacing smile, Guevara now turned to the notary Alfonso de Vergara, a wizened stick of a man, and ordered him to read aloud certain formal papers he had brought, indicting Cortés for the crime of treason and requiring him to submit his person to Narváez.

Sandoval was outraged. The sheer temerity of these bloody Velazquistas! Sheltering behind the governor's power and prestige, they thought they could get away with anything. And perhaps usually they did. But not today, he decided, or at any rate not while he had any say in the matter . . .

Vergara was already pulling papers out of a satchel when Sandoval confronted him: 'If you read those aloud,' he said, 'I shall have you strapped over a barrel and a very large master-sergeant of mine will give you a hundred lashes . . .'

Vergara looked doubtful. 'A hundred lashes? I don't think you have the authority—'

'I most certainly do,' said Sandoval, indicating the grim-faced men of the garrison. 'I have the authority of numbers, and the love our soldiers hold for Don Hernando Cortés, and if I order you lashed, then lashed you shall be.'

Vergara looked from Guevara to Sandoval and from Sandoval to Guevara, swallowed noisily, his Adam's apple bobbing, retrieved an impressive-looking sheaf of documents from his satchel, shuffled one to the top and began to read: 'By order of His Excellency Don Diego Velázquez, whose warrant is affixed herewith—'

'Stop, Señor Vergara!' Sandoval cut him short. 'Desist unless you wish to be flogged! As things stand, I have no idea whether these papers you hold are copies, or originals, or forgeries, and whether, despite your robes, you are really a royal notary or not. If perchance you are not such a notary, but an imposter, then you have no right to read out any documents even if they are genuine. On the other hand, if you are what you appear to be, then you should make your way to Tenochtitlan where you will discover for yourself that Don Hernando Cortés is firmly established as captain-general and chief justice of these New Lands. You may read your documents to him.'

Vergara hesitated – the argument after all was a reasonable one – and slid the documents back into the satchel. Guevara watched him in disbelief, biting distractedly at his lips and now, like a spoilt child, stamped his foot again. '*Why are you even listening to this traitor?*' he bellowed at the notary through a spray of spittle. '*Bring those decrees out at once and read them aloud.*'

Vergara made a peculiar sound, somewhat like a sob, darted his hand back into the satchel, and retrieved the documents. 'By order of His Excellency Don Diego Velázquez,' he began again, 'whose warrant—'

It was enough for Sandoval. His master-sergeant Guillen de Laso, a dour, hulking, loyal brute, whose favoured weapon was the battle-axe, was standing at the ready with half a dozen other toughs. Now, on their captain's signal, they surrounded and laid hands on the three emissaries.

'How dare you!' Guevara screeched. 'Do you not see I am a priest?'

'I do, Father,' growled de Laso, 'and I am a master-sergeant. Struggle some more, why don't you?'

Guevara was a big man and fought with some spirit to break free, at which de Laso delivered a series of hard, rapid punches to his belly that laid him out gasping and puking in the dust.

'Anybody else want some of that?' de Laso asked the other two.

Vergara shook his head and stood slumped between his captors, but the third man, Antonio de Amaya, was still resisting. 'Unhand me,' he demanded, 'or you will be made to regret it. I am the cousin of Don Diego de Velázquez!'

'I don't care if you're the cousin of God himself,' de Laso said. 'One more word from you and you'll join that priest on the ground.'

As Amaya relapsed into a sullen silence, Sandoval thought fast. He had the three envoys in his power but many problems remained, most pressingly the question of Narváez's thousand-strong army – its whereabouts, its disposition, its preparedness for battle, and what was to be done about it. Yet such weighty matters, Sandoval concluded, were far beyond his authority to settle.

His eyes fell on some wooden packing crates used to transport goods back and forth along the road between Villa Rica and Tenochtitlan. They were furnished with sturdy loops of rope along their sides through which carrying poles could be thrust so that each crate could be hoisted and carried on the shoulders of eight bearers. These bearers, called *tamanes* in the local language, were provided to the Spaniards in great numbers by Tlacoch, paramount chief of their allies the Totonacs, who had his seat at the nearby city of Cempoala. At any one time, since the work of fetching and carrying was never complete, it was usual for at least fifty *tamanes* to be present at Villa Rica and fifty would be enough for the job in hand.

Sandoval turned to de Laso. 'Put the prisoners in those packing crates,' he said. 'One in each. Bind them up like bales of goods and we'll send them to Cortés. He'll know what to do with them.'

Weighted down by their burdens, the train of *tamanes* would require four days to complete the journey to Tenochtitlan, but relays of runners could deliver a message there much faster than that, indeed within twenty-four hours. As de Laso saw to the binding and packing of the envoys, and assembled a guard of twenty Spaniards to escort them on the road, Sandoval walked across the parade ground to the weather-beaten shack that served as his office and sat down to compose a letter to the caudillo.

Evening was falling over Tenochtitlan and it was as though some god had reached into the pit of Moctezuma's stomach and twisted his intestines into a knot. Yesterday, after receiving the painted mantle from Cuetlaxtlan, the letter that he and Cuitláhuac had composed to Nar-Vez, the new Spanish commander, had been sent on its way. If the relay system had worked as it should, the codex would certainly have reached Pichatzin in Cuetlaxtlan by now and might reasonably be expected to be delivered to the Spanish camp this evening. There it was to be read aloud in the presence of the commander by one of Pichatzin's scholars and translated by the three soldiers who had defected from Malinche's army.

One concern was that these rough men might, themselves, be unable to understand the subtleties of the message, and might fail to communicate its contents properly.

But it was a greater fear that gnawed at Moctezuma's entrails.

Suppose the letter had been intercepted?

Suppose it had fallen into the hands of Malinche?

If so, the consequences would be severe, since the Great Speaker had kept the news of the arrival of the Spanish fleet to himself. But even worse was the fatal backlash that must be expected if the content of his letter ever became known – for not only had Moctezuma complained bitterly about his treatment and imprisonment at Malinche's hands, but also he had explicitly proposed, if it would please the new commander, to have Malinche seized and sent to the coast dead or alive.

This last bit of bravado had been Cuitláhuac's idea, hastily embraced yesterday in a fit of enthusiasm, but bitterly regretted in the gathering gloom of this evening.

Chapter Nine

—◆—

Monday 25 April 1520–Tuesday 26 April 1520

Past the middle of the afternoon, awakened from his usual siesta by the sweltering heat, Hernando Cortés seated himself at the rather imposing desk he'd had the carpenters knock up for the grand office annexed to the bedchamber he shared with Malinal in his private apartments. Stifling a yawn, he took up a quill and began to go through the draft of his latest letter to King Carlos. Although Pepillo now served as Moctezuma's page, he continued to perform secretarial duties for Cortés and the letter was written in his clear, youthful hand from dictation he'd taken down over the past few days.

There came a knock at the door.

Absorbed in his own prose, Cortés glanced up with irritation and yelled '*Go away!*'

There came another knock.

Now Cortés half rose to his feet: 'Didn't you hear me? I told you to *go away!*'

A third knock. '*Damn!* Enter then!'

By degrees the heavy door creaked open to reveal the pustular, bearded face of Andres Farfan who was on guard duty today. Barely out of adolescence, like so many of the conquistadors, he was actually shaking with nerves. 'Pardon the intrusion, sir – ' his voice was so tremulous as to be almost inaudible – 'but the matter seems urgent.'

Cortés sighed. Everything was urgent! 'Well, speak up, boy!'

'A runner has arrived, Caudillo. He carries a message for you.'

Dripping with sweat, the runner fell to his knees and handed over the scroll. Feigning preoccupied disinterest, Cortés set it aside and had Farfan escort the man out.

As soon as the door closed behind them, however, he snatched up the letter. Yesterday's date, Sunday 24 April, was scrawled on its exterior, together with the words 'For Cortés. Urgent despatch from Villa Rica de la Veracruz'. He broke the seal and with the faintest shiver of apprehension saw that the message had been scrawled hastily in Sandoval's own hand. He forced himself to read slowly and carefully, digesting the implications of every word, but the upshot was obvious from the start! That envious old fool Diego de Velázquez had despatched an army from Cuba, claimed to be a thousand strong, to wrest from him all the gains he'd so painstakingly won in the New Lands. This most unwelcome army – not at all the friendly reinforcements that he continued to hope would be sent from Spain – was under the command of the detestable Pánfilo Narváez who, it seemed, had been appointed captain-general in Cortés's place!

So this was how Velázquez hoped to get his revenge for the humiliation heaped on him the year before! It was inevitable, Cortés supposed, but the big surprise was how soon it had come! Not even six months had passed since he had seized control in Tenochtitlan; he still had his hands full dealing with the Mexica, and yet here was Velázquez – or rather his ugly red-haired proxy Narváez – already knocking on his door!

The intervention could not possibly have been staged at a worse moment.

Hardly more than a fortnight before, Moctezuma had warned Cortés that a war was coming – that the Mexica had been commanded by their priests to end the hated Spanish occupation of Tenochtitlan and to kill all the Spaniards.

The threat was not an empty one, for there was indeed great turmoil in the city and spies reported parties of armed men entering every night by canoe. It was evident that only Moctezuma, claiming to wish to avoid a bloodbath on both sides, was holding the rebels back – and that only on the strength of Cortés's promise to build ships at Villa Rica and sail away.

Of course avoiding a bloodbath was the last thing on Moctezuma's mind; his own survival was all that mattered to him! If it came to fighting, he must know how likely it was he would be killed, so it was in his best interests to edge Cortés out with threats, avoid fighting altogether and thus possibly – miraculously! – to cling on to his throne.

Cortés, on the other hand, was playing for time. He was confident of the martial skills of his conquistadors; they could, he believed, do almost anything. Even so, it was his strong preference that they should not be put to the test by the Mexica yet. The business with the ships he'd commanded to be built at Villa Rica was a charade; they would be built – slowly! – but he had no intention whatsoever of using them to retreat from these New Lands, which he had already privately renamed New Spain. Nonetheless, the longer the inevitable confrontation with the Mexica could be postponed the better, while there was still the prospect that his petition to King Carlos would meet with success and more troops would be sent out to reinforce him and secure his ultimate goal of total domination and conquest.

All these calculations, however – the delaying tactics, the fencing with Moctezuma, the feigned willingness to withdraw – were rendered meaningless at a stroke by Sandoval's news. If Narváez and his thousand had been the hoped-for reinforcements, they might have been sufficient to consolidate the gains of the conquest and render Cortés's control of New Spain irreversible. But instead Narváez was here to steal control from him, and most unfortunately might be aided in this objective by decisions Cortés himself had made! In particular – and it was now a matter for profound regret – he had weakened his force in Tenochtitlan by sending out one hundred and twenty men to prospect for gold, and one hundred and fifty more under Velázquez de Léon to establish a protected harbour and found a colony on the Coatzacoalcos river.

These two scattered units, together with the one hundred and ninety in the Tenochtitlan garrison, totalled only four hundred and sixty men, with an additional seventy or so far off at Villa Rica, bringing his numbers up to around five hundred and thirty, none in battle formation and all – even if they could be concentrated in one place! – massively outnumbered by Narváez's thousand.

As Cortés digested the implications he was suddenly struck – it felt like a physical blow! – by an even more worrying thought. With a curse he jumped to his feet and began to pace restlessly.

In his efforts to bolster the illusion that Moctezuma still exercised genuine control over his far-flung empire, he had allowed the Mexica leader to continue to maintain his own network of couriers. On reflection, that had been a foolish mistake! It raised the horrifying possibility that the Great Speaker might already know of Narváez's arrival – that the two of them might, indeed, already be in contact.

And might not Narváez, as the chosen instrument of Velázquez's vengeance, even be rash enough to attempt an alliance with the Mexica?

Cortés wanted to rush to Moctezuma's quarters at once and confront him, but held himself back. When you're in the lion's den, it's a bad idea to show fear.

As evening once more fell over his city, Moctezuma felt excited . . . and afraid. If the new Spanish commander at the coast had received his message, was it too much to hope that a reply might have been sent immediately and that the runner bearing it might even now be approaching Tenochtitlan?

He fretted through his dinner, shouted angrily at Pepillo when the boy was slow bringing a favoured dish, and shortly afterwards dismissed him for the night.

But it was not seemly for the Great Speaker to shout, and Moctezuma instantly regretted it. His concern was that Pepillo might observe the comings and goings of his couriers and guess the game he was playing, but of course there was no danger of that! Teudile had already given the order that no runner was to be allowed anywhere near the royal quarters while the page was present. Indeed the Great Speaker's closest staff, attendants and confidants were all now under instructions to manage matters such that no Spaniard, either by accident or by design, would ever learn of the secret courier traffic . . .

Some hours passed, during which Moctezuma retired to his bedchamber and sought to amuse himself with three of his most lubricious concubines. For almost a year his *tepulli* had been functional again, but worry unmanned him and before midnight, frustrated and angry, he sent the girls away. He was composing himself for sleep when there came a knock at his door.

'Sire, it is I, Teudile.'

Suddenly aware of the pounding of his own heart, Moctezuma took a deep breath and composed himself: 'Enter then, good steward.'

The hem of Teudile's robe brushed the polished floor as he approached the royal bed. His gaunt features were twisted into a ghoulish smile. 'Master,' he said, 'I bring you good news.'

'A runner has come?'

'Yes, lord, and I have had him strangled . . .'

'Strangled? But I wanted to see him! I wanted to speak with him!'

'My deepest regrets, Majesty, but I remembered your command that we must keep these matters from Malinche. Besides, the man was simply the last of a dozen couriers through whose hands the message passed.

He knew nothing of its content or the circumstances in which it was sent . . .'

'Why have him strangled then?'

'I thought it was what you would wish, lord. Only when a man is dead can we be sure he poses no security risk.'

'Ah! Yes!' Moctezuma giggled. 'I see your point. What's one courier more or less anyway?' He frowned, overtaken by a sudden panic: 'But how are we to understand this message? Neither I nor you can read the language of the Spaniards. Do you know, Teudile, of anyone amongst our own people who has learned their writing who can be trusted to translate this message?'

Teudile's hideous smile had widened. 'That will not be necessary, sire. The message was at first verbal, not written. The Spanish commander has with him those three defectors from Malinche who speak something of our tongue. He addressed Pichatzin in their presence, giving his reply to your own letter, and they translated his words into Nahuatl. Naturally Pichatzin had scribes and artists in attendance and they set those words down on this mantle . . .'

Teudile, who had been fishing in his sleeves for some moments, now pulled out a rolled cloth and unfurled it with a flourish as Moctezuma leaned forward eagerly.

The dominant image at the centre of the mantle was of a huge red-haired, red-bearded and magnificently armoured Spaniard.

'Their commander?' Moctezuma guessed.

Teudile beamed: 'Yes, sire.'

Seated, under a canopy, the imposing commander was shown surrounded by a fawning retinue of other figures – Spaniards and Mexica – with serried ranks of Spanish soldiers beyond them receding to the edges of the mantle. Above and below this scene, translated into Nahuatl hieroglyphs and pictograms, was the commander's reply to Moctezuma:

It pains us to hear, O great Moctezuma, that you are held prisoner in your own city by the renegade Hernando Cortés, who is a thief and traitor to our king. Now our king has learned of the evil things Cortés has done in your country, he has sent me, Pánfilo Narváez, at the head of a very large army to set you free and to capture or kill Cortés. We must consolidate our position here at the coast, and plan strategy with you, but within weeks we will march to your aid. Please be assured that once we have completed our mission, we will leave you and your country in peace.

'It was what we hoped for,' said Moctezuma, rubbing his hands together delightedly, 'and now it is confirmed. With this great force added to our own, Malinche cannot prevail against us.'

'Do you believe, sire, that these other Spaniards will keep their promise to leave?'

'For the present, Teudile, I do not care. Let us prepare another message for this Nar-Vez who offers to come to our rescue. Let's not squander this chance the gods have given us to get Malinche off our backs. Sit with me please – ' suddenly he pointed to a decorative niche in the wall of his bedchamber where a number of pieces of fine sculpture stood – 'but, before you do, kindly bring me that figure of Miclantechutli.'

God of the dead, ruler over the underworld, Miclantechutli was depicted in the form of a human skull, about one-third life-size, carved in exquisite detail out of the most prized translucent jade.

'Beautiful, eh?' said Moctezuma as he took the figure from Teudile. 'I shall gift it to Nar-Vez and inform him in my letter that it portends the death of Malinche.'

The next day, Tuesday 26 April, accompanied by Malinal, Cortés paid his usual morning call on the Great Speaker, who was in his salon taking his breakfast, attended by Pepillo and a bevy of serving maids. The salon overlooked the gardens of Axayacatl's palace, and was furnished with numerous little gaily painted cages in which songbirds trilled. In a corner an elderly musician piped out a plangent tune on a little ceramic flute.

Moctezuma seemed . . . excited and unusually *excitable*. He laughed a great deal, very loudly, and chattered incessantly, often repeating himself, but between bouts of small talk he would from time to time ask a penetrating question – a question that smelled of strategy. For example: 'When do the soldiers who you sent to prospect for gold return?' Or: 'How goes it with Velázquez de Léon?' Or: 'Have you had word of late from Sandoval?' Moctezuma was very good at remembering names, but it was weird that he should bring both Velázquez de Léon and Sandoval up out of the blue like this – since the former had led a large contingent of soldiers out of the city quite recently (was Moctezuma fishing to discover when they, too, might return to bolster the garrison?) and the latter was the very man most likely to get first intelligence of the arrival of other Spaniards on the coast (was Moctezuma fishing to learn if that intelligence had reached him already?).

But Cortés didn't raise these concerns. Catching Pepillo's eye, he turned to the Great Speaker and said: 'Will you object, if I borrow this young man from you for a few hours.'

Moctezuma waved his hand airily. 'You gave him to me,' he said. 'You can take him back.'

'It's only for this morning, I assure you.'

'As you wish, Malinche. Whatever you wish pleases me.'

'What do you think?' Cortés asked as soon as they were safely out of royal earshot. 'Is he hiding something?'

'Definitely!' Malinal replied. 'His eyes – very shifty. And too much laughing.'

'Last night he shouted at me,' Pepillo offered. 'I could see something was eating him. But then look at him this morning, all bright and breezy . . .'

'Has he had any unusual visitors? Any couriers?'

'None that I've seen, Caudillo, but they have their ways of keeping secrets.'

'What about your little friend Tozi? Best damn spy I've ever known. Maybe she can get to the bottom of this for us.'

Pepillo shrugged uncomfortably and looked down at his feet. 'I haven't seen her for many days, Caudillo.'

'That's because she's not in Tenochtitlan,' Malinal added. 'She's gone up north. Some business of her own.'

'I didn't give her permission to leave!' Cortés fumed.

'She no more needs your permission to leave this city,' Malinal said scornfully, 'than the wind needs your permission to blow.'

Cortés was so deeply troubled by Moctezuma's manner that for the second afternoon in succession he found himself quite unable to enjoy his usual siesta. Malinal, on the other hand, had no such problem, and slept deeply beside him, breathing softly, her flank gently rising and falling, her sleek naked back turned towards him. His prick stirred at the smell of sex on her where they'd fallen hungrily into each other's arms a little earlier, but he resisted the temptation to engage in a second bout. Danger was on the prowl and required his full attention.

'Wake up, Malinal!' He gave her a playful slap on the buttocks. 'Time to pay another call on Mucktey.'

Her eyes fluttered open and she half turned towards him. 'What? Hernán . . . ?'

'Time to pay another call on Mucktey. Surprise him! He won't be expecting us to return so soon after our visit this morning. I want to shake him up and see what falls out of his pockets.'

'Shake him up? What do you mean by that, Hernán? You will fight him?' She looked genuinely puzzled. 'And he has no pockets.'

'I'm not talking about a *physical* shaking, my dear,' Cortés laughed. 'Not today, anyway. It's just a figure of speech. But Mucktey's hiding something from us. If we can disturb his balance, maybe even make him think we already know his secrets, I'll wager he'll confess all.'

Although Cortés had not yet shared the news of Narváez's arrival with the rest of his men – even with his most senior captains – he had informed Malinal soon after dismissing the runner the previous afternoon. She was his closest confidante, his 'tongue' in all his negotiations with Moctezuma, so she could not be kept in ignorance. 'You think he knows about the other Spaniard?' she now guessed.

'I'm sure of it! But have they communicated? Have they hatched any plans? At all costs we must prevent Narváez and the Mexica from joining forces against us here. If that happens, we're done for.'

'Done for?'

'Another figure of speech. It means we'll be beaten, defeated, all of us killed.'

'I don't like that . . . figure of speech.' Malinal sat upright, naked and beautiful amongst the crumpled sheets, and added brightly. 'But you are Hernán Cortés, my lord! No man alive can defeat you!'

Pepillo had spent the afternoon in the caudillo's office, making a clean copy of his master's heavily crossed-out and rewritten draft letter to King Carlos. Now Malinal and Cortés came forth from their bedchamber and Cortés beckoned him to follow. 'Come with us, lad! I borrowed you from Mucktey but it is time to take you back.'

'Caudillo . . . May I speak freely?'

'You may.'

'Then please relieve me from my service with Mucktey!' Pepillo placed his hand on the pommel of the sword Escalante had given him: 'I wish to be with the men and to play a man's part in this conquest of ours.'

'This war will not be won by swords alone,' Cortés replied. 'Words and strategy are more important and it serves my strategy to keep you exactly where you are for now. So come! Observe! Take note!'

The walk through the corridors of the palace was short and the guards to Moctezuma's private chambers knew their place. Making no attempt to block the way, they ushered Cortés, Malinal and Pepillo directly into the royal presence.

The Great Speaker was in conference with Teudile and Cuitláhuac. He was seated on a golden stool, they on stools of copper, but the three of them turned as one towards the new arrivals, unable to disguise the expressions of shock and horror on their faces.

'Do we interrupt?' Cortés boomed.

Moctezuma had turned very pale. 'You do not, Lord Malinche! You are always welcome here.' He gestured towards the two men, who rose hesitantly to their feet. 'Besides, my steward and the royal brother are just leaving.' Some whispered words, which Pepillo understood perfectly, followed in Nahuatl. Teudile and Cuitláhuac would return to continue their meeting with the Great Speaker after Cortés and his party had left.

As Malinal gave the gist of this to Cortés, Moctezuma gestured to the two recently vacated copper stools. 'Sit, Malinal! Sit, Malinche!' He paused, suddenly deep in thought, and a cloud seemed to pass over his face. 'To what do I owe the privilege of this visit? It is your second today.'

'I have news from the coast,' Cortés offered. He was just throwing a pebble into the pool to see where the ripples spread, but the effects were remarkable. Moctezuma's waxy pallor at once grew deathly and he rose unsteadily to his feet. 'News?' he asked. 'News?' He hesitated, forced a smile: 'How strange you should say that, Malinche, since I also have news for you.' Babbling now, he summoned a servant and despatched him on an errand. 'You will see, Malinche, it is the best possible news!'

Cortés fixed the Great Speaker with his eye and said nothing. An uncomfortable silence followed until the servant returned carrying a rolled maguey-fibre mantle which, on a further instruction, he spread out on the floor.

'Lord Malinche,' Moctezuma now said, 'not an hour ago a messenger came to tell me that eighteen Spanish ships have arrived in the port where you landed, with many soldiers and horses.' He indicated the painted cloth, which indeed showed eighteen ships, thirteen at anchor and five beached. 'It is all set down here. You must know this already, of course, so I am angry with you that you came to me this morning and failed to tell me.'

Cortés thought quickly. The myth of his omniscience – although largely deriving from intelligence that the now mysteriously absent Tozi had brought him – was an important underpinning of Spanish control in Tenochtitlan and he was therefore loath to give Moctezuma any hint that he did *not*, in fact, know everything!

On the other hand, as events moved forward, might not some strategic advantage be gained by keeping the extent of his own knowledge secret? In an instant his mind was made up. 'My news from the coast,' he said coldly, 'did not reach me this morning, as you imagine, but just now, and having received it – as you can see with your own eyes – I am here directly to tell you.'

Moctezuma's expression was unreadable. 'And does your news confirm mine, Malinche?'

'No, Great Speaker, my news concerns an entirely different matter, but I thought you would be pleased to hear it. My carpenter Martin Lopez has sent a report on the progress of the brigantines we are building at Villa Rica. The work proceeds apace and the ships will be complete, and ready to sail, less than thirty days from now.'

It was a lie, of course! On his own orders almost no progress at all had been made on the brigantines. But the arrival of Narváez, as Moctezuma must realise, changed everything, and matters must now surely move forward – very rapidly – to some climax. Besides, Moctezuma was obviously lying too. The painted mantle had certainly not arrived just an hour ago! The only real questions were how long had it been in the Great Speaker's hands and whether he had yet entered into direct communications with Narváez.

'For my part I am angry with you,' Cortés now said. He glared at Moctezuma.

'Why, Lord Malinche?'

Cortés jerked his chin at the mantle: 'You did not send for me the moment you received this message. Instead you sent for Teudile and Cuitláhuac, with whom I found you in conference here. It seems to me that the three of you would have withheld this information from me if I had not come by.'

'No, Lord Malinche. No! That is not my intent. I wish only to satisfy myself as to the identity and intentions of these new countrymen of yours.'

'And to that end, I'll wager, you've already sent an embassy to them?'

Moctezuma hung his head. 'Pichatzin of Cuetlaxtlan serves as our ambassador, as was the case when you yourself first arrived in our land.'

'And no doubt Pichatzin has been instructed to feed and shelter them and lavish gold upon them?'

'As was the case when you first arrived in our land, Lord Malinche.'

'Ah! So you *have* sent instructions!' Cortés jerked his chin at the mantle again: 'That's not the only communication you've had, is it? There's more! How long has this been going on?'

'Malinche . . .'

'*How long, Mucktey?*'

'I love you very much, Lord Malinche, and I have your best interests at heart, so please do not be angry. Have twenty days yet passed since we agreed that you and your men should leave our land because our priests had incited the people to make war on you?'

'About twenty days,' Cortés conceded. 'And, as you very well know, that's exactly why we're building our brigantines at the coast – so that we can all sail away and leave you in peace here . . .'

Moctezuma suddenly beamed: 'Which is also why, Malinche, I expect that my news of the arrival of these countrymen of yours – ' now it was his turn to jerk his chin at the mantle –'must bring you immense joy! It means you do not have to wait for thirty more days until your own ships are completed! Don't you see? It means war can be avoided. It means you and all your men can leave now, with lives and honour intact, on the ships that your countrymen have brought. You can all return together to the land you call Spain!'

Quite amazing! Cortés thought. The Great Speaker appeared to be completely caught up in this little fantasy he was spinning. In his crude native way, however, he also appeared to be quite skilfully using the arrival of Narváez's ships to call Cortés's bluff about leaving! The one obvious thing was that Moctezuma wanted, nay desperately *hoped*, that he would soon be rid of all the Spaniards – so some confirmation of that might help to play him along and win more time.

Cortés decided on a show of enthusiasm. '*Thank God*,' he now exclaimed in ringing, theatrical tones, '*Who provides for us at the right moment!*'

He paused to let Malinal put his words into Nahuatl and realised how completely he trusted her to convey *only* the words and not the sarcasm in his voice.

Moctezuma's expression was eager and expectant: 'You are thanking your god for what exactly, Malinche?'

'For sending our deliverance in the form of this fleet – ' a glance at the mantle. 'We shall make our preparations to leave immediately.'

Another royal beam from Mucktey: 'I am glad, so glad, that this is your response, Malinche. It would have made me very sad if your people and mine had been driven to war.'

You snivelling, conniving bastard, Cortés thought. *War is coming whether you like it or not.*

But he showed nothing of his real feelings on his face.

The coming of Narváez could not much longer be hidden from the men, so that evening Cortés called an assembly and told everyone of Sandoval's letter and of the arrest of Guevara, Vergara and Amaya, who were even now on their way to Tenochtitlan trussed up in packing cases carried on the backs of porters.

'From the bottom of my heart,' Cortés said after he'd broken the news, 'I wish to avoid a fight with our brother Spaniards. Frankly I doubt the motives of Pánfilo de Narváez. I know him in person and you all, I think, know him by reputation, and he is not a man to be trusted. Worse still, he comes to do the will of Diego de Velázquez who, it seems, is envious of our success and wishes to deprive us of all our gains.'

At this a loud chorus of boos and hoots arose from the assembly.

'Even so,' Cortés continued, gesturing for silence, 'we do not yet know the true purpose of the expedition and we must discover it before taking any precipitate action.'

'Fuck their purpose, whatever it is!' It was Nuno Guiterrez, a big, red-bearded, notoriously profane sailor. He stood up: 'I say we go and fight the fuckers now. These are our New Lands to profit and to gain from, and we've sweated blood and lives for them. No one's going to take them from us.'

Although a few men sat silent, with stony faces, most were excited and angry, and there were several rousing choruses of '*Hear! Hear!*'

When the voices had died down, Cortés addressed Guiterrez directly. 'I remember you!' he said. 'You rowed me in the skiff that night in Santiago harbour in February '19 when I had a falling out with the governor. You did well!'

'It was my honour, Caudillo.'

'And I agree with you now. We *are* going to have to fight the fuckers! But as I often say, strategy is more than half the war, and when we do go into battle I want to be sure it's on our terms not the enemy's. I have a plan, so will you hear me out – ' he raised his voice – 'will you *all* hear me out while I tell you it?'

Cortés knew that the men, even the biggest bitchers and moaners amongst them, respected him as a general and a master strategist. This talk of a plan had immediately made them prick up their ears. Some were leaning forward on the hard benches of the assembly room, others stood and crowded closer.

Cortés sensed his moment. 'Listen to me carefully,' he said. 'This is what I propose we do . . .'

Chapter Ten

Thursday 28 April 1520

Sandoval had sent his letter on Sunday 24 April. Borne by relays of fast runners, it reached Cortés on Monday 25th. The hastily scrawled paragraphs set out the pressing news of the arrival of Narváez and his army from Cuba and informed Cortés that Sandoval had arrested Narváez's emissaries – the priest Antonio de Guevara, the notary Alfonso de Vergara, and Antonio de Amaya, a cousin of Diego de Velázquez's. Sandoval wrote that he had thought it well to have the three of them transported directly to Tenochtitlan, where Cortés would 'know best how to deal with them', and added that he had 'handled them a little roughly' by binding them up in packing crates and loading them, 'like so much freight', on to the backs of native porters who would travel, bearing the load in shifts without stopping for four days and nights. The journey through the mountains would therefore not only be degrading but also excruciatingly uncomfortable.

It was a good strategy! By treating the emissaries so 'roughly', Sandoval had cleverly left an opening for Cortés – should he wish to do so – to present himself as their saviour when they arrived in Tenochtitlan.

And that would be soon. The train of *tamanes* bringing the prisoners had left Villa Rica four days ago, and should even now be approaching the lakeside town of Iztapalapa, whence a causeway six miles long ran arrow straight into the heart of Tenochtitlan. Cortés had arranged for the expedition's chaplain, Father Olmedo, and the tough old soldier Diego de Ordaz, to meet the humiliated envoys on their arrival at Iztapalapa, free them from their packing cases, furnish them with food, drink and clean clothes, mount them on fine horses, and escort them with all honours directly to him.

But why wait? There was so much he needed to do with these men! On impulse, Cortés decided he would meet them on the causeway; it was a little act of chivalry, but he knew it would make a strong impression on them.

Out of habit he called for Pepillo to bring his horse, then remembered with annoyance that the page was still assigned to Moctezuma. Well, damn! – another instant decision – that assignment was going to end tonight. The boy was no longer useful as a spy at Mucktey's sham court since it was obvious the Mexica were on to him, but he'd be needed in the days ahead to keep note of events, and to make drafts and fair copies of the many letters that Cortés expected to have to write. He meant to strike at Narváez, and strike hard, but at a time of his own choosing when it perfectly suited him to do so. Until then his interests were best served by delaying a confrontation – so yes, there would be letters.

He strode to the door of his office and swung it open. Young Andres Farfan, who'd ushered in Sandoval's runner two days before, was on guard duty again today. 'Ah Farfan,' said Cortés. 'Go to the stables and saddle Molinero for me. Bring him to the courtyard. I'll meet you there. Oh, and saddle a horse for Malinal as well – and see if you can find Don Pedro while you're at it . . .'

'Don Pedro Solis, sir?'

Cortés gave him a blank look. Why on earth did the boy think he would be asking for Solis?

'Don Pedro Comacho . . . ?'

'There are many Pedros in my army,' Cortés sighed. 'But it is Don Pedro de Alvarado I wish to see. You know? My second in command?'

Farfan's face brightened in recognition – was he actually stupid or just very nervous? – and he saluted briskly. 'Of course, sir. At once, sir.' He hurried off along the corridor, his boot heels clacking. 'Make haste!' Cortés called after him. 'We're going to take a ride along the Iztapalapa causeway and I want to leave at once.' An afterthought: 'Can you sit a horse, boy?'

Farfan had stopped in his tracks and looked back eagerly over his shoulder: 'Ye . . . Ye . . . Yes, sir.'

'Then saddle one for yourself as well. And bring my standard. You will ride out with us.'

When Cortés and Malinal made their way to the courtyard a little later, Farfan was waiting for them, with not three but four horses, the fourth being Bucephalus, Alvarado's magnificent white stallion.

'You found Don Pedro then?' Cortés called out.

'It was he as told me to saddle his horse, sir. You did not ask that he should join us, but I took the liberty and hope I did the right thing. He'll be along directly.'

Interesting! Despite his unpromising manner, it seemed that Farfan was capable of showing initiative after all.

'You did the right thing,' Cortés said. 'Besides, I shudder to imagine the kicking Don Pedro would have given you if you'd refused to saddle Bucephalus!'

The stallions were both massive beasts and they dwarfed the geldings Farfan had brought along for himself and Malinal – a wise choice since mares could have led to trouble. Molinero was a hulking nineteen hands, but Bucephalus stood a full hand taller, and had a habit of pushing his weight around. A couple of years ago Molinero had made it clear with his teeth that he wouldn't be bullied; there had been an ugly fight and since then the two horses seemed to have got along pretty well. *Although you can never tell with stallions*, Cortés reminded himself. *Or with Alvarado either!*

The Indians called him Tonatiuh, 'the sun', on account of his golden hair. He was a dear friend, but difficult, filled with pride, unpredictable and violent.

'Good afternoon, Pedro,' Cortés exclaimed as his second in command now strolled into the courtyard. 'So glad you can join us.'

Thirty-four years old, broad-shouldered and strong, but light on his feet with a fencer's easy grace, Alvarado wore a low-necked linen chemise, tight-fitting hose that outlined the sculpted muscles of his long legs, a prominent codpiece, and, at his belt, the hefty falchion – more of a cutlass than a sword – that he favoured in battle with the Indians. His hair and his elaborately curled and waxed moustache were thick and blond. He was a handsome man with a firm chin, bright blue eyes, and a duelling scar running from his right temple to the corner of his right eye. 'Us?' he sneered at Farfan. 'Where are we going and why's the boy coming?'

'As my standard bearer,' Cortés replied. 'This is a diplomatic mission, Pedro.'

Alvarado's brow darkened: 'Ah, I see! You're going to ride out and join your stupid welcoming committee for those curs of Narváez's whom Sandoval sent on their way to us?'

Cortés nodded.

'Bad idea, Hernán! To welcome them at all is ridiculous enough – you know my views on that already. But to honour them with your presence?

163

Definitely a mistake! You'll make them think we're afraid and trying to curry favour with their master.'

'My guess is all thought of honour will be very far from their minds. And as to fear, it will be they who are feeling it, wondering what we'll do to them when they get here after their treatment on the way up. Don't forget they've just spent four days bouncing around in packing crates being carried through rivers and jungles in the valleys and over freezing passes in the mountains.'

'Nothing more than they deserve!'

'Come come! They are humble envoys, blameless in themselves, acting on the orders of Narváez . . .'

'Even less reason to honour them!'

'Ah, Pedro! I forget that subtlety is not amongst your many skills. By honouring them I mean to seduce them.'

Alvarado's laugh was broad and sunny – the generous face of Tonatiuh: 'Seduce away then, dear Hernán. Fuck them up their hairy arses if you want to! I should know you always have a plan, though I can't imagine where this one will get you.'

'Observe, be patient and you will see . . .'

The ride through the city in the late afternoon was pleasant enough, the houses with their overhanging roof gardens colourful as ever, the canals between the great avenues teeming with canoes, the markets raucous, pungent and bright – so why, Cortés wondered, was there this keen edge of malice in the air, coming at him like a blade?

He turned to Malinal, riding at his left: 'Do you feel it?'

'Yes.'

'Feel what?' asked Alvarado at Cortés's right.

'War,' Cortés said.

'I love war!' Alvarado exclaimed.

'War is coming, Pedro.'

Cortés hadn't needed to explain to Malinal. They'd both heard Moctezuma's warnings and they'd both talked often enough about the great change in the manner of the people since the year before when the Spaniards had made their first entry into Tenochtitlan along the same Iztapalapa causeway that Narváez's envoys would soon cross.

Then it had been all joy and curiosity – and why not, since Cortés and his men had been invited into the city by the great Moctezuma himself? But after they had taken the monarch prisoner, little by little and day by day, he had become less great in the eyes of his people and started to lose his grip on their superstitious loyalty, and with it all authority and control over them. Something unheard of before in Mexica history was being contemplated – the overthrow of a reigning emperor for weakness and negligence of duty, and his replacement by another, more bellicose man who would honour Huitzilopochtli with all-out war against the Spaniards.

It was the presence of that war that Cortés felt now in the streets – not open war yet, bloody in tooth and claw, but the threat and the strong intimation of war, like some predatory beast that has marked its prey and is patiently stalking it. He could see it in the evil eye of that beggar woman over there, fixing on him with hatred from under her shawl then glancing rapidly away. He could see it in the hand of that butcher at the entrance to his stall, wielding an obsidian knife as though he meant to cut out a human heart, not slice meat. He could see it in the insolence of that knot of a score or so of young men advancing towards them along the centre of the avenue, refusing to give way – something that would have been inconceivable only a few months before.

Alvarado, Cortés and Malinal continued to ride three abreast. About a dozen paces ahead, holding aloft the fluttering standard, was Farfan. Dressed in loincloths and moccasins, flint daggers strapped at their waists, the twenty or so Mexica youths stopped in a block in his path, unyielding, daring him to advance further.

'*Push through, lad!*' Alvarado snapped as Bucephalus ambled into the rump of Farfan's gelding. 'You're a soldier of the Crown. You don't make way for native rabble.'

'This isn't good,' Malinal said. 'These are warriors, Hernán.'

Cortés agreed. He'd been watching the gang. They were purposive and disciplined, eyeing up the huge horses but evidently unafraid of them. No rabble these! Farfan turned with a look of uncertainty.

'*Push through!*' Alvarado yelled again.

Farfan's heels kicked into his mount's flanks and the animal surged forward, half trampling one of the youths, forcing the others to make way. Suddenly he was in the midst of them, and they surged back around him like a returning wave, threatening to bear him down. One made a grab for his reins and others drew their knives as they closed in.

Alvarado's falchion was already out of its scabbard, gleaming in the late sun. '*Santiago and at them!*' he bellowed, the war cry of Spain in its battles against the Moors for seven hundred years, and spurred Bucephalus forward, the great horse seeming to leap from a standstill to a full gallop in an instant, striking the thickly massed Mexica like an avalanche and scattering them left and right. A second later Cortés drew his broadsword and charged Molinero into the melee, heading straight for Farfan, who had been half dragged from his saddle but still doggedly refused to relinquish his grip on the standard.

There were a lot of hands on him! One particularly large warrior had a beefy arm around his head and was set fair to wrestle him to the ground, but none of them was sticking knives into him yet, probably because these idiots, as was the habit of the Mexica, wanted to capture them alive for sacrifice.

Did they really imagine they could get away with that?

Using Molinero's huge mass and weight as a battering ram, Cortés barged forward and plunged the point of his sword down into the soft, unprotected gap between the big warrior's collarbone and his neck. It sunk in deep, finding his heart, and he relinquished his hold on Farfan with a bubbling gasp. From there it was just plain slaughter, delivered as though it were a parade-ground exercise, as Cortés and Alvarado rampaged through the rest of the attackers, leaving a dozen of them dismembered on the ground before the remnant accepted they were beaten and ran. Even Farfan acquitted himself well after his initial panic, drawing his rusty old sword and splitting a fleeing Indian with it.

'That's the way, lad,' Alvarado said, riding up to him. 'Show them no mercy because they'll show you none . . . Your first kill?'

'Yes, sir.'

'Enjoy it?'

'Nuh . . . Nuh . . . No, sir.'

'Well I suggest you learn!'

Hundreds of Mexica who had been passing by when the attack began looked on in stunned silence. Blood pooled on the street, streamed into the drains and spattered the three Spaniards from head to foot.

'It won't do for Narváez's men to see us like this,' Cortés said suddenly. 'I need them to believe they're coming into a calm city where we're completely in control. This gives the wrong impression.'

'You want us to get *changed* for them?' Alvarado asked disbelievingly.

'Yes. We go back to the palace!'

Cortés laid a hand on Malinal's bare forearm, bringing her alongside him, then tapped a heel to Molinero's flank; they set off at a trot after

Farfan with Alvarado taking up the rear. The crowd gave them a wide berth, closing behind them at once and wheeling around the dead warriors.

A great cry of grief went up.

Father Bartolomé Olmedo, Mercedarian friar and chaplain to the expedition to the New Lands of Don Hernando Cortez, strove at all times to be happy. What after all was the point of life without happiness? It defied common sense to imagine that God had put us on this earth to be miserable! Each one of us, each human soul, was here to celebrate joy – and in Olmedo's case joy meant a bottle of good red wine, or preferably several bottles to be had one after the other accompanying an excellent dinner. It was most unfortunate, therefore, that no such joy was to be found anywhere in the New Lands, since the expedition's limited supply, including the special barrels earmarked for Mass, had run out. The only plausible substitute was a fermented local drink called pulque that had happily crossed his path. Being milky white in colour it wouldn't do for Mass, and it had a sour, yeast-like taste that made him shudder at first, but the effect after a few bowls was pleasant enough, so he'd persisted with the experiment and was now even beginning to appreciate the flavour.

A flagon of Olmedo's best pulque, with his drinking bowl half empty beside it, stood on the table before him, attracting worried glances from the servants in the dining hall of Iztapalapa's lakeside palace. He could understand their dilemma; they believed the sacred beverage was forbidden to him as a foreigner, but did not dare to question his right to drink it. He lifted the brightly painted ceramic bowl with its imagery of crescent moons – for some reason the Mexica associated pulque with the moon – drained it, belched, and filled the bowl again from the flagon.

A portly, rugged friar of perhaps forty, Olmedo had a strong jaw which he'd recently taken to shaving clean, and a Roman nose, giving him a somewhat fierce, uncompromising look, greatly softened by twinkling brown eyes. Despite a full tonsure, out of which rose the smooth and deeply tanned dome of his skull, his hair was unruly, reddish-brown in colour, thick and shaggy at the nape of his bull-like neck and somewhat overhanging his brow. His shoulders and chest were massive, and an ample stomach thrust comfortably forward through his habit.

He surrendered to another gulp of pulque; really, the more of the stuff he drank, the better he liked it! Just as well he'd brought along a few flagons, as he had no idea how long he might be sitting here, or whether dour, grey-bearded, cold-eyed, utterly humourless Ordaz sitting opposite him, with whom he'd run out of conversation some dreary hours before, might be transformed into a more entertaining companion if he could get some pulque into him.

Not that there was any hope of that! Ordaz had claimed to be disgusted by the single sip he'd tried earlier and had spat it out explosively on the floor.

That was when Olmedo remembered what was in his satchel. He was something of a herbalist, and it was his practice to collect specimens of interesting plants and fungi wherever he travelled. After coming to Tenochtitlan he'd heard rumours about certain mushrooms that the Mexica called *teonanácatl*, 'the flesh of the gods', said to be intoxicating, and one of his scouts had recently skulked up to him with a linen bag containing a dozen fine large examples. Olmedo had selected one at random and insisted that his scout eat it in his presence, which he did willingly. Observing no ill effect on the man after three hours, other perhaps than some mild disorientation, and having had him return the next day when he proved still to be in good health, Olmedo had concluded that these mushrooms were not poisonous.

With what he hoped was a casual air, he reached into his satchel, found the linen bag with the eleven remaining mushrooms, and transferred it to the sleeve of his white Mercedarian habit. It was the work of an instant, unnoticed by Ordaz, who sat twiddling his thumbs, his gaze fixed on the door.

'Excuse me, Don Diego,' Olmedo now said, rising. 'I'm going to pay a visit to the kitchens and find out how they're doing with the banquet for the men we're meeting . . .'

'Bah! Complete folly that we are here to meet them at all, let alone fretting over a banquet for them!'

'I understand your point of view, Don Diego,' Olmedo replied in soothing, sermon-like tones, 'and most of the other captains share it. Still, we are here to carry out the caudillo's wishes and we must accept, I think, that he knows what he's doing.'

Through until the summer of last year, when he'd taken part in a failed conspiracy at Villa Rica, Ordaz had been – more or less openly – a 'Velazquista', as Cortés termed the supporters of his rival Diego de Velázquez, the governor of Cuba. The conspiracy, which had involved stealing a ship and attempting to make off in it to Cuba, had involved some fifty of the men. Their leader, Juan Escudero, had promptly been hanged, as had the ship's pilot Diego Cermeno, ten of the conspirators had been flogged, and one had the toes of his left foot cut off as an exemplary punishment, but Cortés had generously spared Ordaz, along with all the rest, after which the grizzled old captain had never again faltered in his loyalty.

That was good, Olmedo thought. Unswervingly devoted to the caudillo himself, he valued the same sentiments in others. Nonetheless, the fact could not be escaped that Ordaz was a crashing bore, and if the train of *tamanes* bringing the envoys up from Villa Rica was delayed for any reason – by no means impossible on such a long and difficult road – then he might be obliged to wait here in the old fart's tedious company for hours longer.

The prospect of such *ennui*, Olmedo decided, could not be tolerated.

He made his way to the palace kitchens, returning after an interval accompanied by a serving girl carrying two steaming plates.

'Look here, Don Diego,' Olmedo said as the plates were set down on the table. 'I had them make us a snack. I do hope you might be partial to a rib or two of venison, nicely smoked? Oh, and these very fine fresh mushrooms, sliced and lightly sautéed on the side?'

Ordaz straightened his back, growled with appreciation – a remarkable change from the sullen mood he'd projected all afternoon – and smacked his lips. 'Now you're talking,' he said.

Night had fallen and Tenochtitlan's avenues and canals glittered with lanterns, giving the great city the aspect of a fairytale kingdom, when Cortés and Malinal rode out with Alvarado and Farfan again. They were accompanied this time by a squad of six seasoned killers under Sergeant García Brabo, lean and grey-haired, with a hooked nose and a permanently sour expression. Dressed in filthy clothes, wearing strange combinations of scratched and battered plate and chain mail, and equally scratched and battered helmets, but armed with fine broadswords and daggers of the best Toledo steel, Brabo's men were part of a larger force of twenty-five who'd been doing Cortés's dirty work for years. They were natural foot soldiers but could fight on horseback when they had to and were mounted now for the evening's brisk ride.

The enforced return to the palace, the necessary ablutions to remove the blood, changing clothes, and rounding up Brabo, had all taken much longer than expected. Two hours had been wasted. Cortés couldn't understand why the envoys hadn't already been brought to him. But at the very least, having been met by Olmedo and Ordaz, put at liberty, and given a good dinner in Iztapalapa, they should be on horseback now and well advanced on the final leg of their journey along the causeway, most likely even at the city gates.

They were not at the gates. Once through them, Cortés raised his hand for a halt, his eyes straining to follow the flickering mirage of the causeway, lined by lanterns along its full six-mile length, stretching southward into darkness. There was still some light pedestrian traffic on it, moving in both directions, but no sign of a group of riders and retainers advancing from Iztapalapa.

'You seem deep in thought, brother?' Alvarado observed.

'I'm wondering if we have any cause for concern . . .'

'If you mean, could your precious envoys have been snatched en route by another gang of half-naked indigenes like those we met earlier then, yes, we do!'

'Perchance they are only delayed on the road?'

'Perchance . . .'

Cortés thought for a moment. 'We'll go as far as Iztapalapa. If they're not there we'll send out runners. Most likely it's nothing serious, but we need to know . . .'

He spurred Molinero forward to a trot, then to a canter, then to a gallop. Malinal, who'd become a competent rider in the past year, kept pace on his left. Alvarado on Bucephalus rode on his right. The others followed in a tight group.

The boards of the causeway thundered and echoed beneath their hooves. Ahead of them pedestrians panicked. Some fell and were trampled, others scattered to the sides, many in their haste leaping over the railings and throwing themselves into the lake.

This would do nothing, Cortés thought, to calm the fevered sentiments of the Mexica! On the other hand, the attack earlier had been launched with deadly intent and a harsh response would be expected; indeed, he would look weak if he left the matter unpunished.

He rode down an aged crone, hearing her bones snap like kindling beneath Molinero's iron-shod hooves, and felt no regret.

On his left, Malinal shouted something harsh and wild but her words were snatched away in the wind.

*   *   *

At some unknown interval after eating the mushrooms, which he had divided equally with Ordaz, Olmedo began to notice that he was feeling somewhat strange. In fact, he realised, he had probably already been feeling strange for a while, but time no longer seemed to have any meaning and, besides, this *mushroom* feeling was unfamiliar and insidious, and had rather crept up on him.

He'd been excited when his informants had told him of the *teonaná-catl's* intoxicating properties, which they even described as a kind of drunkenness, and which he hoped might prove as enjoyable as wine. Unfortunately, however – he shook his head violently from side to side to clear it – this didn't feel like alcohol intoxication at all!

It felt like something quite other.

And that something . . . Was it not slightly sinister?

Why, for example, were the walls of the palace dining hall in which they sat actually *breathing*? Walls did *not* breathe! Walls were *not* alive! Olmedo knew this and yet he could swear that the whole huge room was expanding and contracting around him, expanding and contracting like some vast womb about to give birth . . . To what?

To him?

He looked down at his hands. They glowed, surrounded by a foggy nimbus of diffused white light. He remembered his mother, Adelmira, in the brief, sunny, almost forgotten years before he'd been taken into the monastery. He sobbed. Widowed, too poor to raise him, she'd given him up. Suddenly it was brought home to him with the force of a revelation that there was so much *sadness* in the world. How could the purpose of life be the pursuit of happiness when there was so *much* sadness! His long-lost mother's, and his own, were but tiny fragments of an incomprehensibly larger whole – all these human beings, so many of them misguided, afraid, ill informed, foolish, and all of them present together in the joyous garden of the earth and making themselves and everyone else thoroughly miserable.

'None of us have any idea what we're doing here,' Olmedo said suddenly. He spoke so loudly that he startled himself – and Ordaz.

'What? What's that?' muttered the captain, who had slumped forward wordless over the table soon after finishing his plate, falling into a state of withdrawal far deeper than his previous morose silence – an outcome quite the opposite of Olmedo's intentions for this experiment with a novel intoxicant. Now, however, the other man abruptly sat upright, his eyes darting wildly from side to side. 'What? Who?' He half rose to his feet, calloused fingers falling to the pommel of the ridiculous two-handed longsword, known as a *montante*, that he insisted on always wearing, stumbled, tripped between the table and the chair, and fell sideways to the floor with a tremendous clatter of metal and leather.

Rushing to his aid, Olmedo lost his own footing. Goodness! He hardly had his legs under him, an effect that would have taken several bottles of wine to produce! He also felt faintly sick. With much grunting and manhandling, assisted by several servants – why did they all have green skin? – he lifted Ordaz and levered him into his chair, where he promptly slumped forward, seemingly unconscious, over his own folded elbows.

Oh dear! Olmedo thought as he unsteadily returned to his seat. The room simply would not stay still!

And what was that music?

Ah! A flute player. An old, old man, green skin like the rest of them, *huge* wen on the side of his nose, was piping out a haunting tune. Then a tall, ethereal, imperious, Greek-looking woman floated by, wearing a long diaphanous robe, lightning darting from her eyes, and stood over the table staring fixedly at Olmedo. The odd thing – quite bizarre really – was that she was completely transparent and he could see the flute player through her.

Fascinating! How could this be? These mushrooms clearly contained some far from ordinary intoxicant. While aware that he was falling ever more completely under its spell with each passing moment, Olmedo found he still had enough of his reason left to suspect that he had perhaps begun with too strong a dose before he had discovered his measure. Next time – and there would be a next time! – he would start the experiment with just one mushroom, carefully assess its effects on him, then the following day try two, and the day after, if necessary, three. But almost six each in a single serving, as he'd dished out to Ordaz and himself in his fit of boredom earlier this evening, was obviously too many.

As though in confirmation of this, the transparent woman now spoke to him in excellent Latin. 'Olmedo,' she said, her voice, rich and warm, sending chills down his spine and electrifying the hairs on his arms, 'I have work for you to do.'

It was distinctly peculiar that her lips did not move and yet her words rang like a peal of bells inside his head!

More peculiar still, this angel, this vision – *this goddess?* – was changing shape before Olmedo's eyes; not the work of an instant, but a complex, amazing, beautiful and numinous *process*. He could only think of it as a kind of unfolding, like the emergence from the bud of the petals of a flower.

What came forth, however, was no flower, but an immense serpent the colour of rust and mould, a serpent fifty feet long that towered over him, its mouth gaping, its fangs exposed like unsheathed daggers. A ruff of bright feathers adorned its sinuous neck, extending up into a crest that ran the full length of its great head.

'I have work for you to do,' it repeated.

Olmedo had liked the look of the woman, but this nightmarish phantasm was an altogether different proposition. Might it not even be the very serpent that had tempted Adam and Eve in the garden? Was some great temptation about to be offered to him here?

'What work?' he asked suspiciously.

'You'll know when the right time comes.'

The serpent's form shimmered, grew indistinct, returned for an instant in almost complete solidity, blurred again, then vanished. Beyond it the elderly musician was still in place, still playing his little ceramic flute.

Not at all understanding what had happened, but suddenly feeling more or less normal, and that the accustomed balance of the world had in some mysterious manner been restored, Olmedo's eyes and thoughts refocused on Ordaz, whom he'd entirely forgotten in the past moments, but who had, nevertheless, remained in his chair on the other side of the table throughout.

The captain's manner was far from normal, however. Previously slouching, propped on his elbows, he now sat rigidly upright, mouth gaping, wide-eyed and staring – but apparently seeing nothing. Olmedo leaned across and waved, whispered some encouragement, barked a command and finally reached out with both hands and shook Ordaz mightily, but with no discernible reaction.

'Poor man!' the friar clucked. He felt sorry for the old soldier and a little guilty to have inflicted this intoxication on him without informing him. To have endured the storm of visions unleashed by the mushrooms without any preparation whatsoever, or any notion at all of why he was having those earth-shaking experiences, must have been quite devastating. Indeed, apparently it continued to be devastating! The usually stolid and expressionless Ordaz now gave a great shuddering yell, leapt to his feet, again stepped around the table – but this time with remarkable agility – and stood glowering down at Olmedo.

173

'What ho, Don Diego?' the friar asked, attempting to sound cheerful when in truth he was afraid – and for two reasons.

First, to his horror, the room was again contracting and expanding around him like a womb, and he could feel the power of the mushrooms – which had only retreated, he now understood – rushing back with renewed vigour and threatening to undo him utterly.

Secondly, there was the terrible aspect of Captain Ordaz looming over him, sweating beneath the stinking chain mail he seemed never to take off, his face contorted with fury, but also with stark, unabashed terror, his eyes liquid with hatred and fear.

How long, Olmedo wondered in something approaching panic, was this going to last before the mushroom intoxication wore off?

Ordaz's mouth opened and closed, opened and closed, his thin lips making an absurd sound – *clack!* – whenever they touched. '*You!*' he now roared – *clack!* '*You!*' – *clack!* – '*are that beast*'– *clack!* – '*whose name is Leviathan.*' His voice had suddenly cleared, recognition seemed to dawn, and he stooped lower to peer directly into Olmedo's eyes, as though searching for some message there, at last emitting a shuddering roar and announcing: '*You are the devil. You cannot hide from me! I have seen through your disguise!*'

Your lips aren't clacking now, Olmedo thought randomly, but what he said was: 'Come come, Don Diego! Get a grip. This is all intoxicated nonsense you're spouting and you'll be ashamed of yourself tomorrow.'

'*You are the devil, I say!*'

Ordaz was literally beside himself with loathing and fury, Olmedo realised, big veins popping out on his forehead, staring around insanely, so completely in the grip of the mushrooms that he seemed capable of anything.

Could he even be dangerous?

Yes! Because the captain was armed with an enormous sword that he knew how to use and had obviously lost his wits.

'*You are the devil,*' Ordaz repeated, as though in confirmation of something long believed though never before admitted to be true. He hauled the *montante* from its scabbard with a horrible, whispering susurration, and raised it two-handed above his head, but such was Olmedo's faith in his fellow man that only at the last moment did he realise a strike was coming. He squealed and – more by accident than design – ducked out of the way. The blade of the great sword whistled down and embedded itself in the heavy table. Bellowing like a bull, Ordaz struggled mightily

174

to free it and while he was thus occupied, Olmedo darted forward and dealt him a terrific blow to the head.

'Nicely done!' came a familiar voice as Ordaz slumped unconscious to the floor. *The voice of Cortés!* 'Not often I get to see one of my captains knocked out cold by a friar.'

Cortés was somehow here! Malinal was with him. Behind them Alvarado and Brabo, too, and some of his toughs, were crowding through the door, some suppressing sniggers, others openly laughing.

Olmedo reeled. 'Caudillo . . . I . . . I . .' He wanted to explain – although God's blood! How could any of this be explained? – but the power of the mushrooms had now risen to a previously unimagined crescendo. 'I . .' he tried again. 'I . .'

'And not often I find you lost for words, Bartolomé,' added Cortés with a smile. It was particularly difficult to watch this smile since the familiar, bearded face upon which it was fixed was disturbingly mobile, *rippling* in fact, compressed in some directions and stretched in others, with the teeth rather snaggled and long.

Seemingly oblivious to his own process of transformation, Cortés looked down at Ordaz, still senseless, and at the gleaming *montante* still trapped in the table. He raised a quizzical eyebrow: 'Would you like to tell me what happened here, Bartolomé?'

Olmedo hung his head: 'Hernán,' he managed to say, 'I cannot.' Some instinct told him to keep the whole matter of the mushrooms to himself.

'You cannot?'

Out of nowhere, a scheme appeared fully formed in Olmedo's mind. He made the gesture of a man drinking from a bottle and gave a bleary wink: 'Not in my present condition.'

'You're drunk?' When Cortés frowned he looked ugly! He glanced at the pulque flagon, somehow still intact on the table, with the drinking bowl spilled beside it: 'Am I to understand that you and Ordaz got drunk on that native firewater and had a fight? *Am I seriously to believe this?*'

'Yes, Caudillo. I am ashamed.'

'Ha! So you should be! Damned irresponsible of you, Olmedo. If you weren't a friar I'd have you flogged!' He glowered at Ordaz, seemed to consider, then kicked him in the ribs: 'And if he wasn't a captain I'd have him flogged. Truly I'd like to have you both flogged! What did you think you were doing?'

The kick had awakened Ordaz. '*The devil is amongst us,*' he gasped. '*He is a wolf in sheep's clothing.*'

'Gospel of Matthew,' Cortés said, as though speaking to himself, 'Chapter seven, if I remember correctly, verse fifteen.' Ordaz had struggled to his knees and would soon be on his feet, but García Brabo stepped forward and took him by the collar of his jerkin: 'Not so fast, there's a good fellow,' the sergeant said.

The captain thrashed wildly and Brabo's wiry arm snaked around his throat: 'You've been taken unwell, sir. Best if I pop you off to sleep again.' The sergeant squeezed – remarkably little pressure seemed to be involved – and Ordaz's eyes fluttered closed.

'Is he all right?' Olmedo asked.

'Of course he is, Father,' Brabo replied, laying Ordaz down gently on his side, 'and at least he won't be raving about the devil any more.'

Cortés turned to Olmedo: 'Bartolomé, this has been a peculiar business and you look most peculiar yourself.'

Involuntarily the friar brushed at his habit, as though removing crumbs.

'I mean to impress Narváez's envoys,' Cortés continued, 'and win them over to our cause, so I regard it as a matter of great good fortune, indeed of divine Providence, that they have been delayed on their journey and not reached Iztapalapa yet. In the next days I will require a full explanation from you of what happened here, but tonight you must go back to Tenochtitlan, *at once*, and take Ordaz with you . . .'

'But he—'

'No buts! Take him on horseback if he can ride, or trussed up in a hammock and carried by *tamanes* if he cannot. Either way, I want you both gone now. I'll send three of Brabo's boys with you to make sure you stay on your mounts and get back to quarters, but I'll permit you to cause me no further embarrassment here!'

An hour after Olmedo and Ordaz were sent on their way, fortunately without further incident, the runner who'd waited on the road all afternoon to bring advance notice of the envoys' arrival came pounding into the dining hall of the palace of Iztapalapa breathless with news.

He fell to his knees and gave his report – a few words only.

'They're here,' Malinal announced before he was finished. She was already pulling on her cloak.

'Still in their packing crates?' Cortés asked.

Malinal put the question in Nahuatl, heard the answer and laughed. 'Yes, so it seems.'

'What's funny?'

'He said something about the prisoners not even being let out to shit.'

'Uggh. Unnecessarily cruel . . .'

'Like your cruelty in riding down that old woman on the causeway?'

Cortés thought about it. Malinal was intelligent, capable of fine arguments, and she had a point.

'Yes,' he replied, 'perhaps exactly like that. I will not argue with you. But this is war, Malinal, and when I make war I give no quarter.'

'Is it not also war with this – what do you call him? – Nar-Vez?'

'Yes. It is war.'

'Then surely putting his envoys in packing cases was not "unnecessary cruelty" but more like "giving no quarter"? It shows you are strong . . .'

'And it gives me something to bargain with,' Cortés added. Every day his respect for Malinal's political savvy was growing. 'Come now and we'll release those men.'

A hundred torches blazed in the clearing where the three envoys had been brought and set down in their cages – for these packing containers were nothing more than cages, such as one might keep a dog in. Cortés ordered more torches brought until the scene was as bright as day.

Guevara, the fat priest, was in the cage closest to him and was particularly fawning and effusive. Sandoval had described him as arrogant and domineering, but after four days in a packing case, bouncing around in his own shit, he was a changed man.

'You must be Father Antonio Ruiz de Guevara!' Cortés boomed, striding towards the cage.

'I am he,' said Guevara. He pressed himself against the slats in the side of the container, suddenly close to Cortés: 'And you are?'

'I am Hernán Cortés, sir, captain-general for the king, and chief justice in these New Lands, and I have come to set you free.'

At his signal, Brabo's men broke the fastenings of the three containers and brought the captives, hobbling and filthy, out of their confinement.

'Gentlemen,' Cortés said, 'I rushed here to meet you, and to offer my humble apologies in person, as soon as I got word of what had happened. A most unfortunate mistake was made by the commander of my garrison at the coast, Captain Gonzalo de Sandoval, an excellent young officer but sometimes over-zealous. In his treatment of you, he has gone far beyond the bounds of his authority and of all human decency. For this regrettable error you will be compensated, in gold. You have my word.'

'Gold you say.' In his shit-stained robe, the wizened figure of the royal notary, Alfonso de Vergara, was easy to recognise.

'Yes, Señor Vergara. Gold. I am inclined to be generous.'

The third man, Antonio de Amaya, hobbled closer.

'And to you, too, Señor Amaya,' said Cortés, turning towards him. 'I'll see you get satisfaction in this matter . . .'

'My cousin,' said Amaya 'is—'

'I know!' Cortés smiled: 'Juan Velázquez de Léon, like yourself a cousin of Governor Diego Velázquez of Cuba, but also one of my most trusted captains. He is not in the city or I would have brought him here to meet you, but I expect his return soon. You are amongst friends here, Señor Amaya – ' he extended his arms to include the other three but, in their filth, avoided embracing any one of them – 'you are *all* amongst friends here. Now come – the hour is late but we have hot baths, clean clothes, and a banquet prepared for you in our lakeside palace here at Iztapalapa.'

'*Your* lakeside palace, Lord Cortés?' It was Guevara who asked.

'Yes, one of several now in my possession that we hold in the name of the king and for the greater glory of Spain. The best of them is in Tenochtitlan, the capital, where we'll take you tomorrow.' Cortés stepped forward and almost clapped the other man on the shoulder, then thought better of it. 'We enjoy great riches here, Guevara,' he said, 'you'll see. And we are true servants of the Crown—'

'You hold a royal warrant?'

A sharp, legalistic question, for which Cortés had a sharp, legalistic answer. 'We discovered these New Lands for the king and last year we planted a colony here to watch over the king's interests. I am its legally elected captain-general and *justicia mayor*. Now come, let us get you to those baths!'

Chapter Eleven

It was already long after midnight when the three envoys, still not quite believing the sudden change in their fortunes, were shown to their comfortable beds in the palace at Iztapalapa. Leaving them in the charge of García Brabo, Cortés at once rode back to Tenochtitlan, taking Malinal, Alvarado and Farfan with him, ordered Farfan to call a general assembly of all the men after reveille, made certain preparations and finally snatched a few hours of sleep.

His first act in the morning was to have Pepillo summoned from Moctezuma's apartments. 'I'm taking you off Mucktey's staff,' he said. 'You're back with me from now on.'

'Have you informed him, sir?'

'I'll do so in my own good time.'

The assembly was held in the refectory over the customarily lavish breakfast of fruits and roast meats prepared by Moctezuma's palace servants. Cortés waited until every plate was heaped before he stood and pounded the table for attention with the pommel of his dagger.

'We eat well here,' he began, 'do we not?'

Nodding in agreement, a sea of swarthy, bearded, masticating faces gazed up at him and there were shouts of 'We do, Caudillo!', 'Like kings, Caudillo!' and, more raucously, 'We fuck well too, Caudillo! I'm getting more here than I ever got back in Cuba.'

Moctezuma had allocated two hundred 'special girls' to pleasure the men. There were not enough of them to go round, but they were shared on a rota and so far there had been very few fights.

Cortés grinned: 'I'd hazard we all get more of everything here than we did in Cuba,' he said. 'I know we've had to work for it, and that we've had to give up much of what we've earned, but great wealth lies ahead of us and, as a token of that,' he clapped his hands, 'I wish to present every one of you, including our brothers who are not here this morning because of various duties, with a small gift . . .'

It was a dramatic moment. The hand clap was the signal for eight Indian bearers to enter carrying two large and evidently heavy jewel-encrusted chests which, with some ceremony, they placed side by side in the centre of the floor. Summoning the men to gather round, Cortés then flung open the lids of the chests to reveal a cornucopia of gleaming gold and glittering jewels.

There came a loud collective gasp from those nearby; others at tables further away scrambled closer. Cortés waited until enough of them had caught a glimpse of the treasure. None were yet certain how much of it, if any, was their 'small gift'.

'I've been putting pressure on Mucktey these past weeks,' Cortés continued. 'He's a nervous fellow, as you know . . .'

Laughter.

'. . . and it turns out he had some treasure stashed away he hadn't told us about yet.'

More laughter.

'So I persuaded him to part with it – ' a gesture towards the open chests – 'and I thought, since you men have worked so hard, and given up so much, that you should have it all.'

There was a moment of stunned silence as this sank in, then cries of, 'Thank you, Caudillo', and whistles and cheers of appreciation, after which Cortés was lifted up on the shoulders of a number of the burlier soldiers and paraded around the refectory to further whistles and cheers. But when he was set down, and order was restored, questions began to be asked.

'What about the "king's fifth"?' The voice had arisen out of the middle of the crowd; its exact source was impossible to pin down.

'And what about *your* fifth, Cortés?' someone else asked, a trifle sneeringly.

It was impossible to be sure, but it sounded a lot like Alonso de Grado, the on-and-off Velazquista who'd proved to be such a disastrous commander of Villa Rica after Juan Escudero's death that Cortés had been forced to recall him, replacing him – in the nick of time, as it turned out – with the intelligent and efficient Gonzalo de Sandoval, a man who knew how to handle himself in an emergency.

And certainly the arrival of Narváez and his well-armed thousand represented an emergency of the first order, which would have to be fought with every available weapon.

Including, regretfully, treasure.

'I won't be taking my fifth,' Cortés replied. He paused to let this sink in 'and no king's fifth will be levied against you. You have my guarantee.'

Jaws dropped.

'You are to think of this as a bonus, free of all taxes, a very special reward for the very special services you have rendered to this expedition and to the Crown. Be sure you divide it equally so that each of you and each of our absent brothers gets his fair share – the good Diego de Godoy can do the accounting – but other than that . . . *it's all yours, men!*'

Another ragged cheer went up – little wonder since no such bonanza had ever been handed out to the common soldiers since the start of the conquest – and Cortés found himself lifted shoulder-high again.

Might as well enjoy all this enthusiasm and adulation, he thought.

Because he'd paid a stiff price for it.

He'd fabricated the story about the treasure coming from some secret stash of Moctezuma, and instead had raided his personal hoard to fill the two big chests he'd just given to the men. It was a painful sacrifice, and he couldn't even take credit for it since that would mean admitting to false accounting.

On the bright side, what remained of his hoard was still large, far beyond his rightful share as captain-general, even with his – dubious in its legality – extra 'fifth' added. Heaps of gold and jewels that he'd had Brabo keep separate for him in every city along the route of the conquest had never been seen by the royal auditors or shared with the men.

Cortés looked on this king's ransom of sequestered booty as nothing more nor less than his by right, but he also held it as a war chest to be drawn upon in troubled times – times like now, beset on all sides by enemies! For as the old saying so succinctly put it, 'presents make nonsense of troubles' and Cortés intended to be lavish with presents in the days ahead – to the men who'd come with him so far, and risked so much, and also to the new men who'd come with Narváez and whose affections he needed to buy. Since he could not reward the latter without exciting the resentment of the former, it had been necessary to provide for his own men first. Hopefully what he'd given was enough to mollify them while he expended more of his treasure on bribes to corrupt the morale and fighting strength of Narváez's army.

But first he needed the men's help with something else. They were happily biting, holding up to the light, and trying on the many gold chains and bracelets, rings and jewels that glittered and beckoned in the chests – chattering excitedly like the monkeys he knew the Mexica compared them to – so it shouldn't be difficult. A small nightmare of accounting, perhaps, since the division had not been worked out yet, but perfectly possible with goodwill.

'Brothers,' he said. He pounded the table again with the pommel of his dagger: 'Brothers! Listen up. I have a boon to ask you.'

Once more all eyes turned towards him. He could see that the men were in the mood to grant him anything he wanted.

'You'll recall that the envoys of Narváez are on their way here . . . ?'

'Still in packing crates I hope,' someone said, and there was a general burst of laughter.

Cortés waited for silence: 'No! I'm afraid not! It would have been amusing, I agree, to have them brought in before us like baggage, but that wouldn't serve our interests. As I said a few nights ago, we're going to treat them with honour. They're presently having breakfast in Iztapalapa, then they'll be brought here on horseback – I've arranged for them to cross the causeway and pass through the gates of Tenochtitlan at noon. We'll give them lunch and I'll host a grand banquet for them here in our quarters this evening – everything very light-hearted and happy. I want to squeeze as much information out of them as I can about the numbers, morale and combat-readiness of Narváez's force, then I want to send them back to him with three pieces of – how shall I put this? – "misinformation" about us; about our position in the city here. War is certainly coming, so we must do everything we can to mislead our enemy.'

The men were expectant now. The magic of Cortés's plans, and his famously devious strategies, never failed to grip their imaginations.

'First,' he continued, 'these envoys of Narváez must see, and they must understand us to be, completely in control here, even though – ' a broad wink – 'we all know we're not!'

There was laughter, but it was not wholehearted. Every man in the garrison was aware how tenuous their position in Tenochtitlan really was.

Cortés waved for silence. 'Secondly, I want the envoys to see, and to understand us to be, a tight-knit group, with no dissensions amongst ourselves, no Velazquista sympathies – ' he had picked out Alonso de Grado near the back of the hall and now gave him a pointed look – 'and an absolute commitment on the part of every man to hold on to the gains we've made in these New Lands and not be deprived of them by Narváez!'

At this there was more cheering, whistling and drumming of feet.

'Thirdly,' Cortés continued, 'I want them to think that we're *rich*.'

'Ha! How're you going to convince them of that?'

'Well again, I know it hasn't been easy in these New Lands. You've had to sacrifice a lot and some of you have gambled away most of what was left, but I think none of you are entirely without treasure?'

A quizzical look around the attentive men. Shifty, sideways glances in reply.

'By which I mean,' Cortés went on, 'pieces of plate, necklaces, bracelets . . . Some of you have ingots I know . . .' He paused, sensing a fresh current of anxiety in the air: 'Don't worry! This isn't a plot to relieve you of what little you've set aside. You have this new treasure now, after all. Take it! Divide it! My only request, and it may seem strange, is that every one of you should make sure to wear items of value about your persons in the next days while the envoys are here – gold chains, bracelets, jewels, anything that can be put on display. Oh and some of you must gamble in front of the envoys! Wager items of value foolishly – ingots, pieces of plate, worked figures, some fat jewels – and win or lose without seeming to care.'

'You want us to appear so rich that gold is cheap to us?' asked Bernal Díaz.

'Exactly!' said Cortés. 'I want Narváez's envoys to leave here convinced of our great wealth and abundance. It's all part of my plan . . .'

As Cortés had arranged, the envoys were ushered through the gates of Tenochtitlan at noon and thence brought directly to Axayacatl's palace. Their route took them past the Great Pyramid. On its summit, the towering cross that had caused so much anger and unrest amongst the Mexica since it was erected some weeks ago, now seemed to project a silent message to the visitors that conversion – one of the primary goals of conquest – had been achieved here.

If only they knew! Cortés thought.

But all that mattered was the appearance of things, not the substance, and the Great Pyramid, emptied of its idols, washed clean of blood, and holding up the cross of Christ to Heaven, gave a potent appearance of the triumph of the faith.

Luncheon stood waiting in the palace refectory, with the whole garrison other than sentries present to greet the envoys. They were freethinking, outspoken men these conquistadors, blunt and eager in their manners, and several of them took it upon themselves to harangue the newcomers and to quiz them about their mission.

'No offence, señors,' said one, who wore around his neck a prominent gold chain, 'we know it is not your fault, but what's your Captain Narváez even doing here in the New Lands? If his purpose is to join us, then he must come forward and submit to the authority of our caudillo. But if, as we've heard, he's here to challenge us and to take from us everything we've gained, then you should let him know that we will fight him to the death.'

'Narváez is a toy soldier,' said another. On each wrist he wore a massive gold bracelet. He spat mightily on the floor. 'We don't want him here.'

It was the turn of a tough-looking Extremeño to speak. His fingers glittered with thick gold rings. 'We're living like kings and emperors here, thanks to our caudillo. We've made this land our own and fifty thousand Indian auxiliaries stand by to do our bidding. Tell Narváez if he comes against us, we'll destroy him.'

'Enough, gentlemen, enough.' Cortés was on his feet. 'No need for this talk of destruction and war!' He caught the eye of Father Guevara, whom he would have wished to seat next to Father Olmedo, if the chaplain had been present. There was, however, no sign of Olmedo, or of Ordaz! No doubt the two men were still sleeping off their hangovers after their absurd drunken escapade of the night before.

'Father Guevara,' Cortés said. 'It is my understanding that you are the leader and spokesman – ' he nodded towards Vergara and Amaya – 'of your little group?'

The fleshy priest, who was gnawing on a leg of roast turkey, smacked his lips. 'I am.'

Cortés assumed what he hoped was a suitably apologetic expression and bearing: 'For the terrible treatment you received on your journey from Villa Rica,' he said, 'I can only repeat the apology that I offered last night when I met you in Iztapalapa and hope that you will accept, by way of formal welcome to this great city of Tenochtitlan – ' Cortés clapped his hands – 'these small tokens of my esteem.'

The three servants who had been standing by, hiding in the kitchen doorway, now appeared, each carrying an open wicker basket, which they placed ceremoniously on the scarred refectory table, one in front of each of the envoys. In each basket reposed two smaller baskets of precious jewels, two fist-sized gold ingots, three heavy gold necklaces, and a thick gold pectoral five spans wide, fantastically worked in high relief in the Mexica style. Cortés had done his calculations carefully, and knew that if the envoys were to sell their gifts, the proceeds would be more than enough for each of them to buy a manor house and an estate in Castile – every conquistador's dream come true!

All three of them were gaping into their baskets with expressions of mixed disbelief, joy and naked greed. Until last night they'd been treated as common criminals but now, at a stroke, they were wealthy and distinguished men. And who had transformed their fortunes? None other than the chivalrous and benevolent Hernán Cortés!

Plainly overwhelmed, Guevara stood – there even seemed to be a tear in his eye! – and embraced Cortés awkwardly, his very large stomach getting in the way. 'Thank you, Caudillo,' he said.

The embrace was a surprise, but the words contained a more significant concession. Used commonly for Cortés by the men, the title 'caudillo' meant unequivocally 'leader' or 'chief'. Yet Sandoval's letter had also been unequivocal – when the envoys had presented themselves at Villa Rica a few days before, Guevara had spoken haughtily of Cortés as a 'traitor' and demanded his surrender to Pánfilo de Narváez who, he'd claimed, was the legitimate captain-general of these New Lands.

'What of Narváez?' Cortés asked immediately. 'Is he not your caudillo?'

Guevara cleared his throat and looked around the refectory, as though weighing up his audience. He seemed to have a habit, when nervous, of licking his lips – although perhaps it was just the turkey. His tongue, unpleasantly yellow and coated, darted out again. 'Don Pánfilo is a good man,' he said finally, 'and a courageous captain. I hold him in the highest regard. But it is my opinion now, having seen something of this great city of Tenochtitlan, so rich and so peaceful, and how all the land is controlled by you between here and the sea, and how you hold all of it in the name of King Carlos and for the greater glory of Spain, and how you have planted the Faith here so successfully, and how also your soldiers are content and prospering, and how even the natives humbly and with good grace accept your rule, that Don Pánfilo's mission is an unnecessary one.'

What? Cortés blinked.

At the end of that long string of words, had he just heard the envoy correctly?

He'd thought he'd have to work on Guevara for days, but here he was, within an hour of his arrival in Tenochtitlan, proclaiming that Narváez's mission was unnecessary!

Presents, it seemed, did indeed make nonsense of troubles!

Taking care to keep his satisfaction from showing itself on his face, Cortés resumed his seat and waved Guevara to join him. 'And why do you think this unnecessary mission was ever launched?' he asked.

The men nearby all craned their necks to listen.

'It is a project . . .' Guevara said. His tongue licked out. 'It is a project . . .'

Cortés laughed. 'Come come, Father. Don't be shy! We all know already that the Narváez expedition is a project of my good friend, Diego de Velázquez, governor of Cuba, whom we left standing at the quayside looking like a fool when we sailed from Santiago last year. We all know the governor's filled with envy at the great gains we've made for the Crown in these New Lands. And we all know he'll stop at nothing, do any harm and disservice, to punish us and deprive us of our rights.'

While Cortés talked, Guevara had been nodding in agreement: 'Yes. He has it in for you, Don Hernán. Made all kinds of claims and statements about you, hurled all kinds of slanders, called you a traitor, even told us you were setting yourself up as a king here. I can see now that everything he said was false, that it was jealousy speaking, but at the time I believed him and thought the expedition justified.'

'Did you all believe in this when you sailed from Cuba?'

Guevara, who was tucking into another leg of turkey, gave the question some thought before replying: 'No. For most it wasn't a matter of rights or wrongs, or believing this or that, or taking one side or the other. For most it was – ' another pause, as though searching for the right word – 'an adventure! That was why they came. Who wouldn't? Not piracy, which can get a man hanged, but the chance to join a well-funded, well-armed, *legal* expedition, the promise that you and your men were few in number and would be easily defeated, and the promise of gold' – a quick glance at the open, glittering basket on the table before him. 'It's gold that most of the men are after . . .'

'So not many with a burning sense of mission to capture "the traitor", Cortés?'

'They know that's just Velázquez and Narváez beating the drum. Few believe you a traitor, and fewer care! None I think has a personal grudge against you. You're well liked by most, if truth be told . . .'

'But they like gold better?' Cortés offered.

'Regretfully yes.'

186

'Nothing to regret there! If their loyalty was bought with gold, they may be persuaded to sell it again to a higher bidder . . .'

'You are right,' Guevara agreed. A hungry look, furtive and greedy, darted across his eyes like a stoat after a rabbit. 'Narváez is not a popular captain. He thinks too highly of himself and is rude and bad tempered. He has offended many of the men. You would do well, I think, to give some ingots or chains of gold to those who are most disaffected from him . . .'

'And how might these gifts be conveyed to . . . the right individuals?'

'It will be my honour, Captain-General, to serve as your agent in this matter.'

Guevara, Cortés could see now, was going to prove a useful ally – just the right man to conduct an auction of loyalties behind enemy lines! The details, the exact quantity of gold, and the names and ranks of the suggested recipients, would be a matter for private discussion later, but meanwhile Cortés had other questions for the money-grabbing priest.

'Father,' he said, 'I realise you're not a military man and that you may not be able to answer this, but what is Narváez's strength?'

Doubtfully: 'His strength?'

'Yes. His numbers. The size of his army. I'm told it's around a thousand men. Can you confirm that?'

Guevara glanced at his two companions, as though seeking their agreement. Amaya sat tight lipped, counting his jewels, but the notary Vergara, who had now hung his gold pectoral around his neck, gave a wizened smile: 'I can supply you with the numbers you require, Captain-General. Don Pánfilo Narváez sailed from Cuba in eighteen ships, eleven of which are *naos* and the other seven brigantines, carrying in total, in addition to their crews, a little over nine hundred soldiers. Of these eighty are cavalry, all well mounted, eighty are arquebusiers and one hundred and twenty are crossbowmen, and he has in addition a good number of heavy cannon and plentiful supplies of ammunition and military stores.'

Sandoval's letter had already indicated the approximate size of Narváez's force, so the exact numbers came as little surprise. Much more interesting was the willingness of the envoys to share this intelligence. They'd presented themselves to Sandoval as Velázquez loyalists to the core, but evidently the truth was far from that.

Chances were the whole Narváez expedition was riddled with similar contradictions.

Probing further, Cortés now said: 'The one thing that puzzles me, with nigh on a thousand men and orders from the governor of Cuba, is why Don Pánfilo has not attacked us already. Why, for example, did he just send the three of you to Villa Rica, almost inviting you to be taken prisoner, when Villa Rica could not possibly have prevailed against his full force?'

Amaya sniffed: 'Perhaps he prefers to negotiate and save Spanish lives—'

'Nonsense, Alonso!' interrupted Guevara. 'You know as well as I do that Narváez took the decision not to attack Villa Rica because he was afraid.'

'Afraid? What's to fear at Villa Rica?' Cortés asked. 'Sandoval had barely seventy men under his command on the day you turned up there.'

'Our Totonac spies gave us an exact count. But it wasn't the Villa Rica garrison that frightened Narváez. It was the prospect of your Indian auxiliaries. One of your men said it just now – you've got fifty thousand of them you can throw into battle.'

There was some truth in this. Last year, on their march inland through the mountains towards Tenochtitlan, the conquistadors had found themselves locked in battle with the Tlascalans – no friends of the Mexica – who had at first fought them tooth and nail, then joined them. Cortés now enjoyed a strong alliance with Shikotenka, the Tlascalan monarch, and a thousand Tlascalan auxiliaries still bolstered the Spanish presence in Tenochtitlan. There was no doubt, *in extremis*, that Shikotenka could put fifty thousand warriors into the field. He had done so at Cholula in October. But that had been against the hated Mexica. Cortés thought it most unlikely that the Tlascalan king would be so ready to support him in a war against another Spaniard – but of course Narváez, listening to the Totonacs along the coast who rightly feared and admired the Tlascalans, couldn't know that.

Further conversation elicited one more useful item of information from the envoys. A few days before they'd been sent on their mission, Narváez had formalised an alliance with Tlacoch, the same monstrously fat paramount chief of the Totonacs – famously dubbed 'the fat cacique' – with whom Cortés had made a supposedly 'eternal' alliance the year before. Tlacoch was a pragmatist, not a hero. He had no doubt been overawed by all Narváez's men, cavalry, guns and ships, and – seeing a fight coming – had decided to throw in his lot with the side he thought most likely to win. Cortés didn't blame him for this, but it had strategic implications. An immediate outcome, Guevara explained, was that Narváez had moved his entire army from its exposed and essentially indefensible camp on the dunes at Cuetlaxtlan, and had instead taken up residence in Cempoala, Tlacoch's regional capital, which henceforth would serve as his headquarters.

'I shall write to Narváez,' Cortés said, 'and entrust you to deliver my letter to him. So it will be in Cempoala, then, that you will find him?'

'Yes, Caudillo. He has already installed himself there. I will deliver your letter and please be assured – ' he looked at his two companions as though to confirm their complicity – 'that we will do everything in our power to persuade Don Pánfilo to recognise your legitimate authority as captain-general and *justicia mayor* in these New Lands.'

Cortés beamed: 'It is all I ask. But now that we are friends you must not rush away. This evening I have arranged a banquet for you, and tomorrow we will show you our beautiful city of Tenochtitlan, for you have yet seen only a small part of it. The Mexica are a rude and barbaric race, much in need of the word of God, but I think you'll agree they did wonders of civil engineering here . . .'

It was not until after the banquet, well past midnight and more exhausted than he had felt for a long while, that Cortés set out in search of Father Olmedo. The friar was not in his quarters, in the same wing of Axayacatl's palace as his own apartments, but eventually he found him kneeling by the altar of the spacious hall, fitted out as a church, that had served as the conquistadors' main place of worship since soon after their entry into Tenochtitlan. A single candle burned on the altar but otherwise the room was in darkness.

'Good evening, chaplain,' Cortés said quietly, not wanting to startle the other man. 'I was looking for you.'

'I've been here since noon,' the friar announced gloomily, 'praying for forgiveness.'

'And have you been forgiven yet?'

'Well that's the thing, you see,' Olmedo replied. 'You can pray for forgiveness, but it doesn't mean you'll get it. And even if you do get it, you can't know that you've got it. Do you see what I mean?'

'I think I do, Father. May I suggest, as in all matters to do with the mystery of God, that this is why we are enjoined to have faith . . .'

'Yes, I suppose so. I shall simply have faith that I have been forgiven and lo . . . I will have been forgiven! Besides, all this praying is very painful on the knees.'

With great difficulty, leaning on the altar, Olmedo levered himself upright and added: 'Faith subdued kingdoms after all.'

Cortés recognised the quote: 'Hebrews eleven, verse thirty-three?'

'Yes!'

'It's the verse that speaks of the prophets "who through faith subdued kingdoms, wrought righteousness, obtained promises, stopped the mouths of lions".'

'Correct! I forget at my peril how well you know your scriptures!'

'Then take heart from the verse, Bartolomé – ' even in the dim light cast by the candle, Cortés saw how crestfallen Olmedo was – 'for I want you to help me stop the mouth of a lion now . . .'

'You speak in riddles, Hernán . . .'

'I speak of a roaring lion called Pánfilo de Narváez . . .'

'You want me to help you stop Narváez's mouth?' The friar looked genuinely amazed. 'But just last night I failed you very badly with Narváez's envoys. Actually, that's why I've been praying for forgiveness . . .'

'Because you failed me?'

'It's more complicated than that. I didn't only fail you, but I also failed Ordaz and I failed myself . . .'

'By getting drunk? By getting into a fight? Welcome to the human race, Bartolomé! You were an embarrassment, it was good the envoys didn't see you, but let's not make more of it than that.'

The friar seemed not to be listening. 'As you know,' he continued, 'I have been sorely tested since our last supplies of wine ran out.'

'Not you alone, Bartolomé! We all feel the lack.'

'Then I found a new intoxicant . . .'

'That pulque you had on the table last night?'

'Not exactly, Caudillo . . .'

'Well, obviously bad stuff, whatever it was. Look, old friend, we can discuss this another time if you like, but I'm dog tired and have many letters still to write before morning. May I get straight to the point?'

'Of course, Hernán.'

'I'm sending you to Cempoala tomorrow.'

'Cempoala?' There was a look of consternation on the friar's face.

'Yes. I know. It's far and this is unexpected, but Narváez has moved his headquarters there and I need you to pay him a visit . . .'

'And I'm to . . . stop his mouth?'

'Ha! That's the long-term aim of my plan, yes! But for now something less ambitious. First you will carry and deliver a letter to Narváez that I will write to him tonight. Secondly, I will be sending his own envoys back to him very soon. I have been . . . talking with them. I believe we may count on them as allies now, but I want you to observe them closely and confirm this. Thirdly, while you are in Narváez's camp, for however long you are permitted to stay, I want you to sow discord and dissent amongst his men and work to create a favourable impression of us. You will carry other letters that I shall also write tonight to various of his captains, and I ask that you deliver the letters and find an opportunity to speak with those persons in private. I will also furnish you with a stock of gold in easily portable form – chains, medallions, rings, that sort of thing. It will be heavy, but you'll have *tamanes* with you to carry it.'

'I'm just a simple friar,' Olmedo objected. 'What am I to do with gold?'

'You're to buy men's affections, Bartolomé,' Cortés replied softly, 'because each man you buy is a man fewer to confront us in the field. Gold is a weapon of war.'

Chapter Twelve

◄◆►

Sunday 1 May 1520–Friday 6 May 1520

Gold was a weapon of war and, fortunately, Cortés possessed a large secret supply.

On Saturday 30 April, Olmedo left Tenochtitlan for the four-day journey to Cempoala. Cortés provided him with a party of *tamanes* who would carry him in a hammock by night so that no time need be wasted sleeping by the roadside. The friar, however, would not entrust the gold to the porters but distributed it by means of numerous belts, pouches and pockets about his own ample person.

That same day, Saturday 30 April, with stringent steps taken to prevent the embarrassment of further assaults by disaffected Indians, Guevara, Vergara and Amaya were given an extensive tour of Tenochtitlan. Care was taken to ensure they remained unaware of the additional security measures, and saw only the sunny side of the picture, since the aim of the whole exercise was to impress. If Cortés and his tough-looking conquistadors could subdue, and hold in fealty, so splendid a city, then surely they must be men of exceptional mettle whom it would be most unwise for Narváez to attack? The beauties and amenities of the Mexica capital, its pleasant climate, the absence of mosquitos – so different from the coastal region where Narváez and his men languished in hot and humid discomfort – were also constantly and tantalisingly paraded before the envoys' eyes. The hope was that they would talk about what they had seen when they reached Cempoala; with luck their accounts would add further to the restlessness and division within Narváez's ranks.

That night Cortés composed a letter for them to carry to the enemy commander. Quite deliberately, because he wished to keep the other man off balance, it introduced new elements and had a very different tone from the much more conciliatory letter he had sent with Olmedo:

My dear Pánfilo

By now you will have received my previous letter, carried by our chaplain Father Bartolomé de Olmedo, and learned how delighted I am to discover that my old friend from Cuba has arrived in these New Lands!

Welcome then! I greet you heartily! I am astonished that you have been here for some time and have not written to me, but yet have taken the liberty of entering into communication with Moctezuma, the former chieftain I have deposed, it seems, with a view to inciting him to rebel against me and in supporting him in that rebellion!

I am also amazed, my dear Pánfilo, to hear that you have taken unto yourself the title of captain-general, and have appointed captains and magistrates, since these lands now belong to His Caesarian Majesty King Carlos and have already been formally settled and colonised.

It seems to me inconceivable that you are supported by a Royal Commission in these acts and declarations of yours, but if perchance you are, then I require you now to produce it and I will readily submit to your authority.

Until such time as you do, I can view you only as the servant of my rival Diego de Velázquez.

Know that I, for my part, am the servant of the king. It is for the king, not for Diego de Velázquez, that I have conquered this country; and I and my brave followers will defend it for the king, be assured, to the last drop of our blood.

I therefore inform you, on behalf of the king, that unless I receive a satisfactory response from you, I propose to march against you with all the force I have, both native and Spanish.

Cortés re-read the letter and signed off. All bluff, bluster and insinuation, it was just another manoeuvre in the psychological war he'd declared on Narváez before any physical battle was joined. But he also intended that the documents should form the core of the record from which the history of this encounter would eventually be written – a history that would fully reflect his point of view.

The following morning, Sunday 1 May, after attending service, and having said friendly farewells to all the men, the envoys set off for Cempoala. Like Olmedo before them, they were accompanied by *tamanes* so that they could travel without stopping and arrive in four days. Guevara carried Cortés's letter and was authorised to distribute gold chains and plate worth more than thirty thousand pesos to the more purchasable of Narváez's captains and common soldiers; this was packed in saddle bags and loaded on to a mare. Because he suspected that the priest might pilfer, Cortés also sent his clerk, Santos Jimenez, a reliable man, to keep accounts.

With the envoys gone, Cortés spent the afternoon of Sunday 1 May making his plans, and that evening he called on Alvarado in his sumptuous private apartments. The two talked long into the night of the risks and dangers ahead and how best to confront them.

'Velázquez de Léon worries me,' Cortés admitted. 'Actually he worries me more than anyone else!'

'Well, he is the cousin of our dear enemy Diego de Velázquez,' Alvarado agreed. 'And it's said that blood is thicker than water.' He gave a final pass of the whetstone along the wickedly sharp single-edged blade of the falchion that he'd acquired the year before in Cuba after killing the governor's champion. 'By the way, how many relatives can one man have? That envoy Amaya claimed to be yet another cousin of his.'

'The term "cousin" is used loosely by the Velázquez clan – and they really are more of a clan than a family. Nonetheless, Velázquez de Léon's father is the brother of Diego so that does make him a full cousin.'

With a final critical glance at the gleaming blade, Alvarado sheathed the falchion: 'You're guessing he'll hear the call of blood and will desert us when he learns that Narváez has arrived to impose the governor's rule in New Spain?'

'Precisely. And not three months have passed since I last locked him up.'

'Just as well, then,' Alvarado grinned, 'that you released him so quickly.'

Velázquez de Léon had spent only two weeks in chains. It would have been longer, but his groans, echoing down the palace corridors, had been heard by Moctezuma, who had persuaded Cortés to free him. Formerly a staunch Velazquista, imprisoned more than once for his part in the frequent conspiracies during the early days of the expedition, de Léon had been so grateful to be forgiven yet again that he had fallen on his knees before Cortés and kissed his boots. Thereafter his behaviour had been consistently loyal and supportive. At the end of March, Cortés had rewarded him with command of one hundred and fifty men and sent him off with them to found a settlement and build a protected harbour at the mouth of the Coatzacoalcos river.

'I've done him many favours since this expedition began, Pedro.'

'Let's hope he remembers them now. The ungrateful cur! You realise he's almost certainly been in contact with Narváez already?'

'Makes sense. Both their parties are large and they're on the same stretch of coast. I'd be surprised if it were otherwise – so the question really is what transpires from these contacts? Does Velázquez de Léon remain loyal to us, his comrades in the conquest through thick and thin this past year and more – men who've stood by him in battle; some who've saved his life in battle, some whose lives he's saved – or does he throw in his lot with Narváez out of loyalty to his cousin?'

'We're royally fucked if de Léon joins Narváez,' Alvarado reflected. 'The odds are bad enough as it is, but if we're suddenly a hundred and fifty men down and Narváez is a hundred and fifty men up . . . Look, I'm an optimist, but I wouldn't wager a copper maravedi on our chances of winning if that happened . . .'

'My wager is it won't happen. I've written to Velázquez de Léon in three copies carried by different teams of runners, with orders to cease his activities at the coast forthwith and begin an immediate counter-march with his entire force on the route we took through the mountains last year on our way to Tenochtitlan. My intention is to rendezvous with him at Cholula some time between the eighth and tenth of May. I've likewise sent orders to Rodrigo Rangel that he should join us there with his hundred and twenty.'

Alvarado's brow furrowed: 'Rangel is in Chinantla, looking for gold, not at the coast.'

'But Chinantla and Coatzacoalcos are roughly equidistant from Cholula, so Rangel and Velázquez de Léon should get there at about the same time – maybe it will take a little longer for Rangel, since his men are scattered in a dozen different prospecting parties by now . . .'

'Some of them scattered rather far if I recall correctly,' said Alvarado. 'Didn't that prick of an envoy Guevara tell us it was three of Rangel's men, gone absent without leave, who're now serving as "tongues" for Narváez?'

'Yes, and they've done us much harm, which I intend to see them paid out for when all this is over. I've no doubt we'll suffer other deser-tions, too, but if we act swiftly we'll stop the rot . . .'

'So when do we leave for this rendezvous in Cholula?' Alvarado asked.

He had a way of looking eager about almost *everything*. 'I had a girl there I very much enjoyed. Happy for an excuse to get back.'

Cortés had been looking for the right moment but now could delay no longer: 'You won't be coming with me to Cholula, Pedro . . .'

'Eh what? Why not? Some other assignment first, is it? In which case where shall I meet you and when?'

'You won't be joining me on the expedition against Narváez at all, Pedro . . .' Cortés paused to let his words sink in. 'Because I have greater need of your skills here in Tenochtitlan.'

'In Tenochtitlan?' Alvarado looked dumbfounded. 'I don't understand. Why would you have me sit safe here in Tenochtitlan when there's a battle to fight? I am a *warrior*, you know, Hernán? I kill people . . .'

'Better than anyone else . . .'

'Better than anyone else,' Alvarado repeated, very sure of himself. 'And since you recognise that, it's only sensible for you to put me where you need to have people killed.'

'Which is exactly where I'm putting you, Pedro, right here in Tenochtitlan. This city is the soul of our conquest. Should we lose it, the conquest is lost. Therefore, we must hold Tenochtitlan! Hold it at all costs! And we must hold Moctezuma safe and in our hands at its heart, since his people's care for his life remains our best guarantee against attack.'

'I wouldn't be too sure about that last bit,' said Alvarado. 'His people's care for his life has worn a bit thin over the past few months. There's those among them who would happily kill him to get at us.'

'I agree, which is why I need the right man in charge here in Tenochtitlan . . . and have concluded, Pedro, that it must be you. They call you Tonatiuh, the sun, and say that you're always laughing, but they fear you! They fear you more than any other man in this army; they know you have a foul temper, and they know how quickly you resort to violence. Your garrison will be wholly inadequate – I'm afraid I can only spare you one hundred and twenty men – but I'm gambling that the fear you inspire will be enough to stop Mucktey from trying anything foolish, and keep the hotheads amongst the Mexica from chancing their arm.'

Alvarado made a sour face. 'I'd rather be out in the field fighting a real war against Spaniards than cooped up in here nurse-maiding Mucktey and facing down a bunch of savages.'

'Of course. I completely understand that. Yet to hold Mucktey and keep those savages at bay and keep our grip on Tenochtitlan until I've beaten Narváez and can get back here to reinforce you are such vital concerns that all else must be set aside.'

'*If* you beat Narváez.'

Cortés laughed. 'If I don't, then I suppose it will be Narváez who comes to rescue you!'

'But you will beat him, Hernán. You're a winner, and the gods love a winner.'

'We'll *need* the gods on our side to win this one. Narváez can put nine hundred men against us, fresh out from Cuba with good guns and good horses and good supplies . . .'

'And we have . . . What? About five hundred?'

'Less than that. Our forces are already stretched thin. At today's count we have only one hundred and ninety men in Tenochtitlan and I plan to take seventy of them with me when I march to Cholula, which is why you'll be left with just one hundred and twenty . . .'

'Understood. And in Cholula you will rendezvous with Velázquez de Léon and Rangel.'

'Whose forces added together will swell my own numbers from seventy to a magnificent three hundred and forty . . .'

'And then there's Sandoval . . .'

'Indeed there is, and he has seventy-three men with him. I have sent him runners with orders that he's to abandon Villa Rica – he's too easily taken by storm there – and camp upcountry, avoiding contact with Narváez, until I can link up with him.'

'And when you do?'

'When I do, my force will consist of my own original seventy, Sandoval's seventy-three, Rangel's one hundred and twenty, and the one hundred and fifty with Velázquez de Léon – a grand total of four hundred and thirteen. This is less than half Narváez's number, which is worrying in itself, but on the other hand look at the difference in the quality of the men – milksops fresh out from Cuba on the one hand, hardened veterans defending what's theirs by right on the other. It's not a foregone conclusion, but I've taken a few steps to stack the odds in our favour and I think there's a very good chance we can win.'

'Steps such as . . . ?'

'It's well known that "the best captain to obey is the one who gives the best pay".'

'Ha! You're going to bribe Narváez's men to join us?'

'Some of them, yes. Or if not actually to join us, at least to prove

– how shall I put it? – shy to take part in the battle on the day we attack Narváez . . .'

'And what of our Indian allies?' Alvarado asked. 'Shikotenka and his Tlascalan mountain men are real warriors. If you can bring a few thousand of them to the field it would settle the matter.'

'Two days ago I sent a message to Shikotenka asking for five thousand of his men – and we have a thousand Tlascalans already present in Tenochtitlan who'll remain here at your disposal. You'll need them if the city rises against you – but forgive my manners, dear Pedro, I am already assuming that you've said yes to my proposal.'

'It goes against my instincts as a scrapper, but as a thinker I can't deny the logic of your words. I will stay here in Tenochtitlan and hold the city for you.'

'And Moctezuma? Will you hold him also?'

'Can't stand the man. Too slimy and underhand for my taste. But while you're away I'll coddle him, if that's what you want.'

'Show him deference. Let him feel sometimes that he's still the absolute ruler here. It's good for his morale. *Don't* let him get killed – keep him safe at all costs – and keep a close guard on him so that he never escapes. Take care not to agitate the population while we're away, Pedro. I know your love for gold but please restrain yourself. No confiscations – take nothing from anyone. Govern moderately and fairly. Give no man an excuse to rise up against you.'

Alvarado stood and stretched, unsheathed his falchion and began a series of flowing exercises, his feet spread, advancing across the floor in a sequence of sliding, beautifully balanced steps, whirling and pivoting the great blade about his head and body as though it were no heavier than a feather before finally returning it to its sheath.

'Those who rise up against me,' he said, 'I will cut down.'

Through his network of spies, officials and palace servants who doubled as informants, Moctezuma had been monitoring the visit of the three envoys sent by the Spanish general Nar-Vez. Further confirmation that the general and Malinche were enemies came when it was reported that the envoys had first presented themselves at Villa Rica, where they had been made captive and sent on their way to Tenochtitlan bound up in packing cases like common prisoners. Confusingly, however, Malinche himself had met them when they reached Iztapalapa, where he had set them free, and thereafter, during their stay in Tenochtitlan, they had been treated like kings.

What did this mean? Did it mean that Malinche and Nar-Vez were in fact friends and allies and that the Spanish commander in Villa Rica had simply over-reached himself – as Cortés himself had been overheard telling the envoys?

Or did it mean that Malinche was really very afraid of Nar-Vez and wished to appease him for the harsh treatment his envoys had suffered?

Or could there be some other meaning altogether?

On the day following the envoys' departure for Cempoala, where Nar-Vez and his army had recently moved their headquarters, a courier arrived bearing the Spanish general's reply to the last message Moctezuma had sent him. To avoid attracting the attentions and suspicions of Malinche, the courier was not brought to Moctezuma's apartments in Axayacatl's palace, but instead to a discrete villa co-opted for this sole purpose, where the message was taken from him by Teudile. As was standard practice, the courier was then strangled while Teudile made his way directly to the palace with the rolled cloth bearing the message hidden in his voluminous sleeve.

The Great Speaker and the steward, joined now by Cuitláhuac, gazed in puzzlement at the message. It had begun as a spoken address by Nar-Vez, which had then been translated into crude Nahuatl by the three defectors from Malinche, rephrased more fluently by Pichatzin and finally set down in hieroglyphs, pictographs and images by Pichatzin's scribes and artists.

The gist of the message was therefore clear enough, but its content was confusing and extremely worrying.

In his first communications, Nar-Vez had presented himself as a liberator who had come to set Moctezuma free and to arrest Malinche, after which, he had promised, he would sail away with all his men and leave the One World in peace. In this new message he repeated that he would 'release Moctezuma, give him back what had been stolen from him, and not kill anyone,' but now said nothing about sailing away. On the contrary he declared that he was here to 'colonise' the land, a concept with which Moctezuma was quite familiar, since the Mexica had achieved absolute power throughout the One World by populating and inhabiting the lands of other peoples, initially by means of colonies. Despite his earlier protestations, therefore, the truth was that Nar-Vez, like Malinche, was here to plant colonies to spread Spanish power throughout the One World and to end the reign of the Mexica.

The message concluded with a cryptic declaration of an exchange of names. Henceforth Nar-Vez was to be called Moctezuma and Moctezuma was to be called Nar-Vez!

What could be the meaning of this? Teudile, Cuitláhuac and Moctezuma discussed the question at great length. Since it was well known that a man's soul was supernaturally bound to his name, they deduced the declaration to be the first move in a magical attack and, as such, further evidence of the hostile intent of Nar-Vez.

'Sire, may I speak?' Teudile asked.

'Certainly, good steward. I value your counsel.'

'We have been patient long enough, lord. There are now two parties of these Spaniards in our lands. Each seeks to deceive us about the intentions of the other, but both mean us harm. Do you know, sire, that Malinche's forces are presently scattered, with a large detachment sent to Coatzacoalcos, another to Chinantla, and others still at the settlement they call Villa Rica?'

'Of course I know this!'

'But perhaps you have not realised, sire, that as a result Malinche has only one hundred and ninety of his soldiers here in Tenochtitlan as a garrison?'

'Really? So few?' Moctezuma seemed perplexed, then remembered: 'But they are fearsome warriors, not to be counted as normal men.'

'Even the most fearsome warriors can be brought down by superior numbers,' Teudile replied, 'and we have the numbers. I say throw ten regiments against Malinche while he's still here in our capital, and kill him and every one of the hundred and ninety men he has with him before he has time to reunite with his other forces. Let's free Tenochtitlan of this scourge now and then go out in strength to Coatzacoalcos and Chinantla and Villa Rica to slaughter the rest of his men while they're still separated. We mustn't allow them to get together and become strong! Once we're finished with them, and Nar-Vez has seen how terrible our vengeance can be, he won't dare to march on Tenochtitlan.'

'But do you think he will then just sail away?' Moctezuma asked. 'Or will he stay, and perhaps receive reinforcements, and then trouble us further?'

'I believe that he will stay to trouble us further,' Cuitláhuac offered, 'and I for one don't want to see the Spaniards sail away.'

'Tell me why, brother!'

'If they do, it will only be to return next year with more ships and more men. Besides, if we let them go, our gods will be deprived of a sacrifice they have told us they very much desire, namely the hearts of a great number of Spaniards. I therefore propose that we encourage Nar-Vez to come to Tenochtitlan! Malinche and Nar-Vez will then fight one another, and thus weaken one another, or even gather here if that is secretly their intention – what do we care? Let us not be daunted by their fearsome warriors – as Teudile rightly says, we have the numbers – but let us so far as possible bring our enemies together in one place so we can kill all of them at a stroke and be rid of them forever.'

By Wednesday 4 May, Cortés was well advanced in his plans to leave Tenochtitlan with his small force of seventy and, accompanied by Malinal, paid a call on Moctezuma to inform him that he would be departing the following day, Thursday 5 May.

Mucktey looked worried: 'Malinche,' he said, 'as always it delights my eyes to see you, but I have been hearing many things about these new Spaniards at the coast and about how you are going to march out to fight them and how you intend to leave me under the guard of Tonatiuh. Is all this true?'

'It is true. Tonatiuh will guard you well and keep you safe against those of your people who plot against you and seek to take your life. I for my part have a little trouble to attend to at the coast, but it should not detain me long.'

'Malinche, I see your manner these last days, very much preoccupied, and I see your captains coming and going, very much put out, and I hear tidings – for I am not without my sources, Malinche – that you intend to march against those brothers of yours who came on those ships. Tell me all, in case I can help you in any way, which I will do with pleasure; and I am anxious that nothing untoward should happen to you, for you have but few *tueles* and those who have come here are five times more numerous, and they say they are Christians like you and vassals and servants of that emperor of yours, and they have images and they set up crosses and have mass said to them and they publicly say that you are people who are running away from your king and that they have come to seize and kill you. I do not understand you, so see what you can do.'

There were so many layers of subterfuge in the way Moctezuma presented this that Cortés was for a moment taken aback. He recovered quickly: 'These Spaniards are not five times our number but twice our number. They are commanded by a man called Pánfilo Narváez, whom I know very well, and they are indeed Christians after their fashion. But our emperor Don Carlos, being a great sovereign, has under his rule men of many races, and just as in your domains there are savage peoples such as the Otomis and the Chichemecs, so also in his domains is a barbarous race called the Biscayans, and these men under Narváez are Biscayans. They are bad men, untruthful men, and they have come with an evil purpose. That is why I march forth against them tomorrow.'

'I am glad you do not face odds of five to one, Malinche, and I know your men are formidable warriors. Yet still this Nar-Vez outnumbers you two to one by your own admission. I tell you what!' An idea seemed suddenly to occur to him: 'I am concerned for you, Malinche. I am anxious for you. I do not want any harm to come to you at the hands of this wicked Nar-Vez. Will you allow me to send my warriors with you to join your fight against him? I have a hundred thousand picked men I can put at your disposal. They will give you victory.'

After Malinal had interpreted these words she added: 'You know this is a trap, Hernán, don't you? And this concern he's expressing for you – all lies. He wants you dead! Whatever you do, don't accept this offer of men.'

Cortés nodded. Moctezuma's offer was indeed a poisoned gift. Whether he provided one hundred thousand warriors, as he boasted, or just ten thousand, the strategic outcome would be the same – a hostile force in Cortés's camp and behind his lines, in league with his enemy and ready to strike. 'Thank you for your kindness, Great Speaker,' he replied. 'I am truly moved, but I have faith in my God and I know he will give me victory. With no disrespect, therefore, I decline your offer. I ask only that you command your priests to look after the image of the Virgin in the Great Temple and to ensure that she is always surrounded by flowers and by wax candles while I am gone. I trust, also, that you will maintain as friendly relations with Tonatiuh as you and I enjoy between ourselves.'

'I do not like Tonatiuh,' Moctezuma said flatly, 'and he does not like me.'

'For both your sakes, then, it will be important to put your differences aside in the next weeks.'

'I, for my part, will do so,' Moctezuma sulked. 'And I will do it not for my sake, nor for his sake, but for your sake, Malinche, because of the great love I bear for you. I will see to it that Tonatiuh and those who remain here under his command are provided with everything they need while you are gone.'

The Great Speaker paused. His look was suddenly furtive. 'But there is one thing I ask of you in return . . .'

'Ask!' Cortés felt a grand gesture was in order: 'Anything in my power to give I will give you.'

'Each year,' replied Moctezuma, 'we celebrate the festival of Toxcatl to invite the gods to bless us with the rains that fertilise our crops. The preparations, which much involve the sacred precinct, and the pyramid and temple of Huitzilopochtli, must begin three days from now and continue for ten days . . .'

'And then?'

'And then great joy, Malinche! A day of dancing! In the sacred precinct, in front of the great pyramid, the flower of our noblemen will dance to honour the gods. It is truly a beautiful sight, and an ancient festival of our people. I therefore request you to allow this fiesta, and all preparations necessary for it, to take place, and I beg that you instruct Tonatiuh accordingly.'

Cortés thought about it and was inclined to say yes. What was the harm, after all, in an innocent rain festival, even if it honoured pagan gods? There would be time enough to extirpate such practices when he'd settled with Narváez. Meanwhile better not to give the Mexica any reason to feel resentful or rebellious.

'You may proceed,' he said, and saw Moctezuma's face immediately brighten, 'only so long as there are no human sacrifices.'

Immediately the Great Speaker's expression darkened again. 'But we must make our sacrifices to the gods, Malinche! Otherwise they will *not* be honoured but insulted by our festival.'

'Sacrifice corn, fruits and turkeys to them, as Quetzalcoatl himself taught your ancestors, but not humans.'

'Humans eat corn, fruits and turkeys,' said Moctezuma scornfully. 'The gods eat humans.'

Cortés's voice grew firmer. 'As I've taught you many times, it is utterly abhorrent to sacrifice men, women and children to the demons you call gods, and it is forbidden by my God, who is the only true God, and therefore I forbid it. You may hold your festival, but with no human sacrifices. Do you agree?'

Moctezuma sounded weary and wouldn't look him in the eye. 'I agree, Malinche.'

'Very well, then. I shall instruct Tonatiuh accordingly, but see you stick to your side of our bargain, or there will, I promise you, be consequences.'

It was late in the morning of Wednesday 4 May when, after four days of hard travel, Father Olmedo found himself back amidst the familiar tree-lined streets and garden squares of Cempoala, the Totonac regional capital, being greeted warmly by many Indians who'd got to know him the year before, and stood once more gazing up at the city's principal pyramid. Approached by only a single stairway, it was a stepped, steep-sided structure with four distinct levels, and on 30 June 1519 he himself had erected a great wooden cross on its summit. By the grace of God, and Spanish prestige, that cross still stood. The only problem was that the wrong Spaniards – Narváez's Spaniards – were now providing the prestige that kept it in place, strutting everywhere in the town, showing off their weapons, pushing everyone around. The Totonacs were bowing and scraping to them and treating them as overlords, just as they had treated Cortés's smaller army as overlords the year before; there was no doubt, as far as they were concerned, that Narváez was now the man to be obeyed.

And it was surely a sign of the character of Narváez, though it must involve a great deal of inconvenience for himself and everyone required to call on him, that he had established his headquarters in the former heathen temple, now whitewashed and empty, that stood behind the cross occupying much of the summit of the pyramid.

Growing impatient, Olmedo advanced to the base of the stairway, where a pair of guards stood bored and sweltering, their leathers and armour altogether too hot to be endured for very long in this climate. 'Look, just let me go up, will you?' he said. 'I'm a man of God on urgent business.'

'And we told you before, friar,' said the guard on the left, 'that no one goes up without the captain-general's say-so . . .'

'Which I explicitly climbed this monstrous pyramid to obtain for you,' complained the guard on the right through stained and broken teeth. 'So when the captain-general is ready for you, I have no doubt he will summon you, as is his wont, and then and only then, Father, can we permit you to climb.'

'Bah!' Olmedo was genuinely annoyed. 'You see that cross,' he pointed towards the summit. 'I put it there a year ago when you were still in

Cuba, and now you have the nerve to tell me when I can and cannot go up . . .'

'I'm only following orders, sir.'

Suddenly Olmedo relented. The guard couldn't be more than eighteen years old and Narváez's bad manners certainly weren't his fault.

'Where are you from, boy?' he asked.

'Medellín,' the guard replied.

'Ah Medellín, in the north of Extremadura! My own chief Hernán Cortés speaks well of the place – he was born there also, you know?'

'I know.' The guard flushed. 'He's a famous man!'

'And rightly so in the light of all he's achieved. I've heard it said you Extremeños always stick together – so you'll be well in with him!'

'*Ahoy! You there!*' The words, yelled in a patrician Burgos accent, came from a squat, black-haired Spaniard wearing an entirely impractical white ceremonial uniform, who had emerged from the temple at the top of the pyramid. He signalled to Olmedo: 'You there, approach and be quick about it.'

'Is that Narváez?' Olmedo asked the young Extremeño.

'Nah. Narváez has red hair. You'll know him when you see him. That's his deputy, Alonso de Salvatierra.' The sentry lowered his voice: 'Youngest son of a landed family that bought his position for a handsome sum. Spoiled rotten and a nasty piece of work. Look out for that one, Father!'

After trudging slowly up the pyramid's seemingly endless steps, pausing at each level to catch his breath, Olmedo finally attained the summit. There he found Narváez seated at a desk placed in the middle of the spacious, high-ceilinged chamber, formerly the principal sanctuary, lying directly behind the entrance to the temple. Light washed in through the open door and speared down through apertures above in clearly etched individual beams picked out on tiny motes of dust circulating in the air. In one corner stood a narrow camp bed, nicely made with clean, freshly turned sheets. Nearby was a commode.

The general appeared to be about forty years of age and, like his deputy, was wearing an ornate military uniform – blue, in his case, not white – with many ribbons, tassels and medals. Robust and strongly built, with large, muscular hands and broad shoulders, it was obvious, even seated, that he was tall. His clean-shaven features were quite crude – a bulbous nose, somewhat lopsided, a great, thrusting spade of a chin, rather prominent pale blue eyes. His skin was very white, particularly his face, which was framed by unfashionably long curls of red-blond hair.

Seated beside him at the desk, as though the pair formed a committee, was Salvatierra, a swarthy barrel of a man, perhaps in his mid-thirties. Despite a strong build he had a weak chin, a somewhat prehensile upper lip, several boils around his mouth, high, almost Asiatic cheekbones, and close-cropped black hair that formed a sweaty widow's peak over a receding, ape-like brow.

Thus far neither of them had stood. Both remained in their chairs – Narváez upright, Salvatierra somewhat slouched – looking at Olmedo with undisguised hostility. Narváez leaned forward, picked up a quill, dipped it in an inkwell and held it poised over a sheet of paper. 'Let us begin,' he said. 'I am Captain-General Pánfilo de Narváez and this gentleman next to me is my deputy Alonso de Salvatierra. Your name is Olmedo, yes? And the sentry also informed me that you claim to visit us on the business of Hernán Cortés.'

'Yes. That's correct. I am Father Bartolomé de Olmedo and, as you can see from my habit, I'm a friar of the Mercedarian order. I am also chaplain to Don Hernando Cortés, captain-general and *justicia mayor* of these New Lands, and it is he who has sent me to you to discover *your* business here and to deliver a letter that he has written to you.'

Salvatierra bounced to his feet. 'Hernán Cortés is no captain-general!' he blustered, his upper lip curling. 'He is a traitor and an imposter—'

'He's a loyal servant of the Crown,' Olmedo fired back immediately. 'As our properly appointed captain-general and *justicia mayor*, he's the king's representative in these lands, and I'll thank you to speak of him with respect.'

'Respect?' Salvatierra roared. 'Respect for Hernán Cortés? I'll show that mountebank respect! When we have him in chains, I'll cut off his ears and broil them for my breakfast.'

Olmedo made a moue. 'Ah, Señor Salvatierra, now I understand – you are a cannibal! That explains why you seem so at home in this place, where human beings were daily sacrificed and eaten, until our captain-general Hernán Cortés put a stop to such abhorrent practices, brought the word of Christ here and had me re-consecrate this heathen temple as a church.'

Salvatierra's sallow face had turned puce with rage. The cannibal jibe was so offensive that it seemed both he and Narváez had missed the significance of Olmedo's other remark about re-consecration. The deputy strode out from behind the desk – it was more of a waddle really – and stepped directly in front of Olmedo. 'Cannibal? You dare to call me a cannibal?'

'I call you only what you confessed yourself to be, one who relishes the broiled ears of fellow humans for his breakfast – in other words, a cannibal.'

At this Salvatierra lunged forward with both hands and shoved the friar hard in the chest, forcing him back a few paces towards the entrance. Olmedo was the bigger man and braced himself – it seemed possible they might engage in fisticuffs! – when Narváez's voice boomed out: '*Desist!*'

Raised in command, it was a big voice, hollow as if it arose from a vault. It stopped Salvatierra in his tracks.

The general turned his bulging, dead-fish eyes on Olmedo: 'You mentioned, I think, a letter?'

'Yes, Don Pánfilo, I have it here.' Olmedo unbuckled his satchel, produced the scroll that Cortés had given him and held it out.

'You are familiar with its contents?' asked Narváez as he broke the wax seal.

'I am not.'

'Ha!' Don Pánfilo was scanning the letter, his eyes moving rapidly, following the lines. 'Ha!' He threw back his head and laughed. Observing him, it occurred to Olmedo that there was something distinctly theatrical and self-conscious about the man, as though he were performing on a stage, and this impression was enhanced when he began to read passages from the letter aloud, affecting an exaggerated Extremeño accent in an amateurish attempt to imitate Cortés's voice. Olmedo, who was quite the mimic himself, observed the mummery with a critical eye.

'My dear Pánfilo,' read Narváez. He was holding the letter up before his eyes in his right hand, his left placed on his hip, arm akimbo. 'It is my pleasure to welcome you to New Spain where I am, by universal acclaim of the colonists and by blah-blah-blah, and blah-blah-blah, duly elected captain-general and *justicia mayor*. These lands are wondrous and rich and we who are already settled here do not wish to keep them to ourselves, but blah-blah-blah, blah-blah-blah . . .'

Narváez thrust the letter in front of his deputy and stabbed his finger at an offending passage. 'Ha! Look here, Salvatierra! That imp Cortés actually has the nerve to offer us a province of his so-called "New Spain" to settle in!' He held the letter up before his eyes again, began again to read aloud, again trying and failing abysmally to mimic an Extremeño accent: 'Above all it behoves us both to remember that we find ourselves in a hostile land. If there be competition and animosity between us, then we should not proclaim it to the world lest it kindle a spirit of insubordination in the natives and jeopardise all that I and my courageous men have so far secured here, blah-blah-blah. A violent collision between us must be prejudicial even to the victor, and might be fatal to us both. Only in union, blah-blah-blah, can we look to success.' Narváez rolled his eyes: 'Can you believe it, Salvatierra? This Cortés writes like a Parisian whore.' He raised the letter to his nose and sniffed it – 'I'm surprised it's not scented' – sniffed again and resumed reading: 'I am therefore ready to greet you as a brother in arms, my dear Pánfilo, and to share with you the fruits of our conquest and blah-blah-blah, blah-blah-blah, and if perchance you can produce a Royal Commission I am willing to submit to your authority, *blah-blah-blah, blah-blah-blah* . . .'

Narváez was suddenly very agitated. Olmedo guessed why. 'And can you?' he asked.

'Can I what?'

'Can you produce a Royal Commission? Does not Don Hernán, in the line you have just read to us, state plainly that he is willing to submit to your authority if that is the case? So here, now, is the means to resolve all problems that may exist between yourselves. Produce your Royal Commission and Cortés will hand over power to you without dispute. You have his written bond on that.'

'Don Pánfilo has no need of a Royal Commission!' spat Salvatierra. 'He has the commission of Don Diego de Velázquez, governor of Cuba and proxy for the Crown in these parts . . .'

'And besides,' added Narváez, 'what is this "competition" between us that Cortésillo speaks of in his letter? Our force is the superior one. There is no "competition"—'

The mocking use of the diminutive 'Cortésillo' – 'Little Cortés' – had not escaped Olmedo's attention. 'You would do better to say "Cortés the Great",' he interrupted, 'for only through greatness on the scale of an Alexander or a Caesar could any commander have won what Cortés has won here, against overwhelming odds, conquering the warlike pagans who populate this land, making good Christians of them, establishing peaceful and prosperous settlements, and remitting treasure to His Majesty King Carlos in such quantities as have never been seen before . . .'

At this mention of treasure, and of the king, Narváez cast a shifty glance over his shoulder towards the rear of the room, blinked rapidly and gulped, his Adam's apple bobbing. He had a mobile face, on which all his schemes and emotions were writ large – a lack of dissimulation that might have been endearing in a better man, but that in him was repulsive, stemming as it so obviously did from arrogance, self-regard and a deep-rooted sense of entitlement. What Olmedo read on that face was that Narváez was painfully aware how his transparent lack of a Royal Commission (for if he had one he would surely have been waving it around by now) compromised his whole enterprise in the New Lands. Yes, he was here on the authority of Diego de Velázquez; but the position of Cortés, duly elected as captain-general and *justicia mayor* by the citizens of a properly constituted colony, was of at least equal weight. In the eyes of the law, therefore, it was by no means a cut-and-dried affair that Narváez could simply arrive with a large army and overthrow Cortés; indeed, to many, that might look like little more than an act of piracy perpetrated by one group of Spaniards against another. Only a Royal Commission could settle the matter, and a Royal Commission might yet be granted to one of the parties. To which was anyone's guess at this point, but the final decision, in a cash-strapped court, might be subject to *influence* . . .

'Cortés has sent treasure to His Majesty?' asked Narváez with an anxious sneer.

'Shiploads.'

'Shiploads?'

'Yes, shiploads of treasure. Gold and jewels mainly, but some silver plate as well, all now brought safely to Court with letters from Captain-General Cortés to His Majesty. The king will be pleased! We're expecting his reply . . . soon.'

And I'm not even lying, Olmedo reflected, *simply varnishing the truth* – which was that just one ship had been sent, although it had indeed been loaded to the gunwales with the most precious treasure. It was also true that an imminent reply was expected. The treasure ship had, after all, sailed on 26 July of the previous year – so a reply of some sort should have arrived by now! Nor had there been any confirmation that the treasure had been 'brought safely to Court'. Olmedo winced inwardly – *another bit of shameless truth-varnishing there!* Still, he reassured himself, there was a greater and unvarnished truth in all this – which was that Cortés had indeed sent treasure to the king (hopefully it had arrived!), which dwarfed anything that Diego de Velázquez had sent in his nine years in Cuba, while the great Pánfilo Narváez, despite all his huffing and puffing, had not yet sent anything at all. Under such circumstances, with such a head start, Olmedo reflected, any gambling man, and indeed any logical person, would put money on the Royal Commission going to Cortés.

Unless Cortés could be killed quickly – in which case, obviously, he would be in no position to receive a Royal Commission and Narváez could move ahead, without further encumbrances, to seize possession of the New Lands in the name of Diego de Velázquez.

Narváez resumed his seat carrying Cortés's letter with him, looked at it in disgust, then began to study it more closely, taking his time. His lips moved as he read but they weren't saying 'blah-blah-blah'. Olmedo's glance ranged over the desk and fell upon a pile of documents held down beneath a paperweight. His initial impulse was sneak a look at the documents but it was the paperweight that held his attention. There was something very familiar about it.

Salvatierra was still standing and now excused himself, informing Narváez that he 'must see to the guns'. Was this, Olmedo wondered, as the deputy waddled out into the sunlight and began to descend the stairway, some kind of polite Burgos code for taking a piss?

Narváez continued to read and Olmedo narrowed his eyes. He couldn't shake the feeling that he'd seen that paperweight somewhere before! He took a step closer, unnoticed by Narváez, and squinted again. It was a fist-sized chunk of jade, solid, yet translucent, beautifully, delicately and precisely carved into the form of a human skull and it was indeed familiar! The last time he'd seen it, not many weeks ago, it had stood in a niche in the bedchamber of Moctezuma's private apartments, whence he'd been summoned, as the Great Speaker was sometimes wont to do, to discuss an abstruse theological issue.

Was it definitely the same object? Olmedo couldn't be sure but he did know that, amongst the Mexica, the ownership of such precious relics was confined on pain of death to the Great Speakers and their families alone. If that skull had not come from Moctezuma, therefore, then where had it come from?

Still absorbed in Cortés's letter, Narváez had picked up his quill and was underlining certain passages. Olmedo looked around. He hadn't forgotten that shifty glance the general had cast towards the rear of the room, where a corbel-vaulted corridor, with six smaller shrines opening off it to left and right, led to a second large sanctuary at the back of the temple. Olmedo had cleared every one of the shrines and sanctuaries of their idols the year before when he had planted the cross of Christ here and he knew the entire layout very well.

Scrawling and stabbing at Cortés's letter with his quill, what Narváez projected with the whole vainglorious posture of his body was that he was a very important man doing very important things, while Olmedo was of no account, virtually invisible in fact, and could be required at any time to just stand around and wait until, presumably, he was spoken to again or dismissed.

Might as well take advantage of this, thought Olmedo. With no attempt to explain himself he strolled casually and quietly to the back of the room, slipped into the corridor and hurried ahead, only to stop in his tracks at the entrance to the third shrine on the left, bright with the beam of light that poured into it through an aperture in its roof. It had formerly housed an idol of the mother goddess, Tonantzin, the maker of souls, but she was long gone. What stood in her place was a woven native basket covered with a cloth.

Leaning down, Olmedo pulled back the cloth. Nested within the basket, gleaming in the light from above, was a pile of gold chains, gold plate, gold pectorals, gold figures of animals and birds, gold medallions and other fine items of gold – not in huge quantity, but all Mexica work, and of the highest quality. Narváez could not have laid his hands on a hoard like this amongst the Totonacs. Indeed there was only one way it could have come to him so fast, and that was on the direct orders of Moctezuma himself. When considered together with the jade skull, this discovery made it certain not only that Moctezuma and Narváez were in contact, which Olmedo already knew from Cortés, but also – much more sinister – that Moctezuma had begun to give presents of gold to Narváez.

And, as Cortés had rightly said, gold was a weapon of war.

A great bellow of '*What the hell?*', followed by the sound of a chair shoved backwards so hard that it crashed to the floor, was Olmedo's cue to pull the cloth covering back over the basket and dart ahead into the final room of the temple. Although identical in size to the large sanctuary that Narváez had co-opted as his office, it was much gloomier and darker, with no roof apertures, and only such light as filtered into it along the corridor.

'*Where the hell do you think you're going, friar?*' yelled Narváez as he stormed into the darkness. He was so angry, practically bursting into flames with rage, that heat and light actually seemed to be coming off him.

'I swear,' said Olmedo from the corner to which he'd retreated, 'you've made this dull room a little brighter with your fury.'

Narváez advanced upon him, still shouting: 'You have no *right* to be in here!' he bellowed, '*none at all!*'

'I have every right, Don Pánfilo,' Olmedo replied, softly springing the trap he had set in the first moments of their interview. 'I am a man of God and I wish to locate the sacred images I installed here, in this very room, when I translated this pagan temple into a Christian church less than a year ago – a Christian church, need I remind you, that you are now shamefully using as your military headquarters.'

'What?' Narváez seemed momentarily nonplussed. The balance of power had suddenly shifted. 'Other than the cross outside, there was no indication at all that this building is now a church . . .'

'A cross does not indicate a church to you?'

'All churches have a cross, but a cross may stand alone without a church . . .'

'So you didn't notice, then, the statue and images of the Virgin, and of our Lord Jesus Christ, that we had placed here? You just cleared them away without recognising them?'

'No such objects were found, Father . . .'

'We also left a second cross within the church.'

'We did not find it, Father.'

It had been fun having the upper hand – it was a serious matter to desecrate a church – and even the prospect of being accused of such a thing had helped to distract Narváez. But it was time for a softer tone. 'Don Pánfilo,' Olmedo said, 'forgive me. I'm sorry to press you so hard. I don't know what I'm thinking. In my distress I speak out of turn. I realise, of course, that a good Christian gentleman such as yourself cannot have been responsible for this. It must be the Totonacs who abandoned the faith and disposed of our sacred images and symbols, and deconsecrated this church. I should, I suppose, be grateful that at least they haven't moved their idols back in yet! Better you should place your headquarters here than that, eh? Ha ha! Now come, this gloom oppresses me.' He took the other man by his ribbon-bedecked arm. 'Let us return to the light.'

Aware of the eye of Narváez on him as they entered the corridor, Olmedo forced himself not to glance in the direction of the shrine with the gold. The story he'd told of seeking out the images of Christ and the Virgin that he'd left in the inner sanctuary the year before was plausible, and had the merit of being based on the truth. All he really needed Narváez to accept, therefore, was that he had been so single-minded about finding the images – passionate man of God that he was! – that he'd rushed straight through to the inner sanctuary without even looking into the shrines on either side of the corridor.

Of course, Narváez might suspect that he had looked and that he had seen the gold, and guessed its source and would report back to Cortés. He might *suspect*, but he could not *know* for sure. This element of doubt, Olmedo hoped, might be enough to keep him alive for the next days while he was at the general's mercy. Narváez would not want anything to jeopardise the flow of further golden presents from Moctezuma. At the same time, as a good Christian, he would not want to kill a man of the cloth unless he absolutely had to. The doubt could swing the balance.

Narváez returned to his desk and folded himself back into his chair. 'I regret you did not find the sacred images you left here, Father,' he said coldly. He glanced down at the letter from Cortés where it lay scrawled over with his markings, and at once looked up again, his bulging blue eyes beneath his bushy red brows like strange sea anemones in a rock pool. 'I shall be replying to this letter, friar,' he said. 'You will stay with us until I have finished. I'm a busy man as you can see, so I don't know how long that will be. Find Salvatierra. He'll assign quarters to you.'

A wave of the hand and Olmedo was dismissed.

Descending the steep, narrow stairs, he had a bird's-eye view of the two other smaller pyramids that also occupied Cempoala's central square and saw that both of them had been appropriated by Narváez's army. These satellite pyramids were less than half the height of the main *teocalli*, but each also had shrines and temples on its summit which were now being reinforced as defensive positions. Several very large cannon had been trundled into the square while Olmedo had been with Narváez, teams of Spaniards and native *tamanes*, the latter bearing enormous coils of rope, were milling around, and at the nearest of the satellite pyramids the barrel of one of the giant cannon had been successfully lifted off its carriage prior to its being carried up the steps. A small army of *tamanes* swarmed about it; in their midst, screaming curses, was white-uniformed Salvatierra. So 'seeing to the guns' had not, after all, been some obscure argot for a call of nature!

About halfway down Olmedo paused on a stair, recalling the despatch and efficiency with which Francisco de Mesa, Cortés's chief of artillery, had organised the raising of a pair of similar cannon to the summit platform of the great pyramid at Potonchan just before the fiercest of

213

the battles with the Maya in March of 1519. Those cannon – they were called lombards – had inflicted tremendous damage on the advancing Indian warriors who'd come to take Potonchan back.

The prospect of such fire-power being mounted here in Cempoala, and turned against Cortés and his men should they attack, was not a pleasant one. Judging by the shambles Salvatierra was making of 'seeing to the guns', however, it looked unlikely that any of the great bronze cannon would ever make it to the top of any of the pyramids in the square. The deputy seemed to have no management abilities, and the *tamanes* plainly had never been required to shift so heavy an object.

Olmedo resumed his descent. The same sentries he'd spoken to on the way up were still on duty at the foot of the steps. The young Extremeño gave his name as Miguel Ruffo. The other man was Esteban Valdez from Navarre and confirmed, on Olmedo's asking, that he had run with the bulls at Pamplona. Since the friar had visited that northern city a few years before, and witnessed this spectacle, a friendly conversation ensued, and the pair agreed to meet him in the refectory in two hours following the end of their watch.

'What do you think, lads,' Olmedo said, pointing to Salvatierra's work party, 'will they get it done?'

'No, Father,' answered Ruffo. He laughed: 'Lifting the big cannon is skilled work.'

'Rodrigo should be in charge, not Salvatierra,' muttered Valdez.

'Rodrigo?' Olmedo asked.

'Rodrigo Martinez, our chief of artillery. He's a good man but Salvatierra's always pulling rank on him.'

Interesting, Olmedo thought, and mused out loud: 'I must pay a call on Señor Salvatierra . . . He's supposed to assign quarters for me. Who, pray tell, are the other senior officers here?'

Ruffo made a face. 'That would be Juan de Gamarra and Juan Bono de Quejo. We call them the two Juans, Father.'

'And are they good men, these two Juans?'

The sentries looked at one another. There was real eloquence in the way they said nothing.

The refectory, which occupied the ground floor and garden of a requisitioned Totonac palace, was deserted by mid-afternoon when Ruffo and Valdez finished their watch, so Olmedo had the pair to himself for a while. He brought all his experience and charm to bear on them. He was, after all, a holy friar, worldly and well-travelled, with many stories to tell, and they seemed already to be half on his side. If he couldn't win their confidence, nobody could!

There was much laughter and many gasps of astonishment at his accounts of the strange and wonderful adventures to be had in the New Lands. In time, however, quite naturally, Olmedo shifted the focus of the conversation to the two young men themselves. He listened patiently to the shorter stories of their lives, but with great interest and close attention when they spoke of how tough things had been for them since their departure from Cuba. Neither had yet been paid a penny, they complained, their officers were brutes, and the Totonac lands were so poor that there'd been precious little loot.

'But what of the hoard of gold Narváez keeps on top of that pyramid you guard?'

Olmedo had assumed that the presence of the gold had been kept secret, and that his revelation would prove extremely annoying news to the two sentries. But he'd forgotten the air of invincible entitlement that Narváez radiated – entitlement to respect, to power, to treasure – which it seemed had overruled any discretion in the presence of the common soldiers. Exchanging another glance, Ruffo and Valdez leaned forward, their voices lowered to whispers: 'It was brought to him in baskets,' Valdez confided, 'by officers of that savage emperor your Cortés is supposed to have in chains.'

'Moctezuma?'

'Mucktey-something or other at any rate,' said Ruffo. 'And he gave a lot more than gold. There were jewels as well. You didn't see those when you were up there?'

'I did not, but there was little time and it was quite dark in the inner shrines. I could easily have missed another basket.'

'The funny thing is,' Ruffo wasn't laughing, 'that Mucktey-whatsit gave bales of fine cloth too, and whole loads of mantles and blankets. Narváez kept all of those as well.'

'So are you telling me – ' it wasn't difficult for Olmedo to put a disbelieving inflexion into his voice – 'that your captain has not shared *any* of this bounty with you? No gold. No jewels. Not even any mantles or blankets?'

'No, Father. Indeed I overheard him say to his major-domo, "Take heed that not a mantle is missing as I have duly entered down every article". He's quite the miser, Narváez, in his lofty way.'

'My goodness!' Olmedo exclaimed. 'I'm shocked! No half-decent captain would treat his men so shoddily!'

'Begging your pardon, Father, but we don't think Narváez is a half-decent captain.' It was Valdez who spoke. 'Or even a quarter decent . . . He's not decent at all. He's a terrible commander.'

'He's a bully,' Ruffo added. 'And a snob too. But what about Don Hernando Cortés, eh? I've heard talk that he's a generous captain.'

If only you knew! thought Olmedo. But he wasn't here to tell blunt truths about the caudillo's own selfish and miserly tendencies, nor about how he persistently cheated the men by under-reporting the spoils of war and keeping the balance for himself. To err, after all, was human, but to forgive, divine, and Cortés must be forgiven all his petty venality because of the great task he was now performing for the faith. Cortés was human, of course, and filled with error, but he had been selected by God as his Instrument in these New Lands. If he had proved to be a passionless bore, a cold-hearted churchy prude, a bigot, a blowhard or a fairweather friend, Olmedo might have had second thoughts about throwing in his lot with him – divine commission or no! But Cortés was an amusing companion, a gifted raconteur, a red-blooded man of temper and mettle, fair-minded by nature and the most loyal friend that one could wish for. Olmedo loved him like a brother, and would go through fire for him, so when Ruffo asked if the caudillo was generous the answer, of course, was yes!

'Indeed,' said Olmedo, dipping his fingers casually into one of the many pouches deep in the folds of his habit, 'Don Hernando is so generous that when he heard of your expedition, and knowing how hard this land can be, and knowing also the reputation of Don Pánfilo, he grew concerned and felt it would be right to extend a brotherly welcome to those of his fellow Spaniards who might be in need.'

The pouch contained several chunky gold chains valued at five hundred pesos each, a sum of money that common soldiers might hope to earn in five years – if they were lucky enough to be paid at all! Olmedo teased two of the chains loose from the coil, brought them into the light and offered them to Ruffo and Valdez, who gazed at them slack-jawed.

'Well, boys,' the friar said with a grin, 'don't just sit there.'

Ruffo reached forward hesitantly, Valdez followed.

'Go on!' encouraged Olmedo. 'Take them! They're yours. A gift from my caudillo – a gift from the great Hernán Cortés.' He passed the brace of chains over and watched approvingly as they were pushed into grubby pockets. 'Now look,' he added, lowering his voice, casting cautious glances around – although in truth he was happy to be observed and overheard – 'it occurs to me there may be others in your position who are being cheated by Narváez and feeling the pinch. I'd like to meet more of the common soldiers who share your views. Will you make the introductions? And are there perchance also officers who do not love Narváez?'

It was Ruffo who replied: 'Aside from his favourites Salvatierra, Bono de Quejo and Gamarra who claim to love him – though, mind you, even they would knife him if you paid them enough! – I think he's hated by the entire officer corps.'

This was getting better and better! 'Who should I speak to first?' Olmedo asked. He turned to Valdez: 'You mentioned a chief of artillery whom Salvatierra has offended?'

'Yes, Rodrigo Martinez.'

'You should talk to Francisco Verdugo, also,' said Ruffo. 'Oh, and Balthazar Bermudez, the chief constable. I overheard him say he's had enough of Narváez and his little clique of favoured officers.'

Olmedo had met Bermudez before. He was close to Diego de Velázquez, married to one of the governor's many nieces, but he was also a reprobate, a spendthrift, and an eminently corruptible man. Bermudez had been offered, but had turned down, command of the expedition that Cortés had eventually led, and might conceivably be resentful that he'd been overlooked in favour of Narváez for the command of the present expedition.

Much later, well past midnight, in the frankly insulting cupboard Salvatierra had allocated to him for his quarters, Olmedo lit a candle and inventoried his remaining gold. He had parted with more than half of it – an excellent day's work that had allowed him to spread much poison against Narváez and store up much goodwill for Cortés.

He snuffed out the candle, stretched his large, tired body across the verminous pile of skins and blankets that was to serve as his bed, and composed himself for sleep.

Two scenes from the day came back to him in the darkness and he chuckled.

The first was the perfect mess that Salvatierra had made of his project to get the big lombards to the top of the two satellite pyramids. Late in the afternoon Olmedo had witnessed the climax of this stupidity whilst trying to approach the deputy to assign his quarters. By then, in a cat's-cradle of ropes and mats, one of the huge bronze cannon had, with great difficulty, been hauled about halfway up the steep stairs; success seemed just within reach when a *tamane* had slipped and stumbled into the man next to him, who had fallen heavily into another team of *tamanes* working a second rope, and suddenly all control was lost. Breaking loose of its tethers, the lombard tumbled at terrifying speed, somersaulting, bouncing high into the air and finally dropping like some vast improbable spear and embedding itself, the open end of its barrel first, in the soft grass in front of the pyramid. There it would stand overnight until it could be dragged out by a pair of draught horses in the morning.

The second scene was the truly terrible dinner that Narváez had hosted at the 'high table', specially set aside for officers in the refectory. On Narváez's right sat Salvatierra, seemingly growing uglier hour by hour. Next to him was a lean and silent captain of cavalry with thinning hair named Jean Yuste, and Olmedo's old acquaintance Balthazar Bermudez, bustling and self-important as ever, who held the high position of chief constable of the camp. On Narváez's left sat the two Juans – Juan Bono de Quejo and Juan de Gamarra. Next came poised and sophisticated Francisco Verdugo, with his sculpted coif of grey hair, and beside him – wearing a bushy black beard and glaring at Salvatierra with loathing – sat the disgruntled chief of artillery Rodrigo Martinez. Finally, opposite Narváez at the other end of the table, Father Olmedo made up the ninth member of the party.

What was terrible about the dinner was not the food, which was actually quite good, nor the unpleasant tension of the barely disguised hostility amongst the officers, nor even Narváez's lofty declaration that 'the matter of Cortésillo' was 'of too small significance to spoil a good meal discussing'. All of that was merely annoying. But it was the utterly banal dreariness of these men – with the possible exceptions of Bermudez, Martinez and Yuste, who might under other circumstances have had something to say – that Olmedo could not forgive.

Narváez's core group of Salvatierra, the effete, blond Bono de Quejo and the bristling, hog-like Gamarra, seemed obsessed only with wealth, title and possessions, and with retelling gossip, now more than a year old, from the Spanish Court. Despite Olmedo's best efforts, they could not be enticed to express opinions, or even anything approaching a thought, on any matter of the slightest significance. In consequence the conversation dragged, halted, fluttered and finally collapsed in silence like some sad, broken, stamped-upon creature. Narváez attempted to breathe life back into it with a joke that Olmedo simply could not understand but that Salvatierra, Bono de Quejo, Gamarra and Narváez himself all professed to find extremely funny.

There had, however, been a feature of the dinner that redeemed all else.

By the mercy of God, Narváez's ships had been so well stocked on leaving Cuba, and had arrived in the New Lands so recently, that the commander's ample personal supply of fine wines still remained almost completely intact. A barrel of a rather cheeky Galician red had been brought to the table, Olmedo had helped himself liberally and, by the end of the evening, he had ceased to care that he was surrounded by crashing bores.

He'd kept enough of his wits about him, however, to have a friendly word after dinner with Narváez's cellar master, who had sold him half a dozen full wineskins. It was too soon to dispense a bribe, but a month from now things could be very different, and the prospect of a gold chain, dangled only suggestively at this stage, might help to ensure the safety and future ownership of an excellent stock of wines.

He also made a point of complementing Pero Trigueros, the chef who'd prepared the special dinner the officers had enjoyed – far superior, Olmedo had noticed, to the slop served out to the men.

It was difficult, on such short acquaintance, to judge a man's loyalties. Olmedo tried and failed to learn what opinion Trigueros held of Narváez. A lean, scholarly looking fellow with a club foot, the chef was taciturn in the extreme, as placid and as unforthcoming as a stone saint. But there was one sure test.

Reaching into a recess of his habit, Olmedo extracted a single gold ring, fine but not very large, perfectly suited to the task he had in mind.

'Here,' he said, clasping the chef's right hand in both of his as he gently transferred the ring. 'For you, dear boy.' He noted that Trigueros's fingers, dry as parchment, willingly took possession of the gift, and registered the surprise in the other man's eyes as he guessed the value of the present he had been given. None too fine a ring, true, but still worth a year's salary for a man like this.

'To thank you for a very enjoyable dinner,' Olmedo explained as though, despite appearances, he were some great lord to whom rings were trifles. 'I regard myself as a bit of a gourmet and your food gave me the greatest pleasure. Nonetheless, I hope you will allow me to offer a few culinary suggestions – perhaps the next time I dine here?'

'Certainly, Father. It will be my pleasure.'

Once the gleam of gold gets lodged in a man's eye, Olmedo was discovering, it can be relied upon to stay there.

It was the morning of Thursday 5 May, and Cortés was in his apartments, dressing for war, with Malinal fussing around him, finding buckles to tighten here and there, adjusting the gorget, faulds and greaves that he'd opted to wear, and finally giving a polish to his cuirass and backplate.

'You will be hot, Hernán! All this metal. Very uncomfortable. Listen to me!'

'It's not even full armour, but I intend to make an impression when we march out today.'

'You are not *marching*, my dear Hernán,' she giggled. 'I am marching, Pepillo is marching, all your men are marching, but you are sitting on Molinero.'

'Yes, I'm sitting on Molinero! Precisely! And I want to look like the god of war armoured for battle.'

'You will be a very hot god of war,' Malinal warned. 'Will you promise me that you will at least drink? I will speak to the *tamanes* to carry extra water for you.'

'Dammit, woman! You become more like a wife every day!'

'I love you, my lord.'

'I'm not your lord, Malinal!'

'May I say, then – ' she grinned – 'I love you, husband?'

Cortés gave her a level look. This was becoming a tricky issue between them which he preferred not to confront right now. He'd just thought of an argument that might put her off the scent when there came a welcome knock at the door.

'Enter!'

The guardsman this morning was not Andres Farfan, whom Cortés had decided to bring with him on the march, but an older soldier, somewhat grizzled and lame in his left knee, named Alonso Basuto – one of those who would be left behind with Alvarado.

'You have a visitor, Caudillo,' announced Basuto.

'Well? What are you waiting for? Show him in!'

Basuto looked uncomfortable, glanced at Malinal and then back at Cortés: 'He's an Indian gentleman, sir. He's been shown into your audience chamber.'

'An Indian gentleman, you say?'

'Well, more than a gentleman, sir. He's that Indian so-called king we beat last year who joined us as an ally.'

'You mean Shikotenka of Tlascala? He's no "so-called" king! Are you telling me Shikotenka himself is here and waiting like any common ambassador in my audience chamber?'

'Yes, sir.'

'Dear God, man! There should be pomp and ceremony. This is a state visit!'

'But he just turned up unannounced – as I understand it, sir.'

Cortés nodded. It wasn't Basuto's fault. This was, in fact, typical of Shikotenka. 'Very well! I'm on my way. Malinal, I'll need you of course!'

A full week had passed since Cortés had sent an urgent message by relay runners to Shikotenka to beg his support in the looming war against Narváez. After bludgeoning the ferocious battle-king of Tlascala into submission the year before, receiving his surrender on 7 September 1519, the two had become allies and a firm friendship had blossomed. It was testimony to this that a thousand elite Tlascalan warriors commanded by Shikotenka's lieutenants Chipahua and Tree were now permanently stationed in Tenochtitlan, in the midst of their traditional enemies and persecutors the Mexica, to bolster the small Spanish garrison. They would be even more sorely needed here after Cortés marched out later today with seventy of the conquistadors, leaving just one hundred and twenty Spaniards under the command of Alvarado to hold Moctezuma hostage and the city secure!

But what of the five thousand warriors Cortés had asked of Shikotenka to aid him against Narváez?

After a week it was surprising, and perhaps worrying, that there had been no reply, but now, popping up where you'd least expect him as usual, here was Shikotenka himself with his answer!

The audience chamber had been equipped with alien furnishings, Shikotenka couldn't help but notice as he sank uncomfortably into one of the pieces. Malinche's clever carpenters had taught their Mexica counterparts the Spanish style, and now there were these high-backed benches and chairs with feather-stuffed cushions everywhere.

So many things like this had changed in Tenochtitlan in the months since he'd been away – superficial things of no substance. But it was his strong impression, having been in the city since the night before, conferring with Tree and Chipahua, that nothing that really mattered had changed, except very much for the worse. The Mexica, present here in their massed hundreds of thousands, were still as deadly, as cunning and as cold-heartedly ruthless as they had ever been, murderous bullies just waiting for their moment to rampage across the One World once again, enslaving and subjugating everyone in their path. All that stopped them was the despicable fearfulness and indecision of Moctezuma, which Malinche, Shikotenka had to confess, had exploited brilliantly. But how long could the hostage emperor keep the Spaniards safe, when word in the city was that a great rebellion against Moctezuma's reign was brewing precisely on account of the Spaniards, whom the gods wanted dead? Nobody seemed to know yet exactly who was behind all this unrest – there were many rumours – but the mood of the people and the atmosphere of the streets were enough, on their own, to presage the violent upheaval that was certainly on the way.

The big double doors of the audience chamber swung open and Cortés, with Malinal at his heel, strode in: 'Shikotenka! You rogue! Here you are in my city with no word sent in advance to announce your arrival.'

While speaking Cortés had crossed the room and, as Shikotenka rose to greet him, he extended his arms and swept him up in a big Spanish embrace.

Shikotenka, who wore only a loincloth, sandals and a light cloak, felt the cold armour of his friend's cuirass clank against his skin. In some strange way, the embrace was more that of a machine than a man, and he suppressed an involuntary shudder as he stood back and said, in a Spanish phrase that he'd rehearsed: 'It gladdens my heart to see you again after so long, Malinche!'

'Ha! You've been learning our language! I'm impressed. Do you have more?'

Understanding, Shikotenka smiled: 'A little.' He turned to Malinal and switched to Nahuatl: 'Tell Malinche I'm sorry but I prefer my own tongue. We'll speak through you as usual.'

Another exchange followed between Malinal and Malinche, then Malinche addressed Shikotenka again: 'It gladdens my heart to see you too, old friend. Your presence raises my spirits! I can only guess you've received my request for five thousand of your warriors to help me in a little fight I have coming up with fellow Spaniards? And I can only hope, since you have come here in person, that your answer is yes!'

As Malinal put this into Nahuatl, Shikotenka made no attempt to disguise the discomfort he felt. 'Alas,' he replied, 'the opposite is true. I am here in person, to render my apologies to you in person, because I *cannot* grant the five thousand men you ask for.'

'*Cannot?*' Just as Shikotenka had not disguised his discomfort, so too were Cortés's feelings of shock and disappointment written plainly on his face. 'What do you mean, *cannot*? You're a king, for God's sake! You can do whatever you want.'

'You forget the peculiar constitution of Tlascala, Malinche. I am the battle-king only. My father Shikotenka the Elder still runs civil affairs, and both of us are subject to the vote and the final decision of the Senate. In this case, I regret to say, the Senate have refused to agree to my strong request for five thousand warriors – whom I said I would lead myself – to join you in the field against your fellow Spaniards.'

'But why? I don't understand. We have an agreement, Shikotenka! We are allies and we are in the midst of a war. You can't just walk away and leave me exposed like this.'

'I regret it very much, Malinche, but the decision of the Senate on the matter of the five thousand warriors is final. I know this a bitter blow and wish it could be otherwise, but you are wrong if you imagine that any promise is being broken here. The senators reminded me that our agreement and our alliance was never against all-comers, and never envisaged to be against Spaniards, but always and only against the Mexica.'

'Huh!' Cortés grunted. It was an ugly sound: 'Sounds like your senators are all lawyers.'

'They are for the most part old men. They are cautious. Their concern is with the safety and security of Tlascala and nothing else. But also, Malinche, they made a case which I found I could not refute.'

'What is this irrefutable case?'

'Quite simply that we Tlascalans have fought Spaniards before. Indeed, thanks to our war with you last year, we have more experience of fighting Spaniards than any of the other peoples of the One World. The senators' case is that we lost that war against you, that we suffered huge damage and enormous numbers of casualties – our widows and orphans are still grieving – and that therefore on no account must we face Spaniards in battle again. It would be folly to do so, they say, under any circumstances, but against a force twice the size of your own, which did us so much harm last year, it would be sheer madness.'

'You know their numbers,' Cortés said. 'How much else do you know?'

The question seemed at a tangent, but Shikotenka replied: 'As well as the fact that they outnumber you by about two to one, they also have

223

many more riders than you of the animals you call "horses", and many more of what you call "guns" and "crossbows". In general their equipment seems superior to yours. They are telling everyone that you and your men are common criminals and fugitives from justice in your own land and that they have come here to arrest you. The Totonacs are very impressed and have already joined them. Others will perhaps follow. Moctezuma himself, it seems, is in active negotiations with them, which you have been unable to prevent.'

'And yet,' protested Cortés, 'those ignorant cowardly senators of yours imagine my request for help against these Spaniards has no relevance to the safety and security of Tlascala?'

'They see no connection.'

'Well, let me tell you there is a connection, because if those Spaniards defeat me in battle they will certainly enter into an alliance with the Mexica, and if they do then God help Tlascala. I will never forget how you saved us at Cholula, and for that and all your support against Moctezuma, I owe you a lifelong debt of honour. I will always have a special place in my heart for you, Shikotenka, and for Tlascala, and I guarantee your independence. You have my word on that. But this new Spanish general, the one I go to fight, has no special place for you in his heart, owes you no debt of honour, is already in league with Moctezuma, and will take your independence from you like a toy from a child. Don't your senators see that? Don't they see our common interest in crushing this threat?'

'I regret they do not, Malinche. I have been over all these arguments with them, believe me, and they won't budge. Such is the way with old men. But they've agreed to provide you with supplies – twenty loads of turkeys are being prepared – and you may keep the thousand picked men under Tree and Chipahua who are already here with you in Tenochtitlan. While you hold their capital, the Mexica are crippled, abandoned by their gods, and the Senate does at least understand how well this serves the interests of Tlascala.'

'Turkeys?' Malinche exclaimed. 'And the thousand men I already have – on condition I keep them in Tenochtitlan? That's the best proud Tlascala can do for me in my time of need?'

Shikotenka had satisfied honour by coming here to give the bad tidings himself, but he nonetheless felt sad and ashamed to be able to offer so little to his friend. 'I can only again apologise, Malinche. But the matter is out of my hands . . .'

Cortés shrugged. 'What can I say?' The tension seemed to have drained from his body now that he'd accepted the situation. 'I do believe you've done your best for me, my friend. God will watch over me and my men and we will prevail without your help.'

'I see you're dressed for war. You march today then?'

Smiling, Cortés stepped forward and once again wrapped Shikotenka in his iron embrace. 'Within the hour,' he said.

A little later, joined by Tree and Chipahua on the roof of Axayacatl's palace, Shikotenka watched Cortés muster his small band in the sacred precinct.

Although there were five hundred *tamanes*, there were just seventy Spanish soldiers. Seventy! And all on foot! With the exception of Cortés, who was on horseback and clad as he had been this morning, the rest of the men had wisely disencumbered themselves of their armour, shields and supplies – all these were with the baggage carried by the *tamanes* – and wore only light cotton clothing. They were armed with swords, knives, axes and spears.

They were like a pack of wolves, these men, grim, weather-beaten, and battle-scarred, and every Tlascalan knew what formidable and indomitable warriors they were. But why were they so few?

'Malinche got too big for his boots,' explained Tree. 'In recent months he sent out hundreds of men on different missions – find gold, build a town, things like that. Now he's had to recall them—'

'From far and wide,' Chipahua interrupted, 'but the plan is they all meet up in Cholula . . .'

'. . . And then march down to Cempoala by way of Tlascala,' Tree continued. He laughed, something rare for him; a deep, rumbling chuckle.

'What's so funny?' Shikotenka asked.

Another chuckle: 'At least we won't have to deliver the turkeys!'

Tree and Chipahua had been entertained the night before when Shikotenka had told them of the Senate's derisory response to Malinche's request for five thousand men. Like the Senate they did not love Malinche. Like the Senate they supported him in Tenochtitlan only because his presence there kept the Mexica down.

'You feel guilty about this, don't you?' said Chipahua, draping a muscular arm over Shikotenka's shoulders. 'As if you're leaving a friend in the lurch.'

'It's not *as if* I'm leaving a friend in the lurch. Malinche is my friend! I *am* leaving him in the lurch.'

'He'll survive,' said Chipahua. 'He always does.'

There was a commotion below and, looking down from the rooftop, the three Tlascalans saw Moctezuma step out into the sacred precinct from beneath the portico of the palace of Axayacatl. As was customary when he went on foot, he leaned on the arms of Teudile on his left and Cuitláhuac on his right. They were surrounded by a strong guard of Spaniards led by Pedro de Alvarado, whom Shikotenka had once fought hand to hand on the beach at Cuetlaxtlan.

Moctezuma progressed slowly forth, until he was face to face with Malinche. The two spoke, with Malinal urgently giving the translation. Malinche then went to Alvarado and talked with him at somewhat greater length. Finally, splendid in his armour, he mounted his horse, rode to the head of the column and gave the signal to his men to march.

As they surged into motion, fifers and drummers to the front and rear took up the beat, and soon the little troop was on the move – a solid block, ten men deep and seven wide, disciplined, well-ordered, progressing along the flank of the great pyramid, passing the House of Darkness and the House of the Eagle Knights, turning now towards the huge gates of the sacred precinct and marching through them into the city, southwards to the Iztapalapa causeway beyond.

Moctezuma remained on the spot where he had said his farewells until Malinche had passed completely from view, then still leaning on Teudile and Cuitláhuac he turned back, passed beneath the portico and disappeared within the palace. A few paces behind them, Alvarado followed, his hand on the hilt of his sword.

'Tonatiuh will be in command here when Malinche is gone,' said Chipahua, preferring the Nahuatl name many now used for Alvarado. 'He'll have one hundred and twenty Spaniards and our thousand Tlascalans to hold back the entire Mexica nation.'

Shikotenka had reached a decision. 'A thousand and one Tlascalans,' he said. 'I can't leave you boys facing such fearsome odds alone. I'm going to stay and see how things play out here.'

When Cortés left Tenochtitlan on the morning of Thursday 5 May, it was not his intention to mount a forced march to Cholula. For a tough, compact troop like this, even with full packs, the distance of sixty miles could easily be attained in two days. With five hundred *tamanes* carrying all the burdens the time could be shortened, but Cortés had calculated that Velázquez de Léon and Rangel would not reach Cholula before 8

May, and possibly not until as late as 10 May, so for this first leg of the journey he was in no hurry and preferred to keep the pressure off his men and the mood of the march relaxed and light.

There would be hard struggles soon enough.

Heading south along the Iztapalapa causeway, the waters of Lake Texcoco gleaming to either side of them and a merciful cooling breeze blowing in off the distant snow-capped sierra, Cortés remained mounted on Molinero at the head of the column. García Brabo walked alongside him, easily matching the horse's pace. The seventy soldiers, Andres Farfan amongst them, still flushed with excitement at having been selected by the caudillo himself for this mission, followed in a block, keeping formation. Behind them, but ahead of the big, murmuring train of *tamanes*, came Malinal and Pepillo, and bounding and gambolling at Pepillo's feet, sometimes threatening to send him sprawling, was his great hound Melchior.

Cortés had thought long and hard about the expedition's pack of war dogs. After giving good service in the Tlascalan campaign last year, more than eighty of the original hundred still lived. Fed on deer and fowl captured in the hunt, not infrequently supplemented by the corpses of hanged Mexica troublemakers, they were kept in prime fighting condition by kennel-master Telmo Vendabal.

But the ferocious animals were trained to attack Indians, not Spaniards, and this, Vendabal insinuated, could make them unreliable in the coming battle. Besides, Cortés was not sure he wanted to turn the dogs on his countrymen, nor for the monstrous animals ever to get a taste for Spanish flesh. They were very good at killing Indians, and if things went wrong in Tenochtitlan, and Alvarado came under attack, they would be needed there where there would be many Indians to kill.

What if Narváez had dogs?

The good news was there'd been no sightings but, if it turned out, even so, that Narváez did have dogs with him . . . well, in that event Cortés was satisfied his tough, battle-hardened troops would know the remedy.

'You'll be able to deal with dogs if they throw them at us,' he said now to Brabo. It was meant as a question, but came out as a statement of fact.

Brabo stiffened immediately: 'Rather not deal with enemy fucking dogs, sir. Our friendly ones give us enough trouble as it is.'

The reference was to incidents where Vendabal's hounds had attacked and savaged conquistadors: half a dozen men had suffered injuries; one dog, skewered by a sword thrust, had been killed.

'I agree,' said Cortés. 'An absence of enemy dogs is something devoutly to be wished for. But if they come I've no doubt you'll be ready for them.'

'Ready enough, sir. We'll kill men, we'll kill dogs, we'll kill whatever you want us to kill.'

Cortés knew these were not idle boasts. The twenty-five men Brabo commanded, now forming an elite corps stiffening the backbones of the other forty-five Spaniards in the column, were all professional killers; many had been doing Cortés's dirty work for years, and Brabo and he went back to the beginning of the cruel and bloody conquest of Cuba in 1511.

'What about cavalry?' he asked the sergeant now. 'Will you kill cavalry as well?'

'Give us the tools, sir, and we'll get the job done. We've got men as know how to fight cavalry but we don't have the pikes to arm them with.'

It was true. During the course of the campaigns last year, many of the army's pikes – the primary weapons for confronting cavalry – had been shattered. Besides, those they'd brought to the New Lands, based on lessons learned during the conquest of Cuba, were custom-made to break up formations of naked Indian infantry; none were the right length, or strength, to stop an armoured cavalry charge, since it had not been anticipated that cavalry would be encountered. To bring down horsemen, a longer reach and a stiffer shaft were needed.

From astride Molinero, Cortés grinned: 'Now's the time to tell you about my secret weapon then!'

'Secret weapon, sir?'

'You know that Rangel and his hundred and twenty are in the province of Chinantla prospecting for gold?'

'Whence you've summoned them and ordered them to return and meet us in Cholula?'

'The very same, Brabo. But did you also know that as well as for its gold and other metals, including plentiful supplies of excellent copper, Chinantla is famous for the very long and effective lances used in battle by its warriors?'

'I did not, Caudillo.'

'I investigated the matter thoroughly and I was able to see an example of a Chinantla lance brought to Tenochtitlan and they are superb – just the right strength and reach for our purposes. They are usually tipped with obsidian, but I've paid for three hundred of these lances to be made specially for us and tipped with barbed blades of hardened copper. If all is well, Rangel should have them with him when we meet up with his contingent at Cholula.'

'As usual you plan ahead, Caudillo. Saves me and the men the trouble of doing so! But you didn't think to bring our own cavalry troop?'

'It would be a wasted force and I'd rather keep it where it's useful. Narváez has eighty cavalry and we'd be fools to mount a charge against such numbers. Velázquez de Léon is mounted; so too is Rangel; Sandoval when he joins us will be mounted. I sent a mare with Santos and those envoys of Narváez's, and here I am on Molinero – so five of our horses are already engaged. As we close on Narváez, we'll give our scouts the use of them. I've left the other eight with Alvarado, a credible troop to keep the peace in Tenochtitlan where cavalry charges are still feared by the Indians and can clear the streets.'

'So other than a few mounted scouts this'll be strictly an infantry campaign then, Caudillo?'

'I believe so, yes. It must come to hand-to-hand fighting in the end, but I have a few moves to play out first.'

Olmedo had not made the acquaintance of Narváez's envoys Guevara, Amaya and Vergara during their stay in Tenochtitlan. He had, however, observed the threesome from afar, knew that they would have been sent on their way a day after his own departure from the Mexica capital, and was expecting them when, amidst a great commotion, carried in hammocks by exhausted *tamanes*, followed by a grey mare led by Cortés's bookkeeper Santos Jimenez, they arrived in Cempoala on the afternoon of Thursday 5 May.

The envoys were summoned immediately to the headquarters on the summit of the pyramid, where they remained closeted in conversation with Narváez, Salvatierra and Bono de Quejo, for much of the rest of the afternoon. Meanwhile Santos, a lean, clerical-looking fellow with a long nose and a surprisingly obscene sense of humour, took the mare to the stables and was unloading her saddle bags when Olmedo came to him. They knew one another well after more than a year on campaign, and exchanged heartfelt greetings made all the more intense by the subterfuge and potential danger of the mission they shared. To seek to bribe and corrupt the men of a hostile commander like Narváez, to divide them against themselves, and to acquire intelligence on their military preparedness, was undoubtedly the work of spies, not ambassadors. And whereas ambassadors were generally treated with respect – Sandoval's rough handling of Guevara, Amaya and Vergara being the exception that might yet set a new rule – spies, even in a friar's habit, could expect to hang.

Olmedo brought Santos and the bags to his tiny room and they shared a frank conversation about their mission. After his dispensations the day before, further gifts that morning to several of the common soldiers, and a handsome donation to Balthazar Bermudez, with whom Olmedo's prior acquaintance had prepared the way for discussion of acts of sabotage, the friar's stock of treasure was all used up. It was timely, therefore, that Santos had brought much more gold in his saddle bags – thirty thousand pesos' worth, a small fortune, divided entirely into little ingots and chains that recipients could easily carry about their persons.

And who were the recipients to be? It seemed that Guevara, Amaya and Vergara had been entirely won over by Cortés and had nominated several other leading figures in Narváez's camp whose loyalty could be bought with bribes.

'The caudillo told me of this plan,' Olmedo nodded. 'But he was concerned about the trustworthiness of the envoys. They're Narváez's men after all.'

'That priest Guevara and the notary Vergara,' said Santos gravely, 'are raddled whores bought, paid for and fucked by Cortés, and begging for more. I doubted them, too, when we first left Tenochtitlan, but after four days and nights on the road hearing them gush and moon about our caudillo, I'd say he owns them. Amaya I'm not so sure of. Cortés crossed his palm with gold too, but he's the cousin of Diego de Velázquez and a stuffed-up little sodomite to boot. No telling which way he'll end up jumping.'

Olmedo studied the contents of the saddle bags, now spread out glittering on his bed of skins and blankets. 'It's not safe to leave any of that here,' he observed. 'This camp's a den of thieves. The only safe way is for us to carry it ourselves.'

Time was spent dividing the treasure up and carefully secreting it in pockets, pouches, satchels and the now empty money belts that Olmedo had brought with him from Tenochtitlan. Then, weighed down and somewhat clinking, the two sallied forth.

'It is truly Eldorado!' boomed Guevara.

After consuming huge quantities of Galician red, his voice growing louder with every cup, the fat priest had absented himself from the high table during dinner and was now doing the rounds of the common soldiers who listened with rapt attention as he told stories of Tenochtitlan. Narváez looked on with a stony face, plainly furious, but nonetheless laid a restraining hand on Salvatierra's arm when his deputy leapt up, declaring he must silence Guevara. From the urgently whispered exchange that followed, only partly overheard, Olmedo understood Narváez was not too thick-headed to realise that such obvious censorship would only excite the suspicions and curiosity of the men.

'Have any of you seen Venice?' Guevara now bellowed. He was standing in the midst of several of the refectory tables, and soldiers turned in their seats, others craning their necks, others in increasing numbers on their feet and milling around him, their faces filled with curiosity and excitement, to hear what he had to say.

Voices were raised – a number of the men had indeed visited Venice during the Italian wars. 'And it's beautiful, isn't it?' Guevara prompted, waving down cries of assent. 'But let me tell you that that majestic "City of Bridges", that "Floating City", that "Queen of the Adriatic" is as nothing compared with Tenochtitlan; for there, Cortés truly has conquered and has at his disposal the richest and most beautiful city in the whole world.'

He went on to report, quite accurately, that the Mexica capital was built on an island in the midst of a great lake, that it was approached by causeways miles long, evidencing engineering skills far in advance of those of Europe, that its streets and thoroughfares crisscrossed a network of great canals, teeming with waterborne traffic, by means of soaring bridges, that its markets were cornucopias, plentifully supplied with the produce of a vast empire, and that its opulent palaces and lavish mansions outshone even the enchanted castles from the tale of *Amadís de Gaula*.

'Not only that,' Guevara continued, 'but so wealthy has the plunder in these New Lands been, and so generously shared by Don Hernando Cortés with the men of his expedition, that the humblest private can stake his ingot and chain of gold at play, and all revel in plenty . . .'

'But for how long, Father?' asked a soldier in threadbare uniform three tables away. 'What does all that gold serve if those who carry it end up massacred by hostile Indians?'

'That would be most unfortunate, I agree,' replied Guevara, 'but I saw nothing that would suggest it. On the contrary, Cortés and his men live in peace with the Indians; indeed I would say in affection – *amor* – with them . . . Is it not so, Vergara?' He looked to the withered notary at the high table for a response.

Vergara stood and cleared his throat: 'We saw no sign of war or danger,' he confirmed. 'The Indians seemed friendly.'

To Olmedo's surprise, Amaya, who had been attacking the carcass of a turkey, now stood also: 'The city is at peace,' he declared. 'It is rich in gold and jewels. Cortés controls it and everyone is free to come and go as they please.'

'Makes the life of a soldier sound like one long holiday,' piped up a scarred veteran at a nearby table.

'And what a relief,' Guevara added, slapping at a mosquito on his perspiring brow, 'to be freed from the insufferable insects and heat of these coastal lowlands and to find yourself in a highland Venice amidst treasures and splendours beyond your wildest dreams.'

At this point, erupting from his chair, Narváez smashed his fist thrice upon the high table, sending plates and cutlery flying. '*I'll charge you, Father Guevara,*' he roared, '*to say not another word!*'

Olmedo had only been formally introduced to Guevara at the start of the dinner, but sensed a moment of silent recognition of each other's roles. Beyond that peculiar, unspoken complicity across the table, however, he knew nothing of the other man, nor had any special reason to trust him. What was obvious was that he was doing good work this evening! Not only had he painted an enticing picture of life in Tenochtitlan, and of Cortés's bounty, but also he had successfully goaded Narváez out of his earlier prudent silence and into a most unwise intervention.

'Do you not recall, Father,' Narváez now hissed – the man was visibly struggling to keep his voice under control! – 'that Hernando Cortés, whose alleged generosity you so lavishly praise, is a traitor to our patron Don Diego de Velázquez, and to the Crown of Spain?'

Olmedo suppressed an instinct to speak up; the atmosphere in the refectory was already febrile.

Besides, given enough rope, Narváez was one of those who would hang himself. Moments before he'd been holding Salvatierra back, but now, with a shaking, outstretched finger pointed at Guevara, he ordered his deputy to expel the priest from the room.

Salvatierra loved it! He sprang up from his chair at the high table like an evil jack-in-the-box, bounded across the floor of the refectory, and had Guevara in his hands in a trice. The priest turned a baleful, injured look upon Narváez, but his expression was knowing and calculating as he caught Olmedo's eye on the way out.

Composing himself for sleep in the small hours of the morning, once again aided in this task by liberal quantities of Galician red, Olmedo could reflect on another good day's work done and on the extremely useful contribution of Guevara. Indeed, it was quite surprising that Narváez had thus far confined himself simply to throwing Guevara out of the refectory and, in view of the deluge of bribes that had descended on the camp in the past days, that Olmedo himself hadn't yet been arrested.

On the other hand, was it really so surprising that a commander with the Narcissus-like self-absorption of Narváez would be so remote from his men as to overlook the clues? And in just the same way it seemed his deep-rooted arrogance and pride was leading him to overestimate himself and his own capacities, resulting in a false and dangerous sense of security. The silly braying ass felt boastful and supremely confident surrounded by his nine hundred men with all their shiny weapons and big guns; he thought himself invulnerable, and that he could march on Cortés with impunity whenever he wished.

Such complacency, against such an enemy, was foolish in the extreme.

Meanwhile, the outburst this evening had not gone unnoticed by the men. After Narváez and his entourage had swept out of the refectory, there had been animated conversations at all the tables and Olmedo had eavesdropped. There were many who expressed the view that Narváez should reach an accommodation with Cortés. After all, wasn't this country, which seemed to go on for ever, big enough for both of them?

Well pleased, Olmedo had gone in search of Guevara and Santos. By midnight they had enriched Balthazar Bermudez with a further thousand pesos of gold – his services would be invaluable; had sounded out Francisco Verdugo and judged him worth settling a thousand pesos upon, and had held a crucial whispered conversation with Rodrigo Martinez, the chief of artillery, who received gold chains and ingots worth three thousand pesos. None of these men were at this point required to do anything other than swear to be ready to take certain actions in support of Cortés when they received the command to do so – these actions quite explicitly spelled out in each case. If the crisis came before the command could reach them, and battle was joined, they were to act anyway. They would be rewarded further when Cortés had victory.

As dawn broke on Friday 6 May 1520, Olmedo was already up and about, scratching at the fleas that his verminous bedding had infested him with. The last thing Narváez had said to him before leaving the refectory the evening before was that his letter to Cortés was ready and that he should collect it in the morning and leave Cempoala forthwith.

Ah blessed relief! Merciful heavens! It seemed that his prayers were answered! Looking down at the filthy skins and blankets on which he'd slept the past two nights, it occurred to Olmedo, though hoisted on the shoulders of *tamanes* and carried along vertiginous paths, that even the hammock he would retire to for sleep on the journey back through the mountains would be more comfortable than the accommodations he had been provided with here in Cempoala.

He took a full breakfast at the refectory; said his farewells to Ruffo, Valdez, and most of the other common soldiers whose trust he had won; had final words with the officers he'd suborned, and awaited Narváez's pleasure at the foot of the pyramid until he was summoned to ascend.

The commander was in conference, or wished to create the impression that he was in conference, with his close confidants Salvatierra, Bono de Quejo and Gamarra. The four of them were seated around his desk murmuring urgently, but fell silent when Olmedo appeared in the doorway.

'Come!' said Narváez.

Jackass! thought Olmedo as he advanced into the room. *Loves to give orders! Loves to hear the sound of his own bray.*

'As we discussed, Father,' Narváez began, his face corpselike in its pallor this morning, 'I have prepared a reply for you to carry to your master Cortés.'

He picked up a scroll from the table – it was sealed with red ribbon and wax – and passed it over.

'Thank you,' replied Olmedo, as he took it in his hand and placed it in his satchel. 'I'll be off then.'

'Wait!' It was Narváez. 'I know the game you're playing, Father.' Those bulging blue eyes fixed on him with weird intensity.

Olmedo shrugged. 'There's no game, commander. I'm just a simple messenger.'

As he turned again to go, he felt the four men watching him, their stares ripping him apart like instruments of torture, and sweat trickled down his back.

Chapter Thirteen

◆

Monday 9 May 1520–Tuesday 17 May 1520

Melchior stiffened and growled. After four days of easy marching on the busy and well-patrolled thoroughfare south of Tenochtitlan, the column had entered the outskirts of the ruined sacred city of Cholula. The vast bulk of the great pyramid, its summit surmounted by the half-demolished temple of Quetzalcoatl, loomed before them.

Pepillo reached down and gave the dog a pat on the head. He was trembling – not usual for him – and his wiry hair felt hot.

'You OK, boy?' he asked absently, gazing up towards the pyramid.

Melchior whined.

'I know,' Pepillo whispered, 'I can feel it too.'

'You are talking to dog again,' Malinal observed. 'Dog cannot talk back. So please tell me what do you and dog feel?'

'I don't know, exactly,' Pepillo said. 'Something to do with the atmosphere here, after the massacre last October.' Pepillo shivered, though the sun was warm.

On their right, a row of burnt and gutted homes and shops, unrepaired these past eight months, marked just one small corner of the vast destruction unleashed on Saturday 16 October 1519 when Cortés and his Spaniards had corralled the leading citizens of Cholula in the grand plaza around the great pyramid and massacred more than five thousand of them. The fighting, the chaos and the fires had spread far and wide, but the worst destruction had been concentrated within the sacred precinct, into which the column now marched through the huge northern gateway.

When Pepillo had first seen this place the previous October, it had been serenely and majestically beautiful, lined with tall palaces and villas surrounding the great pyramid and the temple of Quetzalcoatl, the city's sacred heart. But in the fighting, cannon fire had brought down the eastern

235

side of the temple, and more than twenty other temples built on top of the smaller satellite pyramids that stood scattered around the plaza had also been destroyed, mostly by burning, and were now reduced to blackened hulks. Again, there had been no serious effort at repair, or even to clean up the mess; the corpses of the slain had been removed, but otherwise things were very much as they'd been left when the Spanish had marched out of Cholula in early November on their way to Tenochtitlan.

'It *is* strange to be back,' Malinal conceded. 'Cholula was such a rich city, and such a lucky one, but now it's all destroyed and broken and its luck has run out.'

'They tried to kill us here,' Pepillo remembered.

'Tlalchi and Tlaqui's bodyguards! You were a hero!'

'All I did was stab one of them through the foot.'

'But that bought us time, Pepillo; we'd be dead now if you hadn't moved so fast.'

The former joint rulers of the city, elderly and eccentric Tlaqui and Tlalchi, had not survived the massacre. Their palace still stood, however, with a new governor in residence, a man called Zolin, appointed by Moctezuma with the approval of Cortés. Alongside the palace were the pair of tall townhouses where the entire Spanish force had been quartered last year. It had been crowded then, but with only seventy to accommodate tonight, space would not be a problem. As the column crossed the grand plaza, however, and the townhouses came into view, it became apparent that there were already Spaniards in residence.

'Velázquez de Léon!' Pepillo said. 'Look, there's his horse!'

The moment he set eyes on Juan Velázquez de Léon's dappled mare, and on the armed Spanish guards posted outside the townhouses, a deep sense of calm descended on Cortés, as he understood that his worst and most haunting fear for the forthcoming campaign had been proved groundless.

That fear had been that de Léon, full cousin and former favourite of Governor Diego de Velázquez of Cuba, would take his detachment of one hundred and fifty men and defect to Narváez. There were many reasons why this might indeed have happened, not least the several previous rebellions against Cortés in which de Léon had played a prominent role, and the several occasions when Cortés had jailed de Léon – for which he might be presumed to bear some resentment. Even more alarming, however, was the fact that, at the end of March, Cortés had sent de Léon and his men far from Tenochtitlan to establish a harbour and settlement on the coast, in a zone very close to where Narváez had landed, so it was likely that there might already have been some communication between the two parties. By the time he led his column into Cholula, therefore, Cortés had braced himself fully for the possibility that de Léon would simply have ignored his urgent summons to meet him there and would instead be with Narváez in Cempoala.

But mercifully it was not so – for not only was de Léon's heavy hunter being brushed down at the edge of the plaza by a groom but, here, now, striding out larger than life from the Spanish quarters, came de Léon himself. Of a naturally loud, vulgar and flamboyant temperament, this big, thick-limbed ox of a man, with his angry green eyes, bushy black beard and aggressive chin, had in the past months taken to wearing about his neck, over his shoulder, and wrapped twice around his arm, a huge chain of looted gold with chunky, heavy links. So distinctive an affectation was it, and with so blatant a purpose, that the men had named it 'the Swaggerer'.

Giving orders for his troop to be at ease, find quarters and see the baggage safely stowed, Cortés jumped down from Molinero, passed the reigns to Brabo and hurried over to greet de Léon, who was so big, in all dimensions, that it was not possible to give him a proper embrace.

'Juan! Here you are ahead of me! I'm so very happy to see you!'

'And you, Hernán! Well met in Cholula, eh? I did the march in double-quick time as soon as I received your orders.'

'You have all the hundred and fifty men you set out with?'

'I've lost eight to dysentery, fever and desertions, so one hundred and forty-two.' De Léon cast his eye over Cortés's men: 'And you have, what, eighty?'

'Seventy.'

A low whistle: 'So, with your seventy, and my hundred and forty-two, we have two hundred and twelve to take on the mighty Pánfilo Narváez.'

'We will be joined here by Rangel with a hundred and twenty more – I hope tomorrow.'

'And Sandoval.'

'He's abandoned Villa Rica on my orders with seventy-three men. We'll rendezvous with them much closer to Cempoala, not here.'

'So it is your firm intention to attack Narváez in Cempoala?'

'It is, unless he chooses to embark all his men and sail back to Cuba at once!'

Velázquez de Léon edged closer, a confidential distance, and lowered his voice: 'I don't think he'll be sailing back to Cuba, Hernán. He wrote to me. His letter gives some idea of his intentions. I have it with me . . .'

'I'm still not certain what did the trick,' Cortés said to Malinal much later. The two were preparing for bed in the comfortable apartments they'd taken within the Spanish quarters at Cholula.

'What trick?' she asked.

'The trick that has turned de Léon from a full-blooded Velazquista ready to do anything to advance the interests of his cousin, into someone who's beginning to look like a real ally.'

'Maybe because you allowed him to keep enough gold to make the Swaggerer?'

It was a serious point.

'Maybe.'

'Or maybe because he thinks you'll win, Hernán?'

'Maybe that too.'

'But do you really trust him?'

'I hope I may.' Cortés sat to pull off his boots. 'He showed me a letter that Narváez wrote to him, appealing to him as the cousin of Diego de Velázquez and offering him treasure and great honour to join him. Indeed, Narváez says in the letter that he's willing to share command with de Léon! Very tempting! So if Juan wanted to betray me, he only needed to make his way along the coast and there would be Narváez waiting for him with open arms, knowing that his defection with so many men would be fatal for our cause. But Juan didn't defect! Instead, he made a forced march inland to bring those men to me and informed me of Narváez's manoeuvres.'

'Poor Velázquez de Léon,' said Malinal. 'So many times you have punished him, but now I think you have to thank him.'

'If his support's real, and not some ploy, then I owe him a great debt of gratitude. It may even be that he's saved New Spain for us.'

'And you think real, not ploy?'

'I *want* to think that. It certainly seems that way. But I'm not a trusting man. I need to test de Léon's loyalty again before I'm ready to put my faith in him wholeheartedly.'

The following day, Tuesday 10 May, Rodrigo Rangel reached Cholula with his detachment of one hundred and twenty, reduced by desertions and two deaths from fever to one hundred and nine. He brought with him in his baggage train the three hundred copper-tipped pikes from Chinantla.

Satisfied that all was now in order, Cortés led the march from the city the day after, Wednesday 11 May. The pace was quicker and more urgent than on the first leg of the journey, as the greatly expanded column, now numbering three hundred and twenty-one men and followed by a large baggage train, struck out into the mountains towards Tlascala and distant Cempoala beyond. They had not travelled many miles from Cholula, however, when a scout, mounted on Rangel's black gelding, cantered back to report encountering a small group of *tamanes* advancing along the road in the opposite direction. Enormous snores, as of a bear in its fury, erupted from a cumbersome burden they carried, which proved on the scout's closer inspection to be Father Olmedo, wrapped in a hammock and perfectly asleep clutching an empty wineskin.

Soon afterwards the two parties converged, exchanging noisy greetings, yet still the sleeper slumbered! Netted in his hammock, reeking of booze, he was lowered to the ground, where he continued to snore mightily, surrounded by a ribald crowd of officers.

Amongst them was Diego de Ordaz, who not many nights before had mistaken the friar for the devil and was now gazing upon him, and upon the empty wineskin, with uncalled-for contempt. 'The man can't hold his drink,' he muttered. Cristóbal de Olid was there too: short, squat and gnome-like, with a wild black beard. His twinkling blue eyes were also fixed upon the wineskin, but not with disapproval, Cortés thought.

Next to Olid was Velázquez de Léon, wearing his Swaggerer as always, and next to him Alonso Davila, darkly handsome and daring, but argumentative, with a habit of disputing every point. Rangel was there, old and grim. Towering over him, a full head taller than everyone else, was Bernal Díaz, twenty-eight years old, heavy built, with solid labourer's muscles like a ploughboy, and a big, sallow-skinned face that was all bony planes and angles. Cortés had promoted him to lieutenant in November, valuing his reliability and common sense as much as his persistence and his courage. Flanking Díaz were the ensigns Alonso de la Serna, a tall, clever, cynical young man with a mop of fair hair, his otherwise handsome face marked by the scars of an old smallpox infection, and Francisco Mibiercas, whose unusually broad shoulders and muscular arms were the result of hours of daily practice with the *espadón*, the long, two-handed sword that hung in a scabbard at his back.

Cortés dismounted and joined the jocular little knot of officers. 'Shush,' he whispered, holding a finger to his lips. He knelt by Olmedo. The friar's snores were truly animalistic, a mixture of snarls, grunts and growls interspersed by percussive bursts of breath.

'Bartolomé,' Cortés said softly.

Nothing.

Louder: 'Bartolomé!'

Still nothing.

Cortés reached down, grasped Olmedo by his surprisingly muscular shoulders, and shook him: 'Bartolomé!'

At this, with a groan, the friar rolled on to his side. Still clutching the empty wineskin, he drew the nozzle to his mouth and sucked upon it.

Cortés tried to snatch it away – '*Bartolomé! Wake up!*' – but the friar clung tight, blinking and grumbling, before finally levering himself upright, relinquishing the skin, shading his eyes from the light and croaking: 'The hammers of hell . . .'

'What, Father?' Cortés strained to listen.

'The hammers of hell are beating in my head.' A sudden smile: 'My goodness, it's you, Hernán!' Olmedo blinked again, still shading his eyes, and squinted up at the officers surrounding him. 'So many of you! Don Diego – there you are, frowning as usual I see. Have you recovered yet from our little . . . outing? Hello, Bernal! Hello, Juan! Hello, Cristóbal, you old rogue!'

With another groan, louder than the first, Olmedo closed his eyes and pressed his palms to his temples. 'The hammers of hell,' he muttered again. 'The hammers and the gnashing teeth of hell.'

'Never mind about the gnashing teeth of hell,' said Olid, who'd taken the wineskin from Cortés and squeezed the last few drops into his mouth. 'I want to know if you've got any more of this nectar, Bartolomé.'

The friar opened his eyes again, a suspicious glare: 'Why do you ask?'

'Why do I ask?' Olid dangled the skin and licked his lips: 'This is the first wine I've tasted for months. Why do you think I ask?'

Olmedo nodded: 'It has been the one joy of my stay in the Narváez camp that a plentiful supply of the commander's personal stock of wines remains. I've made arrangements to secure it when we have victory.'

'And not only for Mass, Father, I'll wager!' The voice came from amongst the common soldiers who were now also pressing around the seated friar.

'Man does not live by bread alone,' Olmedo replied enigmatically.

'Here, give me a hand up.' He reached to Olid and Díaz, allowed them to help him to his feet, and turned to Cortés: 'I have a letter for you from Narváez, Hernán, and news of his sad, sorry shambles of a camp. Shall I unburden myself now?'

'I'll take the letter. I can read it on horseback. The talking can wait until we've completed the day's march . . .'

Olmedo looked anxious: 'You're not disappointed in me, Hernán?'

'To find you drunk again? Perhaps a little, but we're all human, Bartolomé. We each have to take our solace where we can find it.'

There came an aggrieved grunt from Ordaz, which Cortés ignored. Ordaz was a soldier, and drunkenness in soldiers could lead to dangerous derelictions of duty. Olmedo, on the other hand, was a friar, and if he wished to drink himself into a stupor then that was between him and God.

There was trouble in the air. Alvarado had been sniffing it, not quite able to put his finger on it, for some while before the first unmistakable signs began to appear. The Tlascalans had noticed it too, and he'd received several warning messages from their commanders, but had judged them too vague and general to act on.

Then, on Wednesday 11 May, six days after Cortés and his contingent had left the capital, the normal morning delivery of food for the Spanish garrison in the palace of Axayacatl was not made. A pretty Mexica girl, who usually cooked breakfast for the conquistadors and was something of a favourite with them, went out to discover what had happened. Soon afterwards her body was found dumped near the north gate of the sacred precinct, decapitated, her head placed between her legs, and her heart cut out.

By noon many of the other servants had deserted.

In a mood to kill, Alvarado summoned Jerónimo de Aguilar, who'd mastered enough of the foul Mexica tongue to pass for a translator when Malinal was away, and took a stroll in the sacred precinct, in the shadow of the great pyramid, where the preparations for the festival of Toxcatl were well advanced. God how he hated these heathens! He hated the way they smelled. He hated the way they looked. He hated the way they simpered and lied. And he hated their fucking festivals.

On the other side of the square he spotted the distinctive black and red cloaks of a contingent of Tlascalan auxiliaries en route to their wing of the palace of Axayacatl. He recognised their commander Chipahua, a close associate of King Shikotenka, hailed him and met him close to the northwest corner of the pyramid.

This Chipahua was an odd-looking fellow with a big, glistening, completely bald head, smooth and domed on top, narrowing somewhat at the temples but widening again to accommodate prominent cheek bones, a full fleshy face, and what might have passed for sensual, sneering lips had they not been twisted and disfigured by a battle injury that had also left jagged gaps in his teeth.

'Ho Chipahua, greetings!' said Alvarado through Aguilar.

'Greetings to you, Tonatiuh.'

'I have a question if I may . . .' Alvarado was not in the habit of conversing with the Indian auxiliaries. He respected the Tlascalans as fighters, but it would not normally have occurred to him to ask them for advice. Still these were exceptional times. 'I've received your warnings,' he said. 'Do you observe some change amongst the Mexica?'

'No, none,' was the blunt answer. 'They've always been murdering bastards and they always will be.'

'They didn't deliver our food this morning.'

'Ours neither.'

'And they killed one of our cooks – cut off her head, cut out her heart. What do you think it means?'

Chipahua threw back his head and laughed. 'It means that what we've already warned you of many times is now about to happen – the Mexica are getting ready to slaughter us! I can't believe you haven't worked that out yet! They've been making their preparations for days. It isn't just pilgrims who are coming in for Toxcatl, you know. The call has gone out and amongst those crowds on the causeways are thousands of warriors from Mexica vassal states come to save the honour of their precious Great Speaker.'

Alvarado felt the Indian's strong and deeply calloused right hand seize his left arm just above the crook of the elbow and guide him past the corner of the pyramid to an area of the plaza where the paving stones had been ripped up. Here a great many stakes, about the size used for burning heretics in Spain, had been driven into the ground, with one, much taller than the others, at the centre.

'Guess what those are for?' said Chipahua.

'I don't know,' admitted Alvarado. He didn't like the look of them at all. 'Do enlighten me.'

'The big one's for you; the others are for your men. The Mexica plan to capture you, tie you to the stakes and cut your hearts out right there.'

'And you Tlascalans,' said Alvarado, 'what do they intend for you?'

'Oh don't worry,' laughed Chipahua, his gap-toothed face grotesque. 'We're fucked too.'

This Indian might have his own reasons for wanting to stir up a fight between the Mexica and the Spaniards, but Alvarado found he believed him. 'When's all this supposed to happen?' he asked.

'On the feast of Toxcatl itself, six days from today.'

'Thank you for what you have told me, Chipahua,' Alvarado said. 'If it's certain we're to be attacked, then I'd rather get our retaliation in first.'

Aguilar had difficulty translating this phrase, but when Chipahua eventually understood he laughed louder than before. 'Get your retaliation in first! Yes! Very good idea with the Mexica.' A sceptical look: 'But do you have the manpower for it? You are one hundred and twenty since Cortés left? Do I remember right?'

'Yes,' conceded Alvarado.

'And they can throw one hundred and twenty thousand men at you, probably many more by the time they've received all the reinforcements they've asked for from their vassals. What can you possibly hope to achieve against those numbers?'

'At least we can count on you and your thousand Tlascalans,' said Alvarado. 'I'm told that Shikotenka never breaks his word.'

'We won't abandon you,' Chipahua conceded. 'Shikotenka would not accept it. Besides, I'm not even certain we'd be able to leave the city now. The Mexica want us all dead and an attempt to flee – by any of us – might just trigger the attack sooner.'

'I'll think on that,' Alvarado said, 'and we'll meet again and make a plan.'

While the Tlascalans returned to their barracks in the palace, Alvarado continued his walk around the plaza. His eye was caught by a group of women working on the construction of a huge and grotesque figure.

'Any idea what that is?' Alvarado asked Aguilar, who was supposed to be studying the local culture, the better to assist in destroying it.

'It's a figure of their god Hummingbird,' the translator replied. 'They make it specially for this festival every year. It's built up around a wooden frame and then filled with amaranth seed dough.'

Alvarado's mind was buzzing with ideas. Part of him wanted to stop the festival before it got started, but that would only delay the danger.

Wouldn't it be better to let the dancing and the celebration go ahead and then just kill everyone when they were conveniently gathered in this walled and gated precinct around the great pyramid? After all, while telling him to permit the fiesta and to handle Moctezuma gently, Cortés had also informed him that the flower of the Mexica aristocracy would be performing the dances in the square. With Moctezuma already in Alvarado's hands, the festival held out the alluring opportunity to decapitate Mexica society once and for all by removing the rest of the leadership class at a stroke.

The only question was, how would he explain it to Cortés? Alvarado was under strict instructions not to take actions of the very kind he was now contemplating, and to allow the festival to go ahead peacefully, unless there was evidence of human sacrifice. Yet there was only this figure of sticks and dough. 'Seems pretty harmless,' he said, reaching out to touch it.

'Not harmless at all, sir.' As Aguilar replied his lips set into a thin line. 'It is customary for the dough to be kneaded with the blood of recent victims of sacrifice.'

'But we can't know for sure that's happened here.'

'Look further, sir.' Aguilar pointed to a large sewn leather bag on the ground behind the figure. The bag was thickly smeared and crusted with gore and proved on investigation to contain a macabre assortment of human hands and hearts and five heads, all male, with staring, sightless eyes.

Aguilar spoke for some minutes with the women who were making the figure, then turned to Cortés. 'They sew the hands and hearts into necklaces for their effigy. The heads will be strung from a belt. Five men were sacrificed this morning to provide these . . . adornments.'

This was most strongly and definitely contrary to the caudillo's orders, and a clear breach of the agreement he'd reached with Moctezuma allowing the festival to go ahead. Indeed, was it not evidence enough to mete out some exemplary punishment?

Remembering the massacre in Cholula the year before, carried out on the orders of Cortés himself, the exciting idea that was taking shape in Alvarado's mind now crystallised into a definite intention.

'You talked to Alvarado then?'

Shikotenka didn't like to use the popular name Tonatiuh – 'the sun' – for the Spanish captain. He had grudging respect for the man, having fought him and very nearly been killed by him on the dunes at Cuetlaxtlan. But he disliked anything that associated these foreigners with the gods.

'He's ready for a fight any time that one,' said Chipahua, 'but I encouraged him a little . . .'

Chipahua was obviously pleased with himself. Letting him enjoy the moment, Shikotenka asked, 'How?'

'I told him that the posts for the pole-flyer dances were stakes that he and his men were to be tied to for sacrifice. I think he believed me. He's planning – how did he put it? – to get his retaliation in first.'

'The thinking of these Spaniards is not so different from our own,' said Shikotenka. 'By the way, you didn't tell him I'm in the city, did you?'

'I'm not an idiot.' Chipahua looked offended. 'You asked us to keep your stay here secret from the Spaniards, and it's being kept secret.'

The doorway darkened as Tree entered the room: 'Maybe not from the Mexica, though,' he said. 'There's already a rumour in the city that you're here. If things go to shit, expect to be hunted down.'

The letter Olmedo had brought was much as to be expected, all piss and wind, summoning Cortés to submit to the authority of Don Pánfilo Narváez as captain-general of the country and menacing him with terrible punishments if he refused to accept or delayed even for a single day. Cortés was encouraged by the high-handed imperious tone; an enemy who tried so hard to sound confident and strong was most likely, at root, insecure and weak. Summoning Pepillo, he handed the letter to him, telling him to keep it carefully against the day when the history of these events would come to be written.

That night of Wednesday 11 May, after camp had been made, fires lit and a spartan dinner prepared, Olmedo vanished for a few moments amongst his *tamanes* and returned with a bulging wineskin. 'It's the last of them,' he told Olid, who was eyeing him greedily, 'but the Book of Proverbs teaches us that those who are generous will themselves be blessed – so I propose to share.'

'But only with the officers I hope, Father! Share it with the men and we'll not get a thimbleful each.'

'Come, Olmedo, sit with me,' interrupted Cortés, who was nearby with Rangel and Díaz warming his hands at a fire. 'You too, Olid. By God you look like a man who needs a drink! Ordaz! I'd like you to join us. And Juan.' Cortés caught the eye of Velázquez de Léon. 'Father Olmedo has returned from the very belly of the beast – the camp of Don Pánfilo

Narváez, that high-handed interloper, who thinks he can come here and steal from us everything we've won!'

As Cortés spoke, loudly and with deliberate purpose, many heads turned. They'd get no share of the wine, but he wanted as many of the common soldiers as possible to gather close and gain courage from Olmedo's account of the enemy they were marching to fight – an enemy whose camp, the friar had already hinted, was in a state of disarray.

To one who knew Narváez as Cortés did, and was familiar with his irritating habitual tics and his many airs and graces, Olmedo's imitation of the man was little short of amazing. Indeed, in some inexplicable way, the beefy friar seemed almost to change shape, becoming taller and lankier like Narváez, while even his features took on a peculiar resemblance. It was the voice he affected, however – that deep, rumbling voice – that was the most extraordinary part of the mummery since it was, to perfection and without fault, the voice of Narváez himself.

After offering one merciless parody of the man after another for almost half an hour, Olmedo now began to strut back and forth around the fire, one hand on his hip, the other held out before his eyes. It seemed Narváez had adopted this manner while reading aloud to his deputy Alonso de Salvatierra, and to the friar, the first – quite conciliatory – letter sent by Cortés.

'Ha! Look here, Salvatierra!' Olmedo now disclaimed in Narváez's booming voice. 'That imp Cortés actually has the nerve to offer us a province of his New Spain to settle in.'

'Is it true, Caudillo?' shouted a big scarred brute of a soldier in the scrum around the campfire. His voice held a hint of threat. 'Did you offer that cunny some of the land we've conquered, sir?'

Cortés stood to answer the question, remembering, in the same instant, the soldier's improbable name. 'Well, not exactly land we've *conquered*, Angel. I had in mind sharing one of the unexplored provinces with Narváez. Even that, I know, must go hard with you. It goes hard with me too. But let's not forget that the men Narváez intends to put against us aren't Indians or Moors but fellow Spaniards, and I think – don't you, Angel? – that we should make every effort to avoid a war with fellow Spaniards.'

There was a murmur of agreement and cries of, 'You're right, Hernán', and Cortés smiled privately. The truth was he didn't mean it, not a word of it. He had absolutely no intention of sharing anything with Narváez.

All such ideas – and he reserved the right to conjure more of them! – were merely ploys, delaying tactics, until he judged the moment right to crush his enemy.

Still, it was good that Olmedo had chosen to include this land-sharing suggestion in his mummery, because Cortés did in fact want the men to believe he was doing everything in his power to avoid a war! Convinced of that, as they seemed to be now, they would be all the more effective, all the more furious, and all the more murderous when he did send them into battle, justified warriors in a righteous cause, fighting an intractable and arrogant foe who refused every olive branch.

'This Cortés is a traitor to our patron, Don Diego de Velázquez,' boomed Olmedo, in perfect mimicry of Narváez's voice and posture, eliciting an immediate storm of boos and hisses from the assembled soldiery. 'I'm here to arrest him and put him in chains, and set that Emperor Mucktey free and give him all his gold back.'

More boos and hisses. Someone shouted: 'Not if we've got anything to do with it.'

'And then I'm going to bend over,' Olmedo now had Narváez say, 'and let Mucktey . . .'

He stopped, resumed in his normal voice, 'But I must remember I'm a priest . . .'

There were cries of, 'Come on, Father! Give us more!' to which, needing very little persuasion, Olmedo eventually acceded, with imitations of Juan Bono de Quejo, portrayed as a foolish fop, and of Juan Gamarra as an empty-headed glutton. 'The best of them, though,' the friar said, 'truly the prize-winner for ugliness, banality and malice, is Salvatierra, a hideous little man who looks like an ape but fancies himself well-bred and a cut above the rest of us.'

To great hilarity all round, Olmedo told of how Salvatierra had spectacularly failed to hoist two big cannon to the top of a fairly small pyramid, leaving one of them embedded barrel first in the ground. A chorus of angry boos and hisses then erupted when he mimicked Salvatierra's boast that he would cut off Cortés's ears and broil them for his breakfast.

'Just let him try!' someone in the crowd shouted.

'We'll fuck him up!' yelled another.

'But to be serious,' Olmedo continued, again in his normal voice, 'they're all boastful braggarts like that. Narváez is engaged in a deep and passionate love affair with himself, and his officers are flatterers who lack the courage or character to do anything other than minister to his vanity. Partly because they're naturally conceited individuals, but also partly because they bathe one another in a constant unction of praise and self-congratulation, they've become over-confident and actually seem to feel invulnerable. They have no concern with setting proper watches. Sentries are posted but only to stop the men from bothering Narváez. He simply doesn't believe you'll come against him, Hernán!'

'Good!' said Cortés, punching his right fist into the palm of his left hand. 'Let him enjoy that belief, until we fall upon him one dark night when he least expects it and destroy him utterly! Now tell me, Father, what's your view of the state of his troops?' He looked around the flushed, eager faces of the listening men, their eyes glittering in the firelight. 'Are they any match for these heroes, would you say?'

Olmedo threw back his head and laughed: 'No match at all! Our men are honed and battle hardened and they're led – I don't mean to flatter you – by a great commander. Narváez is a fool and his men are soft, untried and inexperienced. And one thing I can tell you about those men, Hernán – amongst them are more than a few who dislike Narváez and who speak well of you and don't want to go to war with you or any fellow Spaniards. I judiciously spread the gold you gave me amongst the members of this faction to stiffen their resolve, and our position was strengthened when the envoys Guevara, Vergara and Amaya returned. I don't know how you persuaded them, Hernán, but from the moment they arrived in Cempoala, they sang your praises and diligently distributed your presents of gold to the officers most likely to support us, and worked in every way to spread poison about Narváez!'

Much later, after everyone else had retired for the night, Cortés and Olmedo continued to talk. Cortés would have preferred that the presents of gold given to Narváez's men had not been mentioned in front of his own exceptionally avaricious soldiers. Nonetheless, the friar had done well: sown dissent in the enemy camp, undermined the authority of its officers, identified and strengthened potential allies, and positioned saboteurs.

Almost equally useful was Olmedo's confirmation that Narváez had received golden treasure and personal gifts from that double-dealing serpent Moctezuma, and that the two had made some sort of agreement, perhaps already now in an advanced state of preparation, to join forces against Cortés.

Olmedo had also seen much else in Cempoala that would be of

strategic value – the disposition of enemy troops, the points of greatest strength and weakness in their defence, the positioning of their cannon, the state of their morale, and so much more whose value a man of the cloth might not even recognise. Patiently Cortés questioned him and, bit by bit, as the stars wheeled above and the last dregs of the wineskin were drained, he extracted the information he needed. When finally he threw himself down on his bedroll, his mental picture of his enemy, and how to defeat him, was clear.

The following day, Thursday 12 May in the late afternoon, one of the mounted scouts returned to the column to report that two Spaniards were lodged in the town of Quechula just ahead. They were, he said, unknown to him and 'definitely not ours'.

Claiming to be notaries, and accompanied only by a small group of *tamanes*, these Spaniards, it transpired, were another delegation from Narváez, sent up into the mountains to find Cortés. Ushering forth into the town square, the senior of the two, small, bustling, energetic, nervous and self-important, with thinning grey hair and a goatee beard, introduced himself as Alonso de Mata and his pale, moist, and somewhat trembling younger colleague as Bernardino de Quesada.

A brace of Spanish notaries travelling the roads alone, unescorted and, apparently, judging by de Mata's satchel, heavily loaded with documents and inkpots, could, Cortés immediately divined, only be here with one purpose. This was, of course, the very same purpose that the priest Guevara and the notary Vergara had tried but failed to fulfil at Villa Rica, namely to serve certain papers, writs and decrees intended to remove him from power, and to require his formal surrender to the authority of Narváez.

Cortés chuckled as he slid down from Molinero.

Mata and Quesada, sweating in their black woollen robes, and each in his different way trying unsuccessfully to look grave, approached . . . and bowed.

Ridiculous! This was the sixteenth century, for God's sake.

Nonetheless, Cortés bowed also. Anything else would have seemed churlish.

Introductions were then made, at which point Mata, unable to restrain himself, imprudently denounced Cortés as a 'pretender', as a 'false captain-general', as a 'traitor to the Crown', and as a 'mere brigand', who had sullied the good name of Spain with his failed attempt at conquest.

Cortés raised an eyebrow: '*Failed* attempt at conquest, you say?'

'Yes! We are *informed*, Senor Cortés, that the natives of this land are in turmoil and open rebellion against you, that your hold on power has failed, and that you cannot finish what you have started in this country...'

Cortés remained outwardly placid, sensing that this was not a moment when anger would serve him. 'And yet,' he pointed out, 'you and your young assistant have travelled here, unarmed and with no escort of soldiers, for many days in complete safety through wild mountains inhabited by ferocious cannibals.'

Mata cautiously conceded that this was so.

'And do you imagine,' Cortés asked, 'that you would have been able to undertake and survive such a journey had I not first subdued the country and made the name of Spaniard a lucky charm here?'

Cortés waited a beat for this thought to sink in, and then struck at what had been the fatal flaw in Guevara and Vergara's case – one that was likely to prove fatal also for whatever case Mata was here to make.

It was a simple question, with a yes-or-no answer.

'Are you a king's notary?' Cortés asked, expecting the answer to be 'no'.

Instead, and it quite shook him, Mata replied 'yes' and, sticking out his goatee, continued rather impudently to arraign Cortés as though he were a felon. When the jumped-up little gnome reached into his satchel, drew forth a sheaf of documents and began to read, however, Cortés raised a hand and loudly commanded: '*Stop!* Show me your title!'

Startled, plainly flustered, Mata dropped the papers. Scrambling to retrieve them, he asked: 'What title?'

'You say you're a royal notary, an *escribano del rey*, not just an ordinary *escribano*, and if you are a royal notary then you have certain rights and privileges – including the right to read those documents to me. So show me your title and I will hear you and consider what will be of service to God and His Majesty.'

'I have ... err ...' Panic wriggled like a worm on Mata's face.

'You have err what?' Cortés demanded.

'I have left my title amongst my other papers at our headquarters in Cempoala.'

'Ah!' Cortés rubbed his hands briskly together. 'In that case, we have a problem. I can't permit you to read these documents to me unless you can attest your right to read them. Also, if you do return with your title, make sure you return with the original documents – I refuse to look at copies – signed in the king's own hand.'

'In the king's own hand?' Mata looked astonished.

'Well you are a king's notary. Should I expect anything less?'

Seeing the hesitation in the other man's eyes, Cortés pounced: 'But you're *not* a king's notary at all, are you?'

With a shamed droop of his head, Mata confessed that he was not. 'I'm sorry, Señor Cortés. I became flustered under your questioning. I am a humble *escribano*.'

'Well, put those papers away, man – let's hear no more about them – and you must join us for dinner.'

Bernal Díaz understood that Cortés had to spend treasure to win enemies to his cause, and knew from Olmedo's stories that gold had already been handed out – by Olmedo himself and by Guevara and Vergara – to a number of Narváez's officers and men. It was always so in warfare, was it not – that buying an enemy cost more than rewarding a friend? Alexander the Great was said to have aroused the resentment of his men on several occasions by giving more gold to those who came over to him than to his own soldiers. So why should Cortés not do the same?

It was remarkable to witness him in action, though!

In the hour before the dinner, Cortés sent word – it was essentially the same order that he'd given to impress Guevara and Vergara – that all the men should wear and put ostentatiously on display as much of their gold and jewellery as they had with them. They complied; in consequence, most appeared with gold on their arms and golden chains and collars round their necks, Velázquez de Léon prominent amongst them with his Swaggerer.

Díaz saw clearly how this public demonstration of wealth, sustained throughout the evening, was having the intended effects on Mata and Quesada. They were transparently impressed and overawed that even the common soldiers in Cortés's army could have got so rich so quickly. Narváez might try to prevent them from sharing their dazzled impressions when they returned to Cempoala, but they would certainly do so anyway, and in the process would spread further poison throughout his ranks.

Díaz nudged the swordsman Mibiercas whom he was seated next to: 'Watch his hands,' he said, referring to Cortés.

'I'm watching.'

Cortés had taken Mata's and Quesada's hands and held them beneath the table. Mibiercas and Díaz leaned forward, peering to look.

251

There came a glint of gold.

'My God,' said Mibiercas, 'are those rings?'

'They are. And I'll wager he won't let them go until their fingers are well-smeared.'

It was all smiles, camaraderie and *abrazos* when Mata and Quesada, thoroughly seduced by Cortés, set off the next day, Friday 13 May, on their return journey to Cempoala. They went by the direct road, while Cortés chose a more roundabout route through Tlascala. Haste led to foolish mistakes and he was not satisfied that he had yet positioned himself strongly or cunningly enough to secure victory against the enemy commander. By visiting rugged Tlascala with his little army in this time of crisis, he still hoped to persuade Shikotenka to thwart the will of the Senate and provide him with five thousand seasoned warriors to throw into the balance against Narváez.

The distance to Tlascala was less than thirty miles, but a tough march of a day and a half through the mountains was required to reach it. Messages had been sent ahead with the scouts and, when Cortés led the column into the populous capital, crowds of spectators were already lining the road, offering a colourful and amiable welcome of ululation, garlands and sweetmeats.

On the approach to the centre, passing the mighty stone temples and the tall pyramid formerly dedicated to the Tlascalan gods but now given over to Christ, Cortés had occasion to reflect how much had changed since the war he'd fought against these courageous and tenacious people the previous summer. Many were pagans no longer; they had proved staunch allies against the Mexica during the past months; the public welcome seemed to indicate – even to reiterate – that their friendship remained strong; and yet they refused to provide him with the aid he'd so urgently called for in his time of greatest need!

Shikotenka's father, Shikotenka the Elder, the civil king of Tlascala, together with his aged and wizened deputy, Maxixcatzin, were at the head of the delegation waiting in the main square in front of the pyramid to greet Cortés. Each now gravely embraced him and looked on, beaming, as a company of nubile, giggling young women draped him in fragrant garlands.

'Great Lord, where is your son?' Cortés asked the aged civil king as soon as he had the opportunity.

Shikotenka the Elder looked puzzled. 'My son is in Tenochtitlan. Did he not meet you there?'

'He did, great lord, but I left the city within hours of our meeting. He gave me no hint that he planned to stay.'

The aged king took Cortés by his right elbow and began to lead him slowly towards the palace. Maxixcatzin, much crippled with rheumatism, hobbled at his left. 'My son did not intend to stay,' Shikotenka the Elder said gravely as they walked, 'but something caused him to change his mind.'

'And I suppose you have no idea what?' Cortés trusted, as he so often did, that Malinal would translate only his words and not convey the irritation in his tone.

'Since my son is our battle-king,' replied Shikotenka the Elder, 'I can only suppose he foresees the coming of a war in which the interests of Tlascala will be involved . . .'

'And yet he tells me that you yourself – you and Maxixcatzin and your entire Senate – see no relevance to Tlascala in the war I'm about to fight with a fellow Spaniard?'

Shikotenka the Elder sighed, and the sound was like the wind whisking autumn leaves out of its path. 'Come, Malinche. I know and regret that we have offended you. Let us talk inside.'

There were constant rumours, mostly spread by the Tlascalan auxiliaries, that a Mexica attack was imminent. Now it was reported that holes were to be hammered in the rear wall of Axayacatl's palace, where it was continuous with and formed part of the boundary wall of the sacred precinct. A second report said that a section of the boundary wall itself was to be undermined instead. Under the ground, sounds of digging had been heard. Then Chipahua came again with credible intelligence of exceptionally long ladders being made and stockpiled so that scaling parties could climb the walls of the palace and rescue Moctezuma.

Alvarado sent out more patrols and set teams of men to work to strengthen the palace fortifications to resist a siege. He also set his factor, Juan Alvarez, to stockpile food, but his efforts were not very successful and he reported great difficulties in the face of growing local hostility and markets often closed against him.

All the more reason to strike and strike hard!

By Saturday 14 May, three days before the fiesta of Toxcatl, Alvarado had already settled all the details of his strategy. The present situation was becoming unsustainable. To flee would be to invite attack on the causeways, where the bridges would be cut; the tiny garrison would be extremely vulnerable and its ultimate destruction more or less guaranteed. The only hope, therefore, was to use Toxcatl itself, and the gathering and concentration of the Mexica elite on that day, as an opportunity for a massacre so savage and complete that it would leave the enemy leaderless and demoralised for a decade.

The fly in the ointment was the possible anger and disapproval of Cortés. Alvarado didn't want to be publicly humiliated by his friend again as he had been at Cozumel in 1519. But the evidence he'd uncovered of continuing sacrifices should surely provide sufficient justification for the massacre?

Alvarado felt uncertainty; it was not a familiar emotion for him. On impulse, he took ten men and marched up to the top of the great pyramid, where he quickly found further proof. There was a pool of blood by the altar and three freshly extracted human hearts sizzled on a brazier.

The great cross that the conquistadors had erected still stood outside the temple, but the images of Christ and the Virgin that Cortés had installed within were gone. In the darkness of the rearmost shrine, twenty prisoners had been herded into a makeshift fattening pen awaiting sacrifice.

As Alvarado freed them and confirmed the removal of the images – sacrilege! – he knew he had the justification he needed for what he planned.

'You have asked us,' said the old king gravely when they were seated in his audience chamber, 'for five thousand warriors to help you against this new Spanish force that has arrived at the coast?'

'That's correct, great lord, and never have I needed the help of staunch Tlascala more than I do today.'

Another of those rattling sighs: 'If you were going against natives of this land such as ourselves, armed as we are, we would help you, and willingly send you more than five thousand warriors, but you have asked us to fight against other *tueles*, Malinche, and against lombards and crossbows and fire-serpents, and this we would be fools to do. We are your allies and we will try to help you in other ways, but we are not prepared to send the flower of our youth to commit suicide in battle for you.'

Like father like son, Cortés thought.

The arguments of Shikotenka the Elder were much the same as those offered by the younger Shikotenka eight days before. But there was one important exception. The battle-king had said nothing to Cortés about fears of a Mexica resurgence, yet the fact that he'd stayed on in Tenochtitlan, the perilous stronghold of Tlascala's traditional enemies and persecutors, suggested some great danger might indeed be fermenting there. Now Shikotenka the Elder confirmed this: 'We have spies everywhere throughout the lands of the Mexica,' he said, 'and everywhere they report mobilisation for war. Certainly that is to be a war against you *tueles*, Malinche, but it will also be a war against Tlascala. It is the unanimous decision of the Senate that we must hold our forces back to defend against this Mexica storm when it falls upon us.'

Using mounted scouts and teams of relay runners, Cortés had maintained sporadic contact with Gonzalo de Sandoval. As ordered, the captain had abandoned Villa Rica at the end of April with his small force of seventy-three men – soon thereafter reduced to seventy-one by desertions to Narváez – and had been leading a nomadic existence ever since, constantly moving and living off the land.

'By all means harass and annoy the enemy if you can,' Cortés wrote to him from Tlascala, 'but under no circumstances engage him. We must keep our forces intact until we can rendezvous, perhaps at Perote – ' he named a town some eighty miles west of Cempoala – 'and come against Narváez in strength.'

The army paused in Tlascala for two full days, taking on supplies in much larger and more varied quantities than the twenty loads of turkeys Shikotenka had spoken of. Short of actual military involvement, it truly was a generous effort, supported by a thousand *tamanes* to carry the bounty.

It was not until dawn on Tuesday 17 May, therefore, with his forces refreshed, that Cortés led the march out of Tlascala, heading out over the mountains towards his distant rendezvous with Sandoval on the coastal plains over two hundred miles to the east.

Chapter Fourteen

---◆---

It was dawn on the day of Toxcatl.

Moctezuma had been awake the entire night in his quarters, shaking with a strange, unsettling mixture of fear and hope, pacing, sometimes sitting, sometimes stretched out groaning on the floor as his mind darted from one possibility to another.

Now in his imagination the battle in the sacred precinct had already unfolded, the *tueles* under the command of Tonatiuh had been defeated, the survivors had been taken captive and were being prepared for sacrifice.

Ah, it was all so . . . satisfying.

But then a different scenario thrust its way to the fore, in which the attack went ahead but the *tueles* were victorious and the sacred precinct was filled with the blood of slain Mexica warriors.

Moctezuma shuddered, recalling the great pleasure Tonatiuh took in inflicting torture. After his failed rebellion a few months before, the Texcocan prince Cacama had been held prisoner in Axayacatl's palace. Believing that the upstart must have a cache of gold hidden somewhere, Alvarado had ordered cooking oil rubbed into the soles of his feet, which were then held to the fire. Despite shattering screams and humiliating pleas for mercy, no gold had been forthcoming. Cacama, who remained a prisoner, was a cripple now, and a shell of his former self.

Unconsciously stroking the bare sole and heel of his left foot, Moctezuma began to contemplate a third scenario in which, obeying his own profound intuition that something terrible was about to happen, he called off the attack at the last moment, the dances simply went ahead, he lived, he was not tortured, Tonatiuh lived, and everything continued as it had been before.

But the plan was a good one, and in a series of urgent and increasingly excited clandestine meetings since Malinche had left for the coast, Moctezuma had allowed himself to be persuaded by Cuitláhuac and

Teudile that it would work. Not since the day the *tueles* had first marched into Tenochtitlan had there been a better opportunity to destroy them. The garrison was now reduced to just one hundred and twenty men – admittedly under the formidable Tonatiuh – with the rest of Malinche's force scattered across the One World and about to be crushed by the much larger army of Nar-Vez.

Not that Nar-Vez was to be trusted! His promises were worthless, Cuitláhuac and Teudile had concluded. The only solution, and the sooner the better, was to destroy him too.

Above all, these *tueles* – these 'Spaniards' – must not be allowed to coalesce into a single large force united in a common purpose. Better to begin their destruction at once, therefore, while they were divided, with the total annihilation of the tiny garrison in Tenochtitlan. Then, after Malinche and Nar-Vez had sapped each other's strength in battle, the Mexica regiments would storm down out of the mountains and crush what was left of them.

As though sensing his inner doubt, his need for reassurance, Cuitláhuac and Teudile now requested entrance to Moctezuma's chambers.

'Everything is ready, sire,' said Cuitláhuac. 'All the six hundred nobles selected to perform the dance today are elite warriors. They've been prepared for the moment and know exactly what they must do. The weapons they'll use, their *macuahuitls* and spears, as well as hatchets and war clubs to arm the spectators, are all concealed around the sacred precinct and in the temple walls and stores.'

'And our Cuahchics?' asked Moctezuma. He had great faith in the warriors of this fearsome class – the best of the best.

'A full regiment of eight thousand, sire,' replied Cuitláhuac in a firm voice, 'to force their way into the plaza and overwhelm any resistance from the *tueles*. A larger number might be more impressive but less effective in so confined an area. More men, a hundred thousand, are in the city to lend support if it's needed.'

Moctezuma had to admit his brother was gaining stature every day! 'The eight thousand who will seize the *tueles* – how are they disposed?'

'They're divided into four companies of two thousand, sire, concealed in the houses and markets adjoining each of the four gates of the sacred precinct. At the instant our dancers begin their attack, Namacuix will blow his conch from the summit of the great pyramid and the Cuahchics will move in to smash Tonatiuh and all his *tueles* and his cursed arse-licking Tlascalans.'

'The *tueles* accepted our invitation, then?' Moctezuma asked. He could not keep the quaver of anxiety out of his voice.

'The formal invitation for Tonatiuh and all his soldiers to attend the Toxcatl celebrations as your guests was extended last night,' Teudile answered, 'and they've accepted. They'll join us in the sacred precinct at noon as the dancers begin to assemble. It's as though they're rabbits throwing themselves willingly into our snare! How convenient to have them with us early so we can overcome them in time to make them ready for sacrifice when the ceremony moves to the great pyramid and the temple of Hummingbird.'

Much encouraged, Moctezuma found his mind filled once again by the glorious scenario of the *tueles* smashed by his brave warriors. 'Very good!' he said. 'May the gods be with us and let us begin.'

He returned to his bedchamber, confirmed that the gilded war club and obsidian-edged *macuahuitl* sword that Teudile had smuggled in for him to defend himself with were still in their hiding places, then summoned his attendants to dress him.

'There's going to be a fight today and it's going to be bad,' Chipahua announced. 'Maybe we shouldn't have stirred things up.'

'It wouldn't have made any difference to the Mexica side of this,' said Shikotenka. 'They're going to go through with their plan whatever we do. Besides, the Spaniards are our allies. They're in great danger here and so are we. We had to warn them about the Mexica preparations. Cortés might have found a diplomatic solution, but Alvarado's not a subtle man and his way is violence . . .'

'Which suits us very well,' said Tree.

'Which suits us very well,' Shikotenka agreed. 'If Alvarado can pull off the massacre of six hundred nobles, then the Mexica will be so fatally weakened that with luck they'll not pose a threat to us again. It's even possible they may never be able to elect another leader.'

'There's Guatemoc,' Tree objected. 'He won't be amongst those they kill.'

'Yes, because he's not here!' Shikotenka shrugged. 'Gone with the wind up north somewhere, perhaps already killed by the Chichemecs . . .'

'Perhaps or perhaps not.'

'But either way not here, which is all we need to concern ourselves with for the moment. We'll deal with Guatemoc if and when we have to, but that shouldn't stop us from delivering a death blow to the Mexica elite now . . .'

'You mean shouldn't stop Tonatiuh from delivering it,' Chipahua observed.

'Yes, while we hold the gates against that mass of Cuahchics they've got hidden out in the town. It's going to be a stiff battle, I would say . . .'

'And you still don't want Tonatiuh to know you're here.'

'I prefer not.'

'It's as though they're pigs hurrying to the slaughterhouse,' said Alvarado to Rodrigo Manusco, his master-sergeant, as the dancers began to assemble in the forenoon of Tuesday 17 May. Sixty of the garrison had been left to guard Moctezuma and the expedition's store of treasure in the palace of Axayacatl; the other sixty were already sauntering amongst the dancers in the sacred precinct, as they'd been invited by the Great Speaker to do.

Though the first performance had not yet begun, the assembling dancers made a dramatic spectacle in their cloaks of rabbit fur and brightly coloured feathers. Their sandals, soled with deerskin and fastened with leather ties, were fashioned from ocelot skin. On their ankles they wore greaves, also of ocelot skin, from which many tiny golden bells were suspended. Their heads were clean-shaven except for topknots, to which they'd attached feather streamers. They wore necklaces of jade and of shells, gold bracelets on their upper arms, leather bands decorated with jade hanging from their wrists, glittering jewels in their nostrils, nose-pieces and ear-pieces of gold, labrets of amber and crystal. Most brandished long bundles of feathers.

The musicians were also assembling, with notes already being blown on flutes, bone fifes and conches. The drummers were taking their places. The air was filled with the smoky sweetness of copal incense.

Alvarado's nose was twitching, but it wasn't the incense, it was the danger. He could smell it on the air like blood, a sour tang. He could see its miasma radiating off each and every one of the dancers, read it in their painted, grimacing leers, in their filed teeth, in their bunched, oiled muscles, in their utter, alien strangeness. His hand itched to draw his falchion but not yet, not yet . . .

Alvarado wore light armour of cuirass and backplate to protect his upper body, cuisse and greaves to protect his legs. He carried his helmet, like all the other Spaniards. War was their purpose, and they were all armed to the teeth with swords, daggers and axes, but they didn't want to look too warlike yet. The Mexica were accustomed to seeing them walking about in armour with their weapons, but they did not usually wear their helmets. For the same reason they had left shields and pikes behind in the palace, but servants would bring those out to them when the killing began.

And Alvarado was very clear that it was going to be a killing that happened here, not a fight between equally matched sides.

A young lad called Mañuel whom he'd appointed as one of his three battlefield messengers now brought him the news that the four squads of ten men he'd posted to guard the four gates of the precinct – the Eagle Gate, the Gate of the Reed, the Jaguar Gate and the Gate of the Obsidian Serpent – were already in position. They were not there to keep additional attackers from outside from entering, for that would be the job of the Tlascalans, but to stop the noble dancers within from escaping the massacre . . .

Moctezuma was together in his quarters with Cuitláhuac and Teudile, watching from a window overlooking the sacred precinct. The two architects of the master plan for the destruction of the *tueles* had just declared their confidence that nothing could go wrong when the opening of the festival was signalled by a blare of conches and a roll of drums.

The six hundred dancers were primed, ready to give homage to the gods. They would complete the first dance, the Serpent dance now underway, and then as they launched into the Hummingbird dance, honouring Huitzilopochtli, half of them would fall bare-handed upon Tonatiuh and his men, beating them down, or at least holding them back by sheer numbers, while the other half rushed to collect their hidden weapons and admit the eight thousand Cuahchics poised outside the gates.

Ah, the Serpent dance! So beautiful! Singing in harmony, the sweet choruses rising and falling, rising and falling, the performers joined hands to form a continuous, sinuous line that swirled in spirals and concentric circles, now expanding, now contracting, around the big *huehuetl* drums. The fifes and conches blew madly. The little bells on the greaves of the dancers jingled.

Moctezuma had begun to savour the moment. How *few* the *tueles* looked as they mingled in ones and twos amongst the dancers, every one of whom was a skilled warrior. Surely, today at least, nothing could go wrong? He was rubbing his hands together in a high state of nervous glee, anticipating the massacre of the interlopers, until he saw Tonatiuh slowly and deliberately place his helmet on his head, draw his sword and shout an order: '*Mueran!*'

It meant, as he immediately understood from his Spanish lessons with Pepillo: 'Let them die.'

Suddenly Moctezuma realised that he had lost sight of many of the *tueles*. A glint at the Jaguar gate caught his eye. He squinted and saw ten of them, armoured, gleaming, standing round it. Their swords, too, were drawn.

At his ear Cuitláhuac gasped, and screams from below commanded Moctezuma's attention. Near the centre of the plaza a squad of twenty armoured *tueles* had rapidly coalesced around Alvarado to attack the noble dancers. The metal swords stabbed and hacked, blood gushed, limbs and heads flew.

There came a ferocious beating at the locked door, the crash of shoulders and boots against it, and it burst open. Eight evil-looking *tueles* entered, weapons drawn, teeth bared. 'Gentlemen,' one of them said, 'I'm afraid you'll have to come with us.'

Alvarado killed and killed again. He loved doing this! The way the heavy blade of the falchion could literally take a man apart, separate his head from his neck, his arm from his shoulder.

And there was barely any fight back!

This was unexpected, because the intelligence of an impending attack to be mounted by these very dancers, all of whom were supposedly warriors, had been convincing. Yet it seemed that most of them simply gave up and resigned themselves to death, as though they were willing sacrificial victims, the moment they themselves were attacked.

With his twenty, Alvarado rapidly carved his way through a great, packed, stinking, painted horde of them, leaving a trail of blood and entrails. His own brutal falchion and his men's swords and axes of Toledo steel had all been honed to a fine edge by the armourers this morning and cut through human flesh and bone as though they had no more substance than cheese.

Ahead lay a mob of screaming, terrified spectators, who'd been waving streamers and throwing confetti a moment ago, but now fled in a mass stampede towards the gates.

'*Mueran!*' yelled Alvarado, and charged in pursuit.

*   *   *

261

Shikotenka was wearing a full Tlascalan war helmet fashioned after the skull of a snarling jaguar. It disguised his face and in addition served the useful function of warding off blows – which he felt sure would soon be coming.

The first phase of the operation had begun with his squad still in barracks and under strict orders not to show themselves – lest they incite the ire of the crowd before the attack was underway. But now, with the body parts of slaughtered dancers littering the precinct, the demon – as the saying went – was out of the bag, so there was no need for further caution. Leaving a reserve of a hundred and fifty in the palace to support the small force of Spaniards there, he'd brought eight hundred and fifty of his Tlascalans out on to the plaza. They at once separated into four streams of two hundred each, heading for the gates to reinforce the Spaniards there, with a fifth group of fifty staying at the centre by Shikotenka's side and ready to do his bidding.

Now it became clear that while many of the dancers had preoccupied the Spaniards by passively allowing themselves to be killed, some of the others had not fled but instead had armed themselves from a hidden source and were returning looking for blood. Shikotenka saw one big Mexica strike a Spaniard in what should have been a killing blow to the chest, but because he was wearing armour, the properties of which the dancer seemed unfamiliar with, the teeth of the *macuahuitl* shattered harmlessly and in the next second the warrior was run through.

Still, there were enough of these returning dancers to cause a problem, and without hesitation Shikotenka launched himself into the fray with his fifty.

The Spaniards had killed several hundred, though not yet all, of the dancers, had thoroughly looted their bodies, and had mown down thousands of spectators – easy meat! – chopping them to pieces, running them through, hacking their heads off until a tide of blood filled the plaza.

All that was very good, but it was not, Alvarado now realised, where the real threat lay.

Proof that the Mexica had indeed conspired to kill him and his men came, according to reports brought by his messengers, in the form of thousands of Moctezuma's best troops presently attempting to stream into the plaza – all four of the gates had already been forced open and in two cases entirely ripped off their hinges. Were it not for the courage and martial skills of the Tlascalans, the attackers would easily have stormed through and might have destroyed the Spaniards.

Moreover, some of the surviving dancers within the plaza were now armed with obsidian-edged broadswords and war clubs, and this, too, meant a conspiracy. Not that they'd gain any ground because of it! Where they'd clashed with Spaniards they'd died, and now a force of fifty Tlascalans under a ferocious-looking fellow wearing a jaguar-skull helmet was systematically hunting them down and killing them.

There came a great shout from the Eagle gate, where a packed scrum of Tlascalan defenders was suddenly and decisively overrun by a huge surge of the attackers from outside the walls. Alvarado was aware of a strange moment when his eyes locked with the eyes of the Tlascalan warrior in the jaguar-skull helmet as they both summoned their squads and raced across the plaza towards the breach.

With the mopping up of the last of the armed dancers, effective opposition within the plaza had ceased, and the defence of three of the gates was also holding well. All would be in vain, however, if the breach at the Eagle gate were allowed to become a flood.

Alvarado and his twenty Spaniards were a little closer than Shikotenka, and hit the mass of the Cuahchics at a run, their shining swords slicing men into hunks of bloody meat as they cut deep into the enemy column, at least two hundred strong, that had forced its way into the plaza. Out of the corner of his eye, as he closed on the column with his fifty, Shikotenka saw with satisfaction that Tree had already retaken the gate with his squad and was holding it against renewed attacks from without.

Still, it was touch and go. Realising they were trapped in the plaza, the Cuahchics fought like madmen, and Shikotenka found himself locked in mortal combat with a muscular warrior who twice nearly took his head off with well-timed *macuahuitl* blows. He allowed the man to circle round again holding his own *macuahuitl* one-handed, moving the weapon constantly, forcing his opponent to watch it, until – *tac tac tac* – he stabbed him thrice in the neck with a short obsidian blade he'd kept concealed in his left hand. Then, as the Cuahchic stumbled he reached out, grabbed Shikotenka's helmet and wrested it from his head.

'*Shikotenka*,' the dying man shouted; his voice was surprisingly loud despite massive blood loss. '*This is Shikotenka, Prince of Tlascala! Take him!*'

With that he fell, choking, but the damage had been done. Looking

263

up, Shikotenka saw he was already surrounded by Cuahchics, maybe a dozen of them, functioning as a distinct unit within the larger column, and every one of them intent on his death.

He swung his *macuahuitl* low, took a man's leg off at the knee, sending him screaming to the ground, fouling the feet of others, and charged into the small gap thus created in their ranks, striking left and right, widening the way. A warrior was coming straight at him. Shikotenka jabbed the heavy wooden tip of his *macuahuitl* into his face, then cut down with the blade of the weapon, slitting his belly, spilling his guts.

The only hope was to keep moving ahead towards the gate – to be fought to a standstill in this melee would be to die – but Shikotenka knew he was badly outnumbered and the Cuahchics were real warriors, not peasants with weapons. There was no sign that any of his men had even noticed his predicament, and he could hardly blame them in the midst of so chaotic and ferocious a battle.

He was, he realised, as he parried a massive blow to his head, almost certainly going to die here. The Cuahchics were closing in on him; so close his *macuahuitl* was useless. He let it go – *tac, tac* – drew his second knife – *tac, tac, tac* – cutting and stabbing, biting somebody's face now, vaguely registering a jolt of pain in his thigh, another in his side, a thumb grinding into his eye, felt a brawny arm circle his throat, lashed out, stabbing its owner, and was released, a scream echoing in his ear.

Shikotenka thrust himself forward again, knowing he'd taken wounds and was losing blood. Five more Cuahchics piled on to him, tackling his legs, bringing him down. He was about to consign his soul to the underworld when he heard a furious roar, saw a glint of armour and then, like a whirlwind, Alvarado was upon them.

At first the big conquistador was alone as he cut the arms off the four men who were holding Shikotenka, beheaded another, smashed the hilt of his sword into another's groin, split a man's skull, but then five more Spaniards came bounding after him, their blades gleaming as they hacked the remaining Cuahchics to bloody ribbons.

Struggling to his feet, Shikotenka saw that Tree still held the gate, and heard the furious war cries, drums and conches of the thousands of Cuahchics beyond. He turned to Alvarado and said in Spanish: 'Thank you. That was well done.'

The conquistador raised his eyebrows. 'A surprise to find you here, Shikotenka. No one told me. And a surprise you speak our language.'

'Only a little.'

It was, Shikotenka thought, a bizarre conversation to be having, at this time and place.

'You fight like a Spaniard though!' Alvarado continued. It was clearly meant as a compliment. He narrowed his eyes: 'You remember our fight on the beach at Cuetlaxtlan?'

'I remember,' said Shikotenka.

'You fight damn well.'

'And you, too, Señor Alvarado.'

The conquistador grinned, and it wasn't entirely nice. 'One day we'll have another bout, man to man, blade to blade,' he said. He patted Shikotenka on the shoulder: 'But not yet, eh? We've got a war to win. You're wounded I see.'

'Flesh wounds only, I think.'

'I'll have our doctor La Peña take a look at you when we get back to quarters.'

Within the hour, because the perimeter of the sacred precinct with its four gates was far too long and porous for such a small force to defend, Alvarado accepted the inevitable and led a fighting retreat across the plaza to the heavily fortified place of Axayacatl. As he and the exhausted column of Spaniards and Tlascalans approached, their countrymen who'd been left in reserve swarmed out to meet them, giving them safe passage into the fortress and firing two falconets loaded with shot into the oncoming Mexica ranks, slaughtering hundreds and bringing them to a halt immediately.

Once all were within, the great gates of the palace barred and patrols posted on the walls and roofs, Alvarado had some moments alone. He was not a reflective man; he knew that. He was a man of action and he had taken decisive action today.

The problem, however, was that the action appeared to have failed.

Its purpose had been to make the Mexica docile by killing their leaders, but the opposite had happened: the Mexica had risen and now the conquistadors were confined to the palace, which they might not even be able to defend, with limited food and also – more alarmingly – limited water.

Through the thick walls there carried the distant furious screams of a great crowd of warriors, and the repeated crashes of a battering ram smashing against the massive doors of the palace. A sortie in force would be required to drive the attackers back and four falconets, loaded with grapeshot, should keep them back.

As Alvarado summoned his picked men, an unwelcome thought crossed his mind. Had the massacre perhaps been a terrible mistake?

Certainly it would have been much more easily explained to Cortés if it had succeeded.

Two days after Toxcatl, Moctezuma, Cuitláhuac and Teudile remained imprisoned in the insalubrious quarters they'd been dragged to, which turned out to be those already occupied by poor, tortured Cacama and more than twenty other rebellious chiefs and vassals who'd fallen foul of Cortés during the past few months. It was not a dungeon – there were skylights high above – but it was cramped, dirty and uncomfortable.

The humiliation of being treated as though he were no better than a common felon, and compelled to bear such crowded conditions, was too much for the Great Speaker, and he withdrew into sullen contemplation, eating little of the foul food provided, making his toilet in a dank corner with as much decorum as he could muster, and refusing to talk to anyone. He heard the sounds of war from outside the palace, the roar of the cannon, the faint screams and battle cries, and knew that his people in their hundreds of thousands had come to rescue him. Yet no matter how furious the assault, it seemed they could not break through.

The night of Toxcatl passed with no let-up in the distant tumult, but there was a long lull the next day, broken only by the sounds of the gruff-voiced *tueles* moving urgently around the corridors of the palace, rearranging things and – judging only from the sounds – knocking a hole in a wall here, building a barricade there.

The other prisoners fruitlessly discussed what this might mean. The fools! How could they know when they were locked in here and given absolutely no information at all about what was happening outside?

A second night passed, almost entirely without fighting, but torn by a vast hullabaloo of wails and screams as the mourning for those killed in the Toxcatl massacre began. The lamentation, which should have begun the night before but must have been delayed because of the fighting, was so immense and so widespread that it clearly involved the entire city.

How many had been killed?

Around noon on the second day after the massacre, after more sounds of fighting in the morning, the door of the prison was flung open and a strong guard of ten *tueles* entered with Tonatiuh at their fore. Even in the half-light it was obvious the golden-haired captain was exhausted. His face was covered in grey dust, there was blood on his shirt and his head was bandaged.

He walked directly to where Moctezuma sat and extended a hand to him. 'Come, Excellency,' he said through the interpreter Aguilar. 'It is not fitting that a great one such as you should be confined in a mean place like this.'

As Tonatiuh helped him to his feet, Moctezuma felt a surge of gratitude. His instinct was to thank the captain for his kindness. Mindful of the eyes of Cuitláhuac and the others upon him, however, he resisted the urge, blinked back tears, and allowed himself to be led from the room with quiet dignity.

Once in the spacious corridor overlooking the palace gardens, filled with barricades and traps and protected by a large cannon, Moctezuma was seized by an expansive sense of joy and freedom. It was a relief to see the door closed and barred on the other prisoners and to know he would no longer have to bear the judgemental stares of Teudile and Cuitláhuac or the injured hate of Cacama.

As they walked, Tonatiuh took him by the arm and said without preamble: 'We imprisoned you, for your own safety, before it had properly begun, so I imagine you'll be wanting to know what happened on Toxcatl.'

'I only know that there has been great loss of life.'

'All caused by you I'm afraid, Lord Moctezuma. If you hadn't incited your people to arm themselves against us and try to kill us, none of this would have happened.'

'How many died?'

'On our side, some injuries – ' he gestured to his head – 'but no Spaniards killed. We did lose some of our Tlascalans, though.'

'And amongst the Mexica?'

'Oh . . . quite a few.'

'How many? I beg you to tell me.'

'Well . . . let's see. Pretty much all of your dancers, so that would be, what, around six hundred? Then there were the spectators. It was hard to count, but we think we killed more than six thousand of them. They've been dragging the bodies out of the plaza for the past couple of days. Still plenty left, though.'

Moctezuma was filled with awe. Six thousand of his people, and six hundred of his leading nobles, all murdered in a single afternoon *and in the precinct of the war god.*

Could this be something, in some unknowable way, that Hummingbird *wanted*?

Was it a sacrifice?

And would the god speak to him again?

As these thoughts flitted through his mind, distracting him, Moctezuma found that Tonatiuh had ushered him back to his own sumptuous quarters, where all his usual conveniences awaited him.

'Don't think of trying to escape,' the captain said. 'We've got scouts on the roof watching the walls outside your quarters, so no one's going to get a ladder up to you, and two of my men will always be at your door. But other than that – ' a yawn – 'we want you to be comfortable . . . Oh – ' he indicated a grizzled elder, Ollin by name, who crouched on the floor – 'and we thought you'd like to hear the record of what happened . . . To bring you up to date.'

Ollin was a Daykeeper, one of the learned college of scribes, astronomers and mathematicians who watched the omens, made the calculations, observed the stars and kept the records of any notable events that had occurred within the borders of the empire. The events of Toxcatl, in the heart of Tenochtitlan, in the sacred plaza itself, were certainly notable; indeed could only be regarded as amongst the most notable ever to have occurred to the Mexica. They would have been set down on a painted mantle, and Moctezuma saw that Ollin – whose name meant 'Movement' – had such a mantle rolled on the floor beside him.

As Tonatiuh and the other Spaniards quietly left the room, closing the door behind them, Moctezuma, in too much haste to wash or change his prison-soiled clothes, sat on his stool and indicated that Ollin should present the mantle, which was duly laid out.

The imagery of slaughter was utterly terrible, too awful to behold. Instinctively Moctezuma averted his eyes. And yet . . . and yet . . . If it were truly an offering required by Hummingbird, then was it not worthy? There could be no doubt, at least, that here was a sacrifice that had cost the Mexica dear. Perhaps it would be enough to satisfy the war god?

Dense rows of hieroglyphs accompanied each of the paintings and spiralled all the way round the mantle, filling every vacant space. 'Read,' Moctezuma commanded.

Ollin coughed to clear his throat, then proclaimed the preamble: '*In which it is told how the Spaniards slew the Mexica, destroyed them, when they celebrated the feast of Huitzilopochtli on the day of Toxcatl . . .*'

'Get on with it, man,' said Moctezuma wearily and, declaiming in a strong, steady voice, Ollin began:

'When already the feast was being observed, when already there was dancing, when already there was singing, when already there was song with the dance, the singing resounded like waves breaking.

'When it was already time, when the moment was opportune for the Spaniards to slay them, thereupon they came forth. They were arrayed for battle. They came everywhere to block each of the ways leading in and out. And when they had blocked them they also remained everywhere. No one could go out.

'And when this had been done, thereupon they entered the sacred plaza to slay them. Those whose task it was to slay them went only on foot, each one with his shining metal sword and his shining metal lance. Thereupon they surrounded the dancers. Thereupon they went amongst the drums. Then they struck the drummer's arms; they severed both his hands; then they struck his neck. Far off did his neck and head go to fall.

'Then they all pierced them, each with their metal lances and they struck them each with metal swords. Of some they slashed open their backs. Of some they cut their heads to pieces; they absolutely pulverised their heads; their heads were absolutely pulverised.

'And some they struck on the shoulder; they split openings, they broke openings in their bodies. Of some they struck repeatedly the shanks; of some they struck the belly; then their entrails gushed forth. And when one in vain would run, he would only drag his intestines like something raw as he tried to escape. Nowhere could he go. And him who tried to go out they there struck; they stabbed him.

'But some climbed the wall; they were able to escape. Some entered the House of Darkness and the House of the Eagle Knights and other sacred buildings around the plaza; there they escaped. And some escaped by disguising themselves among the dead. They got in amongst those really dead but only feigning to be dead. They were able to escape. But if one took a breath, if the Spaniards saw him, they stabbed him.

'And the blood of the brave warriors ran like water; it was as if it lay slippery. And a foul odour rose and spread out from the blood. And the intestines were as if dragged out. And the Spaniards went everywhere as they searched the buildings. Everywhere they went, making thrusts as they searched, in case someone had taken refuge. They went everywhere. They went taking to pieces all places in the buildings as they searched.

'And when the massacre became known thereupon there was shouting: "Oh brave warriors of the Mexica hasten here! Let there be arraying – the devices, the shields, the arrows! Come! Hasten here! Already they have died, they have perished, they have been annihilated, O Mexica, O brave warriors!"

'Thereupon there was an outcry, already there was shouting, there was shrieking, with hands striking the lips. Quickly there was a marshalling of forces; it was as if the brave warriors each were determined; they bore the arrows and the shields with them.

'Thereupon there was fighting. They shot at them with arrows with barbed points, with spears, and with tridents. And they cast at them barb-pointed arrows with broad obsidian points. It was as if a mass of deep yellow reeds spread over the Spaniards who retreated to the palace of Axayacatl. They barricaded themselves within. They resisted our brave warriors.'

Ollin looked up. He had read all the words.

'And now?' Moctezuma barked. He craned forward impatiently, hungry for tidings. 'Two days have passed since Toxcatl! What's happening now?'

'The Spaniards still resist, great Moctezuma. The resistance holds.'

'And who leads our men?'

'The captains of our regiments have done what they can, lord, yet many of our great ones died in the massacre, Cuitláhuac and Cacama are imprisoned, and Guatemoc is gone we know not where. In the streets it is said that only you can lead, yet you are here, so the hope is to free you. Many attempts have been made to storm the palace; all have failed.'

'You are a wise man, Ollin, renowned for your divination. Why do you think Tonatiuh released me from the prison and returned me to my quarters?'

'It is not a natural act for him, sire. It is easy for him to keep you in the prison but here he is put to much inconvenience. He must assign extra guards when his force is already small. I divine you will learn, O great Moctezuma, that Tonatiuh very badly wants something that only you can grant.'

Chapter Fifteen

Friday 20 May 1520–Thursday 26 May 1520

Alvarado woke on the morning of Friday 20 May still furious at the lengths he'd been driven to and at the pretence he'd been required to maintain. He loathed to ask any favour of that cur Moctezuma, but the plain reality was that circumstances might soon force him to do so. That was why he'd released the Great Speaker from prison yesterday, 19 May, and allowed him to move back to his own comfortable apartments. 'It would be wise to let him be informed, by his own people, of what has happened,' Master-Sergeant Manusco had suggested, 'so that he can gain a full understanding of what we're capable of.' It had sounded like good advice, and so Alvarado had given consent for Moctezuma to be presented with the account of the events of Toxcatl that had been prepared by the temple Daykeepers, even though Aguilar's prior translation of it revealed – predictably – that it portrayed the Mexica as innocent victims and said nothing of their own preparations to attack and destroy the Spaniards.

What the account did do, however, as Manusco had foreseen, was vividly to confirm the ease with which a tiny band of determined Spaniards had butchered a multitude; Alvarado had not been exaggerating when he'd told Moctezuma that the slain exceeded six thousand. He wanted the Mexica leader to grasp the meaning of this in a most visceral way – that the Spaniards were not ordinary mortals. They were *tueles*. They were gods. No matter how large, no matter how sustained, they could destroy any force thrown against them.

After all, and Alvarado was very proud of it, his men on the plaza that day, admittedly aided by the Tlascalans, had numbered just sixty but had killed more than six thousand – an average of one hundred per man. Surely even Moctezuma wasn't so dim that he couldn't reckon up the odds? And surely there must be some captain amongst the regiments outside the walls who'd seen what had happened in the plaza and who would realise the terrible slaughter that would ensue if the Spaniards in their palace fortress were ever really seriously pressed.

Because so far, although there had been some tight moments, Alvarado would not characterise the attacks on the palace as truly serious. They'd been brave, screaming, uncoordinated assaults with hundreds, sometimes thousands, at a time, throwing themselves upon the guns and being cut to pieces, but again and again they'd not been sufficiently well organised or sustained to overwhelm his very thinly stretched defenders.

Was it, as the Tlascalans maintained, that the city, preoccupied with mourning for its lost ones, was simply containing the Spaniards with these skirmishes until it was ready to fall upon them with all its might?

Or was this all they had?

On the evening of Friday 20 May, after a forced march of a hundred miles made hazardous by vertiginous passes and heavy, almost unremitting, rainfall, having covered about half the distance to Perote, the army reached Orizaba where the downpour showed no sign of ceasing. Making a virtue of necessity, Cortés decided to pause and take stock.

His first act was to compose a formal letter to Narváez, with a copy for the record to be held secure by Pepillo. Other than goading his enemy further, the purpose of the letter was to provide Cortés with legal justification for the military action that he regarded as unavoidable.

My dear Don Pánfilo

Forgive me for being brief, but you are here in these New Lands that I have conquered and have made certain claims, including arrogating to yourself the titles captain-general and *justicia mayor*. You have sent various embassies and messages to me in which these titles have been repeated, and you have demanded that I surrender myself to you, but, despite my own repeated requests, you have produced no royal commission nor any evidence that you are here on the special orders of His Caesarean Majesty the King.

If you can produce such commission or orders, signed by the king himself, then well and good. If not, then I require you to desist at once from naming yourself either captain-general or *justicia mayor*, and I likewise require you, on pain of condign punishment, not to attempt to exercise any of the functions of those offices.

I therefore command, Don Pánfilo, that you present yourself to me and explain yourself. Know that if you do not do so I shall be left with no choice but to proceed against you with all the force at my disposal.

The letter was carried by Rodrigo Alvarez Chico, one of Cortés's Extremeño friends, and with him – since civil war as well as conquest was governed by law – went Diego de Godoy, the expedition's notary. It was Godoy, after all, whose responsibility it was to read aloud the *Requerimiento* that legitimised battle before every engagement with the Indians. Right and proper, then, that Godoy should be present for this legal manoeuvre as well.

The following day, Saturday 21 May, with Chico and Godoy well on their way, a letter arrived from Narváez, once again in the hands of Guevara, who returned, as he had left, accompanied by Cortés's book-keeper Santos Jimenez and his grey mare. With horses in short supply, the latter was a particularly welcome sight. As to Guevara, he was now thoroughly Cortés's man, bought and paid for. The venal priest, anxious to curry further favours, was plainly embarrassed as he presented Narváez's letter.

'Do you know what it says?' Cortés asked before breaking the seal.

'I do, Caudillo. It's a ridiculous proposal, of course. Despite his bluster, though, I think it's a sign the man is afraid of you.'

Cortés opened and quickly skimmed the letter. He laughed: 'I see what you mean.'

First there were the expected insults and threats: that Narváez was the legitimate captain-general while Cortés was an imposter and a traitor who would be punished, and that Cortés must surrender himself immediately to Narváez and acknowledge his paramount authority in the land or face attack with 'overwhelming force'.

Then, however, came a new approach. If Cortés hoped to avoid the just retribution that was about to descend upon him, then Captain-General Narváez had a proposal that he might be advised to consider. It was extremely simple. Cortés would surrender the entire country to Narváez without further contest, and in return Narváez would guarantee safe conduct to the coast for Cortés, and those of his men who wished to accompany him, and ships in which they might make their escape to wherever they chose to go.

'He can't be serious!' Cortés exclaimed.

'He is clutching at straws, Caudillo. He prefers to bully you rather than fight you. But if you cannot be bullied,' Guevara lowered his voice and leaned closer, 'then his plan is to have you murdered.'

'Ha! And how will he do that?'

'He has asked me to propose, unofficially as it were, that you meet with him, Caudillo – to discuss your differences "as gentlemen", as he puts it.'

'Whatever Narváez is,' Cortés spluttered, 'he's certainly no gentleman!'

'He and his inner clique of officers have planned it this way. They have selected a location some leagues from Cempoala. There is a hill there where they wish the meeting to take place. First safe conducts will be exchanged, then you with an escort of ten picked men will go to that hill and Narváez will do the same. But it will be a trap. Two champions from Narváez's escort will attack you and attempt to kill you on the spot while the others keep your men at bay . . .'

'My men won't be kept at bay!' Cortés said.

'Narváez believes he has foreseen that. A blast is to be sounded from a trumpet the moment the attack on you begins. It will be heard in a coppice on the other side of the hill where Jean Yuste will be waiting with twenty more men. They'll ride in and finish you all off.'

'Jean Yuste?'

'Our captain of cavalry. Not a bad man. An efficient officer. He doesn't like Narváez and he doesn't like this plan, but when the day comes he'll obey orders.'

Cortés embraced Guevara: 'Thank you for being the bearer of this invitation, Father, and for your warning as to its intent. It's said that discretion is sometimes the better part of valour, so I believe I shall avoid this murderous meeting! Besides, Narváez and I have nothing to talk about that can't be resolved on the battlefield.'

Alvarado slept in his armour, as did all the men in the rare intervals when they could snatch a rest, so he didn't need to dress when he was awakened around mid-morning on Monday 23 May by panicked shouts and alarms. After two days and nights of continuous duty, he had allowed himself to fall asleep less than an hour before, and had plunged into blissful dark dreamlessness when the faint sounds of fighting reached him and he was at once alert.

Since the massacre, Alvarado had kept a strong forward guard of swordsmen posted in the plaza in front of the main doors of palace, supported by four falconets to rake any attackers with grapeshot. Now he learned from a panicked and gasping messenger that a sudden concerted incursion by thousands of Mexica warriors had overwhelmed the guard and gun crews. They had withdrawn behind the great double doors of the palace, saving all four of the falconets at the cost of two lives, and now battering rams hammered against the doors as they had last done six days previously.

In tandem a massed onslaught with scaling ladders had been launched against the eastern wall of the southwestern elevation of the palace, where it overlooked the plaza. From there the attackers might gain access to the palace's flat merloned roof and, through the windows and balconies, to every part of the interior. A mixed force of Spaniards and Tlascalans was holding them back with great difficulty and calling for reinforcements.

Alvarado kept a squad of thirty conquistadors – the membership rotated every two days – permanently in reserve to throw into battle where they were most needed. Behind the messenger he registered their grim presence in the corridor awaiting his command.

'Let's go, lads,' he said. He sent ten men up to the roof and ten more to reinforce the guards on the great doors now so thunderingly under attack. The last ten he took with him down to the southern end of the palace, where the sounds of fighting were intense on the second floor with its vast reception hall overlooking the plaza and the great pyramid.

Bursting into the wide, high-ceilinged room at the head of his little squad, Alvarado saw immediately what had happened. Attackers on scaling ladders had torn the shutters off many of the windows and entered in force, half naked, painted, sweating, brandishing their crude stone weapons, before the guard squad – just five Spaniards and five Tlascalans! – had been able to engage them. Now, with a bridgehead won inside the room, many more warriors were swarming up the ladders and pouring through the windows. Three of the Spanish defenders were already down, despite their armour, along with four of the Tlascalans. The two remaining Spaniards and lone Tlascalan were ringed by at least thirty perspiring, glistening, sour-smelling Mexica warriors, wielding their obsidian-edged swords that could take a man's head off at a single blow, or leg off at the hip. They were mercifully ineffective against armour but the Mexica were beginning to learn this, going for weak points such as the ankles, under-arms and neck with increasing success.

'*Santiago and at 'em!*' Alvarado yelled. He wore cuirass, backplates, cuisse and greaves and had donned his helmet on leaving his quarters, but disdained a shield against the stone weapons of the Mexica. He preferred to fill both his hands with blades, his falchion in his right and a long quillon dagger in his left.

With his little squad bunched tightly around him, he hit the intruders eagerly, at a dead run, stabbed a man in the neck with the dagger and brought the falchion smashing down on another warrior's head, snapping his wrist up at the last moment so the heavy blade killed him at that single stroke but didn't get stuck in his skull.

Two warriors, the shaven-headed scum they called Cuahchics, were circling him now, three others visible out of the corner of his eye pressing in from every side; but it was an art, the melee, and Alvarado was like quicksilver, sliding around his opponents, until . . . *Whack* – a man's head suddenly parted from his shoulders; *Whack* – off came an arm; *Whack, Whack* – ribs shattered here, a leg half severed there. '*It's a fucking art!*' Alvarado yelled. He shoulder-charged a dense knot of four Indians and allowed the men next to him to strike them down as they stumbled.

His own target lay dead ahead – tall, older than most, with a silly plume stuck to his painted bald pate identifying him as a captain. Alvarado leapt the last few yards that separated him from the officer, meeting him blade to blade as he swung round with a snarl. The falchion hacked a great splinter out of the hardwood of the unfortunate man's sword and slid down to strip off half of its obsidian teeth before cleanly amputating the fingers of both his hands where they gripped its long hilt. As the warrior dropped the weapon, gazing in disbelief at his bleeding stumps, Alvarado stepped in close and thrust the long blade of his quillon dagger into his beating heart, savagely twisted it, and relished the suction, like a virgin's cunt on his cock, as he withdrew.

Within seconds, with the initial wave of intruders entirely overrun and the second wave smashed, Alvarado led the charge for the windows through which dozens more Indians continued to pour. Amidst grunts, roars and the clash of weapons, a desperate struggle ensued. Some ladders and the men climbing them were thrust down on to the immense howling crowd pressing against the walls below, but others were immediately raised to replace them. Despite a continuous shower of crossbow bolts from above, the climbers kept on coming!

Just as Alvarado was considering the implications of those crossbow bolts – who was firing them? – the ten men he'd sent up to the roof charged into the room and tipped the balance of the struggle at the windows. After that it was just a mopping-up operation, and soon the last of the climbers had been repelled, the last of the ladders thrown down and the carpenters called to secure the windows again.

The roof, it seemed, was commanded by a mixed squad of crossbowmen and musketeers who'd hurried up there on their own initiative as soon as the attack began. It provided a fine platform to fire down on the crowd and was itself still too high to be reached by the scaling ladders of the Indians.

'Still?'

'They're getting longer, sir, haven't you noticed?'

Alvarado thought on it. The Indians' scaling ladders were indeed getting longer. He had noticed, and soon they might be able to reach the roof. The crossbowmen and musketeers working up there were doing a good job, but there weren't enough of them to hold back the tide for ever. Not for the first time he found himself wishing for a technical innovation that would allow the barrels of the garrison's cannon to be depressed sufficiently to fire grapeshot from the vantage point of the roof into the massed attackers in the square. That would clear some ground double quick but was, unfortunately, an impossible dream. Indeed, the only way he could see to end the impasse in the Spaniards' favour was to force the attackers back sufficiently to get an array of cannon out in front of the palace again and enfilade the entire sacred precinct.

An evil thought was taking shape in Alvarado's mind, and he liked it. Indeed, he liked it so much that within ten minutes he'd shared it with Shikotenka – it was a blessing from God that the Tlascalan battle-king was here – and with Telmo Vendabal, the expedition's dog handler. After that he sent a messenger to fetch him a bugle to carry into battle, and summoned his most experienced cavaliers to armour and mount up with him on the eight great destriers Cortés had left with them.

While the horses were being barded at the stables, he ordered Vendabal to do his worst.

'Not all the dogs will come back, Don Pedro,' the ugly little hunchback warned. 'When we call, some will come but some will stay to feed.'

'I don't care. They're used to working with cavalry, aren't they, and if they're not we'll just ride them down with the Mexica scum they're in amongst.'

The dogs were hungry.

They'd been kept on quarter rations – and that sliced from the bodies of dead Indians – since the beginning of the siege six days before. There were more than seventy of them, huge mastiffs and wolfhounds with massive jaws and shoulders, straining at their leashes before the towering

277

doors of the palace which still shuddered with the blows of the battering ram.

A squad of burly soldiers had unbolted, and now with grunts of effort lifted away, the heavy sheet of beaten copper that braced the little wicket gate set low down into the side of the right-hand door. At a nod from Alvarado, Vendabal slipped the wicket open. Grimacing Indians at once appeared in the gap, surged to thrust through, but were smashed back by a volley fired at point-blank range by six musketeers. On Alvarado's command six more musketeers and six crossbowmen stepped forward over the dead, streamed through the wicket, and fired a second volley into the advancing crowd. They were followed at speed by twenty heavily armoured swordsmen, who attacked the battering ram crews, forcing them to drop the huge tree trunk and flee. That accomplished, the swordsmen regrouped to form a defensive cordon flung out in a semi-circle a few paces in front of the gates.

Then the hounds were released, yipping and snarling in anticipation.

Alvarado stayed at the wicket for a moment to glimpse the beginning of the slaughter. The dogs were trained to kill Indians and were all armoured, some with mail, some with plate. It would be extremely diffi-cult for men equipped only with crude stone weapons to fight them off. Besides, unlike the Tlascalans, against whom they'd been deployed the year before, the Mexica had absolutely no experience of dealing with the fearsome animals – which they'd been encouraged to believe were the *tueles'* dragons.

Gruesome screams erupting from all parts of the plaza were music to Alvarado's ears as he ran to the stables and mounted Bucephalus. Minutes later he thundered back to the palace gates with his little troop of riders raising clouds of dust in the courtyard.

Master-Sergeant Manusco was still at the wicket, and reported no enemy now pressing close. The dogs were working them and had driven them far enough back to allow the great gateway to be opened safely.

'Do it!' said Alvarado.

Slowly the towering copper-studded mahogany doors were swung back, each one requiring a team of five Tlascalans to shift it, revealing a hellish scene . . .

'Call in the hounds!' Alvarado commanded, but many of the beasts were feeding, despite the arrows and spears and stone knives of the Indians, and there was almost no response to the whistles of the handlers.

Unable to restrain himself any longer, Alvarado trotted Bucephalus a few paces forward through the defensive cordon, searching for the place to hit where the press of Indians was densest. As the swordsmen made way, the seven other horsemen ranged themselves on either side of him, forming a single straight line of cavaliers, the iron-shod hooves of their destriers ringing on the paving, the steel armour of mounts and men gleaming in the blazing noonday sun.

Alvarado's falchion sprang into his hand and he was already spurring Bucephalus, sensing the other riders do the same.

'*Mueran!*'

With Chipahua and Tree, Shikotenka stood at the head of four hundred Tlascalans, half of his surviving force – for close to a hundred had died keeping the Cuahchics at bay on Toxcatl, and a hundred more had been lost in the fighting since.

'*Mueran!*'

Even as Alvarado yelled his battle cry, Shikotenka urged his men forward. Unless in the utmost extremity, they were not to participate in the attack, for there was a real possibility that war dogs remaining in the plaza – and many still feasted upon the Mexica fallen – would turn upon the Tlascalans as well. As he'd been commanded, Shikotenka therefore drew his men up in front of the yawning gates, ready to hold them against all-comers.

The initial Spanish skirmishers had all returned to the palace, but hidden behind the Tlascalans, framed in the gateway itself, stood a troop of thirty conquistadors in six ranks of five. Metal-clad, their faces barely human beneath their helms, they were armed with diverse instruments of butchery – war-hammers, axes, billhooks, cutlasses, poniards and spears. Their purpose was not military confrontation, for it was not expected that the Mexica would be able to regroup in the next moments, but the simple mass slaughter of enemies already downed and disoriented by the cavalry.

Behind the foot soldiers the gun crews waited – six crews with six of the wicked small artillery pieces they called falconets, and a seventh larger crew with the long-barrelled lombard gun. All, Shikotenka knew, were packed with the little balls of metal and stone called grapeshot.

Chipahua grinned through his broken teeth. 'It's always instructive to watch the Spaniards do what they do best,' he said admiringly, surveying the shambles ahead where dogs feasted on the entrails of the Mexica dead and of the howling, horrified living. Today's attack had been mounted by a crack Cuahchic regiment, renowned for their discipline, yet many amongst the rearmost ranks, pushed back close to the west flank of the great pyramid, seeing what they believed were armoured dragons on the loose and sensing disaster, were already in full-scale, terrified flight. Amidst shouts and wails they could be seen streaming off around the pyramid's south and north faces, where they spread chaos amongst crowds of their own reinforcements.

Meanwhile, at the front, around each of those whom the hounds had fallen upon, other warriors broke ranks in desperate, largely impotent attempts to kill the animals or drive them off. The result, as the Spaniards with their vast experience of war had designed from the outset, was that the massed impetus and cohesion of what just moments before had been the most effective Mexica assault yet, was utterly and irrevocably smashed.

'Mueran!'

Into the densest part of the crumbling ruin of the Cuahchic regiment, the Spanish charge now crashed, an avalanche of horsemen moving at colossal speed – twice as fast as any human could run – their hooves striking thunder and lightning from the paving stones, the great weight of their armour, the momentum of their onslaught and the flashing blades of their whirling swords transforming them into an irresistible, almost supernatural force.

Indeed, it was as though some monstrous harvest of the gods was underway. Men were trampled and scattered in all directions; heads and arms struck off like ears of corn; blood foaming and fountaining from the severed arteries of a hundred dismembered bodies as the Spanish troop hacked a wide, bloody path through the crowd of several thousand Mexica who'd been gathered in front of the palace.

Those fucking Mexica – curse them for their wickedness and their arrogance, Shikotenka thought – had absolutely no idea what they were up against!

The stink of blood rose up from the plaza in a great wave and, as the charge passed entirely through the moiling enemy ranks, close to the western stairway of the great pyramid, the Spanish horsemen split into two files – four of them circling back around the northern edge of what was now a panicking rabble, and four circling south. This was the signal for the foot soldiers hidden behind the Tlascalan ranks to advance, and Shikotenka ordered his Tlascalans to draw aside, a block of two hundred to the left, a block of two hundred to the right, to give them passage.

The Spanish infantry came on at a run, with a great roar of exultation, and were through on to the plaza in an instant as the guns behind them were rapidly trundled out and drawn into place in the gap between the two blocks of Tlascalan warriors.

Shikotenka could feel the pressure as many of his braves pushed forward, already yelling their ululating war cries, eager to take part in the slaughter, but he barged and slapped them back into formation. 'No! Today we guard the gates and guns, nothing more!'

It was what he had agreed with Alvarado and he would stick with it.

Tree was mutinous, swinging his huge club. 'I'm here to break Mexica heads, not do sentry duty.'

'Another day,' Chipahua said, laying a restraining hand on his friend's muscular forearm. 'But now we obey orders and let the Spaniards do what they do.'

'Bah!' Tree shook his arm loose. 'You're a couple of old women.'

But he kept his rank, his club resting on his shoulder, glaring out at the slaughtered and the slaughterers.

Alvarado led the file of four cavalrymen sweeping around the northern edge of the now hysterical and stampeding Mexica, as the armoured block of thirty foot soldiers stormed into the bloody gash through their centre that the riders had carved moments before. On the heels of the infantry came Telmo Vendabal and his gang of handlers with whips, chains and leashes, forcing the half-crazed dogs still at work upon the Indians to disengage and slink back through the palace gates where they were rapidly corralled and confined.

Lost in the ecstasy of murder, Alvarado felt the blossoming of an almost godlike confidence in his own prowess.

Damn, he was good!

And up here on Bucephalus, it was as though nothing could touch him: not the occasional stone-tipped arrows that bounced harmlessly off his cuirass and backplate; not the warriors who reached desperately, like drowning men, to draw him down; not the spear that came flying at him in a blur and that he slapped away with the blade of his falchion. He loved the perspective from the back of the rearing, prancing twenty-hand destrier, the furious, screaming, painted faces swarming round his knees, the shaved, unprotected scalps, the sweating near-nakedness of the warriors' bodies – and the height, speed and leverage to pound them all to bloody meat and splinters of bone.

He rose in his saddle, swung his blade in a beautiful arc, felt it slice through the soft flesh of an oncoming warrior's neck, sensed the jolt and slight slowing as it severed his spine, and then the tremendous release of the follow-through as the blade burst free, taking the head clean off amidst a spattering gush of hot blood.

He charged on, his saddle and cuirass drenched in the other man's gore, took another head, split a skull to the chin and almost lost his falchion, saw two warriors trying to escape and trampled them down. All the other riders were doing the same, playing their part in the plan, rounding up the enemy, driving them in full flight towards the centre and on to the blades of the execution squad there.

Alvarado was reluctant to stop taking heads. He really was having the most enjoyable and absorbing time! He felt . . . drunk! But with huge numbers of Mexica reinforcements still entering the square and throwing themselves into the throng, everything was now in place for the final phase of the battle.

Many years had passed since Alvarado had last blown a bugle, but it was one of those skills you didn't forget. He snatched the instrument to his lips and sounded a long, shrill blast.

It was, Shikotenka decided, as much the coordination and fierce discipline of the Spaniards that brought them success in battle as it was their war animals and their superior weaponry.

That bugle-blast blown by Alvarado initiated a rapid but entirely orderly and obviously well-planned retreat in which the infantry squad withdrew behind the guns while the eight cavalrymen rode back and forth in front of the field of slaughter, taunting the Mexica reinforcements, who already outnumbered the dead and were gathering in fury amongst the shattered corpses.

Finally, with a mocking wave, Alvarado led the cavalry back through the gates to the palace courtyard and, after the clamour and the clash, the battle cries of the warriors and the screams of the dying, a moment of silence fell as each side regarded the other across the dead.

'Now they're really fucked,' Chipahua said gravely. He didn't mean the Spaniards.

They all knew what was coming. Shikotenka pushed a set of cotton plugs into his ears. Chipahua and Tree and most of the rest of the men were doing the same. The gunners were busy around the cannon.

Out through the palace gates, now on foot, his armour painted with blood, sauntered Alvarado.

He nodded to Shikotenka and to the gunners, stepped to the fore through the line of artillery and then – typical Alvarado this! – just stood there, his hands on his hips, his mane of blond hair, released from his helm and now falling to his shoulders, making him the very image of Tonatiuh, the sun. There was not a man in the crowd of thousands who didn't know, or hadn't been told, who he was – that ever-growing, turbulent crowd, which seemed to sprout up like some vast unnatural crop out of the field of the dead and that now surged towards him.

Shikotenka knew they were yelling in fury from the distorted grimaces on their faces, but the ear plugs blocked out much of the background noise.

He did hear what Alvarado said, though, as he sauntered back behind the guns.

'*Mueran!*'

At once the seven cannon opened up, blasting an immense propagating wave of death and destruction across the wide front of the crowd, grape-shot whistling through them, mowing them down in rows, stripping flesh from bones and tearing men to shreds as though they were paper. A big clump of the load from the lombard crashed at about head height against the west face of the great pyramid, bringing down an avalanche of masonry and filling the air with dust that rose to join the plume from the guns. Shot from the falconets had felled men in the farthest corners of the square and everywhere Shikotenka looked he could see only death.

It had been a risk, despite the potentially spectacular effect, to fire all seven cannon at once, and Alvarado had been concerned the Mexica might attempt to storm the guns while they were being reloaded.

Looking out now upon the shattered foe, Shikotenka knew that no such attempt would be made.

Not today, at any rate.

But the Mexica were numberless. They would be back tomorrow.

On Wednesday 25 May, after four further days of forced march, Cortés's army reached Perote, where the jagged and uncompromising mountains at last gave way to gentle foothills and the coastal plains just eighty miles west of Narváez's headquarters at Cempoala. Mounted scouts had co-ordinated the final timing of the rendezvous, and Sandoval's dusty, travel-stained column entered Perote from the east just as Cortés and his larger force entered from the west.

After they had embraced and exchanged greetings, Cortés asked Sandoval: 'Did you suffer more desertions?'

'I did, Hernando. You'll recall I started with seventy-three men. Two have died; one is too ill to fight. Two quickly deserted to Narváez – I notified you of this in a former message – and in the last week five more went over to him.'

'So you have lost,' Cortés counted quickly on his fingers, 'ten men?'

'Let us say nine, since one is sick, not a deserter.'

'Nine men then, and you started with seventy-three, so you bring me sixty-four ready to send into battle?'

'No, Caudillo!' Sandoval grinned. 'Because ours is not the only side to suffer desertions. Five of Narváez's men came over to me! I therefore bring you sixty-nine men ready for battle.' His eyes twinkled: 'And not only men. Two of Narváez's horses deserted to us as well! Remind me to tell you the story later.'

'You got hold of two of his horses, eh? Well done!'

Cortés was delighted at the news. Since leaving Tlascala, wishing to show solidarity with the men, he'd refrained from riding Molinero. Now Sandoval's mare Llesenia and the two additional mounts he'd brought would be added to the little pool of horses available to the scouts, and the army's 'eyes and ears' would be significantly enhanced as a result.

But there were other matters to attend to of at least equal importance, and that evening in Perote, reminding himself that 'presents can break rocks', Cortés took the precaution of distributing gifts of gold amongst the men. His own stock of treasure was still strong, though not limitless, and he'd have to dig deep into it for one further initiative he planned. Meanwhile Rangel's prospecting in Chinantla had met with great success and the old soldier brought several bags of assorted grains and nuggets to add to the war chest. In a grand gesture, somewhat stage managed, Cortés called an assembly of the whole army and shared everything that Rangel had brought. Even though he kept nothing back for himself, or for the king, the total pay-out amounted to less than forty pesos a man. It was not a life-changing sum, but it was an encouraging sum. It helped to reduce resentment at the bribes everyone knew had been paid to suborn the enemy. It strengthened resolve for the coming battle. And it was, Cortés emphasised to the grinning, happy men, to be regarded only as a down-payment, a token, of the vast treasure that would be theirs after Narváez was defeated and the conquest complete – indeed they would reap not merely gold and jewels but also honours beyond imagining. 'You will all be dukes and earls and lords,' he laughed, clapping one on the back here, embracing another there. 'These are not just the New Lands or even New Spain. We're making a New World!'

There was a rousing cheer. As it died down, judging the moment, Cortés waved for silence and said: 'Now, lads, there's one favour I must ask of you tonight. Will you grant it to me?'

Three hundred and eighty eager faces turned towards him.

'I've composed another letter to that dog Narváez, the last that I shall write. It's for history and for the king, so that no one may later say we did not make our position clear, or give our enemy a fair chance.'

Cortés reached down to a satchel at his feet, produced and unrolled a long vellum scroll and proceeded to read its contents aloud. While he was reading there were frequent shouts, and on two occasions full-throated roars, of support. When he was done he held the scroll up to the view of the men. 'My signature is here,' he said. 'And my request is that every one of you, my brothers in arms, should now add your signatures or marks beside mine so that history may understand how we all stood together at this time.'

After the blank space under the letter, and the entire reverse of the scroll, had been completely filled with scrawled signatures, marks, and several fingerprints in blood, and as the men dispersed, Cortés beckoned Pepillo to accompany him, and walked to the simple quarters he'd commandeered for the short stay in Perote. 'I'll be having a few meetings this evening,' he said, 'so make yourself handy. I'll start with Velázquez de Léon. Kindly fetch him for me.'

'What's this about, Hernán?' asked De Léon a few moments later as he plunged into the room without knocking. 'I feel . . . summoned!'

'What has made me summon Señor Juan Velázquez de Léon,' Cortés replied with a smile, 'is a certain report concerning you that I received from Father Guevara when he was with us in Orizaba.'

There was no such report; indeed Guevara had said nothing at all about Velázquez de Léon. Cortés was making this story up because he still did not entirely trust a captain so closely related to his rival, and wanted one further test of his loyalty. If Velázquez de Léon was going to switch sides, then better he do so before battle was joined rather than during the battle, and better he do so as an individual rather than as a commander of an important unit in an already very small army! The simplest solution, Cortés had decided, was therefore to send Velázquez de Léon to Narváez, and to send him, moreover, with all his gold, so that he could defect with a light heart knowing he was leaving no wealth behind amongst those he'd betrayed.

'A report, from that slug Guevara?' De Léon looked affronted. 'What does he know about me?'

'It seems that Narváez says,' Cortés was still smiling, 'and it is a general rumour in his camp, that if you were to go over to him then I should at once be undone and defeated, for they believe you would join with Narváez. For this reason, my dear friend, I have resolved that, for the life of me, if you really love me, you shall go on your good dappled mare, and take all your gold, and your Swaggerer, and all your jewels, as well as some other trifles that I will give you, and you will wear the Swaggerer round one shoulder and arm, and round the other one another chain still heavier that I shall give you. Then you will see how Narváez loves you!'

De Léon clearly understood the intention beneath the pretty words. 'I will not take my Swaggerer,' he said firmly, 'nor any of my own gold; I prefer to leave it all with you for safekeeping. But if you have gold that you wish me to hand over to certain persons, perhaps to buy their affections, I shall be happy to take it to them. Wherever I may go, and whatever it is you wish me to do, please be assured that I am at all times ready to render such service to you, my dear Hernán, as no amount of gold or diamonds could procure.'

'This is my belief,' Cortés replied, 'and with this confidence in you, sir, I send you, but unless you take all your gold and jewels as I command, I do not wish you to go.'

'Whatever your honour commands shall be done, yet I will not take my gold and jewels, sir.'

Eventually, increasingly sure of his man, Cortés agreed that De Léon could leave his own treasure behind. He entrusted him, however, with five good gold chains worth a thousand pesos apiece to buy trouble for Narváez from whichever of his officers and men he thought most likely to be able to provide it. 'I will be sending Father Olmedo with you,' Cortés added. 'He'll carry more gold and he's already established links with many in Narváez's camp.'

Cortés saw Olmedo next, alone, entrusting to him the letter to Narváez, now signed by all the men, and gold rings and chains valued at twenty thousand pesos to distribute as further bribes. 'I'm sending Velázquez de Léon also,' he told the friar. 'He'll keep you safe on the road. It's a journey of eighty miles, time is of the essence now, so you'll both be riding horses.'

'Horses?' Olmedo sounded aghast.

'You *can* sit a horse, I recall?'

'As it happens, I can. But I am not a *cavalier* like Juan. What horse shall I have anyway?'

'I thought the grey mare that Santos Jimenez recently returned to us . . .'

'A placid enough animal, I suppose. But eighty miles, Hernán! You are asking us to ride eighty miles in less than two days. How am I to keep up with Juan over such a long distance?'

'Between you, you will have to manage. There is simply no room in this plan for error. You will leave tomorrow morning, Thursday 26 May, and you must reach Cempoala by the afternoon of the following day, Friday 27 May. You will spend the night there, working what harm you can against Narváez, distributing your bribes, and by the late afternoon of Saturday 28 May, Whitsun Eve, you must rendezvous with me at a certain location – a secret location not three miles from Cempoala – that I will tell you of now.'

'Oooh! A secret location. Sounds very cloak and dagger . . .'

'Ha! Yes. An apt turn of phrase. The cloak to defend and distract. The dagger to stab. I've been showing Narváez the cloak for a good while now and I believe he's distracted sufficiently. It's time for the dagger.'

'And the dagger in this case?'

'We will attack on Whitsun Eve, at dead of night and without warning. Our men must therefore be positioned to launch the attack by the afternoon of Whitsun Eve. That calls for a location close enough to Cempoala to allow a rapid advance on Narváez and yet not so close that we would be seen mustering there. You observed on your last visit, I recall, that Narváez sends out no scouts and keeps no proper guard on the camp?'

'That's right. It's mystifying to me actually, and I am just a humble friar. For a military man like yourself, such lax procedure must seem astonishing . . .'

'Not really. As you saw for yourself, Narváez and his officers suffer from a false sense of security. Since they feel so confident, and so safe, it actually makes perfect sense for them to be reckless and idle. Why should they care or bother when they believe themselves to be invulnerable?'

'So I take it you've already identified your secret location to launch the attack from?'

'I have indeed, Bartolomé, and to that end I shall now ask Sandoval to join us.' Cortés called for Pepillo, who was waiting in the corridor, and sent him to find the captain, then continued: 'Sandoval's suggested the perfect place, a clearing in a little forest by the river three miles northwest of Cempoala, which he says that you and he visited during our operations in that area last year.'

'I remember it,' said Olmedo. 'It's on the south side of the river. The trees around the edges of the clearing are very tall and straight. Gonzalo and I went together and chose one of them to provide wood for the cross I placed on the summit of the Cempoalan pyramid.'

Cortés leaned closer: 'Can you find that clearing again, even the very spot you felled the tree?'

'We could see rapids in the river from where we were cutting and there were some heaps of big boulders nearby. I'm reasonably sure I can find it.'

'Good! That greatly reduces the risk of error. But here's the important thing! De Léon doesn't know this location and I don't want him to know it yet. I've engaged in a little subterfuge by misinforming him of its whereabouts . . .'

'Subterfuge?'

'I've directed his attention to another location. The wrong location. I don't believe Juan will betray us, but if he does then at least he won't be able to lead Narváez to our muster point.'

'A wise but I hope unnecessary precaution . . .' said Olmedo. 'So, if I may summarise, Juan and I are to depart on horseback tomorrow, Thursday 26 May, reach the camp of Narváez on Friday 27 May, and do our work there that night and the next morning, Saturday 28 May, which is indeed Whitsun Eve. Then, on Saturday afternoon, having made every effort to further undermine the enemy's morale and unity, and to suborn as many of his officers and men as possible, and of course after Juan has proved himself true to you, we are to depart Narváez's camp, I'm to explain to Juan that the location you gave him was incorrect – hopefully he will believe me! – and then we make our way directly to the rendez-vous in the forest by the river . . .'

'Where I will be waiting for you with the whole army, keenly antici-pating the latest intelligence you'll bring me of the state of Narváez's camp and the disposition of his forces. I'll make a soldier of you yet, Bartolomé!'

'I gather then that you also leave Perote tomorrow?'

'We march at dawn. The distance, as you observe, is eighty miles.

Although the men are already tired – I confess, Bartolomé, they are *very* tired! – I'm determined we must cover this distance in no more than two and a half days. That means approximately thirty-two miles tomorrow, the same again on Friday, and the final sixteen miles on Saturday to bring us to our rendezvous point, three miles from Narváez, by Saturday afternoon. We've covered greater distances on some of our forced marches in worse terrain. Now at least we're out of the mountains with only gentle foothills and the coastal plains before us.'

With a quiet knock Sandoval entered. He was carrying a large hand-drawn map, on which the location of Narváez's camp in the centre of Cempoala was indicated, along with the outlying areas as far as the river, named locally the Actopan, that flowed some three miles to the south of the town on an approximately northwest to southeast course. 'Come, Bartolomé,' the young captain said, spreading the map out on a table, 'let's make sure we both have the same location in mind. It wouldn't do to miss each other!'

'I dare say the absence of one pot-bellied friar on the night of the attack would not spell disaster for the army . . .'

'But we'd miss the intelligence you'll bring,' said Cortés, 'and I have important work for Velázquez de Léon to do in the attack – assuming he's still with us! – so you'd better be there.'

'I'll be there,' said Olmedo.

He and Sandoval pored over the map a little longer until Cortés was satisfied.

The following morning, Thursday 26 May, at dawn, Cortés had the men form up in the town square to the sound of fife, tambourine and drum. With Sandoval's troop now added, they numbered in total just three hundred and eighty. But with all the heavy baggage carried by *tamanes*, and with no cannon to manoeuvre, it was a light, fast-moving force.

Since leaving Tlascala, the pace of the march had been unrelenting, and there could be no let-up now. As Velázquez de Léon and Olmedo spurred their horses out of Perote on the road to Cempoala, Cortés gave the signal, and, with grim faces, setting a fast, steady, mile-devouring pace, the column followed in their dust.

Chapter Sixteen

Friday 27 May 1520–Saturday 28 May 1520

Velázquez de Léon was a man who loved gold.

Despite all his protestations to Cortés, he had, in the end, brought his Swaggerer with him, packed away in a saddle bag, and produced it at the end of the long day's ride. 'I feel unlucky without it,' he explained to Olmedo, and went to sleep with the chain wrapped around him.

Velázquez de Léon was also a man who farted mightily.

Olmedo knew this from long acquaintance with him, but was forcefully reminded when a series of huge thunder-claps in the pre-dawn awoke him from a fitful slumber.

They had camped overnight in a stinking thicket near some stagnant water, from which swarms of mosquitos arose to torment them, reminding them, if the tropical heat and the luxuriant vegetation had not yet done so, that they had left the mountains with their cold, clear air, and were back on the humid and sweltering coastal plains.

Stunted trees festooned with strangler figs drooped overhead, and a raucous convention of brightly coloured parakeets and jays rustled and whooped amongst the branches.

Emitting another burst of foul gas, Velázquez de Léon rolled on to his side and sat up, rubbing his eyes and disentangling the Swaggerer. 'Morning, Bartolomé,' he croaked.

'Good morning to you too, Juan.' Olmedo had remained prone on his bedroll but now, with a groan, he stood and stretched. The muscles of his thighs ached savagely. He reached to touch a painful spot on his right buttock, only to discover a weeping saddle sore the size of his thumb.

It was the morning of Friday 27 May. A hard ride of many hours lay ahead before they would reach Cempoala.

* * *

After the intense action of Monday 23 May, and the great slaughter of Indians that had taken place then, second only in terms of numbers killed to the bloodbath of Tuesday 17 May, there was an interval of inactivity.

The removal of the bodies by howling relatives was a day-long task with which Alvarado chose not to interfere – who needed thousands of stinking corpses outside their front door, after all? – and when it was complete the plaza was left eerily deserted. Scouts were sent out and reported massed regiments of Mexica warriors drawn up outside the walls of the sacred precinct, but making no move to enter inside.

In the following days there were no further attacks on the palace, and the air was filled with continuous wails of Indian mourning rising up from all quarters of the city.

Stupid beasts!

Alvarado was outraged at their intransigence.

They'd had the good sense to cease their attacks, but didn't they understand that if they wanted to stop being given things to mourn about, what they had to do next was lift the blockade and allow his quartermasters to buy food in the markets again?

On the morning of Friday 27 May, with no change to the stalemate, Alvarado decided to test the resolve of the besiegers by sending out a squad of fifty heavily armed infantry protecting fifty Tlascalan bearers and supported by four cavalry on what he encouraged the men to think of as 'a foraging mission in force'. Their task was to exit the sacred precinct through its northern gate and proceed rapidly due north for half a mile into the vast Tlatelolco market, where they were to seize as much food as the thirty bearers could carry and return at once to safety.

The Mexica permitted the column's exit through the northern gate, and allowed it to proceed a few hundred paces into the city before falling upon it in utterly astonishing and overwhelming numbers from every side street. Two of the cavalry, seven of the infantry and twenty of the unarmoured Tlascalan bearers were lost – though many, including at least six of the nine Spaniards, were not killed but captured by little groups of determined warriors and led away.

Most of the rest who survived the fighting retreat back to the sacred precinct were maimed, and all might have perished if Alvarado and a large force of Tlascalans had not sallied out to their rescue. As they withdrew across the plaza, however, the Mexica pursued them in great numbers and were only finally deterred by a massed salvo from the cannon of the foreguard. There, a few hundred paces from the palace walls, they stopped and menaced the gunners with war cries, daring them to fire again, but Alvarado resisted the temptation. Ammunition and powder were in short supply.

'I have blisters on my blisters,' the swordsman Mibiercas complained.

It was noon on Friday 27 May, the second day of their eastward march from Perote towards Cempoala. With the sun at its zenith, and the enervating heat of the coastal plains enveloping them in its steamy and unforgiving embrace, the three hundred and eighty men of Cortés's army had paused to catch their breath in a clearing amidst a grove of giant Ceiba trees, where countless creeping flowers transformed the branches into bright festoons. Most of the exhausted soldiers now lay sprawled in the green shade of the huge intertwined canopies, gasping for breath, too drained even to contemplate the rations of dried meat that had been broken out for them.

Mibiercas was seated, his *espadón* lay sheathed on the ground at his side, and he had pulled off his cracked and scuffed boots. His large, dirty feet were bloody and blistered. 'All those months in Tenochtitlan turned me soft!' he complained. 'I had hide like an elephant after the Tlascala campaign.'

'Well, you don't exactly have the buttery flesh of a sweet young virgin now,' La Serna observed. He had removed his own boots. He pulled a roll of bandage from his pack and tossed it to Mibiercas: 'Here, bind your feet. And when you're done, I'll do the same.'

'I don't know how I'm expected to fight in this condition,' mused Mibiercas. He laid his hand on the *espadón*. 'Swordsmanship's all about footwork and my feet are fucked.'

'And they'll be more fucked tomorrow,' La Serna added. 'We've got the best part of fifty miles left to march before any fighting gets done at all.'

Listening to his two friends, Bernal Díaz smiled. They could bitch and moan with the best of them, but they were fashioned out of tempered steel. No matter the pain, no matter the hunger, or the thirst, no matter the weariness that settles upon a man when he has endured too much, no matter how fearful the odds that must be faced, Díaz knew from long experience that when the moment came, Mibiercas and La Serna would present themselves eagerly for battle, with shoulders squared and a snarl of defiance rising in their throats, and they would deal out death and destruction to the enemy until the fight was won . . . or lost.

And it *could* be lost. It could be lost so very easily.

Indeed, Díaz reflected, it *should* be lost, given the disparity in numbers.

But wasn't it said that a strong heart breaks bad luck?

And besides, the enemy did not have Cortés.

Díaz felt fatigue press upon his eyes like a draught of opium, and allowed luxurious sleep to cradle him. It seemed only an instant later, however, that fat Canillas, the drummer, began to strut amongst the men beating out a furious, rousing roll.

Cortés stood at the centre of the clearing. '*Up and at 'em, lads!*' he roared cheerfully. 'We've a long, hot afternoon ahead of us. Next rest stop at dusk.'

Since leaving Tlascala, Díaz had noted, the caudillo had forsaken his horse, Molinero, giving the great stallion over to the scouts, and had walked in the ranks like any common soldier. That he was willing to do so, that he endured the forced marches with as much fortitude as the rest of them, that he was never heard to complain, that he made cheerful conversation, and that he unhesitatingly remembered everyone's names, had won him fresh honour amongst the men.

Though strained and grey with exhaustion, their jaws were set as they assembled for the road and a fierce indomitable light burned in their eyes.

The sweltering lowlands seemed to stretch endlessly ahead into the mid-afternoon heat haze of Friday 27 May.

Gonzalo de Sandoval's cavalryman's legs were most unsuited to the task of marching, but his chestnut mare Llesenia had been co-opted by the scouts with the rest of the horses and, despite the discomfort in his knees, he was filled with excitement.

The arrival of Narváez had forced him to abandon Villa Rica, where he had only shortly before been promoted to command. The weeks since, on the run, never stopping longer than a single night in one place, had been immensely frustrating! He had wanted to strike back at Narváez, and had even seen opportunities to do so, but had been obliged to be patient rather than risk destruction at the hands of the much larger force.

There had been some good moments, though! He smiled, remembering the morning when Esteban and Gregorio, two of his darkest-eyed, blackest-haired and most sunburnt men, had come to him with a daring plan that he'd immediately sanctioned. Stripped down to loincloths, their bodies oiled in the local fashion, they'd insinuated themselves into

Narváez's camp, passed themselves off as Indian fruit sellers and spent much of the day gathering useful intelligence. Cheekily they'd sold a plum to the obnoxious Salvatierra and, overhearing him boastfully anticipating the seizure of all the loot won by the Cortés expedition, they'd made sure that his was one of the two horses they stole when they fled the camp that night.

Those horses, together with the few others at the army's disposal, were now proving invaluable to the scouts, who would have been unable to spare the mounts for Velázquez de Léon and Olmedo without them.

Cortés, who'd been a few ranks ahead, held back and now matched his pace to march alongside him. 'Do you suppose they've made it to Cempoala?' he asked.

'Velázquez de Léon and Olmedo? You've just read my mind, Caudillo, for I was thinking of them this moment!' Sandoval glanced at the sun. 'And, yes, by now they should be there, even with Olmedo's poor riding skills.' He lowered his voice: 'I know you have your concerns about Juan's loyalty, with good reason, but I'm quite sure he won't allow himself to be won over by Narváez . . .'

'I can only hope so, Gonzalo. There are so few I really trust.'

'You can trust Juan. He'll be at the rendezvous tomorrow, you'll see.'

'I trust you, Gonzalo! Tomorrow, when we attack Narváez, you will do so in the role of chief constable of New Spain that I now confer on you.'

'But . . .' Sandoval was stunned. 'There are far more senior men, Caudillo – Ordaz, Olid, Juan himself; all of them deserve the honour far more than I do.'

'But none of them have your heart, Gonzalo, or your quick mind, and that will be needed tomorrow when I send you to arrest Narváez. I'll brook no argument on this.'

By mid-afternoon on Friday 27 May, Alvarado was seriously concerned.

This morning's sortie had failed utterly in its primary mission to forage food supplies for the increasingly weak and hungry garrison; indeed it had failed even to get as far as the Tlatelolco marketplace before being turned back by overwhelming Mexica numbers.

Adding insult to injury, the demoralised Spaniards were now obliged to confront yet again the familiar sight of a Mexica regiment arrayed on the plaza within the sacred precinct. Since the cannon salvo, the warriors had attempted no further assaults, but just stood there before the guns, with the west face of the great pyramid rising behind them. The threat was palpable, like a great thunder cloud filled with storm, yet they neither came on, nor retreated, but stolidly held their ground.

It was dangerous ground! Alvarado could enfilade it whenever he pleased with the foreguard's cannons, but the very fact that shortage of ammunition obliged him not to do so revealed his greatest weakness. There might be some amongst the Indian captains who'd worked this out.

Even more disconcerting, was something new. For the last hour at least, while he'd kept the majority of his garrison at the front of the palace – its east side – ready to engage the Mexica regiment at its doors, loud noises of hammering and tunnelling had begun to be heard by the very thinly spread guard of Tlascalans and Spaniards in the palace's western wing, where its rear elevation formed part of the enclosure wall of the plaza as a whole. This was the only sector of the entire structure that directly adjoined the busy streets of the city, and its weakest point, a postern leading into a narrow alleyway that in turn led to the Tacuba causeway, had early been signalled by Malinal.

The postern was heavily barricaded now, and guarded by two Tlascalan spearmen. Accompanied by the translator Aguilar, Alvarado strode along the corridor that led to it. He could hear the banging as a muffled repetitive beat propagating through the palace's thick masonry. Occasionally it was accompanied by rumbling, crashing sounds.

The question was, what, if anything, was to be done about it? Clearly a serious effort was being made to hammer an opening through some part of the rear wall of the palace where it adjoined the street, but he could not tell exactly where. It was also probable that at least some of the sounds were made by Mexica sappers attempting to undermine the foundations. Probably it was both.

The first step was to position a cannon in the corridor to command the postern and to strengthen the guard here. Two Tlascalans were not enough. Even if the postern were somehow opened, however, ten well-armed Spaniards and a falconet stuffed with grapeshot should be sufficient to hold it against all comers. Sending Aguilar to make it so, Alvarado hurried up to the palace roof and asked the guards there – five Spaniards and five Tlascalans – if they'd identified where the sounds, still clearly audible at this remove, were coming from, but they were no help. He walked along the entire parapet of the west wing looking down at the alleys fifty feet below, noting where the postern lay but still seeing no sign of the team of men with picks, hammers and shovels indicated by the sounds.

It was ominous. They must be underground. But where? Alvarado was about to make his way back down the stairs to investigate further when he was distracted by a sudden crescendo of Spanish voices from the front of the palace. He ran to join the roof guards, now lined up along the eastern parapet, gazing down at the plaza and the great pyramid beyond, and was confronted by a repulsive and yet bizarrely fascinating sight.

The crowd had parted, a cruel and deliberate whisking back of the curtains to reveal the six Spaniards captured by the Mexica that morning, bound and standing forlornly near the base of the pyramid with eight or ten Tlascalans. Their bodies were smeared white with chalk and all were naked except for the paper loincloths of sacrifice. The Tlascalans stood silent but the Spaniards cried out pitifully to their brother conquistadors behind the walls of the palace of Axayacatl to save them.

Alvarado considered it for a moment. A chivalric move, no doubt, but not a prudent one under the circumstances. A rushed, unplanned sortie would likely cost more Spanish lives than it would save, and a discharge of the foreguard cannons would kill all the captives anyway.

While he weighed his options, a loud shout from the roof drew his attention. A guardsman stationed on the roof of the north wing was looking towards Tlatelolco and gesticulating wildly.

The target of this morning's failed foraging mission, Tlatelolco was also the location of the royal harbour, where Moctezuma's giant state barges had formerly been kept and where the four brigantines, constructed a few months before to give Cortés mastery of the lake, were now moored. Even before he reached the parapet, Alvarado guessed what had happened. Indeed, the only surprise was that it had not been done sooner. The brigantines were all in flames and crowds of Indians danced around their charring hulks in the distant harbour.

At first, because he did not believe he would ever be forced to flee, Alvarado had not even considered the brigantines as a way out for his beleaguered garrison. As the days had gone by, however, the thought that they might be put to ferrying the men across the lake to a safe shore whence they could make their escape to Tlascala had began to intrude more and more forcefully upon his mind. The problem, as this morning's attempt to reach the market had indicated, was getting to them, but now with the ships burning merrily, their blackened hulks already sinking low in the water, even that faint hope was crushed.

There came another loud collective gasp from the garrison watching the developing spectacle in the plaza from the windows and balconies of the east wing of the palace. Alvarado turned at a run to see that the captives were already being escorted up the pyramid. A large irregular bite had been taken out of the north side of the steps where they'd been blasted with shot by the lombard, but enough of the southern side was intact around the missing section of masonry to allow the prisoners, goaded by guards with obsidian-tipped spears, to struggle on towards the summit.

Truly there was nothing to be done, and a terrible silence fell over the palace as the sacrifices began.

The Tlascalans, fierce and unbowed, were killed first, their breasts split open, their pulsing hearts one by one ripped from their chests and cast down upon the smoking brazier of Huitzilopochtli. The Mexica took their time, as though they relished drawing out the ghastly anticipation for the Spaniards, who huddled together in abject terror near the top of the stairway. '*Show some courage*,' Alvarado wanted to shout, as the first of them, a competent young ensign named Juan Marquez, was dragged weeping to the execution stone and spread-eagled over it. Two priests held his kicking feet and stretched out his legs, two priests held his struggling hands and stretched out his arms to expose his breast. Next, the high priest Namacuix, a filthy-haired apparition dressed all in black, raised the obsidian knife with its cubit-long blade, plunged it into the victim's sternum, sawed upwards from there, found the heart, sliced it free amidst a spray of blood and cast it down upon the brazier. Then the body was rolled off the stone and the butcher priests fell on it to amputate the arms and legs for later consumption in a cannibal feast. Finally, while the second Spaniard was already being stretched over the stone, Marquez's head was hacked off, his smouldering heart was retrieved half cooked from the brazier and both were carried into the temple of the war god.

As Alvarado watched, his hands gripping the parapet, silently vowing bloody revenge and murder upon the Mexica, there came an immense crash of masonry far below and yells from the guard on the roof of the western wing.

Alvarado sprinted to join him, peered down from the parapet, and saw that a section of the western wall of the palace close to the postern had completely collapsed. Amidst the rubble, like demons from hell amidst the dense pall of dust, flitted huge numbers of Mexica warriors.

Taking three of the Tlascalans and four of the Spaniards from the roof with him, desperately sending the fifth to bring a squad of cross-bowmen and musketeers in reinforcement, knowing as he did so that they might not be enough – indeed were pitifully inadequate! – to stem the Mexica incursion, Alvarado thundered down the stairs towards the sounds of fighting.

It was bad, but it could have been worse.

The Mexica sappers digging deep beneath the foundations had collapsed a section of the exterior wall of the palace just north of the postern; however, it had not proved to be load-bearing, presumably because of reinforcing beams further up in the masonry, so neither the upper storeys nor the roof were affected. Indeed what had come down proved on later examination to be only the outer part of a massively thick double wall, thus effectively leaving the palace fortifications unbreached.

That in itself would have been merely inconvenient, were it not for masonry movements around the collapsed section of wall that had twisted the postern partially off its hinges, forcing a gap that the Mexica were able to exploit to cast the gate and its barricades aside and burst into the corridor. There they were confronted by the ten Spanish swordsmen Aguilar had brought, and by the gun crew, who'd trundled the falconet on its carriage the full length of the palace, and were now desperately pulling it into place while loading it and preparing to fire it at the same time.

'Slow down, boys,' said Alvarado, joining them, laying a hand on the barrel of the little cannon. 'Haste makes for sloppy work.'

The corridor gave passage to no more than eight men abreast. Though holding it, their blades licking out, cutting down the dust-covered enemy with great thrusts, the ten Spaniards were being remorselessly forced back by the pressure of hundreds of warriors pouring through the postern.

'We're ready to fire, sir,' the gunner said. He was young for this respon-sibility. Trembling.

'What's your name, lad?' Alvarado asked.

'Alonso Bueno, sir.'

'"Alonso the Good" eh? A pretty name! Well . . . see you do good here.' Alvarado clapped him on his skinny shoulders and stepped forward.

The next bit was going to be tricky. Obviously the Spaniards had to retreat behind the gun before it could fire, but that very retreat would invite the enemy to advance. At all costs they must not be allowed to overrun the falconet.

It was all a matter of timing, but more importantly of musketeers and crossbowmen. Where the *fuck* was the squad he'd sent for? They should already be behind the gun, filling the corridor in two ranks, one kneeling, one standing, ready to fire a massed volley of bolts and bullets into the advancing enemy at the exact moment the swordsmen completed their retreat.

One of the swordsmen was already down, a lucky throw of a lance finding a chink in his armour under his right arm. *Probably fatal*, Alvarado thought abstractedly, as he charged forward with the three Tlascalans and four Spaniards he'd brought from the roof to hold the line.

But it couldn't be held, he sensed it at once, all his years of battle experience coming into play – and where the *fuck* were those musketeers?

'*Alonso Bueno!*' he bellowed, risking a glance back over his shoulder. '*Do you hear me?*'

'I hear you well, sir.'

'Then make ready to fire. I'm going to call the retreat. The instant we're behind the gun, put the match to the touchhole.'

'Yes, sir.'

'*Retreat!*' Alvarado yelled to the men around him, his voice cracking with the strain. 'Get behind the gun! We're going to destroy these Moors.'

They stepped back as one, a perfectly executed fighting retreat that put the falconet between them and the Indians.

Bueno stood ready. He held the match to the touchhole. It sparked as the first rank of Mexica charged in . . . but the spark died and nothing happened.

Suddenly there was hand-to-hand fighting around the gun. Cursing, Alvarado struck a man down, saw that the onrush of braves was overwhelming and, for the first time in his life, looked defeat in the face and did not see how he could snatch a victory from it. Without the devastation that the grapeshot would have wrought, the enemy, numbering in hundreds and filling the entire corridor, were so many that they could not possibly be held back. All the way to the postern, the corridor was filled with ululating, howling warriors brandishing their weapons, and more continuously poured in, forcing the whole furious mass rapidly and threateningly forward.

The only thing to do – and Alvarado could hardly bear it – was to run.

'*Run!*' he yelled. '*Run for your lives!*'

*   *   *

'My buttocks are gruel,' groaned Olmedo. Indeed, his saddle sores had become so severe that he was obliged to half stand in his stirrups, imposing intolerable strain on his thighs, as they trotted into Cempoala around the middle of the afternoon of Friday 27 May. To add insult to injury, having expressed constant frustration at his poor riding skills since they'd set out yesterday, Velázquez de Léon now begrudgingly admitted that they had, after all, made 'rather good time.'

Both men were famous in Cempoala from their stay there the previous year – Velázquez de Léon particularly for his flamboyant style – and now, entering noisily on horseback, they found themselves surrounded by welcoming Indians. Before they reached the main square, word of their arrival had already been rushed to Narváez who – in a spirit very different to his earlier treatment of Olmedo – hurried down to meet them from his headquarters atop the pyramid.

The transformation was remarkable. Far from emanating his usual fetor of hostility, anger and disrespect, the commander, while affecting to ignore Olmedo, was eager to welcome Velázquez de Léon, who he clearly believed was about to come over to him. Amidst a great show of reverence, Narváez embraced De Léon – who looked every bit the courtier with his Swaggerer draped about him – and pressed him to be seated on one of the two chairs that servants had brought out on to the grass at the foot of the pyramid and placed under a hastily erected awning.

While refreshments were brought, Olmedo excused himself. 'I have suffered abrasions on the ride,' he said, 'and must change the dressings. Are my quarters the same as before?'

Salvatierra had joined the throng of officers around De Léon, and his sneering voice now rose in mockery: 'Abrasions? On the ride? That's a pretty way to put it, friar. Don't you mean you've got blisters on your arse?'

Olmedo stared pointedly at the boils around the deputy's mouth. 'Yes indeed, my dear Salvatierra,' he said, 'and as a result my arse now very much resembles your face.'

'Gentlemen, gentlemen,' Velázquez de Léon interjected, 'we are all friends here, I assure you. There is no need for harsh words.'

Half an hour later, after applying balm and bandages to his wounds, Olmedo returned to the square, where something of a party was now in progress under the late afternoon sun. A larger awning had been brought out, and more chairs. Salvatierra, Bono de Quejo and Gamarra had joined Narváez and Velázquez de Léon, and all five were quaffing great bowls of wine from a well-aged barrel that had been rolled out and placed on a stand beside them.

Seeing the friar approach Velázquez de Léon half rose to his feet and indicated an empty chair. 'Join us, Bartolomé! Take your ease. Try some of this fine wine.'

Olmedo winced: 'I think I shall stand – ' a barely suppressed snigger from Salvatierra – 'but a bowl will be most welcome. Is it the same excellent Galician red you offered us before, Don Pánfilo?'

Wine, it seemed, was the one subject that gave Narváez joy, and it had been obvious even on the previous visit that he took great pride in his collection. 'Ah no, not from Galicia,' he now replied, resting a proprietorial hand on the barrel. A dreamy, almost avuncular look passed briefly over his face. He caressed the barrel as though it were his beloved's shoulder: 'This is from Castille. A very fine Tempranillo.'

'Ah! The noble grape.'

A look of surprise: 'You know your wines then, friar?'

'Passably.' Olmedo took a sip. 'And this one is . . . Yes! Very good. Perhaps I might even say superb. I commend your choice, Don Pánfilo.'

Salvatierra nudged Narváez and there was a brief whispered conversation, during which the commander's manner perceptibly changed. Rapidly reverting to type, he held out an imperious hand. 'I believe you bring a letter? From Don Hernando Cortés? Give it to me please.'

Olmedo had the scroll in one of the concealed pockets of his habit, but it suddenly occurred to him that he didn't want to hand it over yet. There weren't enough officers present, and those who were all belonged to Narváez's immediate coterie. It would be good if the whole camp, or at least as many men as possible, could learn of its contents.

'My apologies!' he said. 'How forgetful of me! I left the letter in my quarters.' He was already walking away. 'Forgive me for a few moments while I fetch it.'

Olmedo's mind was racing, but when one is about to do something against all protocol, it is better just to do it! Instead of returning to his room, therefore, he went straight to the refectory, where, since it was now around six p.m., large numbers of Narváez's soldiers, officers and men were congregating for their dinner. He found Balthazar Bermudez, the chief constable – together with Francisco Verdugo and artillery captain Rodrigo Martinez – seated at a table with a great bearded brute of a fellow Olmedo did not know, who introduced himself gruffly as 'Usagre, gunner.'

301

'Diego is part of my team,' Martinez explained. 'He has special responsibility for the long guns.'

'The lombards,' said Usagre. 'We used to have three but that prize prick Salvatierra dropped one off a pyramid, cracked the barrel, and it'll never fire again.'

'Ouch. Yes, I witnessed its fall on my last visit . . .'

'We've had it cleared away since. No use for anything but scrap now. Fucking Salvatierra!'

'As you can see,' whispered Bermudez in Olmedo's ear, 'Diego is of our party.'

'And I'll be sure to welcome him with gold soon, and I have still more gold for you, Balthazar – ' Olmedo turned his smile on the others – 'and for all of you on account of the great services you are going to do for me. But first,' he held up an urgent finger, 'I must conscript your assistance in another matter, which is to witness and hear the public reading of a letter my caudillo Don Hernando Cortés has written to Don Pánfilo.'

'Just tell us where and when.' Bermudez was immediately eager.

'In the main square, on the green in front of the great pyramid, right now. And please, on your way, bring as many other officers and men as you are able to. I want everyone to hear this.'

Olmedo's next call was upon the kitchen, where he sought out the cook Pero Trigueros, whom he'd previously befriended, and asked him to pause his work for a moment to witness events about to unfold in the town square. 'Please bring as many others with you as you can lay your hands on. It's important that everyone hears this.'

Finally, in the garden of the refectory, the friar found the two youthful sentries, Ruffo and Valdez, already wealthy thanks to Cortés's largesse and eager to earn more. He gave the same message to them. 'Come to the square, to the green in front of the great pyramid, and bring as many others as you are able to find, to hear the reading of an important letter from Don Hernando Cortés.'

When all that was done, Olmedo hurried to his quarters, passing others on the way whom he also invited, collapsed gasping, face-down on his bed of skins, counted slowly to two hundred while his beating heart slowed, arose and hurried forth tugging the scroll from his pocket as he walked. Everyone he encountered on the way he asked to follow him, promising 'interesting tidings'.

The sun was still in the sky but had fallen shockingly low to hang off the shoulder of the pyramid – *how long did I take?* Olmedo suddenly wondered.

A surprisingly large crowd had gathered. Beneath the awning, Salvatierra was on his feet, red faced, striding back and forth, shouting incoherently about something, his buttocks wobbling unfavourably in the tight cavalry trousers he had affected that afternoon. Narváez was still seated but his lips were set to a thin line and his bulbous eyes stared furiously ahead.

'*Olmedo!*' The bellow came from Salvatierra, who darted out from under the awning and waddled rapidly towards him. 'How *dare* you behave in this way? Don't you realise Captain-General Narváez has more important things to do than sit here waiting for *you*?' The squat officer was now face to face with Olmedo, emitting tangy whiffs of halitosis with every breath. Involuntarily the friar retreated.

'Don't you back away from me, church mouse!' snarled Salvatierra. 'Give me the letter!'

'This letter isn't for you,' Olmedo replied. He was surprised at how calm he sounded as he sidestepped the captain, shrugged off his restraining hand and progressed beneath the awning to where Narváez, too, was now on his feet.

'Well, friar, here you are at last,' the commander said. His voice was flat and cold. 'I am not a man to be kept waiting.' He extended his hand. 'The letter please.'

'With respect, sir, it is not for you.' Olmedo glanced at the scroll. 'The letter I bear – ' he flourished the scroll – 'is addressed to all the officers and men of this camp, and I am commanded to read it aloud so that everyone who wishes to may hear.' As he spoke he raised his voice, and had the satisfaction of seeing many who had congregated around the awning, as well as others further away, edge closer. Olmedo felt a twinge of conscience, for it was not perfectly true either that he had been commanded to read the letter aloud, or that it was addressed to all the officers and men. These had been his own innovations, but he rather thought that Cortés – a great innovator himself – would approve.

He unrolled the scroll, held it up and was about to read when Narváez, who had been staring at him in disbelief, suddenly exploded: '*Seize that friar!*'

Gamarra, Salvatierra and Bono de Queso actually fell over one another in their haste to implement the order, colliding with Olmedo in a tangled, stumbling tackle. They were so unintentionally funny, like jesters, that he burst out laughing as he used his great weight to resist, at the same time holding the scroll above his head in his right hand while Salvatierra made repeated, unsuccessful lunges for it.

'*Friar!*' It was Narváez again. 'You will hand over that letter at once. Attempt to read it again and I shall have you flogged.'

'*Let the friar read, I say!*'

The voice was astonishingly loud and commanding. Even Olmedo was surprised that it could have emanated from one so small, neat and brisk as Balthazar Bermudez, the bustling and self-important chief constable of the camp.

'What? *What* did you say?' Narváez was staring at Bermudez in horror.

'The friar says the letter is for all of us, officers and men,' Bermudez insisted stubbornly, 'and since many of us are now assembled here, I say let him read.'

'I second that,' growled Martinez, the artillery captain.

'And I.' Francisco Verdugo proved that Cortés's money was indeed well spent, for when he added his voice, a tipping point seemed to be reached and many others began to speak out.

Indecision spread in Narváez's eyes like a stain, and Olmedo could almost see the other man's ugly thoughts taking shape and doing battle. First, and impossible to miss on that furiously affronted face, there was his instinct to lash out – at those of the officers and men who dared to support the reading of the letter, and at Olmedo himself for having engineered this crisis. But the bully was at bay! All his soldiers were watching. They believed the letter had been written to them by Cortés. If Narváez prevented the reading, then resentment and suspicion would inevitably follow. It might even be imagined by some of the men that Cortés, rumoured to be as rich as Croesus, had made some fabulous offer of gold to them which their officers wished to suppress. Wouldn't it be simpler, in the end, just to allow the letter to be heard?

Narváez and Salvatierra were huddled together, whispering urgently. Everyone watched the two men. The pregnant silence seemed to expand. When Salvatierra finally cleared his throat, his voice was strangled. 'Very well, proceed . . .'

'What was that?' Olmedo cupped a hand to his ear. 'I didn't quite catch—'

'I said *proceed!*'

'Ah, good. Yes.'

Striking a pose, Olmedo once again stretched out the scroll, and began to read. He moved rapidly through the opening pleasantries and was soon into the substance of the letter, which was quite obviously written to Narváez himself, and not to his officers and men, and which equally obviously came not only from Cortés but from all his officers and men.

By the time Narváez and Salvatierra had fully grasped this, however, as Olmedo had calculated, it was too late for them to intervene without making matters worse.

'We rejoiced at your arrival, Don Pánfilo,' Olmedo read, 'and at first believed that you had come to aid us here and to join with us in doing great service to our Lord God and to His Majesty, but instead we learned that you call us traitors—'

'Because you *are* bloody traitors,' Salvatierra interrupted.

'. . . we who are loyal servants to His Majesty!' Olmedo persisted, raising his voice to be heard above the interruption. 'And not only that, but also that you have stirred up trouble by the correspondence you entered into with Moctezuma, the great chieftain of this land, who we hold as our hostage and surety against future attack, and from whom we know that you have received rich presents of gold—'

'They were received all right!' It was a voice from deep within the crowd. 'But never shared with us men.'

'*Who said that?*' Narváez was up on his toes and craning his long neck but the speaker remained elusive.

'*Who said that?*'

In the silence that followed, Olmedo continued: 'Moreover, Don Pánfilo, we have begged and entreated you, on behalf of God and of our lord the king, to proclaim to us through a properly appointed royal notary any orders or decrees from His Majesty that you bear with you, or to send us the originals of said orders or decrees, that we might examine them to confirm that they do indeed bear the royal signature, and learn what orders they contain, so that with our breasts bowed before you on the ground we might at once obey you and do all that he should command in his royal decrees . . .'

A grunt from Narváez: 'Royal decrees? Unnecessary. We have the authority of Diego de Velázquez!'

It was not wise to suggest that anything from the king was superfluous. Olmedo fixed the commander with a disapproving glare and carried on reading: 'You, for your part, however, have done neither one thing nor the other, but merely used abusive language to us, stirred up the country against us, and robbed peaceable Indians of their property and possessions.

'It is a grave matter that you have, until the present, failed signally to

305

show us the royal orders and decrees that alone can grant legitimacy and legality to your expedition . . .'

'If, as seems to us now to be certain, you do not in fact possess any orders or decrees from His Majesty – ' at this point hundreds of pairs of eyes turned on Narváez – 'then it will be better for you if you sail back to Cuba at once and cease to disturb this country any more with threats. Should you fail to heed this order we will come against you without warning, in force and in fury to arrest you, and send you a prisoner to our lord the king, because without royal permission your expedition is mere piracy—'

A curse from Narváez: 'Nobody calls me a pirate . . .'

'Ours is the legitimately appointed expedition,' piped up Bono de Quejo, 'Cortés is the pirate!'

Ignoring them, Olmedo finished the reading: '. . . and you have come for no other purpose than to make war upon us and to disturb our cities, and all the evils and deaths and burnings and losses that will follow will be your responsibility and not ours.

'On the other hand . . .' a pregnant pause, 'let it be known that we will welcome and pardon any man amongst you who freely comes over to us before battle is engaged or during battle itself . . .'

'*This is intolerable!*' shrieked Salvatierra.

Narváez was practically foaming at the mouth. 'Arrest the friar,' he barked at his deputy. 'Get him out of here before he causes any more trouble.'

But again, before Salvatierra could act, Bermudez intervened: 'No! No! Wait!'

Verdugo was right behind him, his patrician lip curled in revulsion: 'We cannot arrest a holy friar!'

Finally forsaking the wine barrel, Juan Velázquez de Léon was also on his feet and strode over to stand side by side with Olmedo, wrapping an arm around his shoulder: '*No one is going to arrest this good friar,*' he roared. 'He is here as the ambassador of Don Hernán Cortés, as am I. We come in peace, hoping to avoid conflict between fellow Spaniards – ' he dropped his hand to the hilt of his sword – 'but I am ready for war.'

'Come come, Juan.' It was Bermudez again, now the peacemaker. 'Come, Pánfilo. We must mend this quarrel. Let us for one night at least set all contentious matters aside and simply enjoy one another's company, as Spaniards together in a distant land. A good dinner! More of your excellent wine, Pánfilo, which you so generously share! A night's sweet rest! And then tomorrow, refreshed, we can return to this trying business of diplomacy . . .'

There was no setting aside of contentious matters.

Somehow, since their arrival, and the ingratiating welcome extended to him, Velázquez de Léon had successfully confined his intercourse with Narváez to small talk, pleasantries and insincere statements of mutual regard. He had not yet raised the matter of his own loyalties, yet it was perfectly obvious to Olmedo that this was all Narváez really wished to talk about.

It was inevitable that the subject would come up at dinner, a special event tonight, celebrating the arrival of the famous Juan Velázquez de Léon and offered to the select group of captains and cronies invited to Narváez's high table an hour after the regular service to the officers and men was complete. The refectory remained packed, and a haze of acrid smoke filled the air, as post-prandial cigars of Cuban tobacco were lit and smoked. The Mexica, too, made great use of this herb, Olmedo had observed, and many of the conquistadors had taken it up in the past months. He himself had never been drawn to it. Other than transient dizziness, it had no notable inebriating effects; it seared the lungs, and its taste and smell were repugnant. Nonetheless it was becoming fashionable. Several at high table were partaking even before their dinner was served, and great clouds and billows of stinking smoke rose up from them, adding to the general fug.

Narváez had brought someone new with him to the table: a young man, lumpy and heavy-set in the way of overweight teenagers, with a broad, flat jowly face, suety skin and an infuriating manner of supreme self-confidence – infuriating because it was clearly not based on any achievement or experience but entirely on birth. An ensign, he enjoyed elevated stature and importance in the eyes of this company by virtue of being a nephew and namesake of governor Diego de Velázquez of Cuba. *Yet another relative*! thought Olmedo. It was almost uncanny how everywhere one went – in the islands and now in these New Lands – relatives of the governor popped up, clamouring for attention!

Here, though, was a pretty situation. On the one side the huge, hirsute Velázquez de Léon, on the other this bombastic youth, also bearing the Velázquez name, with barely a hair to his chin, who'd entered the refectory, speaking unnecessarily loudly, and strutted to his place at the table.

Once seated, spotting Olmedo, and without being invited to do so, he had forcefully expressed his opinion on what he affected to view as the 'spiritual deficiencies' of the native peoples of the New Lands. 'One may hardly call them human,' he declaimed, as though he were some acknowledged fount of wisdom and experience, 'so why waste time and treasure trying to convert them to the faith? Might as well preach to pigs or monkeys! What? Don't you agree, friar?'

Olmedo groaned inwardly, but instead of erupting from his seat to box the obnoxious youth about the ears, as he felt very strongly compelled to do, he simply pretended not to hear him, took several gulps of wine, and had already signalled for more when he realised that an interesting change of subject had occurred.

Now Cortés was the focus and, of course, young Diego had a view! Indeed, he was righteously enraged that Cortés had failed to surrender to Narváez. 'He and all his men are worse than thieves or murderers,' the boy stormed, his voice already slurred with drink. 'They are traitors.'

A suspicion presented itself to Olmedo. Had Narváez put Diego up to this deliberately to flush out Juan's true loyalties? If so, the ploy was working, because the big captain, his Swaggerer clanking and his face flushed with prodigious quantities of wine, now surged from his chair, wholly ignoring his youthful relative, and addressed the commander: 'Señor Captain Narváez, I cannot acquiesce in such words being spoken against Don Hernando Cortés, or against any of those who are with him, for it is truly malicious to speak evil of us who have served His Majesty so loyally.'

Narváez's face fell. *Poor fellow*, thought Olmedo. *He's really quite desperate for Juan to be on his side.*

The youthful Diego now also rose to his feet, affecting much injured dignity: 'I am quite content with the words I have spoken,' he said. 'Nay! I take pride in them. But you, my cousin Juan, are upholding a traitor, and you are therefore as worthless as that traitor and condemn yourself by your own words and deeds as a bad Velázquez.'

A bad Velázquez! Olmedo had to choke back his laughter. What a childish turn of phrase, as though this were some fairytale! And besides, could there ever be such a thing as a good Velázquez?

Well, to be fair, Juan was certainly trying to be such a thing. Cortés had fears for his loyalty but Olmedo could see no sign of betrayal. Quite the contrary, the big man's beard was trembling with genuine rage and his hand was now on his sword: 'I'm a better Velázquez than you'll ever be, you jumped-up little whoreson,' he yelled at Diego. 'Better than you and better than your uncle, and I will teach you this lesson outside if Señor Captain Narváez will give me leave.' So saying he drew his sword and stepped briskly towards the youth, whose composure for the first time was visibly ruffled. Indeed De Léon looked so angry, and with the sword in his hand so dangerous, that Olmedo imagined for a moment he might stab Diego there and then. That this did not happen was due to the intervention of several of the captains assembled at high table, who rushed forward to separate the contending parties.

The evening ground to a halt in a welter of drunken acrimony and confusion, with abuse being bellowed back and forth between the senior and junior representatives of the Velázquez clan, three further attempts made by the former to attack the latter, and further childish insults directed by the latter against the former. Evidently still hopeful that he might yet win Juan over, despite his public defence of Cortés, Narváez proposed a further meeting in the morning, in the main square in front of the great pyramid, at eleven a.m. sharp. 'In your honour,' Olmedo overheard him inform Juan, 'I have ordered a muster of all my artillery, cavalry, musketeers, crossbowmen and soldiers.'

'I can't wait,' De Léon replied. He drained off another bowl of wine and belched appreciatively. 'Will you be offering the usual refreshments?'

Narváez's smile was hideous: 'To compensate for Diego's rude behaviour this evening, I shall arrange for a very special barrel to be placed next to your chair.'

'Wonder what that was all about?' Juan asked as Olmedo led him out of the refectory.

'It sounded somewhat sinister, but then Narváez is a sinister fellow.'

Olmedo stumbled and De Léon steadied him. 'Does the thought cross your mind, dear friar, that Narváez might be planning to murder us?'

'Ha! That "special" barrel?' Olmedo replied. 'I for one won't be drinking from it until I see Narváez drink first. But to answer your question, honestly, no, I don't think he'll kill us. He would *like* to kill us – or at any rate me! He's no doubt advised by the viper Salvatierra to kill us. But he holds out hope that you'll come over to him. Probably he aims to impress you with the size of his army and make you mellow with his best wine, so that at the end of the day you'll be his!'

309

'Yet at the end of the day when we ride out of Cempoala he'll be left in no doubt that my loyalties lie with Cortés,' De Léon mused.

'True – and then he may kill us. But sufficient unto the day is the evil thereof. Now, come, Juan. The night is yet young and we have soldiers to bribe, officers to suborn, guns to sabotage.'

'Sabotage the guns? Won't they be guarded?'

'The work will be done by another's hand. In this camp, gold is the key that opens every door.'

It was being hailed throughout the palace as a miracle.

Was it? Might it possibly be? Alvarado was sceptical. More like blind luck! But, because there was nothing like a miracle to lift the men's spirits, he embraced the fantasy, that night of Friday 27 May, as enthusiastically and as back-slappingly as everyone else.

What had actually happened earlier in the afternoon was, he had to admit, a trifle strange.

In that long corridor, so stuffed with screaming, contending men and with the din and collision of battle that its very walls seemed to shudder, with the useless falconet already a hundred paces behind in their rapid flight, and with the enemy far past the gun, coming on in unstoppable numbers, and still pouring in through the postern, all had seemed irrevocably lost.

Hating to flee, and with the sweet consolation that history would remember him as a latter-day Horatius, Alvarado had stopped and turned about, his falchion in one hand, his quillon dagger in the other, to slow the advancing enemy who packed the corridor all the way from the postern, and with whose front ranks he was already trading blows.

That was when the miracle – if it was a miracle – or freak accident – if it was a freak accident – occurred.

Suddenly, with no hint of what was to come, for only Indians were around it and no match was applied to its touchhole, the deadly little cannon discharged its full load of grapeshot. The consequences, in the confined space of the corridor, were utterly devastating. Pretty much everyone in front of the barrel, as far as the postern and beyond, was killed and smashed to pieces in the blink of an eye.

The effects on the forward group of Indians who'd passed the gun to menace Alvarado and the retreating Spaniards were also salutary. They stopped in their tracks at the sound of the blast, turned round, saw how their brothers and friends had been slaughtered by no apparent human agency, wailed in horror and fled as one, over the jumbled corpses and out through the postern, just as a mixed group of Spanish and Tlascalan reinforcements, including musketeers and crossbowmen, came piling in from the east wing, sending a volley of shots after them.

So the day had been saved by a miraculous cannon, and young Alonso Bueno, rather than receiving the thrashing he deserved, was being feted by all as an instrument of divine will.

It was a nice fantasy and the men liked it, but it didn't stop them pressing a case that night, after the fighting had ceased and the postern had been repaired and reinforced, that they'd been making to Alvarado every day since the start of the siege, and that was all the more reasonable and obviously urgent now.

The delegation of two ensigns and five private soldiers was led by master-sergeant Rodrigo Manusco, who was evidently in severe pain from a spear wound to the thigh he'd received that afternoon. 'Captain,' he said, 'this can't go on any longer. We must inform the caudillo of our predicament, for without a relief column we are lost.'

'Sorry to be a bore,' said Alvarado, trying to sound more casual than he felt, 'but we don't even know where Cortés is – and he could be anywhere east of here, perhaps inland, perhaps at the coast along the two-hundred-mile stretch between Coatzacoalcos and Veracruz. We also don't know if he's engaged Narváez yet, and if he has we don't know whether he's won or lost.'

'Still, we must send a messenger, sir. Let him reach Cortés or Narváez – it's of no account – but we *must have help!*'

'We'll get none if Narváez is the victor. He'll tell his friend Mucktey to slaughter us all.'

'Even so, sir, what are we to do?'

Alvarado had given the matter a great deal of thought in the past days. He was quite sure that Cortés *would* defeat Narváez, because Cortés was an evil conniving bastard of the first water.

Nor need it be as difficult as he'd suggested to find the caudillo, whose little army made him much more than a needle in a haystack. Whether at the coast or inland, the Totonacs would know his whereabouts.

No, the problem in a nutshell was Alvarado's honour. Having been entrusted with guarding Tenochtitlan, the soul of the conquest, with keeping Moctezuma secure, and with peacefully holding and protecting the expedition's gains and treasure here, he simply could not bear the humiliation of doffing his cap to Cortés, confessing that he'd made a catastrophic error with the Toxcatl massacre, and begging for help. His every instinct was to delay, to hold out, and eventually to win through on his own proud resources.

'Very well,' he addressed Manusco and the men, 'we'll send a messenger. In fact, we'll send two. But since we don't know where Cortés is, we'll send them to Tlascala instead. Our Indian allies there will surely come to our aid; after all, we have their battle-king Shikotenka here with us! How can they not come?'

'Even if they come, they don't have the force to cross the lake, penetrate the city and defeat the Mexica,' Manusco pointed out. 'They've been fighting them for two hundred years and haven't defeated them yet.'

'Nor been defeated by them,' Alvarado added dryly. 'And they are our best, most immediate hope. We know where they are, they are close, and they dispose of a hundred thousand warriors. Surely you see my point, Manusco?'

A few more moments of blah, blah, blah and it was all settled. 'I'll speak to Shikotenka,' Alvarado said. 'He'll know the best runners to send and the best routes to get them out of the city.'

'Two men!' Speaking through the translator Aguilar, Alvarado was adamant. 'Two of your best men. They should blacken their bodies and go now – just slip out into the night. They won't be seen.'

'The senate in Tlascala already knows we're under attack,' Shikotenka replied wearily, 'and they know by now that I'm here. Our spies will have kept them well informed, so if they wish to rescue us they can try. A message from me will change nothing.'

'I think it will change everything,' Alvarado insisted. 'And even if it doesn't persuade the old women in your senate to act directly, at the very least they can send it onward to Cortés. Surely they'll know where he is?'

Shikotenka showed him the cold face. 'It's a suicide mission,' he said. 'Don't you understand that the Mexica have got this palace sewn up tighter than a water-skin? We're completely surrounded here. I mean *completely*. Nothing gets in or out unless they permit it.'

'I disagree. The night is dark. Two good men lowered on ropes from the roof of the west wing of the palace – I was up there today – can reach the ground and vanish into the streets in seconds. The Tacuba causeway lies just beyond—'

'The Tacuba causeway? You must be mad.'

312

'I insist on this, Shikotenka. We're not having a debate. I'm the commander here and this is my order to you.'

It was an uncomfortable business, Shikotenka thought, dealing with Alvarado. 'If I authorise this,' he said finally, 'I will not tell my men to go by the Tacuba causeway. Too well lit. Too well guarded. Too well watched. It will serve them better to steal canoes and make off directly across the lake.'

'Whatever you decide, Shikotenka. I leave the arrangements to you.'

The bodies of the two Tlascalan messengers were returned soon after dawn the following morning, Saturday 28 May.

Or rather, not their bodies, but their severed heads, their excarnated bones and their dripping, freshly flayed skins. The heads and bones were brought in large, blood-drenched linen bags. The skins were worn as garments stretched obscenely over the arms, torsos and legs of the gyrating, eye-rolling Mexica warriors who delivered the remains to the foreguard outside the palace gates.

Although not a soldier himself, Olmedo had been around soldiers long enough to distinguish their qualities, and was left singularly unimpressed by the muster on Saturday morning, 28 May. To be sure the men of Narváez's army, in total more than nine hundred strong, were well enough turned out, their uniforms clean, their weapons and armour shining. To be sure the massed ranks of the eighty cavalry led by Jean Yuste made an impact; outnumbering Cortés's cavalry by six to one, they had the potential to be a devastating force. To be sure the great block of cross-bowmen, one hundred and twenty strong, could inflict terrible damage on an enemy if properly martialled. To be sure the eighty arquebusiers chilled the blood. A single coordinated volley, properly timed and aimed, would tear through Cortés's infantry like a deadly storm. To be sure, even after the wasteful loss of one lombard, Narváez was still able to parade seventeen cannon – mostly the highly manoeuvrable little falconets that fired one-pound loads of either ball or shot and could be utterly devastating at close range, cutting down great swathes of advancing enemy infantry. To be sure Narváez's own massed infantry, numbering around six hundred and fifty men, and marching through the square with good coordination, should be able to sweep away anything that Cortés could throw at them.

And yet . . .

And yet . . .

It wasn't simply that many of the soldiers were new recruits. While this was true, by no means all were 'milksops', as Cortés had taken to calling them. Stiffening their ranks were hard men who had fought in the Italian wars, or taken part in the conquest of Cuba, or been with Pedrarias for three hellish years in Darién – tough, experienced warriors who knew what they were doing.

Even so, it was perfectly obvious to Olmedo's eye that the possession of superior numbers did not guarantee Narváez the victory he seemed so sure of. Certainly his army could parade; it was much less obvious that it could fight. The problem wasn't the men, but the officers – a very poor set, lacking in all the finer qualities of leadership. They had fostered no *esprit de corps*, commanded no loyalty, lacked practical experience and yet had arranged matters so that nothing could be done without their direct involvement and command. There was no room at all for the men to exercise initiative or deploy their skills. As such, if the officers could be killed, taken prisoner, or otherwise isolated from the men, then it seemed likely that the men would immediately cease to be effective – like some huge armoured beast rendered harmless by a bolt through its tiny brain. Olmedo intended to convey the insight, and the analogy, to Cortés at the rendezvous later today. This was, after all, war, and anything that could bring it to an end quickly, and reduce the loss of life, was to be desired.

Meanwhile, the morale and integrity of Narváez's men had already been deeply undermined by gold, and last night, after dinner, Olmedo and Juan Velázquez de Léon had paid calls on Balthazar Bermudez and Francisco Verdugo, and later on Alonso Cano, the stable-master, who proved particularly susceptible to their proposals. Several other willing conspirators were also visited and rewarded. Finally there was a drinking party with gunners Rodrigo Martinez and Diego Usagre, men who could hold their liquor. Chains and rings and ingots changed hands as the cups were raised amidst empty promises of eternal friendship, and in this way the matter was settled. When the crucial moment came, Narváez's artillery would be crippled; some of the cannon would have their touch-holes stopped with wax; others would be aimed deliberately high, but they would not be permanently damaged as Cortés would surely find use for them in the future.

That was the point in the evening when Olmedo, none too steady on his feet himself, had helped a stumbling and almost incoherent Velázquez de Léon to his bed in the superior apartments allocated to officers. The friar, however, did not immediately return to his own mean room, but paid a visit to the kitchens before finally retiring for the night.

It had been a pleasant surprise to awaken this Saturday morning, evidently as yet unmurdered by a Velázquez henchman and with no very severe hangover. Wiping sleep from his eyes, Olmedo once again made his way from his own cramped and unpleasant quarters to the officers' more salubrious apartments, where he roused Juan from his snoring, farting sleep of the dead and waited while he dressed and adorned himself with his Swaggerer. The two had then taken a fine breakfast, and now here they were, under the awning on the green in front of the great pyramid. They were seated around a low table with Narváez, Salvatierra, Gamarra, Bermudez, Verdugo, the obnoxious youth, Diego Velázquez, and many others, already enjoying a barrel of something quite exquisite and watching the army march by like a colourful but hollow threat.

As the last of the men exited the square, and the cloud of dust began to settle, Juan turned to Narváez: 'You have brought a great force with you,' he said. 'May God increase it.'

'Ah,' Narváez replied in his most patronising tones. 'Now you can see that had I wished to go against Cortés, I should have taken him prisoner, and all of you that are with him.'

'Perhaps,' replied Velázquez de Léon, visibly bridling, 'but it might not have gone as you imagine. We are such men as know how to defend ourselves.'

'"We"? Why do you speak of "we", Don Juan! Am I to understand that you are firmly of the party of Cortés? And if that is indeed the case, then why, pray, did you come to me here at all?'

'I came here only to kiss your hands, Don Pánfilo, and those of all the gentlemen of your camp, to see if Your Excellency and Cortés could agree to keep peace and friendship.'

'What! To make friends and peace with that traitor who rebelled with the fleet against his cousin Diego Velázquez?'

'Traitor?' Velázquez de Léon half rose from his chair, hand falling to the hilt of his sword. 'Last night I warned that impudent child – ' he fixed the youth Diego with a ferocious glare – 'not to use such language in my presence, and I give you the same warning now, Pánfilo. His Majesty the king never had a more faithful servant than Don Hernando Cortés!'

'Be at peace, Juan,' Narváez said, waving a placating hand, his expression at the same time undergoing a ponderous adjustment, like some huge galleon changing tack, hostility and rage giving way to a fawning simper. 'Let us put such matters aside. I value you highly and wish you to join my company. Will you hear my proposal?'

'You are in your own camp, and may speak as you like.'

'The proposal is this. You will return to Cortés wherever he's skulking, and arrange with his followers to give him up to me and to come and place themselves under my command. When that's done and I have Cortés in my custody, I shall make you my deputy and my foremost captain. Well? What do you say to that?'

If Olmedo was surprised at the barefaced cheek of this, and also at its wild implausibility coming so soon after an angry difference of opinion, De Léon was icily furious: 'I hear you and those around you speak easily and often of treason, Don Pánfilo, but it would be a greater treason than any you have imagined here for me to desert the captain – to whom I've sworn obedience during war – and to abandon him in such a scurrilous manner, knowing as I do that what Cortés has done in these New Lands has been in the service of God, our Lord, and of His Majesty . . .'

'I do not trust the friar,' Narváez continued. It was as though he hadn't heard a word De Léon had just said. 'I'll keep him under arrest while you make the arrangements to have Cortés handed over to me.'

Velázquez de Léon was fully out of his chair now, almost overturning the wine barrel.

'I *told you* yesterday!' he roared. '*No one* is going to arrest this good friar, and there will be *no* arrangements to hand over Cortés.' Lowering his voice a fraction, he leaned towards Narváez: 'Can you not finally get it, you dimwit? I am Cortés's man, he is my caudillo; his is the only legitimate ruler in this land and you, sir, are nothing more than an upstart troublemaker whose intervention at this time is most unwelcome.'

Narváez blinked, seeming only now to grasp, or at least to accept finally, that bribery would not work. 'Then I shall arrest you both,' he said, and signalled his officers.

Salvatierra and Gamarra were eager and – Olmedo now noticed uneasily – already had a tough-looking sergeant and a squad of ten men on standby. The younger Diego Velázquez was hopping up and down, almost pissing his pants in excitement at the prospect. On the other hand, Jean Yuste, who had just joined them from parade, appeared discomfited, his features set in a disapproving frown, though he showed no sign of speaking out. Once again, therefore, it was only the vociferous intervention of Bermudez and Verdugo, who'd shared an extra five thousand pesos in gold yesterday, and the smaller but nonetheless numerous voices of other supporters, that saved the day.

Bermudez waxed particularly eloquent, saying he was astonished that Narváez would even consider ordering Juan Velázquez de Léon to be arrested – 'for what could Cortés do against Narváez even if he had another hundred Juan Velázquezes in his company?' Moreover, Bermudez suggested, Narváez should take into consideration the way that Cortés had received all those who had gone to his camp. True the first envoys Guevara, Vergara and Amaya had been roughly handled by the commander at Villa Rica de la Veracruz, but once they'd reached Cortés, they'd been treated like princes, and sent back with many fine presents of gold and jewels. The same went for Alonso de Mata and Bernardino de Quesada, who'd also returned laden like bees to their hives.

In view of this magnanimous treatment it would be barbaric, would it not, and might even be construed as an infamous act, for Narváez to arrest Cortés's envoys, particularly when one of them was so great a captain as Jean Velázquez de Léon and the other was a holy friar. Even in time of war, the niceties must be preserved, and the right thing to do, of course, was to allow the two men to leave, unhindered.

'And do you expect me to give them gold and jewels as well?' Narváez asked.

'No, sir, that will not be necessary. By allowing Juan Velázquez and the friar to leave freely you will satisfy honour.'

Narváez abruptly caved in. 'Very well then.' He waved furiously at Juan Velázquez and at Olmedo. 'Leave! It would be better if you had never come.'

Now was the moment when young Diego Velázquez, who'd clearly been under strict orders to restrain himself this morning, decided he could stand the outrage no more. '*Coward!*' he yelled at Juan. '*Turncoat! Traitor!* You sully the great name of our family.' He lunged closer and spat at the older man but missed.

Velázquez de Léon stood stroking his chin, looking at Diego evenly. 'I swear by my beard,' he said after a beat, 'that I will discover very soon if your courage is as big as your words.'

The threat, Olmedo thought, was all the more effective for being delivered calmly and quietly. 'Come on,' he urged, 'let's get out of here while we still can.' He took Juan by the elbow, surprised to find that the big man was trembling with rage. 'You did well to control yourself,' he whispered.

'Any more of those vaunting words and I swear I would have killed him,' Juan fulminated.

'I'm relieved you didn't! It would have given Narváez just the excuse he needed to arrest us.'

Agreeing to meet at the stables within the half-hour, Olmedo and Velázquez de Léon first went their separate ways about the camp to collect their bags and distribute their remaining gifts. The night before, Olmedo had finalised an agreement with the chef Pero Trigueros, with whom he'd been carefully cultivating a friendship since his first visit to Narváez.

To complete the agreement, three little gold ingots and a large linen bag had to be handed to Trigueros, and this Olmedo now hurried to the kitchens to do this. 'It is all as we discussed last night,' he said, handing over the ingots and the bag.

'And the rest of the gold?'

'I'll give you the other three ingots after the battle, when the job's done. And I will know, Trigueros, whether you have done as I ask you or not.'

Trigueros was peering suspiciously into the bag and sniffing its contents: 'How can I be sure these aren't poisonous?' he asked. 'I don't mind inconveniencing our officers, or taking your gold for doing so, but I don't want to kill anyone.'

Olmedo pushed his hand into the bag and pulled out one of the dried mushrooms at random. There were about a hundred of them in there. He'd had his scouts collect them for him in the couple of days after he'd first experienced their power in Iztapalapa, and they'd assured him that the desiccation process did not in any way affect potency. He popped the mushroom in his mouth and chewed it vigorously – 'there, you see, not poison. But if I were to eat, say, six of these at one time, I'd become inebriated, and that's what I want to happen to the entire officer corps here this evening.'

'So it's as you told me last night? There are enough mushrooms here for all the officers?'

'Yes, definitely. Just cut them up into smaller pieces and throw them into the communal pot . . . What are you giving them tonight?'

'Rabbit stew.'

'Good. It should taste good with mushrooms. Make sure neither you, nor any of the other cooks, nor any of the men, eat that stew. This dish must be for the officers' table only.'

On his way to the stables, Olmedo sought out and was relieved to find Balthazar Bermudez. 'Well met, Balthazar. Suddenly I am in a great hurry, but I have a warning for you.'

'A warning? I'm all ears.'

'At the officers' high table at dinner this evening, the chef will serve rabbit stew. Don't eat any! Likewise, please also warn Verdugo and Martinez and all the others of our party not to eat any. I don't know how you will do this without attracting attention – perhaps the best way would be for some of you to avoid dinner entirely – but if you want to keep your wits about you tonight, don't eat that stew!'

Olmedo and Velázquez de Léon had met with Alonso Cano the stable-master the night before, and had transacted a very specific piece of business with him. Now their horses, fed, watered, brushed down, saddled and ready for the road, stood at the stable door.

Also waiting, bright-eyed, eager-to-please and intelligent, were Ruffo and Valdez. 'Thank God we've found you in time!' said Ruffo.

'In time for what, Miguel?' said Olmedo gently. He liked the two sentries very much. Thanks to them he'd been introduced to, and had successfully bribed, scores of common soldiers whose trust he might otherwise never have won.

'Begging your pardon, Father, but am I correct that you and Captain Velázquez de Léon are about to ride out? And that you are going to return to your camp? To the camp of Don Hernando Cortés?'

'Completely correct, Esteban.'

'In that case be careful, sirs, because we've heard whispers they're readying a troop of cavalry to follow you.'

'They're hoping we'll take them right to Cortés!' snorted Velázquez de Léon. 'Idiots! Come on, let's ride before they've mustered. And if they do follow us, we'll lead them a merry chase!' So saying, with surprising agility, the big man leapt into the saddle of his dappled mare, startling the animal and causing it to rear and wheel spectacularly, scattering gravel. He remained comfortably balanced, watching Olmedo, as the friar, with less physical grace, allowed himself to be helped to mount by Ruffo and Martinez.

The ride out of town took them through the main square – it was unavoidable – and past the awning where Narváez, Salvatierra, Gamarra, young Diego Velázquez and several others sat in the shade drinking and – rather astonishingly under the circumstances – playing cards. The

319

posture and absorbed manner of the officers suggested that Olmedo and Velázquez de Léon were beneath their notice, too unimportant to interrupt their game for, or even to pay the slightest attention to as they rode by.

Olmedo resisted a powerful urge to look back over his shoulder and, following Juan's example, spurred his horse to a canter. He was well bandaged, but it would not be long before his saddle sores reminded him of their presence – indeed, he winced, they had already begun to do so.

And another thing. That single dried mushroom he'd eaten in the kitchen to reassure Trigueros might not, as he'd hoped, be entirely without effect. It was too early to be sure, but he rather thought he might be beginning to feel a little strange.

Cortés had given Velázquez de Léon a false location for the rendezvous. *Good*, Olmedo decided, *since it's likely we're being followed, let's go there first*. Even that was not so simple, however. Juan declared they would not go directly to his meeting point, which lay to the southeast, on the south side of the Actopan river, but would head north instead until they were sure there was no pursuit.

They had left Cempoala in haste around half past midday, much earlier than anticipated, and the rendezvous with Cortés was not scheduled until the late afternoon – so there was time, and Olmedo welcomed it, despite his saddle sores. Though it seemed a petty matter, when so much else of real consequence was at stake, he felt uncomfortable that Cortés had only entrusted the true location to him, and had been worrying about how to break the news to his companion. Juan was a fiery and emotional man. He would certainly be offended that the caudillo had so doubted his loyalty as to resort to such a ploy – and that Olmedo had connived in the gambit.

But now, and God was indeed merciful, here was a potential solution presenting itself, or at any rate a very good reason to postpone disclosure of the vexed matter of the location until Olmedo had time to think up a better story.

If he could think up a better story.

If he could think clearly at all.

Because, without a doubt now, the further he rode in the suffocating heat, the more obvious it became that he had taken some inebriation from the single mushroom he'd consumed. He wasn't seeing visions, and devoutly hoped that none would appear, but he had the distinct sense that the blazing sun overhead was communicating with him – some sublime directive in the language of light that he could almost, but not quite, understand.

Then there was the matter of the trees as they rode by; their weird, stunted shadows, the meaningful way their leaves rustled, the gnarls in their bark, their twisted ancient roots. Suddenly it was obvious to him – how could he have missed it for so long? – that trees were not mere vegetable matter. They were . . . intelligences. Mighty and wise. Watchers upon the earth . . .

'Hey, Olmedo!' Juan's gruff shout jolted him out of his reverie, 'look back! That's a troop of horse!'

Olmedo turned in the saddle and saw a great cloud of dust rising up from the road about a mile behind them, its leading edge moving fast in their direction.

It could only be cavalry.

'Now let's really ride!' cackled Velázquez de Léon.

We're really riding already, Olmedo thought, for it had seemed to him that they were at full gallop. As Juan spurred his horse, however, and his own grey mare surged to follow suit, he realised that there were nuances to galloping, and that they were now flying across the ground, through the trees, over hummocks and into dips, at a speed significantly faster than before. *This is joy!* Olmedo thought. *How exciting!* There was almost no sensation of the animal beneath him at all. The pain of his saddle sores had vanished. *This is what it is to fly!* For it was as though he had taken wings and was soaring and swooping through the lush littoral under his own power.

'*Duck, you moron!*'

Without thinking, Olmedo threw himself forward, clasping the mare's neck as a thick branch swept over his head, leaves slapping at him. He pulled himself upright to see Juan just in front, his horse stretching out again in that effortless, floating gallop. After some minutes, however, he slowed and allowed Olmedo to catch up with him.

'We're not going to be able to lose them,' Juan said in an almost conversational tone. 'Our dust gives us away, just as theirs gives them away, so we're going to have to try something else. Are you all right, Bartolomé? That branch almost took your head off. Were you dreaming? Your eyes look very strange!'

'I'm all right. Just a momentary lapse.'

'Very well, but no more please! Now follow me. Do as I do. Above all, stay alert!'

With that Velázquez de Léon wheeled his horse in a great dust-scattering turn and headed back directly towards the oncoming cavalry.

Olmedo flew after him.

Teudile still languished in the stinking prison alongside Cuitláhuac, Cacama and the rebellious Mexica nobles, but Moctezuma was kept informed by other members of his personal staff, who had remained at their posts during his own period of imprisonment and who continued to serve him now in his apartments. He'd witnessed the second great slaughter in the plaza five days before; his windows offered an excellent view. And he'd been informed of the *tueles'* failed attempt to steal food in Tlatelolco, of the burning of their great boats, and of the attack on the postern. He'd not needed to be told about the sacrifice of the six Spanish captives, because he had seen this triumph for himself from the east window of his audience chamber.

What the *tueles* did not know, though they might suspect it, was that it was he, the great Moctezuma, through his network of staff and spies, who was directing the Mexica encirclement of Axayacatl's palace, and who had been the hidden hand behind every attack since his release from prison. There were some good men out there amongst his captains, but they needed the leadership that only he, the Great Speaker, could provide.

That was why, despite the great danger, he'd agreed to the plan presented to him this morning after the heads of the Tlascalan messengers had been delivered. Within the next week an attempt would be made to snatch him from the grip of the *tueles* and he must be ready. Certain preparations were required.

He requested an audience with Tonatiuh, and the captain quickly appeared, fully armoured, his blond hair gleaming. 'What can I do for you, Mucktey?' he asked. It was the name he used when he wished to insult rather than to flatter.

'I will be in your debt,' Moctezuma replied through the translator Aguilar, 'if you will kindly release my steward Teudile from prison and permit him to reside here with me in my apartments.'

Tonatiuh studied him keenly. 'Teudile? That wily bastard? I'd rather keep him where he is. Why do you need him?'

'To manage my affairs.'

Suddenly interested, Tonatiuh leaned forward and asked: 'What's it worth to you to have him back?'

They settled, eventually, on five hundred chickens and five hundred loads of tortillas.

It was the lean, proper, and primly correct Jean Yuste who led the pursuit – forty men, about half of Narváez's total force of cavalry. That in itself, Olmedo reflected, indicated the amateurishness of the enterprise. Forty was not a sufficient number to come away unscathed if they ran into Cortés – indeed, unsupported by infantry, crossbowmen and gunners, it would be most unwise to go against him with so few. At the same time, however, forty was too many for a clandestine pursuit that might actually hope to achieve the worthwhile objective of discovering Cortés's position so that it could later be descended upon in force. The troop's dust rose high into the air, hanging above and behind them like a swarm of locusts, and would be visible for miles.

Olmedo and Velázquez de Léon, at full gallop, had just entered a wide, upward-sloping expanse of open ground, mostly rocky with low, scattered trees and scrub vegetation, when Yuste and his boys came pouring over the ridge a few hundred paces above them, uttering great whoops and halloos of triumph on sighting their quarry, then at once relapsing into silence as they realised the two men were no longer fleeing but instead riding directly towards them.

In seconds they were enveloped by the entire troop, men with red, excited faces, many with swords in their hands, wheeling around them, enclosing them. 'We just sit,' said Juan, taking Olmedo's reins. 'We do nothing.'

Soon enough, Captain Jean Yuste, flanked by two ensigns, rode through the press towards them. A lean, usually silent man in his early forties, with thinning hair and a permanently tired manner, he seemed almost apologetic now.

'What the *hell* is the meaning of this?' Velázquez de Léon demanded in immediate, incandescent fury. 'You know perfectly well that I and Father Olmedo are the ambassadors of Don Hernando Cortés. We came bearing his message. We attempted, without success, to make peace. But now, as we return to our camp, despite the promise of your commander to give us safe passage, we discover you following us. Explain yourself!'

'I did not hear Don Pánfilo Narváez grant you safe passage,' Yuste said. You could see from his eyes that he knew this was a weak argument.

'But you heard him ordering us to leave,' Olmedo came back at him, 'and you heard the discussion that went before. Your commander did consider arresting us, it's true, but he listened to the arguments of others and, what was the phrase, he "satisfied honour" by releasing us? If that is not a clear offer of safe passage, then I don't know what is.'

Olmedo was amazed he'd managed to speak at all. It was not that his tongue was thick, although it was, but that Yuste's head, his bare scalp glowing pinkly through his thinning hair, was undergoing certain deformations that were most distracting to view. That single dried mushroom had obviously been very potent! But at the same time, Olmedo thought, the effects were definitely more manageable than before. At least he could hold a rational conversation!

Yuste was looking at him as though thoroughly perplexed – how much time had passed? A second? A minute? – when Velázquez de Léon roared: 'Yes. Satisfy honour!' and rode his horse, rather threateningly Olmedo thought, around the cavalry captain, disclaiming in suddenly quieter tones, as though speaking to a child: 'In war, Yuste, it is sometimes necessary for the commanders of enemy camps to communicate with one another by means of envoys. The good friar and I are such envoys. Under the rules of war, you may not arrest us, and by the word of your own commander you must give us free passage. If you do arrest us and should our side prevail, you'll face the death penalty: hanging if you're lucky, something a bit more extended if you're not.'

Looking on, Olmedo saw that Yuste was thinking about it. He was most likely an honourable man. He seemed to stand aloof from Narváez's inner clique. 'Captain Yuste,' the words bubbled up spontaneously, 'I understand that threats don't scare you, and I ask you to release us because you know it's the right thing to do. Very soon, mark my words, you will find your position much changed. In the battle to come, Cortés will triumph. Your commander Narváez will be overthrown and in chains, and any loyalty you may feel to him will be without purpose. I do not ask you to join us now. I merely ask you *do the right thing* and release us as true envoys who must, under the rules of war, be allowed to pass freely.'

'Ride with me,' Velázquez de Léon now said to Yuste, who nodded in curt agreement. The two captains cantered away upslope, a few hundred paces closer to the ridge line and out of earshot, leaving Olmedo surrounded by the cavalrymen.

With the more powerful effects of the mushroom now wearing off, giving way to a pleasant glow, he beamed in an avuncular fashion around him at these rough, for the most part very youthful, soldiers, a few of whom he knew from Cuba and some of the older ones from the Italian wars.

It was one of these, a grizzled forty-year-old called Alvaro Perez, who'd marched beside Olmedo in the terrible retreat from Ravenna in 1512, who spoke up first: 'Hey, Bartolomé! Good to have you with us. It's been too long. But now that you're here and I know you to be a right holy friar who tells the truth: did you really mean it?'

'Did I mean what, exactly?' Olmedo asked.

'Did you mean it when you said Cortés would win?'

'Goodness me yes! Of course I meant it. Your commanders really have no idea of the slaughter they're sleepwalking all of you into.'

Many other heads were turning now, and men clustering close, all wanting to know more about Cortés: 'Father, is it true that fifty thousand savage Indians have joined his army?'

Olmedo laughed the suggestion away. 'Fifty thousand? Nonsense. The real number is much lower – not more than thirty thousand.'

It was perhaps not exactly a lie. Shikotenka could call twice as many if Tlascala's interests were involved. But the truth was that right now there were neither thirty thousand, nor twenty thousand, nor ten thousand Indian auxiliaries in the army Cortés was about to throw against Narváez; in fact there were no auxiliaries at all.

It was, however, unnecessary for these cavaliers to know this.

Another question: 'Father, is it true that in the camp of Cortés, even the poorest man has become rich, and that there's so much gold they make sport with it?'

'If you mean do they chance their ingot or chain of gold at cards, then most unfortunately the answer is yes. The camp of Cortés is no more immune to the vice of gambling than any other – but with one important difference: the men are rich and thus able to replenish their stock from the bottomless supply that the expedition commands.'

'We've heard they have more gold than the royal treasury,' someone offered.

Olmedo shrugged: 'I've heard that too,' he said. 'It could be true. But since I've never seen the royal treasury, I can't swear by the comparison.'

'It's rumoured, Father – ' another questioner – 'that you've been distributing gold to likely lads who might come over to Cortés . . . Care to distribute some to us?'

Olmedo calculated that as many as one hundred and fifty of Narváez's men had, by this time, either been directly bribed by himself or others, or had received their share of a bribe through trickle-down, so it was astonishing that none of these horsemen appeared to have had any.

'Alas all my treasure for today is spent,' he said, 'but you have my word that if you stand down in the battle to come, you'll be rewarded in the days that follow . . .'

'Stand down, Father?'

'I mean simply do not engage. When Cortés attacks, don't engage him; just stay out of it and let those who still love Narváez do the fighting.'

Velázquez de Léon and Yuste came riding back and shook hands formally. Then Yuste ordered his men to form up, and within minutes was leading them away, streaming upslope and over the ridge until the last of them disappeared from view.

'My goodness,' said Olmedo. 'He's letting us go?'

A broad grin: 'Yes. That's the deal. And not only that. If he keeps his word we should face no trouble from his cavalry tonight.'

'Remarkable. He seems such a stickler for the rules and regulations.'

'Every man has his price.'

'You bribed him! How much?'

'I gave him my Swaggerer.'

Olmedo suddenly noticed that the spectacular gold chain was no longer draped around De Léon's neck and shoulders. 'Your Swaggerer!' he said genuinely surprised. 'My goodness, Juan, that's a huge personal sacrifice you're making.'

Another grin, wolfish this time: 'I intend to have it back after the battle.'

Now that the chase was off, Olmedo went through with the charade of allowing Velázquez de Léon to lead him to the place of rendezvous Cortés had agreed with him, about four miles southeast of Cempoala, just south of the Actopan river. In the past days, Juan had so disarmingly and heart-warmingly proved his loyalty to the caudillo that the friar simply could not bear for him to discover how grievously he'd been mistrusted.

'I suppose it's still early,' the big captain mused, scratching his head when, after fording the river with some difficulty, they arrived in the little concealed valley that he believed was the muster point. 'But it's odd. Cortés marches them at a steady pace. They should be here by now.'

Olmedo summoned a mental map of the region. The place Cortés had given him as the true rendezvous point lay three miles northwest of Cempoala, but also on the south side of the river, and they were now four miles southeast of the town. What was interesting was the straight line, seven miles long, that connected the two points from northwest to southeast. On the two-and-a-half day forced march from Perote, the army's route, if extended to the southeast, would bring it to where they were now. Suddenly the entire solution presented itself, perfect and fully formed, in Olmedo's mind. 'I have a suggestion,' he said brightly. 'We know where they're coming from, they're a big column and they'll have scouts out. We're bound to run into them if we just ride northwest.'

'Excellent idea,' Velázquez de Léon said. He was already spurring his horse.

Olmedo followed, his heart beating fast. It was almost touchingly simple and trusting, the way Juan had so easily taken the bait. The deceit was of course sinful but, as he often had to remind himself these days, this was war.

For the last exhausting miles of the march through the long morning and well past noon of that Saturday 28 May, Whitsun Eve, Cortés led the army steadily southeast across the damp and soggy floodplain of the Actopan river. It was not a route that any commander who cared for the comfort of his men would choose. Most now had great clumps of mud gummed to their boots and were dragging their feet the last weary mile through the clinging fen. They were too tired even to curse him, but they should be thanking him – and for two reasons. First, this route kept the river between themselves and Narváez and that, at any rate, would limit the possibilities of him mounting a surprise attack. Secondly, though dry, the direct route into Cempoala, some miles north of the river, was dusty and, if they'd taken it, the great plume they kicked up would long since have signalled their approach.

Besides, even if Narváez was supremely confident of his own strength, as all reports indicated, he would surely at least have posted lookouts along the main road?

Cortés was taking no chances, and the long weary trek was nearly done, with the prospect of some hours of joyous and peaceful rest in the secluded, hidden spot that he and Sandoval had selected, close to the river but on higher, dry ground at the edge of a forest, just three miles from Cempoala. From there, with the men refreshed, and at the hour of his choosing, he would take his army across the river and launch the attack on that pestilential fool Narváez, whose coming had caused so much trouble.

The toe of his boot caught in a tangled patch of marsh grass and he stumbled. Sandoval steadied him. 'Good news, Caudillo,' he said, 'we're almost there. Up that slope and into the forest. A few hundred paces.'

The clearing was as Sandoval and Olmedo had described it. The forest floor was dry and sprinkled with a soft carpet of browning pine needles. There was the stump of the great tree felled the previous year to make the cross. There were the heaps of big boulders. There were the rapids down below, the very sound of the water running over the stones was cooling!

The men needed no instruction. Some scrambled to the river to refill canteens, a few even stripped off and jumped into the icy water with groans of relief, but most threw themselves down immediately to sleep on the soft forest floor in the shady clearing, sprawled out uncaringly, immediately dead to the world.

Cortés looked them over. A fine company. Some of them would be sleeping their last, for there would certainly be deaths tonight. Who could guess? Perhaps he himself would be slain in this foolish battle caused entirely by another's envy and greed? It was well to remember that death could visit anyone at any moment in the melee.

Nonetheless, he did not believe that he would die. He was here, in this New Spain, to accomplish great things, not to be laid in his grave by so inferior a foe as Narváez.

There came a loud 'hello' from below, an exchange of passwords, and the sound of hooves drumming on the slope up to the edge of the forest. One of the scouts reporting back! Cortés walked briskly from the clearing through the trees and met the rider as he came towards him, seeing it was young Farfan. Though a foot soldier, he'd proved himself a good and willing horseman since that night on the road to Iztapalapa and had volunteered repeatedly for scout duties.

'Two riders approaching from the southeast along the riverbank,' he now announced with a smart salute. 'It's Captain Velázquez de Léon, sir, and Father Olmedo! They're back!'

'Thank you, Farfan. This is good news. They are alone, I hope? No sign of any pursuit?'

'No pursuit, sir. We have scouts keeping oversight for ten miles in every direction around Cempoala, south and north of the Actopan. Narváez sent a cavalry detachment out northward a few hours ago, but they returned; since then his whole army have stayed in their camp inside the town . . .'

Cortés was effusive in his embraces of Velázquez de Léon and Olmedo. Moreover, for some reason Juan did not seem to be offended, or even to know, that he'd been given the wrong location for the rendezvous, and jokingly mocked Cortés for being 'so late that we had to come and find you'. A warning glance from Olmedo deterred further questioning.

During the afternoon, heavy rainclouds began to gather, and had completely obscured the sun, bringing a welcome freshness to the air, when another scout rode in at around five p.m. bringing an urgent report. Very rapidly, and giving no prior warning of his intent, Narváez had mobilised almost his entire army, marched his arquebusiers, artillery, horsemen and crossbowmen, as well as his massed infantry, out of Cempoala, and formed them up on flat terrain about a mile east of the town, where they were being kept under observation from two different points by scouts.

Cortés assembled his captains and asked for their thoughts.

'He's obviously challenging us to meet him in battle,' said Ordaz.

'If so, then equally obviously it means he knows we're here,' said Cristóbal de Olid.

'Well certainly he knows,' said Velázquez de Léon. 'He could be in no doubt that my embassy with Olmedo was the last chance for diplomacy.'

'Besides,' offered Sandoval, 'you can be sure local Indians have spotted our advance by now. It would be almost a miracle if he'd had no warning from them.'

'Knowing what we do of Narváez's character,' Cortés mused, 'my guess is that even if they've warned him, he's chosen to disbelieve them – otherwise, presumably, though he'd have to cross the river, he'd be here.'

Velázquez de Léon rolled his eyes. 'Narváez is a madman. Who can say what a madman will do?'

'Narváez is certainly mad,' added Olmedo, who'd been listening in from the sidelines. 'But his behaviour is to some extent predictable. Clearly he's received some intelligence this afternoon that our army is in the vicinity, but I agree with you, Hernán – he's never posted proper lookouts and he doesn't seem to have any use for scouts, so he's not sure where! You're still more like some vague undefined threat to him than a real and present danger that might take him by surprise. Beyond all other considerations, I suspect he longs for a formal battle, fought in chivalric style. The idea of confronting and overwhelming you on an open field with no tricky obstacles for his cavalry to work around is something that's bound to appeal to his sense of order and entitlement.'

Cortés laughed. 'In that case it will please me greatly *not* to give him what he longs for. The fool has formed up in full view of our scouts, so we'll get reports soon enough if he moves. Meanwhile I say let's just leave him where he is while we take our rest.'

He looked up at the darkening sky, now boiling with thick grey clouds, as the first drops of rain began to patter down on the forest canopy and a powerful gust of wind shook the trees.

Chapter Seventeen

Evening, Saturday 28 May 1520–small hours, Sunday 29 May 1520

It was full dark now, with crazed gusts of wind seeming to come from every direction and rain pouring down steadily, but brands had been lit in sheltered spots about the clearing and their guttering glare cast a weird, shifting half-light on the men's faces as they gathered, beneath the canopy of the great trees, listening in rapt attention to the words of their caudillo.

It was not the first such performance Bernal Díaz had witnessed. Indeed, if there was time, Cortés liked to give a speech before every battle and have his secretary Pepillo note his words down for posterity. But the words themselves always seemed to come from the heart and so Díaz, who preferred to keep his life as uncomplicated as possible, appreciated them and was often moved by them.

Tonight, he could see already, was going to be no exception. Cortés was mounted on Molinero in the midst of the throng. 'You will well remember, gentlemen,' he was saying, 'how often we have been at the point of death in the wars and battles we've passed through.'

Cries of 'Aye! You're right, commander.'

'Let me also remind you,' Cortés continued, 'how inured we are to hardships – ' he looked up again at the sky – 'rains, winds and sometimes hunger, always having to carry our arms on our backs and to sleep on the ground whether it's snowing or raining, our skins already tanned from suffering.'

There was a general shuffling and mumbling of approbation.

'And let us not forget our many comrades, more than fifty of them, who have died to get us to this point, nor all of you who are bandaged in rags and maimed from wounds which are not even yet healed.'

Looks of pride and long-suffering fortitude on the men's faces.

'The caudillo's telling it like it is,' Díaz overheard one foot soldier say to another.

'Course he is, you ass! That's why he's the caudillo.'

For that and a great many other reasons, Díaz thought.

Cortés raised himself up in his stirrups: '*Do you remember Tlascala?*' he shouted.

Cries of 'Aye' and 'How can we forget?'

'Then you will remember in what straits fierce Shikotenka placed us, and how they handled us! Yet in the end we prevailed. Do you remember the affair of Cholula? They had even prepared the earthen pots in which to cook our bodies! Then, during the dangers of our entry into and stay in the great city of Tenochtitlan, how many times did we look death in the face? Who is able to count them?'

Cortés paused before coming to his point: 'Consider then the hardships you underwent in discovering this country, and the hunger and thirst of the wounded and the loss by death of so many of your comrades. Will you allow all this to be in vain because of the greed and lust of Diego de Velázquez in Cuba and his agent Narváez, who he's sent here to take what's ours and capture us, and drive us from our property?'

A tremendous, unified roar of 'No!'

'Pánfilo Narváez,' Cortés continued, as the angry shouts died down, 'who marches against us with great fury and desire to get us in his power, calling us traitors and malefactors before he'd even landed, sending messages to Moctezuma to urge him to rise up against us, and now proclaiming war against us from his camp and outlawing us as though we are Moors!

'Imagine, then, our fate, if by ill luck we should fall into his hands. God prevent it! For then all the services that we have done both to God and His Majesty will be turned to disservice; they will bring lawsuits against us, saying that we killed and robbed and destroyed the land when, in truth, they are the ones to rob, brawl and disserve our Lord and king, but they will claim that they have served him.'

'Bastards,' someone shouted from the press of men surrounding Cortés. 'Don't let them get away with it!'

The caudillo raised a mailed fist in acknowledgement. 'As true gentlemen,' he said, 'I believe we are bound to stand up for His Majesty's honour, and for our own homes and property. I am but one and can do no more than one does. Compromises have been suggested to me which were good for me, but only for me; yet, as they were not good for you, I have refused them. You see what the position is; and since this business touches every one of you, let every man say what he feels about fighting or seeking peace; no one will be prevented from doing what he may wish.'

'Seek peace?' said Sandoval. 'Who would want to seek peace with those dogs?'

'*Not I*,' bellowed Díaz, eager to support his good friend, and so many were the voices raised to echo him it seemed that the entire army spoke as one man.

'*We fight!*' roared Velázquez de Léon, and again the shout was taken up by a great number of the officers and men, no one holding back: '*We fight! We fight! We fight!*'

There was a surge towards Cortés; he was lifted bodily out of Molinero's saddle, amidst cheers and claps on the back, and thence carried so many times around the clearing on the beefy shoulders of a pack of infantrymen that eventually he had to beg them to set him down.

When he was back on his feet and standing in the midst of the press, he once again adopted a grave tone: 'Gentlemen, you know there's a saying among soldiers, "At dawn fall upon your enemy"? But if our presence has been detected, as we have reason to believe, then our enemies already await us, and if not, since it will be hard to sleep before a battle, I suggest we use this time for fighting and take our leisure when we've secured our victory. What say you?'

Most of the men had indeed been expecting to attack at dawn; it was something of a tradition – but of course, Díaz reflected, the caudillo was right, as he usually was. Only those who were already dead slept well before a battle! Besides, it was unseasonably cold, wildly wet and very windy, and there was really no purpose to be served in skulking in this forest a moment longer, brooding over the morrow, when the matter could be settled by a swift and unexpected night attack.

'Let's bring them to battle *tonight!*' Díaz found himself agreeing at the top of his voice, and again so persuasive had the caudillo been that the mass of the men were of the same mind.

Out of the black downpour there came a drumming of hooves and a scout, dripping wet, rode in at a gallop. 'Narváez is on the move!' he gasped. 'His whole army. Heading this way.'

'*To arms!*' Cortés yelled. '*To arms!*'

The alarm turned out to be false – or anyway premature.

It was true, after maintaining his formations on the open plain a mile north of Cempoala for some hours as evening gathered, darkness fell and the torrential rain set in for the night, that Narváez had suddenly led his entire force on a rapid deployment towards the south. At first it did look very much like the prelude to an attack. However, a series of further reports from the scouts shadowing the column took the pressure off. The destination was not Cortés's position south of the river, which Narváez still seemed to be unaware of, but the town of Cempoala itself, into which the army quickly disappeared. Dismounting and following the column silently on foot, one of the scouts learned that the motive for the march had been nothing more martial than a desire to seek shelter from the rain and enjoy a good dinner. There seemed to be no suspicion at all that Cortés would try anything so inconvenient as a night attack. A few sentries had been posted, and the artillery had been drawn up in the main square, but Narváez had been overheard to say he was confident that no one would have to fight in the dark, and that everyone should eat and sleep well so they'd be refreshed and ready to do battle at dawn.

'The Lord has delivered our enemy unto our hands,' Cortés said as he shared the news with the men. 'It's greatly to our advantage to attack them in Cempoala, for we know that town far better than they do and, thanks to Father Olmedo and Juan Velázquez, we already have good intelligence of how they dispose their forces there. But I beg you a favour. Surprise is our greatest weapon, therefore keep silent as we approach and when we drive home the attack! No shouting! No battle cries! No clatter of a carelessly dropped shield! We come at them in deadly quiet. Do you agree?'

Who could disagree? Díaz thought. And plainly no one did.

'Another thing,' Cortés continued. 'I know you're all brave men. I know that every one of you wants to push forward among the first to get at the enemy and so to gain honour. But too much of such spirit can make a rabble of an army. Prudence and calculation are at least as important as daring on the battlefield. I therefore propose to arrange you in order and in five separate companies, each with specific tasks tonight.'

The men looked on eagerly. They were the pack and Cortés was their leader. They might dispute with him on other matters, but they knew him to be a master strategist and always left the order of battle entirely to him.

'The first task is to seize their artillery,' Cortés said. 'Our intelligence is that they have seventeen cannon, mostly falconets but a couple of lombards as well, and that we'll find them drawn up in front of the great pyramid where Narváez has his quarters . . . Cristóbal,' he caught Olid's eye, 'you will lead this attack with your company of eighty. Select your men.'

The first man Cristóbal chose was Díaz.

Cortés seemed momentarily lost in thought as Olid's selections continued. 'Our enemy,' he said finally, and every eye was focused on him, 'outnumbers us almost three to one, but they are not so used to arms as we are, the greater part of them are hostile to their captain and we shall take them by surprise. I've heard much of the character of Narváez and his officers from our excellent spy Father Olmedo – ' a glance of acknowledgement at the friar – 'and agree with his conclusion. The men we confront tonight have no stomach to carry the fight without orders and coercion from above, so if we can kill or capture Narváez and his principal captains then the battle will be won . . . Gonzalo – ' he signalled to Sandoval – 'I'm putting you in charge of the detachment of eighty who will seize Narváez, and so that in future there will be no misunderstanding of what was done, I give you this written order.' As he spoke, his secretary Pepillo approached and handed him a scroll, which Cortés proceeded to read out by the light of a blazing torch:

'Gonzalo de Sandoval, Chief Constable of this New Spain, in His Majesty's name I command you to seize the person of Pánfilo Narváez and, should he resist, to kill him, for the benefit of the service of God and the king, insomuch as he has committed many acts to the disservice of God and of His Majesty.

'Given in this camp and signed by Hernando Cortés.'

There were cheers from the men as Sandoval took the order. When they died down Cortés yelled: 'Hey, Farfan, show yourself.'

Out of the crowd appeared Andres Farfan. 'Yes, Caudillo.'

'You'll join Sandoval's eighty. Fight well tonight.'

The next assignment was for Diego de Ordaz, also with a force of eighty. His task was to arrest Narváez's deputy Alonso de Salvatierra.

The fourth company of eighty would be led by Juan Velázquez, also with the objective of killing or capturing officers, and with the specific task of arresting the youth, Diego Velázquez, with whom he'd quarrelled.

Lastly there was Cortés himself, with the remaining sixty men organised as a flying squad that could respond rapidly to any emergency and be brought to bear wherever they were needed. He requested the expedition's two best gun crews to stick with him, putting them under the command of Francisco de Mesa, the chief of artillery. A short stocky, middle-aged professional soldier with thinning hair, a spade beard and a broad, unemotional, sunburned face, Mesa knew more about cannon and how to use them than any other man alive.

'A reward of three thousand pesos to the hero who first lays his hand on Narváez!' the caudillo now shouted. 'Two thousand for the second! One thousand for the third. And look out for those captains! There's a thousand pesos each on the heads of Salvatierra, Gamarra and Bono de Quejo.'

There was a visible stir amongst the men and a hubbub of excited conversation arose. Cortés allowed it to continue for a moment, then waved for silence: 'So, gentlemen, our lives and honour depend, after God, on your courage and your strong arms. I have no other favour to ask of you or to remind you of but that this night will forever be the touchstone of our honour and glory.'

It was close to midnight, every weapon checked, every precaution taken, when Cortés formed the men up in their five companies on the riverbank to begin the crossing. They numbered three hundred and eighty in total, three hundred of them armed with the long, barbed, copper-headed Chinantla pikes against possible cavalry attack.

The first service the pikes gave, however, was on the crossing of the river itself. Close to its south bank there was a sheltered, shallow pool where men had splashed earlier, but beyond that the water deepened and grew faster. On horseback it could be crossed easily if care was taken, and the scouts had done so repeatedly, but men on foot were in places up to their chests in the icy current.

Pepillo bound Melchior to him with a rope tied to the hound's collar and about his own waist, then he and Malinal grasped the stirrups of Cortés's great charger Molinero, and with four soldiers clinging to the cinch straps they entered the river. Pepillo kept as tight a grip on Melchior's collar as he did on the stirrup, and the dog paddled gamely through the rushing flood. All seemed well, if hazardous, and then came a moment of chaos. A foot soldier with no pike to test the depth of the water ahead suddenly plunged beneath the surface, rose up again flailing and gasping for air, and was swept downstream. He was borne past Molinero and through a line of other men, colliding with one who uttered a despairing howl and was also carried away.

Pepillo glanced up at Cortés in the saddle. He'd witnessed the whole

336

incident, but his lips were set and he ordered no rescue attempt, nor did he even look back as he urged the army across the river.

There were no further losses, but a tough trek of almost an hour followed on a road mired with deep mud and tangled brushwood. Not for an instant did the steady, soaking downpour cease. The men marched, their heads down against the storm, gripping their weapons. Then – a miracle! Less than a mile from Cempoala, with the lights of the town already in sight, the column came upon a cross that had been erected by the expedition during its march from Villa Rica to Tenochtitlan the year before. None of the scouts shadowing Narváez had seen it on their way back and forth, yet now here it was! *The caudillo won't waste this opportunity*, thought Pepillo and, sure enough, Cortés immediately dismounted and knelt before the blessed sign, where he proceeded to confess his sins and to declare his great object to be the triumph of the holy Catholic faith. All the men followed in a general confession and received absolution from Father Olmedo, who invoked the blessing of heaven on the warriors and consecrated their swords to the glory of the cross.

Pepillo felt tears spring up in his eyes, and shared the heightened emotion as the tough, ragged, exhausted soldiers rose up from the confession and embraced one another as brothers in a great cause.

Adjoining the road near the cross was a little coppice, quite sheltered from the storm. Here Cortés had his soldiers deposit the baggage and everything superfluous that might encumber movement. All seven of the horses were also brought and their reins fastened to trees.

Cortés summoned Pepillo and Malinal. 'You'll both be staying here,' he said.

'But, sir,' Pepillo began to object. He wore the sword he'd received from Juan de Escalante before his death, and remembered every lesson the good captain had given him in the use of it. 'I want to fight!' he protested. 'I want to do my bit.'

'You'll be doing your bit by staying here, boy.'

'As a caretaker?' Pepillo felt that he was a man now, with manly skills, and was ferociously disappointed to be left out. 'For the baggage?'

'And the horses. But, most important, Pepillo – ' Cortés lowered his voice – 'I need and require that you remain here for our beloved Malinal. A great battle is about to be fought, less than a mile away. We cannot know the outcome of that battle. I believe we will win, but if our side loses, it will go very badly for us afterwards. In that case I charge you with Malinal's safety. You will not take her back to Tenochtitlan, for without my protection the Mexica will kill her. You must take her instead to Tlascala where she will be safe. Shikotenka will give her sanctuary.'

'Always the case with men,' tutted Malinal, who'd heard every word. 'You discuss me as though I'm not here.'

'Sometimes decisions must be made,' Cortés said gruffly, 'and then it's better just to make them and be done.' He stepped forward and embraced Malinal: 'Be safe, my love, I'll see you very soon.'

He shook Pepillo's hand gravely and strode out of the coppice to join the men assembled in battle order. Faintly, from the road, his last urgent command to the army came back to them: 'Everything depends on obedience now. Let no man, from desire of distinguishing himself, break his ranks. On silence, despatch, and, above all, obedience to your officers the success of our enterprise depends.'

The column moved out, quietly, stealthily, the sound of the march muffled by the storm.

In the coppice the horses were restless and Pepillo could not quickly calm them. When he returned to Malinal he found her rigging a length of sailcloth from the baggage to make a shelter – for the rain penetrated even here and dripped from every branch. He hurried to help her; another length of sailcloth was procured to spread on the ground and, in this way, quite soon, they had a makeshift tent.

As they stooped inside and made themselves comfortable, Melchior followed. The great hound was still soaked through from the river crossing and shook himself mightily, showering them with drops of cold water. Oblivious, he sighed and stretched himself out across the opening of the shelter, his massive head and jaws silhouetted against the faint luminance of the night.

The men moved with such stealth and speed, and so silently, thanks to the muffling effect of the rain, that Olid's squad – in the lead – surprised two of Narváez's lookouts at their post on the outskirts of Cempoala. There was a brief fight. One of the spies was captured. The other escaped and fled back towards the town centre crying: 'To arms! To arms!'

Cortés shouldered his way forward through the column, rapidly understood the situation, seized the captured lookout by the throat and began to strangle him. 'Is Narváez in his quarters on top of the pyramid?' he asked. 'Tell me now if you want to live.' He tightened his grip: 'Well? Will you speak?'

His eyes bulging in panic, the lookout nodded his head. 'Speak then,' said Cortés, relaxing his stranglehold.

The answer was yes. Complaining of illness, Narváez had retired for the night to his quarters in the temple on top of the great pyramid. Better still, two of his three principal officers – Bono de Quejo and Gamarra – were with him. They were guarded by crossbowmen on the upper platform, twenty cavalry were below on the patio, and hundreds of infantry were billeted and sleeping nearby.

What a fool Narváez is! Cortés thought. By concentrating so many of his officers in one place, he made it impossible for them to fulfil any useful command functions, and at the same stroke made them much easier to capture or kill. Both of the other, smaller, pyramids in the town's main square were also occupied by his forces, one commanded by Salvatierra, the other by Diego Velázquez, the nephew of the governor of Cuba. But there, too, in most cases, it seemed that the men would be asleep.

Not any longer! Cortés thought. The escaped lookout had already given the alarm. The camp was awake and scrambling to battle positions.

'We all know what to do,' Cortés told the men, 'so let us go and do our duty. Olid, Díaz – the artillery. Sandoval – ' he took the young captain by the arm – 'you see that light there?' He pointed to a lantern glimmering in a high place dead ahead. Sandoval confirmed that he saw it. 'It is Narváez's quarters,' Cortés said, 'on top of the great pyramid. Take that light as your beacon and bring me Narváez, dead or alive.'

Bernal Díaz went in with the first wave of Olid's squad to seize the enemy artillery. Intelligence reports and the information squeezed from the lookout agreed that all seventeen of the cannon would be found drawn up in the central square around the great pyramid. Since the lookout had also revealed that twenty cavalrymen were on patrol in the square, every one of Olid's eighty, including Díaz himself, were armed with the long Chinantla pikes.

Strangely, although the alarm had been given, no opposition at all was encountered for the first few hundred paces into the suburbs. As Díaz would later write in his diary, the escaped lookout's report had – astonishingly! – not been welcomed by the senior officers atop the pyramid, who claimed to be unwell. Narváez had actually taken to his bed and refused to see him! When the lookout insisted, Bono de Quejo stumbled from one of the inner shrines of the old temple and said, in a strange voice: 'You've been deceived by your fears, my man. You must have mistaken the noise of the storm and the waving of the bushes for the enemy.'

The lookout was forthwith dismissed, bewildered, to his own quarters, warning them they would pay a price for their own incredulity.

Nor, it transpired, was this the only warning Narváez had ignored. The local Totonac Indians had known immediately when Cortés and his army had arrived within striking distance of Cempoala on the south bank of the Actopan river. Word had been brought to Tlacoch, the enormously fat paramount chief, and he in turn had rushed to Narváez and upbraided the Spanish commander saying: 'What are you about? You are behaving very carelessly. Do you think that Malinche and the *tueles* he brings with him are the same as you? Well, I tell you that when you least expect it, he will be here and he will kill you.'

The fat chief had been waved away and told to mind his own business on the grounds that Spaniards knew how to defend themselves.

In retrospect, with the benefit of hindsight, it was clear that the mysterious illness Narváez suffered that night, together with his sloth, folly, incapacity and self-pride, doomed him from the outset to lose his contest with Cortés – a man who, unlike him, took no sleep in time of danger. But of course Díaz knew none of this as the attack was pressed home, and was simply grateful to God that the long, wide street on which they were approaching the central square, and where they would be vulnerable to a potentially devastating cavalry charge, was silent and deserted. Indeed, for what seemed an age, though it could only have been moments, he could hear nothing through the howling of the tempest except the rapid, disciplined tread of the squad's own footsteps.

The square ahead cast an eerie light from the many flickering lanterns and sheltered torches distributed around it so, as the men entered, now at a run, they were spotted at once. Gruff shouts and alarums followed, there was a drumming of hooves, one horse reared, almost throwing its rider, and a troop of cavalry swept out across the green towards them as Olid shouted 'Pikes' and the eighty long Chinantla lances were thrust forth with a rattle of shafts. Hearing the thunder of the hooves, feeling the ground tremble under his feet, registering the familiar panicked flutter in his stomach that a charge of heavy horse always provoked, Díaz realised with sudden relief that the threat was incoherent – not the sweeping, coordinated, unstoppable mass he'd been expecting, but something much more like twenty individual horsemen in competition with one another, their approach further disrupted by the many small shrines that dotted the square around the three principal pyramids.

The foremost rider, the rain-starred blade of his sabre gleaming in the torchlight, was coming in fast from the left side of the column, his arm sweeping back for a scything blow. Díaz responded instinctively, raised his long, heavy pike two-handed over his head and jabbed it ferociously at the rider's mouth while he was still five paces distant, connecting joltingly with bone, hooking the man out of his saddle and wrenching the barbed copper blade loose from his shattered face.

Now, from the rank behind him, another pikeman, equally proficient in the arts of strike, swing, cleave, poke and takedown, pitched a second rider off his horse. In seconds twelve of the twenty attackers were on the ground, some dead, some screaming in agony. Díaz braced himself for another onslaught, but none came, and the remaining riders cantered away in the dark as Olid's squad, still without a man injured, closed with the first line of the artillery.

Díaz just had time to note that the rain had abruptly stopped when fire lit the night as every cannon in the square was fired in a massed opening salvo, and the hideous, rolling roar that he'd been dreading since the attack was launched burst out all around him, filling his ears with the horrible whizz of ball and the whirring whistle of grapeshot.

Something struck him hard in the chest. Expecting that his death was upon him, that he was about to be decapitated or rendered to mincemeat, Díaz charged on, levelling his pike at the crew of the nearest gun, who weren't even bothering to reload but at once held up their hands and surrendered. As he twisted the weapon at the last moment to avoid poking the gunner, he suddenly understood from his own obvious lack of injury and the torn strips of burnt wadding clinging to his cuirass that he'd taken a direct hit from a blank! A quick glance confirmed that many of the other pieces in the square must have been loaded with wadding only, while those that had fired live ammunition, producing the familiar sounds of a cannonade, had obviously been aimed high. Only three men of Olid's troop were down, hit and killed by a single lethal one-pound cannon ball, accurately fired, that struck all of them before losing its force. Struggles had erupted around a handful of the guns, but the resistance was quickly overwhelmed; all the rest of the crews had surrendered without a fight and passively allowed themselves to be taken prisoner and bound.

Just then, as Sandoval's squad made their rush for the steps of the great pyramid, another cavalry troop, no larger but better coordinated than before, poured back into the square. Jean Yuste, whom Díaz had known in Cuba and recognised immediately, led the attack; however, he'd come too late to protect the guns from the speed and ferocity of Olid's onward rush, or from the treachery of their own crews. Seeing this, the captain swiftly and efficiently redirected his force, wheeling them right and bringing them down in a direct charge upon the men of Sandoval's column, only a few of whom had yet gained the steps of the pyramid.

'*Stop that cavalry!*' Cristóbal de Olid yelled, and led his troop, pikes bristling, on a rapid sortie to intercept the oncoming horsemen. Again Díaz felt the shock of impact and the satisfying lethal jerk as his pike smashed a rider out of his saddle. He snatched the weapon free and rushed on, trampling the fallen man, feeling teeth break under his boot, noting from the corner of his eye that Velázquez de Léon's squad had entered the square and were also engaging the cavalry.

From the saddle, Jean Yuste hacked at a foot soldier whose shield was broken and who seemed only to have a dagger to defend himself. It was an unequal struggle, and Yuste's sabre cleaved his head. Díaz ran at him as he attempted to rally his few remaining men, but De Léon was faster, suddenly appearing out of the night behind him and planting the barbed copper blade of his pike perfectly in the gap between Yuste's cuirass and backplate. There it lodged securely amongst the unfortunate man's ribs, allowing De Léon to complete the pole manoeuvre known as 'takedown' – reckoned a great physical feat – which required lifting the impaled man out of the saddle like a bale of hay on the end of a pitchfork and throwing him to the ground. The manoeuvre accomplished, De Léon strode forward, leaving the pike in Yuste, for there were suddenly no more cavalry in the square. He looked down furiously at the broken and impaled captain, obviously judged him no longer a threat, yelled something incoherent that included the word 'swaggerer', and hurried away calling his men.

It was strange, Díaz thought. Narváez had eighty cavalry, yet not more than thirty of them could have been deployed tonight. What of the rest? Wherever they were, it seemed improbable that any further charges would now be attempted, with Cortés's men well-armed with pikes and in complete possession of the square. Cortés himself was here, directing the progress of the battle, having thrown his own reserve force of sixty into the fray to support Sandoval on the great pyramid where he clearly judged them most needed. Ordaz had launched a full-scale assault on the western satellite pyramid, where the defenders were reportedly under the command of Alonso de Salvatierra. Velázquez de Léon, his business with Yuste done, now led his squad against the eastern satellite pyramid.

The cavalry was no longer a threat, and the task of seizing the guns was complete. During the afternoon Díaz had talked with his good friend Sandoval, who'd said to him: 'Keep by me tonight and follow me if you're still alive after capturing the artillery.'

The words rang in his ears now as he ran towards the looming mass of the pyramid still clutching his pike, yelling, '*Santiago and at them, Santiago and at them!*' – the old battle cry from the wars against the Moors – hoping the men of Olid's squad would hear him and follow. For at the edge of his attention during the intense activity of the past moments, it had become obvious that even the combined squads of Sandoval and Cortés were losing ground against the defenders and must be urgently reinforced.

Gonzalo de Sandoval always led from the front. He didn't know any other way. But right now, despite Cortés throwing his sixty into the balance, leading from the front meant crossbow bolts skittering off his armour and a fighting retreat down the pyramid steps beneath the savage onslaught with halberds and poleaxes mounted by a hundred of Narváez's troopers swarming from the first level.

Forced to step down again, colliding with others who hadn't grasped the situation yet and were still trying to ascend, using his sword and shield to fend off axe blows to his helmet, Sandoval heard a great cry of '*Santiago and at them!*' from the green below and risked a glance down to see Bernal Díaz running full tilt towards the base of the pyramid, clutching one of the long Chinantla pikes. Following him, urged forward in support by hoarsely shouted orders from Cortés, came Olid and most of the squad assigned to seize the artillery, every one of them armed with pikes which, for speed of movement and manoeuvrability, neither his own nor Cortés's men had brought.

Sandoval half turned to shout an order, stumbled, but regained his balance as something struck him a hard blow in the back. Whatever it was passed through his armour, punctured his skin and lodged itself solidly in the bone of his left shoulder blade. He gasped but ignored the pain and called out: '*Make way below! We need pikemen here at the double! Let them through!*'

* * *

Díaz heard and understood. The problem that must be overcome was that squad of Narváez's men with pole weapons using the advantage of height and greater reach to batter the attackers. But the Chinantla pikes were longer than the pole-arms. Olid rapidly assigned a platoon of twenty to the task, and Díaz led them up the middle of the stairway where the press of men had parted, opening a gap for them and allowing them to fan out behind the two front ranks. Díaz found himself directly behind Sandoval, who had a crossbow bolt sticking out of his shoulder, but seemed oblivious, and had begun a concerted pushback with massed shields against the pole-arm assault.

Pikes were designed for this work, from behind a shield wall, and pikes of the exceptional length of those from Chinantla were exactly what was needed now. One great brute of trooper with an axe mounted on a twelve-foot pole was chopping down relentlessly at Sandoval, and at the man next to him, occasionally using the armour-piercing spike mounted on the end of the haft to jab suddenly rather than to strike. The Chinantla pike was more than sixteen feet long. Díaz hefted it over-head and struck the trooper through the throat, releasing a pulse of arterial blood as he tugged the big barbed blade free, hefted it again and lunged at another trooper. All along the third rank of the assault pikes were thrusting forth over the heads of the first and second ranks, and in an instant half the pole-arm men were down and most of the rest wounded and bleeding. Panic gripped the survivors and they broke forma-tion, some still urging forward, some in pell-mell retreat. It was the end of them. Like a dam breaking, their resistance collapsed in a sudden cascade, and with a great roar Díaz and the attackers surged up the pyramid steps after them, trampling down their remnant and bounding for the next level.✶

After despatching Francisco de Mesa and the two gun crews he'd brought with him to discover which of Narváez's seventeen cannon were still functional – clearly there had been sabotage! – Cortés had thrown almost all his own contingent of sixty into the faltering attack on the main pyramid. He himself remained on the green with half a dozen of his men, all swift runners, to be used as battlefield messengers. Rather than engaging personally in feats of derring-do tonight, which offered high risk and very little gain, it was more important that he keep his finger on the pulse of the fast-moving battle, ready to identify and unleash an immediate response to any emerging threat.

At most a few hundred of Narváez's troops were involved in the defence of the three pyramids in the square, and there undoubtedly remained a great number in reserve – perhaps as many as five hundred, including at least forty cavalry. On the other hand, there were riderless horses randomly galloping here and there across the green and, while some had saddles – the mounts of the men unhorsed by pikes – many others were bareback. Had the bribes paid by Olmedo and Velázquez de Léon worked so well? They'd reported an arrangement with the stable-master, a certain Alonso Cano, who had agreed to cut the girths on the cavalry saddles. When many of the dragoons tried to mount, had they simply fallen to the ground, thus adding themselves to the ranks of Narváez's foot soldiers?

Even so, where were those foot soldiers?

Reluctant to believe his efforts to weaken the enemy had been so successful that they had, at a stroke, deprived him of so many of his men, Cortés remained on edge and vigilant as an arquebus ball fired from the commander's headquarters at the top of the main pyramid whizzed past his ear. Other shots, and showers of crossbow bolts from the same source, were finding targets amongst the squads assaulting the two smaller satellite pyramids, where the defence offered by Salvatierra and by the youth Diego de Velázquez was only desultory. Meanwhile, on the principal pyramid, having swept aside the unexpectedly stiff resist-ance from the lower section of the stairway, Sandoval, Díaz and Olid had now reached the first level and were consolidating their forces there for the next upward push. They too were under a hail of fire and taking casualties.

There was no doubt in Cortés's mind what he must do next. If any of the artillery was still functional – and Mesa would know by now – he would turn it against the garrisons on the three pyramids. The night would not be settled until Narváez and all his senior officers were captured or dead.

The chief of artillery was close, gathered with his crews around a big lombard near the base of the pyramid. 'Mesa!' Cortés's voice carried above the sound of battle: 'a word with you, please'.

'*Charge!*' Sandoval yelled, and with a massed bellow of rage and defiance, under a withering fusillade of crossbow bolts, his reinforced squad poured up the stairway. At the pyramid's second level a company of Narváez's men, armed this time only with swords and shields, braced themselves to receive the assault. At once a dozen were impaled and three hooked from the steps by the pikemen; others attempted to flee but were overrun.

Ignoring the fiery agony of his left shoulder, Sandoval permitted no pause but, with hoarse shouts – bestial to his own ears – of '*Onwards!*' and '*Trample them!*' and '*Faster!*', urged his men to vault the steps at a still more reckless pace, muscles burning, lungs screaming for air, bodies sheened with sweat, sweeping aside the now scattered and diluted opposition, passing the third level, and bowling over the few who confronted them on the way to the fourth.

At the lip of the summit, Sandoval found himself in a scrum with a great hairy bear of a soldier, about twice his own size, who had shit himself copiously. He'd either lost his sword or never had one, and was armed with a short, saw-bladed Toledo dagger. It was a useful weapon at this range, but his opponent was shaking and plainly terrified, his broken teeth bared in a rictus, and was a poor fighter. Sandoval saw an opening to gut him but suddenly found he didn't want to – such an unexpected feeling of compassion! – and clubbed him smartly about the temple with the pommel of his sword instead. The man dropped like a bag of stones and Sandoval strode over him on to the summit platform, where a large force of Narváez's soldiers, perhaps two hundred strong, swords drawn, stood massed before their commander's headquarters in the temple.

Since the rain had stopped, the clouds had begun to clear rapidly, and a chunk of moon scudded through a gap beaming a ghostly radiance upon the scene.

It revealed the strangest thing – Pánfilo Narváez, naked as the day he was born, swinging a great two-handed *montante*. He looked up at the moon and howled.

'*Charge!*' Sandoval yelled.

Only five of the cannon had been disabled. Even they would be easy enough to repair, since wax had simply been poured into their touch-holes. The rest had been loaded with blanks or aimed high. In summary, Mesa said, twelve pieces were ready for immediate use. Of these eleven were falconets and one was a lombard.

Cortés's first thought had been to use the lombard – the big guns, nicknamed 'wall-breakers' were siege weapons – to batter the top of the pyramid, destroy the temple and kill Narváez. But he dismissed the idea when Mesa reminded him that the huge cannon would have to be dragged the best part of half a mile from the square before it could target such a high point. The barrel simply could not be elevated sufficiently from any closer range. Besides, Sandoval, Olid, Díaz and their men had now forced the stairway and attained the summit platform, and a glance revealed a hand-to-hand struggle was underway there. Any cannon fire would kill friend and foe indiscriminately in such a melee.

'And the satellite pyramids?' Cortés asked. 'They're much lower. Can we hit them?'

'Yes. The elevation on the falconets is good enough for that.'

'Then make ready.'

Cortés sent runners to Velázquez de Léon and Ordaz, commanding them to cease further attempts to storm the small pyramids, disengage their forces and draw back a hundred paces while the falconets were pulled into position – five drawn up before each structure. Cortés joined Ordaz first, sending a messenger forward under a flag of truce to give Salvatierra the opportunity to surrender before he and his men were blown to bits.

The messenger was back in a moment: 'Seems Captain Salvatierra is indisposed, sir,' he reported. 'His men say he's not right. Been acting funny all evening, but the moment the attack began he started vomiting and complaining of his stomach. They can't get any sense out of him now. They want to surrender, sir.'

Somehow Cortés was not surprised. He did not know Salvatierra personally, but from what he'd heard the man was a blustering windbag and a coward. 'Very well then,' he said. 'They're to leave their arms behind and come out in single file with their hands raised. Tell them if they make the slightest bit of trouble they'll all be killed, but if they come quietly and hand Salvatierra over to us we'll show them mercy.'

Moments later the entire garrison of the small pyramid – more than a hundred disarmed men – filed out of the temple they'd been defending. Salvatierra, seemingly dead to the world, had been hefted like a gunny-sack over the shoulder of his muscular master-sergeant, who dropped the captain on the ground in disgust before formally surrendering himself and the men to Cortés. 'And we beg you show us mercy,' the sergeant said. He pointed a calloused thumb at Salvatierra. 'A terrible officer! Him and Narváez and that devil of a governor in Cuba – they all misled us. I hope you'll give us another chance, sir.'

Cortés held a lantern over Salvatierra. The man looked ghastly. He wore the lower half of a white dress uniform, now horribly soiled, and no boots. His chest was bare and streaked with gobs of vomit. His eyes were wide open and rolling in opposite directions.

From a few hundred paces away, at the second satellite pyramid, came the thunder of a falconet barrage. On Cortés's orders the same opportunity to surrender had been offered to the youthful Velázquez commanding that pyramid, but it appeared he had not accepted it.

Salvatierra's eyes continued to roll.

Turning his attention to the summit of the great pyramid, bright in the moonlight, Cortés saw that the battle had evolved. The hand-to-hand fighting was almost over. His men had the upper hand and were pressing in close to the temple.

He resisted the urge to join them immediately. Sandoval, Díaz and Ordaz were all competent officers who knew what they were doing. First any danger of a counterattack must be addressed. Hurrying over to join Velázquez de Léon at the second satellite pyramid, he saw at once that its defenders no longer posed any threat; the survivors had come streaming out after the first salvo brought down upon their heads the roof of the temple where they'd barricaded themselves.

'He wouldn't surrender,' De Léon explained, looking down at the bloody and bruised body of his own relative, young Diego Velázquez, the nephew of the governor of Cuba.

'Is he dead?' asked Cortés.

'Not yet,' De Léon replied. 'He's a detestable youth but they say he was brave, so perhaps there's hope for him. A lot can be forgiven in a man if he has courage.'

'Begging your pardon, Captains,' interrupted one of the prisoners sitting bound on the green nearby, 'but it wasn't courage in young Velázquez here, it was madness. You should have seen him! Raving he was. Convinced this was Granada in '92 – before he was born, sirs – and that we were fighting the Moors.'

Stranger and stranger, Cortés thought. Although there had been gossip, he'd shared no details with the men about the bribes he'd paid to undermine Narváez's army. In part this was to avoid inflaming their envy, but it was also so they'd not build up dangerous hopes for a soft and easy battle. Now he wondered if some of his gold might have found its way to the kitchens. It seemed more than coincidence that both Salvatierra and Diego Velázquez should have been taken ill on so crucial a night . . .

Giving orders for Ordaz and Velázquez de Léon to keep the prisoners under close watch and to remain in the square with all their men and all the captured artillery to guard against any possible counterattack, Cortés ran towards the steps of the great pyramid.

Now he would see to Narváez.

The sounds of cannon and the distant clash of blades had ended. Carried on the wind, scattered arquebus shots and faint cries were all that bore witness to the state of the battle.

Beneath the shelter, slumped against a tree, Pepillo had fallen asleep. Melchior too had remained unimpressed throughout. He knew the sounds of war.

Now, however, he whined and pricked up his ears. Malinal reached out her hand, tentatively patted the hound on the head – for she was still a little afraid of him – and his ears at once flattened. 'Are you fine, boy?' she asked, imitating the way Pepillo spoke to him.

Melchior turned and fixed an intelligent amber eye on her for a moment, but something again called his attention, his ears shot back up, he sniffed the air and, with another whine, rearranged himself restlessly across the entrance to the shelter.

Malinal listened intently but could hear nothing. The steady roar of the downpour had ceased a while ago, the wind had lost much of its force, and the only nearby sound was the steady drip, drip, drip of fat raindrops falling from the branches of the trees.

Suddenly Melchior was on his feet, and his whine this time was low in his throat, becoming a growl. Pepillo woke with a start and made a grab for his collar, but too late – the dog was a shadow slipping out into the night. There came a snarl, a harsh scream, a clatter of weapons. Pepillo was already scrambling across Malinal and threw himself from the shelter, drawing his sword.

It had been a most peculiar business altogether, Sandoval thought. The first part of the assault on the pyramid had been strongly contested by Narváez's men, who'd fought with real spirit. Then, thanks to the pikes, they'd been overcome, leaving an almost clear run, with negligible opposition other than horrible but increasingly scattered and ineffective swarms of crossbow bolts.

Once on the summit, though – and Sandoval was happy he'd been able to spare the man who'd grappled with him – the real strangeness had unfolded, to wit Narváez, naked and howling at the moon. He'd got out ahead of the block of his troops drawn up at the entrance to the temple, and there he'd stood, like some figure from myth or nightmare, hirsute, surprisingly well endowed, and swinging a huge long-sword in a practised two-handed grip.

On closer inspection, however, this turned out not to be some unusual berserker pre-battle display. Narváez was doing much more than simply swinging his sword. His movements were rapid – now evasive, now aggressive – his footwork and entire posture that of a man engaged in a fight for his life.

Bizarrely it seemed that he was fighting, on this night of all nights . . . an imaginary opponent!

By itself his nakedness might be excused. Perhaps he slept naked and had been taken so much by surprise he hadn't had time to dress? But this crazed mummery, and that ghastly howling, were aberrations of a different order entirely. It had begun to dawn on Sandoval that there was something seriously wrong with the Spanish commander, when the ranks of those massed on the summit parted, a squad of half a dozen men surged out and in an instant Narváez was grabbed from behind, disarmed, immobilised and carried back, struggling furiously, into the dark depths of the temple.

Every one of the men followed him, leaving their front ranks visible inside, crowding round the door and back into the depths of the room, weapons drawn.

Sandoval was standing beside García Brabo. 'What do you think?' he asked.

'If we storm them, do you mean, sir? Could be costly.'

'Let's try with the pikes,' suggested Pedro Valdelomar. He was a big man with a sour, downturned mouth and hollow cheeks – one of Brabo's squad of twenty-five professional killers. Like the others in the first wave he'd not been armed with a long Chinantla lance, but he'd acquired one now, presumably from one of Olid's men who were oversupplied with them.

The suggestion, Sandoval decided, was a good one. He gave the order and Brabo's squad assembled. Pikes were requisitioned for four more of them from Olid's men and they joined Valdelomar in the third rank. The two ranks in front locked shields, then the whole block of them, five ranks deep, went in fast, a direct attack with the sixteen-foot-long pikes jutting out far ahead, stabbing and hooking.

The effect was devastating. With a clash of arms, and screams of horror from one man who'd been disembowelled, the onslaught drove the defenders back from the doorway and the first three ranks of Brabo's squad, including the pikemen, forced their way inside.

Now, suddenly, Narváez appeared again, erupting from under the six-strong platoon assigned to protect him, thrusting them aside, and shouldering his way forward through the vestige of his panicked, retreating men. '*My God!*' he shouted. '*Can't you see we're under attack? Cortes is upon us!*'

It was a moment of returning lucidity after what had been an inexplicable fugue, but it came too late. Valdelomar thrust forward mightily – a well-aimed poke in the muted light of the temple – and plunged the barbed blade straight into Narváez's head. When he jerked it back at the culmination of the strike the commander's eye came out with it, trailing glistening streamers of gore. '*Holy Mary protect me*,' Narváez screamed, '*I am slain.*'

Blessedly the moon was in the sky, bright through a gap in the clouds. Its beams infiltrated the tree canopy and bathed the scene below, revealing five ragged and filthy Spaniards from Narváez's army, one brandishing a drawn sabre – runaway cavalrymen to judge by their uniforms, no doubt unhorsed by the Chinantla pikes and now hoping to make their escape. A sixth was on the ground, on his back, menaced by Melchior, who stood over him snarling and dripping saliva on his face. Seeing the dragoon with the sabre move up stealthily behind his dog, Pepillo whistled, and immediately Melchior left the man he'd downed and bounded across the clearing to Pepillo's side.

The dragoon, whip thin, moustachioed, fast on his feet, shouted, 'Come on, lads. Let's get him! He's only a fucking boy,' and charged across the clearing, but Pepillo remembered his lessons from Juan de Escalante, who'd taught him that to fight with swords is to dance with life and death. With strong stance, good balance and his centre towards the enemy, he danced aside at the last moment and the other man's blade cleaved empty air. Preferring not to have to kill one of his own countrymen, Pepillo tripped him as he went by, sending him sprawling and his sabre flying. Malinal was on him in a second, her stiletto drawn and pressed to his ear.

The man mauled by Melchior was also still on the ground. With both his hands and forearms shredded by the lurcher's teeth, and a bloody tear out of his shoulder very close to his neck, he wasn't going to be a problem tonight.

Would the other four chance it? Glittering in the moonlight, the blade of Pepillo's sword, held in the deceptively weak position known as the fool's guard, was an open invitation for them to do so. Still none of them moved. Perhaps it was the massive presence of Melchior at his knee, or perhaps Pepillo's handling of the first attack had given them pause for thought, but their hesitation was real.

'We just want your horses,' one of them said. A swarthy, bearded face, baring its teeth, bobbed towards him in the moonlight. 'There's six of us. You've got seven horses so you'll still have one left.' The man was almost pleading. 'We won't kill you if you just let us take them and go.'

'I'm afraid I can't do that,' said Pepillo firmly. The caudillo would never forgive him if he stood by and allowed the horses to be stolen; besides, it would be stupid to trust any promise from these desperate-looking men – so there was no question of a deal. He shifted his balance and raised his guard to the position known as the plough, point angled a little up, hilt held close to his centre, left leg leading, right leg back. 'I tell you what, though,' he said, 'surrender to me now and I'll make sure you're well treated by Cortés.'

Cortés had already begun his ascent of the pyramid when he heard great shouts of jubilation from above: '*Victory! Victory for Cortés! Narváez is fallen! Narváez is dead!*'

Could it really be so? Cortés quickened his pace, his heart pounding, his lungs refusing him the air he suddenly badly needed. He had been constantly on the move during the battle, his armour and his weapons heavy, in a state of unrelieved tension and heightened awareness, and he was paying the price for it. Deliberately he slowed his step, sought to calm his breathing, and when he reached the first level, which was strewn with bodies, he paused.

The only problem was, Narváez was not slain but very much still alive, calling out and protesting horribly, surrounded by his men, who refused to surrender.

Sandoval approached the door waving a flag of truce. 'Let me speak to your commanding officer,' he yelled.

'We don't have one, sir.'

Wishing to prevent further casualties on both sides, he'd pulled Brabo's squad back as soon as Narváez was hit, for without him it was inconceivable his men would go on. But this was now beginning to look like a miscalculation.

'I can hear Narváez!' Sandoval shouted. 'Bring him forth!'

'He's in no fit state, sir. Doesn't even know where he is.'

'What about Bono de Quejo then? He can give your surrender.'

'All due respect, sir, but Captain Bono de Quejo's still talking to God.'

'What do you mean *still* talking to God?'

'Well, he's been talking to him all night, sir, and I don't think he's about to stop now.'

Sandoval had no patience for such an explanation. 'Gamarra, then?' he snapped.

'Says he's not a soldier any more, sir. Can't understand why he ever became one. He's in bed, sir.'

'My God!' said Sandoval. 'What a mess! Surrender, *now*! Let's get this over with.'

'We're afraid if we surrender, you'll kill us, sir.'

'I'll kill you if you don't! Get out of that temple *now* or I'll have a couple of falconets dragged up here to blast you all with grapeshot.'

There came a hideous scream from within. Suddenly Narváez appeared again, still naked, his empty eye socket streaming blood and the big *montante* back in his hands. He padded out of the temple on bare feet before Sandoval could react, and streaked towards him, swinging the huge sword for a killing blow. With a shock, Sandoval realised there wasn't time for him to parry or evade, and that he was going to die here, sliced in half by a madman, when the youth Farfan, whom Cortés had assigned to his unit just before the attack, appeared out of nowhere, intercepted Narváez's headlong charge and bowled the commander to the ground.

'First to lay hands on him!' yelled Farfan triumphantly. 'I claim the three thousand pesos.'

Bernal Díaz was shocked by how ill and tired the caudillo seemed as he reached the summit of the pyramid, sweating and panting for breath. He tried twice to speak to Sandoval but was so winded he was unable to get the words out, finally managing: 'What about Narváez?'

'He's here,' Sandoval replied. 'Here and well guarded.'

'Take care,' Cortés wheezed, but was again stopped by shortness of breath. He doubled over with his hands on his knees but quickly straightened to say: 'Take care, my dear Sandoval, that you do not leave him, and that you and your comrades do not let him break away while I go and attend to other matters. See to it that any other officers who are prisoners with him are likewise guarded in every way.'

With that, and no further explanation, Cortés left the temple. If he was excited or even satisfied at Narváez's capture, he made little show of it. He appeared to be utterly drained, and stumbled dangerously as he reached the edge of the summit platform. Díaz rushed to steady him: 'Let me help you, Caudillo.'

But Cortés shook off his helping hand. 'I'm OK, Bernal, thank you, just a little tired.' He proceeded down the stairs. A short while later, from the square below, Díaz heard the loud voice of a herald issuing an official proclamation:

'*Under pain of death all followers of the defeated commander Pánfilo Narváez must come at once to this place to surrender themselves and their arms, under the banner of His Majesty and in his royal name, to Hernando Cortés, his captain-general and chief justice.*'

As the sun rose on the field of battle on the morning of Sunday 29 May – Whit – Father Bartolomé Olmedo was out and about to make sure his promises were kept. Those of officer class who'd taken his bribes and done their part in undermining Narváez's army – men like Balthazar Bermudez, Francisco Verdugo and the chief of artillery Rodrigo Martinez – had already been plucked from the ranks of the prisoners and were now to be found finishing off a barrel of wine in the refectory with several of Cortés's own officers. No intervention needed where they were concerned then, nor for the rough-mannered gunner Diego Usagre, who turned out to have a brother in Cortés's ranks and had been released into his custody.

But what of Miguel Ruffo and Esteban Valdez, the two young sentries Olmedo had befriended on his first visit to the camp? After a systematic search he found them among the hundreds of Narváez's men who'd been straggling in to surrender all night, and now sat, bound, dejected and awaiting their fate, in a stolid mass on the green in the midst of the square under the towering pyramid. *Just like Mexica sacrificial victims*, the friar thought.

'Come on, lads,' he said. 'Let's go for a walk. I want you to help me find someone.' He stooped, pulled a small knife from its sheath inside his habit and cut their bonds.

'But we can't, Father,' said Ruffo, sitting up and massaging his feet and arms to restore circulation. 'You've cut us loose, and thank you for that. But we're still prisoners.' He nodded his head in the direction of the guards. 'They'll kill us if we walk.'

'No they won't.'

The guards were a tough, unforgiving, cutthroat-looking lot this morning, and Olmedo knew every one of them well. He was a friar, not an ordained priest, but he regarded the difference in time of war as an unimportant technicality, and had agreed many times at their pleading to hear their confessions. A few words with them now set the minds of Ruffo and Valdez at ease. Olmedo put his arms around their shoulders and walked away with them, to a murmur of resentment and angry complaints from the other captives.

'Glad to see you both,' Olmedo said. 'Is all good?' He knew what the answer would be.

'No, Father!' Ruffo replied at once. 'All is not good! You gave us and others gold to stay out of the fight, but your men have taken it all off us along with our weapons. They say it's on the orders of Cortés himself.'

'That's not right and certainly not on our caudillo's orders!' Olmedo exclaimed angrily. 'To your knowledge, has this happened to all the prisoners?'

'Every one of us,' said Valdez. 'If we weren't bound hand and foot, there'd have been a riot. We all feel cheated.'

Olmedo nodded his head grimly. 'I assure you that's *not* what Cortés wants. I'll talk to him and get something done.'

Now that he'd said he'd help, Ruffo and Valdez were both almost pathetically grateful. It seemed they still had complete trust in him as a holy friar and he only hoped he could deliver. But the problem they'd brought to his attention wasn't new. He'd first learned of it a little earlier when he'd found Pero Trigueros, the cook, lying beaten and bound in the kitchen. His gold had been stolen too.

Of course it was completely normal to loot prisoners of war – but these prisoners were different and the word would have to be put out that they should be handled with care. For it remained a discomfiting fact, though victorious in the night, that Cortés's men were outnumbered almost three to one by the captives. This was obvious to all in the daylight, and it was a safe prediction that the prisoners would become difficult to contain and might even break loose and attempt a coup, unless kept permanently tied, or killed or placated in some way.

Olmedo was quite sure that Cortés would placate them, winning their affection with gold and honeyed words, as he usually did. Too many – perhaps fifty of Narváez's men, and fifteen of the caudillo's own – had been killed in the fighting, and as a practical military commander he'd want all the rest alive, well and – above all – *willing* to join his army and help him finish the conquest of New Spain. The looting threatened all that.

'Who do you want us to help you find, Father?' asked Valdez.

'Alonso Cano, the stable-master. He's not amongst the prisoners.'

'Have you checked the stables?'

'I have, Ruffo. Of course. It was the first place I looked.'

'Then he's probably still outside the town, Father. I reckon the best part of five hundred of us slipped away after the attack began. Some didn't trust Cortés. They were going to make for the coast and try to get on board one of our ships. But most of us stayed nearby until we heard about the proclamation, then we gave ourselves up.'

'Nonetheless, humour me. I've got a bad feeling about this.'

Olmedo had the bad feeling because, on his visit to the stables, he'd seen clear evidence that Cano had begun to do what he'd been paid to do. Around half of the makeshift box stalls where the horses had stood were empty, but saddles with cut cinches lay on the floors of most of the rest. However, Olmedo had marched with the men into battle, as he always did, and had witnessed the two cavalry charges – the first, with about twenty troopers who'd been in the square already, more than half of whom had been unhorsed, and a little later a second troop of twenty, led by Jean Yuste, who'd entered the square from the direction of the stables.

That Yuste would bring a cavalry troop of any size into this battle was proof of his bad faith, because he'd taken Velázquez de Léon's Swaggerer in payment for staying out of it! Had he perhaps, like so many others, been awakened from sleep by the attack? And seeing the first cavalry charge defeated, had he rushed to mount up with the rest of his men, only to catch Alonso Cano red-handed cutting the cinches of the horses?

'Do you mind if we check the stables again?' Valdez asked.

'Makes sense,' Olmedo conceded. 'I was only there for a few moments.'

They didn't find Cano at the stables, though they searched every stall again, but nearby in the big trench that had served Narváez's troops as a latrine for the past weeks. Lying on his back, half submerged in shit, enough of the stable-master was still visible to reveal his belly ripped open from groin to sternum and the bloody word 'TRAITOR' incised deeply into his forehead.

'Yuste must have done that,' Olmedo mused.

'Most likely caught him cutting the cinches,' suggested Ruffo.

A wave of remorse washed over Olmedo. 'I was afraid of this,' he said. 'I'm responsible for his death.'

'Because you put him up to it, Father?'

'Yes. If I'd not sought him out, he'd still be alive.'

'But other men would be dead,' observed Valdez.

Olmedo thought about it and it was true. If Yuste had come into the square for that second charge with sixty cavalry instead of just twenty, the impact would have been devastating and many more of Cortés's men would have been killed.

'This is war, Father,' said Ruffo. 'You did the right thing.'

Astonishingly, Cano's bribe of necklaces and ingots could be seen bulging from the pocket of his coat. Yuste must have been so busy executing the man that he'd missed his little hoard of treasure.

'We can't just leave that there,' said Ruffo, with a longing glance into the trench. He didn't mean the body. He extended a hand, 'Valdez, if you grab hold of me, I think I might be able to reach.'

While Dr La Peña, the expedition's surgeon, ministered to their own wounded – including Sandoval, who'd taken a crossbow bolt to the shoulder and continued fighting as though it were no more than a flea bite – Cortés had arranged for Narváez's own surgeon, Maestre Juan, to attend the defeated commander. His right eye was gone, and would never be put back, but, if infection could be avoided, he would certainly live. Indeed, and surprisingly after his bizarre behaviour the night before and the pain he was obviously still in, Narváez now seemed quite his normal self, and was carrying on a reasonable conversation with his doctor about poultices and bandages for his eye.

Cortés slipped into the temple silently around mid-morning, saying nothing, and stood just inside the door, unobtrusive in a patch of shadow. Though he knew Narváez of old, he was curious to look on the face of the foolish, vainglorious and greedy man who'd brought so much trouble to New Spain. He had absolutely no desire, however, to be recognised by him or to speak to him.

There would be time for that soon enough.

But he was observed by one of the doctor's attendants and, before he could signal, the man stooped and whispered in the commander's ear.

Narváez at once raised himself on an elbow from his bed and fixed

Cortés with his bulging blue eye. 'Señor Captain Cortés,' he said in that hollow, booming voice of his, 'you must consider this a great feat – this victory which you have won over me, and the capture of my person.'

Cortés stepped forward to the bedside and looked steadily at the injured man, saying nothing for a moment. Finally, when there was complete silence in the room, everyone waiting with baited breath, he replied: 'I give thanks to God for this victory, and to the gallant gentlemen and comrades of my company who had a share in it, but as to defeating and capturing you, Pánfilo, I consider it as the least of my achievements since my arrival in this country.'

With that he turned his back, strode out of the temple into the sunshine – the sky washed clean after the rain of the night before – and walked jauntily down the steps. Before he'd reached the third level his heart was gladdened to see Malinal and Pepillo entering the square with the seven horses he'd left them in charge of, the hound Melchior and – interesting this! – six docile prisoners, who walked unbound before them and whom they gave over to the custody of the constables.

Things were really looking up!

Chapter Eighteen

Sunday 29 May 1520–Sunday 12 June 1520

At some point during the early afternoon of Whitsunday 29 May, Cortés was in the cool of the commandeered refectory, taking his first refreshment after the battle, when the expedition's foppish and notoriously drunken amateur astrologer Botello Puerto de la Plata came to him, very much in his cups, and requested some moments of his time.

'You've found the wine then, I see?'

'A blessed relief after being *dry* for so long. Father Olmedo has custody of it, but he broke out a couple of barrels of Galician red for a few of us to share.' He belched. 'I've been . . . visited, Caudillo. I don't mean to cause you concern on this day of your triumph, but I've been visited you see . . .'

'Visited? What on earth are you talking about, man? Visited by whom? Where? When? And why must I interrupt my repast to hear about this visit?'

Botello drew himself up to his full height, a little shorter than Cortés. 'I have been visited,' he said, 'by a demon.'

'Before or after you got your hands on the wine this morning?'

'After, Caudillo.'

'Hmm. As I thought.'

'I nodded off in the shade,' the astrologer continued, 'and he came to me and entrusted me with a message that I am to deliver to you.'

'How did he look, this demon?'

'That was the strange thing, Caudillo. He looked exactly like a man. A big, strong man. His hair fair. Big hands. A beautiful, dangerous man.'

Now the astrologer had Cortés's attention. The 'demon' he was describing sounded a lot like his own dreams of Saint Peter. But surely it couldn't be so? Surely the Holy Father, no matter how mysterious his ways, would not seek to communicate with him through a clown like Botello?

'And what message did he give you to deliver to me?' Cortés asked, 'this demon with the looks of a man?'

'Señor, don't delay here long – ' Botello's voice had taken on a stentorian, proclaiming quality – 'because you should know that Pedro de Alvarado, your captain, whom you left in Tenochtitlan, is in great danger. The Mexica have made war against him and have killed some of his men and have even tried to climb into our quarters by ladders and to break down the doors. It would be good, Caudillo, if you were to return to the city at once by forced marches.'

'Nonsense, Botello! If Alvarado was in the kind of trouble you describe, we'd have heard from him by now.'

'Perhaps a messenger is on the way?'

'Then I will act on the message when I receive it. Until then, I have a kingdom to run.'

'A kingdom, Caudillo?'

'This great land. Now's our chance to seize it in a grip that will last a thousand years.'

'Lose Tenochtitlan, lose all, Caudillo. You have been warned . . .'

'Maybe so.' Suddenly Cortés leapt out of his chair and stood face to face with Botello, his voice low and urgent: 'But you'll say no more about this demonic visitor of yours. Such talk will disturb the men.'

'My apologies, Caudillo,' Botello stammered, stepping back, almost losing his balance. 'I meant no harm.'

After the astrologer had left, Cortés thought carefully about the whole incident.

He was much more disturbed by it than he'd revealed, and decided to send a message by runner to Tenochtitlan at once to satisfy himself that Alvarado was keeping the peace there, and in no danger. No sooner had he done so, however, than he was distracted by disturbances amongst the prisoners, still bound and sweltering in front of the pyramid in Cempoala's main square, who'd begun to realise how greatly they outnumbered Cortés's own men.

This commotion, tending towards havoc, was not quickly solved by the release of the prisoners and was laden with much ill-feeling on all sides. Working with Olmedo, it required most of the next day, Monday 30 May, even to begin to approach a workable settlement. Cortés therefore did not immediately have time to consider the implications of the news that was brought to him during the course of that afternoon

– namely that the letter to Alvarado he'd despatched the day before to be carried to Tenochtitlan by relay runners had been returned to Cempoala because the Mexica's sophisticated relay system appeared, for some unexplained reason, to have broken down entirely.

Resolving to send the message in Spanish hands the next day, Cortés returned to settling grievances and soothing agitated feelings.

With the exception of the officer corps – men like Salvatierra, Bono de Quejo, Gamarra, the badly injured Yuste and of course Narváez himself, whose suppurating eye-socket required constant attention – all the prisoners were released and many were rewarded with gold, or given promises of gold to come. Moreover, where the prisoners had suffered looting of their own property by the victorious expeditionaries, notably horses and gold, which were very much in demand, Cortés was assiduous in ensuring its full restitution. Much of the gold had been paid out in the form of bribes from Cortés himself in advance of the battle, and valuable services had been performed for it. A name for giving with one hand and taking back with the other would not win him many new volunteers, and his goal was to have every one of Narváez's men join his army of their own free will.

Returning the looted gold, however, did not go down well with his own expeditionaries, who also likewise resented any promises or gifts of further gold to Narváez's men – feeling that since they had won a victory against perilous odds, it was they, and not those they had defeated, who should now be reaping the reward.

'Our commander,' one of the ringleaders was heard to cry, 'has forsaken his friends for his foes. We stood by him in his hour of distress and are rewarded with blows and wounds while the spoil goes to our enemies.'

Cortés's response was to call together all his expeditionaries for a private meeting. 'Our new comrades are formidable from their numbers,' he reminded them, 'so much so that we are even now much more in their power than they in ours. Our only security is to make them not merely confederates but also friends. Fail in that and we shall have the whole battle to fight over again, and, if they are united, under a much greater disadvantage than before.

'I have considered your interests as much as my own. All that I have is yours. But why should there be any ground for discontent when the whole country, with its riches, is before us, and our augmented strength must henceforth secure the undisturbed control of it?'

*   *   *

361

It was a persuasive argument, thought Bernal Díaz, and, judging from the cautiously welcoming reactions of the men, the caudillo's honeyed tongue had again won the day.

Díaz spent most of Monday and Tuesday, 30 and 31 May, in close company with Cortés, together with Sandoval, Ordaz, Velázquez de Léon, and other captains. And this was interesting because Díaz was not a captain, he was a lieutenant, yet he was being treated with as much courtesy and respect as if he were a captain, and he appeared to have been included, as though this were a perfectly natural thing, amongst the caudillo's group of close and trusted staff officers.

Perhaps a promotion was in the offing?

In his meetings with the expeditionaries during these two days, and with Narváez's men, Cortés wore, over his own clothes, a rich purple Mexica war cloak given to him by Moctezuma some months before. The affectation suited him well, Díaz thought, and added to his presence something of the lofty grandeur of a Roman emperor of old.

Nor was that grandeur undeserved, for the scale of the caudillo's victories, conquering new lands, overcoming all obstacles, was indeed beginning to match the exploits of a Caesar or an Alexander the Great. Not for the first time, Díaz recalled that the Macedonian had likewise been famed for giving more to those he'd vanquished than to those who did the vanquishing for him, had likewise provoked the resentment and hostility of his soldiers, and had likewise talked them round in the end.

Having settled things with the expeditionaries, Cortés turned his attention again to the project of making Narváez's men his own, not just in word, but in their hearts. In the sweetest and most endearing of terms, he begged them to leave behind their resentment over the lost battle and to join his cause. If they did so, he promised, they could expect to be showered with gold and jewels during the further progress of the conquest of New Spain, and could look forward, in addition, to being rewarded with lucrative offices and honours. There was no compulsion, and they were entirely free to go; ships from Narváez's fleet would be provided to those who wished to return to Cuba. But Cortés advised his attentive audience to consider their decision carefully and urged them, one and all, to stay. 'You crossed the ocean to seek a livelihood,' he reminded them, 'and now's your chance! You find yourselves in a country where you can do service to God and His Majesty and make yourselves rich into the bargain. Lads,' he concluded, 'this is a once-in-a-lifetime opportunity. Take it!'

The open vote revealed that every one of Narváez's men had decided to throw in their lot with the caudillo.

'It's your own free choice,' he reminded them. 'I don't want to hear anyone say at some future date that I forced you into it.'

But they remained eager, expressed no doubts, and all affirmed that they were joining the expedition willingly in the hope of wealth and because they wished to play their part, for God and for the king, in this great conquest of New Spain.

If their eyes were not dazzled by gold, Díaz thought, and if they really knew the power of the Mexica – latent, perhaps, but like some rumbling volcano about to explode – then none of them would have wanted to join and all would have fled back to Cuba.

Because there was something about the way Cortés kept going on about this being their free choice, their own willing decision – and he didn't want to hear complaints about the matter later – that aroused a certain suspicious feeling in Díaz.

Did the caudillo perhaps know something about what lay ahead that he wasn't sharing with the men?

It wouldn't be the first time.

Though distracted and fully preoccupied with the pressing need to unify Narváez's forces with his own, Cortés could not forget the equally pressing need to find out what was going on in Tenochtitlan, and he remained troubled by the strange story of Botello's demon. Even in the unexplained absence of the relay runners, he had to admit it was odd that there had been *no* messages from Alvarado – none whatsoever since 5 May. His second in command, to whose sole charge he had entrusted the precious jewel of Tenochtitlan, disliked writing letters, and probably had his hands full keeping the peace in the Mexica capital, but twenty-six days without any communication was beginning to look like cause for concern.

Cortés continued to hope for a messenger, but none came.

And last night, when he had finally taken his rest, he'd prayed that Saint Peter might appear to guide him, but his sleep had been black and utterly dreamless.

That was why today, Tuesday 31 May, he'd sent a cavalry squad on its way to Tenochtitlan to make contact with Alvarado, ascertain his needs, and return. All five of the riders were experts, and to each of them Cortés assigned two spare mounts in addition to their own to speed the journey. The riders, each armed with an arquebus, as well as with the usual sword, spear and shield, were not under any circumstances to become separated from one another, but were to stick closely together for mutual defence. A great deal would be demanded of horses and men, but it was not impossible that they might complete the five-hundred-mile round trip in five days. Even allowing for accidents and delays, they should certainly be back within ten.

Cortés smiled. When Moctezuma's relay system was functioning, messages could travel from Cempoala to Tenochtitlan in just a single day, and a reply could be returned in just two days!

Following in the dust of the five horsemen, already vanishing from view on the road out of town, came an armoured infantry column, moving much more slowly but taking the same route. It consisted of twenty expeditionaries guarding Bono de Quejo, Gamarra, Salvatierra and other senior and potentially troublesome captains from Narváez's army, whom Cortés wished to see securely imprisoned in Tenochtitlan and certainly as far away as possible from the rest of the men.

These coddled, complaining, frankly effeminate officers were all accustomed to the honour of a horse, but Cortés made a point of denying it to them.

They could damn well walk on their own two feet all the way, up hill and down dale, just like the infantrymen guarding them.

Meanwhile Narváez and Yuste, both too badly injured to travel long distances, were sent off to Villa Rica for imprisonment there.

Over the following days, while Cortés awaited news from Tenochtitlan, it became apparent that he had a minor smallpox epidemic on his hands. The disease had ravaged Hispaniola in 1517 and 1518, and had spread to Cuba after he and his expeditionaries had sailed from the island in February 1519, reaching epidemic proportions amongst the native inhabitants whom it slew in great numbers in the latter half of 1519 and into 1520.

It seemed that at least one of Narváez's crew, a sailor named Francisco de Eguía, had brought the infection with him from Cuba, because every member of the Totanac family he'd been lodged with after Narváez had moved his headquarters to Cempoala in May had fallen sick, and very rapidly died, and scores of others were now infected and at various stages of the disease.

Moreover, as had been the case with the spread of the infection amongst the Taino Indians of Hispaniola and Cuba, the Totonacs died not simply of smallpox, as the Spaniards knew it, but of an especially virulent strain of the disease, marked not only by the usual high fever, headache and nausea, but also episodes of blood-filled vomiting and diarrhoea, prior to the outbreak of the pustules which rapidly covered the entire body and were accompanied by a raving delirium that led in every case – so far without exception! – to death.

This was not the pattern in Spain, where smallpox, though feared, was a common, indeed almost universal, childhood affliction that killed only about a third of those it touched. The survivors were left mysteriously strengthened against future exposure to the disease because they rarely contracted it again, even in the midst of raging epidemics, and if they did so it was in a mild, non-fatal form more like chickenpox.

Thus although the Totonac family whose hospitality he shared all died in agony, covered from head to foot in suppurating pustules, Eguía himself had survived the crisis of the infection and was now well on the road to recovery. A few other Spaniards had also developed the disease, but only in its familiar, milder form – fevers, a few pustules, but no great cause for concern. They would live to fight on and advance the great plans Cortés had for the further conquest of New Spain.

Two hundred men escorted Narváez and Yuste to Villa Rica, reoccupying and refortifying the settlement which Cortés now placed under the command of Rodrigo Rangel. 'I'll need you with me as my acting second in command,' he'd explained to Sandoval. Waving down all protestations of modesty from the other man, he'd added, meaning it: 'You're the best captain I have.'

The next assignment went to Velázquez de Léon. Cortés gave him two hundred men and ordered him to settle and secure the Mexica coastal province of Panuco, a few days' march north of Cempoala. To Diego de Ordaz he likewise gave two hundred men, sending him to Coatzacoalcos to complete the project – of founding a harbour and a settlement there – that Velázquez de Léon had begun a few months previously.

Each of the three detachments thus disposed – two hundred to Villa Rica, two hundred to Coatzacoalcos, and two hundred to Panuco – were made up primarily of new recruits from Narváez's army, but stiffened by a hard backbone of twenty of Cortés's veterans.

'Are you privy to the logic of this commission Hernán has given you? Marching to Panuco, securing the province. What's it all about?'

Velázquez de Léon shrugged his massive shoulders, his Swaggerer clinking around his neck. 'I don't know, Bartolomé, truly I don't. I wasn't even aware Panuco needed securing, let alone settling, but I've learnt from long experience that there's usually cunning in the caudillo's orders. These days I just do what I'm told and don't argue.'

'I confess I am puzzled,' Olmedo said. 'Hernán now disposes of a strong force. Not counting Alvarado's contingent in Tenochtitlan, the combination of Narváez's men with our own puts more than twelve hundred able warriors at his disposal. So I understand that he can spare two hundred to send to Panuco, two hundred more to Coatzacoalcos and of course to place two hundred at Villa Rica makes perfect sense. What I do not understand, however, is why he does not also send two hundred men immediately to Tenochtitlan to guard against the eventuality – however remote – that matters might have gone awry there, or even simply to reinforce Alvarado's little garrison. He would still be left with more than five hundred men here! Quite enough to deal with any immediate problems that might arise.'

Velázquez de Léon nodded his head. 'I share your concerns,' he said. 'It is too long since we've had any word, but hopefully those cavalrymen Hernán sent will bring us news soon.'

'Hopefully . . . But I still think he should have sent a strong contingent of two hundred, not just five riders.' Olmedo changed a subject that there was no point in pursuing further. 'I'm glad you got your Swaggerer back.'

'Yes. That cunt Yuste! Excuse my bad language, Father. That arse-wipe Yuste who deceived me had it hidden away. That's the only reason he's still alive.'

'I don't follow, my dear Juan.'

'I had him at my mercy at the end of a pike. Another push and I'd have killed the fellow, but then I wouldn't have known where to find my Swaggerer, so I let him live.'

'You will be rewarded in heaven for showing mercy.'

'Never mind heaven!' The captain lovingly fingered one of the huge golden links of his coveted chain: 'I'll take my rewards here and now.'

They embraced, and Velázquez de Léon mounted his horse, placed himself at the head of his two hundred, and gave the signal. Olmedo watched the departing men, and then their dust, for a long while, as the column marched north out of Cempoala. Deep in thought, the friar wondered if there was anything to be done about Cortés. For it was transparently obvious, in the days after his victory over Narváez, that the caudillo had fallen victim to that well-known malady to which even the greatest leaders were sometimes subject, and for which reason Roman generals embarking on their Triumphs were repeatedly counselled to 'remember you are mortal' – advice they frequently forgot in their subsequent follies of grandeur.

Cortés, it seemed, was suffering from just such a *locura de gradenza*, even affecting a purple cloak like a Roman emperor and behaving in some ways, though perhaps not yet excessively, as though he had been raised to the status of a god – omnipotent, all-seeing and invincible.

He was, undoubtedly, a brilliant military commander, but such delusions would not serve him, or the expedition, well.

It was good to have Teudile back! His calm, efficient presence made Moctezuma feel effective again, and powerful.

Even Tonatiuh must be impressed by the Great Speaker's power now for, in return for Teudile's release, and with no more effort than a snap of his fingers, Moctezuma had been able to give the violent and dangerous captain something he badly needed and was no longer able to obtain for himself – namely, food for his men, admitted through the ranks of the besieging regiment that was now again present in force before the palace doors.

This new ability to bend Tonatiuh to his will was a heady one, and Moctezuma was tempted to use it often to extract other useful favours, but Teudile advised him to wait.

The rescue attempt would take place two days from now, on the day the *tueles* called Sunday, when it was their habit, for an hour, to leave only a skeleton guard, thinly spread around the palace, while the majority of the soldiers assembled in the single room they had consecrated as their temple, before their totem of the cross, to eat the flesh and drink the blood of their god.

Tonight, Moctezuma was to summon Tonatiuh and propose a bargain with him. In exchange for more loads of chickens and tortillas, the royal brother, Cuitláhuac, was to be released from prison and allowed to abide in Moctezuma's apartments, where Teudile was already quartered. The exchange would take place tomorrow, the day before the rescue attempt, so that Cuitláhuac would not be left behind.

Moctezuma found he did not care at all if Cuitláhuac was left behind, but for the sake of appearances agreed to do as he was asked.

* * *

On Saturday 4 June, as negotiated the previous day with that carpet-seller Moctezuma, Alvarado released Cuitláhuac into the royal apartments, reminding him that he, like Teudile and Moctezuma himself, were confined to the palace. Any attempt to leave by any means would be punished by death.

In return the garrison's stores were once again replenished, confirming a suspicion already present in Alvarado's mind that Moctezuma was the real puppet master and orchestrator of the siege. Presumably if he could arrange for food to be delivered so easily, then he could arrange other things as well.

Could he even get the siege called off?

And if so, what was the best approach to take in order to achieve this goal?

Short of the promise of a Spanish withdrawal from Tenochtitlan, which wasn't going to happen, or releasing the Great Speaker and Cuitláhuac from house arrest and returning them to their people, which wasn't going to happen either, Alvarado didn't have anything to trade that Mucktey might want.

Except, he reminded himself, Mucktey's own life . . .

The next morning, Sunday 5 June, at prayer in the great audience chamber that the conquistadors had conscripted as a church, Alvarado was still thinking about it.

Mucktey had to be *forced* to end the siege. Short of Cortés returning victorious from his war with Narváez, there really was no other way. Simple persuasion would not be enough, but a little torture should see to it! Liberally basted, the tender soles of the Great Speaker's pampered feet would feel the teeth of a roasting more than most.

Alvarado resolved to begin tomorrow – since it would not be appropriate to torture on the Lord's day – when there came a tremendous din of shouting and whistles from the guard. Fire had broken out in the southwest wing of the palace facing the great pyramid.

'Fire?' shouted Alvarado, running from the church with the rest of the men to collect buckets of sand, brackish lake water stored in great barrels for this purpose, and other fire-fighting paraphernalia. 'What the fuck? Was it set by the Mexica?'

'Not that we know of, sir. They're still camped on the plaza, thousands of them, but none have advanced past our foreguard. The fire must have started inside, sir.'

* * *

'It has begun, great lord,' Teudile breathed.

'I hear nothing,' Moctezuma complained.

'Listen again, lord.'

Moctezuma cupped his ear, and suddenly he heard it – the distant, hoarse din of shouts and alarums from the southwest wing.

'The fire is a bad one,' said Teudile. 'We paid well for it to be set. They will not extinguish it quickly, but they must if they're to continue to hold the palace. In the confusion our rescuers will come.'

'I still don't understand how they're going to cross the plaza to reach us with their ladders. We can't climb out of these windows and descend to the ground in seconds. We're on the second floor! It will take time! And we've all seen what the *tueles'* cannon can do in just a few moments.'

'This time there will be a distraction.'

'The fire?' Moctezuma was dubious: 'I know it's at the opposite end of the palace. Certainly it will draw some of the defenders away, but I don't think it's enough.'

'Not only the fire, brother,' said Cuitláhuac, who'd worked closely with Teudile on the plan. 'Our signal that the rescuers are coming will be a massed attack on the foreguard, and on the front doors of the palace, by the regiment in the plaza. That's when we go to the windows and wait for the ladders and the brave warriors who'll guide us down.'

The fire in the southwest wing had begun on the second floor, but spread so rapidly up and down the front of the building, quickly reaching ground level, that it could not be extinguished entirely from within the palace. In order to overcome the flames, Alvarado had to take fifty men through the front doors and out into the plaza – a manoeuvre that was itself only possible because of the foreguard with its sheltering artillery cordon. Once outside, however, the fire-fighters came under immediate Mexica attack, so that more than half their number were needed to defend the others while they doused the flames.

As they were thus engaged, a new attack began, this time with at least five thousand warriors surging forward in a mass, screaming their hatred at the foreguard and obviously aiming to storm the massive doors of the palace before they could be closed. They bore down on the guns in an avalanche of sound, war-paint and stone blades, and the guns answered in fire, grapeshot and blood, with a single concerted volley that ripped jagged gashes in the oncoming ranks and slowed but did not stop them. Soon the warriors were in amongst the gunners, but the fifty sent to fight the fire reinforced them, and superior Spanish arms and tactics triumphed over force of numbers. Once again the garrison staged a fighting retreat, and once again they saved all the cannon, although today at a cost of seven men.

It was obvious to Alvarado that his little force could not stand the constant pressure and the high rate of attrition for very much longer. Realising that soon he'd have no men left at all, he concluded reluctantly that some accommodation would have to be reached with Mucktey . . .

But wait! Where was Mucktey in all this? Confronted by the fire in the southwest wing, and the massed assault on the palace doors, Alvarado realised he had forgotten, for some while, the all-important issue of the safety of the Great Speaker in the northwest wing. It was not that he was unguarded. Five sentries were now permanently posted in the corridor outside his apartments. Nonetheless, it occurred to Alvarado, with a dropping heart, that the attacks on the southwest wing and the palace doors could have been diversions when the real purpose of the Mexica today, all along, had been to free Mucktey.

A renewed assault with a battering ram was under way. Ordering Vendabal to release twenty dogs through the wicket to disrupt the ram crew, Alvarado beckoned a dozen men to follow him and pounded up the stairs towards Moctezuma's quarters on the second floor of the northwest wing.

When the assault on the palace began, Moctezuma, Cuitláhuac and Teudile made ready. A window on the northwest side of the apartments, over-looking a quiet corner of the plaza out of sight from the embattled area between the palace and the great pyramid, had been selected for their rescue, and as they looked down a squad of warriors appeared far below.

Filled with fear and hope, Moctezuma was practically gibbering with excitement as the ladder was raised. 'Come on, come on, come on,' he hissed through his teeth as he watched it push up towards him. '*Come on!*' But the ladder was too short and stopped, resting against the wall at a steep angle, approximately the height of a man beneath the sill.

'You go first,' Moctezuma said to Cuitláhuac.

'No, brother, I couldn't possibly. You are the Great Speaker. You must go first.'

'No, one should go,' said Teudile. 'It will not be easy to reach the ladder. Any slip or misjudgement and . . . To fall from this height would mean death.'

'Wait!' Moctezuma was peering out of the window. 'Someone's coming up.'

It was a tall Cuahchic. Standing on the top rung of the ladder, he was able to reach the sill with his hands. 'Come to me, O Great One,' he said to Moctezuma. 'I will bring you down safely.'

Moctezuma looked at him, looked down at his feet, precariously balanced on the top rung, the toes curling. He was obviously a strong fellow, this fine Mexica warrior, but it was not difficult to imagine how quickly and how fatally things could go wrong if some accident were to occur during the process of transferring the royal person from the window to the ladder.

The Cuahchic fixed him with a desperate eye and made urgent, beckoning motions.

'Teudile,' Moctezuma said, wanting to see how it would be done before venturing out himself, 'you go first.'

'No, sire! I cannot. The first to escape must be you, my lord.'

'This isn't a request, Teudile. You will go first.'

'But, sire.'

'Go, good Teudile! Go! And I will follow.'

Teudile hesitated, but Cuitláhuac grabbed him, dragged him to the window and passed him out to the Cuahchic, who clamped him in the crook of one huge elbow and at once began to descend.

Everything was going smoothly, and Moctezuma was cursing himself for not being the first, when something shiny plunged down with a *clang* upon the Cuahchic's bald head and the warrior at once fell backwards off the ladder taking Teudile with him.

It seemed to take unnaturally long for them to reach the ground, but when they did it was with spectacular effect, like two bags of blood bursting.

The Cuahchic stayed silent, but just before the impact Teudile uttered a despairing wail.

On his way up to Moctezuma's apartments, Alvarado met one of the guards from the roof coming down at a run. 'Mucktey was trying to escape, sir,' the lad gasped. 'They had a ladder up for him. But – ' he puffed out his chest – 'I saw them, sir, when they were getting him out of the window and I threw down my helmet, and it was a lucky shot, sir, but it knocked them off the ladder.'

'Them? Please tell me you do not mean Moctezuma himself?'

'Yes, sir!' The idiot boy was still proud. 'Mucktey himself! Reckon I'll go down in history for that.'

Suddenly Alvarado was on him, smashing blows into his face, kicking and pummelling him. 'You're telling me you *killed* Moctezuma? Our one hope of getting out of here alive?'

'Yes, sir.' The little prick wasn't even trying to defend himself from Alvarado's assault. 'Did I do wrong, sir? I only meant to prevent him from escaping, sir.'

'You've killed us all, you fool.'

Alvarado's hand was on the hilt of his falchion. He was dangerously close to committing murder, but he would need every man for the struggle ahead and forced himself to resist the temptation. There wasn't even time to put the cretin under arrest!

Seething with inner fury, his squad pounding behind him, Alvarado resumed his race to Moctezuma's apartments. He feared the worst, but there to his astonishment and immense relief, he found the Great Speaker still very much alive; it had been Teudile, mistaken in his long robes for Moctezuma, who had died. There had been no further attempts to raise a ladder, and sharpshooters on the roof were ready to deter any further warriors who might come forward. Meanwhile, the much larger assault at the front of the palace continued unabated.

Unlike Cuitláhuac, who sat ramrod straight and seemed ready to accept the consequences of his actions, Moctezuma was cowering on the floor, trying to say in broken Spanish that he'd had nothing to do with anything. It had all been Teudile's fault – wretched Teudile, who had now suffered the fate he deserved.

'I don't care whose fault it is,' said Alvarado. He strode across the room, seized Moctezuma by the hair with his left hand, jerked him to his feet, drew his quillon dagger with his right and held it to his exposed throat. 'Do you want to live?' he asked.

'Yes, Tonatiuh.'

'Then . . .'

Alvarado suddenly remembered that he was talking to a savage who barely had a word of Castilian. '*Aguilar! Will someone please bring Aguilar here at once.*'

But the interpreter had anticipated the demand and was already at the door: 'Yes, sir.'

'Tell this clown he must speak to his captains outside and order them to call off the attack, right now. They must make no further assaults against us. They must provide us with sufficient rations of food and good drinking water – all this until His Excellency Don Hernando Cortés returns, at which time everything can be discussed.'

Aguilar put the proposal to the Great Speaker, who seemed aghast and refused.

'We'll see about that,' said Alvarado. He flicked his wrist and the blade of the dagger sliced a figure of eight across Moctezuma's throat. It was carefully judged, cutting just deep enough to draw blood in theatrical quantities, but not so deep as to sever any major vessel.

'*Aaaghhh!*' Moctezuma screamed. Although he was familiar with the sight of his own blood from the many rituals of auto-sacrifice he'd been required to perform since childhood, he'd never seen so much of it, and it had never been drawn by the hand of another. He seemed totally unnerved.

'Tell him,' Alvarado repeated, 'that if he doesn't do what I require, the next cut will kill him.' And he held the dagger up to the Great Speaker's rolling, terrified eyes.

Moctezuma wore his finery of office, but the white bandages round his neck, through which the royal blood was already seeping, must surely reveal to any perceptive eye that he was not master of himself.

Even so, his word was law and his people must obey him.

The *tueles* brought him up to the roof and, taking his arm, Alvarado led him to a point where he looked down directly on the portico, beneath which stood the huge double doors of the palace. There a team of warriors wielded a battering ram amidst a field of corpses both human and animal – for it seemed that some of the unholy dragon-dogs of the *tueles* had once again taken part in the battle.

At Alvarado's urging, Moctezuma climbed unsteadily on to the parapet and showed himself. It required the passage of some moments, but as soon as he was noticed by one warrior – who immediately fell to his knees – it seemed that all the others recognised him as well, and suddenly everyone in the plaza was kneeling.

When he had silence and could feel all their attention focused upon him, Moctezuma reached up to his throat and tore loose the bandages, exposing his bloody wound. 'See, O Mexica! O men of Tenochtitlan! See what they have done to your Great Speaker. Those who can do this can do anything. O brave warriors of the Mexica, hear me! We are not the equals of the *tueles*. Therefore, let the battle be abandoned! Let the arrow, the shield, be held back! We are not their equals. Let there be a cessation of war.'

* * *

373

Alvarado hadn't really expected so desperate a ploy to work, but weirdly it did, and with very few words from Moctezuma.

Within the hour most of the regiment that had threatened them from the plaza had gone, leaving only a token few hundred to mark their continuing presence. These remaining warriors allowed – indeed encouraged – the Spaniards to send out small reconnaissance patrols along the walls of the sacred plaza, which returned to report embankments being thrown up and a mass of Mexica, armed and ready for battle, mustered in the surrounding streets.

The siege, in other words, was as tight as it ever had been. As long as the Spaniards stayed within the sacred precinct, they were not troubled greatly, but if they attempted to stray outside – as further, more forceful, probes in the next days proved – they were attacked with great violence.

Very soon, food became scarce again.

But a new problem, seemingly ridiculous in a city in the midst of a lake, was shortage of water.

The lake was as salty and as undrinkable as the sea, and both the freshwater wells in the palace grounds were close to dry.

By Monday 6 June, Cortés had begun to look out anxiously for the return of his five riders bringing news from Tenochtitlan.

They did not come.

Nor did they come the next day, or the day after.

Finally, however, on Saturday 11 June, late in the evening, two of the cavalrymen, Juan Nasciel and Pedro Morisco by name, rode in to Cempoala. Both were strong young men, but they were bloody and battered, grey with fatigue, filthy and strangely emaciated.

'What of Alvarado?' Cortés asked, striding out to them before they could dismount.

Black haired, a thick, ten-day stubble covering his jaw, his thigh bandaged and caked with dried blood, Morisco confessed: 'We did not see him, sir.'

'You did not *see* him?' Cortés barked, barely able to contain his fury. 'Why not? Explain yourself, man!'

'We couldn't get into Tenochtitlan, sir.' It was the other rider, Nasciel, who replied. Across much of the right side of his head, his red hair had been burned away, leaving the scalp beneath livid and weeping. 'The city's closed tighter than a chastity belt on a virgin's cunt. Four of us were still alive when we got to Iztapalapa. We tried to force entry to the causeway, but the Mexica had warriors stationed there. A lot of warriors. They fell upon us and killed Francisco and Gaspar. Pedro and I barely escaped with our lives.'

'And our men, in the city. What of them?'

'They live, Caudillo!' replied Morisco. 'They still hold Axayacatl's palace.'

'And how do you know this?'

'After we were driven back from the causeway, we rode to a high point nearby and fired our arquebuses in the air. It was a still morning and the lake water helped the sound to travel. Within a minute, sir, there came an answering volley back, and we saw puffs of smoke from the roof of the palace.'

'It can only have been our men, sir,' added Nasciel.

'Yes, of course,' Cortés replied, not hiding his irritation. 'I do realise that the Indians haven't mastered the arquebus yet.'

The rest of the story came out as they sheltered under the awning on the green in front of the pyramid, where Cortés was in the habit of sitting of an evening, dictating letters to Pepillo, holding meetings with his captains and planning the next stages of the conquest. Now a large crowd gathered to hear the disturbing news that Nasciel and Morisco had brought. Although all yet seemed well here on the coast, and the alliance with Tlascala held strong, most of the countryside, particularly in the Mexica mountain provinces and vassal states near to Tenochtitlan, had risen against the Spaniards. In some regions this had meant simple non-cooperation with the riders – particularly the refusal to provide them with food, a problem, previously unheard of in this hospitable country, encountered everywhere they went. But in others they had been viciously and treacherously attacked, losing one of their number to a mob outside Cholula, and then the two more, already told of, as they tried to storm the causeway.

And there was something else. Passing along the floor of a steep-sided ravine on their desperate flight back to Cempoala, Nasciel and Morisco had come across the freshly butchered remains of the slower-moving infantry column conveying the most intransigent Narváez loyalists to Tenochtitlan for imprisonment. The bodies were still warm! All twenty of the foot soldiers and all the prisoners had been killed, but those who died in the fighting had been the lucky ones. The seventeen who'd been captured alive, including Salvatierra, Bono de Quejo and Gamarra, had been staked to the ground through their outstretched hands and crossed feet. Once set in this parody of the crucifix, their hearts had been hacked from their chests and pushed obscenely into their own mouths.

It seemed to have happened less than an hour before. Although vultures were already circling, the corpses had hardly been disturbed by animals yet, and all the signs indicated that the large band of warriors who'd done this had marched east after the killings – precisely the route Nasciel and Morisco needed to follow to get back to Cempoala. Since the consequences of overtaking the murderers were obvious, the riders had chosen to make a long diversion to the south through countryside that was hardly less hostile, and that had cost them an extra day on the journey.

'But now, here you are,' said Cortés. 'I give thanks to God for your salvation and I thank you both from the bottom of my heart for your courage and dedication in bringing us these tidings. Were you able, in your travels, to learn *why* Alvarado is besieged in Tenochtitlan?'

'Neither of us speaks more than a few words of the Mexica language, sir. Still, we learned something from an informant in Iztapalapa who had a little Castilian. It seems there was great trouble in Tenochtitlan. Some kind of fight. We were told it was Tonatiuh as started it, sir – Don Pedro de Alvarado. A lot of Indians were killed. The siege began after that.'

Though he kept his emotions in check, Cortés was inwardly reeling and furiously angry with himself. In his bones he had known it! Alvarado, with his love of gold and murder, had been the wrong man to safeguard the glittering prizes of Tenochtitlan and the person of Moctezuma! It was a bitter blow, truly, just when the whole of New Spain lay within his grasp, to be confronted by such news, but a brave face must be put on it.

Summoning Pepillo with quill and parchment, Cortés called on Sandoval to stand at his side before issuing the only general order that was possible under the circumstances.

'Men!' he proclaimed. 'You have heard the news! Prepare yourselves. Tomorrow we march on Tenochtitlan!'

He paused, looked around the hundreds of soldiers assembled on the green beneath the great pyramid of Cempoala, their faces luridly lit by flickering torches.

'To my veterans in the crowd – you already know what cowards the Mexica are. It seems they've got a little out of hand while we were unavoidably called away on other business – ' a ripple of laughter – 'but when they see us return in all our strength, they'll be bowing down before us, offering us gold and jewels, and garlands of flowers, and sweetmeats, and kissing our feet . . .'

'They can kiss my arse,' a gruff voice shouted.

Shielding his eyes from the glare of the torches, Cortés recognised the speaker. 'If that's the kind of thing you enjoy, Guiterrez, then don't let me hold you back.'

Another ripple of good-natured laughter followed. But it wasn't the veterans Cortés was concerned about, it was the new recruits. In winning them over in the past days, he had used all kinds of persuasions and blandishments and had consistently painted Tenochtitlan as a paradise – 'a mountain Venice', 'an oasis of peace' – where Spaniards were loved and welcomed. Suddenly all his fine words were called into question by the brutal truths of Nasciel and Morisco's testimony, and Cortés knew that he must at once repair the damage or lose men.

'My veterans well understand what they're getting themselves into,' he continued, 'and I know not one of them will baulk at this new challenge. For those of you who have joined us recently, let me repeat, as I've told you many times before, that you're free to go if you wish to.' He grinned: 'But please stay! It will make me very happy, and you very rich, if you will join us in our march to wrest back control of Tenochtitlan from the usurpers.'

Once again Bernal Díaz watched from the sidelines as Cortés the successful general, Cortés the gracious victor, and Cortés the consummate statesman, allowed Cortés the master swindler to come to the fore.

Standing at Díaz's right, his friend Gonzalo de Sandoval, recovering well from his wounds, seemed to read his thoughts: 'Hernán's really good at this!' he observed quietly.

'The best,' Díaz agreed. 'Well, he talked us into it, didn't he?'

It was true. They had both been sweet-talked by Cortés into risking life and limb for him too many times to count. But, Díaz reminded himself, the honeyed words alone could not have done it. There was real substance to the caudillo, real depth to the man: courage and toughness when it was needed, good humour and a gentle side too. Beyond all that, however, Cortés possessed, in great abundance, that special charisma and fortune that the Moors called *baraka*, something that was as much a spiritual as a worldly power, and that had repeatedly brought victory to him, and those who followed him, when any other leader would have faced annihilation.

'Tonight, Saturday 11 June in the Year of Our Lord 1520,' Díaz later wrote by candlelight in his journal, 'our caudillo, Hernán Cortés, talked nine hundred men into a suicide mission. I do not include those of us who long ago threw in our lot with him, for good or ill. We're too deeply committed to pull out now. I speak of the new recruits from Narváez, who have not yet been tested in the fire. Despite being made aware of the uprising in Tenochtitlan, every one of them once again voted to accompany us on what – I have a very bad feeling – will prove to be a march straight through the gates of hell.

'Rangel and his two hundred must stay at the coast to keep Villa Rica secure, but Cortés has tonight sent orders to Velázquez de Léon and Ordaz, with two hundred men each, to rendezvous with us at Tlascala. Even then, however, and adding also the one hundred and twenty men left with Alvarado, the total force that we can bring to bear in Tenochtitlan does not greatly exceed one thousand two hundred men. When we remember that there are, according to Moctezuma's last census, more than half a million Mexica living in Tenochtitlan, and millions more in the towns and villages of the surrounding countryside, the odds against our survival look very slim.

'Yet I put my trust in our caudillo, in God and in my right arm. We have won through when our own numbers were less and against fiercer odds. We shall win through again. Indeed, as my seal upon it, I, Bernal Díaz del Castillo hereby solemnly swear that I shall live until the age of ninety-two and father many children.'

The following day, Sunday 12 June, after prayers, Cortés led the army out of Cempoala. As well as all Narváez's men and all his cavalry, he had all the artillery pieces that the other commander had kindly brought, and these, together with the baggage train, were drawn by more than three thousand Totonac porters.

It would be forced marches, now, up into the mountains and all the way to Tlascala, where they would regroup with Velázquez de Léon and Ordaz before the final push on Tenochtitlan.

Was Alvarado alive or dead? Cortés was so incensed with his childhood friend for losing control of the Mexica that he found he didn't care, so long as enough of the garrison were still alive to hold out and had not yet been killed or fled the city.

Part III

Chapter Nineteen

Friday 24 June 1520

'I've never seen him in such a foul temper,' Pepillo said, 'and I've seen him in some foul tempers.'

'In his sleep,' Malinal offered, 'he grinds his teeth and calls out for Saint Peter.'

It was an hour after dawn and the column was well advanced on its six-mile march along the causeway connecting the lakeside town of Iztapalapa with Tenochtitlan. Last night, and again this morning, Cortés had ordered trumpets to be blown and ordnance fired, the din rewarded on both occasions with an answering roar of cannon from the palace of Axayacatl in the heart of the city.

Malinal looked over her shoulder at the long column of marching men and horses. The Spaniards alone stretched over a mile behind, but the rearguard, after the Tlascalans and the baggage train, was almost three miles further back. 'All these lives depending on him,' she said, 'too much responsibility! That's why he's bad tempered; that's why he doesn't sleep well.'

Pepillo was not oblivious to the enormous pressure his master was under, and understood his bad mood. In the moment of his triumph, when he should by rights have been enjoying the laurels of a tremendous victory, he had been failed, and failed dismally, by his second in command and closest friend, Pedro de Alvarado. The country had risen against them, and every day on the long, hard road from Cempoala they had expected to confront an enemy army.

Then, after an exhausting series of forced marches through the mountains, there had been the interval in Tlascala. There Velázquez de Léon and Ordaz joined them, bringing two hundred men each and swelling the number of Spaniards marching on Tenochtitlan to more than a thousand. These included eighty cavalry, eighty arquebusiers and close to one

381

hundred and fifty crossbowmen. In addition Cortés asked Shikotenka the Elder and Maxixcatzin for two thousand elite Tlascalan warriors. They had refused to help when his fight was with a fellow Spaniard, but now that a decisive battle loomed against their age-old enemies the Mexica, they showed no such reluctance. It seemed the battle-king Shikotenka the Younger had remained in Tenochtitlan after his meeting with Cortés in early May, and had been present in the city, at the head of the further one thousand Tlascalans stationed there, ever since.

Beyond Tlascala, though the troops were rested, well fed and well supplied, thanks to five days spent gathering their energies, the road became difficult again and, entering once more into territories under Mexica hegemony, they found everywhere that the people turned their faces against them. Nobody picked a fight – who would against an army as formidable as this one? – but the enmity of the country was so intense, and so openly expressed, you could almost touch it. Whereas before the Spaniards had been greeted with smiles and garlands, and offered food and hospitality, now there were no greetings and no hospitality. Food was provided when it was demanded, but it was of poor quality and always offered with bad grace.

Draining in itself, this all-pervasive atmosphere of loathing, threat and danger compared very poorly with the images Cortés had summoned up in the minds of Narváez's men of a country, bounteous and at peace, eagerly welcoming them to dip their fingers in its limitless cornucopia of gold and jewels. Moreover, the hostility seemed to intensify, the closer the army approached to Tenochtitlan.

Last night they had slept in the lakeside town of Iztapalapa, occupying the palace, which they found utterly deserted, and pitching tents in its grounds to accommodate the entire army. It was not a good position, vulnerable both from the lake and from the land, and they placed a strong guard. Again, however, no attack came, nor any contact of any kind with the Indians. Not only had all the palace staff deserted, but the whole town of Iztapalapa was void of population, its streets and its markets empty, and there was no food to be had there at all.

The same eerie and inexplicable silence accompanied them across Lake Texcoco. When the conquistadors had first marched the length of the Iztapalapa causeway in November of the previous year, it had been lined with huge crowds of friendly, inquisitive, cheering people, and the waters of the great salt lake had been gay with brightly coloured pirogues packed with eager sightseers. Today there were no watercraft, no people and no cheers – just the *tramp, tramp, tramp* of marching feet and the forlorn, high-pitched calls of multitudes of water birds.

'What do you make of it?' Pepillo asked Malinal. 'The silence, I mean. I didn't expect it to continue all the way into Tenochtitlan.'

'I don't like it,' she replied. 'I think they've sent women, children, the elderly, the sick – everyone who can't fight – up into the mountains, but the warriors have stayed behind to kill us in Tenochtitlan. That's why we've not been opposed anywhere on our march – in fact they're making it easy for us to come here. But once we're inside the city – it's so obvious really! – they'll aim to finish us off.'

'So the caudillo's doing exactly what they want. Have you talked to him about this?'

'Yes, Pepillo, but he won't listen. He says that all the warriors of the Mexica won't be enough to kill us now that we're so many, and that he'll soon have the city by the throat again. Do you think he's right?'

Pepillo shrugged. 'Let's pray to God he is.'

Tonatiuh did not follow through on his threat of punishment by death for attempting to escape from the palace. Not that Moctezuma ever for a moment admitted that escape had been his intention! The story was that both he and Cuitláhuac had been the victims of an unauthor- ised scheme by Teudile who, rightly, had paid the price for it. Perhaps Tonatiuh had been convinced, or perhaps he had other reasons, but he had allowed both Moctezuma and Cuitláhuac to remain quartered in the Great Speaker's apartments, and had continued to permit Cuitláhuac to come and go within the bounds of the palace on Moctezuma's business.

Through the few remaining kitchen staff and servants, a tenuous connection was maintained with the captains outside the walls, and little by little the plot was evolved. It was learned that Malinche had triumphed over his enemy Nar-Vez, and incorporated the soldiers of Nar-Vez into his own army. That army contained more than a thousand *tueles* – indeed, all the *tueles* in the One World except those already in Tenochtitlan, reduced now to about one hundred, and the two hundred at the settle- ment on the coast called Villa Rica. Every *tuele* must be killed, Cuitláhuac had urged Moctezuma to agree, and there could be no better killing ground than Tenochtitlan itself, to which the larger part of Cortés's army was now willingly marching.

Even as they advanced along the six-mile causeway from Iztapalapa this morning, the Daykeeper Ollin was summoned to describe their progress, and the measures taken to defeat them.

'As Malinche descends upon us he brings with him many Spaniards and many Tlascalans – very many,' Ollin declaimed. 'They not only are coming! They are coming to war. They come provided with devices, they come arrayed for war, each one with his shield and his sword. They have stirred up columns of dust on their march. Their faces are covered with dust; indeed each is cloaked in dust.

'We have evacuated the city to receive them and are ready to fall upon them, sire. Only warriors now remain. If the Spaniards could see how many of our brave fighters are assembled together in places of conceal-ment, they might guess what we have planned for them and would know in their hearts that only death awaits them here. But our warriors are well hidden, watching them through holes pierced in walls, awaiting your order to strike.'

'Not yet,' said Moctezuma. He had noticed that Ollin, and Cuitláhuac too, had stopped referring to the *tueles* by that Nahuatl word that meant 'gods', and preferred to call them Spaniards instead. He resolved never to call them *tueles* again, since they certainly were not gods and did not even deserve to be dignified by the title of men. 'We will allow the Spaniards to enter the city in peace. Let them withdraw into the palace of Axayacatl. We will give them a night for their confidence to grow, then we'll lift every bridge on the causeways, trap them in the sacred precinct and slaughter them for Huitzilopochtli.'

Seven moons earlier, Guatemoc had concealed himself here, in this coppice on a deserted hilltop outside Tacuba, just west of Lake Texcoco, to observe the first entry of the white-skins into Tenochtitlan. He'd chosen the very same spot for reconnaissance today, and watched grimly across the sparkling waters as Malinche again led an army along the Iztapalapa causeway. It was a greatly enlarged force, perhaps three times more numerous than before, but Guatemoc was undaunted. Moctezuma's star had been falling for a long while, and his was on the rise.

He touched Tozi's elbow. 'I've seen enough,' he said. 'You should go into the city now. I'll get back to the men.'

The 'men' being his army – ten times the size of Malinche's expanded force! – left camped an hour's march north of Tacuba.

Oh, what a race Guatemoc had run in the last seven moons, only to return here in the end! With his five knife-brothers, Starving Coyote,

384

Fuzzy Face, Big Dart, Man-Eater and Mud Head, he'd trekked north through Chichemec canyon country on a quest for the lost land of Aztlán and the Seven Caves of Chicomoztoc, the home of the gods, the mystic place of origin of the Mexica and all other Nahua peoples, where legends spoke of masters of wisdom and workers of magic who they hoped might weave for them the spells of a new dispensation.

They had sworn a blood oath to see this quest through to its end and return to purge Tenochtitlan or die in the attempt. But the Opata, a truly wild and ferocious Chichemec tribe, had got in their way, pursuing them into what had turned out to be a box canyon, where a great crowd of braves had blocked their exit while others swarmed down ropes from the clifftops to surround them.

They'd looked hungry, Guatemoc remembered, and it had been uncomfortable to be menaced by the filed teeth and obsidian daggers of a gang of furious cannibals! Not that he wasn't partial to a bit of human flesh himself, but the way the Chichemecs were rumoured to do it, relishing the meat raw and bloody, carved off the living bone and seasoned with the victim's terror, was frankly barbaric.

'Reckon they're going to eat us,' Big Dart had observed. 'Not the end I had in mind for myself.'

'Just let them fucking try,' said Mud Head, brandishing his *macuahuitl*.

Guatemoc was ready to trade blows with the primitives – truly a thing was not over until it was over – when the one he assumed to be their leader spoke to him in Nahuatl. 'You are Mexica?'

What turned the statement into a question was the tone, which the savage did well.

'You've spent time in Tenochtitlan?' Guatemoc guessed.

The Chichemec's face was a flat, blank slab. The small, slanted eyes glittered like dark jewels. 'My father sent me for one year to the *telpuch-calli*. Besides, our tongue is not so distant from yours.'

The *telpuchcalli*, 'house of youth', was the name given to the schools that all Mexica boys were required to attend to learn the basics of history, religion and the art of war. There were levels of education far beyond this – the *calmecac* and the *cuicacalli* – that Guatemoc had mastered, but the fact that this Chichemec had attended school at all marked him as much more than the simple killer he appeared to be.

'May I know your name?' Guatemoc asked. There was something faintly absurd about this conversation but it seemed wise to persist with it.

'I am Kasakir, son of Hedia, chief of the Opata Chichemecs. And you?'

'I am Guatemoc, son of Cuitláhuac.'

Kasakir's eyes narrowed. He adjusted his grip on the handle of his *macuahuitl*. 'It would be well for you to speak the truth.'

'I do. I am Guatemoc, prince of the Mexica.'

'We heard the true Guatemoc was wounded in battle by Shikotenka of Tlascala . . .'

'I was fatally wounded but I was healed by the goddess Temaz and lived.'

With that Guatemoc opened his tunic and showed the puckered line of scars across his belly. To his astonishment the response of Kasakir was to fall to his knees. The obeisance was followed by all the other Chichemecs.

'I know I've got a beautiful body,' Guatemoc whispered to Big Dart, 'but isn't this going a bit far?' He reached down to Kasakir, raised the warrior to his feet and asked, confidentially, 'What's this all about? Why did you kneel?'

'Sir, we are the paid men of your father Cuitláhuac. He sent us to find you. You are to make us into an army that can overthrow Moctezuma and rescue Tenochtitlan from the white-skins he protects.'

And so it had begun.

Guatemoc was astonished to learn that his habitually rubbery, subservient and appeasing father was at last showing some sign of a backbone. It was not clear when this new, firmer, more decisive Cuitláhuac had first appeared, but it had certainly not been before the day of Moctezuma's kidnapping by the white-skins – because, on that day, warned by Tozi, Guatemoc had fled just before a squad of fifty men sent by his father had burst into his quarters to arrest him.

Whatever had happened since then to change Cuitláhuac's heart was welcome – and never more so than at the bottom of that desert canyon in Chichemec country when, at his father's behest, a gang of cannibals had offered themselves to Guatemoc as his private army! That was when he'd realised – and it had come to him with the force of divine revelation – that he had fulfilled his quest, honoured his blood oath and found what he was looking for.

The Chichemecs, after all, were the rude stock out of which the fine vine of the Mexica had sprung. Were they not, therefore, the living embodiment of the mystic origin places of Aztlán and Chicomoztoc? In the savage purity and simplicity of the Chichemecs might there not, indeed, be found the wisdom from which a new dispensation could emerge? And who was to say, once they had been properly trained, that they might not work magic?

Tozi, with her own kinds of magic, had come later, when Guatemoc's Chichemec army was already beginning to take shape, bringing him news of Tenochtitlan.

He did not profess to understand her strange powers – the power of invisibility, the power to call animals, the power to drive men to madness and, surpassing all that, the power to heal that had brought Guatemoc back from the edge of death and restored him to health and strength again.

For a long while he had really believed she was the goddess Temaz! Then he had begun to suspect that she might be a human woman with great powers – perhaps a witch. Finally, on the first and only night they'd made love, she'd told him her true name – Tozi! – and confessed that she was indeed a witch. She had feared he would despise her, but he'd told her that it made no difference to him, and when she'd revealed that it was she who'd been driving Moctezuma mad, he'd told her that he loved her even more for that.

What Tozi had not done that strange night in Chapultepec nearly nine moons before was renew her attempts to persuade him that the white-skins were the companions of Quetzalcoatl and that their leader, the bandit Malinche, might even be Quetzalcoatl himself, returning to the One World to reclaim his throne as he had long ago promised.

Her other bizarre fixations, still present today, included her hatred of Lord Hummingbird and of human sacrifice, but she had not urged either of them on Guatemoc that night, or since. He had seen her again two moons later when she returned to Chapultepec, just ahead of the arrest squad, giving him time to escape.

Then five more moons passed – the quest to the north, the encounter with the Opata Chichemecs, the making of an army – and suddenly Tozi had returned to his life, leaving Tenochtitlan, crossing the deserts and finding him in the wilderness preparing for war.

In her usual way she had simply materialised at his side, emerging out of invisibility. 'I was wrong about Malinche,' she said without preamble. 'He is not Quetzalcoatl. He is a man from a country called Spain, as he himself says, and he's not here to bring peace; he's here to conquer our land by violence and destroy us completely. He must be stopped.'

'That's quite a change of view!'

'I entered his dreams,' Tozi said. 'He is a far more faithful and effective servant of Hummingbird than Moctezuma ever was. Indeed, he is the chosen one of Hummingbird.'

'But he prevented the sacrifice of those ten thousand girls.'

'He might easily not have done. He seized Moctezuma when he did for other reasons. The freeing of the girls wouldn't have happened otherwise. Cortés is a killer.'

'A man like me then?'

'He says he's against human sacrifice,' Tozi continued, the words spilling out of her. 'He's taken some actions to stop it, but still human sacrifices are performed in Tenochtitlan, to which he continues to turn a blind eye. His own religion performs human sacrifices by means of burning to death! In his wars of conquest across the One World, he himself has sacrificed thousands of lives – those of the Maya, those of Tlascala, those of Cholula – and he holds the great city of Tenochtitlan in his thrall. I believe now that I have divined his ultimate purpose.'

'Which is?'

'I don't think even Malinche himself is fully aware of it yet, but his ultimate purpose, the reason he was summoned to the One World, the reason he has been *protected* during his time here, is to offer Hummingbird the greatest sacrifice of all – the sacrifice of every man, woman and child living in Tenochtitlan. All are to die.'

'I cannot believe that my Lord Hummingbird would demand such a sacrifice!' Guatemoc had protested.

'Then you do not know your lord at all.'

'And you do?'

'Better than any other, for I owe my own powers to him.'

'Yet you do not serve him?'

'I will never serve him. That's why I can no longer help Malinche.'

'Then will you help me to destroy Malinche?'

'Yes, it's part of what we have to do . . .'

The matter of Tozi's powers, and how they might most usefully be applied, needed to be approached carefully. At the side of Cortés, after all, was the woman Malinal, whom Tozi loved. Buying time, Guatemoc had changed the subject. 'How did you find me here?' he asked.

Tozi had indicated the valley below, where thousands of Opata Chichemecs were being schooled in military techniques by Starving Coyote, Mud Head and the others. 'Your father has been very cunning,' she said. 'He's told Moctezuma nothing about this army, or his plans for it. But he has associates, fellow conspirators . . .'

'Conspirators?'

'Yes, Guatemoc! I know you think your father's weak and stupid, but this *is* a conspiracy against Moctezuma and Cuitláhuac *is* behind it. He knew he couldn't depend on the other noble houses in Tenochtitlan, or on the generals, or hope to persuade the masses to rebel against their precious Great Speaker. He therefore decided to recruit an army of his own – this one! It seems the idea had been growing in his mind for some time, because a few years earlier he arranged for Kasakir to attend a *telpuchcalli* in Tenochtitlan, but it is only in recent months that he's started to bring the whole scheme to fruition. That's how I found you – by spying on your father in his meetings with other conspirators. He informed them of your presence here with the Opata. He takes great cheer from it. He says there's no better general than you to get the job done.'

It was true. Guatemoc was by far the best of all the Mexica generals. Other than that, however, with which he could hardly disagree, he'd liked very little of what Tozi was telling him. Because, as the months had passed, he had become ever more firmly entrenched in the conviction that the twelve thousand Opata warriors Kasakir had brought him, and to whom he was devoting great efforts to train, were *his* army – funded by Cuitláhuac by all means, but to be used for Guatemoc's purposes. Kasakir had given him no reason to believe otherwise, but now here was Tozi with the annoying reminder that 'his' army in fact belonged to his father and that his own role was simply to 'get the job done'.

'And what is that job?' he'd asked.

'He hasn't told you?'

'I have the general idea, but communications have been difficult. Since you already know exactly what he intends, kindly enlighten me!'

'First the white-skins must be destroyed. Your father's intention is to leave that to Mexica regiments. Every one of them will be brought into Tenochtitlan when the time is right. The fighting will be very severe – the white-skins know how to defend themselves – and many warriors, many from the noble families, many of the generals, will be killed. It cannot be known if Moctezuma will live or die, but certainly there will be a time of chaos after the fighting. That is when your father wants you to come, with your Chichemec mercenaries, to impose order, to kill Moctezuma if he's not already dead, and to place Cuitláhuac himself on the throne.'

'An interesting idea,' Guatemoc had admitted after a moment's reflection. 'My father continues to surprise me.'

'In all this – ' a strange, faraway look had come into Tozi's eyes – 'if we make our own plans with care, we may find the seeds of a new dispensation.'

Guatemoc had pricked up his ears. The notion of seeking out a new dispensation – a new order of things, even the beginning of a new age of the world – had been at the forefront of his mind since he'd left Tenochtitlan on his quest, and it felt somehow deeply meaningful to hear the same phrase on Tozi's lips now.

'What do you have in mind?' he'd asked cautiously.

'That army – ' Tozi had nodded in the direction of the men in the valley – 'Cuitláhuac paid for it, but I'll wager *you* have the loyalty of the men.'

'I do. They love me like a brother.'

'And will do as you order them?'

Grimly: 'Yes. They'll jump down the throat of hell for me.'

'Would they kill your father for you?'

'What?' Guatemoc was momentarily taken aback at the changes Tozi had undergone in the past months – from gentle goddess of healing and love, to enchanting witch, and now to this ruthless, calculating, obsidian-edged young woman.

'If he gets in our way,' Tozi clarified. 'If he doesn't serve the new dispensation.'

Guatemoc thought about it. He liked this new, manipulative Tozi, and he wanted to make changes – big changes – when he came to power. Fast, sweeping changes would be needed to adapt to the new reality that Malinche signified. For even with Malinche himself and all his men dead and gone, the land he came from would still be there, and its people would not lose their ability to build ships, and they would therefore be back. A new world in which the inevitable encounter with these powerful foreigners could be made from a position of strength, rather than from the present position of weakness, was therefore the goal, but Cuitláhuac was a traditionalist. He might have accepted, reluctantly, the need to depose Moctezuma, but in all other matters he would block change.

'Don't worry,' said Guatemoc, 'I won't let him get in our way.'

That was when he'd noticed he'd started talking about 'we', 'us', 'our', not 'me' and 'mine'. When had he become an 'us' with Tozi? When had they become a 'we'?

He suspected that it went all the way back to the miraculous healing she'd brought him, but whenever it had begun, the feeling that they were not just lovers but a team, and that they shared a common purpose, had only grown and consolidated in the past two moons. There was still much they disagreed on – the subject of human sacrifice was particularly vexed – but that sense of being on the same side, serving the same cause, helped to overcome these problems.

And this morning, as they'd promised one another, they'd looked upon Tenochtitlan once again and were ready, with an army, to do battle for the future of the world!

The spies reported that Cuitláhuac was still in the palace of Axayacatl, where both he and Moctezuma were under house arrest. And now, as Guatemoc and Tozi had seen with their own eyes, Malinche was marching into the city in his strength and splendour along the Iztapalapa causeway. All the pieces and the players were being moved into position by the puppet-master gods and soon a great conflagration must unfold . . .

Guatemoc touched Tozi's elbow again; she was lost in thought. 'We should go,' he reminded her.

She smiled, but there was sadness in it, and pointed down at the Tacuba causeway, the route she would take from the west side of the lake into Tenochtitlan – much shorter, and much closer to their present position than the Iztapalapa causeway used by Malinche and his men at the southern side of the lake. 'It was by the Tacuba causeway that Malinal and I made our escape on the night we were to be sacrificed to Hummingbird. If there's to be a new dispensation, Guatemoc, if it's really to work, if we are to make the One World strong to resist the invader, then human sacrifice must cease.'

Guatemoc groaned. 'Not now, Tozi!'

They'd had the conversation a hundred times.

'It must cease!' Tozi repeated. 'Any new world we create will be rotten at the core if human beings continue to be murdered for the gods.'

'Let us first rid ourselves of Moctezuma and Malinche,' said Guatemoc wearily.

That wistful smile again: 'We will. It's what we're here to do. But know this, Guatemoc. When you become Great Speaker, if you fail to abolish human sacrifice, I will leave your side and you will never see me again.'

With that, saying nothing more, Tozi vanished.

Guatemoc sighed. She was sometimes very difficult. But they'd already made all the necessary arrangements. She would go into Tenochtitlan now, quietly, invisibly, in her way, before he entered it in force. She would find the master-spy Huicton, her mentor, observe and assess the disposition of Mexica regiments and of the Spaniards in the city, and return with the detailed, fresh intelligence that Guatemoc would need.

For the march along the silent causeway and across the empty lake into Tenochtitlan, Bernal Díaz had placed himself alongside his friends Mibiercas and La Serna. Thirty paces ahead, Cortés, riding his dark chestnut stallion Molinero, led the column.

'I feel embarrassed for the caudillo,' Díaz said. 'On the march I heard him often boast to Narváez's men, glorifying himself, telling of how he ruled absolutely over the great Moctezuma and over all his captains, telling of the veneration and command that he enjoys amongst the Indians of Tenochtitlan, and how they would turn out to receive him and celebrate the occasion and give him gold.'

'And now we find everything to be the complete opposite,' said Le Serna. 'They haven't even given us food to eat.'

'Probably why he's in such a bad mood today,' offered Mibiercas.

Díaz had seen how the caudillo was this morning, covering up his shame at the way the Indians had failed him by being irritable and haughty towards any Spaniards who crossed his path, and otherwise appearing very sad and fretful.

The march into the heart of the city beyond the end of the causeway continued silent and uneventful. No Mexica – warriors or otherwise – were to be seen anywhere, and yet Díaz had the strong sense that the Spanish column was being watched, and watched closely, every step of the way. Quite possibly, if they were to send a squad into any of the large buildings lining this avenue, they would find hordes of armed warriors gathered.

The suspicion only grew stronger, the creeping sensation down his spine only more pronounced, as they approached the massive south wall of the sacred precinct, with the great pyramid looming behind it. For a moment all seemed deserted of life, and yet filled with maleficence, but then along the top of the wall cheering Spaniards began to appear, men they recognised, friends waving their arms and bellowing cries of relief, joy and welcome.

Díaz waved back, returned the excited cries, and was enjoying strong, heart-warming feelings of solidarity and renewal when he caught a flash of movement out of the corner of his eye in a high window of one of the great mansions lying around the sacred precinct. He was almost certain that what he had seen was an Indian painted for war, but the apparition was already gone.

'Did you see that?' he asked La Serna. But the other man was still happily greeting the Spaniards on the wall above and asked: 'See what?'

'Probably nothing. I'm jumping at shadows.'

Though its margins had been churned by innumerable feet, and there were signs of recent fighting, including blackened and collapsing buildings demolished by fire and cannon shot, the streets in front of the south gateway were completely, mysteriously empty.

'Is it like this around the other three gateways, lads?' Cortés asked the lean and ragged conquistadors lining the wall above. 'No Mexica warriors to greet us?'

'No fucking Mexica at all! They were occupying the plaza, camped right in front of the palace doors, until the small hours of that morning, then suddenly they began to move out. Very quiet about it they were. At the same time, the regiments in the streets melted away as well. Looks like you've scared them off, Caudillo!'

Díaz was not convinced. The city did not have the atmosphere of ruin and abandonment that usually accompanies a fleeing army. Rather, the feeling in the air was one of tightly sprung readiness, like a trap poised to snap shut.

And where was Don Pedro de Alvarado?

Privately Cortés agreed with the soldier on the wall. Whatever catastrophic mistake Alvarado had made here, no matter how much hostility he'd stirred up, the arrival of this new, greatly enlarged and well-equipped Spanish army had terrified the Indians. They had fled the city in fear and in shame, but they'd be back on their knees in a few days begging for forgiveness.

Still, it was odd that no food at all had been made available in Iztapalapa – forcing the conquerors to go hungry yet again. He'd make the bastards pay for that insult.

As the southern gateway swung open, Cortés entered the sacred precinct at the head of his army, made his way past the great pyramid, and arrived before the doors of Axayacatl's palace, where Alvarado, looking thin and shamefaced, waited to greet him. Cortés dismounted and embraced the other man. He would not, yet, show his anger.

'So you have held the city, Pedro, after a spot of bother, I understand.'

'Yes. There was trouble. I'd like to explain . . .'

'And I would like that also, Pedro.' Cortés was smiling, although inside he felt coldly furious. 'But first there are more pressing matters to attend to. You've been under siege for a long while. What's your most urgent need here?'

'It's food, Hernán. The last fighting was more than two weeks ago. Mucktey ordered them to stop and they stopped, but since then we've been under a tight blockade. They won't give us any food and they won't allow us to buy any in the markets. Our magazines are empty. The truth is we're close to starving.'

Cortés nodded his head. It all made sense. 'For the last three days of our march on Tenochtitlan, local supplies of food dwindled almost to nothing, and last night in Iztapalapa we could find none at all either to buy or to commandeer. There's clearly a policy to starve us.'

'Then it's Mucktey's policy. He's behind everything.'

'How about drinking water?'

'The palace wells have run dry, but a week ago – some say it was a miracle – we dug a hole in the courtyard and fresh water flowed up into it, even though the ground is salt. It's kept us going.'

Behind Cortés, amongst the men, a murmur of conversation suddenly arose. Curious, he looked up and saw Moctezuma, in full ceremonial robes, coming forth to greet him through the big double doors of the palace. The Great Speaker was in such a hurry, it seemed, that he had dispensed with the usual custom of leaning on the arms of two courtiers and walked alone.

Cortés waited until he was close, and they looked upon one another, then pointedly turned his back. '*What have I to do with this dog of a king*,' he roared, '*who suffers us to starve before his eyes?*'

The words and theatre surrounding the snub were for the benefit of the men, but Cortés saw Moctezuma blink when he called him a dog and knew he'd been perfectly understood.

Tozi found Huicton in the simple shack he still occupied near the closed and utterly deserted Tlatelolco market. Though stooped with age, the poor blind beggar, who'd adopted Tozi many years before when a mob killed her mother, was neither poor nor blind. He had served as a spy for the late King Neza of Texcoco, and for his son Ishtlil, who'd rebelled against Moctezuma's rule.

'So,' he said now, greeting her as though she'd been out for an hour

394

to buy vegetables, and not on a dangerous two-month mission to Chichemec country, 'did you find Guatemoc?'

'I did, and have returned with him and twelve thousand men to cleanse the city.'

'Oh dear,' said Huicton. 'Yet another force of cleansers. The Spanish say they're here to cleanse the city of its old gods. A dozen Mexica regiments say they're here to cleanse the city of the Spaniards, and now Guatemoc is here—'

'To cleanse the city of its vile past and bring a new order of things to birth . . .'

'Do you really believe that Guatemoc can do that? Or are you just infatuated with the boy?'

Tozi felt herself blush. 'I love him not because of what he is but of what he can become.'

Huicton focused those milky-white eyes of his on her: 'I suppose you're the one who will bring about this miraculous transformation in him?'

'He's a good man, Huicton. A good man at heart. I've been working to change his mind and, you know, *pushing* him just a little.'

They both knew what 'pushing him' meant. It was the word they used for Tozi's power of mental dominance – her ability to bend others to her wishes and make them want what she wanted.

'And how does he respond to being *pushed*?'

'Not well,' Tozi admitted.

'Come, daughter,' Huicton stood, held out his arms. 'It is so good to see you again.'

They embraced and when they stood apart Huicton said: 'Everything is upside down, my dear, and I confess I no longer know right from wrong, or whose side I am supposed to be on. After Neza, I accepted Ishtlil as my master and spied for his cause against both Cacama and Moctezuma. Cortés has imprisoned Cacama in the palace of Axayacatl, with many of Moctezuma's other favourites, and he has placed Moctezuma himself under house arrest, and clipped his wings, so I see nothing wrong in that. Since my master Ishtlil remains Malinche's ally, I suppose this should make me Malinche's man . . .'

'But . . .'

'Yes, beloved Tozi, there is, as you discern correctly, a but . . .'

They talked urgently, but in whispers, through what remained of the still late morning, hearing the constant clamour of the newly arrived

Spaniards half a mile to the south as they reinforced their garrison in Axayacatl's palace, and occupied and took possession of all the buildings of the sacred plaza, including the great pyramid itself. The harsh foreign voices of the soldiers, and the confident din of their armour, weapons and devices, hinted at their fatal strength and power. All around them, silent as death, the city waited.

When Tozi left, making her way invisibly south towards the sacred plaza itself, she understood everything that had happened in Tenochtitlan since her departure. A giant force was about to be thrown against the Spaniards. The attack would be on a scale they had never encountered before, even in Tlascala. All would be killed and, amongst them, singled out for special punishment, would be Malinal, the hated 'tongue' of Cortés. Through intermediaries, Moctezuma and Cuitláhuac were directing matters from Axayacatl's palace, where they were held under house arrest. They'd issued special orders that Malinal was at all costs to be taken alive when the Spanish were overrun. They wished her to be partially skinned – as large a surface area as possible, short of actually killing her, was to be removed – prior to sacrifice.

All this placed Tozi in a terrible dilemma. She'd seen through Cortés. She'd long ago understood he was not Quetzalcoatl. And the truth was now obvious. Despite saving the ten thousand young girls who were to have been sacrificed for Hummingbird's birthday, Malinche had come to bring war, not peace, to the One World, and with it cruelty, murder, and the extinction of hope for all its peoples.

Just as it was Tozi's mission to fight and bring down Moctezuma, she'd accepted for some time that it was also her mission to fight and bring down Cortés – to fight him with all her magical weapons and to kill him if possible. The inner conflict that she felt arose not from that, but from her love for Malinal and Malinal's love for Cortés. Somehow they must be disentangled – for how else was Tozi to ensure that her friend would survive the inevitable destruction and death about to be visited on all the Spanish forces, and escape the wicked retribution planned by Moctezuma?

Some hours passed in giving orders and making plans to extend his control outwards from Tenochtitlan to all of New Spain, so it was not until the early afternoon of Friday 24 June that Cortés found Alvarado in the courtyard of the palace, took him by the arm and said, 'Walk with me.'

'I know you're very angry, Hernán,' Alvarado said in a lowered voice. 'I'm grateful to you for not humiliating me in front of the men as you did at Cozumel, but I think on this occasion it would be a good idea, and would serve our cause, if you were to show your anger . . .'

'I don't understand.'

'You know, Hernán . . . Make a scene! Shout at me! Threaten to have me arrested!' Many of the men who were here with me through the siege feel it's the least I deserve. Perhaps it will placate them to see me chastised.'

'Pedro . . .' Cortés paused then continued in a near whisper. 'How can I put this? The very *least* you deserve is imprisonment, but it decidedly will *not* serve our cause if any dissension is observed between us. Now come, let us walk amicably to my quarters and we will talk the matter through there.'

Soon after, in his office, Cortés heard Alvarado out.

Suggestions had already been whispered in his ear by a number of expeditionaries that the massacre of 17 May, which had sparked all the trouble, had been carried out because Alvarado had been greedy for the gold worn by the dancing nobles. Nor was this impossible, given Alvarado's love of treasure and disdain for human life, and indeed it was evident that gold and jewels had been looted from the bodies of all the slaughtered Mexica nobles. Equally evident to Cortés, however, was that this could not have been Alvarado's primary motive, since the action was risky and jeopardised the vastly larger treasure that the expedition as a whole had accumulated in the past year, which he was charged to guard. Listening to his friend, it was obvious he had absolutely believed he was about to be attacked, and his tiny garrison overwhelmed, by the Mexica, and had seized the opportunity of the Toxcatl festival to decapitate their leadership at a stroke.

'I wasn't going to just stand around waiting for the Indians to attack us!' Alvarado said defensively. 'When they didn't take the first step, we took it ourselves. He who begins the battle wins.'

'Except you didn't win, did you?' Cortés replied. And although he kept his voice low, he didn't disguise the scathing tone. 'I found you here out of food, almost out of water, twenty of your men dead, many more injured – and that certainly doesn't look like any kind of victory to me. You have done badly, Pedro. You have been false to your trust. Your conduct has been that of a madman—'

'But—'

'No!' Cortés held up his hand to silence the other man. 'No more talk. Kindly leave me now, go about your work, and for God's sake let's not discuss this matter again . . .'

Alvarado looked hurt, like a puppy that's been wrongfully kicked, and left without a further word.

Watching his friend's retreating back, Cortés didn't really blame him. It had always been Pedro's policy to get his retaliation in first, and Cortés had known this before entrusting him with just one hundred and twenty men to guard Tenochtitlan and hold Moctezuma hostage. That something might go wrong under such a volatile commander in such a dangerous situation had been entirely predictable, and it was not necessarily the case that a different man – Ordaz, say, or Olid – would have done a better job.

No! The real responsibility for the appalling situation that now confronted him lay squarely with that bastard Diego de Velázquez and his bum boy Pánfilo Narváez. If it hadn't been for the Narváez intervention, Cortés was certain he could have followed through his originally bloodless coup against the Mexica to acquire total control of New Spain without a further life being lost. War had come only because the arrival of Narváez, and Moctezuma's duplicitous dealings with him, had shifted the balance of power in Tenochtitlan and provoked the Indians to rebellion.

It was a sign of God's grace, therefore, that it was this very army of Narváez, with its great numbers, that gave Cortés the force he needed to threaten the Indians, intimidate them and bring them to heel.

So far, with no sign of enemy aggression in the sacred plaza or anywhere in the surrounding streets, it looked like the threat might be working.

Malinal was in the playroom with Coyotl and little Miahuatl. She liked to spend as much time as she was allowed with the two adopted innocents, because they reminded her that there was life beyond war, and that it was only the force of love, not more violence, that could bring the cycle of death and destruction to an end.

Suddenly Malinal gasped, holding her hand to her throat, her eyes focused on a shimmer in the air just ahead of her. Her heartbeat quickened.

'Tozi?' she said cautiously.

Miahuatl looked up from her play and asked: 'Tozi?'

Coyotl began to skip around the room: 'Tozi! Tozi! Tozi!'

The air shimmered again and Tozi materialised slowly into form, looking older and stronger than when she'd left the city two months before, but also fiercer, more determined and – Malinal had to admit – somehow more terrifying.

Because there *was* a terrible aspect to Tozi the witch, and her face glowed and her eyes blazed as she told her tale.

It seemed that all was arranged. Tomorrow, on the orders of Moctezuma and Cuitláhuac, an overwhelming force of Mexica warriors would enter the sacred precinct, bring the Spaniards to battle, and fight until all the interlopers were killed. There would be great mutual slaughter and, since most of the leadership class of the Mexica had already died in the Toxcatl massacre, the battle would be followed by a vacuum of power.

Into that vacuum would step Prince Guatemoc, who now waited nearby with an army of twelve thousand men. In some magical but unexplained way, once he had installed himself as Great Speaker, the prince would then bring about what Tozi called a 'new dispensation', in which human sacrifice would be abolished and a kinder, stronger society would emerge, which could more effectively combat any return of Spanish forces in the future.

Malinal heard her friend out, but discounted much of what she said. Tozi was plainly in love with Guatemoc – madly, irrationally in love; the sort of love that blinds the eye. She simply could not see how improbable it was that this murderous, bloodthirsty sacrificer would ever be transformed into the person she imagined. To get rid of Moctezuma and Cuitláhuac and replace them with the arrogant prince would not usher in a new dispensation – just many years more of the same bloody and arrogant Mexica behaviour that had been the problem all along.

Much more alarming and immediate, however, was Tozi's warning that an attack was to be mounted on the Spaniards the next day. Malinal had already been convinced that something of the kind was planned, but had failed to persuade Cortés of it; rather he stubbornly continued to maintain that he had enough soldiers to deal with any eventuality.

Tozi was still talking, apparently oblivious to the turmoil she'd caused in her friend's heart. 'I can get you out of here,' she said now. 'You and me, Coyotl and Miahuatl. I can fade us all and we can simply walk out of here, walk across the Tacuba causeway – remember, like we did last year! – and go to Guatemoc. He'll keep you and the children safe from whatever's going to happen. He'll protect you afterwards. He's given me his word on that.'

Malinal was suddenly furious. 'Do you not understand,' she said, 'that I love Hernando Cortés? *He is my man!* If he's to die, then I will die proudly by his side, not creep away in secret like some coward to seek the protection of a Mexica prince.'

Tozi took a step back, gave Malinal a long, level gaze: 'Then we are no longer on the same side,' she said.

'After so many adventures together, it seems very sad that we should not be,' Malinal replied. 'If the aim of your side is to overthrow Moctezuma and his vile regime and find a better way, then there is no quarrel between us and of course I'm with you. But if your side aims to kill my man then, Tozi, I promise you, I will fight you to the death. *Leave my man out of this!*'

'Your eyes are blinded by your love for him,' Tozi said, using the exact phrase that had been in Malinal's mind moments before, 'but he can't be left out of this. He and all his men must die for the great sins and evils they've committed in the One World . . .'

'Including,' Malinal objected, 'saving the lives of ten thousand virgin girls like Miahuatl who would otherwise have been sacrificed?'

'Cortés did a good thing. I accept that. I'm even grateful to him. Nonetheless, for the future of the One World, he and all his men have to die. Not one of them can be allowed to live to carry the news of their destruction back to their own land. Please, Malinal, I beg you, let me get you and the children out of here!'

'*No!*' Malinal shouted. She was surprised by how loud she sounded, and how sure she was. '*Stay away from me.*'

In the background, in concert, Miahuatl and Coyotl began to cry. Tozi was already fading, the air shimmering around her, when Malinal reached out and touched her arm. 'Wait!' she said. 'Don't go! There's something I have to tell you.'

It was late afternoon and Cortés sat in his office preparing a short despatch to Rangel in Villa Rica, informing him of the army's safe arrival in Tenochtitlan, and requesting that he send heavy chains and other items of ironware from Narváez's ships, as well as ropes and sailcloth. The top priority was to secure the lake, and since the four brigantines Cortés had previously built for that purpose before had all been burnt, he would need to have Martin Lopez build four more of them – and perhaps even eight or ten. The salvaged ironware from Narváez's ships would prove invaluable in this task.

He sealed the despatch and placed it on his desk. It was too late to send it today, but he would have a fast rider with a couple of spare horses take it at dawn tomorrow. He had Farfan in mind for the mission. The lad had proved himself in the battle at Cempoala, and was eager and willing. Also he'd been paid the three thousand pesos bounty for being the first to lay hands on Narváez. Easy money! Now he could bloody well do some work for it!

Next on the agenda that afternoon of Friday 24 June, Cortés had arranged for his principal captains to call upon him – Sandoval, Ordaz, Velázquez de Léon, Olid, Davila and, despite his epic failure, Alvarado. Cortés had also asked for Bernal Díaz, whom he planned to promote to captain, to be there and, last but not least, the invaluable Father Bartolomé de Olmedo. Pepillo would also be present to keep the minutes.

The purpose of the meeting was to address ways and means to meet immediate needs – most notably food – but also to make plans and dish out assignments for the colonisation and settlement of New Spain, and for the rapid dissemination of the Holy Catholic faith. 'Gentlemen,' Cortés said, when they had taken their seats, 'as you will have seen for yourselves by now, we reached Tenochtitlan in the nick of time to end the uprising here. It was not the welcome I expected when we returned to our city, but it is better that the Indians hide from us in fear and shame than attack us.'

'With respect, sir . . .' It was Sandoval.

'Yes, Gonzalo. Feel free to speak.'

'We do not know that the Indians are hiding from us in fear. Isn't it equally likely that they're preparing to attack us?'

Cortés suppressed a pulse of irritation. He did not appreciate being contradicted. Nonetheless, Sandoval was a good man, perhaps his best officer, so his mind should be set at rest.

'No, there's no danger of that, Gonzalo. I know these people! They are cowards. Look! They couldn't even overrun Don Pedro here – ' a glance at Alvarado – 'when he had just a tiny garrison. Now we are ten times that number, and very well supplied with cannon, crossbows and cavalry. That's why they haven't attacked us, and that's why they will never dare to attack us. It may take some time to restore friendly relations, but I'm confident, if we're patient, that we must succeed.'

There came a knock at the door.

'Enter!' said Cortés, making no effort to hide his irritation. He was just getting started and there was much more to say.

'You have a visitor, sir,' the guard announced. 'It is the lord Cuitláhuac. Shall I admit him?'

Cortés thought about it only a moment. The most pressing need was to get the markets of Tenochtitlan reopened and food flowing in for his hungry army again. It was all very well commanding a great force more than one thousand two hundred strong, but that also meant one thousand two hundred stomachs to feed and water every day, something impossible in the midst of a salt lake, in the heart of an island city, without the full cooperation of the locals.

Cortés glanced around his captains. It was obvious they were interested in what Cuitláhuac had to say. 'Very well,' he told the guard, 'admit him.' He turned to Pepillo: 'Can you translate for us, or should I send for Malinal?'

He hoped he would not have to send for Malinal. She was in the adjoining room, their bedchamber, where she had retired in tears an hour earlier, having failed to persuade him that a Mexica attack was imminent.

'I can translate,' Pepillo replied.

With a rustle of robes, Cuitláhuac entered. A tall, gaunt man with high cheekbones, a long nose, a delicate chin, a vaguely apologetic air and eyes that never looked directly at you, he was the Great Speaker's younger brother, next in line of succession to the Mexica throne after Moctezuma himself.

He looked around the faces of the assembled captains with something like dismay, and spoke a few words in Nahuatl.

'The lord Cuitláhuac greets you all,' Pepillo said.

'Yes, yes,' Cortés was becoming increasingly annoyed. 'Let's not waste time on formalities. We're in the middle of a meeting here, so can he please get to the point?'

Pepillo explained. Cuitláhuac seemed to understand and began immediately: 'My brother, the Great Speaker, is offended,' he said. His voice was surprisingly strong, but when he looked at Cortés, his eyes skittered off to the side as usual. 'When he came to greet you earlier in the courtyard, you shamed him. Nonetheless he requests, because of his great love for you, that you attend him now in his audience chamber so that any differences between you may be resolved.'

'Pepillo,' Cortés said quietly, 'I want you to translate every word I'm about to say, exactly as I mean it, and don't spare the bastard's feelings. Got me?'

'Got you, sir!'

'Very well.' Cortés glared at Cuitláhuac, turned his gaze to the seated officers, and made a gesture with his hands, palms up, that was meant to signal weary contempt. '*Did not the dog Moctezuma,*' he suddenly boomed, '*betray us in his communications with Narváez? And does he not now suffer his markets to be closed and leave us to die of famine?*'

As Pepillo finished the translation, Cortés turned fiercely again to Cuitláhuac and thundered: '*Go tell your master and his people to open the markets, or we will do it for them at their cost!*'

'I will convey your message,' Cuitláhuac said. His features were set and gave away nothing of his feelings. 'Will the captains be so kind as to await my return?'

'We'll be here,' Cortés growled, 'but be quick about it.'

To his surprise, while Cuitláhuac was gone, Velázquez de Léon, Sandoval, Ordaz and even Díaz all sought to persuade him to honour Moctezuma with a visit. To be sure the Great Speaker was duplicitous and tried to act in the interests of his people; this was only to be expected. But over the months he had also shown great generosity to the Spaniards; it was also possible that the Great Speaker's love for them was all that was preventing the Mexica from launching a massive attack.

'Bah! Love for us? I've never heard such nonsense,' Cortés laughed. 'The only thing that keeps Mucktey bending the knee, and stops the rest of them slaughtering us, is their fear of us. *Fear*, boys! Remember it! We rule them through fear, not through being nice, not through following protocol, but by *fucking terrifying* them!'

'Wait! Don't go,' Malinal said. 'There's something I have to tell you.' But Tozi was so angry that she didn't wait, didn't even speak, but completed her fade and left her friend.

She remained in the palace of Axayacatl for some while longer, invisibly haunting every room, understanding the disposition of Spanish forces, observing the sloppy watch they kept, gathering intelligence for Guatemoc. She attended the meeting of Cortés and his captains but, following little of their language, was about to drift through to the bedchamber where she knew Malinal lay – reminding herself that she still loved her friend, even though she was misguided – when Cuitláhuac was suddenly ushered into the room.

Tozi listened with scorn to Cuitláhuac's address, and to Pepillo's translation into Nahuatl of the reply given to him. Would they open the markets, she wondered, or would they go through with their plans to annihilate the Spaniards? When Cuitláhuac left to report to Moctezuma, she followed him to find out.

Very soon it became clear that plots were afoot within plots.

Cuitláhuac conveyed Cortés's message accurately enough – the Spaniard had named Moctezuma a dog, demanded that he reopen the city's markets and threatened violence if he failed to do so.

'We must play for time,' the Great Speaker replied, 'so Malinche takes no action before our warriors are ready to attack tomorrow. Go back to him, good Cuitláhuac. Tell him that since I am his prisoner, there is nothing I can do. He must either free me to make the necessary arrangements, or at the very least summon the leading nobles and citizens to the plaza so that I can address them from the roof of this palace as I've done before.'

'He will not free you, brother!'

'Of course. But the second proposal will take time to organise. In the interval, the attack can be launched.'

'You speak wisely, lord. It shall be as you say.'

Tozi followed Cuitláhuac when he left the Great Speaker and returned to Cortés and his captains. There, speaking through Pepillo, he said: 'I have talked with the lord Moctezuma. He regrets that the great fear his people have of Spanish arms has led so many of them to evacuate the city. This is why the markets are closed. This is why you have received no food. The lord Moctezuma apologises for the inconvenience, but cannot be active or effective from his place of imprisonment in bringing the people back and getting the markets opened.'

'So what are we to do?' Cortés asked. 'Set him free?' He laughed, an ugly sound. 'Because that's not going to happen.'

'The Great Speaker understands that you cannot release him in the present circumstances,' replied Cuitláhuac. 'He has suggested, therefore, that you free me. In his name and acting on his behalf, I can take all the measures you require.'

A heated discussion followed, which Tozi, with only a few words of Spanish, could not understand. It seemed to her, though, that whatever point of view the captains were arguing was opposed by Cortés, who at one point raised his voice to a shout and became rather red in the face. Finally, it was evident he'd been won round – though reluctantly and with bad grace. He turned to Cuitláhuac. 'Very well,' he said. 'On the advice of my captains, who are more generous and trusting than myself,

I'm going to release you.' He paused for Pepillo to give the translation, then continued: 'Go from this place immediately. Call your people back into the city; we will not harm them. And let us at least have some semblance of a food market tomorrow so we may replenish our stores. Do all this and we will have peace. Fail to do it and I promise you, Cuitláhuac, I will kill your brother Moctezuma and I will destroy Tenochtitlan completely, so that nothing remains of it but mud and burnt sticks.'

Tozi followed Cuitláhuac when he left the palace.

He went alone to the district of Atzcoalco, less than half a mile north and east of the sacred precinct. Directly and purposively he slipped through the empty city until he came to a great, shuttered, silent mansion. Overhanging the street from six storeys above, the flowers of its roof garden glowed and flamed in the sun's last rays as the sky darkened towards evening.

For a long while the door was not answered. Just as Cuitláhuac was about to knock again, however, it was cracked cautiously open by a clerk wearing the livery of the Tlatocan, the great governing council of the Mexica. There was immediate recognition. 'Lord Cuitláhuac,' the clerk said, dropping to his knees. 'You are free!'

'So it seems,' Cuitláhuac replied, stepping past him and into the vast, echoing hallway. 'Is the full council assembled to plan tomorrow's attack?'

'Yes, sire.'

'Good! Then let us go to them.'

In the hour that followed, Tozi witnessed a side of Cuitláhuac that she had not guessed at during their previous encounters. Then he'd been very much under Moctezuma's thumb. Now he'd come into his own.

What he did was unprecedented.

Taking advantage of the meeting that had already been called to co-ordinate the attack planned for the next day, and with remarkable simplicity and eloquence, Cuitláhuac persuaded the Tlatocan to depose Moctezuma – not out of anger towards him but simply because, as a prisoner of Cortés, he could no longer fulfil his role or meet his responsibilities towards the Mexica people at this vital time. Cuitláhuac himself was immediately elected to take Moctezuma's place. The formal investiture would be held, after the passage of five days, at a ceremony presided over by Namacuix, the high priest. In the meantime, however, Cuitláhuac was immediately confirmed with the full powers of the Great Speaker, and asked to direct tomorrow's attack.

Events appeared to be moving fast towards some sort of resolution. Though Tozi was far from done with Malinal, and still believed she might win her friend round, her priority now was to get back to Guatemoc and tell him everything she'd learned.

Invisible and unseen, she slipped out of the council chamber, down the stairs and out into the empty streets.

It was late, close to midnight, before Cortés, finding Malinal still awake to translate, was free to seek out Shikotenka. As they walked through the corridors of the palace, talking in hushed voices, she again implored him to ready his men for the attack that would surely come tomorrow, and again he dismissed her concerns: 'The Indians are too afraid to attack,' he said, 'and we've just marched hundreds of miles through the mountains to get here. I don't want to disturb the men with false alarms. I think everyone deserves a rest.'

Privately he wondered: *Is something wrong with her?* Usually so steadfast and unafraid, Malinal was more nervous and jittery tonight than he had ever seen her.

They had reached the palace courtyard. Near the improvised well which, thank God, still gave a little water, they found the Tlascalan leader seated, smoking a pipe of fragrant tobacco.

'Ho, Shikotenka,' Cortés said as they embraced. 'Forgive me for not seeing you sooner but I've been kept busy the entire day. I want to thank you for your part in fighting off the Mexica. I understand from Alvarado he'd have been overrun if it hadn't been for you and your men.'

Shikotenka had one of those unblinking stares, like a reptile, and it was fixed on Cortés now. 'I'm told,' he said coldly, 'that you released Cuitláhuac tonight.'

Beside him Cortés heard Malinal gasp. She'd been in their bedchamber during the meeting, and he hadn't informed her about what he'd done.

'Yes, I've released Cuitláhuac,' Cortés replied cheerfully. 'He's to arrange food for us, reopen the markets, help us get things back to normal here.'

The corners of Shikotenka's mouth curled down: 'You should have talked to me first, Hernán.'

'Why?' Cortés asked. *Damned savage* was what he was thinking.

'Because you've just made a most unfortunate mistake. You're no longer holding the Great Speaker of the Mexica hostage.'

'Rubbish, man! What are you talking about? Of course we're holding him hostage.'

'No, Hernán! You're holding Moctezuma hostage, but he is no longer the Great Speaker of the Mexica. That honour, I can assure you, will have been transferred to Cuitláhuac somewhere in this city tonight. Moctezuma is of no use to you now, and we'll be fighting Cuitláhuac tomorrow.'

Cortés was greatly taken aback. He still refused to believe there was any real risk of a Mexica attack tomorrow or any other day, but it was galling to be taken to task for his decisions not only by Malinal but now by Shikotenka as well. What was the matter with these people? Why were they all so nervous? Couldn't they see that the wheel of fortune had turned and that, after the hard knocks, hard marches and hard rations of the past two months, a bright and inviting future lay ahead?

Chapter Twenty

Saturday 25 June 1520

Soon after dawn on Saturday 25 June, with the streets of Tenochtitlan still utterly silent all about, young Andres Farfan cantered out of the south gate of the sacred precinct carrying the despatches for Villa Rica. The enthusiastic youth, ever eager to please, was provided with a fast horse and two spare mounts. As a sop to the fears of imminent attack that so many were expressing, Cortés had added a postscript to the despatch he'd written, requiring Rangel to send him not only chains and ironware from the beached ships, but also five falconets and additional powder from the settlement's armoury.

Farfan had not been gone a half-hour before he came galloping back through the same gate with blood streaming down his face from a scalp wound, his left eye swollen closed and his shirt slick with blood from an arrow lodged between his ribs. His two spare horses were nowhere to be seen, and the mare he rode was so deeply gashed across the withers that she collapsed and died in the shadow of the great pyramid.

A crowd of soldiers gathered round Farfan, who'd stumbled off the horse as it fell and now slumped to the ground himself. Olmedo and Sandoval were with him, and Dr La Peña had been called when Cortés reached the scene. A stretcher was rigged and Farfan was carried into the palace, with Cortés at his side.

'I'm so sorry, sir,' Farfan said. 'I failed you.' His voice was weak, almost inaudible, and his breathing ragged.

'Nonsense, lad. No failure that I see. La Peña will get that arrow out of you, but first I must understand what happened. Can you talk?'

'I rode south, sir,' Farfan said, 'heading for the Iztapalapa causeway.' His voice was so low that Cortés had to put his ear close to his mouth to hear him at all. 'The streets were deserted. I was cantering down the long avenue, the one they name the Street of Flowers after the roof gardens on the houses, when a shower of stones came from above. I was struck on the head. I looked up. I saw warriors there, on the rooftops. Too many warriors! They threw more stones so I took off at a gallop, but crowds of warriors came suddenly from all directions, sir. Where the city seemed empty a moment before, now every side street was filled with them. They blocked the avenue ahead. I tried to push my way through but they were too many, jostling me, grinning at me and showing their teeth in that evil way they have. I was hit by this arrow, sir. My spare mounts were torn from me and slaughtered. I turned about to get back to the palace. My mare they struck with one of their obsidian-edged swords, but she was a spirited one and we burst right through the pack and came back at a gallop, sir.'

Cortés laid his hand momentarily on Farfan's shoulder. 'You've done well, lad. Let's get you patched up.' He turned to Sandoval: 'Gonzalo. Go at once and triple the guard around the walls and gates of the precinct.'

Sandoval had great faith in Cortés, and his love and admiration for the man were undiminished. Still, it had been obvious to him from the moment of their return to Tenochtitlan yesterday that the balance of the caudillo's mind had been disturbed by the events of the past weeks. Truly it had been a superhuman task to take on, undermine and defeat Narváez, but it seemed that the victory had gone to Cortés's head, blinding him even to the possibility that the seemingly empty and inviting island city might be nothing more than a huge killing trap.

Sandoval mounted the stairs to the top of the great wall that enclosed the sacred precinct. On its western side, rising much higher than in other sectors, the perimeter was continuous with the rear elevation of Axayacatl's palace. But the northern, eastern and southern sectors of the wall were all of a level, surmounted by a parapet, lined with sentries, along which Sandoval now walked.

Silence enshrouded the deserted geometry of the criss-crossing streets and avenues looking north towards the district of Tlatelolco. Looking east it was the same story. And when, eventually, Sandoval came to the south wall and walked the parapet over the southern gateway through which Farfan had entered, he again saw only empty streets.

'Any sign?' he asked a sentry.

'See for yourself, sir. There's nothing.'

What Sandoval saw didn't feel right. Contrasting with its seeming emptiness and silence, a thick and almost palpable emanation of evil arose like a vapour from the city, filling the air with menace.

What was this? The past year had been spent in almost continuous danger, yet in none of the battles with the Tlascalans and the Maya, nor in the build-up to the recent fight with Narváez, had Sandoval ever felt such a deep and ominous sense of oppression. Was it just imagination? Were his nerves playing tricks on him? He narrowed his eyes, scanned the streets, seeing nothing of the crowds of warriors Farfan had spoken of.

But, wait . . . Sandoval cocked his head.

Just at the edge of perception did he hear something, some strange sound, some whisper, something like a murmur?

Bernal Díaz had ascended to the roof of Axayacatl's palace, the highest point in the sacred precinct after the summit platform of the great pyramid, which blocked his view of the city to the east. From this vantage point, however, he had clear sight of the major streets surrounding the plaza on its west, north and south sides.

He saw . . . nothing.

But he heard . . . something – a faint, chaotic, unidentifiable something, becoming deeper, more throaty, more sullen and terrible by the moment, building at an alarming pace until it resembled the roar of an immense river in flood that carries all before it. Hideous in its intensity, it nonetheless seemed diffuse in its origins, arising from all directions at once.

That was when Díaz saw movement amongst the bright roofs of the great villas lining the principal avenues around the precinct. The hairs on the back of his neck stirred. The hanging gardens had seemed empty just an instant before, but now, as though by sorcery, they were all filled with half-naked, painted warriors, screaming and brandishing weapons.

Díaz shook his head, closed his eyes and opened them again. The warriors were still there.

Then, down at street level, something else! A muscular surge of movement, coupled with an impression of great weight and mass.

At first he couldn't quite grasp what it was. But like the awful roar of all-encompassing sound arising from it, this new spectacle had a dark, roiling, chaotic, amorphous quality, as though some turbulent black tide were welling up out of the lake and surging through the city towards him. It raged closer, moving at tremendous speed, and soon Díaz was able to resolve details within it – the raven hair, the grimacing faces, the body paint, the obsidian blades, and the pounding, naked legs of an uncountable mass of Mexica warriors.

One of the roof sentries had joined him at the parapet. 'God help us,' he said.

'The Lord is my shepherd,' Díaz replied, 'I shall not want. He maketh me to lie down in green pastures: he leadeth me beside the still waters . . . Yea, though I walk through the valley of the shadow of death, I will fear no evil: for thou art with me; thy rod and thy staff they comfort me.'

Cortés was with Alvarado and Ordaz in the plaza, assessing the defence – even with more than a thousand Spaniards at his disposal, and three thousand Tlascalans, the sacred precinct was so large that they were stretched thin. It was already obvious that a mighty struggle would be required to defend the walls, extending more than seven hundred paces on each side, and to keep an intact perimeter.

That fucking, perfidious Mucktey! Cortés thought. *He planned this all along!*

He felt nothing but cold, hard hatred and revulsion towards the Mexica ruler, but beneath the anger, other feelings moved. Most forcefully, he realised, and immediately accepted, that he'd been stupid, brash, and irresponsible to allow himself to be lured into such an obvious ambuscade. Malinal had warned him, so too Sandoval and Shikotenka, but he'd ignored them all.

In many respects, Cortés realised, his worst nightmare on first entering Tenochtitlan, observing the ease with which the bridges along the causeways could be removed, had now come true. It had happened because he had underestimated the Mexica. He resolved, if he lived through this, that he would never do so again.

And he *would* live through it! They all would! Because, on every occasion when they had been confronted in open battle, his conquistadors had proved themselves superior to any Indian enemy, regardless of the numbers.

There came a volley of arquebus shots as the mass of advancing braves were given their first taste of Spanish defiance by the army's eighty musketeers posted on the perimeter wall. They were interspersed amongst the hundred and fifty crossbowmen who, though their work was silent, would be sending forth storms of iron-tipped bolts and doing terrible damage. Cortés now greatly regretted, in his complacency of the day before, that he'd not had the foresight to order cannon moved to the lower sections of the wall, where their barrels might be depressed sufficiently to bear, if not upon the foremost ranks of the Mexica, then certainly upon the mass of warriors in the streets beyond.

This had been a grave oversight; instead the twenty-three cannon Cortés had taken from Narváez sat within the plaza, lined up impressively, but uselessly, in front of the palace of Axayacatl, where they could presently be brought to bear on . . . no one at all. The entire perimeter wall, except the higher section on the west side formed by the rear of the palace, was now an active combat zone, and some Mexica had succeeded in scaling it, despite the deadly hail of arquebus and crossbow fire, only to be laid low when they reached the parapet by fast-moving bands of Tlascalans armed with spears, clubs and *macuahuitls*. Until the attackers retreated, there would be no possibility of manhandling any cannon up there.

'Ordaz,' Cortés said, and the grey-haired captain in his old-fashioned chain-mail armour, his huge double-handed *montante* slung across his back, turned towards him. 'We must teach these savages some manners.'

'High time, Caudillo. What's your pleasure?'

'I want you to lead a sortie – in force.'

'Now you're talking!' said Alvarado.

'Take two hundred and fifty infantry,' Cortés continued, 'well-armoured if you please, one hundred and twenty of our crossbowmen and thirty of our musketeers – so you'll be a column of four hundred foot. Vendabal will go with you with forty of his hounds. In addition I'll give you an escort of forty cavalry, twenty under Pedro here and twenty under young Sandoval. That should be enough, don't you think, to do the enemy some serious harm?'

Cortés had expected resistance from Alvarado, until now his unquestioned second in command, who might have hoped to lead the entire sortie, not just twenty horse. But Pedro seemed content. 'Time to cleave some heads and have some fun at last,' he said, loosening his falchion in its scabbard.

With his comrades in arms, Alonso de la Serna and Francisco Mibiercas, Bernal Díaz volunteered to join the sortie. His hoped-for promotion to captain had not yet been offered – perhaps it never would be – and was of small account to him anyway. He'd come to New Spain for adventure, and to make his fortune, but he stayed because of the love and loyalty he felt towards his friends.

They were all lined up now, the infantry organised into four squares.

Each square was a hundred strong and disposed in ten ranks of ten, the outer ranks carrying big *adarga* shields, others deploying long Chinantla pikes, brought with them from Cempoala, to protect the musketeers and crossbowmen. At Ordaz's signal, all would sally forth together through the south gate of the precinct – the same direction Farfan had taken this morning. The objective was to proceed as far as the entrance to the Iztapalapa causeway, engage the enemy wherever he could be found, and inflict such heavy punishment upon him that he would cease his attacks. There was every reason to expect success. After all, the column was almost the same size as the entire force with which Cortés had defeated the Maya and the Tlascalans the year before, and made such a great show that he was able to enter Tenochtitlan unopposed, so why should it not succeed?

Still, Díaz was reassured to see so many shooters going out with them – the thirty musketeers and one hundred and twenty crossbowmen taken from the walls made the column truly formidable, but left only fifty of the former and thirty of the latter along the perimeter. To fill the gaps, Cortés had sent almost the entire remaining Spanish force up to join them, dividing the command between Olid and Davila while he himself kept his twenty-five picked men under García Brabo as a flying squad to deal with any emergency.

With shouts and whistles, teams of *tamanes* applied themselves to the thick guide ropes, and the great southern gateway of the sacred precinct began to creak inwards. Ponderously it opened a span, then a cubit, admitting an incoherent explosion of sound, at once followed by the bare legs of warriors, hands brandishing weapons, and furious faces thrust into the gap. In the same instant, sweeping the *tamanes* aside, the gates were borne fully back and inward by the immense weight of the Mexica hordes pressing against them from without, and warriors poured into the breach, which was immediately filled by the solid mass of the Spanish column surging forward on the signal from Ordaz.

The two forces collided with a tremendous roar and a clash of weapons but, as always, the Indians with their stone blades and cotton armour were no match for the Toledo steel and disciplined thrusts of the Spanish soldiers. Those of the Mexica who did succeed in slipping past them into the plaza were immediately surrounded and killed by a squad of five hundred Tlascalan auxiliaries under Shikotenka, brought to the gate for this express purpose.

'Cordon!' Ordaz yelled. It was a prearranged command, and the

413

Spaniards smashed into the dense scrum of attacking Mexica, sweeping them aside, seizing and holding the ground, the squares keeping perfect formation as they deployed into a cordon fifty paces in front of the yawning southern gateway.

Díaz, defending himself and Mibiercas next to him with the shield in his left hand, hacked down on a bare, painted head with the edge of his sword, felt the skull split and the blade lock in the bone, shook it free with an immense heave of his shoulders and immediately plunged the point into the heaving guts of another screaming warrior.

For a few seconds no one came at him, and Díaz had a moment of clarity as he took in the scene ahead – a great ceremonial avenue, five hundred paces wide, running west to east and bordered on its south side by two immense terraces of flat-roofed townhouses. Separating the terraces was the entrance to the Street of Flowers, which arrowed due south, dead straight towards the Iztapalapa causeway. On every roof there were hundreds of warriors. And ahead across the width of the avenue, the Mexica were packed and advancing from all the side streets in their thousands and tens of thousands, some waving flags and standards of bright feathers, all howling in fury and brandishing weapons, rushing forward with impetuous carelessness for life.

It seemed to Díaz then a foolish and chimerical quest that Cortés had led them all on – at the end of which lay no Holy Grail but only certain death here in the city of the Mexica; trapped, massively outnumbered, and with no hope of relief. A big warrior came at him with a spear but he caught its tip on his shield and ran the man through. Behind him, well-protected, aiming over the heads of their comrades, the musketeers and crossbowmen opened fire. Ten of the soldiers in the square were trained pikemen, armed today with the long Chinantla lances, jabbing down overhanded, killing three and four ranks back in the enemy mass as the shooters reloaded.

'*Dogs!*' shouted Ordaz, and Vendabal and his handlers came forth with forty slavering and armoured hounds, which they led through the gaps between the squares and unleashed upon the Mexica. As they attacked, snarling, jaws agape, the huge animals spread terror and confusion amongst the foe, and for a moment the massed assault upon the squares faltered.

'*Cavalry!*' It was the third prearranged command, and the two troops of twenty horse under Alvarado and Sandoval trotted out behind the shelter of the cordon.

'*Now!*' Ordaz roared. Again with perfect coordination, the squares briefly redeployed to allow the cavalry through at a full gallop, in a single mass of forty that was immediately among the enemy, pummelling through the gaps torn in their ranks by the monstrous dogs.

But the charge bogged down within a hundred paces, as though they'd ridden into quicksand. Entirely filling the wide avenue, the Mexica had come in numbers so vast as to be beyond comprehension, and Alvarado, who'd advanced too far in his excitement, found himself surrounded. He had reason to be grateful that he'd armoured himself fully this morning, wearing a gorget of multiple, articulated steel plates around his throat, and a gleaming open-faced helmet called a sallet, with flaps at the side and back to protect his neck. Beneath his cuirass and backplate he wore a shirt of chain mail – a hauberk – that fell to his thighs. It had mailed sleeves, but over them he wore *paludrons* of steel plate to protect his shoulders and armpits, *rerebraces* to protect his upper arms, articulated metal joints called *couters* to protect his elbows, forearm guards called *vambraces*, and gauntlets cunningly fashioned from leather, plate and mail. *Cuisses*, *polyns* and greaves protected his thighs, knees and shins and mailed *sabatons* covered his boots.

Bucephalus was also fully barded with a *chanfron* and hinged cheek-plates protecting his head, a *crinière* of segmented steel plates covering his neck, a *croupier* over his hind quarters, *flanchards* over his flanks and *peytrals* on his chest. Even his reins had riveted steel plates attached so they could not be cut, and Alvarado held these reins in one gauntleted hand, using the white stallion's massive power and armoured weight as a battering ram, laying about him with the heavy blade of the falchion, now smeared from grip to tip with gore and brain matter, cutting a way through the Mexica quagmire. Arrows and sling-stones clanged off his helmet and backplate, a flint knife shattered against his steel-sheathed thigh, a big warrior brought his *macuahuitl* down with immense force on Bucephalus's neck but its obsidian blades were stopped and broken by the *crinière*.

As Alvarado hacked off the attacker's head – *leave my horse alone!* – he risked a glance around and saw that all the other riders had likewise become separated from one another in the charge and were also now surrounded by raging knots of warriors. It felt disturbingly like the outcome of some strategy on the part of the Mexica. And damn! Far over to his right, a cavalier in Sandoval's squad was pulled from his saddle while, much closer, some savage had succeeded in bringing down another rider's horse amidst pitiful screams, thrashing hoofs and a fountain of blood. This was nothing short of disaster! For to see the previously terrifying and invulnerable cavalry of the conquistadors stopped in its tracks in this way, defeated by a mob of savages with riders and mounts dying, sent a potent signal across the battlefield that was obvious to both sides.

'*Santiago and at them!*' Alvarado yelled, wheeling Bucephalus in a tight, rearing turn, back towards the sacred precinct, taking advantage of an opening in the press to nudge the stallion into a canter and then into a soaring jump that carried him clear over the heads of the warriors who surged forward to stop his escape. But the Mexica were everywhere, and, with a tremendous crash and shock, horse and rider smashed down in the midst of another throng, crushing and scattering men in all directions while more ran in to fill the gaps, stabbing and thrusting with lances and knives.

The precinct's southern gateway had been closed and barred again behind the infantry cordon, and all along the wall Spaniards and Tlascalans battled with Mexica climbers, who ascended like seething swarms of cockroaches on the hunt, jamming dagger and spear points into cracks in the masonry as hand and toe holds. Still the defence appeared to be holding; there was no reason why Ordaz should not now throw his foot soldiers into the battle – this was supposed to be a fucking *sortie* after all! – and Alvarado saw with relief that the four squares were at last on the move, surging forward into the swarming enemy and dashing them aside.

But something terrible had happened. With fury and a sense of deepening horror, Alvarado saw that Bucephalus was badly wounded. Some fucking savage had slipped the blade of a knife between the plates of his *crinière* and opened a blood vessel in his neck, out of which his life now gushed.

If the purpose of the sortie was to impress and terrify the Indians, Díaz thought, then it had already failed. Because the only lesson the Mexica would take from this battle was that the Spanish were not after all invulnerable but could – albeit at great cost – be overwhelmed and defeated.

Across the whole surging battlefield in front of the south gate of the sacred precinct, many, perhaps the majority, of the forty cavalry who'd ridden out were now down, and the others were separated and fighting for their lives. The first objective was to rescue the survivors and get them to the safety of the precinct, but that could not be done without forcing back the Mexica horde.

And therein lay the problem. For although the unarmoured enemy, with their primitive weapons, were easy to kill, their great numbers, and their absolute willingness to die – literally throwing themselves on to the conquistadors' swords – constituted, in itself, an effective tactic that hindered and slowed the advance, so that every step had to be taken in the midst of a churning, moiling bloodbath. Díaz felt his sword arm grow tired and weak from hacking and thrusting, felt the muscles of his legs burn and his breath grow short with the constant shoving and pushing of the melee.

But little by little Spanish discipline, skill at arms, and the tight coordination of the advancing squares allowed some headway to be made, and the four hundred conquistadors cut a path deep into the midst of the enemy, destroying his formations, and offering haven to the fleeing cavalrymen.

Some twenty paces ahead of his own square, Díaz saw blood pumping from the neck of Alvarado's great white stallion Bucephalus, which now foundered and fell, the conquistador leaping clear at the last moment with a furious yell.

What had begun as a confident charge was ending as an ignominious and costly disaster.

Gonzalo de Sandoval sat firmly in the saddle of his chestnut mare, Llesenia, given to him by Cortés after the great battles at Potonchan the year before. Half his squad were already down: some riders who'd lost their mounts had taken shelter in the infantry squares; others tried to fight their way back to the gates. Alvarado's squad had suffered even worse damage, and Alvarado himself was down, with Bucephalus dead under him.

Díaz's square was close but Sandoval was closer. He spurred Llesenia to a charge, cutting his way through the ring of whistling, ululating warriors surrounding Alvarado, who defended himself with great scything sweeps of his falchion.

'*Santiago and at them!*' Sandoval yelled, and saw that Alvarado had heard him. Hacking and slashing, his sword arm drenched in blood, he smashed through the last of the encircling warriors and, guiding Llesenia only with his knees, reached for the other captain, who took his hand and jumped lightly up into the saddle behind him.

'Fuckers!' Alvarado said. 'They killed Bucephalus.'

Even in the heat of battle, Sandoval was astonished to see tears in his friend's eyes, but he also saw the rage and madness of the man, and bore him through the press to the edge of Díaz's square, where he leapt down into the front rank, and with a great roar immediately resumed his onslaught on the enemy.

The young battlefield messenger had come in at a run, blood seeping from multiple flesh wounds to his head and arms. 'Captain Olid sent me,' he gasped. 'The north wall has come under heavy attack. The captain says we can't hold it much longer. He begs you to send reinforcements, sir.'

In a heavy sweat under his hauberk and cuirass, somewhat shaken and dizzied by a slingshot that had caught his exposed brow just below the rim of his sallet, Cortés nodded grimly and set off across the plaza at a sprint, followed by Sergeant García Brabo and his twenty-five toughs. Despite the almost unimaginable numbers of warriors swirling round Ordaz's column, there had been no lessening in the ferocity of the general assault on the sacred precinct, and Cortés had come under intense, unceasing pressure as he raced from point to point with his flying squad shoring up the crumbling defences.

Pounding now along the east flank of the great pyramid, with the north wall a few hundred paces ahead, he saw the heave and glitter of the tremendous fight unfolding there. It looked as though at least a hundred Mexica warriors, highly visible in their feathers and body paint, had got in amongst the Spanish and Tlascalan defenders. In minutes they'd be overwhelmed.

'*Charge!*' he yelled. '*Santiago and at them!*'

The press of warriors had severely disrupted battlefield communications, but the bugle call just sounded from Ordaz's square was another of the pre-arranged signals. Díaz understood its meaning clearly enough, and passed on the order to his hundred. The captain was determined to continue the sortie the full length of the Street of Flowers, as far as the opening to the Iztapalapa causeway half a mile to the south.

There was some logic to this. With the cavalry neutralised by the enemy's numbers, and the surviving riders absorbed into the infantry squares, it was essential to punish the enemy for their audacity or they'd be back again tomorrow. Somehow a victory must be snatched from the jaws of this humiliating defeat. But surely more such fruitless battling and struggling through a vast and violent Mexica sea was not the way to do it?

Díaz suddenly felt weary of fighting, weary of the battlefield smells of blood and shit and sulphur, weary of the constant din and danger. Amidst a rising chorus of hoots, whistles and yells from the enemy, his square, and the other three in formation behind it, had now advanced so close to the terraces of townhouses on the south side of the wide avenue bounding the sacred precinct that missiles thrown from their roof gardens were already doing damage. A stone dinged off his helmet, setting his ears ringing, and an obsidian-tipped javelin whizzed past his shoulder, striking the man behind him full in the chest but shattering against his cuirass.

Then, surprisingly, as Díaz's square battered open the way into the Street of Flowers, the entire column was allowed to follow unopposed, the warriors ahead seeming shy of combat, melting into the side streets. With a sinking feeling, Díaz counted a hundred paces, two hundred, three hundred, thinking *this is too easy* when, out of every side street ahead boiled a seething mass of howling warriors. He looked back the way they had come and saw fresh Mexica squadrons pouring in to block their route of escape to the sacred precinct.

From the roof gardens above showers of stones, javelins and arrows poured down on them.

Winded from the long run in armour, culminating in a pounding rush up the stairs to reach the parapet, Cortés found himself immediately in the midst of five of the shaven-headed Mexica warriors known as Cuahchics – supposedly the best of their best. By the time he'd killed one with a thrust to the throat and hacked the legs out from under another, he'd been wounded again – somehow inside his shield a blade had found his left hand. A *macuahuitl* slammed into his backplate, jolting him, and, as he whirled to face the grimacing Cuahchic wielding it, his vision blurred and darkened and his head swam. Gasping for breath, lathered in sweat, he spent the last of his strength stepping in on the man, gutting him from groin to sternum with an upcut just as Brabo reached his side, coldly and efficiently spearing the two remaining warriors.

'You wait here, sir, there's a good officer,' said Brabo. Leaving five men with Cortés, he led the other twenty in a silent, determined, deadly charge along the parapet, to the point where the defenders were heavily engaged with large numbers of Mexica already on the wall and many others pouring over it.

His head swimming, Cortés doubled over and vomited.

Alvarado was in an ecstasy of rage. The fuckers had killed his beautiful Bucephalus and he was going to make them pay. He'd been integrated into Díaz's square, which had been in the van when they were heading south along the Street of Flowers, but now – as Ordaz's bugler sounded the inevitable retreat, and showers of missiles rained down upon them from above – they formed the rearguard.

The bugle blew again, signalling the squares to merge, a difficult manoeuvre they'd practised a hundred times that would transform them from four distinct groups into a single armoured mass twenty men wide and twenty men deep, with those bearing shields deployed to provide protective cover for those without them.

Seizing his chance, Alvarado pushed forward, shouldering men aside, until he was once again in the van.

He carried no shield. Though poor defence against the showers of stones falling all around him, his falchion in his right hand and his quillon dagger in his left were quite sufficient for what he had in mind.

What mattered, really the only important thing, was the safety and security of Tlascala. Were that not implicated, Shikotenka reminded himself, he wouldn't even be here, let alone have been drawn in to this mess of a battle, regardless of his alliance with the Spaniards.

The thought passed through his mind because he saw that Cortés was in trouble on the north wall. He'd taken his brutal little flying squad up there to reinforce the hard-pressed defenders, but way too many Mexica were pouring over the parapet. If Cortés was lost, it would only be a matter of time before the battle was lost, and if the battle was lost then Tlascala's long war with the Mexica was lost also and a terrible bloodletting would ensue . . .

Shikotenka wished the Senate had granted him more men. Two thousand of his Tlascalans were already deployed around the wall in support of the Spaniards, and fighting a losing battle there; five hundred were in his own flying squad, and the last five hundred were still within the palace in reserve. He gave terse orders to Tree to fetch all the reserve to the north wall, and, as the big captain pounded off, summoned Chipahua and the rest of his squad.

'Well, lads,' he bellowed, 'what are you waiting for?' and led the charge northward across the plaza.

Having marched in the front rank of the vanguard entering the Street of Flowers, Díaz found himself at the rear of the rearguard on the retreat. This meant turning about to face the hooting and whistling mass of the enemy pressing them from behind, walking backwards while fending off thrusts, blows and clouds of sling-stones whistling in at them from street level, and the constant hail of larger, heavier rocks and rubble thrown down from above that piled up haphazardly across the road. The men nearest the flanks of the column had to contend with the same set of challenges while shuffling sideways and, for all concerned, there was grave danger of a misstep, when to lose one's footing here and fall from the embrace of the square meant immediate capture by the enemy, who had already borne off three screaming Spaniards to the horrible fate of sacrifice.

Thus, though strong in defence, the square was far from ideal for the present purpose of driving a wedge through the massed foe across the distance of more than seven hundred paces that now separated the column from the sanctuary of the sacred precinct.

'Fuck you,' Díaz heard La Serna snarl through gritted teeth as he smashed his shield into the face of the fat, shrieking warrior who was clawing at him, seeking to drag him out of the square. 'And fuck your mother,' he added, battering the clinging attacker again, shoving him away and hacking a huge gash in the side of his neck with his broadsword. In the same instant the man at Díaz's right – one of Narváez's soldiers whose name he didn't remember – was struck a crushing blow by a great clump of broken masonry hurled from above. He fell without uttering so much as a gasp, instantly dead, his head and helmet mashed together into a bloody, twisted wreck, one eye forced from its socket and his brains seeping out through split and gaping rivets.

A knot of howling warriors hit the line at a run, laying about them with heavy battle clubs, more effective weapons against armour than their obsidian-bladed swords. At his left Mibiercas swung his *montante* in a great gleaming arc, neatly dividing a warrior's skull and splitting him to the midriff, so that the two halves of his upper body peeled away from the blade. In a single, flowing follow-through, the tall swordsman jabbed the massive point up through the throat and into the brain of another attacker, lifting him spitted off the ground.

Everyone knew it would mean the end if the enemy were allowed to divide and scatter the retreat. The rear half of the column must not, under any circumstances, become separated from the van. Still keeping up the steady, exhausting backward shuffle needed to hold the formation, Díaz stumbled on a pile of loose stones, struggled to regain his balance, and discovered to his alarm that a pair of hands were locked round his left ankle.

He'd been seized by a beefy, naked Indian who must have slipped to the ground, snaked through the press to reach him and now threatened to tug him off his feet. Díaz struck down wildly with the edge of his sword, slicing off the warrior's nose, cheek and ear. His teeth and skull gleamed white through the bloody meat, but the blow was not mortal and failed to dislodge his grip. At the same time other hands clamped his right leg, immobilising him as though he'd become stuck in deep mud.

Díaz struggled mightily, but fell. More hands were upon him and, with a pulse of dread, calling out to Mibiercas and La Serna for aid, he felt himself borne away into the Mexica ranks.

Sandoval had become unhorsed from Llesenia, didn't know if the mare had been killed or if she yet lived, and was now fighting in the van of the great square, two ranks behind Alvarado, deploying one of the long Chinantla pikes to probe deep amongst the howling Mexica squadrons seeking to block their path.

His face, helmet and armour drenched in blood, apparently not much of it his own, Alvarado had seemed possessed by a holy fury since losing Bucephalus. This made him dangerous, Sandoval realised, not only to the enemy but also to his comrades in the front line, whom he now left unprotected as he saw an opportunity, and without hesitation broke ranks. One of the armoured war dogs had appeared out of nowhere, like a shining, blood-smeared demon, torn out the throat of a Mexica officer and seized the head of the warrior next to him, bearing him to the ground amidst terrified screams and a froth of blood. A ragged breach in the enemy ranks was thus created, and it was into this that Alvarado now stalked, a master swordsman at the peak of his powers, unleashing slaughter, hacking at heads and ribs with his huge falchion, plunging the point of his quillon dagger into an eye here, a bare chest there, and all the time laughing like a madman, '*Hahaha-hahaha . . . haha . . . haha.*'

Perhaps it was because of his fearsome reputation, or because of the almost supernatural force and power of his swordsmanship, or because so many still superstitiously believed him to embody their sun god Tonatiuh – but, for whatever reason, Sandoval saw that Alvarado's onslaught was having an effect, causing consternation amongst the Indians confronting him, some of whom began to scatter in disarray.

Ordaz saw it too, and reacted immediately. '*Forward!*' he shouted. His bugler blew the advance and the entire column, twenty ranks deep from van to rearguard, surged ahead, as though energised by Alvarado's momentum, seeking to widen the small breach he'd opened and cut their way through to the sanctuary of the palace.

Alvarado was in the thick of it, still hacking his own path, still a full five paces ahead of the Spanish front rank and completely surrounded by the Mexica. He had the grim, determined manner of a woodsman with a forest to cut down, but he was so focused on the work of thrusting and hacking that he'd failed to notice two big warriors working their way round behind him in the melee. One was armed with a mahogany club, the other held a net – a combination of weapons favoured by sacrificial snatch squads.

Mahogany Club was the nearest of the two, just within range, getting into position to stun Alvarado with a blow to the head while his comrade threw the net over him.

Not on my watch! Sandoval thought.

He raised his pike high, two handed, and plunged its hardened copper point into the back of Mahogany Club's thick neck, feeling it separate the vertebrae where the spine entered the base of his skull, sensing the immediate slump of death. Net hadn't given up, and Sandoval had to step through into the front rank to strike him as he was poised to throw, the thick shaft of the pike transfixing the man's torso, its bloody copper point protruding an arm's length out from the front of his chest.

So quick was the momentum now, so rapid the forward rush, that Sandoval simply strode on, reached down, grasped the pike just behind the point and drew the long shaft out through Net's dead body as the column surged ahead. Moments later, the entire van burst free of the narrower confines of the Street of Flowers and into the wide avenue south of the sacred precinct.

The great southern gateway, heavily under siege, lay less than five hundred paces ahead, with the perimeter wall on either side of it black with thousands of climbers. Seeing fighting all along the parapet, Sandoval wondered – *Are we exchanging the frying pan for the fire?* But there was really no alternative. Those outside the Spanish fortress and those within must reunite or they would all be destroyed.

Responding to piercing cries and conch blasts from the Mexica battle leaders, several of the squadrons besieging the gate now wheeled to reinforce the attack on Ordaz's column.

Clearly the enemy would do all in their power to prevent the consolidation of the Spanish forces and, as a new mass of warriors whirled round them, the momentum of the huge square once again began to slow. Alvarado was still out ahead but now, reading the change in the weather, he reluctantly allowed the front rank to catch up with him and took his place in the line.

Cortés and a handful of his men – three still standing but wounded, two already down – appeared to have become separated from the rest of their unit but, for some minutes, had held the top of the stairway to the north wall, denying the Mexica access to the plaza below. Their defence was spirited but hopeless, since hundreds of warriors had poured over the wall and were preventing other Spaniards along the parapet from coming to their rescue.

Shikotenka hit the stairway at a run, bounding up three and four flights at a time, and threw himself immediately into the fray, his flint dagger licking out too rapidly for the eye to follow, slaughtering four of the vile Mexica thugs in the space of a heartbeat – *tac, tac, tac, tac*. He found himself momentarily side by side with Cortés, saw his pallor, his sweat-sheened face, the huge livid bruise on his temple, the blood dripping down his shield arm from a wound to his hand, but also saw the fanatical gleam in his eye, the determination and the courage in the set of his mouth, and knew, whatever else might happen, whatever might afflict him, that this man would never back down.

Seeing the new force of Tlascalans streaming on to the north wall encouraged the hard-pressed defenders, and a ragged cheer went up as Shikotenka's five hundred, soon supported by five hundred more brought fresh from barracks by Tree, streamed along the parapet, killing Mexica warriors in droves and eventually joining up with Brabo and his squad, who'd ranged almost to the northeast corner of the perimeter.

'Thank you, Shikotenka,' Cortés said formally when the last of the attackers had been pitched from the wall. 'Once again I owe you my life. I'll not forget it.'

Shikotenka understood the Spanish words perfectly and knew in his heart that Cortés would forget the debt the instant it suited his purposes to do so.

More climbers were ascending, but in much smaller numbers than before, easily contained by the reinforced defenders, when from the opposite side of the plaza around the besieged southern gateway came a great swell of noise and a desperate series of bugle calls summoning help from all quarters.

Díaz fought with the fury of the damned as the crowd of warriors sought to carry him off along the Street of Flowers, cruel hands gripping him, lifting him to shoulder height. He heard his own voice in his ears, screaming, shouting hoarsely, as he struggled to resist the Mexica. In the chaos, ignoring his kicks and struggles, they began to pass him overhead like a parcel from man to man. Panic filled him. Then – a stroke of luck – some portion of a great mass of rocks cast down from above fell amongst the Indians carrying Díaz, braining two, knocking another off his feet, shaking loose their hold on him. He'd lost his sword but got his right arm free. He wrapped it round a warrior's muscular neck and hurled his body sideways, bearing the man to the ground, snarling and biting at his face as they fell. More stones pelted down, other warriors tumbled on top of them, and then – Díaz could not be sure – more still seemed to scramble over them in a great rush along the street in the direction of the sacred precinct.

The weight of the scrum of braves pressing down on him was now so immense, his chest so crushed, his nose and mouth so blocked by rank Mexica flesh, that Díaz was suffocating in black darkness. Some of those piled over him were certainly dead, killed by the avalanche of stones, but others were alive and struggling to their feet. Feeling the weight around him shift, he found a gap, drew a deep, shuddering breath, got his knees under him, lunged for a patch of light above, lunged again, gave a mighty heave and burst forth through the dead to witness a square of twenty Spaniards led by Mibiercas and La Serna hacking their way freely towards him, confronted not by any great throng but only by small knots of braves whom they felled and scattered.

Mibiercas reached down a big, calloused hand. 'Come on, Bernal,' he said. 'We haven't got all day.'

'Thought you might want this back,' added La Serna, passing him his sword. 'I found it sticking out of one of the heathens.'

After the noise and fury that had accompanied the sortie from the outset, it felt strange to be suddenly in the midst of a pocket of silence, surrounded by dead and dying braves with none left to come at them. La Serna explained that in the last moments, just after Díaz was taken, the column had surged forward a distance of several hundred paces. Most of the Mexica in the Street of Flowers had followed in hot pursuit.

Lulls like this, Díaz knew, were a random part of every battle. You couldn't predict when they would begin or when they would end. The only certainty was that they never lasted very long.

'Gentlemen,' he said to his rescue squad, 'I thank you all from the bottom of my heart, but now let's get the fuck out of here.'

Silent, grim faced, announced by whistles and more showers of stones from above, Díaz led his little square back along the Street of Flowers at a run, descended like a storm upon the horde of warriors harrying the Spanish rearguard, cut them aside, smashed them down and trampled them as the column opened and they reintegrated themselves seamlessly into its ranks.

The van was already far out into the avenue, heading for the southern gateway to the sacred plaza, but had seemingly become bogged down again by the press of warriors. Meanwhile the rear dozen ranks or so remained fully within the Street of Flowers and subject to the unremitting hail of missiles from above.

Simply by throwing rocks from the rooftops, Díaz thought miserably, the Mexica had taken more Spanish lives in this single day than had been lost in the whole of the rest of the conquest. It was a formidable new tactic, and a way would have to be found to combat it if there were to be any hope of ever escaping from Tenochtitlan.

But what if Cortés didn't want to escape? Only this morning Díaz had overheard him say he'd rather be cut to pieces than evacuate the city.

And what if it was too late? With so many warriors assaulting the sacred precinct, its defences might already have been breached and overrun. What if the column was retreating not to succour amidst comrades in arms within a secure perimeter, but to final destruction amidst numberless foes?

Alvarado's rage had subsided somewhat, cold clarity and calculation seeping back to reoccupy the space it had left.

Thousands of braves had been detached from the Mexica assault on the wall and thrown at the column to block its path to the south gate and the safety of the sacred precinct.

But what safety?

Because even as more warriors left the wall to join the attack on the column, others, fresh and as yet unblooded, could be seen pouring in to take their places through the great avenues lying to the east of the precinct where there'd been no action as yet. Damn Cortés! Damn him for failing to set out cannon yesterday. For now these new fighters, in a great, howling inchoate mass, began to spread out everywhere, like a stain that would soon engulf the entire precinct, a great block of at least five thousand of them, bristling with stone blades, supported by *tamanes* carrying ropes and long ladders, heading straight for the southern gateway.

The enemy strategy was obvious. Anyone in their position would do the same. At all costs they must try to prevent the two separated halves of the Spanish force – those within and those without the precinct – from joining up.

Each must be massacred separately.

Over my dead body, Alvarado thought as he neatly and economically struck off a Mexica head with a single blow of his falchion.

That was the way these things were done.

With Shikotenka, Olid, Davila and Brabo at his side, Cortés stood atop the parapet of the southern gateway looking down upon the boiling ocean of Mexica warriors extending in all directions as far as the eye could see around the sacred precinct. On a section of wall fifty paces west of the gate, he saw lines of dozens of climbers, knives gripped between their teeth, swarming up improvised stairs of blades and spears thrust into cracks, only to be clubbed over the head by the squad of Tlascalans awaiting them on the parapet. All around the perimeter, other equally suicidal climbers, in utterly appalling numbers, continuously overtopped the walls and were continuously thrown back. The defence held, but was everywhere under relentless and overwhelming pressure.

'Drink, Caudillo?' Brabo offered, discreetly passing Cortés a battered canteen. Cortés took it, swilled the brackish, briny scum through his teeth, its bitterness reminding him of yet another looming crisis – for there was almost no potable water left within the precinct for the Spaniards to drink. The well dug in the palace courtyard a month earlier now gave only a trickle, and the few other accessible sources were either barren

427

or foul. Half a mile north of the precinct, in the great square of Tlatelolco, there was, of course, plenty of water, gushing in fresh and clear along the twin aqueducts carried overhead from the springs at Chapultepec, but it might have been on the other side of the earth for all the hope there was of reaching it.

Cortés's lungs still heaved, sweat still poured from him, and a wave of dizziness and nausea shook him, threatening once again to lay him low. It was not fitting in a commander to show weakness, but it was only with the greatest difficulty that he mastered himself. The slingshot that had struck his temple seemed to have addled his brains and, for the first time in his life, he was uncertain what he should do.

The problem, however, was clear enough. Although Ordaz's column had inflicted heavy losses on the enemy, probably killing thousands, their numbers had already been replenished by fresh squadrons of warriors. It was not difficult to see where these were coming from. Drawing on all the resources of their own empire, of their vassal states, and the Chichemec and Otomi mercenaries they'd hired in recent years, the Mexica, *in extremis*, could mobilise as many as half a million men – and clearly they judged the slaughter of the Spaniards occupying their city as worthy of such a mighty effort.

That was why they could afford to throw wave after wave of warriors at Ordaz, while constantly bringing in fresh squadrons to dispute every inch of the walls, not caring how many lives it cost them, knowing that in the end, by force of numbers, they would wear the Spaniards down.

The immediate crisis, and the reason Cortés had been summoned to the south wall, was the predicament of the column. Its rearguard was still within the Street of Flowers, vulnerable to missiles thrown from the roofs, while its van had already partially traversed the avenue, five hundred paces wide, that separated the Street of Flowers from the south gate of the precinct. There all further forward progress had been halted by the scale and ferocity of the Mexica attack.

At the same time – and this was sinister – a new, seemingly highly disciplined troop of Indians, almost naked, with distinctive black and red body paint, had reinforced the warriors still assaulting the south wall. Although they carried ropes and grappling hooks, these newcomers had not yet joined the assault but had interposed themselves in a solid block between the south gate and the vanguard of Ordaz's column.

'Who are they?' Cortés asked Shikotenka.

The Tlascalan leader's Spanish was hesitant, but good enough for his answer: 'Chichemecs. Maybe Guatemoc bring. Big trouble.'

Guatemoc! That firebrand!

Needing to know more, Cortés sent a battlefield messenger to summon Malinal to the wall and told Davila to assemble a column of two hundred Spaniards just inside the south gate.

'That'll be two hundred fewer men to defend the perimeter, Caudillo,' Davila reminded him.

'Just do it,' said Cortés. He turned to Shikotenka: 'And I'll need five hundred of your Tlascalans as well.'

The speed and efficiency with which the new force of braves in their distinctive red and black body paint had formed up to block the column's retreat to the south gate was alarming. Alvarado had fought many Indian armies, including some damn good ones like the Tlascalans, but he'd seen nothing like this before.

He spat. Even so, they were just painted savages. It was *intolerable* that they should get in his way. Relapsing suddenly and completely into the berserk rage that had seized him earlier, blood pounding in his temples, spittle foaming at his mouth, he heard himself, as though from a great distance, shout '*Santiago and at them!*', and then he was bounding forward, leaping high, quillon dagger in his left hand, falchion in his right, and the Mexica were falling before him in geysers of blood, as though it was the sun god himself who slew them.

'*Santiago and at them!*' Sandoval yelled. It was the second time in this battle that he'd seen a kind of divine madness descend upon Alvarado, and it would be foolish not to harness it.

'*Santiago and at them!*' bellowed Ordaz, who clearly had the same idea.

'*Santiago and at them!*' The whole column took up the cry and surged forward in a massed, armoured shove against the enemy.

The men in the front rank were now too close to use their swords. Depending absolutely on the ranks behind for protection, they braced their big *adarga* shields double-handed as they piled in to the foe, the wide, blunt end of a steel-clad battering ram, propelled by all the weight and momentum of four hundred desperate but disciplined soldiers moving in perfect coordination to scatter and dismay the enemy.

*   *   *

Coming to his senses as quickly as he'd left them, Alvarado heard the infantry behind him hit the enemy ranks in a hard, compact mass. *Well!* he thought, *That's going to be bloody!*

Not that it wasn't bloody enough here in the midst of five thousand crazed savages, painted like grubs, and clearly in possession of some rudimentary notions of tactics. They'd already proved themselves significantly harder to kill than other Indians during the first few paces of his crazed charge, and they had a worrying inclination to work together in coordinated teams.

With a casual flick of his falchion, he batted aside a spear that was coming much too fast at his face, transformed the motion into a lunge to the heart of a sweating warrior who sought to bar his way, severed another man's jugular with the edge of his dagger as he strode past him, and came almost within striking distance of his target – the leader of this formidable band, a handsome and muscular young prince in splendid regalia who stood in the midst of his officers, watching the battle closely, giving orders, sending messengers here and there.

The good news was that the advance of the Spanish column had not slowed. Alvarado was too closely engaged with a team of five warriors who seemed to be trying to throw some sort of net over him to risk a glance back, but if his ears did not betray him, the front rank was very close. Soon, perhaps already, he'd be back under the aegis of the pikes again, always a good place to be when your enemies had a nasty habit of sneaking up on you from behind.

'Hey, you!' he yelled, and saw he'd got the prince's attention. '*Fight me!*'

And why not? He was the famous Tonatiuh, after all. What man of blood and honour would not wish to fight him?

The young warrior shouted a reply – meaningless of course – then made a motion with his hand, and immediately the braves pressing round Alvarado drew back.

'*Fight me! Just you and me!*' Alvarado attempted to mime two men fighting a duel.

Again the prince replied, and again Alvarado could make no sense of it, but now more and more of the warriors on both sides were watching rather than trading blows while the front line of the column was no longer under attack at all and had come to a halt. Something like silence descended, freakish and fleeting, and in it Alvarado clearly heard Malinal's voice.

'*His name is Kasakir,*' she yelled from the parapet over the south gate where she stood with Cortés and others. '*Prince of the Opata Chichemecs. He says he knows of you by reputation and will be honoured to fight you.*' The silence had deepened while she spoke, but now, as she gave some longer oration in the barbarous tongue of the Mexica, all fighting ceased. It seemed the entire battlefield was looking on.

Guatemoc wore no finery – he'd left all that to Kasakir – and was dressed simply in loincloth and moccasins like the rest of the Opata. This was not, he had to remind himself, because of any modesty on his part, but because Tozi had asked him to do so. He'd wondered why. He was, after all, a famous man, and everyone knew him – regardless of the clothes he wore. But she'd been adamant: 'Let those who do *not* know you think you just a humble soldier, with Kasakir the leader of this band.'

'What about those who *do* know me?' he'd asked.

'Let them be puzzled,' Tozi had replied gravely. 'Let them be confused.'

She was his witch; she had access to uncanny sources of knowledge and Guatemoc trusted her instincts. That was why he wore only a loincloth and moccasins, now, while Kasakir, who was in fact a chief, strutted around in the full chieftain's regalia, which he was entitled to but usually never wore.

All that had been agreed in advance – part of a series of distractions and disguises.

What hadn't been agreed, however, was this outrageous proposal for single combat between Kasakir and the Spanish warrior Alvarado. It wasn't even Kasakir's fault, because the proposal had come first from Alvarado, and thereafter Kasakir had been honour-bound to accept it. Still, Guatemoc felt a twinge of jealousy as the two men squared up in the strip of clear space that had now opened between the Chichemec and Spanish ranks.

That should be me, he thought.

Alvarado had hoped to drive a bargain with the Indians – how about allowing the Spanish column to complete its retreat if he won this fight? – but no one seemed interested in talking any more. Instead here was the barbarian prince squaring up to him, a great lump of a man, eyes like two gimlets in a slab of meat, swinging his silly wooden paddle with its even sillier obsidian blades that were sharp enough to shave with, but which shattered on contact with armour.

Hadn't they even *heard* of armour? Hadn't the word got around?

Alvarado understood that the Mexica squadrons were made up of men from many different regions of a far-flung empire, and that most of those here today had never seen, let alone fought, Spaniards before. Still, it was amazing, and enormously to his advantage, that so many of them – including the feathered dolt prancing round him now – didn't seem to have a clue about the properties of steel.

'*Ordaz!*' he roared. '*Sandoval! Be ready. I will make an opening. Use it!*' And with that he strode in on Kasakir, ignoring the hard but harmless *macuahuitl* blow that the other man struck at his cuirass, indifferent to the stone dagger that shattered against his gorget, gripping his quillon dagger in his left hand, his falchion in his right, but not using them yet, instead hoisting the overbalanced warrior under the armpits, lifting him clear of the ground and, with a tremendous burst of strength, throwing him back into the mob of painted savages behind him.

'*Santiago and at them!*' Alvarado roared.

The situation was fluid, with everything happening so fast, and so many Opata braves separating him from the action around Kasakir, that Guatemoc was unable to intervene. It was obvious immediately, however, that the Spanish warrior was a powerful athlete, a master of blades and entirely without fear.

Guatemoc had never fought Spaniards before, never seen or studied their way of battle, never confronted their weapons, so what happened next was . . . instructive.

First Kasakir's knives and *macuahuitl* were impotent against the gleaming armour of his opponent. Alvarado simply allowed himself to be hit, suffering no hurt from the killing blows, stepped in on the chieftain, crowded him, overbalanced him and, without letting go of his own weapons, picked Kasakir up, pitched him bodily into the ranks behind, bellowed some hideous imprecation and continued his advance.

Now a lesson in butchery. Kasakir was momentarily helpless, sprawling, held up by the stumbling Opata mercenaries he'd been thrown amongst. Alvarado came on, the arc of his huge metal blade catching the sun, and struck the chieftain a massive blow diagonally across the chest, hacking off his entire left arm and shoulder. The blade flashed again, off came the right shoulder and most of poor Kasakir's head. A third flash and Alvarado was in amongst the surrounding mercenaries, more like some deadly mechanical device of slaughter than a man, dancing the long dagger and the sword through bones and flesh, a near-visible wave of fear and uncertainty spreading round him and opening a zone of weakness in the Opata ranks that the armoured Spanish column now hit at a charge.

The tremendous crash and roar of the impact signalled a rapid, almost uncontested advance, which brought the entire column out of the Street of Flowers and its van within seventy or eighty paces of the south gate, before the press of warriors bogged it down again. Alvarado was still out ahead, completely surrounded, but had come within range of half a dozen sharpshooters on the south parapet, who were picking off the warriors around him with carefully aimed arquebus and crossbow shots.

Such cover could not be provided for all, and the possibility remained strong that Alvarado and the entire column behind him would be massacred out there in the open without ever reaching the sanctuary of the precinct.

Leaving Olid in command on the parapet, signalling Brabo, Shikotenka and Malinal to follow, Cortés hurled himself down the stairs to take charge of the two hundred men Davila had assembled. Waiting with them were Brabo's little squad and five hundred of Shikotenka's Tlascalans.

'What's the plan?' Shikotenka asked.

'We're going to make a sortie and open a cordon so Ordaz's column can get through. All the warriors out there are focused on him. They think they've got us pinned down here and they won't be expecting an attack.'

'But they *have* got us pinned down here,' Davila objected. 'It's all we can do to hold the perimeter. Weakening it now is sheer folly.'

Cortés sighed and tentatively adjusted his grip on the handle of his shield, slippery with the blood that still guttered from the wound he'd taken. A knife or spear point – he didn't know which – must have done the damage, somehow slipping past his guard to impale his left hand between the metacarpals, and smashing his middle two fingers on the way through. The pain was so severe that he could barely hold the shield, yet to go out there without it was obvious madness, so he must simply grit his teeth and press on.

The *tamanes* were already drawing back the gates and the immense throng of braves on the other side became visible. 'You stay here with your five hundred,' Cortés told Shikotenka. 'A great many of the enemy are going to get past us when we go out, and the gates have to stay open so we can get back in, so your job is to hold the breach. Hold it at all costs.'

Suppressing another wave of nausea, his sweat clammy on his brow, Cortés stepped into the front rank alongside Davila and nodded to the bugler to signal the charge. The gates continued to swing inward, giving clear passage to a few dozen enemy braves who slipped through to either side before the advancing column blocked the way, but not one of these first intruders survived the Tlascalan clubs.

Cortés knew that the only hope lay in joining forces with Ordaz very rapidly. For this reason, while lining the outer edges of the moving square with shield-bearing swordsmen, his main force, in the centre, was a corps of one hundred and forty pikemen, deploying the long Chinantla lances and able to reach as many as six paces deep into enemy ranks. Cortés hoped to emulate the 'push of pikes' that had been used so famously during the Italian wars at the battle of Ravenna. In theory, if the swordsmen could prevent the enemy disrupting his pikemen, then he could use them and the armoured mass of the entire square to force his way through to Ordaz. Pushing has its limits if it's just hand to hand, but when what's pushing at you are the pointy ends of an array of sixteen-foot-long pikes, it's another matter entirely.

And at Ravenna, there had been pikes and armoured men on both sides, while here only the Spaniards had them . . .

Guatemoc had brought five thousand of his Opata Chichemecs to the battlefield today, without the knowledge or agreement of his father, for the sole purpose of testing them against the Spaniards. Logistically it had been easy; so many different vassal peoples and mercenary bands had answered the Mexica call that one more regiment amongst the myriads filing into the city attracted no attention. Nor had Guatemoc found it difficult to disobey his father. The notion that he should hold the Opata in reserve until after the Spaniards and Mexica had destroyed each other, and then claim the city for Cuitláhuac, had become repugnant to him, and he refused to be bound by it. His only regret was that he'd left the rest of his force – seven thousand men – sitting idly an hour's march north of Tacuba.

Flanked by Starving Coyote, Fuzzy Face and Big Dart on his left, Man-Eater and Mud Head on his right, Guatemoc was poised by the gate. He ordered in the skirmishers as soon as there were gaps for them to squeeze through, and waited with two thousand of his men whom he'd called away from the assault on the column to see what new tactic the Spaniards were going to try.

They came out in a bristling mass, in a rush, like some monstrous porcupine.

Guatemoc recognised the distinctive lances that gave them this spiny look – the bastards must have got them from Chinantla – but had never before seen them used the way the enemy were using them now.

Right there beside him, Fuzzy Face was amongst the first to die. The lance that killed him was wielded by a tall Spaniard, three ranks back from the edge of the advancing square, who hoisted the long shaft of his weapon overhead and plunged its barbed metal point down into the soft chasm of flesh at the base of Fuzzy's neck, behind the collarbone, thrusting it through to his heart before ripping it free again in a burst of blood. A blink of an eye later, Mud Head went the same way, and Guatemoc himself only narrowly avoided impalement, by twisting his body to the side as a lance sought him out.

The natural instinct was to scramble back, which Guatemoc, Starving Coyote, Big Dart and Man-Eater all now did – only fools or madmen would stay still to be spitted – stumbling over one another in their haste like everyone else around them. Meanwhile, the Spanish squad thrusting all those points forward continued to do so with such perfect, unbroken coordination, harnessing the strength and momentum of every one of its two hundred men, violently pushing anyone coming at them from any side, leaving their swordsmen to slaughter those who slipped in close beneath the reach of the lances.

It was, Guatemoc had to admit, incredibly well done. And, while it was undoubtedly the case that such a small force would sooner or later be overwhelmed, the fact remained that they'd seized the initiative with this new tactic.

He for one was not about to throw himself screaming at the lances.

No need to squander life for glory today when tomorrow would be soon enough to settle the score.

Pepillo, only lightly armoured, his sword strapped at his side, had joined Malinal on the parapet whence she'd returned the moment Cortés and his two hundred were out of the gate. He'd been involved in the fighting from the beginning; his face was smoke blackened and he was cut deeply, but not critically, with a bleeding gash in his side and another to his thigh. 'The caudillo told me to look after you,' he said. 'I'm to take you back to the palace.'

'No!' Malinal shook off his insistent hand. 'No, Pepillo. I will wait here. I must know the fate of my lord.'

'He'll survive this, Malinal! He always does. It's you he's worried about!'

'Still I must know.'

She turned from him to look out at the scene of battle again, her ears assaulted by the furious din, her eyes fixed on Cortés at the head of his two hundred, everywhere beleaguered, but everywhere pushing forward with incredible speed. She knew that he was just a man, with all the frailties and viciousness of men, and certainly no god as she'd once believed him to be. Nonetheless she loved him with all her heart, and surely only a man who had been touched by the gods could have done what he had done, achieved what he had achieved, and won such victories against fearful odds?

He was sick from the heat, and shortage of water, dazed from his head wound, and in terrible pain from the injuries to his hand, which she'd bandaged and helped him bind to his shield. Nonetheless, she knew he would find victory again today. It seemed impossible, but somehow Hernán would do it and, as though to confirm this, she saw him hack his way through the last of the Chichemec resistance to join forces with Ordaz.

There was an immediate shuffling and rearrangement of the lines. 'What's happening?' she asked Pepillo.

'They're going to make a cordon of pikes for Ordaz's men to retreat through,' the page replied. He pointed below to the rearguard of Cortés's square, only a few paces in front of the yawning gates where Shikotenka's large force of Tlascalans, supported by a handful of Spaniards, were mounting a furious defence. It was the Chichemec squadron that had engaged them, but in the last moments, thousands of Mexica, detached from the attack on Ordaz, had also thrown themselves into the fight here. Malinal had seen enough of battles to know that the Mexica and the Chichemecs weren't working well together today; the two peoples often cooperated, but it almost seemed as though the Mexica felt usurped and were now reclaiming what was theirs by right, attempting to thrust their barbaric northern cousins out of the way. Some fights had even broken out amongst them, and all this aided Cortés.

The concept of a cordon of pikes was unfamiliar, but Malinal had no need to ask Pepillo what it meant as, with a mighty struggle, the six

436

hundred Spaniards outside the gate redeployed, opening up a heavily armoured corridor of swordsmen, backed by two ranks of pikemen offering temporary safe passage through the gates and into the sacred precinct.

'I have to get you out of here *now!*' Pepillo insisted. '*Please*, Malinal. The caudillo will kill me if I fail him in this. You have to come with me!'

'But why? Look! This cordon of pikes is working. I will wait until Cortés comes through the gate, then I go!'

'*We're going now!*' roared Pepillo. He picked her up bodily, slung her over his shoulder and carried her down the stairs, seemingly indifferent to her fists pummelling at him. 'I'm sorry, Malinal,' he said, 'but I have to get you inside the palace. Cortés's orders.' She felt him zigzag right and left, as though avoiding some obstacle, then saw behind her that a Mexica warrior lay dead on the ground with the huge Tlascalan called Tree looming over him holding a bloodstained club.

'The perimeter's too big to hold,' Pepillo said, 'and with six hundred of our men to bring through the gates, the caudillo's certain we'll be overrun. He's just thinking ahead – getting you inside. That's where we'll all be going.'

He set her down amongst the cannon drawn up before the gates of the palace, where two scared-looking young Spaniards stood on guard. The guns themselves, Malinal noticed, were untended, as though no one expected to use them and, indeed, while the fight remained outside the sacred precinct, there *was* no use for them. That would change completely, however, if the fight moved inside the precinct, and didn't Cortés's horrible certainty that they'd be 'overrun' mean exactly that?

She heard a great shriek of triumph from the Mexica; looking back she saw the south wall being abandoned, its gates gaping wide and countless warriors pouring through – so it was happening already, and happening fast.

Pepillo had sprinted off to join the defence there, but what about these cannon still sitting idle in the plaza? Might they not be redeployed? Remembering that she'd seen Francisco de Mesa, the chief of artillery, amongst the defenders on the north wall, Malinal made an instant decision to find him and bring him and a few of his crews to the guns.

And of course, it occurred to her as she ran, she'd also have to bring everyone else off the north wall. With the south wall entirely breached, the walled perimeter could no longer be maintained, and the only hope of safety lay in a rapid retreat to the palace.

* * *

Shikotenka was bitter at the losses amongst his men. Hundreds had died this day who might have survived if they'd been issued with armour like the Spaniards.

He understood there wasn't sufficient steel to go round, but still it didn't feel right for only Spanish hides to be protected while Tlascalan skins were punctured with impunity. He'd have a word with Cortés about it, he decided, if any of them lived beyond the next few hours.

That, however, seemed increasingly doubtful.

On the one hand the caudillo had just succeeded in bringing the last of his six hundred Spaniards – or what was left of them after the beating they'd taken – through the south gate and into the sacred precinct. That was good. On the other hand, however, the gate could not be closed behind them and thousands of Mexica and Chichemecs were pouring through.

'Gods,' said Tree. 'What a mess.'

There was no longer any question of holding the perimeter, and those few who hadn't already deserted the south wall were now dead men, cut off from their comrades' fighting retreat across the plaza towards the palace of Axayacatl. The focus of everyone's attention was on the zone of contention that had now opened up within the plaza itself, between the south gate and the palace, and lapping around the south and west sides of the great pyramid. It was this route that the Spaniards must traverse to reach the relative safety of their quarters, though harried every step of the way by the Chichemec and Mexica squadrons.

But no one, let alone Cortés, who was so preoccupied with other matters, seemed to have thought of the longer route to the palace around the east and north sides of the pyramid – no one, that is, except the warriors pouring through the south gate, from whose midst a large squadron now detached itself, at once heading north and east at a run.

'With me!' Shikotenka shouted, and took his squad of five hundred north and west towards the palace, leaving the Spaniards to fight their own battle in the plaza. He heard angry shouts behind him, one from Cortés himself, but closed his ears. Explanations could come later. All that mattered now was to deploy his men in front of the palace doors before any of the Mexica pounding round the long way could reach them.

The defence of the north wall had crumbled. There were still a few men there, Mesa amongst them, but they held only the sector east of the stairway and were being beaten back by huge numbers of Mexica climbers.

'*Get out of there!*' Malinal yelled when she reached the foot of the stairs. '*You must all get back to the palace. We're being overrun.*'

She was well liked by the men of the original expedition, enough of whom, including Mesa and two of his crews, were here to persuade the others that her word could be trusted.

As they fled, with the Mexica right on their heels, literally breathing down their necks, Malinal realised they'd never make it. Then out of nowhere came Shikotenka, with five hundred of his mountain men, in a great flying wedge that smashed into the pursuers, and drove them back in a violent, grinding surge almost as far as the wall.

'Come, Mesa!' Malinal said, tugging at the artillery chief's arm. 'You must make your guns speak.'

Cortés was raving at the betrayal – *Fucking Shikotenka! Deserting in the heat of battle! He'd hang for this!* – only to discover that the Tlascalan's quick thinking had once again saved the day. By throwing his five hundred in front of the palace in the nick of time, he'd given the men on the north wall breathing space to retreat without significant losses, driven off wave after wave of Mexica attackers advancing around the east and north flanks of the pyramid, and allowed Mesa to prime the cannon.

Placing the palace wall at their back, Cortés deployed his men side by side with the Tlascalans in a great ark protecting the guns. The Tlascalans had suffered terrible losses during the defence of the perimeter, but must still number close to two thousand. Meanwhile, despite casualties amongst Ordaz's column, and his own, the total muster of Spaniards within the sacred precinct still certainly exceeded a thousand. With such numbers now concentrated in one place, and with the great guns about to unleash hell, Cortés still felt confident he could prevail.

More crews were being assembled from their scattered remnants, after this morning's fruitless sortie which many of the gunners had joined. Until then, with thousands of the enemy pressing every inch of the line, single volleys of around eight cannon at a time were the most that Mesa and his two available crews could achieve.

'We're ready, sir,' the artillery chief whispered in his ear, and on Cortés's signal, relayed by the bugler, the Spanish front line stepped back behind the guns and there came the massive rolling thunder of one of the great lombards, accompanied by the sharper reports of seven falconets and the hideous whine of the grapeshot that exploded from the barrels into the heart of the enemy advance.

439

At once there arose from the Indians a piercing wail, and the clouds of smoke cleared to reveal hundreds mowed down at a stroke, with broken and dismembered bodies lying scattered in viscid clumps everywhere.

What was also obvious, however, was that the slaughter had not halted or even slowed the enemy advance – for striding forward over the corpses of their comrades, and from all directions, fresh squadrons of Indians had appeared, with seemingly limitless numbers of them stretching away as far as the eye could see, all around the great pyramid and across the plaza.

With screams of defiance and hatred they threw themselves again at the Spanish line, at several points breaking through and isolating guns before being killed by the defenders. Meanwhile, attempting to reload a few paces back, Mesa and his crews came under fierce attack from a group of enemy slingers, experts in their craft, whose stones flew like bullets, hitting man after man with unerring accuracy, while dense showers of arrows and spears descended all around as though the sky had opened.

The melee was so close, the oppression of the missiles so great, that it was only possible to fire two more guns, and those at point-blank range, before the Spanish line was overrun everywhere by the massed enemy.

'*Retreat!*' Cortés shouted. '*Into the palace. Bring all the powder and ammunition. Bring three falconets.*'

In the few minutes they had, it was the most they'd be able to carry through the gates amidst the chaos of the retreating army.

Díaz was with Sandoval, Mibiercas, La Serna and two hundred others in a mixed force of swordsmen and pikemen who'd fanned out in front of the palace doors to keep the enemy at bay while the cascading, increasingly panicked and disorderly retreat continued.

Then he saw something that chilled his blood.

A large band of Indians had got hold of one of the lombards left stranded thirty paces to the south of the doors. There were so many of them that they'd easily lifted the huge bronze cannon off its cradle. Now holding it in the manner of a battering ram, they charged at the palace wall. They backed up and repeated the manoeuvre.

Díaz summoned a battlefield messenger, showed him what was happening. 'They're going to break through,' he said. 'It's only a matter of time. Go and find the caudillo – your life depends on this; all our lives depend on it. Tell him there's about to be a breach, and where it is, and that there'll be hundreds of Indians through it. He must send a force to stop them or we're all dead men.'

Cortés had already seen it and anticipated what the messenger was going to say.

It was no great problem in itself that the Indians had now overrun and had possession of most of his cannon. Lacking powder and ammunition, and with no knowledge of gunnery, they'd be unable to use them – and, besides, the savages were present in such great numbers, all of them so eager and urgent to die, that the possession of these weapons no longer conferred any special advantage on the Spaniards. Yes, they could slaughter hundreds of Indians at a time but there were always hundreds more where they came from and no amount of losses, it seemed, was too great for them to bear.

And now the bastards were improvising! The messenger was right. They were using a lombard as a battering ram and they were going to knock a hole in the palace wall. The retreat still continued, and many of the men had taken shelter in the relative quiet and safety of the courtyard, nursing their wounds. 'No such luck, lads,' Cortés announced. From their number he quickly gathered fifty musketeers and fifty crossbowmen and hurried south through the inner galleries to the point where he'd calculated the breach would be made.

Another tremendous crash and a cloud of dust confirmed they were in the right place. Ignoring a savage jolt of pain in his hand, Cortés had the shooters form up in ten ranks – a line of crossbowmen followed by a line of musketeers, followed by another line of crossbowmen, and so on – with the van about a dozen paces from the now cracked and sagging wall.

'Hold your fire,' he said. 'Not a shot until I tell you, and here's how we're going to do it.' He spoke for a moment longer as two more great blows battered the wall. At the third, the massive barrel of the lombard burst right through, causing a general collapse of the masonry across a front about a dozen paces wide, revealing an immense crowd of painted Indians rushing at the breach.

'*First rank fire!*' roared Cortés.

Click . . . whoosh was the sound death made as the ten crossbowmen in the van let fly into the massed enemy. Immediately they retreated through the square, a manoeuvre they'd practised a hundred times, which brought them to the rear to reload, as the second rank – composed of musketeers – stepped forward to take their places and fired.

These two volleys of crossbow bolts and lead bullets heaped up a great pile of enemy dead across the breach. Those from squadrons pressing in behind leapt over the obstacle, only to fall, flailing and screaming, as the third and fourth ranks of crossbowmen and musketeers did their work.

The butchery continued. Within moments all the Spaniards had stepped into the firing line, killed and retreated, so that the original front rank of crossbowmen was once again in the van and ready to start the cycle again. Now, however, the heap of the dead and dying was so high and wide as to form a wall of sorts itself, and there was no longer any question of the enemy simply sweeping through the breach and into the palace. The pile of corpses prevented that, and men snaking over it in ones and twos were for some moments more efficiently picked off by snipers – quickly assigned to the task – than by volleys.

Through the smoke and dust, over the squirming mound of the injured and the dead, the Spaniards looked out defiantly, daring all-comers to do their worst. Night was falling, the sky dark. Across the plaza, the House of the Eagle Knights had caught fire during the fighting, and immense flames gushed forth from it, casting a lurid, flickering glow through the breached wall of the palace of Axayacatl and on to the faces of the defenders.

There came a great yell from outside and a new squadron of Indians hit the heap of bodies at a run, seeking to drag enough of them out of the way to clear a path through which they could enter.

Cortés walked sternly amongst his men. They were nervous and some had itchy fingers. 'We'll give them some more volley fire by ranks,' he said, 'but don't touch those triggers till I give the word.'

'Sir! They're coming.'

'Hold your fire, I say! We'll kill more of them when there's more of them to kill.'

Cadavers were being cast aside, the mound began to collapse, and suddenly a gap opened through which a rush of Indians poured.

'*Front rank fire!*' roared Cortés.

It seemed the Mexica preferred not to fight at night, for soon after the second wave of intruders had been shot down at the breach, the entire attack on the palace ceased. The breach was still guarded by a force of musketeers and crossbowmen, and the Indians were still just outside, filling the plaza in an uncountable, sullen mass, but they had withdrawn twenty paces and now, with the stolid, business-like manner of a besieging army, set about making camp for the night. The cannon they'd captured were all hauled away, cooking fires were lit here and there and, in full view of the defenders on the roof, hundreds of water-skins were brought in by teams of *tamanes* and shared amongst the warriors.

The sloshing sounds of the skins, the sight of fresh, cool water carelessly tipped over men's faces, and swilled down throats with exaggerated glugs and gasps of satisfaction, was maddening to the parched Spaniards – as, of course, it was intended to be.

And soon enough, even before the worst of the injured had been properly tended to, the complaints and bellyaching began. As Cortés had expected, none of it was from his veterans, who had known all along what they were getting themselves into. But Narváez's men, lured by images of a magical highland Venice, exotic bedmates, a life of luxury, and heaps of gold, were out in force to reproach him and demand that he do something about the terrible predicament they now found themselves in.

The charge was led by Balthazar Bermudez and Francisco Verdugo, the latter's coif of grey hair very much awry and bloodstained, the former uninjured – quite an achievement in itself on such a day.

'Hernán, you have deceived us,' protested Bermudez. 'I speak for all the men who sailed with Narváez when I say that if we'd known what awaited us here in Tenochtitlan, we would never have come.'

'You did know,' Cortés replied flatly. 'You were informed that the Indians had risen against the small garrison I left here while I was obliged to divert my main force to Cempoala to deal with Narváez.'

'But you gave us to believe,' Verdugo objected, 'that this rising in Tenochtitlan was a mere trifle that might be subdued by your presence alone. You spoke of the mighty emperor Moctezuma, and your control of him, and of how everything would soon be well . . .'

'As it will be, I promise you, if we can just hold our nerve. What cannot be undone, however – ' and now, suddenly, Cortés found himself very angry – 'is the *disastrous effect that your fucking expedition with Narváez has had on the whole course of the conquest.*'

Verdugo took a step back. 'It was not *my* expedition,' he hastened to explain.

Cortés wiped a gob of spittle from his cracked lips. 'Yet you joined

443

it, you supported it, you probably contributed to funding it, you took part in it, and if you'd defeated me at Cempoala you'd be quite happy to see me and all my veterans dead . . .'

'That's not true!' soothed Bermudez. 'All we're saying is – you got us into this, Caudillo, and we expect you to get us out of it.'

The temerity of the man! Cortés felt his anger rise again: 'Do you realise, *you worm*, that before the disastrous intervention of Narváez – for which I hold you personally responsible – we had dominated the Mexica by fear alone, without ever having to fight them? *We took this city without shedding any Spanish blood!* Everything could have been achieved here for God and for the King, *and achieved peacefully*, if you and others like you hadn't given Narváez, and that swine Velázquez behind him, the means to meddle.'

Cortés stepped forward, seized Bermudez by his throat with his uninjured right hand and roared in his face: '*I should fucking kill you, you little toad!*' Then, lowering his voice to a confidential hiss, he added: 'You dare to say you expect *me* to save you? Are you a child? Take responsibility for your own decisions like a man and save yourself – as we all must.'

He shoved Bermudez away and addressed the room. 'Gentlemen,' he said, 'our predicament is as it is, and there you have it. We must try to make the best of it. Our salvation lies, as it always has, in our unity, our discipline, our courage and our faith in God.'

Around midnight, Cortés called a muster to assess the cost of the day, instructing Pepillo to keep the record.

Shikotenka had already reported more than a thousand of his Tlascalans lost.

Now the count revealed that seventy-three Spaniards were missing, some confirmed dead by their comrades, others carried off alive, presumably for sacrifice. In addition, and more troublesome because they required care, and above all water, which was in extremely short supply, close to six hundred of the conquistadors had been injured, more than a hundred of them severely.

The high number of injuries was at first surprising amongst well-armoured men, but as Cortés inquired into the matter he found that a great many – indeed hundreds – had been caused by stones and rubble thrown from above.

Nor was it difficult to understand why, by contrast, the number of

Spanish dead was relatively low. Wherever possible throughout the battle it seemed that the Indian warriors had sought to grapple and capture rather than kill on the spot.

As Cortés spent the night restlessly moving around the defences, supervising the construction of a new wall to block off the breached gallery, talking to some of the real heroes amongst the injured, he continued to be haunted by the thought of those missing men.

He did not sleep, and in the morning the sacrifices began.

Chapter Twenty-One

Sunday 26 June 1520–Wednesday 29 June 1520

'It is everything we promised we'd fight to bring to an end.'

Dawn had broken, and Malinal stood with Tozi on the roof of Axayacatl's palace, transfixed by the grizzly scene unfolding at the base of the great pyramid a hundred paces to the east. Directly ahead, on the pyramid's western flank, its lower northern side blasted by cannon fire, but enough of the south side intact to give passage to the victims who would soon be climbing to their deaths, lay the wide stairway leading to the western edge of the summit platform. Because of the pyramid's immense mass and steep slope, the platform itself, on which perched the temple of Huitzilopochtli, was set back about another fifty paces eastward. It overlooked the palace but was too far off for Mexica slingers and archers to hit the roof from there, and even too far for Spanish crossbowmen and musketeers positioned on the roof to hit them.

Tozi was at Malinal's side, where she'd suddenly reappeared moments before, lean and fierce but flushed as though in a fever. 'This is the way the great plan fulfils itself,' she replied finally. There was a pompous, self-assured boom to her voice. 'Don't you see? The Spaniards *have* to die. The gods command it. It's the final sacrifice; only then can the reign of peace begin.'

Malinal felt nothing but immense sadness for her very young friend. 'No sacrifice can ever bring peace,' she said. 'Only love can do that.' She looked out over the great pyramid. 'Don't you remember, that night when we climbed, waiting our turn to reach the execution stone and die?' She gestured to the miserable huddle of thirty-eight Spaniards at the base of the steps, crying out piteously to their brothers for help, naked but for the white paper loincloths of sacrifice, their hair and scalps basted with molten rubber, into which clumps of turkey feathers had been set. 'Do you imagine that those men feel any differently from the

446

way you and I felt then, or have any less of a desire to live than you and I had then?'

'I have told you,' Tozi insisted stubbornly, 'but you refuse to listen. The Spaniards *must* die to prevent a greater sacrifice. If they're allowed to live, the time will come when they'll slaughter every man, woman and child in Tenochtitlan.'

'And how do you know this?'

'I have seen the future,' Tozi replied.

She seemed about to say more when there came a terrible groan from the conquistadors who, in the last moments, had assembled in great numbers on the roof. Below on the plaza, the aghast and stooping victims, many of them with bruises and stab wounds livid on their white skins, were being goaded to the steps by brutal Mexica guards armed with obsidian-bladed spears.

The guards were taunting them. 'The gods have delivered you at last into our hands,' one of them boasted in a loud voice as the first of the prisoners reached the steps and began to climb, the rest following in single file. 'Huitzilopochtli has long cried out for his victims. The stone of sacrifice is ready. The knives are sharpened. The wild beasts in the zoo are roaring for their offal.'

Now Namacuix, the high priest, appeared on the summit of the pyramid in front of Hummingbird's temple. 'And you false sons of Aztlán,' he roared, addressing the many Tlascalans who had also been drawn to the roof to witness the spectacle. 'Don't imagine your brothers we captured yesterday have escaped. They're a bit lean for our taste but, rest assured, we will fatten them until they make a respectable offering.'

The man at the head of the file of prisoners, now about halfway up the steps, was named Alonso de Valbuena, one of Narváez's soldiers. Malinal remembered a conversation with him on the long march from Cempoala to Tenochtitlan. He'd talked of his wife and children, left behind in Spain, and his hopes for the future.

There came a burst of arquebus fire as musketeers lining the parapet took aim at the guards forcing the prisoners upwards, and in the same instant Cortés was suddenly on the roof, his presence bringing an unmistakable frisson even before he spoke: 'What the *hell* is going on here?' He rushed to the parapet, took in the smoking muskets, the scene on the stairs: 'You're shooting at our own men?'

The prisoners were closer now than they would be when they reached the summit, but, as the smoke cleared and pathetic cries arose from the stairway, the outcome of the volley was seen. Only one guard had been hit. By some freak chance, most of the bullets had dropped amongst the Spaniards, wounding five of them, though none fatally, and they continued to be driven upwards.

'It can't be tolerated, Caudillo,' answered one of the musketeers. 'We were aiming for the guards but the range is too long.'

'Besides, sir,' said another, 'it is better our boys die at our hands from gunshots than have their hearts cut out by these devils.'

'But you haven't killed any of them,' said Cortés, looking out with disgust at the limping and bleeding victims. 'You're wasting bullets from here and only increasing their suffering. Come with me, lads! Let's make a sortie and see what we can do.'

He paused at the top of the stairs. His eye caught Malinal's and fell to Tozi. A black look settled on his face. Then he was gone, pounding down with a clatter of armour, almost all the men on the roof following.

Tozi felt deeply uncomfortable, knowing she had not told Malinal everything. For although it was true that Guatemoc was determined to kill all the Spaniards, she hadn't agreed that the means must be by human sacrifice. Let them die in battle, or by execution, she'd argued, not under the obsidian knife, and not to gratify the gods.

He'd objected there was no difference – they died either way.

She'd tried to teach him what she'd learned on her vision quests.

The offering up of lives to the gods, as the Mexica did in such huge numbers, had caused a rift in the universe and corrupted the deities, transforming them into hungry vampires who lusted after human blood. It was the deliberate magnification of terror in the sacrificial ritual that had allowed the rot to enter, and only by ending it entirely could its fatal consequences be reversed. Then, starved of fear, the demonic aspect of the gods would retreat into the shadows, and only their benign manifestations would appear to teach and inspire men. In this way the epoch of darkness that was the reign of Huitzilopochtli would end and the age of light that was the reign of Quetzalcoatl would begin.

Guatemoc had yawned, saying he had other problems to deal with – and it was true, he did. Cuitláhuac, who had taken upon himself the full authority of the Great Speaker, and who only awaited his official consecration in the coming days to be confirmed publicly in that role, had been outraged by Guatemoc's intervention on the battlefield yesterday and had required his rebellious son to keep his Chichemecs out of Tenochtitlan, as they'd previously agreed, until he himself called for him.

Would Guatemoc abide by this restriction?

Most unlikely, Tozi thought.

But at least it meant he wasn't atop the great pyramid this morning, taking a hand in the sacrifice of the miserable Spaniards now climbing to their deaths. If he had been there, she would have had to leave him, as she'd promised she would.

Beside her Malinal gasped and, directly below, emerging from the wide portico, Tozi saw a strong squadron of Spanish soldiers emerge, perhaps a hundred of them, all heavily armoured, a great mass with long lances waving above their heads, others with crossbows and muskets, surging across the plaza at a fast run. For some reason – Guatemoc would never have allowed it – the Mexica ranks were still drawn back twenty paces from the palace wall as they had been during the night, and this new manoeuvre seemed to take them so much by surprise that Cortés and his men were not at first seriously opposed as they charged towards the pyramid.

There came a great shout from the summit platform, and Tozi looked up to see that the first in the line of prisoners had reached the top and was now being spread-eagled over the execution stone. He lay absolutely still, unresisting, seemingly unafraid, gazing upward towards the heavens. Two black-robed priests, oblivious to the Spanish advance far below, stood nearby conferring with another man, very tall, wearing the purple mantle of . . . the Great Speaker! With a shock Tozi recognised Cuitláhuac, and saw him now seize the sacrificial knife, stride to the execution stone and plunge it into the Spaniard's chest.

The victim made not a sound as his heart was plucked out and cast steaming on the brazier. But the next man was different – a screamer, a pleader, a struggler – and his terror was a contagion for the others lined up waiting their turn. Some of them tried to run down the way they'd come, or break off to the side, only to be jabbed ferociously back into place by the guards. One succeeded in throwing himself off the precipitous steps, and fell tumbling and bouncing to his death – reminding Tozi with a pang that on the night she and Malinal had escaped the knife there had been a similar suicide.

Suddenly she was repulsed at herself for being on the side of the sacrificers, and remembered the hope with which she'd once greeted the arrival of the Spaniards, believing them – wrongly! oh so wrongly! – to

449

be harbingers of peace. Though she'd long since learned the truth, she couldn't in all conscience hate them now for intervening to prevent sacrifices, since this was what she'd always asked them to do, even if those they sought to save today were from amongst their own number.

She reached out and tentatively took Malinal's hand. Her friend was trembling.

Malinal did not know what to do with this new Tozi, who seemed complacent of human sacrifice, but she loved her all the same and was warmed by the pressure of her hand.

Out in the plaza her man, her hero, was fighting for his life, and for the lives of those poor Spaniards now about to be sacrificed. In the last few moments five more of them had died, Cuitláhuac finally passing the knife over to Namacuix to continue the work, and even the last man in the line was now more than two-thirds of the way up the stairs, and very far from any hope of rescue before his turn came.

Though surrounded by a howling mob of Mexica warriors, Cortés and his squad continued to move forward so rapidly, using push of pikes, that they very soon reached the base of the steps. There they met with massed resistance from a force of Cuahchics, also armed with long lances, who had the advantage of height. They defended the narrowest part of the stairway, at the base, where a large chunk of masonry had been removed by cannon fire. Meanwhile, from the palace, hundreds of other Spaniards had poured forth, and spread themselves out in an armoured cordon, challenging the Mexica ranks ahead.

For the moment, however, the two sides stood apart and there was no mass engagement.

All eyes were focused on the struggle for the pyramid where, out of the temple of Huitzilopochtli and other structures on the summit, now suddenly appeared a black cloud of warriors, thick as a swarm of ants. With a roar, a great mass of them charged down the stairs and past the few remaining victims awaiting sacrifice, to support the lancers holding back Cortés. At the same time, from the Spanish ranks, rose up a storm of crossbow bolts that smashed into the defenders, tearing a great hole in their midst which the pikemen widened and the swordsman in the van smashed through.

Now the Spaniards climbed unimpeded for a dozen steps or more, before a new squadron of warriors descended from above and once again contested the way. Malinal saw Cortés clearly, in the front rank. This morning it had not been she – for he had gone out so suddenly – but perhaps Pepillo, who had strapped his shield to his left arm and bandaged together his bloody and broken fingers around the handle. She hoped the job had been done well, and that the bindings would hold long enough for him to survive the fight – for even from here it was obvious he was in the thick of a ferocious melee, taking massive blows on his shield from a huge warrior above him wielding a club; but now, with a crafty lunge, Cortés cut the man's legs from under him, so that he was instantly trampled beneath the onrushing armoured mass of the Spaniards.

Malinal wanted to cheer, but when Tozi beside her said, 'They are devils', she knew she wasn't referring to the Mexica.

'They are the very same devils,' Malinal again felt compelled to remind her friend, 'who stopped human sacrifices on the great pyramid entirely, who rededicated the temple of Hummingbird to their own god—'

'Ha! Their own cruel and murderous god who demands that those who do not believe in him be burned to death. We should stick with our own gods, Malinal. If we become better people and deny them sacrifices, then they will become better gods.'

With Cortés's squadron fighting its way upwards and still twenty steps from the summit, the last of the captives was spread hurriedly over the execution stone, his heart cut out, his head hacked off and carried into the temple, his limbs butchered and set aside for later consumption, and his torso added to the mound of Spanish carcases piled up at the top of the steps.

Malinal knew what was coming next and she felt Tozi tense beside her as a gang of black-robed priests, their long, tangled hair matted with blood, got their shoulders against the heap and shoved. There was a moment of stasis, much grunting and yelling and then, with a horrible rumble, clearly audible from the palace roof, the gruesome remains tumbled amongst the ascending Spaniards, scattering them and exposing them to a flight of arrows that felled three in the blink of an eye.

Malinal heard Cortés's harsh commands as he at once forced the men back into order and fought to resume the ascent.

And now a new Mexica tactic. Huge tree trunks that must have been hauled up to the summit platform during the night by the eastern stairway – out of sight of the palace of Axayacatl – were brought forward to the lip of the western stairway and cast down upon the Spaniards. It would have been devastating if the logs had rolled sideways, as was certainly intended, sweeping the Spaniards off the full width of the steps, but instead, a miracle! Both turned on end and slid past the conquistadors, missing them entirely but gaining momentum, finally bounding into the air as they approached the plaza, cartwheeling and smashing down on the front ranks of a grim throng of Mexica troops – more than two thousand of them, Malinal thought – who'd quietly assembled at the base of the western stairway to cut off any Spanish retreat to the palace.

That was when, right at the edge of vision, she saw that fresh hordes of Mexica warriors had swarmed into the plaza and had begun to climb the northern and southern stairways of the great pyramid, with more, no doubt, ascending the eastern stairway out of sight from the palace roof.

Malinal called out 'Trap!' just as Cortés, with Alvarado the slayer to his right, and brave, dependable Díaz to his left, smashed their way through the last Mexica defenders at the top of the western stairway. The rest of the squad followed with a yell of 'Santiago and at them!' and overran the summit platform, some of them, including Cortés, rushing into the temple, many raising a great lament around the sacrificial stone, others seizing and binding two of the black-robed sacrificial priests who'd been caught before they could flee. One of the pair was Namacuix, the other his deputy. But of Cuitláhuac there was no sign.

'Trap!' Malinal screamed again, and again the warning went unheeded. By now, thank God – inadvertently she crossed herself – Ordaz had seen the danger and ordered a huge squad of five hundred men, bristling with pikes, to advance on the pyramid and harry the Mexica in the plaza, still leaving a cordon of four hundred to defend the palace.

The distance between the base of the great pyramid on its west side and the east wall of Axayacatl's palace was just a hundred paces, and the Spaniards were so many and so well prepared for battle today, despite the fearful beating they'd taken yesterday, that they rapidly cleared and held the ground, opened a wide, well-defended cordon between the palace doors and the western stairway, and sent a mixed force of fifty pikemen and fifty skirmishing swordsmen racing up the steps to hack into the mass of Mexica who'd gathered there to deny the Spanish retreat and who now found themselves suddenly under deadly assault from behind.

'What's the point?' Tozi asked. 'I understand their attempt to rescue their comrades, but they've failed and now there's just more slaughter.'

Her inner turmoil was growing, roiling like a hurricane. No matter how hard she tried, she couldn't reconcile her love for Guatemoc, a man who was devoted to sacrifice, with her love for Malinal who hated it, and also with her own strong convictions on the matter. Likewise, she couldn't reconcile her own hatred of the Spaniards, and her absolute certainty that they would bring doom to the One World if they were allowed to remain here, with Malinal's cloying love for them, which caused her to see only the good and none of the bad.

'They haven't failed!' her friend exclaimed now. 'They've succeeded! They've showed the Mexica they won't tolerate human sacrifice and that they're prepared to die themselves to prevent it.'

'But don't you see how crazy that is?' Tozi protested. 'Death to prevent death?'

'There's nothing crazy about cheating the gods of these vile offerings,' Malinal replied. 'That's the very cause that brought us together.'

Tozi could think of no suitable response, so she just stood there on the roof, breathing in Malinal's heady scent, with her eyes locked on the struggle between worlds, between realms, between realities, unfolding on the great pyramid. Cortés and others who'd run into Hummingbird's temple now burst forth again, alerted by calls from Ordaz's bugler and the shouts of their comrades. Some reverently cradled the severed heads of recently sacrificed Spaniards but, seeing the new danger now confronting them, they cast these down and in an instant fell into rank for the descent of the western stairway. Others had seized the high priest Namacuix and his deputy – they would make useful hostages – hurrying them into the midst of their column.

For the first dozen steps on the way down they were unopposed, and then the solid mass of Mexica ascending from the plaza hit them at a run. A great fight began in which the long lances the Mexica had cleverly equipped themselves with today – clearly they were not *all* idiots as Guatemoc maintained – were confronted by the long lances of the Spaniards.

It was an unequal struggle.

The conquistadors had the momentum of descent as well as the advantage of fighting from an elevated position, and they were all armoured from head to toe in metal. The Mexica had all the disadvantages, fighting from a lower elevation, struggling up a steep slope, unarmoured, and evidently lacking the skill and coordination in the manipulation of the lances that the Spaniards effortlessly demonstrated.

453

Worse, the other block of Spaniards climbing from the plaza had now reached the Mexica rearguard and begun to hack their way through it with terrible speed and efficiency. Simultaneously, however, a few dozen paces higher up, the Spanish rearguard also came under powerful attack as a new tide of Mexica warriors foamed over the lip of the summit platform and down the western stairway to engulf the retreating conquistadors.

For a moment they were surrounded, above and below, and even down the steep, glassy sides of the pyramid beyond the stairway, by countless attackers, so numerous that they seethed like flies upon a carcass. Tozi felt Malinal stiffen beside her as the Spanish column all but disappeared, then heave a sigh of relief as Cortés came into view again, fighting with demonic strength, smashing his shield into the face of the man ahead of him, bringing down his sword on the neck of another. Tonatiuh, who'd slain the sorcerer Acopol, was beside him, cutting a red path, and it seemed obvious to Tozi then that such great warriors would never be stopped by the Mexica under Cuitláhuac's insipid leadership.

Only Guatemoc had been touched by the gods, and with him alone lay all hope for the defence and renewal of the One World.

If he were here today, Tozi felt sure, he would have devised a strategy to foil the killing machine of whirling blades and plunging lances on the western stair as Cortés and his men, fighting their way down, reached the second group of Spaniards fighting their way up, slaughtered the last of the Mexica who'd got between them and, with a triumphant shout, joined forces. Now, while their crossbowmen and musketeers poured withering volleys into the far larger numbers of Mexica who continued to stream down from above, a clear route of escape lay before them through a heavily armed cordon all the way to the palace doors.

Very rapidly and efficiently, though surrounded on all sides and under a continuous barrage of arrows, spears and sling-stones, the Spaniards began their withdrawal through this cordon.

Tozi turned to Malinal. 'Looks like your man will survive,' she said.

A shrug: 'He always does.'

'But you must know he can't win here! The Mexica will never permit it. Guatemoc will never permit it. I won't permit it!'

'Cortés does not simply do that which is permitted, like other men. He does that which is not permitted. You may do your worst, you and Guatemoc. See if you can defeat Cortés! You will find it can't be done!'

'It *can* be done, Malinal, and it will be done. Please at least let me get you out of the city. Coyotl and Miahuatl too. No need for those poor children to suffer what's going to happen here.'

Malinal didn't immediately answer her. When finally she spoke, her voice was small, barely audible. 'Remember yesterday that there was something I wanted to tell you but you didn't stay to hear it?'

'I was angry with you,' Tozi said.

'Do you want to hear it now?'

Tozi wasn't sure she did. She'd resisted reading her friend's mind, but sensed there was a sharp edge to this news, whistling towards her like a blade. Her instinct was to duck and weave. Instead she said: 'Tell me.'

'I carry the child of Cortés in my womb.'

Tozi's head swam. 'How long?' she breathed.

'About two months . . . I haven't kept careful count.' A wan smile: 'It's exciting, isn't it? That I will be a mother?'

Below, as the last of the Spaniards made their escape through the cordon, the Mexica squadrons in the plaza followed them, pressing them close, the action rapidly escalating into a full-scale assault on the palace and its defenders.

On Monday 27 June, the day after the battle at the great pyramid, with almost all of his men now injured and with the supply of drinking water so critically limited that everyone was thirsty, all the time, Cortés was forced to withdraw the squad of four hundred he'd intended to keep permanently posted in the plaza. The attacks upon them, and all along the palace façade, had become so intense, so heated and so sustained that the men would have been overrun if he'd waited a moment longer. Even so, more than twenty were lost in the pell-mell retreat, and the entire east wall of the palace was again subject to direct assault and attempts to burn it, undermine it and batter a way through it.

Learning a thing or two from the Indian way of warfare, the Spaniards on the roof of Axayacatl's palace greeted the enemy sappers, engineers and demolition crews approaching the wall with showers of stones and rubble thrown down upon them in great quantities. The technique proved as effective against the Mexica as it had against the Spaniards. Nonetheless, as a further deterrent against encroachment, Cortés took the risky step – risky because it might cause the whole building to collapse – of having his stonemasons and carpenters cut and then reinforce ten embrasures in the wall at ground level, facing east across the plaza towards the great pyramid. Three falconets had been saved from the rout on Saturday, and seven more of the deadly little cannon, part of the armoury Alvarado had been left with in May, were still within the palace. So it was these ten guns, loaded with grapeshot, that went into the embrasures. Just the tips of their barrels pointed forth when they fired, and swordsmen were assigned to stand each side of each gun as they were drawn back to reload. The embrasures were too narrow for the enemy to take by storm; they could slip through them in ones and twos but were easily killed by the swordsmen.

Despite the additional slaughter worked by the cannon, there was no let-up throughout the whole of the day in the scale or the ferocity of the Mexica attacks, and when there were lulls the warriors taunted the Spaniards. One, with the loud voice of a herald, was frequently heard and was particularly eloquent and insulting. Malinal translated his latest tirade for Cortés: 'Defend yourselves well, Spaniards! You have need to. Were it not for your fire-serpents, that palace you cower in would by this time have been destroyed, and yourselves cooked, though you would not have been eaten; for we tried your flesh yesterday and it tasted bitter, so we should have thrown your carcasses to the eagles, pumas and snakes, which would have eaten you for us.'

'Filthy heathen,' commented Alvarado, who was listening in.

But the Mexica wasn't finished. 'All the same, if you don't free Moctezuma soon, you'll be properly killed and cooked with chocolate. We shall do this because you seized our Moctezuma and touched him with your filthy hands, Moctezuma who was our lord and God.'

'I note the use of the past tense,' Cortés said to Malinal. 'Moctezuma who *was* their lord? So that's pretty much official then? Cuitláhuac's the Great Speaker and Mucktey's been deposed?'

'Yes. That's how it is.'

'But surely they still retain some affection for Mucktey? Some respect? Surely his word must still count for something with them? After all, they seem to want him freed.'

'They're tricky,' Malinal sighed wearily. 'They're liars and deceivers and they can't be trusted. What do you have in mind?'

Cortés turned to Alvarado. 'You got him up on to the roof, didn't you? When you were hard pressed?'

'It was the fifth of June or thereabouts. I had him speak to the people. Didn't think it would make any difference, but it worked like a magic charm. All he had to do was tell them to stop fighting and they stopped.'

456

'Do you think it'll work again?' Cortés asked Malinal.

'Honestly, no, Hernán. Things have changed. It's as Shikotenka told you. Cuitláhuac is leading the attack on us now, and Moctezuma no longer holds any power.'

'I'm going to give it a try anyway,' Cortés said, as sounds of renewed fighting struck home to the depths of the palace. 'We can't take much more of this battering. Come with me, Malinal. You too, Pepillo, but first go and find Olmedo and bring him with you. He's always got along well with Mucktey and his presence will be soothing.'

All the fine cloths and soft furnishings from Mucktey's apartments had been commandeered for the makeshift hospital, and the echoing suite of rooms that he'd occupied since being taken hostage in November had a sad, desolate and abandoned air – as did the man himself, Olmedo decided.

For the Great Speaker, once a towering and terrifying figure, had truly collapsed as a personality since the friar had last seen him in early May.

But that, of course, had been before the Toxcatl massacre, before the Narváez episode, before this latest bout of horror in Tenochtitlan and – the decisive point – before Cuitláhuac had been seen during yesterday's battle for the great pyramid, not only directing operations and performing sacrifices, but also wearing the formal mantle of office of the Great Speaker.

Cortés, in a rage after the fighting, had taken the decision that Moctezuma should be informed of all this, and the whole story would certainly also have reached him through his own network of informants as well. One therefore didn't have to be a genius to work out the main reason for Mucktey's present self-pitying funk. He had been replaced, made obsolete, and rendered utterly impotent by his own despised younger brother. No wonder his spirits were low!

Olmedo felt compassion for the man who had agreed to speak only through him, who, in his fatally injured dignity, was presently refusing even to acknowledge that Cortés was in the room, and yet whose entire concern was with Cortés.

'What more does Malinche want from me?' Moctezuma now asked, pointedly addressing the friar but nonetheless waiting while Malinal gave the translation. 'I neither wish to live nor listen to his sweet words, to such a pass has my fate brought me because of him.'

'You can continue to speak with me,' Olmedo said, 'and you know I'll lend you a sympathetic ear. But here's what is required of you. You must allow us to escort you upstairs to the roof, Excellency, and there you must address the warriors of the Mexica who are even now attacking the palace in huge numbers, and you must order them to end their war against us.'

Moctezuma made the face of a man who has tasted something foul. 'I believe I shall not be useful at all for stopping this war,' he said, 'for they have already raised up another lord and are determined that you should not leave this place alive, therefore I believe that all of you will have to die.'

'Come, that will not be necessary,' Olmedo objected, 'for if all of we Spaniards have to die, you can be assured that many thousands of the Mexica, and you yourself, Moctezuma, will also have to die, and that the lord Malinche will destroy your city entirely, regardless of its beauty, leaving not a stone standing upon a stone.'

'Thousands have already died,' said Moctezuma in a sepulchral voice, 'the city is already destroyed and I myself am already dead.'

'Even so, for the sake of peace, can you not, once more, ascend to the roof and speak to your warriors and require them to desist their attacks upon us and give us safe passage? If they do, because of the great love he bears you, and because he does not wish to see Tenochtitlan destroyed, the lord Malinche authorises me to say that we Spaniards will quit the city forthwith and without further dispute.'

Only after much further persuasion, in which Pepillo and Malinal also joined, did Moctezuma agree, but when he did so it was with a sudden boyish joy. 'Very well, then, I will try it!' he said. 'I shall wear my robes of proclamation . . .'

The clash and clamour of battle, the crash of battering rams and hammers, the bark of the muskets, the roar of the cannon, the war cries of the Mexica, the hoarse shouts of the Spanish soldiers, the rumble of rocks thrown from the roof, the screams of those they fell amongst – all these sounds of war and danger contrasted peculiarly with the scene of Moctezuma in his dressing room, preening and primping. His valet had long since fled the palace, so Pepillo did the honours of helping him into the splendid imperial robe that was traditionally worn by the Great Speaker when he issued a proclamation to his people.

'Does it look well on me?' Moctezuma asked, as Pepillo draped the white and blue *tilmatli* about his shoulders and fastened its rich turquoise-inlaid clasp.

'Magnificent, Your Highness.'

The robe, which fell almost to Moctezuma's golden sandals, was studded with large emeralds set in gold. Pepillo did not doubt that Cortés, who was looking on, was assessing their value.

'Now your headdress, sire? Which shall it be?'

'Only the *copilli* is suitable for an occasion such as this.' Moctezuma pointed – 'That one, with the *quetzal* feathers.'

Pepillo fetched the massive but surprisingly light contraption, which somewhat resembled a papal mitre. Upon it, in the deep crosswise cleft between the two peaks, was mounted a spectacular fan of blue *cotinga* and brilliant green *quetzal* feathers, with sewn-on gold detailing.

Reaching up, Pepillo set the *copilli* on Moctezuma's head.

'Is the effect impressive, do you think?' the monarch asked.

'You look, sire, as you are – a great king about to address his people.'

A squirm of anxiety twisted Moctezuma's smooth features. 'I fear my people will reject me, Pepillo. Such humiliation will be more than I can bear, but I do this – ' he turned at last to Cortés – 'out of the great love I bear for Malinche and in the hope that further bloodshed and suffering may yet be avoided . . . Shall we go? I am ready.'

With that, Moctezuma swept from the room. Waiting in the hallway was an escort of half a dozen conquistadors. They were bruised and battered, these men, from days of fighting and constant danger, short of food, almost no water. They each carried spears, and big *adarga* shields.

'I'm assigning these soldiers to protect you while you address your people,' Cortés told Moctezuma. 'Sling-stones and arrows from the plaza can reach the roof where you'll be standing and there may be some out there who wish you dead.'

As Malinal gave the translation, Moctezuma's face twisted again. 'My people wish me dead?' he asked.

His tone was that of a man who has never before considered such a possibility, yet, upon doing so, has found it to be entirely realistic.

In a time of chaos there is a need for order.

Cuitláhuac was doing well, within his limits – far better than Guatemoc had ever imagined he would; he was minded, for the moment at least, to allow his father to remain in the position of Great Speaker. After the costly but interesting and instructive intervention two days before, he'd agreed to keep his little army of Opata Chichemecs out of the battle until Cuitláhuac himself called for them.

That did not mean, however, that he, Guatemoc, a prince of the blood, must abjure the fighting. After Cuitláhuac had exhausted his rage at the unauthorised intervention, he suddenly and surprisingly reached out to Guatemoc and wrapped him in a heartfelt embrace. 'I know we haven't seen eye to eye in the past,' his father said, 'but I embrace you and welcome you now as my beloved son and heir. We need your military genius, Guatemoc. But we need it in a planned and coordinated way. For this reason I am giving you command of a special regiment I've assembled, composed entirely of eagle knights and jaguar knights. I invite you, my son, to take this regiment and join our fight against Malinche and let us do everything in our power to destroy him and that evil witch Malinal, after whom he is named.'

Ha! thought Guatemoc. *Witch! If you think Malinal's a witch, wait until you meet Tozi.* For he had told his father nothing about his strange new lover.

'She had a consort,' Cuitláhuac continued. 'A filthy little beggar girl. The night Malinal was to be sacrificed, she was there. They climbed the steps to the execution stone together. Moctezuma was performing the sacrifices but then the madness came and he released them both. He said that Hummingbird himself had intervened to spare them, but I know the truth. Malinal wrapped him in her web of illusion. She deceived him with her sorcery . . .'

Guatemoc knew the story well, for he had heard it not only rumoured around Tenochtitlan in the months after it happened, but also later, and in a great deal more detail, from Tozi herself. He had shared none of this with his father. Some things were best left unsaid.

So Guatemoc had accepted command of his newly assigned regiment of eagle and jaguar knights and had spent the entire day attempting a variety of assaults and strategies against Axayacatl's palace and the Spaniards entrenched within it. But in their armour, and behind their battlements and earthworks, hastily erected where walls had been destroyed, they continued to be extremely difficult to kill.

Around noon, using his hand-sling, he had brought down an archer – often the simplest weapons were the best! The Spaniard had been shooting and killing all morning from the shelter of a balcony overlooking the plaza, picking off men one at a time. Guatemoc had waited his moment, whirled the leather sling around his head and let loose, hitting his target on the brow, causing him to tumble from the balcony to the paving, where his broken body still lay amidst heaps of rubble earlier thrown from the roof to prevent an attempt to batter down a section of the palace wall.

The second Spaniard killed that day had been one of the defenders on the roof, hit by a lucky arrow fired this afternoon by a man from another regiment. The arrow slipped through a gap in the Spaniard's throat armour and drew a great burst of blood as he fell. The kill could not absolutely be confirmed, but it was most unlikely that he would survive.

And that was it! Two Spaniards, and one of those not definite, had died throughout this whole long day, while the Mexica had paid a vastly heavier price – many hundreds amongst the attacking regiments had lost their lives or been maimed during the three direct frontal assaults they'd attempted against the palace with ladders, battering rams and fire. It was the enemy's carriage-mounted guns, bearing directly on the plaza through holes smashed in the palace walls, that had done most of the damage. Inspection of the dead had revealed that these guns fired a mass of small metal balls, which spread out across a wide area on leaving the barrel, mowing down huge numbers of men.

In Guatemoc's view any further such attacks against such weapons would be equally fruitless and costly in life. A far better solution, though it affronted his warrior pride, was simply to blockade the bastards in the palace so tightly that not a man could sneak out, and then . . . just wait. Soon hunger and thirst would kill them or weaken them so greatly that their resistance would crumble.

The sun was setting in a sky filled with smoke – for parts of the palace were still smouldering, though the Spaniards had succeeded in extinguishing the flames with heaps of earth. The effect was to transform what might, at other times, have been the first pink blush of evening into a wound in heaven, lurid and threatening, seeping blood.

The day's fighting was over – although, defying the open mouths of the cannon and the ever-present danger of rubble thrown down from the roof, the Mexica front line was still close to the palace walls. It was time to learn lessons and put them into practice so, that evening, Guatemoc resolved, he would sit at dinner with his father and advise patience, not impetuosity. It would be quite a reversal of their normal roles – but these were not normal times; the old order of things was everywhere being upended. After blooding his Chichemecs two days before, and learning something of the Spaniards' arms and way of battle, Guatemoc knew them to be a very serious, very deadly enemy, unlike any the Mexica had ever confronted. Nonetheless they were men, not gods. They ate food, they drank water, and time would kill them just as effectively as weapons.

He was about to issue the order to draw his regiment back the usual twenty paces for the night when a great gasp went through the crowd. Looking up, somewhat silhouetted against the setting sun, a feather headdress came into view beyond the battlements on the roof. The wearer of the headdress was hidden by a merlon but, as he progressed towards the next crenel, he became briefly visible from head to waist.

Dressed in the full ceremonial regalia worn by the Great Speaker when important pronouncements were to be made, it was none other than Moctezuma! Was he there against his will? No knife or spear was held to his throat, but behind him, gazing around watchfully, came an escort of six Spanish shield-bearers.

The little party now advanced to the widest of the crenels, midway along the battlements, an overlook that in the old days Moctezuma's late father Axayacatl himself had used for pronouncements. There Moctezuma paused, gazing down at the ocean of his warriors lapping against the palace walls.

Unthinking and obsequious mental slaves to the aura of power that even now surrounded the monarch like a nimbus, many prostrated themselves, or bent the knee. But those of Guatemoc's regiment were not amongst them, and he quietly ordered a dozen of his archers and a dozen of his slingers to stand with him and be ready.

Complete, unbroken silence had fallen all across the plaza and, after one nervous clearing of his throat, Moctezuma addressed the crowd in a loud, clear and commanding voice. Standing back from the parapet's edge, Malinal whispered the translation to Cortés and the assembled Spaniards.

'Why do I see my people here in arms against the palace of my fathers?' Moctezuma asked in what Cortés took to be fine rhetorical style. 'Is it that you think your sovereign a prisoner, and wish to release him? If so, you have acted rightly. But you are mistaken. I am no prisoner. The Spaniards are my guests. I remain with them only from choice, and can leave them when I wish. Have you come to drive them from the city? That is unnecessary. They will depart of their own accord if you will open a way for them. Return to your homes then. Lay down your arms. Show your obedience to me who have a right to it. The white men shall go back to their own land; and all shall be well again within the walls of Tenochtitlan.'

Two Mexica nobles, formerly favourites of Moctezuma, stepped forward from the crowd and one of them addressed the monarch. 'Oh Great Sovereign,' he said, and his tone, Malinal confirmed, was genuinely sorrowful, 'please know how all your misfortunes and injuries afflict us. Nonetheless, we are obliged to inform you that we have raised one of your kinsmen, your revered brother Cuitláhuac, to be our lord now. And while we hear and respect your words, oh great Moctezuma, it is also our sad duty to tell you what the gods demand, which is that we continue this war until every one of the Spaniards is dead. We pray daily to Hummingbird to guard you free and safe from the Spaniards' power, and when this war ends in our favour, be sure that we will hold you in higher regard than we did before.'

At this there came a gruff yell of protest from the crowd: '*What is that which is being said by that scoundrel of Moctezuma, whore of the Spaniards, and these other whores who soothe him with soft words?*' The speaker, a splendid young warrior wearing the uniform of a jaguar knight, leapt out of the ranks and swept his helmet off his head, allowing his long black hair to fall to his shoulders, showing his face clearly.

'Who's that?' Cortés asked.

'It's Prince Guatemoc,' Malinal replied. Cortés issued an immediate order to a musketeer to shoot him.

'*You have the soul of a woman,*' Guatemoc addressed Moctezuma directly, '*and you have abandoned your empire out of fright. We'll never obey you because you're no longer our monarch.*' So saying, with incredible speed, he produced a hand-sling from behind his back, whirled it round his head and let fly at Moctezuma, the round, egg-shaped stone smacking into the deposed monarch's right temple with a tremendous *clunk*. Even as his knees went out from under him and he began to fall, two other slingshots and an arrow fired by Guatemoc's little squad also hit him, and a general rain of stones, arrows and *atlatl* darts poured down upon the Spaniards on the roof, causing the shield-bearers to scatter back, the musketeers to miss their aim and all present to seek shelter.

When the storm ceased, Moctezuma was found prostrate and comatose, with a massive bloody bruise darkening his temple, another the crown of his head where his beautiful *copilli* had been knocked loose, and a third his shin. The arrow that had hit him had penetrated his right shoulder, not very deeply, and Dr La Peña removed it on the spot before the limp body of the broken emperor was carried down from the roof and into the quiet of his apartments, where he was laid out upon his bed, seemingly a corpse were it not for the tiniest rise and fall of his chest and the faint wheeze of his breath.

'Oh dear,' said Olmedo. 'It looks very much as though we're about to lose our hostage.'

'Hostage?' answered Cortés. 'He's no hostage if his people don't want him. I'm tempted just to finish him off now.'

'Please do not do that,' said Olmedo quietly. 'It gains us nothing and will not sit well with God.'

They left Moctezuma under the eye of Pepillo, who was to call Dr La Peña if there was any obvious deterioration in his condition.

'I'd like to show you something,' Olmedo said to Cortés once they were out in the hallway. 'You, too, Malinal; it's important you know about this.'

'I have many other matters that demand my attention,' Cortés objected. 'Can it wait?'

'No, Hernán. It's urgent. It has implications. You must take this into consideration now.'

'Take what into consideration?'

'A smallpox epidemic has begun today amongst our men. It shows every sign of ravaging them.'

'Oh that!' said Cortés. 'It started in Cempoala. I wouldn't use the word *ravaging* to describe some fevers and a few pustules. Most of the men aren't affected at all.'

'I'm not referring to Spaniards, Hernán. I am speaking of our Tlascalan allies. I have been discussing the matter with La Peña, and he and I are agreed that the first signs of smallpox usually appear between eight and twelve days after encountering an infected individual. There are variations, some longer, some shorter, but that is the norm.

'We arrived in Tlascala on the afternoon of the fourteenth of June and we left on the seventeenth of June. Today is the twenty-seventh of June and the first signs of infection – very severe ones – appeared amongst our Tlascalan allies this morning. Eight have already died. More than thirty are in the sick room. Most likely they contracted it from our Totonac bearers on the fifteenth or sixteenth of June while we rested in Tlascala. There was much mixing and dancing between Tlascalans and

Totonacs then and, though I am sure you have not had time to notice, most of our Totonacs have since perished. We can safely say that the disease will take the same course amongst the Tlascalans as it has amongst the Totonacs – in other words, everyone amongst them whom it infects will certainly die.'

The makeshift hospital was already filled with groaning Spaniards and Tlascalans, whose injuries in the battles of Saturday and Sunday still incapacitated them. This was not where the smallpox victims were being kept. La Peña had insisted that their sickroom be separate, and had co-opted a large, windowless store in a near-deserted wing of the palace for the purpose.

Olmedo paused before opening the door. 'It is not a pretty sight,' he said, 'but you need to understand what we're dealing with.'

Cortés had spoken to Malinal frequently of hell, the place in the Christian religion, corresponding somewhat to Mictlan, to which the souls of the wicked were consigned after death. And just as there were tortures and ordeals to be faced on the soul's passage to Mictlan – flesh-scraping knives, clashing mountains, ferocious jaguars, a river of blood – so too the Christian hell was filled with torment and suffering.

This terrible room, into which Olmedo had brought Cortés and Malinal, seemed to her the perfect vision of hell. Blazing torches set into brackets on the wall reminded her of the fires Cortés had described that consumed the damned, while the damned themselves lay everywhere before her eyes: some groaning, some crying out in delirium, some lying on soiled mats, some crumpled on the floor amongst the pools of blood, vomit and faeces that lay scattered about everywhere.

Suddenly one of the Tlascalans staggered to his feet and into the full glare of the torches. He wore only a filthy loincloth, so Malinal could not avoid seeing the weeping pustules that covered his entire body and face, swelling his eyes almost closed, eating at his lips.

And then she recognised the smashed teeth behind the lips.

'Chipahua!' she said. 'Is it you?'

'Quite a pretty sight, aren't I?' Shikotenka's trusted lieutenant replied. 'Dying for your fucking lover . . .' He turned to Cortés and spat. 'Dying of your demon disease.'

While he'd spoken, Malinal noticed, Olmedo had quietly stepped in front of her, partly obscuring her view of Chipahua. Now, gently but firmly, even as she gave the translation, he pushed her back towards the door.

The Tlascalan was still raving. 'So cunning, you Spaniards – to summon disease demons that spare you and kill only the peoples of Aztlán. How did you do it, eh? What price did you pay?'

From the doorway Malinal gave the translation. When she was done, as though he'd been waiting for her to finish, Chipahua doubled over, groaned and vomited copiously on the floor.

'Come on,' said Olmedo. 'I think we've seen enough. Let's get out of here.'

Only when they were in the corridor did Cortés wipe Chipahua's spittle from his face. 'I had a dose of smallpox when I was a child,' he said. 'Just as well, or I'd be a dead man walking now.'

That night, for the first time since November, Saint Peter appeared to Cortés again in a dream.

The previous encounter had been very strange, for in it he had seen the Holy Father briefly assume the general form of the monstrous demons worshipped by the Mexica, perhaps even of Huitzilopochtli himself – slouching and misshapen, coarse-featured, great fangs and tusks sprouting from his mouth, a necklace of human hands and hearts around his neck.

The little spy Tozi had also appeared in the same dream. She'd taken the form of a winged angel and the saint had fled before her.

But now the rock on whom Christ had built his church was back, striding through Cortés's dream in his more familiar form as a tall and robust man, clean-shaven and fair-haired, perhaps forty years old, dressed in a simple hemp tunic and yet, as ever, projecting an unassailable aura of charisma and authority.

Cortés found that he was standing in a grassy meadow, with a brook of sparkling water bubbling nearby. 'Well met,' said Saint Peter, 'for I have come to strengthen your hand in your fight against the Mexica.'

Cortés fell to his knees: 'Holy Father, you are generous. I fear our struggle to expand the kingdom of God goes badly here. Tell me what I must do.'

'You must ensure the Mexica are infected with smallpox.'

Even in his dream, Cortés was puzzled. 'But we can't hold out much longer, Father. They'll overrun us before the disease can harm them.'

'I said I would strengthen your hand, not save you in Tenochtitlan. Your mission in this land is not over yet, my son, but in the next year, I promise, you will see the fruits of my counsel.'

'Most likely the Mexica have already been infected, Holy Father. They've captured some of our Tlascalans and are fattening them for sacrifice, so there will have been contact.'

'You have failed to listen to me carefully, Hernán. I said *you* must *ensure* the Mexica contract smallpox. It's not good enough if it's just *likely* they will – even if it is *most likely*. For the disease to spread with its full virulence as I intend, it must be energised by malice, intent and cunning. That's why I require you personally to be involved if I'm to make this plague a weapon for you. Do you agree?'

'Yes, Holy Father, I agree, and with all my heart.'

'Good.' The saint laid a reassuring hand upon Cortés's head: 'Then this is what you must do.'

Before dawn, Cortés was awake. Taking Malinal to translate, he went straight to Shikotenka.

The Tlascalan leader didn't like the idea, but came round to it when Cortés convinced him that all his infected men would die anyway, not in the glory of battle, but in the agony and dishonour of a hideously disfiguring disease. 'I'll put it to Chipahua,' the battle-king had said. 'I think he'll agree.'

On leaving Shikotenka's quarters on the morning of Tuesday 28 June, Cortés dismissed Malinal, whose mood had become burdensome to him. 'I hate this ungodly plan,' she told him in the hallway.

'Nothing ungodly about it,' Cortés replied. 'Sometimes we have to be cruel to be kind, but it will further God's work here. You'll see.'

Malinal merely shrugged and walked off along the hallway.

What on earth is the matter with the woman? Cortés thought.

He suspected the influence of her friend Tozi, with whom he'd seen her just before the battle for the pyramid on Sunday, but put the problem out of his mind as he made a complete circuit of the defences of the palace. There were no new breaches, the sentries were alert, and outside in the plaza the sullen regiments of the Mexica remained camped, their front line some twenty paces back from the palace walls, showing no inclination either to attack or to withdraw.

Just waiting, Cortés thought. *Patiently. As a cat waits for a bird.*

He laughed. *But today they're going to catch much more than they've bargained for!*

By ten in the morning he'd reached the roof, the final station on his rounds, and there he found Malinal, once again in the company of the spy Tozi. Immediately his mood darkened, for he did not like the part this peculiar young woman had played against Saint Peter in his dream, he did not like her influence on Malinal, and he did not like that she had absconded for many months, without his permission, and had now returned equally without a by-your-leave.

Bizarrely, both women were crying as Cortés strode up. 'What's this about?' he barked.

'Nothing of importance to you,' Malinal answered with defiance in her tone.

Somehow her tear-streaked face angered him. It was only with difficulty that he restrained himself from striking her and turned his fury on Tozi instead.

'You!' he said. 'What do you think you're doing, skulking around our defences again? You spied for us once. Maybe you're spying for the other side now.'

'*Stop it, Hernán!*' Malinal shouted.

She was really angry, Cortés realised, for she rarely raised her voice. But then he was angry, too, dammit! Alvarado was looking on, Sandoval and Ordaz also, and at least twenty of the men. He simply could not allow his mistress and her little friend to show him up in so public a place.

'I want to know who she's working for,' Cortés insisted. 'Is she on the side of the Mexica or on our side? Put the question to her.'

Malinal spoke for some moments in Nahuatl and Tozi replied.

'She says she's not on our side and not on their side either. I've told you, Hernán, she comes and goes as she pleases.'

'Good! But if she wishes to continue to do so, then I require her to spy upon the Mexica for us. I have a mission for her this very night.' Seeing Malinal's hesitation, he barked: 'Translate what I said!'

Again a lilting exchange followed in Nahuatl, and at one point Tozi laughed as she gave her answer.

'What's she saying?' Cortés demanded.

'You will not like it, Hernán. Shall we go inside, where we're not under the eyes of so many?'

'No! I want to hear it now.'

'Then it is this, Hernán. Tozi says that she will not spy for you upon the Mexica because, although the Mexica are bad, you are worse, and she says she will continue to come and go as she pleases and you won't be able to stop her.'

'Oh really!' Cortés was stunned by the answer. 'We'll see about that.'

He turned to Sandoval: 'Gonzalo! Bring two men at the double and arrest this little bitch.'

Tozi was already backing away.

'No you don't,' Cortés said. He ran to take hold of her but then – the strangest thing! Just when he thought he had her, the air around her shimmered and . . . she was gone!

He blinked. There were gasps from the men. What had happened made no sense, and what happened next even less so – because, suddenly, Alvarado's quillon dagger was snatched from its sheath and seemed to float through the air, moving so fast that it reached Cortés before he could react. The point came to rest against his throat and made a deliberate nick, drawing a trickle of blood. The dagger was then cast to the ground, a girl's voice, coming, it seemed, from nowhere, said a few words in Nahuatl, there was that mocking laugh again, and then only the stunned silence of the soldiery.

'What did she say?' asked Cortés.

'She said that she can kill you any time she likes,' Malinal replied, 'but she does not do so for my sake.'

Even as she spoke, the palace doors could be heard opening below, and Cortés broke away to peer down over the battlements. A moment later, as Shikotenka had promised, a file of Tlascalans emerged from under the portico. Naked but for loincloths and the simple maguey-fibre caps that marked them as devotees of the god Nanahuatzin, the suppurating pustules covering their bodies and faces were obvious to all. Though many were stumbling and obviously weak, each was armed with a good *macuahuitl* and a shield, and each would have been persuaded by Shikotenka that it was better to die a warrior's death, or on the stone of sacrifice, than by the teeth of this hideous new disease.

'*Oh Mexica*,' called out a firm, commanding voice from below. Looking down, Malinal saw that Shikotenka himself had emerged from the portico and stood behind the squad of Tlascalans. '*These twenty young warriors, whom Nanahuatzin has marked as his own, wish to offer themselves to you for sacrifice to the gods.*'

'What's he saying?' demanded Cortés. 'Is it as we agreed?'

'It's as we agreed,' Malinal replied.

There came a murmur of interest from the massed Mexica regiments. Shikotenka's announcement could hardly fail to get their attention, since Nanahuatzin played such a special and revered role in the shared pantheon of Tenochtitlan and Tlascala. In all the ancient texts and traditions, he was portrayed with his body and face covered in weeping pustules, exactly as the Tlascalans looked this morning. He was the god, humble and of despised appearance, who was worshipped and thanked daily for having sacrificed himself to place the sun in the sky and begin the present age of the earth. All subsequent holocausts offered by humans were modelled on his, and indeed were understood to nourish and sustain the sun, which had already grown ancient and would otherwise wither and perish.

It would, therefore, be extremely difficult for the Mexica to resist the offer of twenty victims who had been specially marked by Nanahuatzin as his own. Nor, given their martial pride, could they conceivably reject the single condition that accompanied the offer and that Shikotenka now announced.

'Oh, Mexica,' he said. 'Our warriors who are to die ask only one thing of you in return for their sacrifice, and that is that you take them first in combat.'

At that Chipahua raised his *macuahuitl*: '*Fight us if you're not cowards*,' he yelled, his voice surprisingly firm: '*Fight us for honour! Fight us for the gods!*'

Down in the plaza, Malinal saw Tozi. She'd made herself visible again after leaving the palace and was speaking urgently to Guatemoc, tugging at his arm. She would be warning him that this whole Nanahuatzin gambit was a trick – that the Tlascalans were truly sick with a new and deadly disease and that their intention was to pass the contagion on to the Mexica. She'd be telling him, because Malinal had told her – though it was a betrayal of Cortés – that under no circumstances must he or any other accept the Tlascalan offer of combat, and that it would be death to touch these men even on the stone of sacrifice.

But she was too late. Chipahua's challenge, laden with the taunt of cowardice, had energised the Mexica in the plaza, who were on their feet and roaring their assent as the Tlascalans spread out to form a defensive circle.

Guatemoc shoved Tozi aside and strode towards them, swinging his *macuahuitl*.

Cortés was in a cold, hateful fury at the way Tozi had publicly discountenanced him. It was also obvious the girl was in league with the enemy and, moreover, a damned witch – for only a witch could manifest such powers. Resolving not to rest until he'd burnt her at the stake, he looked out on the plaza where Saint Peter's holy strategy for the defeat of the Mexica was unfolding as it should.

Having made a circle, shields braced, obsidian-edged swords raised, the smallpox carriers now shouted their war cry three times – '*Tlascala! Tlascala! Tlascala!*' – and gave a great roar.

Shikotenka's heart felt gashed and torn at the pass he'd been brought to – where he could so easily be convinced that it was right to send his own men out as sacrificial victims.

And yet it *was* right, because it gave his beloved friend Chipahua and the other heroes with him a chance to die swiftly and with honour, rather than in the drawn-out agony and shame of sickness.

It was right, too, because it would now bring this curse down upon the heads of the Mexica, as well as upon the Tlascalans, the Totonacs and other peoples of the One World whom it had already afflicted. Somehow the Spanish were not subject to it – because it was they, many now believed, who had conjured this disease demon into existence – but under no circumstances was Shikotenka prepared to allow the Mexica to escape.

Weak, stumbling, physically shattered, but with his warrior spirit yet unbroken, Chipahua had agreed. 'If it means I get to die in battle rather than on this fucking shit-smeared floor, then my answer's yes.' It had taken very little effort to persuade those of the others in the sickroom who were still able to walk to join in, and now, deployed in a defensive circle, surrounded on all sides by rank upon rank of Mexica warriors, the tiny band of Tlascalans faced their final battle.

'*Come on, you monkey-fuckers!*' taunted Chipahua, '*what are you waiting for?*'

'*They've not got the stomach for the fight!*' guessed another member of the squad, a brave young warrior named Xolotl whom Shikotenka had known since he was a child.

'*Fucking cowards!*' yelled a third.

Looking out at the Mexica, it was obvious the provocations were working. Many amongst them were shouting bloodcurdling war cries while others blew skull-shaped death-whistles that produced a horrifying sound, like the scream of a thousand corpses.

Soon! Shikotenka thought as he stepped back through the immense palace doors which were immediately barred closed behind him.

Running now, he made his way into the building and up the flights

471

of stairs to the roof. When he reached the parapet to stand alongside Malinal and Cortés, battle had already been joined.

Truly the Holy Father was a genius! For in the boiling melee that had now engulfed the Tlascalan warriors, it was inconceivable that the infection would *not* be passed. Shikotenka's men were not only fighting like devils, but some were vomiting, some shitting through their loincloths, while those who were seized and dragged away for sacrifice all sought to clasp the Mexica close, to rub them with their bodies, and to breathe and cough upon them as they'd been taught. In the last seconds their leader, the one called Chipahua who'd assailed him last night, had struck five Mexica dead but was now himself killed, his great ball of a head hacked off by a jaguar knight's sword.

Beside him, Cortés heard Shikotenka utter a groan. It was understandable. Chipahua was his friend, after all. Still, he'd died in a good cause.

In minutes it was all over. Eight of the Tlascalans had been killed outright and twelve survived to be stretched over an execution stone hastily brought to the plaza for this purpose. Guatemoc looked on, but it was Cuitláhuac himself who snatched up the sacrificial knife, splitting the victims' breasts and tearing out their hearts. His long grey hair was matted with clots of their blood, it dripped into his mouth, it rimmed his eyes, and his entire body was bathed in it.

Did he wonder why the Spanish marksmen weren't taking this opportunity to shoot him dead when he was in range and made an easy target?

Apparently not, for he seemed transported in an ecstasy of murder, as did all the raving and screaming Mexica around him. It would be easy for Cortés to order his musketeers and archers assembled on the roof to fire down on them, and many were itching to do so, but he'd issued firm orders that they must not. Why risk scattering the crowd by killing a few tens or even hundreds of them with gunshots and bolts when the disease the Tlascalans were passing on would kill tens of thousands, or hundreds of thousands, or perhaps even millions?

In the Mexica way of things, sacrifice was usually followed by butchery and dismemberment, but today the bodies were kept intact.

'Why?' Cortés asked Malinal.

'Because they want to wear the victims' skins,' she replied tersely, as though the answer were obvious.

Olmedo had quietly joined them at the battlements. 'In the pustules of the victims it may be they're seeing not only to Nanahuatzin,' he now explained, 'but also Xipe Totec, another of their gods associated with disease, and with boils and pimples in particular. At his festival, sacrificial victims are flayed and their fresh, still bleeding skins are then worn for twenty days by the sacrificers as they go about in public. By then the skins are rotten and falling away, revealing the fresh, clean skin of the sacrificer beneath. By some twisted reasoning, it's supposed to symbolise the rebirth of nature.'

'Disgusting,' said Cortés. 'But it serves our purpose. In twenty days those who wear the skins will spread the infection to countless others.'

'You did this deliberately, didn't you, Hernán,' Olmedo asked. 'You got the idea when I showed you the sickroom last night and you thought – why not give smallpox to the Mexica?'

'Exactly, Bartolomé! That's what happened,' Cortés replied. He'd decided on the spur of the moment – he wasn't sure why – not to share the inspirational part Saint Peter had played in devising this strategy.

'You should be ashamed of yourself for ever conceiving such a wicked idea,' the friar said and abruptly turned his back.

'Shame on him who thinks evil of it,' Cortés snapped.

Olmedo could think what he liked and judge him as he wished. Cortés found that he no longer cared.

He watched, fascinated, as the Tlascalan bodies in the plaza – not only those sacrificed, but also those killed in battle – were rapidly and expertly skinned, while hordes of Mexica warriors, now in a profound and terrifying frenzy, thrust themselves forward, eager for the honour of wearing the bloody pelts.

Twenty men were selected.

They removed their loincloths.

Then naked, with shrieks of triumph and joy, they reverentially received the skins and carefully slipped them on, arms into arms, legs into legs, until, though somewhat gashed and bloody, they became complete, close-fitting body suits.

That night Tozi lay with Guatemoc in the bedchamber of the townhouse he'd co-opted in Tenochtitlan.

Against her advice he had involved himself in the slaying of the sick Tlascalan warriors sent out by Cortés to infect the Mexica. There was no doubt whatsoever that he would also have performed the sacrifices himself, had his father not claimed priority. But Guatemoc had needed no persuasion to stay away from the victims' vile, pustulant skins, no matter what associations they might have with the gods. He was far too fastidious about his personal hygiene even to consider such a thing.

He slept now, and Tozi lay with her arms and legs wrapped about him in the heat of the night, under a thick pile of blankets, searching out sickness in his body, sending the ancient magic of healing to him which, with the right intent, carried on the right song, could cure all ills.

The song was coming to her now; she could feel it rising within her like the waters of a spring, and quietly, almost in a whisper, she began to chant, while all the while fiercely embracing Guatemoc and holding him so close that soon their bodies seemed bonded in heat and they were both lathered from head to toe in sweat.

Guatemoc did not wake and Tozi did not move, but she continued to sing softly into his ear the whole night through.

In the morning he rose, fresh and strong, invigorated and radiant.

Tozi knew then that no matter how many others were struck down by the disease demon of the Spaniards, her beautiful prince would never be one of them.

The day of Wednesday 29 June passed in a series of ferocious battles, all focused on the two-mile long causeway connecting Tenochtitlan to the western shore of Lake Texcoco.

Not only were the island city's two other principal causeways – that to Iztapalapa, and that to Tepeyac – much longer than the Tacuba causeway, but also exploratory probes in the morning, not much opposed by the Mexica, had shown that neither was functional at all. Their first sections had been deliberately demolished, and while the further sections all appeared to be intact, it seemed that the bridges had been lifted between every one of them. Only the Tacuba causeway, with its eight bridges still in place, remained functional and provided a thoroughfare for all traffic moving in and out of Tenochtitlan.

With the wells now dry and the last of their drinking water stored in barrels that were for the most part also empty, it was obvious to Cortés that he must abandon the city, and let all its glittering prizes go, if he hoped to save the lives of enough of his men to return with him, once they'd licked their wounds, and take everything back. His strategy there-fore – and, like the earlier probes towards Tepeyac and Iztapalapa, it was not at first seriously opposed by the Mexica – was first to seize and hold all eight of the bridges on the Tacuba causeway, so that he and his entire army could retreat safely across them and on to the mainland, where their predicament, while still extremely dangerous, would be far better than in this present hellish prison.

At first all seemed to go well. Sandoval and Alvarado, with six other riders, succeeded in getting as far as Tacuba itself, and returned with flowers from the mainland to prove their success. Cortés didn't like it. 'Roses and nosegays,' he said, 'are no plumes for war helmets, and you'd better be quiet rather than irritate the enemy with your light-hearted ways.'

Matters soon became much more serious as Cortés ordered four hundred more conquistadors out from Axayacatl's palace. They marched through the Mexica cordon which again, mysteriously, did not oppose them, and on to the causeway. Their mission was to secure and hold the eight bridges, but no sooner had they occupied the first than the causeway and the waters beneath it were filled with great masses of warriors on foot and warriors in pirogues, sending showers of sling-stones, *atlatl* darts and arrows their way.

Four bridges were eventually captured at a cost of many injuries and some loss of life, but just at the moment when Cortés was about to urge the assault forward on the fifth, a terrified Mexica runner came bearing an astonishing message. It seemed that Cuitláhuac, in his capacity as Great Speaker, was prepared to offer a complete and unconditional peace to the Spaniards.

Was it a ruse?

Cortés didn't think so. After days of slaughter, the Indians must be tired, and – no matter how ferocious their passions – they were not a people who were notable for their persistence. Of course they were ready to make peace!

The message requested that he return to the palace to meet with certain Mexica officers and finalise the details of a lasting truce. Cautiously optimistic, Cortés rode off at once, flanked by Sandoval and Alvarado and accompanied by forty other horsemen – almost all of his remaining cavalry. They were not attacked anywhere along the route, another re-assuring indication that the proffered peace was genuine.

On reaching the plaza, although neither Guatemoc nor Cuitláhuac were present, Cortés was greeted by a number of very senior Mexica officers, some of whom he knew personally. Malinal came forth to trans-late and their words provided further reassurance. If Cortés would release the high priest Namacuix and his deputy, captured on the day of the battle for the great pyramid, and if he gave his word that the warriors who'd participated in the rebellion wouldn't be punished for what they'd done, then the Mexica would raise the siege, replace the bridges, repair the roads and serve the Spaniards as they had before.

'Can this be true?' Cortés asked Malinal.

'No,' she replied, 'it is certainly a lie.'

But Cortés preferred to believe it, gave his word, and released the two priests on the spot.

By nightfall, after hours of renewed fighting, all four of the bridges that the Spaniards had captured along the Tacuba causeway were back in Mexica hands, a dozen more conquistadors were dead, and the rest of the force sent out to secure the causeway had to fight its way back to the palace under a continuous shower of insults and missiles.

Bitterly disappointed, for there had been a moment today when he'd believed his troubles were over, Cortés made his way to the roof, Malinal at his side, to look down on the plaza as the campfires of the Mexica were lit and the regiments renewed and tightened their siege.

A voice wafted up to them – a strong voice with a mocking tone, a voice he'd heard before. Guatemoc!

For a moment the painted face of the prince became visible in a flicker of firelight and then he was gone, but his words continued, Malinal whispering the translation. 'Hey, Spaniards,' he was saying, 'we want to thank you for giving us our priests back. We needed them to sanctify the consecration of my father, Cuitláhuac, as the Great Speaker.'

'*Your father promised us unconditional peace!*' Cortés roared.

'Ah yes, but he did so as our Great Speaker when he had not yet been consecrated as such. Now that he is in fact the Great Speaker, he has rescinded that offer.'

There was much laughter amongst the Indians, but the night passed without further attacks, although everywhere the siege pressed close. It was, however, the shortage of water amongst the conquistadors that was now the biggest threat. Rationing meant there was not a drop left to drink through the whole of that long parched night.

The next mouthful for each man would be in the morning.

Chapter Twenty-Two

———◆———

Thursday 30 June 1520

On the morning of Thursday 30 June, Cortés came across the astrologer Botello Puerto de la Plata weeping in the palace courtyard. They had not spoken since Cempoala, when Botello had given him true tidings of Alvarado's plight in Tenochtitlan that he'd ignored to his cost. The astrologer had claimed to be guided by a 'demon'. If he'd listened to him then, and returned to the city to relieve Alvarado so much the sooner, things might have been very different today.

'Ah, sir,' Cortés asked, 'is this a time to be crying?'

'Don't you think there's every reason to?' Botello replied, red eyed. 'I tell you that by the morrow not a man of us shall remain alive unless we find some way of escape.'

'And what do you advise?' Cortés asked, half seriously.

'The same demon who visited me in Cempoala has visited me again. He warns our only hope is to leave this very night. Then you will save some of the men, though I myself will not be amongst them.'

'And did he speak of me,' Cortés asked, 'this demon of yours?'

'He said only this, Caudillo – that you will be reduced to the furthest extremity of distress, but that in time you will come to great honour and fortune.'

'Well I can only suggest, Botello, that you look after your own life carefully, because I find myself in complete agreement with your demon. We will quit the city this very night at midnight by the Tacuba causeway. I've already passed the order to my captains and told them to prepare. Do then go freely and announce your prophecy amongst the men. I'm told that some of them imagine themselves safer here, within these walls, than facing a fighting retreat to the mainland. Perhaps you can persuade them of the folly of their ways.'

Botello's prophecy spread rapidly through the army, because most of the men were already convinced, as Cortés was himself, that their last stand in Tenochtitlan had taken on the dimensions of a supernatural battle of good against evil into which hosts of demons, witches, saints and angels had been drawn.

Cortés had been told that Saint James had been seen riding his white charger into the thickest press of the foe to open a path for a group of Spaniards who'd been surrounded and cut off. There had likewise been multiple apparitions of the Virgin Mary.

But such uplifting sightings were much less common than encounters with evil.

Many of the soldiers claimed to have felt the maleficent presence of the demon Huitzilopochtli, stalking the corridors of the palace, tainting every battle.

There was also the matter of the witch Tozi, and the truly diabolical manner in which she had simply *vanished* on the roof yesterday, later re-appearing in the plaza to converse brazenly with the enemy prince Guatemoc.

And there were the spectres of human heads floating through the air, groaning corpses, and a frightful decapitated man, recognised by the Tlascalans as a Mexica ghost called Night Axe. This apparition careened around the palace, making hideous sounds as its gaping chest, the breast-bone split for heart sacrifice, snapped open and closed.

Even so, and despite the exhortations of Botello, noon came and went with more than a hundred men, those most severely injured and those most afraid, still preferring to remain in the palace, with all its privations, than risk the horrors of a midnight retreat across the causeway. They sent a deputation of the most able amongst them to inform Cortés of their decision.

'I'll not mislead you, boys,' he said when he'd heard their speech. 'To stay here after the rest of us have gone means certain death for you. You'll never hold the palace. You'll be overrun in minutes.'

'It's our decision, sir. We're all agreed.'

Cortés shrugged: 'I will exercise no compulsion. At a time such as this it's right that you make up your own minds. Still, I urge you to reconsider, make whatever preparations you can to ease your journey, and be ready to join the retreat tonight.'

He hoped that none of them would do so.

Those who were severely injured – the stretcher cases rather than the walking wounded – would require constant assistance, care and attention. Better to leave them behind, where they might at least serve to delay and distract the enemy, than allow them to divert sounder men from the more urgent tasks of defending the column and getting the treasure out of Tenochtitlan.

And as to those who chose to stay in the death-trap of the palace because they were afraid – better, too, that they should remain behind rather than endanger others with their cowardice.

All that Thursday morning and throughout the afternoon, with no further Mexica attacks and noticeably fewer warriors than usual occupying the plaza, Cortés was able to keep a large team of men at work under the direction of his chief carpenter and shipbuilder, the exceptionally skilled and able Martin Lopez. Since every effort to seize and hold the bridges on the Tacuba causeway long enough to evacuate the army across them had been frustrated by determined Mexica counter-attacks, and since it was highly probable that the enemy would seek to destroy the bridges themselves the moment an evacuation was attempted, he had come up with the idea of building a portable bridge. In order to span the gaps in the causeway, and in three of the city's canals that would have to be crossed before reaching the causeway, it must somewhat exceed five full paces in length and breadth, and it must be rigid and sturdy enough not only to be carried, but also to bear the weight of the cavalry, the marching men, the baggage train, the ammunition wagons, the treasure, and the cannon – for all must pass across it.

The ceilings of many of the great rooms and galleries of Axayacatl's palace were supported on massive wooden beams. After some extensive demolition work, enough of these were sawn to measure and joined crossways and lengthways to provide the strong framework that such a bridge would require. To this armature, sturdy floorboards were then firmly nailed.

The result, when complete, looked solid enough, but also cumbersome.

Its weight was tremendous. Forty bearers crammed around its sides were required to lift and move it. Hungry and thirsty as they were, they could not carry it far. Though it took precious manpower away from other tasks, Cortés assigned four hundred bearers to the bridge, ordering them divided into ten separate gangs and to relieve one another in shifts.

Around mid-afternoon, just as he was settling all this, Pepillo came to him with the news that Moctezuma had regained consciousness and was asking to see him.

'I don't have time for that dog,' Cortés snarled, and indeed he did not, for his next task was to secure the expedition's treasure, the full extent of which, up to now, only he knew. The men had been told there was much less of it in the strongroom than they would see tonight as they packed and carried it out of Tenochtitlan.

Would they notice the discrepancy amidst such an emergency and wonder at its implications for their share?

Probably not, though they were an avaricious lot.

But Gonzalo de Mexica, the officially nominated account-keeper for the king's fifth, had not been back in the strongroom since January – and he would certainly see some differences!

When Pepillo returned to Moctezuma's bedchamber, he was surprised and concerned to see that Tozi had entered the room. She could not have been admitted by the guards since they were under orders to arrest her on sight, so once again this was evidence of the extraordinary powers she'd first revealed to him in Cholula the year before.

Malinal was with her and the two of them sat on either side of Moctezuma's bed.

'May the gods protect us,' Pepillo said, speaking fluent Nahuatl. 'You can be here, Malinal, but Tozi – are you mad? If Cortés catches you, he's sworn he'll have you burnt as a witch.'

'*Witch?*' breathed Moctezuma. He was still conscious. His eyes, filled with terror, darted from side to side, now looking at Tozi, now Malinal. 'I remember you,' he croaked. 'You were there, on the great pyramid, the night my downfall began.'

'We were there.'

Eerily, Malinal and Tozi had spoken in unison.

They turned to Pepillo.

'You should leave now,' said Tozi.

'Yes,' said Malinal, 'you should leave.'

'But what are you going to do?'

'You should leave,' Malinal repeated. 'But I ask as a personal favour that you wait for us in the corridor.'

'Why?'

'To keep watch. If Cortés comes before I tell you we're finished, you must warn us.'

After Pepillo had gone – giving no promise to stand guard – Malinal and Tozi had Moctezuma to themselves.

'Why do you torment me?' he groaned. He had a livid bruise on his temple, a great lump on the top of his head and a bloody bandage on his shoulder, but when Tozi searched him with her magic, she saw at once that none of these wounds was fatal.

That was good, because if anyone had earned the right to kill this venomous toad, it was she and Malinal. More than a year ago they'd promised one another they'd do it, and now they were here to keep that promise, not by stealth, not by a garrotte, or by poison, but face to face, with eyes open and Moctezuma fully conscious.

Tozi had brought the knife, the very same instrument, procured from a secret priestly cache, that the Great Speaker had wielded the year before when she and Malinal had faced and escaped sacrifice at his hands.

'It was the god who saved you,' he now said, as though reading her mind. His voice was faint but a little firmer than before. Then suddenly he giggled – a terribly discordant sound. 'I'd have had your hearts out in a trice if Hummingbird hadn't stopped me.' He paused, seemed to reflect: 'You must be very special to him, the two of you. He's cast me aside now – no more use for me, I expect – but I'm certain he has great plans for you both.'

'Everyone feared you,' Malinal intoned, as though reading a list of charges: 'You killed people for tiny and imaginary offences, or none at all, just because it suited you to get them out of the way. The whole world lived in terror of you . . .'

'You were a bully,' said Tozi, 'you were a murderer. You deserve to die.'

'I am already dead,' said Moctezuma. 'I've been dead for some time.'

'No you're not,' said Tozi. 'You're alive! You can't escape responsibility for your crimes.'

'But what have I done? Did I sacrifice humans? All my forefathers did that too. Did I make war upon my neighbours? All my forefathers did that too. Did I inspire fear amongst them, and hatred of the Mexica? All my forefathers did that too.'

'Because your forefathers did wrong things,' said Malinal quietly, 'is no reason for you to repeat them.'

'I am proud to have done as my forefathers did . . .'

'Shame on you!' snapped Tozi. 'By doing as your forefathers did, you continued to spread hatred and fear throughout the One World; by doing as your forefathers did, you continued to make war upon your neighbours and to sacrifice their children. You failed to confront the threat of the white-skins because you refused to change. That's your real crime, Moctezuma.'

Tozi had taken the obsidian knife from beneath her blouse. Now, as she pulled it from its sheath, its black blade glittered wickedly.

Moctezuma shuddered. 'Are you going to kill me then?' A tear appeared at the corner of his eye.

He turned towards Malinal: 'We have spoken together many times,' he said. 'You are kind and you are also a Christian now and the Christians speak much of mercy, do they not? Therefore I beg you, dear Malinal, have mercy on me today.' He cast a sideways glance at the obsidian knife in Tozi's hands and added: 'I am terribly afraid of pain.'

'*But you didn't mind inflicting it on others, did you?*' screeched Tozi.

Moctezuma seemed taken aback: 'My hand was always swift.'

'As ours will be,' said Tozi. Standing, she held the hilt of the knife out towards Malinal. 'Come, friend. Let's do this together.'

Malinal hesitated. She'd agreed to this, but she didn't like it. Her grudge against Moctezuma and all he stood for seemed old and used up now as she viewed the ruin of the former monarch. To plunge a knife into his breast had once seemed so right – the only appropriate way to repay him and the Mexica for the terror they spread, for their bullying and arrogance, and for the countless indignities they'd heaped not only upon her, and upon Tozi, but upon all the subject peoples of the One World.

So why, then, as the blade of retribution was offered, did she find herself reluctant to accept?

'Take it!' hissed Tozi.

Malinal reached out both her hands, enclosing Tozi's fingers and the hilt of the knife in a gentle grip. Quite suddenly, with absolute clarity and conviction, she knew what she had to do.

Unmanned by fear, frozen beneath the blade, Moctezuma sobbed.

'If we kill him,' Malinal whispered, looking directly into Tozi's eyes, 'Hummingbird wins. Is that what you want?'

'I'm here for vengeance. Nothing more.'

Another sob from Moctezuma.

'Why slake a thirst for vengeance if it gives Hummingbird a victory? Don't you see, Tozi? Moctezuma is already crushed. He's already paid the heaviest price for his misdeeds. To kill him now just lowers us to his level and makes a mockery of all our noble ideas of a world without sacrifice or cruelty.'

'But it is *right!*' Tozi's fingers, gripping the knife, strained within Malinal's enclosing hands, and the blade was pushed down.

Malinal pushed back. 'It is *not* right, Tozi. We must not do this. *You* must not do this. If we forgive, we win. Take revenge and we become Hummingbird's creatures.'

'I'm already Hummingbird's creature!' snarled Tozi. 'Don't you remember? He told me I was his when he renewed my powers.'

'That doesn't make you his, Tozi! Only your own choices can do that. Do you choose Hummingbird?'

'And do you choose the tortured god on the cross? Is he any better? Look at what your precious Spaniards do in his name!'

Their eyes had remained locked. Malinal saw her friend's fury and felt her strength. Supine beneath them, Moctezuma lay as though paralysed, or – the thought crossed Malinal's mind – as though he had finally resigned himself to his fate.

'Let me go!' snarled Tozi. Again her hand struggled against Malinal's. 'Be a Christian if you wish, but I'm going to kill him.'

As she spoke the door burst open and Pepillo appeared. His eyes widened as he took in the scene. 'The caudillo's coming,' he gasped. 'You've got to hide!'

With a screech of frustration, leaving the knife in Malinal's hands, Tozi vanished.

'Were you about to do away with him?' Cortés asked as he took in Malinal's wild look and the glittering obsidian blade. The notion did not seem to distress him very much.

'I was,' Malinal replied levelly, 'but I changed my mind.'

'Why?'

She remembered something she'd heard Olmedo say: 'Forgive and ye shall be forgiven?'

Cortés nodded: 'Luke chapter six, verse thirty-seven. You're becoming quite the Bible scholar, Malinal! But there is a time for all things and this is not a time for forgiveness. Moctezuma played us foul with Narváez and he's played us foul with his own people, urging them to make war while pretending he wants peace. I've washed my hands of him.'

He turned to Pepillo. 'The day Mucktey got hit on the head he was wearing a rather fine robe. Blue and white? A lot of emeralds and gold?'

'Yes, sir. His *tilmatli*.'

'I don't care what it's called. When we're done here, find it and bring it to the strongroom. All the treasure's being packed to leave and I'll need your help with the inventory. There are some discrepancies.'

'You don't wish me to remain with the Great Speaker, sir?'

'What Great Speaker?'

'Moctezuma, sir.'

'Oh . . . him? He's not the Great Speaker any more, Pepillo, and he's of no further use to us. I've sent the guards away – it's a waste of manpower to keep them at his door. I'm relieving you of all your duties to him as well.'

'But his spirit's broken, sir, and he can't fend for himself. All his retainers have fled. If we leave him here, he'll die.'

'I'm not planning to leave him here, lad!'

A clank of armour and a tramp of boots announced the arrival of men in the hallway. 'Is that you, Sergeant?' Cortés called.

'Yes, sir.'

'Well, what are you waiting for? Come ahead.'

García Brabo limped in. His knee was swollen to almost twice its normal size by a bad slingshot wound. There was blood on his battered cuirass, in his hair and on his face. Grime and dust covered him from head to foot. Four other lean and exhausted soldiers followed, all equally bloody and bruised. Their collective smell was rank and feral, as though some scavenging beast had entered the room.

Moctezuma remained prostrate and seemingly lifeless until they laid hands on him, a man taking each limb, and hoisted him like a sack of cocoa beans. Then, pathetically, he struggled. 'Malinche!' he called out, catching sight of Cortés as they carried him from the room. 'What is this? Where am I being taken? What is to be done to me? Even on my deathbed can I not be left in peace?'

Cortés ignored him, and the sounds of protest rapidly receded as Moctezuma was borne off along the corridor.

'Where are they taking him, Hernán?' Malinal asked.

'To prison, with the other Mexica lords, where he should have been all along.'

Malinal knew her lover's face very well. She saw something furtive and cruel in it as he spoke, but he was clearly in no mood to explain. 'There's a rainstorm coming in,' he said, 'a big one by the feel of the air. I want to pass a message to the Mexica before it breaks. Come with me to the roof; I need you to translate.'

Pepillo had brought the *tilmatli*.

'Take it to the strongroom,' Cortés told him. 'Add it to the rest of the treasure and make sure what's there tallies with the inventory, if you get my drift. When I left it was a bloody mess – the king's fifth, my fifth, my regular share, the men's shares, Gonzalo de Mexia stamping about blaming everybody for everything. In this madness nobody knows what's what.'

Malinal noticed that Cortés made no mention of the large chest of gold and precious jewels – additional to his specially allocated fifth, and to his regular share as captain-general – that he kept hidden under blankets and furnishings in their quarters. It was filled with plunder that he'd been quietly setting aside for himself for more than a year. A second, smaller chest had been emptied in the past weeks during the campaign against Narváez.

When the white-skins took Moctezuma, grabbing him with their filthy hands, carrying him slung by the arms and legs like a sacrificial victim, Tozi followed.

The loss of the knife was no obstacle; there were a hundred other ways to kill. But something about Malinal, and what she'd said, or perhaps the way she'd said it, had troubled Tozi deeply. She remembered that night on the great pyramid more than a year ago, when Hummingbird had saved her from death by the same knife that she'd brought today, held then in Moctezuma's hands. She remembered how the god had multiplied her powers. And, with a shiver, she remembered the words he'd spoken to her: '*You're mine now!*'

The squad of Spanish soldiers had reached the door to the fetid room, set aside as the jail for Cortés's high-ranking Mexica prisoners. Cloaked in invisibility, Tozi had visited it two days earlier, had left quickly, and had not felt the need to return. She cared nothing for Cacama, the deposed monarch of Texcoco, or Itzququhtzin or Atlixcatzin or any of the other arrogant bullies rotting in there.

The room itself was lit only by narrow skylights but now, as the Spaniards swung the heavy door wide, Tozi saw it was much more crowded than it had been before. She recognised two of Moctezuma's wives, his ailing son and his three daughters amongst the newcomers revealed in the spill of light from the hallway. There were others there who she did not know. All but a handful sat, or slouched, or lay huddled on the floor. All were exceptionally dirty. Most had been beaten and it looked as if about half had been tortured. Tozi had not noticed the terrible injuries done to the soles of Cacama's feet on her last visit, but she did now. The only explanation was that he must have been held over a fire.

Some of the prisoners groaned as the door was opened. In the bowels of the room another howled like a dog and a third laughed maniacally. There were cries of recognition from the children as Moctezuma was seen, his face bobbing, pale as a ghost, and a further chorus of shrieks and gasps as the Spaniards threw him down. It was only then, as the back of his head bounced off the shit-smeared floor, that Tozi understood what was intended here. An instant later, when the squad of soldiers drew their swords and hefted their hatchets and hammers, everyone else understood too.

There were close to thirty Mexica in that dreadful room, mostly men, but now also some women and children, all in very poor health. There were eight Spaniards – the four who'd carried Moctezuma, their mean-faced sergeant, and three more. They began the butchery at once, grim and silent except for the bestial grunts some of them made as they hacked their blades and smashed their bludgeons down on Mexica heads. Most of their victims were already on the floor, which made the task of slaughtering them so much easier, but even those few who were standing were too weak and terrified to fight, and the Spaniards cut them down in an instant.

Soon the whole room was a shambles of blood and guts and amputated limbs and struck-off heads. A few of the prisoners still showed signs of life, writhing or crying out, but a soldier with a spear and a cruel laugh finished them off one by one.

Moctezuma they kept until last, and it was the sergeant who killed him, thrusting a dagger five times into his chest, impaling the thin, graceful, fluttering hands he raised in a final, hopeless attempt to defend himself, and finding his heart.

The late afternoon sky was darkening towards evening, and thick rain clouds scudded through the heavens driven on strong winds, as Cortés stood with Malinal on the roof of Axayacatl's palace looking out over the sacred precinct. Behind them, Velázquez de Léon, Alvarado, Olid, Ordaz and a number of other captains had gathered, with perhaps twenty of the men, all curious to see what might happen next.

Cortés turned to them and winked: 'Don't believe a word I'm going to say here, boys. It's all a ruse.'

The day had passed without a single attack being launched, and with nothing like the usual press of Mexica warriors occupying the plaza between the walls of the palace and the great pyramid. At one point that afternoon their number had fallen as low as a few dozen, almost as though they no longer cared to keep the siege. Cortés knew that impression to be false, however. The entrance to the Tacuba causeway was half a mile away, and lookouts confirmed that regiments still occupied every street between it and the sacred precinct. Regardless of how many warriors were camped right outside the palace, therefore, whether very few or a great many, the siege remained effective, and there was no hope of slipping away quietly.

The number of warriors in the plaza had risen since this afternoon's low to perhaps a thousand men. 'Do they have a worthy captain or general amongst them?' Cortés asked Malinal. 'Cuitláhuac, perhaps, or Guatemoc? I should not wish to treat with a lesser officer.'

An exchange followed in Nahuatl with a hunched, elderly warrior who'd stepped forward from amongst the Mexica.

'None of their great chiefs or captains are here,' Malinal said finally. 'This man is something like one of your sergeants.'

'Which means what?'

'Which means there's no point trying to negotiate anything with him, because he's not senior enough to make decisions.'

'Can he get a message to Cuitláhuac?'

Another exchange in Nahuatl.

'Yes,' Malinal replied. 'He says tell him your message and he'll take it to Cuitláhuac right away.'

'Very well. The message is this. I wish to quit the city, but many of my soldiers are too badly injured to walk. We need eight days to tend to them and prepare them for the journey to the coast, after which we will withdraw peacefully from Tenochtitlan. If Cuitláhuac agrees and offers us safe passage for the evacuation, then I promise to return to him all the gold and jewels we received from Moctezuma during our stay here.'

After the Mexica sergeant had hurried off to find Cuitláhuac and deliver the message, Cortés and Malinal left the roof. 'What is a ruse?' she asked.

'What we just did there – tricking them, misleading them, putting them off the scent. Whatever happens, whether they believe anything I said or not, we're still getting out of here at midnight, so please, Malinal, go to our quarters now and make everything ready for the evacuation. Arrange things exactly as we discussed.'

No further explanation was needed. In every place of danger where they'd stayed together in the past year, Cortés had always had an evacuation plan. Certain objects, certain papers, and the treasure chest, must be saved.

It was Malinal's responsibility to see that all was as it should be and to make everything secure for travel.

'We'll meet again later,' Cortés said. 'See me in the courtyard half an hour before midnight. I'll find you a sheltered spot in the column.'

The butchered bodies of the murdered Mexica nobles, Moctezuma's amongst them, were removed from the prison room, carried down the stairs and heaped up in the palace courtyard like so much offal. Tozi followed, invisibly observing, curious as to what would happen next. Even amongst the Spaniards, she saw, there were those who seemed horrified by the killings, some crossing themselves, muttering under their breath, others looking away and giving the mound of corpses a wide berth.

Malinal should see this, Tozi thought. Would she still speak of Christian forgiveness then?

But there was no sign of her friend and, as dusk settled over the palace, the bleeding bodies were one by one dragged to the great doors and shoved out through the wicket into the portico. There, as the brutal-ised remains again began to pile up, they attracted the attention of the Mexica in the plaza. Carrying burning brands that penetrated the gloaming with a lurid flickering light, several of them came forward to examine the dead.

Cortés stood in whispered conversation with Alvarado and Velázquez de Léon in a shadowy corner of the torch-lit strongroom, where the final inventory and division for carriage of more than eight tons of treasure proceeded at a frantic and chaotic pace. Under Pepillo's close supervision, a dozen clerks and notaries pored over the heaps of gold and jewels, separating them for transportation into smaller piles according to type, value and weight, while Gonzalo de Mexia, the officer responsible for calculating the king's fifth, stormed back and forth, fuming, biting his lips, constantly and loudly proclaiming that things were not as they should be.

'I had Brabo's squad kill them all,' Cortés whispered.

'All? Even Mucktey?' It was De Léon who'd asked the question about the prisoners but he didn't seem to like the answer.

'Even Mucktey,' Cortés confirmed. 'Besides, he's more useful to us dead than alive.'

'Last time I checked,' Alvarado said dubiously, 'he was more useful to us alive than dead.'

'That stopped when Cuitláhuac replaced him. But Mucktey's not without importance. He *is* a former Great Speaker, and custom says they must cremate him and begin the mourning immediately after his death. Same goes for his wives and children and for all the other nobles.'

Understanding dawned on Alvarado's handsome, dirt-smeared features. 'That's true!' he conceded. 'I remember the wake after the Toxcatl killings. The whole city went mad with grief.'

'The prisoners' bodies will have been passed through the wicket and dumped in the portico by now,' Cortés said cheerfully, 'so we can count on more grief tonight – enough, I'm calculating, to serve as a distraction while we make our escape.'

'You're saying you killed Mucktey and all the prisoners as a *distraction*?' Again, Velázquez de Léon seemed taken aback by the idea.

'Well yes, more or less.'

'So how does this fit with the bogus peace deal you offered them from the roof not half an hour ago? Surely killing their nobles sends the opposite message?'

'Juan,' said Cortés, 'that's exactly my strategy! My aim is to confuse them, keep them guessing as to our real intentions, on the one hand seeming to seek peace, on the other seeming to invite war, when all along our only plan – which they must not divine! – is to make our escape tonight.'

Pepillo had approached as they talked and now coughed to announce his presence. 'Caudillo,' he said, 'please forgive me for interrupting you, but there is a matter that requires your attention.'

Behind him, so red in the face that one could almost imagine smoke pouring from his ears, stood the gnome-like figure of Mexia.

There was history between Velázquez de Léon and Mexia.

Pepillo recalled how the two had come to blows in January, when Mexia had accused Léon of keeping certain pieces of gold plate aside for himself before they were submitted to the royal stamp, thereby depriving the king of his rightful fifth. The pair had succeeded in stabbing each other then, fortunately not mortally, and Cortés had briefly jailed Léon for his part in it, before releasing him after an appeal for clemency by Moctezuma. But the bad blood remained and, over the caudillo's shoulder, Pepillo saw Léon edge closer, his hand dropping to the hilt of his sword, his Swaggerer wrapped flamboyantly around his neck and shoulders, glittering in the torchlight as an ever-present rebuke to Mexia and everything he stood for.

'Is there some problem here, Gonzalo?' Cortés asked.

'Some problem?' Mexia spluttered. 'Much more than just *some* problem.' He whisked a sheaf of documents from a satchel at his side. 'Here,' he said, 'I have a fair copy, certified by yourself, Don Hernando, of the full inventory of the expedition's treasure as it was set down . . . let me see – ' he glanced at the papers – 'on the twentieth of January this year. The inventory records a treasure valued at a grand total of 235,000 pesos consisting of 160,000 pesos of gold – ' he waved the papers theatrically – 'and 75,000 pesos of fine ornaments, jewellery and silver plate. The problem that I have, therefore, is that I and my assistants have now assayed all the treasures in this room, and we find that they approach much more closely in value to one million pesos than to the mere 235,000 pesos against which the king's fifth was levied.'

Pepillo wondered absently how the caudillo was going to get out of this. He knew perfectly well that his master had under-declared the amount of treasure in the strongroom, keeping the lion's share of it separately with Brabo's squad and waiting until after the completion of the 20 January inventory to place it with the rest.

But Cortés answered Mexia smoothly. 'Fie, Gonzalo! What are you suggesting?'

'That you have under-declared our treasure in order to defraud the king of his fifth.'

Cortés's face darkened. 'That's a very serious charge, Gonzalo. I don't care who you are. Be careful what you say.'

'It is my duty to say it. The inventory is clear: 235,000 pesos. That is what the king's fifth was calculated upon in January. Our assay today is also clear: one million pesos. The difference between the two sums is 765,000 pesos, against which the king's fifth has never been assessed – and, I avow, never would have been assessed if this emergency had not arisen.'

'Avow all you wish, sir,' Cortés replied, 'but you slander me. Has it somehow escaped your notice that in the months since that inventory was taken we have been rather preoccupied? Has it somehow escaped your notice that we have fought a war against fellow Spaniards in those months, and been obliged to deal with the most pressing emergencies here in Tenochtitlan? All this time, Gonzalo, treasures have continued to flow into our strongroom – more presents from Moctezuma to ourselves, the presents also that Moctezuma sent to Narváez, tribute and booty from Mexica vassals, and so on . . .'

'*Hunnh!*' Mexia made a peculiar sound when he cleared his throat. 'What do you mean "and so on"? Am I seriously expected to believe that these bits and pieces of presents and booty that have dribbled, not "flowed", in over the past five months somehow add up to the astronomical sum of 765,000 pesos?'

'That is what happened, Gonzalo, and that is certainly what I expect you to believe. If you continue to insult me with your disbelief, we can always step outside now and settle the matter with swords.'

'You see!' said Mexia, suddenly very flustered. 'You people are all the same.' He glared at Velázquez de Léon. 'Whenever you're caught with your fingers in the king's fifth, you draw your swords and harm innocent men . . .'

'I have no wish to harm you, Mexia,' Cortés said quietly. 'But truly now is not the time for us to have this out. My only concern is with the safety of the men during tonight's evacuation. It will be fraught with danger and difficulty, and I won't allow myself to be distracted by you and your quibbles. You are quite wrong, I assure you, and deeply unjust, and if we survive the night we will sit together and I will put your mind at rest on everything, I promise you.'

'No!' Mexia protested. 'That's not good enough.'

'What will satisfy you then? And be quick, man. We don't have much time.'

'We agree that the discrepancy is 765,000 pesos?'

'It's not a discrepancy.'

'Whatever we call it, I propose we forthwith set aside one fifth of it, 153,000 pesos, for the king. It will be added to the treasure allocated to him in the January accounting, the whole amount will be loaded on to a wagon, you will post a strong guard upon it in the midst of the column, and in this manner we will at least get what belongs to His Majesty safely out of Tenochtitlan.'

'And my own fifth? And the shares of the men?'

'These are not my problems, Don Hernando, but I am sure you will arrive at some solution.'

Looking at Cortés, knowing his master very well, it crossed Pepillo's mind that Mexia might not be long for this world.

* * *

Somehow Tree had kept back a gourd of pulque. Now, Shikotenka shared it with his old friend on the roof of Axayacatl's palace under the scudding, rain-heavy clouds, through gaps in which a half-moon from time to time appeared.

'Chipahua died a good death,' Tree said. 'To sacrifice himself like that – for us, for the others. The gods will honour him.'

'I don't think the gods will honour any of us,' Shikotenka replied after a moment's reflection. 'We're all terrible human beings doing terrible things here. We should have found another way.'

'Ha! What other way? We tried to fight the Spaniards and it didn't work. We made common cause with them against the Mexica and that hasn't worked either.'

'Perhaps we should have tried love?'

'Love?' Tree laughed bitterly, as though the very idea were offensive. 'Love who? Love what?'

'I don't know. The Mexica, the Spaniards, everybody. We're good at loving our own families, our wives, our children – so why shouldn't we love strangers the same way?'

'Sounds like the Christians have been getting to you, brother!'

Shikotenka wasn't going to bother denying it. He did find some of the Christian teachings interesting, but what couldn't be escaped from was the obvious fact that the Christians themselves were every bit as cruel, greedy and murderous as the Mexica.

He voiced none of this. 'I just think we missed an opportunity here,' he said, taking another swig of pulque and rolling it around his mouth before swallowing. 'You know? The historic meeting of two peoples? So much good could have come of it.'

'In your dreams,' said Tree.

Of the three thousand Tlascalans who'd stood with Cortés to defend Tenochtitlan, more than two thousand had been killed or captured for sacrifice in the battles since they'd reoccupied the city. Amongst those who survived, hundreds were injured, and more fell sick every day with the mysterious 'Spanish disease' that Chipahua had sacrificed himself to pass to the Mexica, but that the Spaniards seemed invulnerable to.

Cortés had asked Shikotenka to provide five hundred of his best men to support the rearguard during tonight's evacuation.

'I don't even have five hundred men left who can fight,' Shikotenka had said.

'How many can you give me?'

'Four hundred – maybe a few more. Many are injured but they're up to the task. I'll lead them myself.'

Shikotenka took another gulp of pulque and gazed into the black night.

Lightning sparked and there came a roll of distant thunder.

The sense of a vast storm about to break was overwhelming.

It would not be long now.

Night brought a lull. The movable bridge had been built. Everything that could be stowed away in the baggage to be carried by the remaining *tamanes* had been stowed away. The treasure still had to be carried down from the strongroom, but the wagons to transport it were drawn up ready in the courtyard, with *tamanes* to pull them.

Cortés had announced a general muster of the entire army in the courtyard at eleven of the evening – just an hour before the evacuation would begin.

In the interim, some time after nine, Díaz and Sandoval repaired to the roof, where they couldn't help overhearing the conversation of the group of soldiers already gathered there. There'd been much talk about the fight they'd face – no one was in any doubt it would be bad – but now treasure was the subject. Many of the men wanted to carry their own shares and not entrust them to the baggage train.

Díaz strolled over to them: 'Lads,' he said, 'sorry to be the cold voice of reason, but you do realise this will be a *fighting* retreat tonight, in the dark, across water deep enough to drown in, with spears and sling-stones flying at us?'

They were mostly from Narváez's army, these men. They lacked the savvy and hard-bitten edge of the veterans and looked at him blankly.

'So you'll need your hands free to fight with,' Díaz continued. 'You know, one for your sword, the other for your shield?' As he turned to rejoin Sandoval, something else occurred to him. 'My advice is carry only what you can wear, and only if it's light enough to run and fight with. Leave everything else behind.'

They looked at him as though he was mad.

Or, worse, as though he secretly sought to defraud them.

'Idiots,' he said to Sandoval, in a tone too low to be heard by the others. 'They're lucky Cortés offered them shares at all since they joined us so late.'

'A lot of the veterans resent it. They're worried it might affect their share . . .'

'Which of course it will. I had such concerns myself, but I've thought it through, Gonzalo, and truly, if I'm left alive and with my wits and limbs intact after tonight, that'll be share enough for me.'

'How very virtuous of you, Bernal!'

'I suppose the prospect of imminent death focuses the mind on the essentials.'

They were standing at the gap in the battlements, directly overlooking the portico into which the bodies of Moctezuma and the slaughtered prisoners had earlier been thrown. They'd not been left there out of sight. The first of the Mexica to inspect them had dragged them out into the open, heaping them up on the plaza itself.

'That was a bad business,' Sandoval now said.

Neither of them had been informed of the plan to kill the prisoners, learning of it only when the bodies had been brought to the courtyard and dumped through the wicket.

'Cortés told me he had no choice,' Díaz offered. 'He said he couldn't spare the men to guard them.'

'Probably true, but he still didn't have to kill them. He could have left them locked up for their own people to find.'

They both fell silent, and into that silence, across the plaza, where the number of warriors had fallen rapidly after nightfall to less than a hundred, they saw the flicker of braziers and torches approaching and heard the murmur of voices and the shuffle of many feet.

At first it was shadows and echoes only, spilling around the sides of the pyramid, but soon the nature of the crowd became clear.

These were not soldiers.

These were not priests.

These were women.

A great crowd of many hundreds of women.

'Hey, Shikotenka,' Sandoval called, for the Tlascalan leader and his friend Tree were also on the roof, 'what do you make of this?'

Both warriors uncoiled from the patch of darkness they'd been sitting in and strode over to the parapet.

Tree spoke no Spanish and Shikotenka claimed only to have mastered a few words. Still, what he said was enough to make sense of the spectacle unfolding on the plaza below.

The women were the wives, mothers and other kin of the murdered prisoners, come to take their bodies for cremation. Scores of guttering torches and glowing braziers lit their way as they gathered round the heaped corpses and began to search through the bloody remains for recognisable parts of their relatives. A chorus of terrible groans and wails rose up, rapidly rising in scale until it amazed the ears.

From the group of former Narváez soldiers, one hurried to the battlements, looked out and gasped. 'You should see the hell and flood of tears over here,' he told the others.

A hell indeed, Díaz thought, as more of them came forward, jostling one another on the parapet, and as the volume of screams, moans, ululations and piercing howls from the mourners continued to mount.

Hell had many mouths, but this was one Cortés had deliberately chosen to open by murdering helpless captives. Truly it was a dishonourable act, and it would, Díaz felt sure, have ignoble consequences. He shivered as he realised that never once, despite all the dangers he'd faced since the start of the conquest, had he been as afraid as he was now, confronted by that awful lamentation.

Tozi could not rid herself of her dark fascination with Moctezuma, in whose fattening pen, and at whose hands, not so long before, she'd been held awaiting sacrifice like an animal – the fattening pen where she had met Malinal and where the whole strange adventure of the past sixteen moons had begun.

And tonight?

What did that great butcher Moctezuma amount to tonight?

What was left of the proud oppressor after the loathsome Spaniards had done with him?

She looked at his ruined corpse, lying crumpled and alone now on the plaza, just a fetid bag of blood and shit, punctured, leaking putrefaction. The bodies of his wives and children, and of all the other lords, had been taken up and reverentially carried away, but the wreck of Moctezuma himself still lay there, shunned and untended.

It was not until after the great mass of mourners had departed, their cries rising to the gods, that four priests gathered round Moctezuma's corpse, wrapped him in a thick maguey-fibre sheet, hefted him on their shoulders, and carried him silently out of the plaza.

Cloaked in invisibility, Tozi followed.

The streets of the city were filled with squadrons of warriors moving northward towards the district of Tlatelolco. From snatches of conversation, Tozi gathered they were going to honour the murdered lords whose funeral service and mass cremation were about to take place in the great square there.

Moctezuma's little cortege was headed in the opposite direction, the black-robed priests pushing through the crowds. When they were asked where they were going, or whose body they carried, they made no reply but stared fixedly ahead and quickened their pace. Somehow, however, a rumour arose that the corpse in the sheet was indeed that of the former emperor, and a procession of curious and prurient hangers-on began to form.

The destination, it soon became clear, was the district of Capulco, the scene of fierce fighting a few days earlier between the Mexica and the Spaniards. There the cortege entered the wide, torch-lit courtyard of a part-demolished royal palace, where more priests were at work placing the last cords of wood on a low and mean funeral pyre.

Moctezuma's body was laid upon the stack so roughly that his winding sheet fell back to reveal his pallid, blood-streaked face, his eyes wide and staring, his mouth unhinged in a final gape. There were gasps of recognition from the gathering crowd and someone cried out as an acolyte approached with a blazing torch.

Standing in a pool of deep shadow, Tozi allowed herself to materialise into full visibility; when she stepped out in plain view, she was just another unremarkable young woman mingling with the bystanders. No one here knew her. No one was hunting for her. No one cared.

The torch touched the base of the pyre, once, twice, three times, and the fire crackled, seeming to flare up. Many tongues and sprigs of flame arose from it, and soon Moctezuma's body lay sizzling, his hair burned away, his flesh blistering.

Was she mistaken, Tozi wondered, or was there a foul smell?

She looked around. Others were holding their noses, pointing at the corpse as it cooked in its own fat.

It should have been a triumphant moment, but somehow it wasn't. Instead Tozi felt only sadness and confusion. All her old certainties had collapsed. The terrifying figure of Moctezuma had been revealed as an illusion. She hated human sacrifice, but loved Guatemoc who practised it. She and Malinal, once so close, had chosen men who were enemies to the bone, and in the process had grown distant from one another, becoming almost enemies themselves.

There and then Tozi decided she could no longer allow the remnants of her love for Malinal to influence her judgement on the matter of the Spaniards. It had been obvious to her for some hours that they intended to evacuate the city tonight, and part of her wanted them to succeed so that Malinal could escape with them.

But this was wrong thinking, and the realisation brought Tozi back to the intimations of a dark future, linked inextricably to the white-skins, that increasingly haunted her. If she had been asked where the knowledge came from, she would not have been able to explain; nonetheless she knew with certainty that if the Spanish snake was allowed to slither away now, if its head was not struck off tonight, here in Tenochtitlan, then doom would follow for all the peoples of the One World.

She'd delayed too long. Guatemoc must be told what Cortés planned, and told immediately.

Tozi went directly to the great square of Tlatelolco, for that was where Guatemoc must be tonight, Cuitláhuac too, honouring the funeral of the murdered lords. They'd use the occasion to stir the people up to new heights of hatred towards the Spaniards. Meanwhile, cunning Cortés intended to use the distraction, and the cover of night, to flee the city.

Cloaked again in invisibility, Tozi caught sight of Guatemoc seated with his father and other chiefs under an awning erected against the rainstorm that still threatened but had not yet broken. A few tens of paces in front of them, surrounded by scaffolding, stood the immense funeral pyre on to which the bodies of the murdered Mexica nobles, gathered in winding sheets, had been laid. Clustered close were hundreds of their kin. Beyond them, packing every available space to the edges of the huge square, were tens of thousands of warriors.

Suddenly cautious, remembering Guatemoc had not spoken to his father about her yet, Tozi edged closer. On that dreadful night of blood sixteen moons ago, when she'd escaped Moctezuma's knife on the great pyramid, Cuitláhuac had been there. He detested her, and rightly believed her to be a witch, so he was hardly likely to accept military advice from her if she appeared in front of him unannounced.

But why did she need to appear at all when invisibility served her better? There had been so many omens in the past years, so many apparitions, so many disembodied voices prophesying true, that if she spoke openly but was *not* seen then she was much more likely to be believed.

When Cuitláhuac stood to give his oration, she didn't hesitate, but darted to his side and loudly proclaimed: '*The Spaniards plan to escape the city tonight! You must stop them!*'

The newly consecrated Great Speaker stumbled back, fumbled his own opening words, fell silent and turned towards her, at first in fury but then in confusion when he saw nobody there. Several of the princes who had been seated nearby were on their feet, weapons drawn, looking around fearfully.

'O valiant warriors of the Mexica,' Tozi added a throaty cadence to her chant. 'What are you doing? Will you allow those whom the gods wish us to kill to get away from us? Stop the Spaniards, oh Mexica! The gods demand it.'

She had a momentary qualm about Pepillo. Must that gentle boy also die tonight? But she hardened her heart. She'd done what she could to send death to all the Spaniards. She would save Coyotl and Miahuatl, and Malinal if she would allow it, but Pepillo would have to fend for himself.

Guatemoc remained outwardly calm but his thoughts were in turmoil.

He had seen very little of Tozi in the past three days, but he would recognise her voice anywhere, whether she cloaked herself in invisibility or not, and knew she would not have come here to deliver such a message unless it was true.

His father and the other chiefs were impressed too. Well, who wouldn't be by a voice speaking prophecy out of nowhere? But they were bound by protocol. The state funeral of the murdered prisoners, with all their relatives and so many warriors present, was too far advanced to be halted – for in the last moments the acolytes had come forward and put their torches to the pyre, and now the flames soared up and the bodies began to smoulder.

A great roar of sorrow arose from the mourners; the rites had to follow. It would be sacrilege to dispense with them. As Namacuix the high priest began the invocations, Guatemoc stood to go, but Cuitláhuac, always a stickler for the rules, laid a restraining hand on his arm and urged him back to his seat.

The final muster was complete and the order of march had been settled when distant sounds of lamentation filled the air and a flickering orange glow lit the sky, reflected off the underside of the massed clouds that loomed over the northern sector of the city. 'Right on schedule,' Cortés said. 'That's our safe passage out of here, boys. We go now, while they're busy burning their dead. It's our best chance of getting to the causeway unopposed, and perhaps all the way across it.'

He paused, signalled to Brabo. 'But there's one more thing.'

From the palace a long line of tamanes came forth carrying a dozen large wooden crates which they placed on the ground. The crates were open and filled with jumbled heaps of gold and jewellery that glittered alluringly in the light of the blazing torches.

Cortés called Mexia to stand beside him and pointed to the baggage wagons, pulled by *tamanes*, and to the seven wounded and lame horses, loaded with saddle bags filled with ingots, that were placed behind the wagons. 'Bear witness for me,' Cortés said, 'that distributed there amongst the wagons and the horses are the king's fifth and the shares of all the men.'

'I confirm it,' Mexia said. 'I supervised the loading myself before the muster.'

'Bear witness for me also, please,' Cortés continued, 'that – excepting what we can carry on our persons – this is all the treasure we are physically able to transport, and that my own fifth and my share as captain-general are left behind here with the residue.' He gestured towards the six open wooden crates in the courtyard.

'I confirm it,' said Mexia again.

'And bear witness finally that you have no objection if I now give this gold, which otherwise will be lost to the enemy, to any soldiers who care to take it.'

'I confirm it,' said Mexia.

'Well, there you are, boys,' Cortés laughed, 'help yourselves.' There was a stir of excitement amongst the men. 'But be careful not to overload yourselves. He travels safest in the dark night who travels lightest.'

The Mexica called gold *teocuitlatl*, literally 'the shit of the gods', but even in the face of death, Pepillo saw how his fellow Spaniards hungered for it and lost their reason on account of it.

So they did now, in these last moments before midnight. Despite their bandages, despite their wounds, despite their hunger and thirst, despite their fatigue, despite their pallor, many of the soldiers – mostly Narváez's men, it soon became clear – grew wildly excited and flushed in the face at the prospect of the instant, unbelievable wealth to which they'd just been invited to help themselves. Eager hands reached out, fists closed around necklaces and rings, pockets bulged. Shirts, helmets, life-saving armour, all were turned into receptacles for loot and, not content with what they could accommodate on their persons, men stowed more of the treasure away in sacks and boxes, which they somehow imagined they'd be able to transport.

Amongst the veterans, Velázquez de Léon was as covetous as any of the newcomers. Despite his great Swaggerer and other chains of gold wrapped flamboyantly around his massive neck and shoulders, he dipped his hand into the crates with a roar of enthusiasm and filled a satchel with ingots.

Others were more restrained. Bernal Díaz took no gold at all, but only four of the small green stones called *chalchihuites* that he was able to place easily beneath his cuirass.

Pepillo followed suit. Like Díaz, he knew that these curious little stones were much more highly prized amongst the Indians than gold, and would more readily buy food and lodging in times of need.

Pepillo reached down to pet Melchior.

It was a miracle he still lived, for the other war dogs had all perished in the sorties and during the siege, but he had done all in his power to keep Melchior safe from the madness.

Now Cortés approached with Malinal on his arm. 'You and your hound protected my lady in Cempoala,' he said, 'and I ask you to protect her again tonight.'

'It will be my honour,' Pepillo replied.

All the soldiers in the courtyard, heads bowed, were gathered round the kind-hearted priest, the one called Olmedo, who appeared to be offering up some kind of prayer to the god of the white-skins, no doubt seeking his protection from the terrors of the night ahead. When he was done, Cortés signalled for the gates to be opened.

Tozi watched, and followed, as the Spaniards marched out, their feet and the hooves of their horses bound in cloth to hush their tread, the wheels of their wagons muffled.

With their baggage and the need to heft the heavy wooden contraption they'd built, they still made a great deal of noise, but there was no one in the sacred precinct – not a single warrior! – to say halt to them.

It seemed the warning she'd given at the funeral had been ignored. And as a further proof that some god was tilting the balance in the Spaniards' favour, the heavens now opened and lightning flickered. With a tremendous crash, the rain that had threatened all day came down in a roaring flood.

Chapter Twenty-Three

——◆——

The Night of Sorrows: Midnight, Thursday 30 June 1520–dawn,
Friday 1 July 1520

Superstitiously impressed by the disembodied voice, and convinced by the warning it had given of an imminent Spanish escape, Cuitláhuac reluctantly permitted Guatemoc to slip away from the funeral before the closing rites – with their tedious choruses and pointless repetitions – were completed.

With Guatemoc's Mexica regiment in attendance, Starving Coyote, Big Dart and Man-Eater were waiting nearby. He beckoned them: 'Get the men in formation, fast. If the gods are with us after this ridiculous delay, I want to put some squadrons between the Spaniards and the Tacuba causeway.'

'So you believe the warning?' asked Big Dart.

'I do.'

'The voice didn't say anything about Tacuba, though,' objected Man-Eater.

'But we've made sure it's the only option for the Spaniards by removing the opening sections of the Iztapalapa and Tepeyac causeways and letting them see we'd done so. Besides, Tacuba is the obvious choice. It's the shortest and most direct route to the mainland and they've already signalled their intent to use it by trying to seize the bridges.'

'It was damned difficult to dislodge them from those bridges,' grumbled Big Dart, who'd been shot by one of the Spanish 'guns'. A little ball of metal, no larger than a fingertip, had been removed from his shoulder. Amazingly, when these tiny projectiles touched vital organs they killed.

'So what we have to do now,' Guatemoc continued, 'the very first thing, is destroy the bridges. Are there six of them, or eight?'

'Eight,' confirmed Starving Coyote.

'Very well. Man-Eater and Big Dart, take four hundred men in the

501

war canoes to tear the bridges down. You must start with the first bridge on the causeway if the Spaniards haven't reached it yet – the one nearest to the city – and work your way towards Tacuba from there until you've wrecked them all. Make sure they're completely destroyed, so no one can use them, then turn back in your canoes along the sides of the causeway until you come to the battle – wherever it's got to – and re-inforce us there.

'Starving Coyote – you're with me. We'll take the rest of the regiment to try to stop the Spaniards in the city. Before they even reach the causeway, they have to cross three canals. Not sure how they're going to do that, since the bridges over all the canals were removed days ago, but it's bound to slow them down. If we're lucky we can catch them there; if not, and they've reached the causeway, we'll pursue them until we find them stopped at a gap by Man-Eater and Big Dart's bridge breakers.'

'And all the other regiments, under Cuitláhuac, under the other generals: are they going to be part of this?'

'We're the vanguard. They'll follow as soon as they're done with their muttering around the dead.'

As Guatemoc spoke, lightning forked through the heavens, the clouds ruptured, and rain poured forth from them with startling force, hitting hard like stones in its first hissing rush, bouncing off the paving, forming pools in an instant.

There was a general movement of mourners out of the square, where the pyre had succumbed to the downpour, but it wasn't Cuitláhuac's regiments coming to fight. Most of the soldiers who'd attended the funeral hadn't heard the disembodied voice, knew nothing of what was planned and had no expectation of a battle tonight.

Their only thought was to seek shelter.

Sandoval was given charge of the vanguard, consisting of three hundred foot soldiers and twenty cavalry, every man – and every horse! – wounded but able. He also had a pair of falconets on wheeled carriages, the crews to fire them, and a small ammunition wagon drawn by *tamanes*. He found himself somewhat embarrassed when Cortés assigned the vastly more senior Diego de Ordaz as his second in command. What made it worse was that Sandoval was on horseback, though not on his dear Llesenia, lost in Saturday's battle, whereas Ordaz was on foot.

The point of a vanguard was to be at the forefront, but that was not at all the case tonight. Crab-walking awkwardly ahead of them as they marched out of the palace and across the deserted, rain-swept plaza, under the glowering bulk of the great pyramid, was the first shift of forty *tamanes*, carrying the hulking movable bridge. The plunging rain, and tendrils of fog curling up from the ground, were blessings that muffled the sounds of the escape, but they also caused men's hands and feet to slip. Twice before reaching the west gates of the sacred precinct, which hung ajar, the bridge was dropped, making a colossal din and maiming several of its bearers.

There was still not a sound from the Mexica, not a war cry, not a death whistle, and not a sight either of scouts or of regiments. For the first time Sandoval began to entertain the heady and almost unbelievable hope that he might survive the night.

A wide, empty avenue lay beyond the gates, and stretched westward from there for a little less than half a mile to its junction with the Tacuba causeway. This avenue was part of the solid ground of the island on which Tenochtitlan was built, and it was crossed by three deeply dredged canals that allowed the water traffic of Lake Texcoco to come and go. The bridges had recently been removed from the canals, and it was to span these gaps that Martin Lopez's portable contraption had primarily been conceived. Thereafter it was to be hoped that the eight bridges of the Tacuba causeway on its two-mile run to the mainland were still in place, as had certainly been the case until this afternoon. Should any have been removed, the portable bridge would have to serve to span them too.

With another mighty impact, the *tamanes* dropped the massive contraption again; even in the drenching rain the sound echoed up through the funnel of the tall townhouses lining the avenue, seeming, in Sandoval's imagination, to stun even the sky. Yet still, amazingly, no alarm was raised! A fresh shift of bearers from the reserve of four hundred hurried forward out of the column, hoisted the bridge again and moved on.

After another hundred paces, peering through the curtain of rain over the heads of the *tamanes*, Sandoval saw they were approaching the first of the canals and heard Martin Lopez call a halt.

The carpenter, known for his obstinacy as well as for his shipbuilding genius, had insisted on overseeing the operations of his bridge himself. There was a tense moment as he peered down into the watery gap, seeming to measure the distance, but then he called together a hundred of the *tamanes*, giving them instructions in signs and grunts that they seemed to understand. Fifty dived into the canal and reappeared on the other side ready to receive the bridge. Mibiercas and La Serna followed with twenty skirmishers to protect them. The other fifty edged the bridge forward with great care. Finally it was set down, perfectly in place.

'A miracle, Martin,' Sandoval said as he urged his gelding across, its iron shoes, muffled by rags, making barely a sound in the rain.

'Not a miracle,' the carpenter replied, 'but strong joints.'

The bridge would need both, Sandoval thought. Close to a thousand Spaniards had survived the past days' fighting in Tenochtitlan, along with around seven hundred Tlascalans and some twelve hundred Totonac bearers. All these, together with ten cannon and a mass of baggage and treasure, would have to cross Lopez's bridge on this soaking, dangerous night – and not simply once but several times.

Amongst the three hundred foot soldiers of the van, Díaz, Mibiercas and La Serna led a special unit of forty skirmishers. Armed with swords and light *rodelero* shields, their task was aggressively to attack, disrupt and drive back any enemy squadrons that got too close to the bridge while it was being transported, set in place, crossed, lifted and moved again.

'Well, that was easy,' said Mibiercas, after the whole army had passed over the first of the canals at a quick march without accident and without any challenge from the Mexica.

At the second canal, their passage muffled by rain, partly hidden by the rising fog, they again crossed without difficulty.

Now many were openly excited. Congratulations were being passed around, backs slapped, but Díaz didn't like it. It gave him a bad feeling, and that feeling grew into an ominous watchfulness as the third canal was reached and once again the army began to cross.

As they'd done on the two previous crossings, Mibiercas and La Serna swam the canal with twenty skirmishers and stood ready on the other side, swords drawn, shields up, as the *tamanes* wrestled the bridge over the gap, grunting and heaving in the streaming rain. A fragment of moon glared from behind thick cloud, shedding a baleful glow on the struggling men and reflecting ominously off the black waters of the canal, before being snuffed out again.

Still there was no opposition.

The rest of the van crossed, together with the three hundred *tamanes* not immediately involved in moving the bridge.

Next came the 'Battle', the middle of the army. There Cortés, mounted on Molinero, supported by Olid, Morla and Davila, also on horseback, had placed himself with a flying squad of a hundred picked foot soldiers, ready to hasten to whichever part of the column most needed reinforcement.

Directly behind the Battle, with Pepillo and Olmedo flanking her, Díaz was relieved to see Malinal and the two little children she'd adopted. This was a good position she'd found. Olmedo was unarmed but a strong man in a melee, and Pepillo, though young, wielded his sword like a master. His hound Melchior, fully armoured tonight, was at their side.

Díaz felt great tenderness towards Malinal. Indeed, he admitted to himself now – as he had done on numerous previous occasions – that he loved her. Of course he could never declare himself to the caudillo's woman! He loved her chastely, therefore, and from afar. If he were Cortés though, Díaz thought, he would have surrounded this treasure with a strong guard of soldiers, not just a page, a priest and a dog!

Behind Malinal's little group, protected by a mixed force of a hundred Spaniards and two hundred Tlascalan warriors, came the entire baggage train of wagons and overloaded horses, heaving with gold and ammunition, and the eight falconets that Cortés had brought but would not deploy tonight.

Next came a large block of two hundred of Narváez's men, some of the most useless in the army, with a hundred brave Tlascalans to stiffen their backbones.

Alvarado and Velázquez de Léon, both on horseback, commanded the rearguard, consisting of two hundred Spanish infantry, with strong contingents of pikemen, crossbowmen and arquebusiers, four hundred of the fittest and most able amongst the Tlascalans, and the remaining fifteen cavalry.

Alvarado was riding the fine mare he'd had to settle for after the loss of Bucephalus. He passed Díaz and his twenty *rodeleros* on the city side of the bridge, where they remained to defend the *tamanes*, whose next task was to push the heavy contraption across to their workmates and the rest of the army on the causeway side.

'Doesn't look like you're going to get much skirmishing done tonight, Bernal,' Alvarado said to Díaz, looking back over his shoulder as he crossed the bridge. 'This infernal rain's made all the Indians stay at home.'

Against his better judgement – perhaps things really were going to be all right after all? – Díaz was about to make a joke of it, when a mournful and horribly familiar sound pierced his ears.

It was a conch being blown, it was very close, and as it fell silent a loud voice roared out a furious threat. Díaz spoke enough Nahuatl to get the gist of it: '*Death to the wicked men who have done us so much harm*.'

Other voices – thousands of them – joined in the cry while, across the whole city, out to its furthest edges, conch blasts rose up everywhere, and a war drum, deep and loud, began to beat out from the top of the great pyramid. Suddenly arrows and spears began to fall amongst the conquistadors, slingshots whizzed through the air, clanging off armour and helmets, and through the pounding rain Díaz heard the rush and pad of the moccasin-shod feet of an immense mass of men moving directly towards his small party of skirmishers – who were now, he realised with alarm, the only Spaniards remaining on the city side of the bridge.

The first priority was to save the bridge, in case it was needed on the causeway. Díaz just had time to place his *rodeleros* in a semicircle to protect the *tamanes* as they struggled to lift it and shove it over to the other side, before a great mass of Mexica warriors came screaming out of the darkness, brandishing clubs and *macuahuitls*.

Instantly a very hot fight erupted – these Mexica were disciplined and determined – and as Díaz thrust his sword through a man's belly, smashed his shield into the face of another, and trampled a third, he saw out of the corner of his eye that Alvarado had dismounted. Better still he was striding across the bridge with Mibiercas and La Serna and the other twenty *rodeleros* in support!

Alvarado was a whirlwind of malice and deadly energy, and Mibiercas swung a sword so long and heavy that it could split a man from crown to arse. Very quickly they drove the Indians back, allowing fast-moving teams of skirmishers to dart in amongst them and cut their formations to pieces.

But the Mexica were relentless and suicidal. In a face-to-face fight, their weapons were almost useless against armour and Toledo blades. When enough of them clung to a man's arms and legs, however, they could pull him to the ground, separate him from his companions, and murder him at their leisure.

In the next moments, Díaz lost three of his *rodeleros* this way, and there was no avoiding it. Whether they were killed on the spot or held for sacrifice made no difference. The numbers of the enemy were so great it would have been madness to try to rescue them.

He became totally absorbed in the fight, lost track of the passage of time, struck a man down and was working his way around behind another when he heard Mibiercas shouting, '*The bridge is jammed. We'll have to abandon it.*'

Díaz blinked and saw La Serna, who'd lost his helmet, wrestling with a big Indian. A dagger flashed and the warrior fell back dead, but La Serna was also hurt, doubled over, holding his hand to his belly, losing a lot of blood. It looked bad.

In the same instant, Díaz understood what Mibiercas was shouting about. After taking the weight of the whole army, the portable bridge had become jammed in place and was now so firmly wedged across the last of the canals that it could no longer be lifted up and moved forward to span any further gaps that might be encountered. With arrows dropping down all around him, Martin Lopez joined the *tamanes* and a few dozen Spaniards and Tlascalans in attempts to rock it free, but to no avail. The bridge was going nowhere. The attack intensified.

'Are you all right, Alonso?' Díaz asked, taking La Serna's arm.

His friend was trembling. Blood streamed from beneath his cuirass.

'I don't think so, Bernal.' La Serna showed him the weapon he'd been stabbed with, wrested from the warrior who'd attacked him. With a shock Díaz realised this was no crude stone blade but a broadsword of Toledo steel.

And why not? It made perfect sense. Many swords had been looted from Spaniards killed and captured in the fighting of the previous days, so it had only been a matter of time before they turned up in the hands of the enemy.

Out of the dark and the rain Mibiercas appeared and took La Serna's other arm. 'Come on,' he said, 'across the bridge. We're to abandon it – Cortés's orders!'

Galloping back and forth along the column, now everywhere under ferocious attack by squadrons of Indians boiling forth from the side streets, Cortés reined in Molinero as the skirmishers fought a rapid retreat.

Catastrophe loomed.

Before Sandoval and the van could secure the permanent bridge joining the western end of the avenue to the eastern end of the causeway, a large, well-organised party of Indians in canoes had demolished it. The portable bridge could have spanned the gap. The weight of the men, horses, guns and wagons passing over it hadn't broken it – Martin's handiwork was too good – but instead had forced it down and wedged it so firmly into the dikes on either side of the canal that no amount of force could now budge it.

A return to the palace was inconceivable, and besides was absolutely blocked by the Mexica squadrons pouring in to fill the avenue all the way back to the gates of the sacred precinct. In consequence, Cortés realised with horror, the entire army now found itself packed dangerously in the dark, its movements and the transmission of orders confused by falling missiles and the enormous rainstorm, into the final stretch of the avenue between the canal and the now inaccessible causeway. Lined by looming townhouses, from the roof gardens of which mobs of Indians hurled down a deadly barrage of broken rubble, it formed a perfect death-trap, about five hundred paces in length, with side streets that allowed the enemy to reinforce and to harass the column's vulnerable flanks.

Already discipline and order were breaking down. Yes, the van was still the van – Cortés had left Sandoval in charge at the front – but the van's skirmishers were now mixed up with the rearguard; to try to move them forward through ranks that were rapidly deteriorating into a chaotic rabble would only make things worse.

That was when it occurred to Cortés that – even if the portable bridge could have been lifted one more time – the overwhelming scale and ferocity of the Indian attack would have made it impossible to move the structure forward to the causeway. It had been a chimerical idea all along, workable only in perfect conditions, a phantasm of his imagination that could not stand up to reality.

Spurring Molinero, smashing a knot of Mexica warriors aside, his sword a flash of silver in the rain as the moon again burst through the clouds, Cortés galloped back towards the head of the column.

A new idea had occurred to him, and this was no chimera.

All was not yet lost if Sandoval would only listen to reason.

We all die here, Sandoval thought gloomily as he plunged the point of his lance into a snarling Mexica face. With his twenty cavaliers, supported on Cortés's command by Olid, Morla and Davila, he'd been making charges all along the flanks of the column, aiming to break up and drive back the fresh squadrons of Indians pouring into the avenue from the side streets. And they could be broken up, and they could be driven back, but there were always more – so many more!

Where the dark, constricting avenue came to an end between the last of its looming townhouses, the army's advance had been halted at the edge of Lake Texcoco. There was a gap, five paces wide, previously spanned by the bridge that the Mexica had just destroyed. Beyond it, sturdily constructed of massive blocks of stone solidly founded on the lake bed, spacious enough for ten people to pass comfortably abreast, and raised to twice the height of a man above the open waters, the causeway stretched away towards Tacuba.

Unless by some miracle the portable bridge could be brought forward – and there was no sign of it yet! – that gap might as well have been five miles wide as five paces, for all the hope there was of getting the Spanish army across it. On the other hand, with no armour or baggage to weigh them down, several hundred Indians were already occupying the first section of the causeway, and canoes were speeding across the lake bringing further reinforcements from the city.

Although it was too wide for a man to jump, the gap wasn't wide enough to prevent arrows, slingshots and spears from flying across and finding their targets. Unable to attack, the van should have drawn back so that it was not under direct fire. This, however, was impossible, because the rest of the army – the Battle, the baggage, the Narváez block and the rearguard – was still pushing forward under intense Mexica pressure from the city side of the avenue.

That forward impetus would already have shoved everyone in the van into the lake if Sandoval hadn't deployed fifty pikemen to hold back the oncoming ranks, causing confusion that soon degenerated into fury. All in all, it was a desperate situation, and the more he thought about it, the less likely it seemed that the portable bridge could be brought forward through the panicking, tightly packed army. Yet without it, even if the baggage was abandoned, how many men would survive a mass plunge into Lake Texcoco, in the dark, under fire, to haul themselves up on to the first section of the causeway, where the Indians were already in possession and would easily destroy them?

We all die here, Sandoval thought again gloomily. He was about to make one more sally against the Mexica squadrons harrying the flanks of the column, when Cortés rode in from the rear at a gallop.

A glint of moonlight showed the caudillo's face covered in blood and a strange glint in his eyes.

Cortés looked like Satan this night, and Sandoval knew at once that what he had just acceded to was a deal with the devil that would haunt him for the rest of his life.

If he lived.

But what changed everything was the news that the portable bridge was wedged in place over the last canal and could no longer serve its purpose. If immediate action were not taken, it was certain that every man in the army would be massacred in this 'death-trap of an avenue' as Cortés had called it just before he rode back to his place at the centre of the column, with Olid, Morla and Davila flanking him.

Though it maimed his spirit to do so, therefore, Sandoval issued the command exactly as the caudillo required. Three hundred of the four hundred Totonac *tamanes* assigned to the bridge were embedded with the van and would not now be needed to take further shifts. Giving no explanation – but then who ever bothered to explain anything to *tamanes*? – he ordered them out of the column and forward to the very edge of the avenue. From there it was a sheer drop of about twelve feet to the waters below, and those closest to the edge cried out in fear and tried to struggle back.

The whole group of Totonacs now formed a frightened, milling huddle between the Spanish front rank and the fall to the lake. There, across the gap, they came under heavy bombardment from the massed Mexica warriors on the causeway.

'*Pikemen stand back!*' Sandoval roared, and suddenly the tremendous forward pressure of the whole army, held in check only by the pikes and by Spanish discipline, was released. Remorseless as a tidal wave, a great surge of men and baggage swept up the helpless *tamanes* and toppled them rank after screaming rank into the lake. There they fell promiscuously upon one another – those who could swim mixed with those who could not – but all drowning regardless because of the avalanche of men continuing to tumble down from above, crushing them, breaking their bodies and their heads, forcing those who went first deep into the thick mud beneath the water.

Lake Texcoco was everywhere quite shallow. In most parts men could stand up in it with the water rising to their chests or throats. Though it was no deeper than that here, a hundred *tamanes* were not enough to fill the gap.

Two hundred were not enough.

But perhaps fifty of the Totonacs remained alive when the mound of the dead and the desperately struggling had risen sufficiently high to form a bridge of sorts, and they were thus shoved forward over that bridge of bodies into the teeth of the Mexica squadrons awaiting them on the causeway.

510

Unarmoured and unarmed, they all died within moments, adding their corpses to the grotesque but increasingly solid human bridge across which, in great disorder, the entire army now struggled. Bizarrely and unexpectedly, although it required some clambering over, and sometimes settled alarmingly, pitching the unwary into the water, the slimy and slippery bridge of flesh held in place even as the army fell apart. Sandoval saw that his vanguard, now hopelessly mixed with the ranks behind, had ceased to function as an effective force. In the din of battle and the continual hiss of the rain, he was no longer able to give orders that would be heard or acted upon.

Then Cortés appeared, dismounted, at the head of his flying squad of a hundred skirmishers. Somehow he'd kept them in order in the midst of the madness and they now plunged across the bridge of bodies and threw themselves into the massed Mexica squadrons occupying the first section of the causeway.

'*Cut them to pieces!*' Cortés yelled.

Which was exactly what *rodeleros* like these did best.

Cortés had chosen the men well. Brabo and his lethal little squad – reduced now from twenty-five to just sixteen men – were there. But all the rest were hard cases, too: tested skirmishers, with years of brutal experience in the Italian wars, who worked together in gangs to disrupt and scatter the enemy formations.

The Mexica on the causeway, despite support from hundreds of archers and slingers in canoes, were no match for a team like this and were soon cleared. While Sandoval attempted to restore order in the van, Cortés took his hundred forward at a run, quickly covering the full quarter-mile to the second bridge.

Watched over by a tall but entirely deserted guardhouse, it was still in place!

Could it be, in their enthusiasm for what must have looked like a certain kill in that death-trap avenue, that the Indians had either forgotten or failed to see the need to destroy the rest of the causeway's eight bridges?

Whatever the explanation, Cortés knew he must seize the moment, and raced back to find the bridge of bodies connecting the city to the causeway heaped even higher. In the melee, and the unending barrage of missiles and rain, an ammunition wagon, five of the falconets, and a dead horse had become embedded in the gap, over which the army continued to flee.

Olid, Davila and Morla were there, with Velázquez de Léon holding the reins of Molinero and of Alvarado's new mare. The cavaliers had made themselves useful by pulling aside all the other horsemen as they came across – fewer than thirty survived – so that they now looked again almost like an effective mounted force. Gratefully Cortés climbed back into Molinero's saddle just as Alvarado, Díaz, Mibiercas and La Serna crossed the bridge of flesh with the last of the rearguard.

Cortés spoke briefly with De Léon and Alvarado. 'Stick with the rearguard,' he said. 'Whip them into some sort of order if you can, and keep the fucking Indians off my back while I get our people to the mainland.'

Even as he spoke, he realised how ridiculous it was to talk of order when in fact the column had long since lost any semblance of an order of battle. Not only ranks but whole sections had become incoherent, separated in some cases and intermingled in others. In the dark and the rain and the Indian onslaught, it was impossible to exercise any kind of discipline or control, and if it was not yet quite a case of every man for himself, it would soon come to that.

The only solution was to keep pushing fast towards Tacuba, taking the whole causeway by storm while the bridges were still in place. Alvarado and Léon were already about their business with the rearguard, but the rest of the cavalry would have a vital role in sweeping the enemy off the causeway.

'Forward!' Cortés yelled, and the bruised and battered column lurched into motion. Swarms of missiles continued to soar up from the flotillas of canoes that darted along the sides of the causeway, but only a few squadrons of warriors challenged the march. A single cavalry charge swept them aside and Cortés again reached the second bridge, this time posting a strong force to hold it as the army came on and began the crossing.

Man-Eater and Big Dart had disobeyed him, destroying Bridge One but then throwing themselves and their men into the fight instead of destroying Bridge Two. It was poor discipline, but Guatemoc couldn't fault them for their eagerness, and anyway they were his friends.

He crouched in the big war canoe from which he was directing the battle, looking back at the causeway over the waters of Lake Texcoco. Man-Eater, Big Dart and Starving Coyote, also in canoes, had paddled out to join him. In the past moments the rainstorm's power had been transmuted into a soft drizzle. Ragged gaps were beginning to appear in the clouds, and the moon shone through, revealing the extraordinary scene of the rout.

The fleeing white-skins had reached Bridge Two. Preceded by the compact, fast-moving troop of horsemen led by Cortés himself, who'd so contemptuously brushed aside Guatemoc's warriors on the causeway, around four hundred Spanish foot soldiers, hundreds of Tlascalans and some baggage – almost half the army – had already crossed. The rest hastened to follow.

'I'm going to get over there with a few thousand men and fuck them up,' said Guatemoc. 'Starving Coyote, you're with me again. Big Dart and Man-Eater, I want you to go after Bridge Three. Some of the Spaniards will already be at it by the time you reach it – but so will we, so leave us to do the fighting and just make sure you get that fucker down as fast as you can. Then Bridge Four. I forbid you – *I absolutely forbid you* – to rejoin the fighting until you've destroyed all the bridges. Understood?'

'Understood, boss.'

There was no time for Guatemoc to explain. If the gods blessed his plan, the portion of the Spanish army that had already crossed Bridge Two behind Cortés would be over Bridge Three before the teams with Big Dart and Man-Eater could complete their demolition work. Meanwhile, Guatemoc and Starving Coyote would fall on the remnant as it tried to follow and block its passage until Bridge Three was down.

In this way, Guatemoc hoped to split the strong Spanish force into two weaker parts. Those in the lead could be surrounded and destroyed further along the causeway, most likely between Bridge Three and Bridge Four. Meanwhile, those between Bridge Two and Bridge Three would be unable to advance further if Big Dart and Man-Eater did their work, unable to seek safety and escape in the water – for it seethed with canoes packed with slingers, spearmen and archers – and unable to retreat because of the mass of Cuitláhuac's warriors at last spewing out from the city to reinforce Guatemoc's thinly stretched regiment.

Anyway, that was the plan . . .

The moon looked down through a great rent in the clouds and cast a faint, scudding glamour over the third bridge and its towering guard-house. The bridge was blocked by a shadowy mob of ululating Mexica warriors hurling insults and missiles.

'*Santiago and at them,*' Cortés yelled, spurring Molinero from a canter to a full gallop, delighting in the urgent vibration and rumble of the causeway beneath the great stallion's iron-shod hooves as the other thirty cavaliers followed suit.

Harnessed by the skill of the riders, the speed and the weight of the huge armoured beasts gave tremendous momentum to the charge, which smashed into the Indians on the bridge, scattering them. Many were thrown into the water, and others were trampled, as the flashing swords and lances of the cavaliers hacked down and lunged forth, whirling and scything. It was as though some terrible threshing engine of the gods had got in amongst the Mexica, efficiently separating their souls from their bodies.

Cortés wheeled Molinero amidst the butchery, found a grimacing warrior gripping his stirrup, trying to unhorse him, and plunged his sword into the man's neck, releasing a gush of hot blood. An instant later the obsidian tip of an arrow shattered against his helmet. He looked up to find the guardhouse occupied by the Mexica, and was about to yell a warning when he saw that Brabo and his skirmishers, armed with swords, a few of them hefting long Chinantla lances, had already forced the door.

Minutes later, protected by a platoon carrying big *adarga* shields to deflect the infuriating barrage of projectiles hurtling from the war canoes on the lake, Cortés made a quick inspection of the bridge. So far it appeared serviceable, but more canoes had got under it like an infestation, and there were the sounds of gangs of men hacking lustily at the pilings and substructure.

Cortés posted thirty archers, thirty *rodeleros* and twenty pikemen to disperse the sappers and to defend and hold the bridge while the army crossed. He then led those who had already crossed – all the cavalry, more than four hundred Spaniards, hundreds of Tlascalans and Totonacs, the two falconets that had been with the van, an ammunition wagon, more than half the baggage and treasure wagons, and several of the lame horses carrying treasure – on a pell-mell rush through the darkness towards the fourth bridge.

It was obvious now that the Mexica intended to destroy *every* bridge, which meant that *every* bridge would have to be seized and held if the army were to have any hope of reaching the mainland.

Once your eyes got used to the dark, and more so now with the moon sometimes appearing, it was amazing what you could see. The solid stone mass and the clean geometrical lines of the causeway rising above the water were impossible to miss, providing a natural focus to the eye, while the hordes of Spaniards moving upon it were faintly silhouetted against the sky – easy targets, though their armour continued to make them extremely difficult to kill.

'Let them have Bridge Four,' Guatemoc said suddenly.

Starving Coyote didn't like it. 'Why in the name of the gods would we do that?'

'Trust me,' Guatemoc replied, 'I've got a plan.'

At the crossing of the fourth bridge, Cortés was exultant. There was solid opposition from Indians in canoes, who fired on the column from the water and leapt screaming on to the causeway in fruitless attempts to bar their path, but no demolition crew lurked amongst the pilings.

Cortés cleared the bridge, posted fifty men to defend it, and pressed on at once. In the dark and the frenzied confusion of the retreat, however, with all his men and horses already injured, and all suffering new wounds from the constant fire of the Indians, it was impossible to keep control over the army.

Unlike the avenues of the city, the causeway was too narrow and too packed with frightened, fleeing Spaniards to allow effective cavalry charges along the flanks of the column. That same crazy, panicked flight, and the relentless attacks of the Indians, also meant no battlefield communications were getting through. Of the three messengers Cortés had sent out, two hadn't come back, while the third had been snatched from the causeway in plain sight, dragged into a canoe and paddled off before he could be rescued.

The sky was brighter now than it had been when they'd left the palace; the rain had stopped and a burst of moonlight showed Cortés the hunched, shadowy forms of hundreds of his men pressing forward, almost at a run now, along the causeway. He stood in Molinero's stirrups as the throng parted around him and looked along the column. It stretched back into the darkness as far as the eye could see, ten men abreast, rank after weary rank of hobbling, wounded soldiers, defending themselves as best they could against the missiles and the raging Indians who swarmed the causeway from the lake in fleets of canoes and fell upon them in suicidal waves.

There was nothing to be done but continue this unbroken rush hell for leather to Tacuba, secure every bridge, and save as many lives as possible.

*   *   *

515

'I don't understand why you changed the plan,' objected Starving Coyote.

They were talking amidst the carnage at Bridge Three, where the entire Spanish garrison had just been wiped out.

'Right there,' Guatemoc answered, 'is why I give orders and you take them . . . Look, it's really very simple. For whatever unfathomable reason of their own, the Spaniards have decided to do our work for us, dividing themselves up into smaller units that are easier to kill. So I say, let's allow them to put fifty men at every guardhouse along the causeway – because that's obviously *their* plan. They think they're going to hold those bridges to allow their army to pass through safely, but we've just proved that fifty Spaniards at a time are much easier to kill than hundreds of them together.'

'Actually, it looks like fifty at the other bridges but it was more like eighty here.'

'Which only strengthens my point. Out on the causeway, in the dark, with their discipline breaking down, cut off from all support, the white-skins aren't that hard to kill.'

'We still lost at least a thousand men killing eighty of them – mostly not our crew, I hasten to add – but, nonetheless, killed is killed.'

'We have the numbers,' Guatemoc replied with a shrug, 'so please take another of my father's regiments by canoe to kill the garrison of white-skins at Bridge Five, hold it so that Big Dart and Mud Head can tear it down, and then get the other side of the gap and defend it with your lives. I don't want a single one of the Spaniards on this side of it to get through.'

'What about the later bridges? Six? Seven? Eight? Do we take them too?'

'Yes! Send squads to take them all. Kill their garrisons or capture them for sacrifice, I don't care which. Your men do the fighting. Mud Head and Big Dart do the wrecking.'

Breaking the final bridges was a safety precaution, a contingency plan in the unlikely event that any of the Spaniards from the rearguard were able to fight their way through. Nonetheless, Guatemoc was determined that the real kill zone should be here, between Bridges Three and Five, where roughly half the Spanish army would be trapped the moment Bridge Five fell.

The beauty, in the darkness and confusion, was that Cortés wouldn't even know it had happened. According to Guatemoc's scouts, who moved back and forth constantly in fast canoes, the Spanish war leader was already far past Bridge Five with half his army and would soon cross Bridge Six.

Supporting La Serna between them, an arm over each of their shoulders, Díaz and Mibiercas had crossed the third bridge. Finding themselves in a lull, facing only light and sporadic attacks, they'd moved ahead with the rest of the column, which increasingly resembled a mob of frightened refugees. The fourth bridge was held by the fifty soldiers Cortés had wisely placed in the guardhouse, some of whom came forth to greet them as they passed, when a great splashing of paddles was heard from the lake and a terrifying horde of Indians shot forth out of the darkness in an armada of canoes. They assailed the column on both sides with a squall of missiles, and swarmed on to the causeway itself in such numbers, and with such furious violence, that the last semblance of order was lost, discipline was abandoned and panic blazed through the scattered and hopelessly uncoordinated ranks.

Díaz and Mibiercas defended themselves, and in the scrimmage a big Mexica warrior grabbed La Serna firmly by the hair, dragged him violently towards the edge of the causeway and pulled him into a canoe.

It was a sad night, Díaz reflected, when the best that you could hope for a dear friend was that he would die of his injuries before he could be sacrificed.

Out of the corner of his eye, he saw Alvarado and Velázquez de Léon ride by at a gallop, heading towards the fifth bridge. Minutes later, however, as the dismayed and broken column continued to file past, they forced their way back through the throng with the desperate news that the bridge had been sabotaged.

Where it had stood there was now only a plunging gap, five paces wide, into the waters of Lake Texcoco. Beyond it, bristling with weapons, hosts of warriors occupied the Tacuba side of the causeway, while others, slingshots and bows at the ready, watched the gap from a fleet of war canoes.

It was amazing, Alvarado thought, after their brief reconnaissance, how rapidly the quarter mile between the fourth bridge and the now-demolished fifth bridge had filled up with Indians swarming on to it from canoes on the lake. They were so thickly packed that he and Velázquez de Léon were both obliged to dismount. As they did so he noticed for the first time how heavily loaded Juan's saddle bags were.

517

He even had a fair-sized strongbox strapped to his horse's back. And amazingly, in the heat of battle, not only was his massive Swaggerer wound twice around his neck and shoulders, but also two more very long and heavy gold chains.

'You're wearing the price of a ship and an estate in Castile, Juan,' Alvarado said. 'Mind you don't end up in the water or the weight will drown you.'

Securing a strap on a saddle bag, Velázquez de Léon didn't seem to hear him although, for a moment, it was as if they and the horses stood in the eye of a hurricane. On the Tenochtitlan side, Díaz and Mibiercas, with a handful of the skirmishers from the van, some units of the Spanish rearguard, and a wedge of Tlascalan warriors, held back the onrushing Indians. Meanwhile, enough of the retreating column, with much of the baggage, had pushed forward over the fourth bridge to match the numbers of the Indian squadrons on the Tacuba side.

Somewhere up ahead, Alvarado knew because he'd seen them pass, were two falconets that had originally been with Sandoval and the van, but had now become absorbed into the general stampede. In the chaos, nobody seemed to have thought of loading them with grapeshot and bringing them to bear on the Indians on the causeway. Leaving De Léon with the horses, Alvarado drew his falchion and barged forward through the crowd.

Passing so many injured men, some crying out in pain, some trembling and weeping like girls, others plainly on their last legs, with hardly the strength to take another step, it occurred to Alvarado that he might not survive the night. The prospect of death wasn't terrifying – in truth he never thought about it – but he would slit his own throat rather than be hauled off for sacrifice.

He was forcing his way through the packed middle of the column. Everyone wanted to be there, as far from the Indian spears as possible, so men pushed back and snarled as he shoved them aside. When one of the fools tried to wrestle with him, Alvarado yelled, '*I don't have time for this*,' and plunged his quillon dagger into the man's eye, sending him reeling and screaming to the ground, where he fell under the onrushing feet of the mob behind.

Passing Malinal, Pepillo, his dog, a couple of native brats, and Olmedo, Alvarado saw that even the friar had armed himself tonight. Somewhere he'd picked up one of the Indians' mahogany war clubs and used it to brain a brace of Mexica warriors who audaciously thrust themselves into the midst of the column and tried to drag Malinal away. As Pepillo gutted another man with that fine sword Escalante had given him, Alvarado asked: 'Have you seen the falconets? Our lives depend on it.'

'Right there,' the boy gasped, 'just past those wagons.'

Alvarado jogged forwards again. Pulled by *tamanes*, there was a knot of baggage, treasure, and ammunition wagons ahead, so close together that their wheels banged and jostled. He threw himself into a running jump, landed high up on a stack of boxes, pushed off from them over the heads of the *tamanes* and came down lightly on the balls of his feet in front of them.

Pepillo was right. The falconets were here with their crews, but with Spaniards in front of them and no orders, they hadn't known what to do.

Alvarado took charge at once.

In her invisible state, the bonds that connected Tozi to the material world were loosened. Her clothes and the contents of her pockets and anything she carried always faded with her and, if she focused her will, she was able to spread the field of magic to other things and to the people around her. She could pick up objects and use them if she chose to do so, but she was also able to make herself as insubstantial as thought and flow in this form through the air, into the sky, and even through solid matter. The keys to control were always the same, focus and intention, so she focused now as she slipped invisibly away from Malinal, Pepillo and the children. Since they hadn't yet suspected her presence, they would hardly notice her gone.

The Spanish retreat was immense, strung out, haphazard, and under ferocious attack on every side. It was a miracle that all were not already dead, for here in the dark, in the narrow confines of the causeway, in the midst of a great lake of salt water, the discipline they prided themselves on, and that kept them alive on the battlefield every bit as much as their armour, had almost entirely collapsed.

It wouldn't be long before Guatemoc had the victory Tozi so much wished for him. Yet, flowing invisibly along the causeway, free as a bird in her movements, she saw only the terrible and immediate danger in which Malinal and the children now found themselves.

First, they were trapped between Bridge Three, which was in Mexica hands, and Bridge Five, which had been destroyed.

Secondly, they were with only a rump of the army – for hundreds of men, including Cortés himself, were nowhere to be seen. Had they been killed already? Or were they somewhere much further ahead? Either way, they would not be coming to the rescue.

Thirdly, and most urgently, Malinal was a famous woman, the consort of the self-styled conqueror, and several Mexica snatch squads had already made attempts on her. It was obvious they'd been sent out specifically to seize her and carry her off for sacrifice.

Surely Guatemoc, who knew Tozi's feelings for Malinal, couldn't have ordered this? Such petty vindictiveness smelt more of Cuitláhuac's hatred and resentment. But it made no difference who was behind it. If Malinal stayed in this maelstrom, she'd certainly be taken. Therefore, she must be removed from it, and since she'd rejected all offers of help, she'd have to be removed from it against her will – something she might never forgive. The really tricky bit, though, would be projecting a field of magic that would enfold her and the children without at the same time enfolding Olmedo, Pepillo and Pepillo's dog. This would work best if Malinal could be persuaded to hold the children while making no contact with the others, but Tozi knew her friend would never agree to that.

She returned to Malinal to find her again under attack. A snatch squad of five braves had broken through into the midst of the column. They had their hands on her, one of them punched her hard in the face, knocking her senseless, and they sprinted to make off with her. The Spaniards on either side fled by with their eyes averted, but the dog reacted instantly, sinking its teeth into the loins of one of the Mexica and bearing him to the ground. In the last moments, Olmedo had somehow lost his club, but he waded unarmed into the other four, wrestling with them, breaking their grip on Malinal, pounding one with a bunched fist, taking another by the throat while Pepillo darted round the edges of the scrum, lunging once, twice, thrice, four times, and killed them all. 'Good boy,' Tozi heard him say as he turned to see the hound with its snout in the bloody entrails of the fifth man, and at once raised his sword as another squad came pounding in.

There were eight of them this time, a gang of burly, hard-bitten Cuahchics, but they hadn't come to snatch.

Armed with *macuahuitls*, they'd come to kill.

The blow had knocked Malinal out, and consciousness returned as though through a deep and turbid fog filled with roaring, incoherent noise.

The din began to take shape – men shouting, a clash of weapons, grunts and cries – and Malinal's eyes fluttered open in the darkness to the realisation that she was face-down on the paving of the causeway. Miahuatl and Coyotl lay pressed against her, both whimpering with fear. Standing over the three of them, Pepillo and Olmedo fought desperately to hold back a gang of Cuahchics, while other Spaniards hurried by as though it was none of their business.

That was when, distinguishing itself from all the other sounds, Malinal began to detect the cadences of a guttural, throaty chant – an eerie, rough, whispering snarl that had the rhythms of magic and that she would know anywhere.

Coyotl and Miahuatl were already holding her, and as the field of Tozi's magic began to crackle and sparkle all around them, she reached out her hands and took Pepillo and Olmedo by the ankles.

By brute force, not hesitating to strike fellow Spaniards with the flat of his falchion when they failed to get out of his way, threatening death to any who gainsaid him, Alvarado forced the *tamanes* and crews to wrestle the two falconets to the front, where a block of pikemen were doing a reasonable job of holding back the enemy.

They immediately saw the point of the falconets, orders were barked, and Alvarado instructed the teams to bring the guns through the ranks on their wheeled carriages, with a small ammunition wagon between them, so far as possible keeping them concealed from the Indians ahead.

Packed with double loads of grapeshot, lethal at close range, the cannon were primed and ready to fire. The crews rolled them forward until their barrels jutted through the front rank of pikemen and their black mouths bore directly on the raging mass of the enemy.

'*Mueran!*' shouted Alvarado. He dodged a spear that stung his cheek as it brushed past, and with a prodigious, deafening crash that made his ears ring, both the falconets fired at once, their barrels belching yellow flame into the night and throwing up a dense pall of sulphurous smoke.

When it cleared, nothing but beautiful devastation lay ahead. As though a ripe crop had been struck by some huge rushing wind, Indians lay scattered everywhere along the best part of a hundred paces of the causeway, some in their ranks where they had fallen, some in groaning, bleeding heaps, those nearby so filleted and dismembered by the storm of shot that their bodies were barely recognisable as human.

The moonlight showed swarms of other Indians leaping on to the causeway from their canoes, but they hesitated when they saw the carnage, their faces aghast.

'*Mueran!*' yelled Alvarado, and led the charge that scattered them, bringing the squad of pikemen in a single muscular surge to the brink of the gap where the fifth bridge had stood. The dark waters of the lake below were already choked with bodies, mostly Spaniards gazing up sightlessly at the moon. For a moment Alvarado couldn't understand how they'd got there, but then remembered the garrisons that Cortés had left at the third and fourth bridges.

Obviously Hernán was garrisoning every bridge. Equally obviously – with the exception of the fourth bridge, left untouched deliberately to make enough space for the front and rear of the Spanish army to become separated – the Indians were going to wipe out every one of these garrisons.

But would they also succeed in wiping out what was left of the rump, presently stuck between the third and fifth bridges? The poor, shattered, devastated rump that it was Alvarado's dubious honour to lead?

'*Mueran!*' he yelled, and the falconets poked through the ranks of pikemen and vomited flame again, this time blasting across the gap into the massed ranks of Mexica warriors occupying the next stretch of the causeway. As before, the butchery was immense, and as before the dead were rapidly replaced by fresh squadrons of Indians swarming out of their canoes and on to the causeway.

Alvarado was about to order the pikemen back and some shield bearers forward to protect the gun crews from slingshots and arrows, when there came a sudden tremendous surge of movement, with those behind shoved violently forward against those in front. Such surges happened in battle, and often you never learned why, but this one was so forceful and so fast that Alvarado only escaped it by leaping up on to the parapet as the first three ranks of pikemen, the ammunition wagon, both the cannon and most of their crew were pitched into the gap. Some lay smashed and dead in the fall amongst the guns, sinking to the bottom of the lake, others drowned, others struggled to climb the slippery pilings in their wet clothes and heavy armour but were dragged down again by Indians, who clubbed them over the head, hauled them into their canoes and paddled off triumphantly into the dark.

Alvarado thought quickly. There were no *tamanes* here to sacrifice, as Sandoval had done at the first bridge, so if there was another surge, many more Spaniards were going to end up in the water. There were, however, *tamanes* with the baggage wagons, not so far back, and the wagons themselves might fill the gap if enough of them were pitched into it.

It was difficult to make himself understood in the confusion, but with punches and kicks and the edge of his sword he urged the wagons forward, and one after the other the *tamanes*, unarmoured and taking fearful losses under the unremitting hail of missiles, shoved them through the gap. On top of the bodies, the cannon and other debris already down there, three loaded wagons packed with bulky baggage were sufficient to make a platform, across which foot soldiers could scramble with difficulty.

But then out of the night, with a great thunder of hooves, scattering men, a runaway horse appeared, its eyes rolling, bleeding from a great gash in its neck. De Léon's dappled mare! Heavily burdened as it was, it plunged into the gap with terrified screams, foundered, broke a leg with a sickening snap amongst the shattered wagons, tumbled sideways breaking another leg, and lay kicking spastically, deeply embedded in the midst of the pile of rubble, the bellows of its breath heaving, surrounded by a great spray of spilled jewels and ingots, like false promises glittering in the moonlight.

And now here came Juan after his treasure!

Being a man who liked gold himself, Alvarado could understand the big cavalier's haste. But gold could be won and lost and won again, while life, once lost, was lost forever, and for no quantity of treasure would Alvarado have done what Juan did next, which was to leap into the perilous gap, on to that toppling, shifting mound of bodies and baggage and guns and broken wagons, and there to unstrap the strongbox from the back of his still pitifully whinnying and struggling mare. He had it off in a moment, though, and was about to hoist himself up to the causeway again when a second surge, not as forceful as the last, pushed a dozen more men into the choked and treacherous gap on top of him. Most scrambled out, cursing, and joined the fight on the causeway, but some lay where they'd fallen, already trampled deeper into the mound by the ranks behind, who in turn were followed by more waves of men.

Velázquez de Léon, Alvarado saw, had become part of the bridge now, a corpse stretched out beside his dying horse, jostled by other dead men, his Swaggerer still wrapped around his neck, while the rump of the army stamped over him regardless and got to grips with the enemy.

Alvarado didn't need to urge them on because they were all fighting for their lives. Every foot of the causeway would be contested, and every broken bridge would pose a fresh challenge, to which they'd have to find a solution or die. But it was a foolish army, even in a rout, that failed to keep its rearguard strong, and those surges suggested some extraordinary pressure.

What was the state of the rearguard now? Had it been broken?

Against the tide of fleeing men, Alvarado turned back towards the fourth bridge to find out.

So rapid was the advance led by Sandoval and Cortés that they passed the fifth, sixth, seventh, and eighth bridges before any of the Indians could get to them in their canoes. Sandoval's mind was still reeling at how Cortés had talked him into marching hundreds of *tamanes* to their deaths at the first bridge. He could only hope that the garrisons of fifty men posted at each of the remaining bridges would make any further such actions unnecessary.

The most obvious immediate outcome of leaving the garrisons, however, was that the large contingent of four hundred men or thereabouts – with which they had reached the fifth bridge – had been reduced to just two hundred men – more or less – by the time they'd passed the eighth bridge. And those two hundred with whom they limped into Tacuba were all so exhausted and in many cases so severely injured that they could do nothing except drop to the ground like the dead beneath the huge ceiba tree at the centre of the deserted main square. Though they were in the extremities of thirst, few even had the strength to ask for water, so Sandoval ordered a squad to raid neighbouring houses for suitable vessels and to bring refreshment for all from the town spring.

Mounted on Molinero, Cortés trotted up out of the darkness. Around him, also on horseback, were Olid, Davila and Morla. Cortés cast a glance in the direction of the causeway. Very faintly, as though coming from a great distance, sounds of fighting carried across the water. 'Something's gone wrong,' he said. 'Let's go and see if we can help.'

There was no question, Sandoval thought, of taking any of the wounded, bone-weary foot soldiers. They could not move another step if their lives depended on it. It was miracle enough that in the rapid dash to the mainland they had got as many as two hundred away, with some of the baggage and close to thirty horses. Now the most immediate danger was that the Mexica would pursue them to Tacuba, though there was no indication of that yet. Perhaps they were too busy fighting the remnant

524

of the army still battling along the causeway. Or perhaps they would come at any moment and massacre the weary refugees prostrated beneath the tree.

'I'm not talking about a rescue mission,' Cortés continued, 'but I for one cannot have it said that we fled and left them at the bridges. Olid, Davila and Morla are with me. Will you join us also, Gonzalo? A quick gallop along the causeway to see if all is lost, or if we may yet salvage something from the wreck.'

'I'm with you,' Sandoval replied as he mounted the good gelding with which he'd replaced Llesenia. This horse, like all the others that had survived the exodus from Tenochtitlan, was winded and leery, bleeding from numerous flesh wounds, legs bruised and swollen by slingshots, but still capable of walking, perhaps even a canter, though he doubted a gallop would be possible. Still, Sandoval's gelding, and the mounts ridden by Olid, Davila and Morla, were in better shape than most of the rest, which would need days of rest and healing if they were ever to take part in a cavalry charge again.

Ordaz seemed at death's door from his wounds, his face ashen, blood dripping from beneath his armour, but he stirred himself when he was told what was planned and accepted command of the fugitives beneath the tree. 'They cannot just be left there to sleep,' Cortés urged. 'Do what you can. Post scouts. Organise defences. Another attack may come at any moment.'

Then together in a tight group, moving at a gentle trot and picking up the pace as they left the square, Cortés and Sandoval, Olid, Morla and Davila took the avenue that led down to the causeway. The rainstorm had completely cleared, the wind had broken up much of the cloud cover, and a baleful glow radiated from the chunk of moon now far over in the western sector of the sky, and perhaps an hour from setting, just as the first faint glimmer of a false dawn showed in the east.

Privately Olmedo was not immune to doubts over the truth of his most deeply held beliefs. In his darkest hours, he had even been known to wonder if there was a God at all.

But no longer – for his faith had been renewed! This night he had witnessed and participated in a miracle, and it was rightly said that all miracles worked by a mortal saint come ultimately from God.

When they were in the gravest of danger, pressed closely by Indians on every side, little Tozi had appeared out of nowhere and spirited them away. Somehow, as though it were projected by her voice, emerging from her throat in an uncanny, guttural chant, a transparent, filmy screen had formed around them, spreading out rapidly into a sphere, enclosing and protecting them. They could not reach beyond the margins of this sphere – for Pepillo had tried and failed when his dog was left behind – and it seemed that within it they were invisible to those outside.

What else, then, but the power of God could have accomplished such a marvel, and what else could Tozi be but a saint?

Carried along in her bubble of light, with Miahuatl and Coyotl uttering delighted cries, they had first soared above the embattled causeway, and then raced at dazzling speed along its full length towards Tacuba, where finally the sphere had dissolved, spilling them out in a pool of deep shadow on a side street near the square. The two children winced when harsh words in Nahuatl, a language in which Olmedo was gaining some proficiency, were exchanged between Malinal and Tozi. They spoke too fast for him to follow it all, but the gist was clear enough – and passing strange and most unsaintly. Tozi was angry with Malinal for loving Cortés and Malinal was angry with Tozi for rescuing her!

'Shut up the pair of you,' Pepillo interrupted in his own good Nahuatl. 'I didn't ask to be rescued either!'

'I, for my part,' Olmedo felt compelled to add, 'am very happy and grateful to be rescued and count young Tozi amongst the blessed saints for doing so.'

As he spoke, another miracle! With the same mysterious shimmer of air that had announced her presence when she appeared, the girl simply vanished again – vanished on the spot, without a trace, and was gone.

Olmedo blinked and looked around. At the end of the street, he realised, torches were already blazing, men and horses moving, weary Spanish voices raised. Thanks be to God – the final miracle! – it seemed the army's vanguard must have made it safely across.

Would they send help back to the others, still beset out on the lake?

Even as the thought came to him, Olmedo saw several men on horseback detach themselves from the rest and enter the avenue that led to the Tacuba causeway.

Pepillo turned in the same direction and hurried off.

'Where are you going?' Olmedo called.

'To find my dog,' the boy replied.

* * *

Díaz was weary of life, weary of death, weary of fighting.

How many hours – or weeks, months, or *years* of night – had passed since they'd marched out of the palace? He could not even guess how long it had been since a great onrush of fresh Mexica warriors had pushed him, Mibiercas and what remained of the fragmented rearguard off the fourth bridge and a dozen paces closer to the fifth bridge in a matter of seconds. But they'd dug their heels in there, fighting every step of the way to hold ground so that those in front might have a chance to escape.

A second surge pushed them back again, but soon after that Alvarado joined them, coming up suddenly out of the night, bringing fear to the enemy. He'd been at their side, a reassuring warrior presence, as they'd held the rear of the fighting retreat all the way back across the fifth gap in the causeway, choked with the dead now, and to the edge of the sixth, where more corpses lay entangled – Spaniards, Totonacs, Tlascalans, Mexica, all tossed together in a heap, but not yet high enough to allow a rapid crossing.

Still, many must have crossed – for the bodies of slaughtered Indians lay strewn between the parapets of the otherwise deserted stretch of causeway on the Tacuba side of the gap. Of the column itself, however, there was no sign.

How had it got so far ahead?

Or had it been wiped out to the last man?

Either way, the result was the same. A dozen Tlascalans led by Shikotenka, and just eight Spaniards, including Alvarado, Díaz and Mibiercas, were all that remained of the rearguard – which was no longer guarding anything and had been reduced to a tiny, isolated, no-account gang of desperate scrappers at the edge of a difficult gap.

'I'll hold them here,' Alvarado growled, looking back at the horde of Mexica warriors rushing them from the Tenochtitlan side of the causeway. 'You boys get across. I'll follow after.'

'Are you mad?' asked Díaz. 'If you stay here you'll die.'

'And if someone doesn't hold the gap, we'll all die. Anyway, I'm spoiling for a fight.'

'Go!' Shikotenka told Díaz, intervening suddenly. It was always a surprise to remember that the Tlascalan chief spoke a little Spanish. 'I will stay with Don Pedro and six of our warriors.'

Díaz considered a heroic moment – should he volunteer for this suicide mission? – but rapidly decided against it. He'd satisfied honour enough tonight; now it was time to get out of here.

*   *   *

527

The first bridge on the Tacuba side of the causeway – the eighth if you were travelling from the direction of Tenochtitlan – had been destroyed in the interval of an hour since they'd crossed it. The garrison of fifty men Cortés had left in the guardhouse there had been slaughtered. He counted thirty-two mutilated bodies; the other eighteen had certainly been carried off for sacrifice.

Alerted by cries he looked up and saw a stampeding herd of Spanish soldiers, more than seventy of them, he thought, but fewer than a hundred, running and stumbling along the causeway towards them from the direction of the next bridge. They might have been fleeing from the devil himself to judge by their terror, though there was no immediate sign of pursuit.

Without hesitation they threw themselves into the gap (the water was not deep), scaled the pilings and climbed out on the Tacuba side.

'What's happening?' Cortés demanded as the first few of them drew level with him where he was seated on Molinero.

'It's a bloodbath, sir. The garrisons you left at all the bridges were massacred, and those of us in the column, sir, we were trapped on the causeway. Hundreds were killed or dragged off for sacrifice.'

'Does Don Pedro de Alvarado still live?' Cortés asked.

'I can't say as I know, sir. But I pray that he does.'

'And are there other survivors like yourselves?'

A shrug. 'I never had time to look back, sir. But I pray that there are.'

'Well, make your way ahead, up into the main square. You'll find two hundred survivors there. Report to Don Diego de Ordaz. He'll tell you what to do.'

Cortés turned to the other cavaliers. 'Gentlemen, it is unnecessary for you to proceed further. You will be putting yourselves in grave danger for no good reason, for I fear there is very little any of us can do.' Dismounting from Molinero, he handed the reins to Sandoval. 'Keep an eye on him for me, Gonzalo.'

'But where are you going, Caudillo?'

'To find Don Pedro. I put him in charge of the rearguard and, if I know him well, he'll be the last man of our army off the causeway.'

'But do you yourself have to go, Caudillo? Is it wise? Can you not send others?'

'No,' Cortés replied. He'd already thought about it and rejected it. 'This is something I have to do alone.'

Moments later, having stripped off much of his armour except his

528

cuirass and backplate, he strode into the stinking, salty goo of Lake Texcoco, which rose no higher than his chest, clambered up on to the causeway and began to jog towards the next bridge.

This was something that he had to do alone, but it wasn't really about rescuing Alvarado.

This was penance for his own terrible mistakes.

It was almost unbelievable, but nevertheless true, Guatemoc realised, that he had lost control of the battle because of a combination of Mexica greed and his father's unexpected lust for sacrificing Spaniards.

On this night, when the only goal should have been the complete annihilation of the white-skins, Cuitláhuac had squandered a great deal of time and manpower on some mad project to capture as many as possible alive so that they could be offered up as a mass sacrifice on the great pyramid.

Worse, Guatemoc had discovered that his father had assigned no less than ten snatch squads to capture or kill that filthy bitch Malinal. He had no problem with killing her, although Tozi wouldn't like it, but it was a diversion tonight when killing Spaniards should have been the entire focus.

Worst of all, however, was the rowdy and undisciplined behaviour of the Mexica regiments around the causeway. From the moment the white-skins' baggage had begun to spill, the now bright and unwavering moon had revealed a dazzling bounty.

Here was the wealth in gold and jewels that they had stolen from the court of Moctezuma!

Here were the strange and mysterious possessions of the Spaniards themselves – objects never before seen that must surely possess enormous power!

And here were many highly prized Spanish weapons!

All in all, it was easy to see why warriors found it difficult to resist such rich and curious temptations, but the result had been a shameful frenzy of looting into which thousands had become drawn.

Idiots! Guatemoc thought. Of course they should have resisted! Because the damage caused by their failure to press the enemy was immense. Reports from the scouts left no doubt that Cortés had already got around two hundred of his men across to Tacuba, and others, perhaps as many again, were now pouring off the end of the causeway to join them there. Yes, hundreds of the bastards had been killed! Yes, many had been taken alive and were even now being prepared for sacrifice! Yes, they had been separated from much of what they'd stolen!

But none of that mattered in the least.

What mattered, the only important thing, was that hundreds of them still lived, amongst them Cortés himself! If they were allowed to escape tonight, how long would it be before they were back bearing a grudge and seeking revenge?

Yet Guatemoc did not see how he could prevent their escape, for as the men of the Mexica regiments finished looting the bodies and wagons along the causeway, the great majority of them were drawn back to Tenochtitlan by the news that a large party of Spaniards had been left behind to defend Axayacatl's palace. Cuitláhuac had ordered that they were to be rooted out at once and that until that was done all other operations were to cease.

What fucking stupidity! Guatemoc thought.

Some of his men, a few hundred, were still on the causeway, in the stretch between Bridge Six and Bridge Seven, finishing off the last of the Spanish rearguard. Those few hundred men would not be enough to take on the white-skins in the numbers now reported to be assembling at Tacuba, and nor did Guatemoc intend that they should. It was, he realised, an act of the gods that Cuitláhuac had confined his Chichemecs to their camp outside Tacuba, because now they were just an hour's march away and could be deployed against the surviving Spaniards by the morning, even if Cuitláhuac himself required the entire Mexica army to witness the sacrifices in Tenochtitlan.

Jogging towards the gap formerly spanned by the second bridge from the Tacuba side – the seventh from the Tenochtitlan side – Cortés passed many more groups of stragglers. It was hard to keep anything like an exact count, but he guessed perhaps another eighty men fled by, all running in the greatest haste and dread, and every one of them injured, bleeding and exhausted.

As he reached the gap, which was choked though not filled with bodies, another large party of Spaniards fled across it, some losing their footing and falling amongst the corpses, only to be stamped and crushed by other men coming behind. Those who clambered out safely included Díaz and Mibiercas, with a few of the Spaniards and Tlascalans from Alvarado's original rearguard.

'Where's Don Pedro?' Cortés yelled.

It was Díaz who replied: 'He wouldn't run. He made us leave him at the sixth bridge with Shikotenka and some of the Tlascalans. He said he was spoiling for a fight, sir.'

More men were struggling across, too many for Cortés to force his way through, so he jumped into the lake and began to wade around the side of the gap, intending to climb out on the other side of the causeway. The water was a little deeper here, almost up to his neck; he hoped not to have to discover whether it was possible to swim in even the minimal armour he was wearing now. As he took another step forward through the cloying mud, he felt a pair of strong hands grip his ankles and then, to his horror, pull his legs from under him, pitching him into the lake.

Cortés seemed intent on retracing the night's route along the causeway, and that was Pepillo's intention too, at least until he found Melchior, so he followed the caudillo, finding his presence ahead reassuring.

When Cortés went in the water, Pepillo waited for an interval before jumping in too. He didn't want his master to see him and send him back. But in that interval, at the edge of vision where the night met the lake, a flash of paddles caught his eye. A sleek canoe shot stealthily in, out of the darkness, passing very close to Cortés, yet unseen by him. From the canoe, a naked man slipped soundlessly into the water, while four others stayed behind, crouching in its belly, eagerly watching.

Pepillo had seen enough snatch squads in action during the retreat to begin to guess what would happen next. He ran along the parapet twelve feet above the canoe, and when Cortés was pulled beneath the water, he leaped directly down into it, striking it amidships and capsizing it. The four warriors spilled out and, at the same time, in a great upward surge, Cortés broke the surface, gripping his attacker by the throat and thrusting his sword repeatedly into his belly.

The other four men clustered round now. Pepillo had never learned to swim and the water here was deeper than before, but he was tall for his years and succeeded in keeping his head above it as he found himself back to back with the caudillo.

'What are you doing here, lad?' Cortés asked.

'Came to find my dog, sir.'

Their assailants moved closer and it seemed they must face a tough fight in a difficult place, when suddenly two big Tlascalans came leaping down from the causeway and ended everything in seconds.

'Shikotenka!' Cortés said with a grin. 'I do believe you've just saved my life again.'

When Cortés and Pepillo hauled themselves out of the lake with Shikotenka and Tree, they were on the Tacuba side of the causeway, but could now see Alvarado clearly where he remained on the Tenochtitlan side swinging his falchion. 'Come on you fuckers,' he yelled at the band of warriors who confronted him. 'Let's see what you've got.'

'*Get out of there, Pedro!*' Cortés shouted over the gap, and it did sound like a tremendously good idea, but how was he to accomplish it with this screaming horde around his ears and a deadfall half clogged with bodies to negotiate.

The deadfall was just five paces wide, and suddenly Alvarado remembered a conversation he'd had the year before with Sandoval and Olid when they'd first crossed the Iztapalapa causeway where the bridges spanned much wider distances. He'd boasted he could jump the width of one of those big bridges so, certainly, he should be able to jump this one – though the lack of space for a run-up, the weight of his armour, and blood loss from the many cuts he'd suffered, threatened the enterprise.

He was just thinking it would have to be the water for him, when he spotted one of the long Chinantla lances discarded amongst other debris of war on the causeway. He gave a great roar and charged his attackers, sweeping the blade of his falchion in wide, scything arcs to force them back, then, at the last moment – and in a way he hated to do it – he turned tail on them and ran.

There was an instant of shocked silence before the Indians surged after him, but by then Alvarado had picked up the lance, darted forward, planted the end of the sixteen-foot weapon firmly on the pile of corpses and vaulted over the gap.

'Nice to have you back with us, Pedro,' Cortés said. 'For a moment you had us worried there.'

A blare of sound emanating from Tenochtitlan carried clear across the waters, conch after conch blasting a terrible intuition into the night.

And then, mournful and deep, hollow and gut-wrenching, beating out from the top of the great pyramid and seeming to clutch at the heart, came the sound of the snakeskin drum – the sound that always announced the commencement of the most important sacrifices to the gods.

At once the warriors who'd been about to cross the gap in pursuit turned back towards Tenochtitlan, or slipped over the sides of the causeway into waiting canoes which whisked them off. In moments, all of them were gone, and what was left was only the terrible cadence of that drum and the first clear light of the true dawn seeping into the sky.

An hour later, as the day brightened, the horrifying drumbeats continued, and Cortés learned the cost of this night of sorrows. Miraculously, Malinal and the children she'd brought with her had survived, but more than six hundred Spaniards had been killed or dragged away for sacrifice during the exodus along the causeway, all but twenty of the Tlascalans and almost all the Totonac bearers. All the cannon had been lost. Of the thirty horses that had survived the crossing – themselves a mere remnant of the eighty that had proudly trooped into Tenochtitlan on 24 June – seven were permanently lamed. Since they would never work again, their throats were cut on the spot and they were butchered, roasted and eaten by the hungry men.

Mexica scouts were seen from time to time, flitting around the edges of the square, and when one of these was captured and tortured, he confessed that an attack was imminent.

Cortés needed no further urging. He'd had his fill of city fighting in the past days; if he were to be brought to battle again soon, he preferred it to be in the open with his forces deployed on a high place.

He would not contemplate defeat. What had happened in Tenochtitlan was a reverse only, brought about not primarily by his own failings, nor even by Alvarado's penchant for violence, but entirely by that bastard Diego de Velázquez and his bum-boy Narváez. They were the ones who'd caused all the trouble and broken the firm grip Cortés had previously held on the Mexica capital. Absent their intervention, he was certain he would have been able to extend his control over the whole of New Spain without bloodshed.

But all that was past history now, and the future lay ahead. That six hundred had been lost was a tragedy, but that four hundred had survived was a triumph, and Cortés intended to use them as the nucleus around which he would build a new army to reconquer Tenochtitlan.

Shikotenka, whose generosity of spirit he would never forget, had offered them sanctuary. They would be exposed to Mexica attacks on the march, but now they were out in the open Cortés was confident they'd survive them and reach Tlascala to lick their wounds, rebuild their strength and soon – perhaps even this year – take their revenge.

Though he had been brought to the furthest extremity of distress, Cortés still believed his chances were good, and that he would come to the great honour and fortune that Botello had prophesied.

He had a plan and was ready to follow it through, but one important element was as yet unsettled. If tonight's harsh lesson had taught him anything, it was that to have victory over the Mexica he must control their lake. But if he was to control their lake he must have ships. And if he was to have ships, he must have Martin Lopez, his shipbuilder.

Before ordering the column out of Tacuba, Cortés sent Pepillo, who was mourning the loss of his dog, to make enquiries. The boy returned to report that Lopez had been badly wounded but that Dr La Peña was sure he would live.

Cortés looked down from Molinero's saddle and smiled as he signalled the advance. 'Well, let's go then,' he said, 'for we lack nothing.'